A TIMELINE OF MILESTONES IN THE

Shown here (and on the inside back cover) are a number of key figures and events in the development of Organizational Behavior. These events, which appear in chronological order, represent some of the important milestones in the history of the field. (Space limitations prevent the inclusion of additional important people and advances.)

1911

Development of scientific management
Frederick W. Taylor developed principles for maximizing human efficiency on the job (see chapter 1).

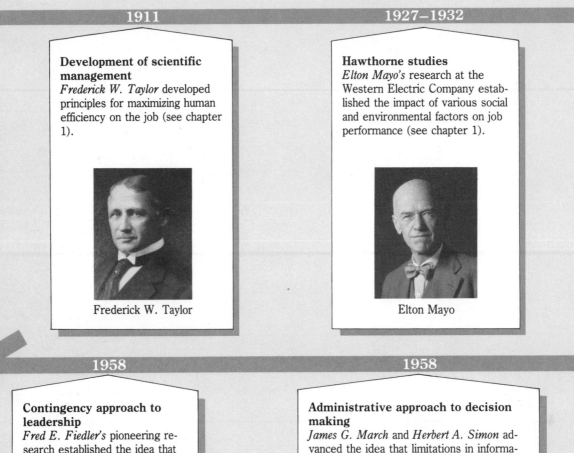

Frederick W. Taylor

1927–1932

Hawthorne studies
Elton Mayo's research at the Western Electric Company established the impact of various social and environmental factors on job performance (see chapter 1).

Elton Mayo

1958

Contingency approach to leadership
Fred E. Fiedler's pioneering research established the idea that different leadership styles are appropriate for different situations (see chapter 11).

Fred E. Fiedler

1958

Administrative approach to decision making
James G. March and *Herbert A. Simon* advanced the idea that limitations in information-processing ability lead people to make less than optimal decisions (see chapter 14).

James G. March   Herbert A. Simon

FIELD OF ORGANIZATIONAL BEHAVIOR

1947

Bureaucratic organizations advocated
Max Weber's writings on bureau-cracies stimulated the study of the formal structural characteristics of organizations (see chapter 15).

Max Weber

1951

Ohio State leadership studies
Ralph Stogdill and his associates distinguished the major dimen-sions of leadership behavior (see chapter 11).

Ralph Stogdill

(Continued on inside back cover)

1959

Dimensions of job satisfaction
Fredrick Herzberg and his associ-ates described factors that con-tribute to job satisfaction and dis-satisfaction (see chapter 5).

Fredrick Herzberg

1959

Bases of social power
John R. P. French and *Bertram Raven* identified the bases of social power wielded by individuals (see chapter 12).

John R. P. French   Bertram Raven

(Continued on inside back cover)

BEHAVIOR IN ORGANIZATIONS:
Understanding and Managing the Human Side of Work

Third Edition

Robert A. Baron
Rensselaer Polytechnic Institute

Jerald Greenberg
The Ohio State University

Allyn and Bacon • Boston • London • Sydney • Toronto

Series Editor: John-Paul Lenney
Production Editor: Susan McIntyre
Developmental Editor: Hannah Rubenstein
Text Design: Glenna Collett
Photo Research: Laurel Anderson/Photosynthesis
Cover Coordinator: Linda Dickinson
Composition Buyer: Linda Cox
Manufacturing Buyer: Bill Alberti

Library of Congress Cataloging-in-Publication Data

Baron, Robert A.
  Behavior in organizations : understanding and managing the human side of work / Robert A. Baron, Jerald Greenberg.—3rd ed.
      p.   cm.
    ISBN 0-205-12161-6
    1. Organizational behavior. I. Greenberg, Jerald. II. Title.

HD58.7.B37 1989
658.3—dc20   89-35252
                                                                   CIP

Printed in the United States of America

10 9 8 7 6 5 4 3 2   93 92 91

PHOTO CREDITS   Page 7 Jim Brown/Offshoot. Page 8 (left) Seth Resnick/Picture Group; (right) George Hall/Woodfin Camp & Assoc. Page 37 (left) Peter Vadnai/The Stock Market; (right) John Curtis/Offshoot. Page 44 Richard Howard/Offshoot. Page 52 (left) Michael Mauney/Click-Chicago; (right) Sygma. Page 80 Doug Menuez/Picture Group. Page 85 (left) Christina Rose Mufson/Comstock; (right) Topham/The Image Works. Page 119 Jon Riley/Click-Chicago. Page 156 Russ Schleipmen/Offshoot. Page 166 (left) Dan McCoy/Rainbow; (right) Max Hirshfeld/Folio Inc. Page 172 JP Laffont/Sygma. Page 198 David Dempster/Offshoot. Page 211 David Dempster/Offshoot. Page 212 David Dempster. Page 227 Robert Frerck/Click-Chicago. Page 237 (left) Nik Klienberg/Picture Group; (right) P. Perrin/Sygma. Page 262 (left) Jim Pickerell Photography; (right) Dick Durance II/Woodfin Camp & Assoc. Page 275 (left) Jim Pickerell Photography; (right) Duomo/Dan Helms. Page 285 (left) Jim Pickerell Photography; (right) Jeffrey Blackman/The Stock Market. Page 296 Gabe Palmer/The Stock Market. Page 301 David Dempster/Offshoot. Page 333 (left) Charles Harbutt/Actuality Inc.; (rignt) Spencer Grant/Photo Researchers. Page 335 (left) Comstock; (right) Chuck O'Rear/Woodfin Camp & Assoc. Page 353 Miro Vintoniv/The Picture Cube. Page 373 John Goell. Page 398 Superstock. Page 414 Shostal Associates/Superstock. Page 428 Russ Schleipman/Offshoot. Page 445 Shepard Sherbell/The Picture Group. Page 450 Lorraine Rorke/The Image Works. Page 467 David Dempster/Offshoot. Page 483 Tony Stone/Worldwide. Page 489 John Blaustein/Woodfin Camp & Assoc. Page 533 Yang Putao/Eastfoto. Page 535 (left) David Wells/The Image Works; (right) Jose Azel/Contact Press. Page 561 (top) Bill Campbell/The Picture Group; (bottom) Ira Wexler/Folio Inc. Page 566 Peter Yates/The Picture Group.

DEDICATION

To David, a fine young man who has the ability to
be anything he wishes to be
and
To Stuart, whose enjoyment of life is matched
only by his outstanding good judgment (i.e.,
he has the good sense to see the world very
much as I do!)

—R. A. B.

To Carolyn, whose tireless dedication to her own
career has been a constant source of inspiration
to mine (although the fruits of my labor are far
less delicious)

—J. G.

CONTENTS

Preface: A Strategic Plan for Improvement   *xi*

Acknowledgments: Some Words of Thanks   *xv*

1 THE FIELD OF ORGANIZATIONAL BEHAVIOR: AN INTRODUCTION   1

The Field of Organizational Behavior: A Working
Definition   *4*

Organizations: Their Basic Nature   *7*

Organizational Behavior: A Capsule Memoir   *10*

The Search for Knowledge: Research Methods in
Organizational Behavior   *18*

Using This Book: A Displaced Preface   *26*

SPECIAL SECTIONS

OB: An International Perspective   Product Quality
in the United States and Japan   *17*

OB: A Research Perspective   College Students as
Subjects in Organizational Research: Some Pros
and Cons   *24*

CASE IN POINT

Management Misunderstanding at Winebago   *31*

EXPERIENCING ORGANIZATIONAL BEHAVIOR

OB versus Common Sense: A Demonstration   *33*

2 LEARNING: ADAPTING TO THE WORLD OF WORK   35

Theories of Learning: An Overview   *38*

Reinforcing Desirable Organizational Behaviors   *44*

Discipline: Eliminating Undesirable Organizational
Behaviors   *58*

SPECIAL SECTIONS

OB: An International Perspective   Training
Managers for Overseas Assignments: Bridging
the Culture Gap   *55*

OB: A Research Perspective   Vicarious
Punishment in Action: Learning What *Not* to Do
by Watching   *62*

CASE IN POINT

Improving Sales Performance: Organizational
Behavior Management in Action   *68*

EXPERIENCING ORGANIZATIONAL BEHAVIOR

The Reinforcing Value of Social Approval   *71*

3 MOTIVATION IN ORGANIZATIONS   73

The Nature of Motivation in Organizations   *75*

Theories of Motivation   *78*

Techniques for Enhancing Motivation   *91*

SPECIAL SECTIONS

OB: An International Perspective   Work Values
behind the Great Wall   *77*

OB: A Research Perspective   Procedural Justice:
Do the Ends Justify the Means?   *87*

OB: A Management Perspective   The Language of
Motivation: It's Not What You Do, But What
You Say, That Counts   *102*

CASE IN POINT

Successful Uses of Job Redesign: Three
Organizational Examples   *108*

Problems Implementing Merit Pay Plans: Two
Organizational Examples *110*

 Motivating Mr. Gillett: Mixing Business
with Pleasure *112*

EXPERIENCING ORGANIZATIONAL BEHAVIOR
Goal Setting and Personal Productivity *113*

4 PERCEPTION: UNDERSTANDING AND
EVALUATING OTHERS **114**
Perception: Some Basic Features *117*
Social Perception: Understanding Others *121*
When Social Perception Fails: Errors in Our
Efforts to Understand Others *129*
Social Perception and Organizational Behavior: Its
Role in Job Interviews and Performance
Appraisal *136*

SPECIAL SECTIONS
OB: An International Perspective Nonverbal
Communication during Negotiations: When
Cultural Differences Really Count *128*
OB: A Management Perspective Conducting
Effective Appraisal Interviews: Some "Do's"
and "Don'ts" *142*

CASE IN POINT
Hidden Traps in Performance Appraisal *148*

EXPERIENCING ORGANIZATIONAL BEHAVIOR
The All Too Powerful Impact of Stereotypes *150*

5 WORK-RELATED ATTITUDES: THEIR
NATURE AND IMPACT **152**
Attitudes: Their Basic Nature and How They
Can Be Changed *154*
Job Satisfaction: Attitudes toward One's Work *160*
Organizational Commitment: Attitudes toward
Organizations *173*
Prejudice: Negative Attitudes toward Other
Organization Members *176*

SPECIAL SECTIONS
OB: A Research Perspective When Professionals
Perform Non-Professional Jobs: Loss of Work-
Related Status and Job Satisfaction *167*
OB: A Research Perspective Employee Stock
Ownership Plans: Their Positive Impact on
Organizational Commitment *175*

CASE IN POINT
Walt Disney World: A Magical Place to Work *185*

EXPERIENCING ORGANIZATIONAL BEHAVIOR
Getting What You Expect: Anticipated Compensation
of Women and Men *187*

6 PERSONALITY: INDIVIDUAL
DIFFERENCES AND ORGANIZATIONAL
BEHAVIOR **188**
Personality: Its Basic Nature *190*
Work-Related Aspects of Personality *193*
Measuring Personality: Some Basic Methods *210*

SPECIAL SECTIONS
OB: An International Perspective Type A's and
Type B's on the Job: Evidence from Two Different
Cultures *195*
OB: A Research Perspective Personal Motives and
Presidential Politics: Does Having the Right
Motives Make a Leader Great? *209*
OB: A Management Perspective Putting Personality
Measures to Practical Use: Assessment Centers
and the Identification of Managerial Talent *211*

CASE IN POINT
David and Debbi: Two Very Different Cookies *218*

EXPERIENCING ORGANIZATIONAL BEHAVIOR
Are You High or Low in Self-Monitoring? *220*

7 STRESS: ITS CAUSES, IMPACT, AND
MANAGEMENT **222**
Stress: Its Basic Nature *224*
Stress: Its Major Causes *226*
Stress: Some Major Effects *235*
Individual Differences in Resistance to Stress:
Optimism, Pessimism, and Hardiness *243*
Managing Stress: Some Useful Tactics *245*

SPECIAL SECTIONS
OB: A Management Perspective Sexual Harassment:
An Especially Objectionable Source of Stress at
Work *231*
OB: A Research Perspective Stress and Decision
Making: Poor Choices, Bad Strategies *239*
OB: An International Perspective Managerial Stress
in Different Cultures: Evidence from
the United Kingdom and Singapore *242*

CASE IN POINT
The Unexpected Stress of Success *253*
Burnout Blues *255*

EXPERIENCING ORGANIZATIONAL BEHAVIOR
Personal Characteristics and Resistance to
Stress *256*

CASE IN POINT
Corporate Culture at Ben & Jerry's Ice Cream:
Tutti Fruitti? *326*
  Corporate Culture at SAS *329*

EXPERIENCING ORGANIZATIONAL BEHAVIOR
Personal Values throughout Life *330*

**8 GROUP DYNAMICS: UNDERSTANDING
GROUPS AT WORK** **258**
Groups at Work: Some Basic Issues *260*
The Structure of Work Groups *267*
Task Performance: Working with and around
Others *278*

SPECIAL SECTIONS
OB: A Management Perspective Guidelines for
Creating Effective Work Teams *266*
OB: A Research Perspective Social Loafing on a
Judgmental Task: The Importance of Feeling
Dispensable *282*

CASE IN POINT
The Rogers Commission: An Insider's View *291*

EXPERIENCING ORGANIZATIONAL BEHAVIOR
The Social Loafing Effect: A Classroom
Demonstration *293*

**10 COMMUNICATION IN
ORGANIZATIONS** **331**
Communication: Its Basic Nature *334*
Major Influences on Organizational
Communication *342*
Overcoming Communication Barriers: Enhancing the
Flow of Information *354*

SPECIAL SECTIONS
OB: A Research Perspective Written or Spoken
Communication? Matching the Medium to the
Message *340*
OB: A Management Perspective Managing the
Hidden Messages behind Corporate
Relocations *360*

CASE IN POINT
How Communication Saved Lives, a Popular
Product, and a Company *366*

EXPERIENCING ORGANIZATIONAL BEHAVIOR
Becoming an Active Listener *369*

**9 THE COURSE OF WORKING LIFE:
ORGANIZATIONAL CULTURE,
ORGANIZATIONAL SOCIALIZATION,
AND CAREER DEVELOPMENT** **294**
Organizational Culture: Its Origins, Nature, and
Effects *296*
Organizational Socialization: The Process of
Joining Up *302*
Careers: How Work and Work Experiences
Change throughout Life *311*

SPECIAL SECTIONS
OB: A Management Perspective Imposing a
Corporate Culture: When Saying
Isn't Doing *301*
OB: A Research Perspective Realistic Job
Previews: What Type Works Best? *304*
OB: A Management Perspective Effective
Socialization Programs: Some Basic
Guidelines *307*

**11 LEADERSHIP: ITS NATURE AND
IMPACT IN ORGANIZATIONS** **371**
Leadership: Its Basic Nature *373*
Leader Traits and Leader Behaviors *376*
Major Theories of Leadership: The Contingency
Model, Normative Theory, and Path-Goal
Theory *384*
Additional Perspectives on Leadership: The Vertical
Dyad Linkage Model, Substitutes for Leadership,
and Situational Leadership Theory *396*

SPECIAL SECTIONS
OB: A Research Perspective Charismatic Leaders:
A Closer Look *383*
OB: An International Perspective Getting on the
Fast Career Track in Japan: The Role of
Leader-Subordinate Exchanges *397*

CASE IN POINT
Leadership by Example 405
Leadership at Price Waterhouse 407 (CNN)

EXPERIENCING ORGANIZATIONAL BEHAVIOR
Can Everyone Be a Leader? 408

12 POWER, POLITICS, AND ETHICS IN ORGANIZATIONS 409

Power: The Capacity to Influence Others 411
Organizational Politics: Power in Action 420
Ethics: Moral Constraints on Organizational Behavior 428

SPECIAL SECTIONS
OB: A Research Perspective Using and Avoiding Power in Crisis Situations 416
OB: A Management Perspective Coping with Organizational Politics: Some Techniques 427
OB: An International Perspective Corporate Morality: Facing the Challenge of the Global Economy 434

CASE IN POINT
Hollywood: Where Dreams Can Be Deadly 440

EXPERIENCING ORGANIZATIONAL BEHAVIOR
What Are Organizations Doing to Promote Corporate Ethics? 442

13 COOPERATION AND CONFLICT: WORKING WITH OR AGAINST OTHERS 443

Prosocial Behavior in Organizations: Beyond the Call of Duty 446
Cooperation: Mutual Assistance in Work Settings 449
Conflict: Its Nature and Causes 458
Conflict: Its Major Effects 466
Conflict: Its Effective Management 467

SPECIAL SECTIONS
OB: A Research Perspective Prosocial and Noncompliant Behavior at Work: Some Personal Factors 448
OB: An International Perspective Conflict in International Joint Ventures 465

CASE IN POINT
Unfriendly Skies/Friendly Freeways 476

EXPERIENCING ORGANIZATIONAL BEHAVIOR
Personal Styles of Conflict Management 478

14 DECISION MAKING IN ORGANIZATIONS 481

Organizational Decision Making: Its Basic Nature 483
Individual Decision Making in Organizations: An Imperfect Process 489
Group Decisions: Do Too Many Cooks Spoil the Broth? 497

SPECIAL SECTIONS
OB: A Research Perspective Identifying Differences in Decision Styles 495
OB: A Management Perspective Guidelines for Improving Group Decisions: A Checklist 509

CASE IN POINT
Coke's Fizzled Decision Making 514

EXPERIENCING ORGANIZATIONAL BEHAVIOR
Making Decisions in Nominal Groups 517

15 ORGANIZATION DESIGN: ENVIRONMENT, STRATEGY, TECHNOLOGY 518

Organizational Structure: Its Basic Dimensions 521
Basic Organization Designs: Functional, Product, Matrix 527
Environment: How External Conditions Shape Structure, Function, and Strategy 532
Technology: How Tools Shape Structure 542

SPECIAL SECTIONS
OB: A Research Perspective Strategy and Structure in Large Manufacturing Firms: When Divisionalization Affects Diversification 526
OB: An International Perspective The Present and Future Form of Organizations: Convergence or Divergence? 540

CASE IN POINT
Organization Design for Effectiveness: Promoting Teamwork 552
Casey at the Bat: Prodding the Post Office to Efficiency 554
Internal Structure in a Changing Organization 556 (CNN)

EXPERIENCING ORGANIZATIONAL BEHAVIOR
Competition, Strategy, and Structure: A Personal Perspective 557

16 ORGANIZATIONAL CHANGE AND DEVELOPMENT   559

Organizational Change: Some Determining
  Factors *562*

The Process of Organizational Change: Some Basic
  Issues *570*

Organizational Development: The Implementation of
  Planned Organizational Change *576*

SPECIAL SECTIONS

OB: A Management Perspective Overcoming
  Resistance to Organizational Change: Some
  Guidelines *575*

OB: An International Perspective Cultural
  Barriers to Effective OD Interventions: The
  Importance of Matching OD Values and National
  Culture *586*

CASE IN POINT

Changing Agendas *592*

   Keeping Xerox Successful: Changing,
  Not Copying *595*

EXPERIENCING ORGANIZATIONAL BEHAVIOR

Facing Resistance to Change *596*

PREFACE:
A STRATEGIC PLAN
FOR IMPROVEMENT

Every significant undertaking should proceed in accordance with a plan. Worthwhile plans possess two key components: (1) clearly established goals and (2) specific strategies for attaining them. Our primary goal, established nine years ago during preparation of the first edition, remained unchanged—to produce an OB text that is:

1. broad and up-to-date in coverage,
2. balanced in terms of its emphasis on research and application, and
3. interesting and comprehensible to students.

In this third edition, however, we added the following key objective to our list—*to improve the new edition as much as possible*. In our efforts to reach our goals, we drew heavily on our combined teaching experience of more than thirty-five years. In addition, in order to attain our new key objective, we developed the following strategy: *obtain as much feedback from colleagues as possible, and then follow this input as carefully and thoroughly as feasible*. We devised this strategy before writing a single word, and adhered to it very closely throughout the project.

How did we go about securing and using such feedback? First, we designed a questionnaire dealing with many aspects of the text and our tentative plans for the new edition. This was distributed to several hundred colleagues—both those who had used the previous editions and those who had not. The items on this survey dealt with a wide range of issues, from the nature of various types of special inserts and pedagogical aids, to the inclusion of specific topics or issues. On the basis of this initial feedback, we formulated specific plans for the new edition and began drafting chapters. The most important changes suggested by the results of our survey—ones which we incorporated into out writing efforts—fall under three major headings: changes in content, changes in special features, and changes in ancillary materials.

Changes in Content

The new content of this edition is apparent both in an entirely new chapter and in the addition of many new topics to existing chapters.

A New Chapter on the Course of Working Life One point that virtually leapt out at us from the survey results was this: a large majority of our colleagues endorsed the inclusion of a new chapter dealing with such topics as *organizational socialization*, *organizational culture*, and *career development and planning*. On the basis of this input (and of our own agreement with it), we decided to include a new chapter titled *The Course of Working Life* (chapter 9). Given the wealth of recent research on the topics listed above, plus growing recognition of the importance of career management, we feel that this is an important addition to the text.

Inclusion of Many New Topics Other results of our survey suggested the desirability of adding many new topics to the text, and of expanding the coverage given to many others. Perhaps the most important of these was a clear mandate to include more information on *ethics*. Consistent with this advice, we added this topic as a major section in chapter 12. Among the many other new topics suggested by survey respondents, reviewers, or our own knowledge of the field were those listed below. All of these are new to the third edition.

Product Quality in the United States and Japan

Improving the Accuracy of Performance Appraisals

Nonverbal Communication during Negotiation

Perceived Similarity and Performance Appraisal

Implicit Theories of Personality

Performance Appraisals and Escalation of Commitment

Employee Stock Ownership Plans and Organizational Commitment

Physical Aspects of Work Settings and Job Satisfaction

Sexual Harassment

Self-Efficacy and Task Performance

Self-Monitoring and Job Performance

Optimism and Resistance to Stress

Stress and Decision Making

Managerial Stress in Different Cultures

Whistle-Blowing

Prosocial and Noncompliant Work Behaviors

Interpersonal Causes of Organizational Conflict

Destructive Criticism

Escalative Interventions and Conflict Resolution

Organizational Socialization

Organizational Culture

Career Management

Charismatic Leaders

Situational Leadership Theory

Strategy and Organizational Structure

Environmental Uncertainty and Boundary Spanning Activities

Work Values in Chinese-Speaking Nations

Procedural Justice

Pay-for-Performance

Two-tier Wage Structures

Creating Effective Work Teams

Stages of Group Development

Informal Communication Networks and Turnover

Technology and Communication

Office Design and Communication

Coping with Organizational Politics

Political Gamesmanship

Reasons for Unethical Organizational Behavior

Individual Decision-Making Styles

Cognitive Framing and Heuristics

Cultural Barriers to Effective Organizational Development

Planned and Unplanned Organizational Change

Changes in Special Features

Previous editions of this text contained several types of special inserts. On the basis of our survey and comments from reviewers, we changed the nature and content of these significantly. The present edition now contains the following three special features:

OB: A Research Perspective These sections describe the results of recent studies that we perceive as being on the cutting edge of research progress in the field.

OB: An International Perspective These sections describe research conducted from an international perspective. Our survey indicated that internationalizing the OB curriculum was seen as a growing concern, prompting us to include numerous *International Perspective* inserts.

OB: A Management Perspective These sections present specific suggestions for applying the principles and findings described in the text to actual management contexts. In short, these sections are designed to help illustrate the practical value of OB to managers.

Changes in Illustrations

Our survey also indicated a preference, among our colleagues, for a somewhat different "mix" of illustrations than was present in previous editions. We were encouraged to increase the number of bar graphs illustrating research findings and the number of flow charts illustrating conceptual frameworks. Both these recommendations were carefully heeded as the book took shape.

Addition of Cases and Experiential Exercises

As we note in chapter 1, there is often a great deal to be learned from careful study of specific situations in specific organizations. Reflecting this belief, we have added a number of cases to the text. These cases, which appear at the end of each chapter, are based on real events in actual organizations, and are tied very closely to chapter content. We believe that they help illustrate the relevance of OB concepts, and that students can learn a great deal about the application of such concepts from them. (All cases were prepared by Suzyn Ornstein, Suffolk University.) An additional set of cases has been prepared by the authors. These cases are based on CNN video interviews and appear in selected chapters. We have included a number of experiential exercises. These, too, appear at the end of each chapter and are labeled *Experiencing Organizational Behavior*. As this title suggests, these exercises are designed to give students first-hand experience with key processes and principles discussed in the text. They provide a useful means of demonstrating and elaborating on concepts presented in the text.

Resource Materials for Students

A Student Study Guide: This item is designed to help students master the topics and information presented in the text. Among its useful features are the following: detailed learning objectives, definitions of key terms, a variety of review quizzes, further sources of information, and a fill-in-the-blanks guided review.

Resource Materials for Instructors

Instructor's Edition
Test Bank
Cases and Exercises (Ready-to-Duplicate Materials)
CNN Videotapes
Allyn and Bacon Business Line

Our Strategic Plan Revisited: Have the Goals Been Reached?

As we're sure is now apparent, the third edition represents a major revision in every sense. Have we accomplished our major goals—or at least made progress toward them? We have no doubt on this score: in our view, the third edition is *much* improved over the previous versions. Its content, special features, perspective, pedagogical aids, and even its appearance all represent substantial progress. We realize, however, that this is merely a belief—and a personal one at that. Only additional feedback provided by you, our students and colleagues, can close the loop and inform us as to the accuracy of these perceptions. We conclude, then, with a plea for your input. We want to know what you like or dislike about our efforts, and whether you share our view that the text is indeed much improved. We'd appreciate hearing from you and learning of your reactions. We can't guarantee that we'll agree with every suggestion you offer or institute every change you recommend. But we can promise to listen—and listen carefully—to everything you have to say. Thanks in advance for your help.

Robert A. Baron

Robert A. Baron (seated)
Department of Psychology
   and School of Management
Rensselaer Polytechnic Institute
Troy, New York 12180

Jerald Greenberg

Jerald Greenberg
Faculty of Management and Human Resources
The Ohio State University
Columbus, Ohio 43210

ACKNOWLEDGMENTS:
SOME WORDS OF THANKS

Writing is a solitary task. Converting authors' words into a book, however, requires the efforts and cooperation of many individuals. In preparing this text, we have been assisted by a large number of dedicated, talented people. We can't possibly thank all of them here, but we do wish to express our appreciation to those whose help has been most valuable.

First, our sincere thanks to the colleagues listed below who read and commented on various portions of the manuscript. An additional group of colleagues responded to an in-depth questionnaire which assisted us in formulating plans for the new edition. Their suggestions were invaluable, and helped us in many ways.

Reviewers

Debra Arvanites
Villanova University

Maureen Fleming
School of Business Administration
University of Montana

Mark Miller
Department of Psychology
DePaul University

Jack Kondrasuk
School of Business Administration
University of Portland

Jane M. Berger
Department of Psychology
Miami-Dade Community College

Charles Regan
Social Sciences Division
Manchester Community College

Bruce Kemelgor
Department of Management
University of Louisville

Suzyn Ornstein
Department of Management
Suffolk University

Angelo DeNisi
Institute for Management and Labor
Relations
Rutgers University

Hal W. Hendrick
College of Systems Science
University of Denver

Survey Respondents

Jack Croxton
SUNY, Fredonia

Ron Di Battista
Bryant College

Betty Woody
UMass, Boston

John Sample
Slippery Rock University

Kevin Mossholder
Auburn University

Mario Sussman
Indiana University of Pennsylvania

Arthur Darrow
Bowling Green State University

Floyd Willoughby
Oakland University

Charles Kaufman
University of South Dakota

John Drexler, Jr.
Oregon State University

Dennis L. Dossett
University of Missouri

Mary Burton
*California State University,
Northridge*

Joseph Garcia
Western Washington University

Lynn Johnson
North Texas State University

Bob Giacolone
University of Richmond

Tom Case
Georgia Southern College

Walter Smock
Rutgers University

John Mack
Salem State College

Jeff Fahrenwald
Central University of Iowa

Samir Ishak
Grand Valley State College

Paul Keaton
University of Wisconsin-LaCrosse

John Bunch
Lehigh University

James Welch
William Penn College

Donna Randall
Washington State University

Dean Frost
Portland State University

Paula M. Popovich
Ohio University

Barbara Hastings
University of South Carolina

Robert Vandenberg
Georgia State University

John Kmetz
University of Delaware

Robert Taylor
Memphis State University

George Lyne
Appalachian State University

Dale Dickson
Mesa College

Harriet Kandelman
University of Portland

Donald Bowen
University of Tulsa

Robert MacAleese
Spring Hill College

Mary Elizabeth Beres
Mercer University

Michael Burke
New York University

Steven Field
University of West Florida

Bruce Meglino
University of South Carolina

Hevng-Gook Kim
Ann Arbor, MI

Joe Lovell
California State University

Gregory B. Northcraft
*College of Business and Public
Administration
University of Arizona*

Eser Belding
University of Michigan

John Koziell
Merrimack College

Walter Green
Pan American University

Fraya Andrews
Eastern Michigan University

Harold Carrier
Rensselaer Polytechnic Institute

Robert Liden
Georgia Institute of Technology

Alan Weinstein
Canisius College

Gene Burton
California State University, Fresno

Alexander McEachern
UCLA

Gary Gordon
SUNY College at Oswego

Fileman Campo-Flores
California State University, Long Beach

Bonnie Allen
Warner Pacific College

Betty Yantis
University of Nevada, Las Vegas

Vincent Palacino, Jr.
American International College

Beth Martin
Shaker Heights, OH

Esther Hamilton
Pepperdine University

Robert W. Moore
Boulder City, NV

Gary L. Fischer
Madonna College

Richard Melucci
Adelphi University

Michael McCuddy
Valparaiso University

Daniel Barber
California State University, Long Beach

Robert Barbato
Rochester Institute of Technology

Allen Bluedorn
University of Missouri

William Stratton
Idaho State University

Thadeus Stupi
Sidman, PA

Edward Adedji
CUNY
Medgar Evans College

Second, we wish to express our appreciation to John-Paul Lenney, our editor at Allyn and Bacon. His enthusiasm for the project was contagious, and his constant support and good humor certainly helped us to bring it to completion in a timely and enjoyable manner.

Third, our sincere thanks to our production editor, Susan McIntyre, who copyedited the entire manuscript with intelligence, sensitivity, and kindness(!), helped us resolve many problems concerning illustrations and other text elements, and assisted us in preparing the endsheets. It has been a pleasure working with her, and, as a fellow author, she provided a degree of understanding and empathy that is rare indeed!

Fourth, our thanks to several other people who contributed to various aspects of the production process: to Laurel Anderson for outstanding photo research, to Glenna Collett for a very attractive design, and to Linda Dickinson for an appealing cover.

Finally, we wish to thank Suzyn Ornstein for preparing an excellent set of cases, Angelo DeNisi and Robert Goddard for their outstanding work on the Instructor's Manual, and Don Eskew for his help in preparing the *Test Bank*.

To all these truly outstanding people, and to many others, too, our warm personal regards.

CHAPTER ONE

THE FIELD OF ORGANIZATIONAL BEHAVIOR: AN INTRODUCTION

CHAPTER OUTLINE

The Field of Organizational Behavior: A Working Definition
Organizational Behavior and the Scientific Method
Individuals, Groups, and Organizations: Three Levels of Analysis within OB
OB in Action: Putting Knowledge to Work
OB: Why It's Needed

Organizations: Their Basic Nature
Organizations as Open Systems
How Organizations Shape Organizational Behavior

Organizational Behavior: A Capsule Memoir
Scientific Management: The Beginnings
Human Relations: Social Factors in Work Settings
Organizational Behavior: An Overview of Its Current State

The Search for Knowledge: Research Methods in Organizational Behavior
Natural Observation
The Case Method: Generalizing from the Unique
Systematic Observation: Survey Techniques and Correlation
Experimentation: Knowledge through Intervention
Theory: Essential Guide to Organizational Research

Using This Book: A Displaced Preface

Special Sections

OB: An International Perspective
Product Quality in the United States and Japan

OB: A Research Perspective
College Students as Subjects in Organizational Research: Some Pros and Cons

LEARNING OBJECTIVES

After reading this chapter, you should be able to:
1. Define the field of organizational behavior and describe its three distinct levels of analysis.
2. Define the term *organization* and indicate how organizations shape the behavior of individuals.
3. Describe the major events and developments that led to the emergence of an independent field of organizational behavior.
4. Describe several major characteristics of the modern field of OB.
5. Explain key methods of research in OB (e.g., systematic observation, experimentation).
6. Explain the central role of theory in organizational research.

"Well, so much for *that* magic formula," Susan Devon, a senior vice president at Consolidated Stores, comments in disgust. "Concrete goals; hmmph! We call in those experts, we listen to their advice, and what do we get for our trouble? Nothing!"

"Yeah, it sure is disappointing," Paul Petrakis, her assistant, replies. "You'd think that by now we'd see *some* improvement. They tell us to give people specific goals to shoot for, and we do. But look at these figures: sales are flat and returns are up. I just don't understand it."

"Sure looks like we wasted our time and money," Susan adds. "I don't know why we even bothered."

At this point, Ellen Reilly, a younger member of the team, enters the conversation. "You're both right; it *is* disappointing. But are we really being completely fair in judging the program?"

"What do you mean?" Paul answers, a note of irritation in his voice. "They said 'Give people goals,' and we did."

"Right," Ellen agrees. "We did. But do you remember what else they said—that it's important to get people *committed* to the goals? I'm not sure that really happened."

"But they voted for 'em in each department. What more could we do?" Susan asks, a puzzled look on her face.

"I'm not sure. I'm no expert," Ellen answers, "but I have the gnawing feeling that no one really felt committed to the goals; they just seemed to be there, floating in space. They were something to refer to, but not something anyone really ought to shoot for."

"I can't believe it's that simple," Susan replies, shaking her head. "A goal is a goal, right?" After a moment's thought, she continues, "And yet, maybe, just maybe, you've hit on something. . . ."

"What's the problem out there anyway?" Jim Koslowski asks, scratching his chin. "Forty-two percent turnover; that's more than twice the company average."

"It's strange, all right," Tamika Jones replies. "And at one of our best operations, too. A beautiful new building, a great location. Beats me why so many people want to leave."

"I may have an idea," Hal Cohen replies. "It all seems to center around feedback."

"What do you mean?" Tamika asks. "All our units use the same performance appraisal system, so how can things be different out there?"

"Yeah, we all *do* use the same appraisal system. But that's only part of the picture. A lot of feedback comes on a day-to-day basis, informally. And I think they do *that* differently."

"How? What do you mean?" Jim asks.

"There seems to be a feeling out there that it's important to be really tough on subordinates—to rake them over the coals every so often just to keep 'em on their toes. I was there for a couple of weeks last year, and I heard some wild conversations."

"No kidding!" Tamika exclaims. "Tell us more."

"For one thing, they use a lot of threats. I heard one Division Head tell her Deputy 'Next time that happens, out the door.' You can imagine how he reacted! And they do the same thing in their written memos. They'll write 'This stinks,' or 'Try thinking a little next time' on reports. It's weird, but that's how they operate."

"Wow!" Jim comments, shaking his head. "No wonder they have problems. How'd they ever get started on that anyhow? It sure wouldn't fly around here."

"Beats me, but it might be one reason why they lose so many good people. I know *I* wouldn't stay around long for that kind of stuff!"

Something is seriously wrong in both of these organizations. In the first, efforts to enhance employee motivation have failed, and disappointing productivity continues. In the second, a somewhat unusual organizational climate has developed in an important branch operation. This climate, which encourages destructive types of feedback to subordinates, seems to be contributing to the loss of valuable personnel (see Figure 1.1). In short, both organizations have problems that interfere with their efficiency, performance, and effectiveness. Moreover—and this is the key point—these problems do *not* stem from poor equipment, faulty technology, or lack of needed supplies. Rather, they center around *people*—the human side of work mentioned in the subtitle of this book. They involve key aspects of human behavior (e.g., motivation), relations between people (e.g., communication), or the impact of organizational structure and function (e.g., organizational climate) on them.

As you probably already realize, such "people problems" (or, more appropriately, people-*centered* problems) are far from rare; indeed, they often play a crucial role in the success and profitability of many organizations. How can these problems be solved, or at least alleviated? The field of **organizational behavior** (OB for short) provides

"Perhaps, sir, your rhetoric was a little too harsh."

FIGURE 1.1 Organizational Behavior: One Potential Source of Problems

An organizational climate that encourages harsh, biting criticism of subordinates may have adverse effects on both morale and productivity. This is one of countless problems related to the "human side of work." (Source: Drawing by Lorenz; © 1986 The New Yorker Magazine, Inc.)

one potential answer. Basically, OB suggests that the best approach to solving such problems involves the application of the knowledge, findings, and methods of the **behavioral sciences** (e.g., psychology, sociology). In short, it proposes that applying the largely scientific approach of these fields may yield valuable new information about organizations and the complex processes within them. This knowledge can then be used to solve a wide range of practical problems.

Has this approach succeeded? The pages of this text will, we believe, offer a very positive answer. In recent decades, OB has developed into a diverse and vigorous field. At present, it is actively studying virtually every imaginable aspect of organizations and behavior within them.[1] Moreover, the results of this systematic research have already contributed greatly to making organizations more effective, as well as better places in which to work.[2] To be up-front about our own personal biases, we are highly optimistic about the potential and actual contributions of OB.

In the remainder of this chapter we will provide you with the background information you will need for understanding the scope of OB and its potential value to you as a future manager. First, we'll offer a formal definition of OB, indicating what it is and what it seeks to accomplish. Second, we'll comment on the nature of organizations and the ways in which organizations shape the attitudes, actions, and values of persons in them. Third, we will briefly trace the origins of OB from its emergence to its modern form. Fourth, we'll consider the methods OB uses in carrying out one of its major tasks—adding to basic knowledge about organizations and the behavioral processes within them. Finally, we will describe the structure of this book and call attention to several of its special features. Then we'll be ready to move on to the main body of the text and our primary task: enhancing your understanding of the human side of work by providing a broad overview of the field of OB and its major findings.

THE FIELD OF ORGANIZATIONAL BEHAVIOR: A WORKING DEFINITION

We'll begin with a definition of the field, and then offer some clarifying comments on it. *The field of organizational behavior seeks knowledge of all aspects of behavior in organizational settings through the systematic study of individual, group, and organizational processes; the primary goals of such knowledge are enhancing organizational effectiveness and individual well-being.* This definition is complex, so please bear with us while we clarify several of its key points.

Organizational Behavior and the Scientific Method

Earlier, we noted that the field of OB rests firmly on the findings and methods of the behavioral sciences. Given this fact, it should not be surprising that modern OB, like these closely related fields, is scientific in orientation. It, too, seeks increased knowledge through an empirical science-based approach. We will have more to say about this strategy later in this chapter. For the moment, we simply wish to add that while OB is certainly scientific in orientation, it is far from rigid in this regard. Most practitioners in the field fully agree that carefully conducted research, performed in accordance with basic scientific principles, is the best single way of adding to our store of knowledge about behavior in organizations. At the same time, they recognize the complexities of applying such methods in actual organizations, and the limitations this may imply.[3] Further, many believe that important ideas and valuable insights can sometimes be gained through other means (e.g., from the comments of experienced, practicing managers; from information about the conditions present at the time some important event or change occurred).[4] Please don't misunderstand: such sources are *not* viewed as a substitute for the findings of systematic research. There is some feeling, though, that they *can* sometimes be useful as preliminary input and should not be totally ignored. As noted recently by Lorsch, a well-known researcher in the field, OB now accepts the view that qualitative data, too, are sometimes useful, and may supplement purely quantitative data in some instances.[5] In our view, this is an important "plus."

Individuals, Groups, and Organizations: Three Levels of Analysis within OB

Next, let's address our contention that OB focuses on three levels of analysis: individuals, groups, and organizations themselves. Why this complexity? The answer is straightforward: in order to understand behavior in organizational settings, all three levels are essential. To see why, let's return to the two opening cases on page 2. The first illustrates a process centering primarily on individuals—*work motivation*. After all, it is individuals who demonstrate high or low motivation to work on their jobs. Yet, consider the following question: why didn't employees at Consolidated Stores become committed to the goals selected, even though they voted on them? To answer, we must know something about their perceptions of the process through which these goals were selected, something about their interpersonal relations (how they get along with one another), and something about the informal norms within this organization concerning output and cooperation with management. To fully understand work motivation, we must consider all three levels: individuals, groups, and the organization itself.

The same point can be made about the second case. Here, the major issue is *communication*—the manner in which managers at a branch operation deliver informal feedback to their subordinates. This is clearly a process involving two or more persons. Yet, to fully understand its impact, we must also consider (1) the emotional and cognitive reactions of the persons receiving such feedback, and (2) the organizational factors that led to the emergence of a harsh style of feedback in this particular plant.

To make a long story short, most OB specialists now concur that in order to fully understand why people think and act as they do in organizational settings, we must acquire information about their reactions as individuals (e.g., their attitudes, perceptions, motives), the groups to which they belong (e.g., communication between them, formal and informal norms affecting their behavior), and the organizations in which they work (e.g., their culture, values, structure; see Figure 1.2). Careful attention to all three levels of analysis is a central theme in modern OB, and will be fully reflected throughout this text.

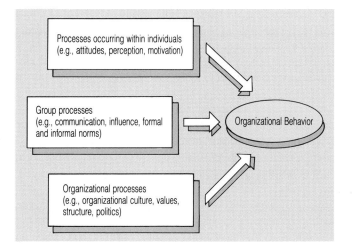

FIGURE 1.2 OB: Three Levels of Analysis

To fully understand organizational behavior, we must consider processes occurring largely within individuals, processes occurring between two or more persons (i.e., in groups), and the nature and functioning of organizations themselves.

OB in Action: Putting Knowledge to Work

Living as we do in the era of the "information explosion," the view that knowledge is a wonderful thing has taken on new significance. And knowledge that can be *used* is even better! While this sentiment is not an official motto for OB, it is certainly one of its guiding themes. There is general agreement in our field that knowledge about organizations and organizational behavior, once acquired, should be put to practical use. Further, there is agreement that it should be used to enhance productivity or efficiency on the one hand, *and* the quality of working life on the other. Please note that there is no necessary contradiction between these two goals. On the contrary, they often go hand in hand.[6] So, where OB is concerned, there is often no sharp distinction between basic knowledge and application; in actual practice, the two tend to be closely intertwined.

OB: Why It's Needed

Before concluding this discussion, we should comment on one additional point: Why is the field of OB, as we have defined it, necessary? Our answer consists of two parts relating, in turn, to the imperfect nature of "common sense," and to the increasing complexity and competitiveness of the modern economic world.

OB and common sense. Over the course of history, human societies have gathered a great deal of informal knowledge about organizational behavior and processes. Some of this information was useful, allowing specific organizations to attain great success in reaching their stated goals. For example, the Roman army succeeded in conquering much of the known world, despite its relatively small size. This success was due only in part to the possession of superior military tactics and weapons. It also stemmed from the army's highly efficient internal organization. Similarly, the construction "industry" of ancient Egypt left us with an enduring legacy of architectural treasures over which we continue to marvel (see Figure 1.3).

Despite these accomplishments and the practical experience on which they were based, informal knowledge about organizational behavior was, and remains, incomplete. What kind of leadership is best? Should decisions be made by groups or individuals? What tactics are most effective in bringing negotiations to a successful conclusion? Common sense offers only fragmentary and inaccurate answers to these and many other crucial questions. To pursue one of these examples a bit further, consider the following: in the past, it was widely held that committees are less likely than individuals to go off the deep end and make high-risk decisions. Yet, it is precisely such groups that have been responsible for selecting some of the most disastrous courses of action in recorded history (e.g., the decision by the Japanese high command to attack Pearl Harbor; the repeated decision by groups within the U.S. government to continue escalating the Vietnam war). How can this apparent contradiction be explained? Only, it appears, through systematic research designed to determine precisely *when* and *why* groups are more likely to make extreme decisions than individuals. (See chapter 14 for a discussion of this topic.)

In sum, common sense often fails as an accurate guide to understanding key aspects of organizations and behavior within them. It does not offer consistent answers to our questions concerning motivation, leadership, power, conflict, and scores of other issues. OB, with its reliance on scientific methods, is better able to provide such answers. And this, in turn, provides strong justification for its existence.

OB and the world economy. But why, precisely is such information needed? The answer to *this* question should be obvious. We live in a time of increasing complexity, and increasing economic competition. As a result, success (and even survival) will go

FIGURE 1.3 Organizations in
the Ancient World: Some of
Their Achievements Were
Impressive

Ancient societies possessed
much practical knowledge
about organizational processes
and structure. However, this
information was fragmentary
and incomplete at best.

only to the most fit—to those organizations (and national economies) most capable of
competing effectively. Clearly, the information provided by OB is one essential ingredient in this equation. Potential benefits include the development of techniques for
enhancing employee motivation, commitment, and satisfaction, for resolving costly organizational conflict, and for improving communication,[7,8] all of which can contribute to
the economic success not merely of specific organizations, but of entire industries and
even national economies. To conclude: if ever the need for OB and the knowledge it
provides was great, it is *now*.

ORGANIZATIONS: THEIR BASIC NATURE

The name of our field has two distinct parts: *organization* and *behavior*. In our comments
so far, we have focused on the latter. At this point, we will restore the needed balance
by focusing directly on organizations themselves. In this context, we'll address two
basic questions: (1) What, precisely, are organizations and (2) how do they shape the
behavior of the persons within them?

Organizations as Open Systems

Which photo in Figure 1.4 (on page 8) shows an organization? The answer is both of
them. This is so because both meet the following definition: *an organization is any
social structure or system consisting of two or more persons who are somehow interdependent and who work together in a coordinated manner to attain common goals.*[9] In
other words, organizations consist of persons who interact with one another (directly
or indirectly), whose fates are somehow linked (what happens to one affects what
happens to the others), and who work together in order to reach shared goals.

We should add that many scholars believe it is useful to view organizations as a
special type of *system*—an **open system**.[10,11] Open systems (like all systems) consist
of interrelated components. However, they also show several distinct and interesting
properties. Several of these are summarized in Table 1.1 (on page 8). As you can see,
open systems receive *input* from the external environment which they then transform,
through internal processes, into *output*. Their exchanges with the environment are
cyclic in nature, and throughout the process, they tend to maintain a constant internal
state; in short, they are self-sustaining. If successful in these tasks, open systems
grow, and tend toward greater internal differentiation (e.g., various components tend

FIGURE 1.4 The Many Sizes and Forms of Organizations
Which of these shows an organization? In fact, both do. Both represent social structures or systems in which two or more persons work together to attain common goals.

to specialize in different functions). Indeed, this description seems to fit many modern organizations. It is also interesting to note that the properties that distinguish open systems from simpler ones (e.g., *control systems* such as the one that regulates the operation of furnaces or air conditioners) are the same properties that distinguish living organisms from inanimate objects. Life, too, is self-sustaining, engages in cyclic exchanges with the external environment, and so on.

One final point: because of its deep commitment to the practical use of knowledge, OB usually focuses on work-related organizations. For this reason, we will concentrate mainly on such organizations throughout this text. However, many of the principles and findings discussed apply to organizations generally, and may extend beyond the world of work.

TABLE 1.1 The Properties of Open Systems
Open systems have properties that allow them to be self-sustaining and permit them to grow and change under appropriate conditions. These same properties distinguish living organisms from inanimate objects.

PROPERTY	EXPLANATION
Importation of Energy	Energy is imported from the external environment.
Through-put	Open systems transform the energy they import.
Output	Open systems export some product to the external environment.
Cyclical Nature	The pattern of energy exchange with the environment is cyclical in nature.
Steady State	The system is maintained in a relatively steady state.
Trend toward Differentiation	Open systems tend to become more differentiated and elaborate.
Equifinality	Open systems can reach the same final state from differing initial conditions and in many ways.

(Source: Based on suggestions by Katz & Kahn, 1978.)

How Organizations Shape Organizational Behavior

An executive known personally to one of the authors frequently remarks: "A business is only as good as its people." What he means is that the actions, motivation, and commitment of the persons in an organization determine its fate. Certainly, this is true; organizations are indeed composed of individuals. Yet, this is only part of the picture. While individuals shape organizations, they, in turn, are often profoundly affected by being in them. There are several reasons this is so.

Organizational structure: The formal dimensions. First, organizations have a formal **structure**—an internal arrangement of divisions, departments, work teams, and so on.[12] This internal structure, which is often represented by an *organizational chart* such as the one shown in Figure 1.5, indicates how tasks and responsibilities are to be divided, how communication is supposed to take place, and where power or authority rests. This internal structure often profoundly affects the persons within the organization, determining the kinds of work they do, with whom they come in contact, and to whom they report. Although every organization has some form of internal structure, it varies greatly. For example, some adopt a system in which few intermediate levels separate the lowest rung on the career or corporate ladder from the highest—their *chain of command* is short. In contrast, others develop a structure in which many levels separate such positions; their chain of command is long. Similarly, in some organizations, many subordinates report to a single supervisor—the *span of control* is wide. In others, only a few subordinates report to a single supervisor—the span of control is narrow. Organizations also differ in many other aspects of internal structure; we'll consider a number of these in chapter 15. Here, we wish to emphasize that the way a given organization is structured can greatly affect the persons within it.

We should add that often, the formal structure of organizations is shaped by two factors: *technologies* and the *external environment.* Technologies refers to the knowledge, processes, equipment, and facilities used by an organization to produce desired outputs. The external environment refers to the economic, social, and legal context in which it operates. We'll examine the impact of both groups of factors in chapter 15.

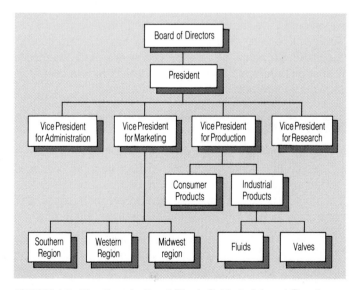

FIGURE 1.5   The Organizational Chart: Guide to Internal Structure
The formal structure of an organization is often represented by an *organizational chart.* Here, part of the internal structure of one large organization is represented.

Organizational structure: The informal dimensions. As anyone with actual work experience well knows, the formal organizational chart is only part of the total story. Many informal networks and structures exist as well. Moreover, in many instances, these are actually more important, in certain respects, than the formal ones. For example, information frequently flows much more quickly through the informal "grapevine" than through more formal channels of communication.[13] Similarly, persons who appear to have authority over others on the organizational chart may be mere figureheads, with little influence or power. Such informal structures and systems constitute a second important way in which organizations shape the behavior and attitudes of individuals. (We'll consider these effects in more detail in chapters 6 and 10.)

Organizational culture. A third major way in which organizations affect the behavior and attitudes of their members is through **organizational culture.**[14,15] This term refers to beliefs, values, attitudes, and expectations shared by most (if not all) organization members. As we will see in chapter 9, such views can profoundly affect persons entering an organization. Indeed, new organization members often find that they must make many adjustments to their new work setting, changing everything from their style of dress to their views on various issues. Only if they adapt in this manner can they become fully accepted members of the organization or work group. While organizations obviously can't think or feel (these processes occur only within individuals), the impact of organizational culture is powerful and real.[16] Further, organizational culture can persist over long periods of time, being passed along from one "generation" of organization members to the next. As a result, such shared beliefs and values may remain quite stable even as large numbers of persons join or leave the organization. (See chapter 6 for more information on organizational culture and *organizational socialization*—the process through which individuals become fully functioning members of organizations they have recently joined.[17])

ORGANIZATIONAL BEHAVIOR: A CAPSULE MEMOIR

In the late 1980s, the importance of the human side of work (and organizations) is far from controversial. Most people realize that communication, motivation, cooperation, power, and many other person-based processes play a key role in organizational functioning and success. It is surprising to learn, therefore, that this idea is relatively new. It took form only during the present century, and did not gain widespread acceptance until recent decades. Why was this the case? How did this idea—which is central to OB—finally emerge? It is on these questions that we will focus next.

Scientific Management: The Beginnings

How can productivity be improved? This has been a central issue in most organizations since ancient times. In one sense, emergence of OB as a distinct field can be traced to efforts to answer this question. To understand why, we must return to the closing decades of the nineteenth century, a period of rapid industrialization and technological change. At that time, the prevailing view of work was much as it had been throughout recorded history. The jobs being performed were what really mattered; the people performing them were much less important. Accordingly, engineers set about the task of applying the new technological knowledge at their disposal to the development of ever-more efficient machines. The rationale behind such efforts was straightforward: if the means of production were improved, efficiency, too, would automatically rise. Much to their surprise, this was *not* so. In some cases, new and presumably more efficient machinery enhanced productivity, but sometimes it did not. Faced with such outcomes, a growing number of managers reached a new conclusion: while machines and equipment *are* important, they are not all that matter. The people who run them, too, must be considered. Efforts to apply this basic idea soon led to *time and motion studies*—attempts to design jobs so that they could be performed in the most efficient manner possible.

The process did not stop there, however. Growing concern with the human side of work soon paved the way for emergence of a major new approach—one known as **scientific management**. Although it was practiced by many persons, its most famous advocate was Frederick W. Taylor. In a book entitled *The Principles of Scientific Management,* Taylor outlined the key features of his new approach.[18] It, too, was concerned with maximizing efficiency and getting the most work possible out of employees. Thus, scientific management emphasized the importance of effective *job design*, efforts to plan work tasks in a systematic manner. In addition, it contained two new features that, together, focused attention on employees as well as on their work.

First, Taylor suggested that workers be carefully selected and trained for their jobs. In this respect, he broke with the traditional view that employees are basically interchangeable cogs and can easily be shuffled from job to job. Second, he recognized the importance of motivation in work settings. Indeed, he firmly believed that efforts to raise worker motivation might result in major gains in productivity. His view concerning the basis of such motivation was, by modern standards, quite unsophisticated. Briefly, he assumed that work motivation stems mainly from the desire for monetary gain. Today, in contrast, we realize that people actually seek many goals through their work—everything from enhanced status to personal fulfillment. While he was mistaken about the nature of motivation in work settings, Taylor *did* grasp the importance of this key factor. This was certainly a major step forward.

To repeat: scientific management was primarily concerned with raising efficiency and output—*not* with enhancing worker satisfaction or morale. But it did begin to recognize the importance of considering people in work settings, especially the abilities, training, and motives of individual employees. This encouraged further attention to the human side of work, and contributed to an intellectual climate that ultimately paved the way for an independent field of OB.

Human Relations: Social Factors in Work Settings

While scientific management directed some attention to the importance of human behavior at work, it did not go far enough in this respect. Good job design and high motivation are indeed important factors where productivity or output is concerned, but performance is also strongly affected by many other factors including relations among members of work groups, the quality of leadership they receive from supervisors, and their perceptions that they are being treated fairly or unfairly by management.[19] Today, these facts seem so obvious they hardly bear repeating. In the past, however, this was not the case. In fact, it took some dramatic and unexpected research findings to call the complex, social nature of work and work settings to the attention of practicing managers. The research most directly responsible for this shift is known as the *Hawthorne studies*. Because this research played an important role in the emergence of our field, it is worthy of our attention here.[20]

The Hawthorne studies: An overview. In the mid 1920s, a series of fairly typical scientific management studies were begun at the Hawthorne plant of the Western Electric Company outside Chicago. One purpose of the research was to determine the impact of level of illumination on worker productivity. Several groups of female employees took part. One group worked in a *control room* where the level of lighting was held constant; another worked in a *test room* where the level of lighting was systematically varied. Results were baffling: productivity increased in *both* locations! Further, there seemed to be no orderly link between level of lighting and performance. Output remained high in the test room even when illumination was reduced to that of moonlight—a level so dim that workers could barely see what they were doing!

Puzzled by these findings, Western Electric officials called in a team of experts headed by Elton Mayo. The results they uncovered contributed to the emergence of an independent field of OB.[21] In an initial series of studies (known as the *Relay Room experiments*), Mayo and his colleagues examined the impact of thirteen different factors on productivity. These included length of rest pauses, length of work day and work week, method of payment, place of work, and even a free mid-morning lunch. Subjects were again female employees who worked in a special test room. Once more, results were mysterious: productivity increased with almost every change in work conditions. Indeed, even when subjects were returned to initial standard conditions, productivity continued to rise (see Figure 1.6).

As if these findings were not puzzling enough, additional studies soon added to the confusion. For example, in one investigation (known as the *Bank Wiring Room study*), male members of an existing work group were carefully observed by members of the research team. No attempts were made to alter the conditions under which they labored, but they were interviewed by another investigator during non-work periods. Here, results were quite different from those in the earlier studies. Productivity did *not* rise continuously. On the contrary, it soon became apparent that workers were

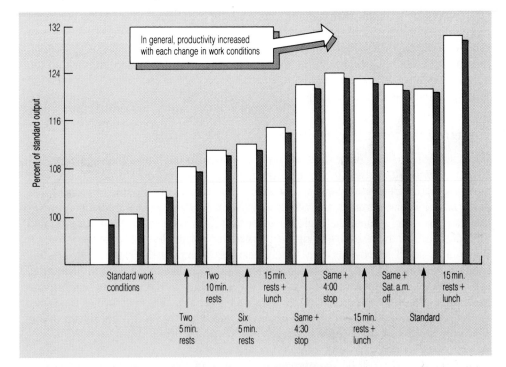

FIGURE 1.6 The Hawthorne Project: Some Puzzling Results

In one part of the Hawthorne project, female employees were exposed to several changes in work conditions. Surprisingly, almost every one of these alterations produced an increase in productivity. (Source: Based on data from Roethlisberger & Dickson, 1939; see Note 20.)

deliberately restricting their output. This was revealed both by observations of their work behavior (e.g., all men stopped work well before quitting time) and by interviews (almost all admitted that they could easily do more if they wished). Why was this the case? Why did these workers restrict their own output while those in the Relay Room experiments did not? Gradually, Mayo and his colleagues arrived at the following answer: Work settings are actually complex *social systems*. In order to fully comprehend behavior in them, it is necessary to understand worker attitudes, communication between workers, and a host of other factors.

Armed with this insight, Mayo and his associates were soon able to interpret the puzzling findings of their research. First, with respect to the Relay Room experiments, productivity rose because subjects reacted favorably to receiving special attention. In short, they knew they were being studied, and because they enjoyed this attention, their motivation—and also their productivity—rose. In contrast, output was held low in the Bank Wiring Room study because the men in that group feared that high productivity would lead to an increase in the amount they were expected to produce each day, and might even cost some of them their jobs. The result: they established informal rules (*norms*) about behavior on the job—rules that reduced production.

The Hawthorne studies: Their implications and impact. By modern research standards, the Hawthorne studies were seriously flawed. For example, no attempt was made to assure that participants were representative of all workers in their plant, or all manufacturing personnel generally. As a result, findings could not readily be generalized from the specific groups studied to other groups of employees. Similarly, no efforts were made to assure that the rooms in which participants were tested were identical in all major respects to those in other parts of the plant. As a result, changes in performance could have stemmed from differences in this regard, rather than solely from changes in working conditions (e.g., the level of illumination, length of rest pauses). Also, different groups of employees were exposed to contrasting conditions, or tested in different ways. Thus, all employees in the Relay Room experiments were females, while all those in the Bank Wiring Room study were males. Did this factor contribute to the different patterns of findings obtained? From the procedures employed by Mayo and his colleagues, it is impossible to tell. (See the discussion of experimentation on page 22.)

Despite these flaws, the Hawthorne studies exerted several lasting effects relevant to the development of OB. Together, they underscored the fact that full understanding of behavior in work settings requires knowledge of many factors ignored by scientific management and earlier views—factors relating to complex aspects of human behavior. As recognition of this basic principle grew, a new perspective known as the **human relations approach** took shape.[22] This perspective devoted far more attention to human needs, attitudes, motives, and relationships than previous ones. In addition, it recognized the fact that lasting gains in productivity and satisfaction can be achieved only through appropriate changes in these and related factors. In this way, it established a close link between the emerging field of OB and several behavioral sciences (e.g., anthropology, psychology, sociology)—a link that has persisted to the present. While the human relations perspective itself was gradually replaced by even more sophisticated views, several of its ideas and concepts contributed to the emergence and development of OB. Since OB, in turn, has greatly influenced the practices adopted by many organizations, it is clear that the workers in the long-vanished plant outside Chicago probably had greater and more lasting effects on the entire world of work than most of them would ever have dreamed possible.

(Incidentally, we should add that the original topic of the Hawthorne studies—the impact of levels of illumination on productivity—has continued to be the subject of research attention. Studies on this topic suggest that the precise level of illumination best for a given job depends on many factors, such as the nature of the work being performed, other environmental variables such as temperature, and even the color of the walls in the room.[23,24])

Organizational Behavior: An Overview of Its Current State

The realization that behavior in work settings is shaped by a wide range of individual, group, and organizational factors set the stage for the emergence of an independent, science-based field of organizational behavior. And such a field was not long in taking shape. Although no ribbon-cutting ceremonies were held to mark its appearance, significant events suggest that it began to emerge in the 1940s. The first doctoral degree in organizational behavior was granted in 1941.[25] The first textbook on this field was published in 1945.[26] By the late 1950s and early 1960s, it was very much a going concern. By that time, active programs of research designed to increase our understanding of such key processes as leadership and motivation were well established, and important studies on the impact of organizational structure and design had already been conducted.[27] (Please see Figure 1.7 for a summary of some of the key events in the development of OB.)

Since its emergence, OB has continued to develop in many respects. Currently, it is as diverse and varied as the processes it seeks to clarify. Here, briefly, is an overview of some of its major characteristics as we enter the 1990s.

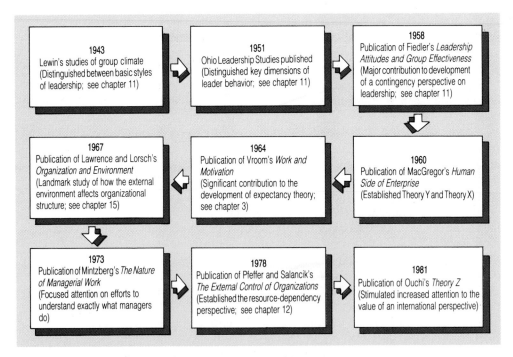

FIGURE 1.7   Major Contributions in the History of OB

The events shown here are among those that have contributed to the development of OB as an independent field of study. (Source: Based on suggestions by Lawrence, 1987; see Note 5.)

OB and the human resources model. Suppose you approached a large group of managers working for a diverse group of companies, and asked them to describe their basic views of human nature. What kind of answers would you receive? Unfortunately, even today many of the replies would be negative. Some of the managers might suggest that human beings are basically lazy and irresponsible. Further, they might note that the key task of managers is giving such persons direction—keeping them on track, so to speak. This traditional view, often known as **Theory X**, has prevailed for centuries and is still very much with us today.

In contrast, other persons in your sample might report a more positive view of human nature. These managers would reject the notion that most people are basically lazy. Instead, they would note that human beings are as capable of working hard and accepting responsibility as they are of "goofing off." What's crucial in determining their reactions is the work environment in which they are placed. If conditions are such that working hard will pay off (i.e., yield rewards they value) *this* is what they'll do. If, instead, conditions are such that effort is not rewarded, it would be foolish to expect much from them. Managers who accept this more optimistic view—which is often known as the **human resources model** or **Theory Y**—might add that the key task for supervisors is assuring that the right conditions exist, *not* "riding herd" on employees and goading them on to hard work.

Which of these perspectives prevails in modern OB? As you can probably guess, the second. Most persons working in this field currently believe that employees can indeed demonstrate many desirable behaviors at work, provided appropriate conditions exist. But please note: acceptance of this human resource perspective does *not* imply a Pollyanna-like belief that employees will always, or even usually, act in productive or responsible ways. Rather, it simply recognizes the fact that human beings do indeed respond to their work environments. If these are favorable (e.g., employees are treated fairly and with respect by their managers), they will work hard, become committed to their organizations, and develop many other desirable behaviors. If, in contrast, conditions are negative (e.g., they feel exploited, lack confidence in their supervisors), they may adopt far less positive patterns of behavior. In short, modern OB does not view the world of work through rose-tinted glasses. What it *does* assume is that there are no intrinsic reasons why work settings cannot be pleasant and satisfying or why employees cannot be encouraged to act constructively on the job. In a word, it is basically optimistic, but not naive, in its approach to behavior in work settings.

OB and the contingency approach: Realizing that there are no simple answers. What style of leadership is best? What is the most effective means of motivating employees? What is the best technique for reaching complex decisions? At first glance, these questions may strike you as both intriguing and reasonable; indeed, you might assume that they are close to the core of modern OB. In fact, however, there is one basic problem with all of them: they seem to imply the existence of simple, unitary answers. In other words, they suggest that there is indeed *one* best style of leadership, *one* best technique for enhancing motivation, or *one* best procedure for reaching decisions. It is a basic assumption of modern OB that such an approach is inaccurate and simplistic. Where behavior in work settings is concerned, there are (alas!) no simple answers. The processes involved are far too complex and are affected by far too many factors to permit us this luxury. Recognition of this fact is often known as the **contingency approach**, and is a hallmark of OB as we enter the 1990s.[28] According to this approach, behavior in work settings is a complex result of many interacting forces. Personal characteristics (e.g., attitudes, values, beliefs), situational factors (many aspects of a specific work setting), organizational culture, present and past relations between individuals and groups, and existing organizational structure may all shape and influence what happens at a specific time in a specific location (see Figure 1.8).

Because it attempts to deal with such complexity, the answers offered by the contingency approach—and modern OB—often include such phrases as "under some conditons . . . ," or "all other factors being equal . . ." Some persons, hoping for simple "cookbook" formulas for dealing with organizational behavior, find such replies disappointing. Indeed, they often grumble about the inability of OB to offer "straight answers." While we understand the reasons behind such complaints, we feel they are unjustified. People and organizations are complex, so expecting simple answers about them is unfair and a bit naive. Even more important, accuracy, not simplicity, is the ultimate goal of our attempts to understand the human side of work. In the chapters that follow, therefore, we will reflect the prevailing approach in our field. We will do our best to avoid superfluous complexity, but will also steer clear of conclusions that are misleading because, in the quest for simplicity, they overlook much.

OB and the international perspective. A third characteristic of modern OB worthy of mention is its growing adoption, in recent years, of an *international perspective.*[29] This shift involves efforts to understand differences between work settings in various nations and the effects these have on both employees and organizations. In addition, it includes sophisticated attempts to understand how these differences relate to the culture and history of different societies. One well-known example of the latter approach is provided by Ouchi's book, *Theory Z.*[30] In this text, Ouchi first described several major differences between Japanese and American corporations—differences he felt were related to contrasting levels of productivity in these organizations. (Some of the differences noted by Ouchi: guarantees of long-term employment are more common

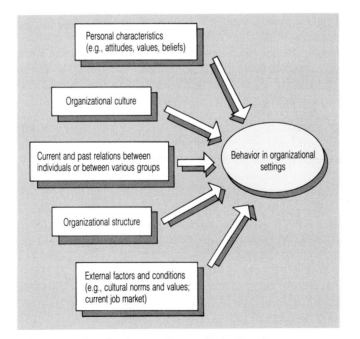

FIGURE 1.8 The Contingency Approach: An Overview

Contingency theory holds that behavior in organizations is a complex function of many interacting factors, processes, and conditions. Because of this, there are usually no straightforward or simple answers to many of the questions investigated by OB.

in Japanese than in American companies; decision making is more likely to be by consensus in Japanese companies; performance is evaluated over longer periods of time in Japanese companies.) Then he related these differences to various cultural and historical factors (e.g., Japanese industry emerged suddenly, out of an essentially feudal society, while American industry developed gradually, in the context of markedly different social conditions). Whether or not Ouchi's conclusions are accepted, there can be little doubt that his book stimulated many persons, including practitioners of OB, to focus more attention on the role of cultural factors in organizational effectiveness.[31]

Given the fact that the economies of most nations are becoming increasingly interdependent, an international perspective seems likely to become an increasingly important aspect of OB in the years ahead. (For an example of the kind of research currently being conducted on international issues, please see the **International Perspective** section below.)

OB: AN INTERNATIONAL PERSPECTIVE

Product Quality in the United States and Japan

In recent years, Japanese products have gained increasing popularity in the United States. Most cameras, virtually all videocassette recorders, and a substantial proportion of automobiles sold in the United States are manufactured in Japan. While price and product design clearly play a role in these trends, another factor seems especially important: quality. Many consumers believe that Japanese products are much more reliable, and much less likely to suffer from defects, than corresponding products manufactured in the United States. Is this actually the case? And if so, what factors are responsible for such differences? A study by Garvin provides some intriguing answers.[32]

In this investigation, product quality was studied at nine U.S. and seven Japanese companies involved in the production of room air conditioners. To assess actual product quality, several measures were employed (e.g., number of assembly-line defects per 100 units, service calls per 100 units during the first year of use). Together, these measures painted a discouraging picture for the American companies: in all cases, the products manufactured in Japan were clearly superior (see Table 1.2). Moreover, this was true even when such comparisons involved only the best American companies.

To determine exactly why these differences existed, Garvin asked first-line supervisors at all the companies to provide information on the causes behind any quality problems they experienced, and also to rate the importance of various manufacturing objectives within their companies. These results, too, were revealing. With respect to the causes of

TABLE 1.2 Product Quality: The Differences Are Real

Air conditioners manufactured in Japan showed much fewer defects than those manufactured in the United States. This was true even when Japanese plants were compared only with the best U.S. plants.

	ASSEMBLY-LINE DEFECTS/100 UNITS	SERVICE CALLS/ 100 UNITS (FIRST YEAR)
Japanese Plants	0.95	0.6
Best U.S. Plants	9.00	7.2
Worst U.S. Plants	135.00	22.9

(Source: Based on data from Garvin, 1986; see Note 32.)

quality problems, Japanese managers were much more likely than their U.S. counterparts to pinpoint faults in materials or purchased parts. In other words, they perceived quality problems as originating outside their own operations. In contrast, U.S. managers were much more likely to attribute such faults to poor workmanship, a problem within their companies. Turning to the relative importance of various manufacturing objectives, Japanese managers indicated that their companies placed great emphasis on producing high-quality (defect-free) products. American managers reported this goal as considerably less important. Conversely, American managers reported a heavy emphasis on meeting production schedules; Japanese managers noted that this goal as somewhat less important in their companies (see Figure 1.9 on page 18).

In sum, Garvin's findings suggest that perceived differences in product quality between Japanese and U.S. companies are indeed real, and that the basis

FIGURE 1.9   Contrasting Views about Quality in U.S. and Japanese Companies

Japanese managers reported that producing defect-free products was more important to their companies than did U.S. managers. In contrast, U.S. managers reported that meeting production schedules received greater emphasis in their companies. (Source: Based on data from Garvin, 1986; see Note 32.)

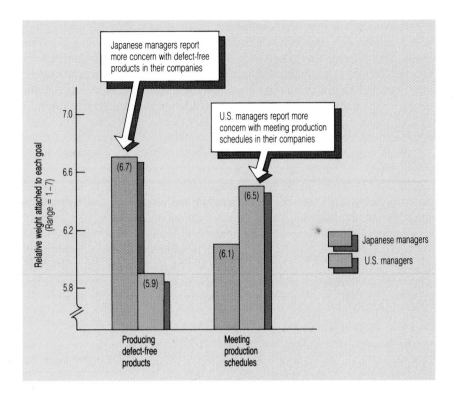

for these differences lies in several causes (e.g., greater concern with quality among Japanese workers; greater emphasis by Japanese management on defect-free products as an organizational goal). In view of these results, Garvin suggests that the key to higher quality in American companies lies not in better equipment or more modern plants (although these are certainly important). Rather, it involves key attitudes held by employees and management alike. As he puts it, ". . . without a management and workforce dedicated to quality, little is likely to be accomplished" (1986, p. 669).

THE SEARCH FOR KNOWLEDGE:
RESEARCH METHODS IN ORGANIZATIONAL BEHAVIOR

OB, we have already noted, is essentially scientific in orientation. Thus, in its efforts to add to our knowledge of organizations and behavior within them, it relies heavily on scientific methods widely employed in several other fields. In this section, we will briefly describe some of these techniques. Our goal here is not to turn you into an expert in such research methods, but simply to provide you with a basic grasp of the logic underlying these techniques and an introduction to how they are actually put to use in systematic efforts to understand important aspects of organizational behavior. We believe that such information will prove useful to you in several respects.

First, it will help you to understand the discussions of specific research projects and their findings presented at many points in this text. Second, it will enable you to evaluate the many statements about work-related behavior you are certain to encounter in your future career. Once you know how research on organizational behavior *should* be conducted, you will be better able to judge whether such statements rest on relatively firm or shaky foundations. Finally, having a basic grasp of the research methods used in OB will enhance your ability to communicate with persons trained in this field, should you encounter them in your own organization. (This is not at all unlikely; persons with advanced training in OB and related fields often work in organizations or are hired as outside consultants to assist with problems relating to employee motivation, organizational conflict, and many other issues.) So, having a working knowledge of the basic research methods used by OB will arm you with one more skill that may prove useful in many ways throughout your own career.

Natural Observation

The simplest, and in some ways most obvious, techniques for acquiring information about organizational behavior is **natural observation**. As this phrase suggests, this approach involves spending time in an organization and simply observing the events and processes that take place. For example, suppose an investigator wanted to determine how employees react to a forthcoming merger with another company. Information about this issue could be obtained by visiting the organization in question and observing what employees say and do in the days or weeks prior to the merger. Further, their behavior could be compared to that during some base line period, before news of the merger was announced. In a variation on this basic theme, known as **participant observation**, an investigator could actually be hired by the organization, and could then observe it from the inside, as an actual member.[33]

Direct observation of organizational behavior offers several obvious advantages. It is applied to actual work settings, and can be used without disrupting normal routines. Further, almost anyone—including persons already employed by the organization—can be trained to use it. On the other hand, it suffers from several limitations. Being so close to the daily functioning of the organization may make it difficult for observers to remain impartial; they may become friendly with several persons, and be strongly affected by such relationships. Similarly, since most of what takes place in organizations is fairly dull and routine, there is a natural tendency to focus on unusual or unexpected events—with the result that observers' conclusions can be distorted by them. Finally, as we will see in chapter 3, all human beings—even the keenest and most observant— have a limited capacity to notice, process, and store incoming information. Accordingly, observers may miss much that is important and reach conclusions that are biased by their selective sample of information. For these reasons, natural observation is not generally viewed, in OB, as a basic method for acquiring scientific knowledge about behavior in work settings. Rather, it is seen as a starting point in this process—a basis for insights and ideas which may then be studied by more systematic means.

The Case Method: Generalizing from the Unique

Suppose that in the study of mergers noted above, an investigator decided she would not simply observe employees in the days or weeks prior to a merger. Instead, she would interview them, focus on specific potential changes (e.g., a rise in experienced levels of stress, the initiation of wild rumors), and in general, use a more detailed and systematic approach. Here, she would be using an approach known as the **case method**. The basic idea behind this strategy is as follows: by studying one organization in depth, we can learn much about processes occurring in many others, and so increase our knowledge of organizational behavior. The case method, too, rests on observation of ongoing events and processes. In contrast to natural observation, however, it involves active questioning of employees and other procedures for gaining information about them, their reactions, and their company.

Because it may involve detailed interviews and the use of questionnaires for measuring attitudes and intentions, the case method often yields more quantitative data than natural observation. However, it suffers from some of the same drawbacks (e.g., investigators may become so involved with a particular organization that they lose some of their objectivity). Further, since each organization is in some way unique, it is not clear that findings and principles can be generalized to others. For these reasons, the case method, too, is often viewed as only the beginning of the research endeavor; it can provide intriguing hypotheses and insights which are then subjected to testing through other, more systematic, methods.

Systematic Observation: Survey Techniques and Correlation

The shifts toward increasing detail and precision mentioned in connection with the case method reach their full development in a third research method—**systematic observation**. This is one of the two major approaches used by modern OB to increase our scientific knowledge of the human side of work, and is currently being applied to virtually every topic considered in this book. In essence, this approach consists of three major steps: (1) identifying **variables** (aspects of people, organizations, or the environment) that might potentially affect organizational behavior; (2) measuring these variables as precisely as possible; and (3) determining whether they are related to one another in any manner.

Deciding which variables are the relevant ones is a complex process, in which researchers draw on previous research, theories of organizational behavior, and even, occasionally, hunches or informal observations. (See our discussion of the role of theory in OB below.) Measuring such variables often involves the use of **surveys**—questionnaires completed by participants in a research project, on which they provide information about their own behavior and their organization. The specific questions asked are chosen or prepared so as to measure the variables of interest. Finally, the data provided by participants are carefully analyzed by statistical procedures, to determine whether these variables are related. Here, the central question is whether changes in one variable are associated with changes in one or more others. The strength of such relationships is often expressed in terms of **correlation coefficients**. These can vary from −1.00 to +1.00; the greater their departure from 0.00, the stronger the relationship between the variables in question. For example, if one variable tends to increase as another rises, this would be reflected in a *positive correlation* (e.g., +.30, +.82). If, instead, one variable decreases as another increases, this would be reflected in a *negative correlation* (e.g., −.18, −.57). Why are correlations useful? Because the stronger the correlation between two variables, the more accurately one can be *predicted* from the other. Thus, for example, if we discover that job satisfaction and voluntary turnover are strongly correlated in a negative direction (the higher employees' job satisfaction, the lower their rate of quitting), we can predict changes in rate of turnover from changes in employee satisfaction in an accurate manner. Let's look at a concrete example of how systematic observation (or the *correlational method,* as it is sometimes termed) might be used.

Imagine that an OB researcher wanted to gather information on the following possibility: interviewers' moods affect the ratings they assign to the job applicants they interview. Specifically, the researcher has reason to suspect that the more positive interviewers' moods, the higher the ratings they assign and that, conversely, the more negative interviewers' moods, the lower the ratings they assign. Together, these predictions constitute the researcher's **hypothesis**—the as yet untested prediction this person wishes to investigate. How could this issue be studied by means of systematic observation? One possibility is that since the researcher has already identified the variables of interest (interviewer's mood, ratings of applicants), she or he would proceed to the next step: devising ways of measuring these variables. Thus, the researcher might develop a brief rating scale on which interviewers (e.g., persons working in the Human Resources Department of several organizations) report their own current moods. Similarly, the researcher would devise questions for assessing the ratings assigned to job applicants by the interviewers (see Table 1.3 for samples of both measures). He or she would then arrange for a large number of interviewers to complete the mood scales each day, before they begin interviewing applicants, and perhaps at the end of each day as well. The same persons would also complete the questionnaire on which they report their ratings of each job candidate. (Of course, no names would be attached to these ratings; the privacy of job applicants would be carefully protected.)

In the final step, the researcher would apply appropriate statistical procedures to the data collected, to determine whether, in fact, ratings assigned to the job candidates do vary with the interviewers' moods. If this analysis yielded a positive correlation (e.g., +.43), evidence supporting the initial hypothesis would be obtained: the more positive interviewers' moods, the more favorable their ratings tend to be.

Corresponding methods can be applied to virtually any aspect of organizational behavior, from leadership effectiveness to the effects of exposure to prolonged job-related stress. Thus, systematic observation is a very valuable research method; indeed, it is one of the most frequently used approaches in OB today. The advantages it offers are both obvious and impressive: it can be adapted to almost any topic, used in many actual work settings with minimum disruption, and is often quite efficient (a large amount of information can be collected relatively quickly). Further, it can be extended to include many variables at once. For example, in the study mentioned above, such variables as interviewers' years of experience, the level or importance of the job in question, and the sex and age of the applicants could all be included in the study. Through statistical techniques known as **regression analysis**, the extent to which each of these variables is related to ratings of the job applicants, and the extent to which considering each variable adds to our ability to predict such ratings, could be assessed. These are very important techniques and are used frequently in research on organizational behavior.

Unfortunately, despite such advantages, systematic observation suffers from one important drawback: *the findings it yields are not conclusive with respect to cause-and-effect relationships*. For example, consider the study described above. Suppose that the correlation between interviewers' moods and ratings of job candidates was +.92. Does

TABLE 1.3   Sample Items in Survey Used for Research Purposes
Items such as these might be used to assess interviewers' current moods (left-hand items) and their ratings of job applicants (right-hand items). Information on both factors (variables) would be required in a study concerned with the possible relationship between them.

Please rate your current mood below. (Circle one number for each)							Please rate the applicant you just interviewed on each of the following dimensions. (Circle one number for each)						
							Suitability for the position in question						
Sad						Happy	Low						High
1	2	3	4	5	6	7	1	2	3	4	5	6	7
Bad						Good	Motivation						
1	2	3	4	5	6	7	Low						High
Tense						Relaxed	1	2	3	4	5	6	7
1	2	3	4	5	6	7	Background/Experience						
							Low						High
							1	2	3	4	5	6	7

the existence of this strong relationship indicate that changes in interviewers' moods *cause* changes in their ratings of employees? This seems like a reasonable conclusion, but in fact, it is impossible to tell. For example, isn't it also possible that when interviewers are in a good mood, they act in a friendlier manner toward applicants than when they are in a bad mood? This friendly treatment, in turn, might put applicants at ease, helping them perform better during the interview. Thus, it may actually be friendly treatment, not the interviewers' moods themselves, that produces the observed effects. In other words, if interviewers treated applicants in a friendly manner, even if they were *not* in a good mood, these persons would perform better and receive higher ratings (see Figure 1.10). Because of such uncertainty, it is important to avoid interpreting even a strong correlation between two variables as evidence for a direct causal link between them. A cause-and-effect relationship may indeed exist, but a correlation between two variables does not guarantee that this is so. Since establishing such causality is one of the key tasks of science, researchers in OB sometimes turn to another approach which does permit such conclusions.

Experimentation: Knowledge through Intervention

The research method referred to above is known as **experimentation** (or the *experimental method*) and many people mistakenly believe that it is both complex and mysterious. In fact, the basic logic behind it is surprisingly simple and involves only two

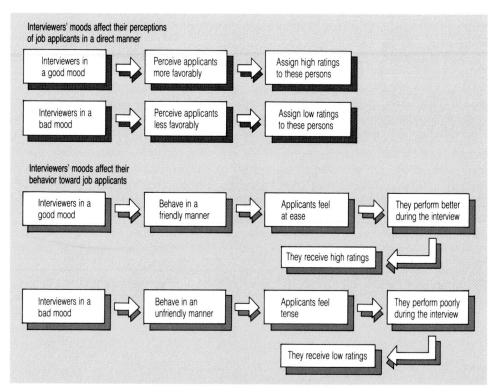

FIGURE 1.10 Why Correlation Does Not Guarantee Causation
The fact that interviewers' moods are correlated with the ratings they assign to applicants does not guarantee a direct causal link between these factors. Interviewers' moods may indeed affect their perceptions of applicants directly. However, it is also possible that good and bad moods affect interviewers' behavior toward applicants, and that this factor, *not* mood, is the crucial one. (If this is so, then interviewers who behave in a friendly manner may rate applicants more highly even if they are not in an especially good mood.)

major steps: (1) the presence or strength of a factor believed to affect some aspect of organizational behavior is systematically varied, and (2) the effects, if any, of such variations are assessed. The idea behind these steps can also be simply stated: if the factor varied does indeed affect organizational behavior, then persons exposed to different levels or amounts of it should also show differences in behavior. For example, exposure to a small amount of the factor in question should result in one level of behavior; exposure to a larger amount should result in a different level, and so on. Generally, the factor systematically varied by the researcher is termed the **independent variable**, while the aspect of organizational behavior measured is termed the **dependent variable**.

In a simple experiment, then, subjects in different groups are exposed to contrasting levels of the independent variable (e.g., low, moderate, high). Their behavior (the dependent variable) is then carefully measured and compared to determine whether it does in fact vary with different levels or amounts of the independent variable. If it does, and if all other factors that might also affect this aspect of behavior are held constant, it can be tentatively concluded that the independent variable does indeed affect the aspect of organizational behavior under investigation. Since our comments up to this point have been somewhat abstract, perhaps a concrete example would be helpful.

Let's return to the study described above—the one concerned with the impact of interviewers' moods on their ratings of job applicants. How could this be investigated by means of experimentation? One possibility is as follows: participants in the project might, as before, be professional interviewers. Now, however, these individuals are randomly assigned to several contrasting conditions in the study. One group is exposed to procedures designed to make their moods more positive (e.g., they are given positive feedback about their performance on some task). A second group, in contrast, is exposed to procedures designed to make their moods negative (e.g., they are given negative feedback on the same task). Finally, a third group is given no feedback; no attempt is made to shift their current moods. Following these procedures, subjects in all three groups interview one or more job applicants who are, in reality, assistants of the researcher. Such persons are carefully trained to behave in a neutral manner, so that what they say and do during the interviews will have minimal impact upon the ratings they receive. This gives any effects of the interviewers' moods on such ratings an opportunity to emerge. After each interview is completed, subjects rate the applicants on several dimensions (e.g., their motivation, suitability for the job, intelligence). In a final step, the data collected are subjected to statistical analysis to determine whether interviewers in the three groups do, in fact, assign contrasting ratings to the applicants. If interviewers in a positive mood rate them highest, those in a negative mood rate them lowest, and those in the *control group* (subjects who receive no feedback) rate them in between (see Figure 1.11 on page 24), support for the hypothesis under study is obtained. (By the way, several studies quite similar to this imaginary one have actually been performed. In general, their results support the hypothesis described above.[34,35])

Because it yields firmer evidence about causal relations between variables, experimentation is often useful to researchers in OB. However, it also has several important drawbacks. First, in order to obtain careful control over factors other than the ones of interest, it is often necessary to conduct such research under artificial conditions, in laboratory settings. As a result, whether, and to what extent, results can be generalized to functioning organizations remains uncertain. (In some cases, it is possible to conduct experiments in natural settings. Such *field studies*, of course, are not subject to the criticism we have just described.) Second, since subjects usually know that they are participating in a study, their behavior may be altered by this fact. For example, they may bend over backwards to present themselves in a positive light or impress

FIGURE 1.11
Experimentation in OB:
A Simple Example

Interviewers placed in a positive mood rate job applicants more favorably than those in a neutral mood. Those placed in a negative mood assign the lowest ratings of all. These findings offer support for the hypothesis that interviewers' moods affect their perception of job applicants. (Note: the applicants in this study were accomplices of the researcher, specially trained to behave in the same neutral manner in all cases.)

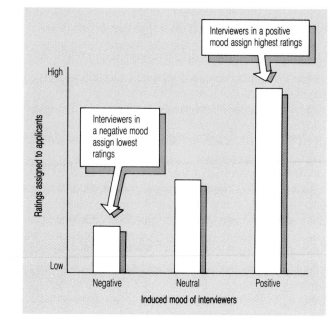

the researcher, and fail to reveal reactions or behaviors they would show under other circumstances. To the extent these effects occur, generalizability of the obtained results is also problematic. Despite such potential problems, however, experimentation remains a basic research tool in OB. When carried out with skill and precision, the results it yields often add substantially to our understanding of organizational behavior and processes. Thus, we will consider many research projects employing this method throughout this text. (Must the persons participating in research projects in OB come from the groups to whom we wish to generalize? Or can valuable information be obtained from other groups, like college students? For some contrasting thoughts on this issue, see the **Research Perspective** below.)

OB: A RESEARCH PERSPECTIVE

College Students as Subjects in Organizational Research: Some Pros and Cons

Have you ever participated in a research project conducted by faculty or graduate students at your university? If so, you know that many studies of human behavior—including organizational behavior—are conducted on college campuses. When such studies are performed to investigate basic aspects of behavior (e.g., memory, personality), few questions about their usefulness are raised. After all, there is no reason to assume that, within limits, findings about such processes obtained with one group of people would not generalize to others, or even to all human beings. When laboratory studies of organizational behavior are conducted with college

students, however, such questions *are* frequently raised. Students, it is argued, have often had little experience working in actual organizations. Moreover, they may be different from employed persons in several respects (e.g., they are younger, hold contrasting attitudes, and so on).[36] As a result, findings gathered from them may not readily generalize to the groups with whom OB is really concerned: persons working in functioning organizations. And indeed, recent studies of this issue suggest that when students and employed persons participate in identical research projects, their behavior sometimes differs in various ways.[37]

In response to such criticisms, other OB researchers have offered the following arguments.[38] First, while college students do indeed differ from persons working in organizations in some ways, they will soon be employed themselves. Thus, the similarities between the two groups are probably much greater than their differences. Second, conducting OB research with employed persons does not, in itself, guarantee generalizability. In fact, in many OB projects, the persons taking part may be less representative of all working people than college students (e.g., in most samples, participants are mainly male, have professional or technical training, and are very homogeneous). Third, and perhaps most important of all, the purpose of experimentation in OB is to study the *processes* affecting behavior in work settings. Information on such matters can be obtained from students as well as from other groups. For example, if we wish to study how individuals combine information to reach complex decisions, we can investigate this topic as readily with college students as with practicing managers, for there is no reason to assume that the underlying processes are radically different in these two groups.

As you can see, there are compelling arguments on both sides of the issue. Where, then, does this leave us? Our view is as follows: when the purpose of research is understanding basic processes in organizational behavior, valuable information can be obtained from a wide variety of participants, including college students. However, it is then the researcher's obligation to establish generalizability by assuring that the groups studied and employed persons do not differ in theoretically important respects, and by replicating the study with persons who *are* representative of the groups to whom results will, ultimately, be generalized.

Theory: Essential Guide to Organizational Research

By this point, you should have a solid grasp of the basic methods of research used by OB. You may still be wondering, though, about where the ideas for specific research projects come from. The answer is: from several sources. On some occasions, the idea for a study is suggested by informal observation of organizations and the activities within them. On others, ideas are suggested by the findings of previous research which yielded puzzling or unexpected results. Perhaps the most important source of research ideas, though, is **theory**. Briefly, theory represents attempts by scientists to answer the question "Why?" It involves efforts to understand precisely *why* certain events occur as they do, or *why* various processes unfold in a specific manner. Thus, theory goes beyond mere description; it seeks explanation. The formulation of comprehensive, accurate theories is a major goal of all fields of science, and OB is no exception. Thus, a great deal of research in our field is concerned with efforts to construct, refine, and test such frameworks. But what, exactly, are theories? And what is their value to OB? Perhaps the best means of answering both questions is through a concrete example.

Imagine that we observe the following: when individuals are given concrete goals, their performance on many tasks improves. (We'll return to this topic in detail in chapter 3.) This observation is certainly useful by itself. After all, it allows us to predict what will happen when goals are introduced (performance will increase), and it suggests a useful means for improving performance in a wide range of settings. These two accomplishments—*prediction* and *intervention* (control)—are major goals of science. Yet, the fact that concrete goals enhance performance does not explain *why* this is so. This is where theory enters the picture.

In older fields such as physics or chemistry, theories usually consist of mathematical equations. In OB, however, they generally involve verbal assertions. For example, a theory designed to explain the impact of goals on performance might read: "When individuals are given concrete goals, they know exactly what they are supposed to accomplish. This increases their motivation and helps them to choose the best strategies for reaching the goal. As a result, performance increases."

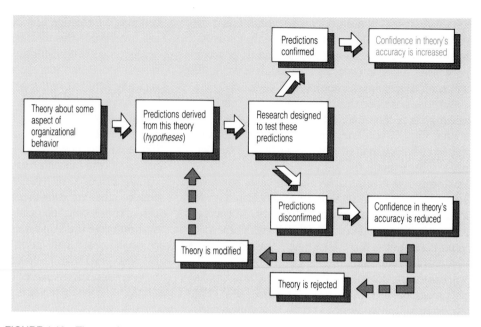

FIGURE 1.12   Theory: An Important Guide to Research in OB
Once a theory has been formulated, predictions derived from it are tested through direct research. If these are confirmed, confidence in the theory's accuracy increases. If they are disconfirmed, confidence in the theory's accuracy diminishes. Then, it may either be modified so as to generate new predictions or, ultimately, be rejected.

Note that this theory, like all others, consists of two major parts: several basic concepts (goals, motivation, task strategies), and assertions concerning the relationships between these concepts.

Once a theory has been formulated, a crucial process begins. First, predictions are derived from the theory. These are developed in accordance with basic principles of logic and are known as *hypotheses*. Next, these predictions are tested in actual research. If they are confirmed, confidence in the accuracy of the theory increases. If they are disconfirmed, confidence in the theory may weaken. Then, the theory may be altered so as to generate new predictions and these, in turn, are tested. In short, the process is continuous, involving the free flow of information between a theory, predictions derived from it, and the findings of ongoing research. (See Figure 1.12 for a summary of this process.)

We will consider many theories in later portions of this book. As each is presented, try to keep these two points in mind: (1) such theories are designed to explain key aspects of organizational behavior, and (2) they should be accepted as valid only to the extent that predictions from them are confirmed in careful research.

USING THIS BOOK: A DISPLACED PREFACE

Before concluding, we would like to comment briefly on several features of this text. Such information is usually included in a Preface, but since people often ignore such notes from authors (!), we chose to insert our comments here.

First, a word on the text's overall organization. It begins by focusing on processes centered mainly on the behavior of individuals (e.g., motivation, attitudes, perception). Next, it shifts to processes occurring in groups (e.g., influence, communication, leadership). Finally, it turns to processes involving entire organizations and the way in which they shape the actions of people working in them (e.g., organizational design, organizational change).

Second, the text contains several features designed to make it easier and more convenient for you to use. Each chapter is preceded by specific learning objectives (goals you should seek to accomplish while reading) and an outline showing the major topics covered. All chapters end with a summary of major points, followed by a glossary of key terms and concepts. These terms are printed in boldface type the first time they are used in the text.

The book also contains three distinct types of special sections. These occur in each chapter (when appropriate) and are clearly cited in the text. The first type, labeled OB: AN INTERNATIONAL PERSPECTIVE, calls attention to differences between organizations in various cultures. Inserts of this type are designed to help you appreciate how such factors influence both individual and organizational outcomes. The second type, labeled OB: A RESEARCH PERSPECTIVE, describes the findings of recent projects in OB or issues relating to the conduct of organizational research. The third type, labeled OB: A MANAGEMENT PERSPECTIVE, indicates how the findings and principles of OB can be applied to management practice to enhance its effectiveness.

Finally, all chapters are followed by several questions for discussion, one or more cases, and an experiential exercise. The discussion questions will help you check your understanding of the key concepts presented, while the cases will assist you in seeing how these concepts and ideas apply to actual work settings. All cases have been carefully prepared to illustrate major points made in the text, and are based on real events in actual organizations. The experiential exercises are designed to provide you with opportunities to see the principles and findings discussed in actual operation.

That concludes this "displaced preface," and our introduction to the field of OB. Now that you know what it is, where it comes from, what it hopes to accomplish (and how), you are ready to consider the core of the field itself—its major findings and principles. Good luck, and may you benefit greatly from the new insights into the human side of work you are certain to acquire.

Summary and Review

The Field of Organizational Behavior. Organizational behavior (OB) seeks knowledge of all aspects of behavior in organizational settings through the systematic study of individual, group, and organizational processes. It uses this knowledge to enhance organizational effectiveness and individual well-being. Because it relies on scientific methods, OB provides much more accurate and systematic knowledge about many aspects of work behavior than does common sense.

The Nature of Organizations. Organizations are social structures or systems in which two or more persons who are somehow interdependent work together to attain common goals. It is sometimes useful to view organizations as **open systems** which receive input from the external environment and then transform it into output through internal processes. Organizations are self-sustaining, maintain a relatively constant internal state, and have both formal and informal internal structures.

Development of the Field of OB. OB can trace its roots to work on **scientific management**, which focused on efficient job design. It was strongly affected by the **human relations approach**, which recognized that work settings are actually complex social systems in which individuals' behavior is affected by a complex interplay between many different factors. It emerged as an independent field of study in the 1940s and 1950s (the first doctoral degree in the field was granted in 1941). However, its major growth and adoption of its current multi-disciplinary approach took place in the 1960s.

Modern OB accepts a **human resources perspective**—the view that under appropriate conditions, most people will work hard and accept responsibility. It is the manager's task to establish such conditions. OB is also characterized by the **contingency approach**—a view recognizing that behavior in work settings stems from so many factors and processes that there are no simple answers to important questions about such behavior. In recent years, OB has adopted an increasingly international perspective on organizations and work settings.

Research Methods in OB. In order to acquire accurate information about behavior in organizational settings, OB employs several methods of research. **Natural observation** and the **case method** are generally viewed as starting points—sources of ideas for further study. In **systematic observation**, potentially important variables are identified and then measured precisely to determine if they are related to one another in any manner. In **experimentation**, one or more independent variables are systematically altered by a researcher in order to determine whether such changes affect one or more dependent variables (usually, aspects of organizational behavior). Much research in OB is carried out to test hypotheses derived from **theories**—efforts to explain specific aspects of organizational behavior or organizational processes.

KEY TERMS

behavioral sciences: Fields such as psychology and sociology that seek knowledge of human behavior and human society through the use of scientific methods.

case method: A method of research in which one organization is studied in detail in order to establish general principles about organizational behavior or organizational processes.

contingency approach: A perspective suggesting that organizational behavior is affected by a very large number of interacting factors.

correlation coefficient: A statistical measure of the extent to which two or more variables are related.

dependent variable: The variable in an experiment that is measured in order to determine whether it is affected by variations in one or more factors.

experimentation: A method of research in which one or more factors are systematically varied to determine if such changes have any impact on one or more variables.

human relations approach: A perspective on organizational behavior that recognizes the importance of social factors and processes in work settings.

human resources model: A view suggesting that under appropriate circumstances, employees are fully capable of working productively and accepting responsibility.

hypothesis: An as yet unverified prediction concerning relationships between specific variables. Such propositions

may be derived from existing theories, or suggested by the findings of previous research or informal observation.

independent variable: The factor in an experiment that is systematically varied by the researcher.

natural observation: A method of research in which an investigator simply observes events and processes occurring in an organization. The observer makes every effort possible to avoid affecting these events or processes by his or her presence.

open system: A self-sustaining system that uses energy to transform input from the external environment into output, which the system then returns to the environment.

organizational behavior: The field that seeks increased knowledge of all aspects of behavior in organizational settings through scientific methods.

organizational culture: The shared beliefs, values, and expectations held by most persons within a given organization.

participant observation: Natural observations of an organization made by individuals who have been hired as employees for the purpose of observing the organization.

regression analysis: Statistical techniques indicating the extent to which each of several variables contributes to accurate predictions of another variable.

scientific management: An early approach to management and organizational behavior emphasizing the importance of effective job design and employee motivation.

OB versus Common Sense: A Demonstration

33

Experiencing
Organizational
Behavior

EXPERIENCING
ORGANIZATIONAL
BEHAVIOR

Over the years, we have sometimes heard students (and others) remark: "Sure, OB is interesting. But isn't it just common sense? Didn't we know all this stuff before there ever was a field of OB?" If you hold such views, or if you know someone else who does, try the exercise below.

Procedure

Read each statement listed below. Then, for each, indicate whether you feel it is true or false. Indicate your answers by inserting a T (for True) or an F (for False) in the spaces provided. Also, rate your confidence in the correctness of your answer on a seven-point scale (1 = very low confidence; 7 = very high confidence).

1. In most cases, leaders should stick to their decisions once they have made them, even if it appears that these decisions are wrong.
   Answer: _____ Confidence: _____
2. When people work together in groups and know that their individual contributions can't be easily observed, they each tend to put out less effort than when they work on the same task alone.
   Answer: _____ Confidence: _____
3. The best way to stop a rumor is to present convincing evidence against it.
   Answer: _____ Confidence: _____
4. As morale or satisfaction among employees increases in an organization, overall performance almost always rises.
   Answer: _____ Confidence: _____
5. Relatively few top executives show the Type A behavior pattern (extreme competitiveness, time urgency, aggressiveness).
   Answer: _____ Confidence: _____
6. Providing employees with specific goals often interferes with their performance; they resent being told precisely what to do.
   Answer: _____ Confidence: _____
7. In most organizations, the struggle over limited resources is a far more important cause of conflict than other factors such as interpersonal relations among organization members.
   Answer: _____ Confidence: _____
8. In bargaining, the best strategy for maximizing long-term gains is seeking to defeat one's opponent.
   Answer: _____ Confidence: _____
9. Even skilled interviewers are sometimes unable to avoid being influenced in their judgments by factors other than applicants' qualifications.
   Answer: _____ Confidence: _____
10. In general, groups make more accurate and less extreme decisions than individuals.
    Answer: _____ Confidence: _____
11. Most individuals do their best work under conditions of high stress.
    Answer: _____ Confidence: _____
12. In general, women are higher in self-confidence than men, and for this reason, expect greater success in their careers.
    Answer: _____ Confidence: _____

Points to Consider

Our suggested correct answers to these questions are listed below. How did you do? If you are like most students in our classes, you probably missed at least several items.

Was your confidence lower on these items than on the others? Perhaps not, because most people think they know more about organizations and behavior in them than they actually do.

Here is another point to consider: the answers listed below really *are* only suggestions. Each of these questions involves complex situations and processes. Thus, in a real sense, there are no simple answers to them. For example, consider question four. Our suggested answer is False, because contrary to what common sense might suggest, research findings indicate that the relationship between job satisfaction and performance is complex. Under some conditions, increments in satisfaction are related to enhanced performance. Under other conditions, this is not the case. So, in a sense, the most accurate answer to this question is really "It depends."

The same general point could be made about many of the other questions posed above. As we noted earlier, where organizational behavior and organizations are concerned, there really are no simple answers. We hope this exercise helps to emphasize that important point.

Correct Answers: T,T,F,F,T,F,F,F,T,F,F,F

CHAPTER TWO

LEARNING: ADAPTING TO THE WORLD OF WORK

CHAPTER OUTLINE

Theories of Learning: An Overview
Classical Conditioning: Learning by Association
Operant Conditioning: Learning through Rewards and Punishments
Observational Learning: Learning by Modeling Others

Reinforcing Desirable Organizational Behaviors
Schedules of Reinforcement: Patterns of Administering Rewards
Organizational Behavior Management: Positively Reinforcing Desirable Organizational Behaviors
Training: Learning and Developing Necessary Job Skills

Discipline: Eliminating Undesirable Organizational Behaviors
The Uses of Discipline
The Impact of Discipline: What Makes Punishment Effective?

Special Sections

OB: An International Perspective
Training Managers for Overseas Assignments: Bridging the Culture Gap

OB: A Research Perspective
Vicarious Punishment in Action: Learning What *Not* to Do by Watching

LEARNING OBJECTIVES

After reading this chapter, you should be able to:
1. Understand the concept of learning and how it applies to the study of organizational behavior.
2. Identify and describe the three major approaches to learning and how they apply to understanding behavior in organizations.
3. Name and distinguish between various schedules of reinforcement.
4. Appreciate how principles of reinforcement may be used in organizational behavior management programs to improve organizational functioning.
5. Understand the principles of learning that make organizational training effective.
6. Describe the conditions necessary for effective use of discipline in organizations.

It was only lunch time, but Jane Sullivan's first day on the job was already over-whelming. There were lots of new things to figure out—everything from who was really in charge and how to use the new equipment, to where the rest rooms were. "I know I'll get the hang of this place eventually," Jane said, frustrated. "The first day at work sure can make your head spin."

"I can understand how confusing it must be for you," said Jane's new coworker, Marge Clayton. "There are a lot of things to learn when you start working at a big company like Peacock Industries. I remember my first day, and it wasn't much better."

Jane nodded as she sipped a well-deserved cup of coffee with her lunch. *Just finding this lunch room was an accomplishment*, she thought to herself. *Hopefully, I'll be able to find my way back to Section B–3 in Building 2. Or was it Section B–2 in Building 3?*

Luckily, after lunch Jane ran into Ted Schmidt, the accounting supervisor she had met earlier in the day. "Going back to the office?" he asked.

"Yes, I am," Jane replied. The whole way back she felt lucky to be spared the embarrassment of admitting she was lost. *First day or not, even in a gigantic place like Peacock*, she thought, *getting lost just isn't acceptable once you're more than eight years old.*

Back at her desk, anxious to return to work, Jane faced a stack of balance sheets she had to audit. *No problem*, she thought. *I've done these before on my last job.* So, she turned to her computer terminal, but to her surprise, a strange image appeared on the screen.

Oh no, I'll have to ask for help on this system, she mused, *but not without first trying it myself.* After about ten minutes, though, all she could do was log onto the system; she couldn't get it to work.

Her frustration must have shown, because Bob Herrington, at the next desk, offered to help. "Let me show you how to use this thing," he volunteered. "We have our own software designed for us here at Peacock; nothing out of the can for us. But you'll get the hang of it."

A few hours later, Jane seemed to catch on fine and had gotten through a few accounts when suddenly, the system froze and the cursor disappeared off the monitor. *Now what*, she asked herself. *Bob looks really busy, and I don't want to be a pest. I know. I'll just re-boot the system and do some word processing. After all, I have some reports to write for the accounts I just audited.*

Fortunately, the word processing system was like the one she had used before. *Nothing to it*, she thought, and worked the rest of the afternoon on her reports.

Before long, it was time to go home. *I'll just print out my reports*, she thought. *But how do they want me to save the file? It's confidential, so perhaps I should lock the data in my computer. But then Ted wouldn't be able to check my work like he said he would. I just don't know.*

In her frustration, Jane did the one thing she shouldn't have—she just switched off her terminal. Gone for good were four hours' worth of words and numbers, vanished into the vast electronic graveyard. "I can't believe it," she grumbled aloud. "I just threw out half a day's work."

I just gotta get out of here, Jane thought. *I can't afford to do any more damage.* So she packed up her belongings and began to leave.

As Jane passed by, Marge said, "Good night, Jane. Hope you had a good first day."

"Good night, Madge," Jane answered. "See you tomorrow."

"It's Marge," she replied.

"I'm sorry," Jane said, blushing. "It's been a really rough first day for me, Marge.

I'm so confused, I can hardly remember my own name." All Jane could think about was what a tough day she'd had and how difficult it was getting used to her new job.

At least I can find my way out of the building, Jane reassured herself. *Now, if I can only remember where I parked my car. . . .*

Surely you can relate to the frustrations Jane is having on her first day at work. Exactly what am I supposed to do? How do I go about doing it? Where do I go? These questions are typical of the challenges people face as they confront new environments. As time goes on, no doubt, Jane will become expert in the things that so confuse her now—her way around the building, the operation of the company's software, the names of her coworkers, and even the best places to park her car. With a little experience, she will surely acquire the skills and knowledge needed to function in the complex world she faces on the job. It is easy to conclude that Jane has lots of things to learn about her new job. Whether we're talking about technical skills, other job knowledge, or study skills, the basic processes of learning are the same (see Figure 2.1). As we will show in this chapter, **learning** is a fundamental process, relevant to many aspects of organizational behavior.[1]

We may define learning as *a relatively permanent change in behavior occurring as a result of experience.*[2] An important element of this definition is that some kind of change in behavior must be evident for us to say that learning has occurred. This change must be more than temporary, and it must be the result of experience—continued contact with the world around us. In other words, the temporary performance changes

FIGURE 2.1 Learning: A Basic Part of Daily Life
There is something in common happening in both of these scenes. In each, someone is in the process of *learning*. The principles of learning explain a variety of human activities.

often brought about by illness or fatigue would not be taken as evidence of learning. Learning cannot be directly observed, but we can infer that it has taken place on the basis of a fairly permanent change in behavior. In our opening example, Jane is in the process of learning how to use her new company's accounting software, her way around the corporate complex, the desired procedures to follow, and the names of her co-workers. Relatively permanent changes in the ways Jane does things on the job because of her experiences may be taken as evidence that she has learned.

Hardly any process is more basic than learning. It is not only responsible for acquiring job skills, but also for attaining such vital information as who really has the power in an organization, how to get things done most effectively, and what you can get away with, to name only a few things. For this reason, we have chosen to cover the topic of learning very early in this book, beginning with a review of some of the most prominent theories of learning advanced in the social sciences. Then, we will apply this information by examining some of the ways learning can be used to help manage desirable behaviors and eliminate undesirable behaviors, showing that the sound application of learning principles is the key to effective management of people in organizations.

THEORIES OF LEARNING: AN OVERVIEW

Several theoretical approaches to learning have developed during this century. Each has its own ways of explaining the learning process, and each focuses on a different set of behaviors. The approaches we will consider are known as **classical conditioning, operant conditioning,** and **observational learning.**

Classical Conditioning: Learning by Association

Imagine, if you will, the following situation. You've always disliked the smell of paint; it makes you sick. After many years of hard work, you've just been promoted to a junior executive position. Congratulations! You now have the power, the prestige, and the fancy office to go with it. Only one problem: the maintenance crew just repainted your newly assigned office, and it's making you ill. The aroma nauseates you for the first few days it lingers in the air. Then, a funny thing happens. Even though the smell is gone after a few days, you have associated the way the office looks and nausea. Now, you feel sick whenever you enter your office. Is this any way for a new executive to act? Actually, it's not at all strange. You're merely the victim of a very strong and well-known type of learning known as **classical conditioning.**

This type of learning was discovered by the Russian physiologist Ivan Pavlov at the beginning of the twentieth century. You are probably already familiar with Pavlov's discoveries concerning a dog's salivation in response to a bell. Pavlov noted that a certain stimulus (known as an *unconditioned stimulus*), such as food, would elicit a naturally occurring reflexive response (known as an *unconditioned response*), such as salivation. Over time, if that unconditioned stimulus was paired with another, neutral stimulus (known as a *conditioned stimulus*), such as a bell, that stimulus would come to elicit a response similar to the naturally occurring, unconditioned response (known as a *conditioned response*)—in this case, salivation. This process of classical conditioning—also known as **Pavlovian conditioning,** after the scientist who first studied it—takes advantage of the natural tendency for some stimuli to elicit some responses automatically, reflexively. By pairing an unconditioned stimulus with another, neutral one, that previously neutral stimulus brings about the same response as the original stimulus. Recently, scientists have noted that this conditioning occurs as a result of a set of cognitive processes. Specifically, as the conditioning proceeds, people respond to the conditioned stimulus because they develop an *expectancy* that it will be followed by the unconditioned stimulus.[3] Just think of how it whets your appetite when you merely see the name and description of your favorite food. Reading the words makes you think about the food, which triggers your appetite. A summary of the classical conditioning process is shown in Figure 2.2. The example on the left shows the process in operation for Pavlov's dogs; the example on the right shows the process in operation in the case of the foul-smelling office.

The process of classical conditioning may help explain a variety of organizational behaviors. For example, workers who have witnessed dangerous industrial accidents after certain warning lights have gone on may be expected to feel fear the next time those lights begin to flash. As another illustration, imagine that you have just been praised by your boss, making you feel good, while standing in front of a new employee unfamiliar to you. Now, whenever you see that new employee, you will associate him or her with the praise you received, and will likely feel good once again. In fact, research has shown that the classical conditioning process actually does operate in this manner in organizations. Specifically, it has been found that we tend to like, and evaluate highly, coworkers we associate with praise we have received ourselves.[4]

Although classical conditioning explains some types of learning in organizations, its usefulness is limited. It deals only with behaviors that are *reflexive* in nature—that is, they are involuntary and occur automatically. The illness experienced at the formerly smelly office, the fear experienced in response to the warning light, and of course, the salivation of Pavlov's dogs are all examples of simple reflexive behaviors. Of course, many behaviors learned on the job are far too complex to be explained in terms of classical conditioning. The next type of learning we will describe, operant conditioning, better explains how we acquire more complex forms of behavior.

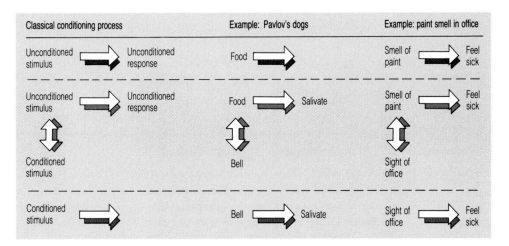

FIGURE 2.2 The Classical Conditioning Process: An Overview
The process of classical conditioning is based on the tendency of some naturally occurring stimulus (the *unconditioned stimulus*) to elicit a reflexive response (the *unconditioned response*). By pairing a previously neutral stimulus (the *conditioned stimulus*) with the unconditioned stimulus, it will eventually elicit a response similar to the unconditioned response (known as a *conditioned response*).

Operant Conditioning: Learning through Rewards and Punishments

Imagine you are a copywriter working at an advertising agency. The vice president just assigned you to an important new account. If you can write the perfect radio script and get it in on time, the company stands a chance of gaining a lot of future business. Knowing it's important, you stay up all night working on it. The next day you present it and . . . finish the ending yourself. Either the client loves it, and your grateful boss gives you a large raise and a promotion, *or* the client hates it, and your angry boss gives you two weeks severance pay and fires you. Regardless of how the story ends, one thing is certain: whatever you do in this situation, you will be sure to either do it again (if it succeeds), or avoid doing it again (if it fails).

This story nicely illustrates an important principle of **operant conditioning** (also known as **instrumental conditioning**)—namely, that our behavior usually produces consequences. If our actions have pleasant effects, then we will be more likely to repeat them in the future. If, however, our actions have unpleasant effects, we are less likely to repeat them in the future. This phenomenon, known as the **Law of Effect,** is fundamental to operant conditioning.[5] As you may know, our knowledge of the operant conditioning process comes from the work of the famous social scientist B. F. Skinner. Skinner's pioneering research (initially with animals, although also with humans—including his own daughter) has shown us that it is through the connections between our actions and their consequences that we learn to behave in certain ways.[6] See the summary of this process and the example shown in Figure 2.3.

One of the things we learn is to engage in behaviors that have positive results, actions that are pleasurable. For example, employees may find it pleasant and desirable to receive monetary bonuses, paid vacations, praise and recognition, and awards. The process by which people learn to perform acts leading to desirable outcomes is known as **positive reinforcement.** Whatever response led to the occurrence of these positive events is likely to occur again, thus strengthening the response. For a reward to serve as a positive reinforcer, it must be made contingent upon the specific behavior sought. An employee may be rewarded for his or her good attendance by receipt of a monetary bonus. But, that bonus is only a positive reinforcer when it is clearly tied to the desired behavior. Employees who do not perceive a link between the good at-

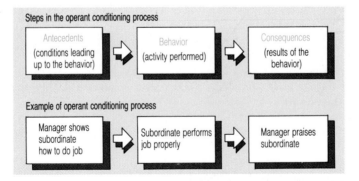

FIGURE 2.3   The Operant Conditioning Process: An Overview

The basic premise of operant conditioning is that people learn by connecting the consequences of their behavior with the behavior itself. In the example shown here, the manager's praise for the subordinate increases the subordinate's tendency to perform the job properly in the future. Learning occurs by providing the appropriate antecedent and consequent conditions.

tendance record and the reward will not be reinforced for their good attendance. Consider the example that opened this section, in which you were an advertising copywriter. If your script is well received, you will probably try that same approach on another campaign. The fact that it was positively reinforced—that is, linked to desired rewards—"teaches" you to make that same response again.

Sometimes we learn to perform acts because they permit us to avoid undesirable consequences. Unpleasant events, such as reprimands, rejection, probation, demotion, and termination, are some of the consequences faced for certain actions in the workplace. The process by which people learn to perform acts leading to the avoidance of such undesirable consequences is known as **negative reinforcement,** or **avoidance.** Whatever response led to the termination of these undesirable events is likely to occur again, thus strengthening that response. For example, imagine that you are involved in a very boring business meeting. When you can no longer stand it, you begin to gather your belongings and recommend breaking for lunch. As everyone concurs and begins to get up, it appears that you have escaped the boredom you faced. You were negatively reinforced for your act of recommending a lunch break, and you will be likely to do the same thing again the next time you are involved in a boring meeting. You learned how to avoid the aversive situation.

Thus far, we have identified responses that are strengthened because they either lead to positive consequences or the termination of negative consequences. However, the connection between a behavior and its consequences is not always strengthened; the link may be weakened. This is what happens in the case of **punishment.** Punishment involves presenting an undesirable or aversive consequence in response to an unwanted behavior. A behavior accompanied by an undesirable outcome is less likely to occur again if the person eventually learns that the negative consequences are contingent upon the behavior. For example, if you are chastised by your boss for taking long coffee breaks, you are considered punished for this action, weakening your tendency to repeat it in the future. It is important to note that punishment is *not* the same as negative reinforcement. Whereas negative reinforcement *removes* an aversive stimulus, thereby increasing the strength of the response that led to its removal, punishment *applies* an aversive stimulus, thereby decreasing the strength of the response that led to its presentation.

The link between a behavior and its consequences may also be weakened via the process of **extinction.** When a response that was once rewarded is no longer rewarded, it tends to weaken; it will gradually die out, or be *extinguished.* Suppose that for many months you and the members of your weekly planning group met in your office for breakfast, and being a congenial host, you supplied the donuts. Your colleagues always thanked you for the donuts, and jealously fought over favorite kinds (i.e., you were positively reinforced through their social approval). Now, however, your colleagues are realizing that they may have eaten too many donuts and have all begun dieting. This time, when you open the box of donuts, nobody says anything. The donuts are tempting, but your colleagues' willpower prevails and the donuts remain in the box, uneaten. If this happens a few more times, you will no longer bother to purchase donuts. Your once-rewarded behavior is no longer rewarded and will eventually die out. This is the process of extinction.

The various relationships between a person's behavior and the consequences resulting from that behavior—*positive reinforcement, negative reinforcement, punishment,* and *extinction*—are known collectively as **contingencies of reinforcement.** The four contingencies discussed are summarized in Table 2.1 (on page 42). As we will see, these contingencies have very important effects on many types of organizational behavior. Selectively reinforcing (either positively or negatively), punishing, and extinguishing behaviors are very effective tools for managing employees.

TABLE 2.1 Contingencies of Reinforcement: A Summary

Here, the four reinforcement contingencies are defined in terms of the presentation or withdrawal of a pleasant or unpleasant stimulus. Positively or negatively reinforced behaviors are strengthened; punished or extinguished behaviors are weakened.

STIMULUS (PRESENTED OR WITHDRAWN)	DESIRABILITY OF STIMULUS	CONTINGENCY	STRENGTH OF BEHAVIORAL RESPONSE
Presented	Pleasant	**Positive reinforcement**	Increases
	Unpleasant	**Punishment**	Decreases
Withdrawn	Pleasant	**Extinction**	Decreases
	Unpleasant	**Negative reinforcement**	Increases

Observational Learning: Learning by Modeling Others

Although operant conditioning is based on the idea that we engage in behaviors for which we are directly reinforced, many of the things we learn—especially on the job—are not directly reinforced. For example, imagine that you're new to the job. On your first day, you see many of your coworkers complimenting your boss on his attire—"Nice suit, Mr. Johnson, looks good." Each time someone says something flattering, the boss stops at his or her desk, smiles, and acts friendly. They're reinforced for complimenting the boss by his return of social approval. Chances are, by observing this, you too will eventually say something nice to the boss, hoping to receive similar social approval. Although you may not have experienced it directly, you would expect those consequences in return for your actions on the basis of what you've observed happening to others.

This example describes another kind of learning, known as **observational learning,** or **modeling.** It occurs when one person acquires new information or behaviors *vicariously*—that is, by observing what happens to others.[7] The person whose behavior is imitated is called the *model*. For someone to learn by observing a model, several processes must occur. (See Figure 2.4.)

First, the learner must pay careful *attention* to the model. Learning will be most effective when models get the attention of others. Models can purposely call attention to themselves in order to facilitate learning. When one worker trains another on the job, he or she may call attention to job performance by asking the trainee to "pay attention, and watch carefully." Second, workers must have good *retention* of the model's actions. The person learning to do the job must be able to develop some verbal description or mental image of the model's actions in order to remember them. If the learner can imagine himself or herself behaving just as the model did—a process known as *symbolic rehearsal*—then learning will be facilitated. Third, there must be some *behavioral reproduction* of the model's behavior. Unless workers are capable of doing just what the model does, they do not have any hope of being able to learn observationally from that model. Of course, the ability to reproduce many observed behaviors may be quite limited initially, but can improve with practice. Finally, there must be some *motivation* to learn from the model. We don't emulate every behavior we see, but focus on those we have some reason or incentive to match—such as actions for which others are rewarded.

Interestingly, in observational learning, the learning process is controlled by the learners themselves. What you learn is, of course, based on what you observe and

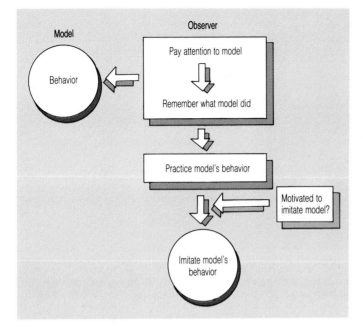

FIGURE 2.4 Observational Learning: An Overview
The process of observational learning requires that an observer pay attention to and remember a model's behavior. By observing what the model did and rehearsing those actions, the observer may learn to imitate the model, but only if the observer is motivated to do so (i.e., if the model was rewarded for behaving as observed).

desire to learn. The more you observe others and carefully attend to what happens to them, the more you can learn from them. You can reward yourself by carefully imitating the successful behavior of others. In many cases, the desire to feel that you have successfully taught yourself something constitutes the only reward received. For example, one of the authors knows someone who used to work for a large commercial bakery, making some of the company's delicious candy products. Every day she observed the pastry chefs working nearby as they made their elaborate cakes and tarts. She diligently watched them mix the various ingredients, bake, assemble, and decorate the cakes. In time, she learned to make them herself, just by watching and practicing on her own. Today, she makes them very well. She was not directly reinforced by rewards offered on the job, but by her own self-approval (feeling good about acquiring her new baking skills).

A great deal of what is learned about how to behave in organizations can clearly be explained as the result of observational learning (see Figure 2.5 on page 44).[8] On the job, observational learning occurs both formally and informally. As we will see, observational learning is a key part of many formal job instruction training programs.[9] Workers given a chance to observe experts doing their jobs, followed by an opportunity to practice the desired skills, and feedback on their work, tend to be very effectively trained. Of course, observational learning also occurs in a very informal, uncalculated manner. Workers who experience the norms and traditions of their organizations, and who subsequently incorporate these into their own behavior, have also learned through observation. In chapter 9, we will show that observational learning is responsible, in part, for the ways new employees are socialized into their organizations (i.e., how they "learn the ropes") and how they come to appreciate their organization's traditions and ways of doing things (i.e., its culture).

FIGURE 2.5 Observational Learning: Learning by Watching and Doing
Many job skills are acquired through the process of observation. The young apprentice shown here can learn a great deal by watching and trying to imitate his more experienced coworker.

REINFORCING DESIRABLE ORGANIZATIONAL BEHAVIORS

One of the most useful purposes of learning in organizations is assuring that desirable job behaviors (e.g., high quality performance, safe job behavior, high attendance, etc.) are developed and maintained. As we have just discussed, an effective mechanism for getting people (and animals, too) to behave in a desired fashion is through reinforcement. A **reinforcer** is any event (a pay raise, praise, etc.) that increases the probability of the behavior preceding it. For example, praising an employee for superb performance on a special project positively reinforces the employee's good work. In other words, it increases the chance that he or she will do just as well the next time a similar project comes along (see Figure 2.6).

For reinforcement to be effective, it must be properly administered—which is easier said than done. Indeed, companies sometimes make the mistake of inadvertently

FIGURE 2.6 Praise: An Important Organizational Reinforcer
Praising employees for their good work is an effective way of ensuring that they will continue performing well in the future. It would probably work in this case, if only Ralph weren't so impatient and insulting. (Source: Reprinted with special permission of NAS, Inc.)

reinforcing the very behaviors they wish to eliminate (e.g., some companies may reinforce the wasting of money by raising the budgets of departments that spent all their money the previous year).[10] On the other hand, proper use of a reinforcer, such as a supervisor's praise, is credited for saving one large company, Emery Air Freight, $3 million in a three-year period.[11] Management's recognition of and praise for good employee performance lowered turnover and improved productivity, resulting in Emery's dramatic financial gain. Obviously, it is important to consider how to use reinforcement effectively in organizations. Our discussion of effective reinforcement practices includes two systematic approaches to reinforcing desired behavior: **organizational behavior management** programs, and **training** programs. First we will take a closer look at the patterns of reinforcement administration, better known as **schedules of reinforcement.**

Schedules of Reinforcement: Patterns of Administering Rewards

Although rewards may help reinforce desirable behavior, it is not always practical (or, as we will see, advisable) to reward employees for everything they do that may be worthy of reward. Rewarding *every* desired response made is called **continuous reinforcement.** Unlike an animal learning to perform a trick, people on the job are rarely reinforced continuously. Instead, organizational rewards tend to be administered following **partial reinforcement** schedules—that is, rewards are administered intermittently, with some desired responses reinforced, and some not. Four varieties of partial reinforcement schedules have direct application to organizations.[12]

1. Fixed interval schedules are those in which reinforcement is administered the first time the desired behavior occurs after a specific amount of time has passed. For example, the practice of issuing pay checks each Friday at 3:00 P.M., or receiving pay raises once a year on the anniversary date of hiring are good examples of fixed interval schedules. In both instances, the rewards are administered on a regular, fixed basis. Fixed interval schedules are not especially effective in maintaining desired job performance. For example, clerical workers who know that their boss will pass by their desks every day at 11:30 A.M. will make sure they are working hard at that time, and will surely avoid taking an early lunch. However, without the boss around to praise or reprimand at other times, they will be less likely to work as hard because they know that positive reinforcement or punishment will not be forthcoming.

2. Variable interval schedules are those in which a variable amount of time (based on some average amount) must elapse between the administration of reinforcements. For example, a bank auditor who pays surprise visits to the various branch offices on an average of every eight weeks (e.g., visits may be six weeks apart one time, and ten weeks apart another) to check their books is using a variable interval schedule. So, too, is a boss who passes the desks of his or her employees at unannounced times once a day—perhaps 9:30 A.M. on Monday, but 4:30 P.M. on Tuesday. Because the staff members in both examples cannot tell exactly when they may be rewarded, they will tend to perform well for a relatively long period. They may slack off after they have been reinforced, but they cannot stay that way for long because they don't know how long they'll have to wait until they are reinforced again. It may be sooner than they think.

3. Fixed ratio schedules are those in which reinforcement is administered the first time the desired behavior occurs after a specific number of such actions have been performed. For example, migrant farm workers are often paid a certain amount based on the number of boxes or pounds of fruit or vegetables they pick. In fact, any type of *piecework pay system* constitutes a fixed ratio schedule of reinforcement. As another example, employees may know that they will receive a monetary bonus and/or praise from their boss each time they exceed a certain level of production or sales. Immediately after receiving the reinforcement, work may slack off, but it will then pick up again as workers approach the next performance level at which the reinforcement is administered.

4. Variable ratio schedules are those in which a variable number of desired responses (based on some average amount) must elapse between the administration of reinforcements. For example, a salesperson might receive a sizeable bonus every time an average of twenty sales are made, but sometimes the bonus may be given after only fifteen sales, sometimes after twenty sales exactly, and others after twenty-five. As a result of not knowing how many desired responses are necessary in order to be rewarded, salespeople may work diligently in the hope of being reinforced for their next successful job performance. A classic example of the effectiveness of variable ratio schedules is playing slot machines. Since these devices pay off after a variable number of plays, the gambler can never tell whether or not the next coin inserted and pull of the handle will hit the jackpot. It is this lack of knowledge about what will happen that makes the variable ratio schedule so effective in maintaining performance.

As we have described them here, the various schedules of reinforcement have a number of important similarities and differences. We have summarized these in Table 2.2. As you review this table, it is important to keep in mind that these schedules of reinforcement represent "pure" forms. Used in actual practice, however, many reinforcement schedules may be combined, thereby making complex new schedules. For example, a company's promotion policy may require that promotions be given only after a fixed interval of time has passed (e.g., five years of job experience) *and* a fixed amount of successful performance is demonstrated (e.g., $1 million in sales). In such a case, the reward (the promotion) is based on both a fixed interval and fixed ratio schedule. Whether they operate separately, or in conjunction with one another, it is important to be aware that different schedules of reinforcement can exert strong influences on organizational behavior.

Research has shown that people perform quite differently in response to various schedules of reinforcement. For example, Saari and Latham compared the job perfor-

TABLE 2.2 Schedules of Reinforcement: A Summary

The four schedules of reinforcement summarized here represent different ways of systematically administering reinforcements intermittently (i.e., according to a partial reinforcement schedule).

SCHEDULE OF REINFORCEMENT	DESCRIPTION	EXAMPLE
Fixed interval	Rewards given after a constant amount of time has passed	Pay check given the same time each week
Variable interval	Rewards given after a variable amount of time has passed	Bank auditor visits branch offices an average of once every eight weeks, but not on a fixed schedule
Fixed ratio	Rewards given after a constant number of actions performed	Pay of $1.00 is given for every five boxes of fruit picked and packed
Variable ratio	Rewards given after a variable number of actions performed	A slot machine pays a jackpot, on average, one time per million plays

mance of beaver trappers working for a paper products company in the Pacific northwest who were paid under different schedules of reinforcement.[13] Before the study began, the trappers were paid a flat rate of $7 per hour, regardless of their job performance (i.e., their reward was administered *noncontingent* on performance). The experiment augmented their base salary in one of two ways contingent on their job performance— following either a continuous reinforcement schedule, or a variable ratio schedule. Those receiving continuous reinforcement were paid $1 for each beaver they caught. Those on a variable ratio schedule were given $4 whenever they caught a beaver *and* then twice correctly predicted an odd or even outcome on two consecutive rolls of a pair of dice. Because the chance of making these predictions correctly is one in four, the workers paid on a variable ratio basis had, over time, the opportunity to earn the same amount of money as their coworkers paid $1 per beaver caught. Despite this, those paid using the variable ratio schedule were over 70 percent more productive than those paid according to a continuous reinforcement schedule. (By the way, you may find it interesting to know that the trappers went along with these unusual pay plans because they supplemented the base pay normally received.) After either contingent pay plan was introduced, the level of productivity almost doubled (see Figure 2.7).

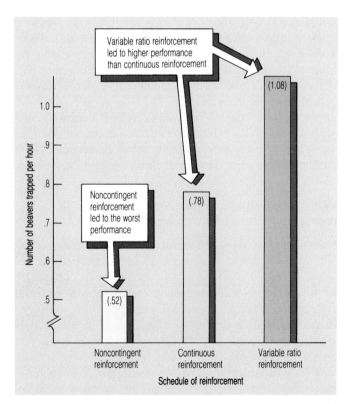

FIGURE 2.7 The Effectiveness of Variable Ratio Schedules: An Experimental Demonstration

An experiment compared the job performance of beaver trappers originally paid on a noncontingent (flat salary) basis with their performance after a contingent pay schedule (either a continuous reinforcement schedule or a variable ratio schedule) was introduced. As the results described here show, making pay contingent upon performance improved individual productivity. The improvement was greater when the payment was made on a variable ratio schedule compared to a continuous reinforcement schedule. (Source: Based on data in Saari & Latham, 1982; see Note 13.)

Findings such as these provide a good example of the effectiveness of contingent reinforcement, especially variable ratio schedules of reinforcement. In general, research has found that many kinds of organizational rewards (e.g., praise, time off) made contingent on the performance of specific desirable behaviors (i.e., employees paid according to ratio schedules) tend to be effective in raising performance. In contrast, rewards contingent on the passage of time (i.e., interval schedules) tend to be less effective in enhancing performance.[14] Certainly, this makes sense. You would probably find yourself working harder if your pay raises were based on how productive you were than you would if you knew that the same pay raise was automatically forthcoming regardless of your productivity. As a result, it is not surprising that many previously hard-working employees tend to become less productive when pay plans that make their pay contingent upon job performance (known as *merit-pay* plans, or *pay-for-performance* plans) are eliminated in favor of systems in which raises are given on the basis of seniority.[15]

Another well established finding is that, in general, partial reinforcement schedules tend to make learned behaviors more resistant to extinction than continuous reinforcement schedules.[16] In other words, once rewards are no longer administered, the previously reinforced behaviors will continue for a longer time after intermittent reinforcement than after continuous reinforcement. This makes sense given that persons receiving continuous reinforcement would sooner detect the lack of reinforcement than those who did not expect to be reinforced for every desirable action. As an example, imagine that Latham and Saari stopped paying their beaver trappers contingent on their performance. If this occurred, we would expect to find that those paid on a variable ratio schedule would continue working longer than those reinforced continuously. Although this was not done, partial (or intermittent) reinforcement schedules are well known for producing greater *resistance to extinction* than continuous schedules, and this represents one of the major advantages of using them.

The central point of our discussion is that job behaviors can be influenced by the selective application of learning principles. Given this, we will now direct our attention to systematic attempts at using principles of reinforcement to induce desirable organizational behaviors, a practice known as **organizational behavior management.**

Organizational Behavior Management: Positively Reinforcing Desirable Organizational Behaviors

Earlier, in describing operant conditioning, we noted that it is the consequences of our behavior which determine whether we repeat or abandon it. Behaviors that are rewarded tend to be strengthened, repeated in the future. Accordingly, it is possible for us to selectively administer rewards to help reinforce behaviors that we wish repeated in the future. This is the basic principle behind **organizational behavior management** (also known as **organizational behavior modification,** or more simply, **OB Mod**). Organizational behavior management may be defined as *the systematic application of positive reinforcement principles in organizational settings for the purpose of raising the incidence of desirable organizational behaviors.* We will begin our presentation of organizational behavior management by reviewing the steps for successfully implementing such programs. We will then discuss some actual programs that have been used in industry. Finally, we will conclude this section by considering the ethical implications of organizational behavior management programs.

Steps in program development. In order to be effective, organizational behavior management programs must follow certain steps in their development (see Table 2.3).[17] The first step involves *pinpointing the desired behaviors.* It is easy to say that you want

**TABLE 2.3   Developing an Organizational Behavior Management Program:
Some Basic Steps**

The general steps of an organizational behavior management program are
listed here, along with an example of how each step may be applied in the case
of improving secretaries' typing speed.

STEP	EXAMPLE
1. Pinpoint the desired behavior	Improve typing speed
2. Perform a baseline audit	Currently typing at 50 wpm
3. Define criterion standard	Desired typing speed is 65 wpm
4. Select a reinforcer	Praise improvements in typing speed
5. Selectively reward desired behaviors approximating the goal, until it is reached	Praise when performance improves to 55 wpm, again at 60 wpm, and again when the goal of 65 wpm is met
6. Periodically re-evaluate	Monitor typing for changes in performance; alter goal and/or administer new reinforcers as needed

job performance to improve, but it is important that you first specify exactly what aspect
of performance you want to see changed. For example, instead of saying you wish to
improve customer service, it would be better to say that you will answer your customers' inquiries more quickly.

The second step is to *perform a baseline audit*. This involves determining the rate
at which the desirable (i.e., pinpointed) behavior already occurs. It is, of course, necessary to identify the baseline rate of desirable behaviors so that any changes in these
behaviors resulting from the reinforcement can be identified.

Third, *define a criterion standard*. Precisely what performance goal is being sought?
What will constitute the level of performance desired from your employees? For example, do you want them to increase their wearing of hard hats by 20 percent, 40
percent, or more? The exact performance level desired must be specified.

Fourth, *choose a reinforcer*. What will be the consequence of performing the desired
behavior? This is an important decision. Whatever it is, the reinforcer should be something that supervisors can deliver in a timely fashion immediately after the desired
behavior. After all, for a reward to reinforce behavior, the connection between the
desired behavior and the reward must be made. Praise is commonly used as a reinforcement in many organizational management programs. So, too, are rewards such
as time off from work, small gifts, and the like.

Next, it is considered useful to *selectively reward desired behaviors that approximate
the criterion standard*. In other words, it would speed the learning process if employees
were reinforced for improving their behavior in the general direction of the desired
standard. The process of selectively reinforcing behaviors approaching the goal is known
as **shaping.** For example, imagine that the baseline rate of wearing safety goggles on
the job is 62 percent, and you wish to raise it to 95 percent. After a few days, the rate
of wearing the goggles increases to 71 percent. Although the desired rate has not been
met, it has improved, and the employees should be praised for moving in the right
direction. Saying, "I'm really glad to see you're wearing your goggles; keep it up" would
surely help. (Although this may sound hokey to you, subordinates tend to be quite
sensitive to the praise they receive from their superiors, and may find such remarks
highly reinforcing.) Then, you would only give more praise when the rate of goggles-
wearing has increased more and more until the desired goal is reached.

Finally, after the desired goal has been attained, it would be useful to *periodically
re-evaluate the program*. Is the goal behavior still performed? Are the rewards still

working? It is not unusual to expect some changes in these events over time. As a result, it is important to audit the behavior in question. Without careful monitoring, the behaviors you worked so hard to develop may change.

Organizational behavior management in action: Some examples. Research has shown that principles of reinforcement have been used effectively to improve a variety of organizational behaviors.[18] The technique has been used in a wide range of organizations, such as Michigan Bell, United Airlines, Chase Manhattan Bank, IBM, Procter & Gamble, and General Electric, to cite just a few well-known companies.[19]

As one example of an effective organizational behavior management program, let's consider the bonus system used by the City of Detroit to improve the performance of its garbage collectors in the early 1970s.[20] The city was interested in reducing the costs of its refuse collection operation, and with the cooperation of the unions involved, instituted a bonus system to reward the workers for increased efficiency. The plan established a pool of savings based on reductions in the numbers of hours worked, reductions in overtime costs, the percentage of routes completed on schedule, and the cleanliness of the routes serviced. The city and the refuse workers agreed to split the savings on a 50–50 basis. The program was considered a great success, as improvements were found on all the criterion measures. Everyone benefitted: in 1974, the city saved $1,654,000; each employee received a bonus of $350; and citizen complaints decreased markedly.

Another successful example of an organizational behavior management plan in operation can be found at Diamond International of Palmer, Massachusetts, a plant with 325 employees that manufactures Styrofoam egg cartons.[21] In response to sluggish productivity and strained relations with employees, a simple but elegant and effective reinforcement system has been put into place. Any employee working for a full year without an industrial accident is given twenty points. Perfect attendance is given another twenty-five points. Once a year, the points are totalled. When workers reach one hundred points, they get a blue nylon jacket with the company's logo and a patch indicating their membership in the "100 Club." Workers earning over one hundred points receive extra rewards. For example, in exchange for 500 points, workers can select a blender, a set of cookware, a wall clock, or a pine cribbage board. Although the workers can well afford these inexpensive prizes, they recognize these items as tokens of appreciation. This plan has helped improve things at Diamond International dramatically. Compared to before the reinforcement program was initiated, productivity improved 16.5 percent, quality-related errors were reduced 40 percent, grievances decreased 72 percent, and time lost due to industrial accidents was lowered by 43.7 percent. The result of all of this has been over $1 million in gross financial benefits. Needless to say, here is an example of a very simple and very effective organizational behavior management program.

These are only a few examples of many effective organizational behavior management programs that have been employed (for a summary of several others, see Table 2.4). Although other programs may have brought about less spectacular results, most organizational behavior management programs have been quite successful. Research has found such programs to be effective in improving the quantity and quality of performance, reducing absenteeism, improving employee safety, reducing waste and theft, and improving customer service.[22]

Before concluding this section, we should note that not all reinforcement contingencies need to be administered by supervisors. Some theorists and practitioners, inspired by the observational learning approach, have recognized that employees may be able to improve their own behavior by rewarding themselves appropriately.[23] The key is for employees to catch themselves performing correctly, and to praise or somehow otherwise reward themselves for doing so. One recommendation for doing this is

TABLE 2.4   Organizational Behavior Management Programs: Some Success Stories

Although not all organizational behavior management programs are as successful as the ones summarized here, many have been extremely effective in bringing about improvements in desired behaviors.

COMPANY	REINFORCERS USED	RESULTS
General Electric	Praise and constructive reinforcement	Productivity increased, cost savings resulted
Weyerhauser Co.	Contingent pay, and praise/recognition	Productivity increased in most work groups (18–33 percent)
B. F. Goodrich Chemical Co.	Praise and recognition	Production increased over 300 percent
Connecticut General Life Insurance Co.	Time off based on performance	Chronic absenteeism and lateness drastically reduced

(Sources: Based on Hamner & Hamner, 1976, Note 19; and Frederiksen, 1982, Note 14.)

that employees carefully observe and keep a record of their own job performance. Workers must systematically monitor their performance (e.g., words per minute typed) in order for them to recognize and feel good about improvements. Through observation, and trial-and-error, improvements in performance may be noted. Once this happens, workers can reward themselves. They may, for example, praise themselves, or allow themselves to put off doing a less preferred job. Although the effectiveness of such *self-managed reinforcement plans* has yet to be firmly established, they represent an interesting new direction for the field of organizational behavior management. If nothing else, such research shows that the management of organizational behavior may be the result of not only operant conditioning principles, but observational learning principles as well.

A question of ethics. Despite their apparent effectiveness—or, perhaps, because of it—organizational behavior management programs have generated some criticism. One of the primary criticisms is that such programs tend to be too demeaning, manipulative, and "controlling" of human behavior, and as such are unethical.[24] Although we encourage you to make up your own mind on this issue, it is certainly important to put a few key issues in perspective.

No doubt, positive reinforcement is a form of manipulation, but as Skinner reminds us, we are all constantly influencing (hence, manipulating) each other, and such impact is inevitable. Hence, the key question is *not* whether we influence each other through our actions, but whether such influence is constructive.[25] In the case of organizations, the proper use of reinforcements may not only improve profitability for the organizations involved, but for employees as well. This is certainly true in the case of the studies we have reviewed here. It is probably rare that managers would somehow misuse reinforcement contingencies to control employees in any inappropriate ways. Indeed, it is doubtful that employees would allow this to happen, making the manager's questionable actions self-defeating. Thus, we believe that organizational behavior management is, like any other technique used in the social sciences, inherently neutral. It is only as "good" or "evil" as the person using it.

Thus far, we have been relatively vague about the processes through which employees learn to perform the skills needed to do their jobs. Systematic efforts at establishing needed job skills are referred to as **training.**

Training: Learning and Developing Necessary Job Skills

One of the most obvious uses to which principles of learning are applied in organizations is that of *training*. Training may be defined as the process by which people systematically acquire and improve the skills, abilities, and attitudes needed to improve job performance.[26] Just as your classroom training in school is designed to prepare you for basic life skills, the training of employees is designed to prepare them to operate with maximum effectiveness on the job. Training can be used not only to prepare newly hired individuals for the jobs they are about to face by teaching them the required skills, but also to upgrade and further develop the skills of existing employees (see Figure 2.8). Thus, training is an extensive, ongoing activity in most organizations. As evidence, consider this statistic reported by the Carnegie Foundation: American industrial corporations spend more than $40 billion annually on training their employees.[27] Obviously, then, we are talking about a process that has great relevance to organizations—a process which, when effective, puts to practical use the various principles of learning we have described thus far.

Identifying training needs and objectives. Given the staggering sums of money spent on industrial training, it is no wonder organizations are interested in identifying the people and situations that would most benefit from training. Certainly, not everyone can be trained in everything. So, to determine who should be trained in what skills, organizations typically perform a *needs assessment*—a systematic procedure for diagnosing required areas of training. This may be done in many ways: asking managers to identify those areas in which their work force is most deficient; asking trainees to identify areas they wish to learn more about; checking company records for evidence of problems (e.g., high accident rates may indicate the need to train employees in safety measures).

After a training need has been identified, it is helpful to identify a specific behavioral objective, or goal, that is sought from the training. For example, supermarket employees being trained in the store's inventory may be required to correctly identify the aisle location of 95 percent of the items carried. This goal would help focus on the exact kinds of things trainees should know and help identify the extent to which training

FIGURE 2.8 Training: Some of Its Many Forms
A wide variety of training techniques are used to improve the skills of employees.

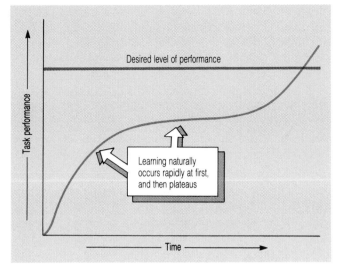

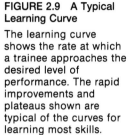

FIGURE 2.9   A Typical Learning Curve

The learning curve shows the rate at which a trainee approaches the desired level of performance. The rapid improvements and plateaus shown are typical of the curves for learning most skills.

was effective. Specifying such goals helps trainers identify the specific content areas to be covered. Without specifying this in advance, it is easy to waste time training people to perform skills that may not be relevant to their jobs.

Principles of effective training. Once it has been determined exactly what trainees are expected to learn, it is possible to design a training program using one or several of the methods we will describe shortly. Regardless of what method is used to teach the job skills, it is important to understand that the aim of any training program is to get trainees to perform at the desired level (i.e., to reach the stated behavioral objective) as quickly as possible. It is a basic principle of training that learning does not take place evenly. Instead, it occurs in bursts and plateaus. This tendency may be observed in what is known as a **learning curve**—a graph showing the rate at which learning occurs. Although different skills are acquired at different rates and follow different patterns, it is instructive to look at a typical learning curve, such as the one shown in Figure 2.9. This diagram shows that learning may, at first, be very rapid, and then level off, or plateau. Then, after repeated training over time, the rate of learning will raise up again. The aim of training is to get the trainee's performance up to the desired level as quickly as possible.

If you try to recall the things that have helped you learn various skills, such as how to study, type, or drive, you can probably appreciate some of the principles that help make training effective. Four major principles are most relevant.

1. *Participation* occurs when trainees are actually involved with the desired skills. People learn more quickly, and tend to retain the learned skills, when they actively participate in learning. For example, students who actively participate in class may be more effective learners than those who just sit passively. Similarly, although there is something to be learned about swimming by reading about it, there is no substitute for participation.

2. *Repetition* of the desired behavior has been shown to improve learning. Although it isn't always fun to memorize a poem or a script, the process of constantly repeating it certainly helps you learn it. It works! After all, that's how you learned the alphabet and the multiplication table. In learning many job skills, research has shown that practice makes perfect.[28]

3. *Transference* is the degree to which what is learned during a training program can be applied to the job. The more closely a training program matches the demands of the job, the more effective training will be.[29] It is with this principle in mind that very elaborate simulation devices are used in the training of astronauts and pilots. By using sophisticated computer-based techniques to carefully simulate real flight conditions, trainees can learn what it is like to manipulate their craft safely, without actually having to risk the loss of their lives and expensive equipment. The same principle applies as well to more "down to earth" jobs. For example, the greater the similarity between the cash register you learn to use during a training session and the one you use on the job at the checkout stand, the more your training will effectively transfer to the new job.

4. *Feedback* is the process of giving trainees progress reports on the effectiveness of their training.[30] For learning to be more effective, trainees must be told how well they are doing. Knowing what you are doing right and wrong is important in helping you keep up the good work and avoid repeating mistakes. Just as you need test grades to gauge the effectiveness of your learning in this class, employees need to know how well they're doing. For example, persons being trained as word processing operators will certainly find it useful to know how many words they have typed per minute in order to judge whether they have improved.

These principles—participation, repetition, transference, and feedback—are the key to the effectiveness of any training program. The most effective training programs are those that incorporate as many of these principles as possible. A variety of methods for conducting training programs exist. These range from the most simple, "show and tell" approach of job instruction training, to very complicated simulation devices used off the job. We identify and summarize some of the most commonly used job training techniques in Table 2.5. Please review this table carefully. We think you'll find it in-

TABLE 2.5   Training Techniques: A Summary of Some Popular Methods

As shown here, employee training can take many forms, some very simple, and others quite elaborate. The techniques may be distinguished with respect to whether the training takes place on the job or off the job.

TRAINING METHOD	DESCRIPTION
On-the-Job Methods	
Apprenticeship programs	An inexperienced trainee works alongside a senior coworker for a certain number of years; often accompanied by formal classroom training; used to train skilled trade workers (e.g., carpenters, electricians)
Job instruction training	Trainees are told about the job, instructed on how to do it, allowed to try out the job, given feedback, and then permitted to work on their own (with someone nearby to help, if needed)
Off-the-Job Methods	
Films/video presentations	Complex procedures not easily demonstrated in person may be shown on film or videotape. Because questions cannot be asked, presentations are often used in conjunction with a live lecture by a knowledgeable trainer
Simulations	Simulations may range from the most simple procedures, such as cases and role-playing exercises used to train managers in interpersonal skills, to the most complex computer-assisted simulations used to train astronauts for space flights

teresting to see the range of methods used to train workers. (Although these training methods can be used for a variety of purposes, some types of training are designed for specific purposes. In the **International Perspective** section below, we describe and compare the effectiveness of some training techniques used for a highly specialized, important purpose, preparing managers for overseas assignments.)

OB: AN INTERNATIONAL PERSPECTIVE

Training Managers for Overseas Assignments: Bridging the Culture Gap

In this era of multinational corporations and the growing global economy, more organizations are doing business abroad than ever before. One of the most important challenges this creates is preparing workers for assignments in other nations. Cultural differences may impose a potent barrier between people trying to conduct business, an impediment that goes beyond speaking different languages. As one American business executive learned the hard way, it is crucial to know a people's social traditions as well as their language. While attending a party with his business cohorts in the Middle East, an American manager casually asked his native colleague how his family was doing. Because this culture permitted these kinds of inquiries among only the most intimate of associates, the American unknowingly committed a serious social blunder that alienated his native colleague.[31] Difficulties in adjusting to different cultures may be responsible for as many as 30 percent of the unsuccessful foreign placements made by American multinational companies.[32] So it is important to consider how persons doing business abroad can avoid culture shock and minimize the chances of offending foreign hosts by learning about the other culture in advance of their assignments.

What training methods are most effective in preparing people for intercultural work assignments? A recent study by Earley reveals some potentially useful answers.[33] Eighty managers employed by an American electronics firm, who were about to spend three months in Seoul, South Korea, participated in this investigation. One group of managers received advance training in the form of practice in interpersonal relations. They learned about South Korean culture through several methods, including participating in a simulated cocktail party in which persons knowledgeable about South Korean culture worked with them on appropriate types of interaction (e.g., greetings and introductions, types of

conversations). In addition, managers trained via this *interpersonal approach* also visited an Asian community near their homes to help further familiarize them with the culture in which they would be living. In contrast, those trained by way of the *documentary approach* studied Korean culture by reading about it in printed materials prepared from various books and reports. Although their training covered much the same material as that in the interpersonal approach (e.g., the tendency for Koreans to make eye contact with others only when responding to a superior), they received no hands-on experience. There were two additional groups in the study—one receiving both types of training, interpersonal *and* documentary, and a control group receiving *no training* at all. After being trained, the managers went to Seoul to work. How well did these various groups adapt to their new environments? The results are summarized in Figure 2.10 (on page 56).

One of the key measures of the effectiveness of training was how well the managers' supervisors thought they were performing their jobs. As you can see from the left side of Figure 2.10, the interpersonal approach and the documentary approach were approximately equal in effectiveness. However, the two approaches used together were more effective than either one used alone. Also measured were the managers' own assessments of the difficulties they had in making the adjustment to their new culture. The data summarized on the right side of Figure 2.10 show that managers receiving both types of training found it easier to adjust to their new culture than those receiving just one type of training (although either type of training was far more effective than no training at all).

These results show that training for intercultural assignments can help workers ease their transition into their new cultures and also perform their jobs more effectively. Hands-on training in interpersonal customs and simply reading documentary material

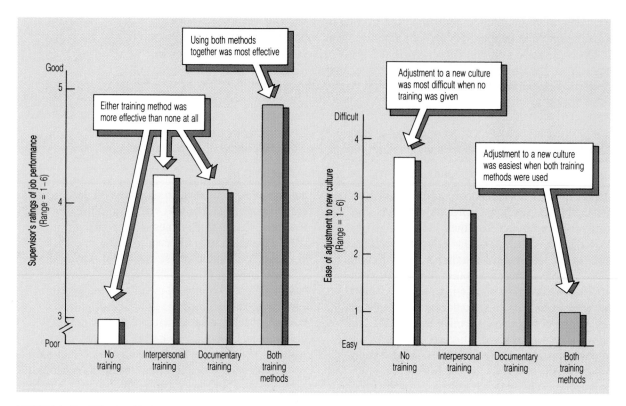

FIGURE 2.10 Effective Methods of Avoiding "Culture Shock": Empirical Evidence

As shown here, research has demonstrated the effectiveness of using both interpersonal and documentary approaches for preparing managers for overseas placements. Used together, these techniques not only eased workers' adjustments to their new cultures, but also improved their job performance. (Source: Based on data in Earley, 1987; see Note 33.)

about the host nation's culture were each effective in promoting cultural awareness. However, the best results came when both techniques were used together. Such evidence makes a very strong case for the value of carefully training workers in advance of overseas assignments. The time and effort spent in such training clearly pays off—for both the company and the workers themselves.[34]

Training through observational learning. It should be apparent that the use of positive reinforcement is an important aspect of any effective training program. Trainees certainly benefit from the effective use of reward. Most often, this takes the form of social approval from the trainer, reporting that they have done well. However, it would be misleading to imply that the only source of positive reinforcement in employee training comes from trainers. Indeed, the observational learning concept described earlier in this chapter implies that people can also learn by reinforcing their own desired behavior.

The fact that observational learning goes on in employee training has been demonstrated in a study of forty male supervisors working for an international company located in the northwestern United States.[35] The study was designed to determine whether supervisors' interpersonal skills could be improved by the process of observing effective behaviors by models and practicing these behaviors. The company was interested in training its supervisors to do a better job of dealing with problem employees and correcting their work habits. Different training techniques were compared. One group's training consisted of: (a) viewing a film depicting a supervisor model effectively handling a problem employee, (b) reviewing the key things done correctly by the model, (c) discussing with others the effectiveness of the model's behavior, (d) practicing the desired behaviors of the model, and (e) receiving feedback on how well they emulated the desired behaviors. Another group was only told what an effective supervisor is supposed to do, but was not given an opportunity to observe and practice emulating a model's behavior. Finally, for comparison purposes, a control group was used, whose members received no training at all.

Did the training work? In other words, did the opportunity to observe and practice a model's effective supervisory behaviors make the managers more effective supervisors on their own jobs? The answer is *yes*. One year after the training, those who received it were judged by their superiors (superintendents) to be more effective supervisors than either those who were merely told but did not observe and practice effective supervisory techniques, or those who received no training at all. Apparently, the company was justified in using the observational learning approach to train their supervisors. Although using this technique was more difficult than merely telling supervisors what to do, it was clearly more effective. This study provides excellent evidence that observational learning is an effective mechanism of employee training. (For a more humorous look at learning by systematically noting the behavior of successful models, please see Figure 2.11.)

Evaluation: The important final step. Before concluding this section, it is important to note one final step in the training process—**evaluation.** A critical step in any training program involves testing the effectiveness of the training. Did it work? In other words,

"Gentlemen, let us open to page 82 of our Iacoccas."

FIGURE 2.11 Training through Observation

For observational learning to be effectively used in training, trainees must carefully attend to and practice the behaviors of an effective model. That's what seems to be going on here.
(Source: Drawing by Ziegler; © 1986 The New Yorker Magazine, Inc.)

did the training successfully influence job performance (as it did in the above example)? By systematically comparing critical job behaviors before and after training programs, administrators of training programs can gain valuable insight into the effectiveness of their efforts. This, of course, constitutes feedback. So, just as feedback is an important part of training workers to do their jobs, it is also an important part of determining the effectiveness of the training efforts themselves.[36]

DISCIPLINE: ELIMINATING UNDESIRABLE ORGANIZATIONAL BEHAVIORS

Thus far, this chapter has focused on the ways desirable organizational behaviors may be reinforced. Although it is very important to get employees to behave appropriately, it is sometimes also necessary to get them to stop behaving in some undesirable ways. Indeed, it is not too difficult to imagine how problems like absenteeism, lateness, and drug and alcohol addiction cost companies vast sums of money.[37] Managing such problems involves the use of **discipline**—the systematic administration of punishment. As you may recall from our earlier discussion, punishment is the process through which an undesirable outcome follows the performance of an unwanted behavior, thereby reducing the strength of that behavior. It is important to keep in mind that an unpleasant stimulus is not by itself a punishment; an unpleasant stimulus may be considered a punishment only when it suppresses an unwanted behavior.

Our discussion of discipline will focus on two important issues. First, we will review the various ways disciplinary measures are used in organizations. We will then discuss the factors that make discipline effective.

The Uses of Discipline

Disciplining problem employees in one form or another is a common practice in organizations. In fact, a survey of one hundred organizations found that discipline, or the threat of discipline, was used by 83 percent of the companies in response to undesirable behaviors.[38] Although some believe punishment produces undesirable side effects (such as aggression and withdrawal), it is a process that is commonly used in organizations in one form or another.[39] Many types of disciplinary problems exist in organizations, some of a personal nature (e.g., alcoholism, emotional disorders), and others more directly job-related (e.g., incompetence and insubordination).[40] Although some of these problems may be temporary and others more chronic, they are likely to have profound effects on the whole organization (e.g., poor morale, decreases in production, interpersonal conflict), and are therefore frequently punished.

Disciplinary actions in organizations vary greatly. At one extreme, they may be very formal, such as written warnings that become part of the employee's permanent record. At the other extreme, they may be quite informal and low key, such as friendly reminders and off-the-record discussions between supervisors and their problem subordinates. An interesting field study by Beyer and Trice reported the frequency with which different types of disciplinary actions were taken by a large sample of managers in dealing with their problem subordinates (a large proportion of whom had alcohol addiction problems).[41] Specifically, they found that 95 percent of the managers first discussed the problem informally with their subordinates, with most of the discussions covering both constructive topics (e.g., ways to get help with their problems) and confrontive topics (e.g., possible disciplinary steps, and the effects on their work record). More formal, and more punitive, written warnings were given by 49 percent of the managers. Suspension without pay (for an average of four days) was used by 27 percent of the managers. Finally, only 3 percent fired the problem workers.

The large organization studied in this research used punishment *progressively*—that is, starting mildly, and then increasing in severity with each successive infraction. This is the idea behind **progressive discipline**—the practice of basing punishment on the frequency and severity of the infraction.[42] For example, for some offenses, such as unauthorized absences or tardiness, a progressive discipline program might begin by giving the employee an informal spoken warning. Then, with the next offense, the employee would have a formal meeting with his or her supervisors and be given a more formal spoken warning. A third offense would result in a formal written warning that becomes part of the employee's personnel record. Fourth offenses would result in several days' suspension without pay. Finally, if the problem continued after all this, the employee would be dismissed. For more serious offenses, such as gambling, the program would eliminate some of the more preliminary, informal disciplinary actions and begin with a formal written warning. The most serious offenses, such as stealing, falsifying information, or destroying company property, would result in immediate dismissal. Companies using progressive disciplinary programs can adjust the punishments given to reflect how serious they believe the infraction is. They can also publicize their punishment rules in company handbooks in order to communicate to their employees the kinds of behaviors they will not tolerate.

As you might imagine, managers may be predisposed toward using different disciplinary measures and corrective actions in response to different employee problems. A survey of managers from one hundred companies located throughout the United States asked what techniques they used in dealing with four crucial problems—alcoholism, use of marijuana, use of hard drugs, and serious emotional illness.[43] The results (summarized in Figure 2.12 on page 60) show employees with alcohol problems were likely to be disciplined and counselled rather than discharged, whereas those using hard drugs were more often discharged. Such findings reveal a great deal about the extent to which managers believe they can and should do something about their subordinates' various personal problems. Companies appear to be willing to help employees eliminate their serious personal problems, but at the same time, reserve the most serious disciplinary actions for incidents in which these personal problems directly result in poor job performance.[44]

Of course, not all inappropriate actions are punished all the time. There are several reasons for this.[45] For one, many supervisors may feel constrained against using punishment, either because of limitations imposed on them by labor unions or by their lack of formal organizational authority. Not surprisingly, it is sometimes easier for managers to just sit back and hope the undesirable behavior will go away—especially when they feel their hands are tied. Another factor restricting the use of punishment is that supervisors may believe their use of punishment is not supported by company policy. Punishment is most likely to be used when organizations support the use of disciplinary actions through specific programs outlining the appropriate actions to take.[46]

As we have shown here, managers may be willing to use some forms of punishment under the appropriate circumstances. Obviously, much care is needed for punishment to be used as an effective managerial tool.

The Impact of Discipline: What Makes Punishment Effective?

Punishing others is a tricky business, at best. Those who administer punishment may dislike doing so, much as those who are disciplined dislike being punished. Although it might not be exactly accurate for the punishment giver to tell the person being punished that "this is going to hurt me more than it hurts you," it is safe to assume that few of us enjoy making others feel bad—even if it's for their own good. One reason supervisors find administering punishment so undesirable is that they anticipate the strong negative

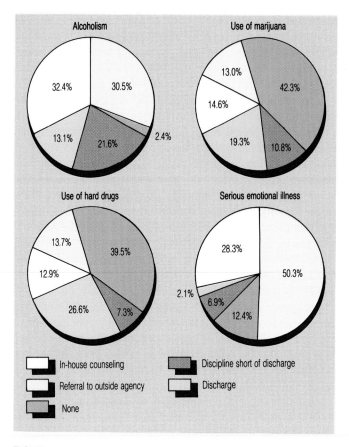

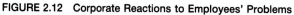

FIGURE 2.12 Corporate Reactions to Employees' Problems
Survey results show that companies are likely to take different disciplinary actions for the different personal problems of its employees. The relative use of various actions is shown for four serious employee problems. (Source: Based on data reported by Miner & Brewer, 1976; see Note 38.)

emotional reactions the punished individual may display. They may also fear revenge or retaliation on the part of the disciplined employee (e.g., industrial sabotage). Fortunately, much of the research and theory on the use of punishment has pointed to some ways of avoiding these problems, while at the same time making punishment an effective method of eliminating undesirable organizational behaviors. Our presentation will center around several very useful principles for effectively administering punishment.[47] A list of guidelines for using punishment based on these principles is presented in Table 2.6.

Principle 1: Deliver punishment immediately after the undesired response occurs. When the undesirable consequence is delivered after the undesirable behavior is performed, workers are more likely to make the connection between the two events. Hence, the undesirable event will serve as a punishment, thereby reducing the probability of the unwanted behavior. The more time that separates the undesirable behavior and its consequences, the weaker the association between them will be. So, for example, supervisors should immediately show their disapproval to employees who arrive for work two hours late. The same disapproval given later in the day would surely be less effective in reducing subsequent tardiness.

TABLE 2.6 Using Punishment Effectively: Some Helpful Guidelines
Although it is difficult to administer punishment effectively, many of the pitfalls
can be avoided by following these rules.

1. Punishment should be *immediate*.
2. Punishment should be *moderately intense*—not too weak, and not too harsh.
3. Punishment should *focus on the undesirable action*, not the personality of the individual being punished.
4. Punishment should be *used consistently* for all workers, by all supervisors, all the time.
5. The reasons for punishment should be *clearly communicated*.
6. Punishment should *not be weakened with rewards* given out of feelings of guilt or remorse.

Principle 2: Give moderate levels of punishment—nothing too high or low.
Punishment that is too weak (e.g., rolling your eyes to show disapproval when someone makes an error) is not likely to work, as employees may easily get used to the mildly undesirable consequences. On the other hand, if the punishment is too intense (e.g., immediate dismissal), it is unlikely to work because other employees are likely to reject it as unfair and inhumane, and may resign. For these reasons, it is important that the progressive discipline programs described earlier in this chapter do not start with punishments that are too weak or too strong.

Principle 3: Punish the undesirable action, not the person. It is important to keep in mind that it is the employees' undesirable acts that are being punished, not the individuals themselves. Indeed, this needs to be communicated clearly to the workers involved. As such, a supervisor should not feel uneasy about disciplining a coworker with whom he or she has developed a friendship. Good punishment is impersonal. It should not be treated as an act of revenge, or a chance to vent frustrations. When discipline is handled impersonally, the punished person is less likely to feel humiliated, and as a result, the administrator is less likely to be the victim of revenge. To punish impersonally, supervisors should focus their remarks on the employee's behavior instead of his or her personality. For example, in response to a tardy employee a supervisor should *avoid* saying something like, "Sam, your kind of laziness and irresponsibility will not be tolerated around here. You better show up on time, or else!" It would be much better to say, "Sam, lateness costs this company a lot of money each year. All employees are expected to help us by showing up on time."

Principle 4: Use punishment consistently—all the time, for all employees.
Unlike the intermittent schedules that so effectively reinforce desirable behaviors, punishment is most effective when it is administered according to a continuous reinforcement schedule. As such, it is important that *every* undesired response be punished every time it occurs. The manager who, out of a sense of kindness, turns a blind eye to an infraction may be doing more harm than good by inadvertently reinforcing an undesirable behavior. Consistency is also important in punishing all employees. Everyone who commits the same infraction should be punished the same way by any of the supervisors in charge. Fairness demands that supervisors show no favoritism. If one supervisor is very lenient, and another very harsh, what the subordinates will learn to avoid is not the undesirable behavior, but the harsh supervisor! Similarly, discipline that is believed to be uneven, the result of not being "in" with the supervisor, will not work because it does not link the disciplinary actions to the undesired behavior.

Principle 5: Clearly communicate the reasons for the punishment given.
Making it clear exactly what behaviors led to what disciplinary actions greatly facilitates

the effectiveness of punishment. Clearly communicated explanations can only help strengthen the connection between the behavior and its consequences. Wise managers use their opportunities to communicate with subordinates to make it clear that the punishment being given does not constitute revenge, but an attempt to eliminate an unwanted behavior (which, of course, it is). It would also be useful to explain how others who have engaged in similar infractions have been similarly punished in the past. Indeed, it is not just the actions themselves, but the explanations given for those actions, that influence others.[48]

Principle 6: Be careful not to follow punishment with noncontingent rewards. Imagine that you are a supervisor who has just written a formal letter of discipline in reaction to a serious infraction of the rules by a particular subordinate. The disciplined employee is feeling very low, which makes you feel remorseful. Feeling bad, you reduce your guilt by telling the worker he can take the rest of the day off with pay. Although this may make you feel better, it poses a serious problem. You have inadvertently rewarded the person for the unwanted behavior. His serious infraction was punished by the letter, but rewarded by the time off. As a result, the effect of the punishment may be greatly diminished. More seriously, such an action sends the wrong message out to the other employees. Soon, they too would learn that they could get you to give them time off if they display the proper degree of dejection. For punishment to be most effective, it is important not to inadvertently reward undesirable behaviors.

If, after reading all this, you are thinking that it is truly difficult to properly administer rewards and punishments in organizations, you have reached the same conclusion as experts in the field of organizational learning.[49] Indeed, one of the key skills that makes some managers so effective is their ability to influence others by properly administering rewards and punishments. (Although learning is often the direct result of punishments administered by supervisors, the **Research Perspective** section below shows that not all punishment is the result of direct experience. Some punishments appear to operate vicariously, through the process of observational learning.)

OB: A RESEARCH PERSPECTIVE

Vicarious Punishment in Action: Learning What *Not* to Do by Watching

Imagine that you have just observed your coworker being chastised by your boss for returning from lunch late. "Mr. Townsend, we don't pay you to take two hour lunch breaks around here at Scrooge Industries. You owe this company an additional hour's work, and by golly, I'm going to see to it that you give it to us!" Although chances are good that poor, embarrassed Mr. Townsend will not return late anytime soon, it may very well be that he was not the only one who learned something from the boss's disapproval. He was directly punished, but because you observed the event, you, too, would now be unlikely to commit this undesired act. In other words, you may have been punished *vicariously*. Earlier in this chapter, we described the process of vicarious reinforcement, but now we are considering whether people can also learn *not* to perform undesired acts through the process of observational

learning. In other words, might someone be vicariously punished in a work setting? The results of a recent study suggest that the answer is *yes*.[50]

The subjects were college students hired on a temporary basis to perform a clerical task (copying stock market quotation information onto specially prepared coding forms). Unknown to them, they were actually participating in an experiment designed to study the effects of vicarious punishment. After performing the clerical task for several hours and handing in their work, some of the participants witnessed one of their coworkers (actually an accomplice who was part of the experiment) punished. The experimenter told this alleged employee that she was performing poorly and would, as a result, have her pay cut from $5.00 per hour to $3.50 per hour. In another condition, the experimenter merely threatened to cut this person's pay, but did not do so. Finally, in a control condition, nothing was said. The researchers' question was: how was observers' performance influenced by the threat of punishment or actual punishment they witnessed? The results are shown in Figure 2.13.

As you can see, although observing a coworker being threatened had little effect on the observers' job performance, seeing a punishment actually given had a marked effect—it led to an increase in performance of approximately 33 percent. Importantly, watching another's criticism did not have detrimental effects on workers' morale. Even those who observed another's punishment remained as satisfied with their jobs as those who did not. Apparently, the effects of punishment are not limited to only direct experience (as in operant conditioning), but are also affected by the process of observational learning.

You may have heard the expression, "praise in public, criticize in private." The idea behind this advice is that chastising another in public may cause undue embarrassment and lower morale. Despite this, the experiment described here suggests not only that observing punishment does not lower morale, but that it actually improves observers' job performance. Indeed, punishment may be used most effectively when it eliminates the unwanted behavior of several people at once. Seeking such efficiencies, however, remains a potentially dangerous business. Should those observing the punishment feel that it was too harsh or unwarranted, chances are that the undesirable side effects may multiply by the number of observers. For this reason, we recommend that you pay careful attention to the suggestions for administering punishment described in the text. Punishment—whether experienced directly or vicariously—can be a powerful and effective management tool if used properly.

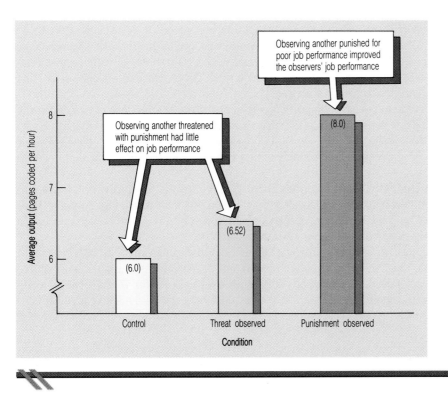

FIGURE 2.13 Improving Performance through Vicarious Punishment: An Experimental Demonstration

Research has shown that employees observing one of their coworkers being punished tended to improve their own performance. Merely observing another threatened with punishment had little effect. These findings show the effects of vicarious punishment. (Source: Based on data in Schanke, 1986; see Note 50.)

SUMMARY AND REVIEW

Theories of Learning. The concept of **learning** refers to a relatively permanent change in behavior occurring as a result of experience. One theory of learning, **classical conditioning,** explains the learning of automatic, reflexive behaviors in terms of pairing a previously neutral stimulus (*conditioned stimulus*) with a stimulus (*unconditioned stimulus*) that naturally elicits a certain response (*unconditioned response*). After pairing the conditioned stimulus with the unconditioned stimulus, the conditioned stimulus comes to elicit a response similar to the unconditioned response (known as a *conditioned response*).

In the **operant conditioning** approach, individuals learn to perform actions based on the consequences of those actions. Stimuli that increase the probability of the behaviors preceding it are known as **reinforcers.** Reinforcement may be either *positive*, if it is based on the presentation of a desirable outcome, or *negative*, if it is based on the withdrawal of an unwanted outcome. The probability of certain responses can be decreased if an unpleasant outcome results (**punishment**), or if a pleasant outcome is withdrawn (**extinction**).

Observational learning involves learning by modeling the behavior of others. By paying attention to and rehearsing the behaviors of others, we can learn vicariously, i.e., through the model's experiences.

Learning Desirable Organizational Behaviors. The rules for systematically applying reinforcements are known as **schedules of reinforcement.** These may either be *continuous*, in which every desired response is rewarded, or *partial*, in which case not all desired responses are reinforced. Behavior may be rewarded on the basis of a fixed or variable number of desired acts performed (*fixed ratio* and *variable ratio* schedules, respectively), or after the passage of a fixed or variable amount of time (*fixed interval* and *variable interval* schedules, respectively).

Organizational behavior management represents a systematic attempt to apply principles of reinforcement to the workplace, so as to improve organizational functioning. Studies conducted in a wide variety of organizations have found that reinforcing desired behaviors can greatly enhance productivity, raise attendance rates, and improve adherence to safety practices.

Reinforcement is also an important part of **training,** the process of systematically acquiring and developing job skills. Training is most effective when trainees actively participate in the learning process, repeat the desired behaviors, receive feedback on their performance, and learn under conditions that closely resemble those found on the job.

Reducing Undesirable Behaviors through Discipline. Discipline, the systematic application of punishment, is widely practiced in organizations in forms ranging from the very mild and informal (e.g., displays of disapproval) to the very severe and formal (e.g., suspension without pay, or even termination).

The effects of discipline are most beneficial when punishment is: applied immediately after the undesired activity, moderately severe, focused on the undesirable action instead of the person, applied consistently over time and for all employees, clearly explained and communicated, and not weakened by the use of inadvertent rewards.

KEY TERMS

avoidance: See *negative reinforcement.*

classical conditioning: The form of learning in which a stimulus, initially not capable of eliciting a specific response, is paired with another that can elicit this reaction. As a result of such pairings, the first stimulus gradually acquires the capacity to elicit reactions similar to those elicited by the second stimulus.

contingencies of reinforcement: The various relationships between one's behavior and the consequences of that behavior—positive reinforcement, negative reinforcement, punishment, and extinction.

continuous reinforcement: A schedule of reinforcement in which all desired behaviors are reinforced.

discipline: The process of systematically administering punishments.

evaluation: The phase of a training program which assesses a program's effectiveness in bringing about the desired training goals.

extinction: The process through which responses that are no longer reinforced tend to gradually diminish in strength.

fixed interval schedule: A schedule of reinforcement which dictates that after a reinforcement is administered, a fixed period of time must elapse before another response can be reinforced.

fixed ratio schedule: A schedule of reinforcement in which a fixed number of responses must be performed before reinforcement is administered.

instrumental conditioning: See *operant conditioning.*

Law of Effect: The basic law of operant conditioning, which operates on the observation that behaviors with desirable consequences are strengthened, and behaviors with undesirable consequences are weakened.

learning: A relatively permanent change in behavior occurring as a result of experience.

learning curve: A graph showing the rate at which the learning of various skills occurs.

modeling: See *observational learning.*

negative reinforcement: The process by which people learn to perform acts that lead to the removal of undesired events.

observational learning: The form of learning in which people acquire new behaviors by systematically observing the things that happen to others.

operant conditioning: The form of learning according to which people associate the consequences of their actions with the actions themselves. Behaviors with positive consequences are acquired; behaviors with negative consequences tend to be eliminated.

organizational behavior management: The practice of systematically reinforcing desirable organizational behaviors through operant conditioning and observational learning principles.

organizational behavior modification (OB Mod): See *organizational behavior management.*

partial (or intermittent) reinforcement: A schedule of reinforcement in which only some desired behaviors are reinforced. Types include fixed interval, variable interval, fixed ratio, and variable ratio.

Pavlovian conditioning: See *classical conditioning.*

positive reinforcement: The process by which people learn to perform behaviors that lead to the presentation of desired outcomes (i.e., rewards).

progressive discipline: The practice of gradually increasing the severity of punishments for employees who exhibit unacceptable job behavior.

punishment: Decreasing undesirable behaviors by following them with undesirable consequences.

reinforcer: Any event that increases the probability of the behavior that preceded it.

schedules of reinforcement: Rules governing the timing and frequency of the administration of reinforcement.

shaping: The process of selectively reinforcing behaviors that approach a desired goal behavior.

training: The process of systematically teaching employees to acquire and improve job related skills and knowledge.

variable interval schedule: A schedule of reinforcement which dictates that after one reinforcement is administered, a variable period of time (based on some average value) must elapse before another response can be reinforced.

variable ratio schedule: A schedule of reinforcement in which a variable number of responses (based on some average value) must be performed before reinforcement is administered.

QUESTIONS FOR DISCUSSION

1. Describe the concept of learning and discuss the ways it is applied in the field of organizational behavior.

2. Give an example of learning occurring in organizations that exemplifies each of the following: classical conditioning, operant conditioning, and observational learning.

3. Describe four different schedules of reinforcement and give an example of how each may be used in organizations.

4. What is organizational behavior management? Describe the principles of learning that make this practice effective.

5. Describe the steps needed to institute an effective training program in organizations.

6. What are the advantages and disadvantages of using discipline in organizational settings?

7. Argue for or against the advice, "praise in public, criticize in private." Give evidence in support of your position.

NOTES

1. Weiss, H. (1990). Learning and industrial/organizational psychology. In M. D. Dunnette (Ed.), *The handbook of industrial/organizational psychology* (2nd ed.). Palo Alto, CA: Consulting Psychologists Press.

2. Atkinson, R. C., Herrnstein, R. J., Lindzey, G., & Luce, R. D. (Eds.), (1988). *Steven's handbook of experimental psychology* (2nd ed.), vol. 2. New York: Wiley.

3. Hall, J. F. (1989). *Learning and memory*. Boston: Allyn & Bacon.

4. Scott, W. E., & Podsakoff, P. M. (1985). *Behavioral principles in the practice of management*. New York: Wiley.

5. Thorndike, E. L. (1911). *Animal intelligence*. New York: Macmillan.

6. Skinner, B. F. (1969). *Contingencies of reinforcement*. New York: Appleton-Century-Crofts.

7. Bandura, A. (1986). *Social foundations of thought and action: A social cognitive theory*. Englewood Cliffs, NJ: Prentice-Hall.

8. Manz, C. C., & Sims, H. P., Jr. (1981). Vicarious learning: The influence of modeling on organizational behavior. *Academy of Management Review, 6,* 105–113.

9. Goldstein, I. L. (1986) *Training in organizations: Needs assessment, development and evaluation* (2nd ed.). Monterey, CA: Brooks/Cole.

10. Kerr, S. (1975). On the folly of rewarding A while hoping for B. *Academy of Management Journal, 18,* 769–783.

11. Anonymous. (1973). At Emery Air Freight: Positive reinforcement boosts performance. *Organizational Dynamics, 1*(3), 41–50.

12. Luthans, F., & Kreitner, R. (1985). *Organizational behavior modification and beyond*. Glenview, IL: Scott, Foresman.

13. Saari, L. M., & Latham, G. P. (1982). Employee reactions to continuous and variable ratio reinforcement schedules involving a monetary incentive. *Journal of Applied Psychology, 67,* 506–508.

14. Frederiksen, L. W. (1982). *Handbook of organizational behavior management*. New York: Wiley.

15. Heneman, R. L. (1984). *Pay for performance: Exploring the merit system*. New York: Pergamon.

16. See Note 2.

17. Miller, L. (1978). *Behavior management*. New York: Wiley.

18. O'Hara, K., Johnson, C. M., & Beehr, T. A. (1985). Organizational behavior management in the private sector: A review of empirical research and recommendations for further investigation. *Academy of Management Review, 10,* 848–864.

19. Hamner, W. C., & Hamner, E. P. (1976). Behavior modification on the bottom line. *Organizational Dynamics, 4*(4), 8–21.

20. See Note 17.

21. Anonymous. (1985, May 15). Hot 100: A million dollar incentive plan. *Business Week*, p. 52.

22. See Note 15.

23. Kreitner, R., & Luthans, F. (1984). A social learning approach to behavioral management: Radical behaviorists "mellowing out." *Organizational Dynamics, 12*(3), 14–19.

24. Ashby, E. (1967, February 2). Can education be machine made? *New Scientist*, pp. 18–22.

25. Skinner, B. F. (1972). *Beyond freedom and dignity*. New York: Knopf.

26. See Note 7.

27. Eurich, N. P. (1985). *Corporate classrooms*. Princeton, NJ; Carnegie Foundation.

28. Schendel, J. D., & Hagman, J. D. (1982). On sustaining procedural skills over a prolonged retention interval. *Journal of Applied Psychology, 67,* 605–610.

29. Baldwin, T. T., & Ford, J. K. (1988). Transfer of training: A review and directions for future research. *Personnel Psychology, 41,* 63–105.

30. Ilgen, D. R., & Moore, C. F. (1987). Types and choices of performance feedback. *Journal of Applied Psychology, 72,* 401–406.

31. Baker, J. C. (1984). Foreign language and predeparture training in U.S. multinational firms. *Personnel Administrator, 29,* 68–72.

32. Henry, E. R. (1965). What business can learn from Peace Corps selection and training. *Personnel, 42,* 17–25.

33. Earley, P. C. (1987). Intercultural training for managers: A comparison of documentary and interpersonal methods. *Academy of Management Journal, 30,* 685–698.

34. Tung, R. L. (1988). *The new expatriates: Managing human resources abroad*. Cambridge, MA: Ballinger.

35. Latham, G. P., & Saari, L. M. (1979). Application of social-learning theory to training supervisors through behavioral modeling. *Journal of Applied Psychology, 64,* 239–246.

36. Latham, G. P. (1988). Human resource training and development. *Annual Review of Psychology, 39,* 545–582.

37. Hellervik, L. (1990). Dealing with marginal and ineffective performance in work settings. In M. D. Dunnette (Ed.), *The handbook of industrial/organizational psychology* (2nd ed.). Palo Alto, CA: Consulting Psychologists Press.

38. Miner, J. B., & Brewer, J. F. (1976). The management of ineffective performance. In M. D. Dunnette (Ed.), *The handbook of industrial/organizational psychology* (pp. 995–1029). Chicago: Rand McNally.

39. Katz, D., & Kahn, R. L. (1978). *The social psychology of organizations* (2nd ed.). New York: Wiley.

40. O'Reilly, C. A., III, & Weitz, B. A. (1980). Managing marginal employees: The use of warnings and dismissals. *Administrative Science Quarterly, 25,* 467–484.

41. Beyer, J. M., & Trice, H. M. (1984). A field study of the use and perceived effects of discipline in controlling work performance. *Academy of Management Journal, 27,* 743–764.

42. Oberle, R. L. (1978). Administering disciplinary actions. *Personnel Journal, 18*(3), 30–33.

43. See Note 34.

44. Podsakoff, P. M. (1982). Determinants of a supervisor's use of rewards and punishments: A literature review and suggestions for further research. *Organizational Behavior and Human Performance, 29,* 58–83.

45. Arvey, R. D., & Jones, A. P. (1985). The use of discipline in organizational settings: A framework for future research. In L. L. Cummings & B. M. Staw (Eds.), *Research in organizational behavior*, vol. 7 (pp. 367–408). Greenwich, CT: JAI Press.

46. See Note 40.

47. Arvey, R. D., & Ivancevich, J. M. (1980). Punishment in organizations: A review, propositions, and research suggestions. *Academy of Management Review, 5,* 123–132.

48. Bies, R. J., Shapiro, D. J., & Cummings, L. L. (1988). Causal accounts and managing organizational conflict: Is it enough to say it's not my fault? *Communication Research, 15,* 381–399.

49. See Note 2.

50. Schanke, M. E. (1986). Vicarious punishment in a work setting. *Journal of Applied Psychology, 71,* 343–345.

Improving Sales Performance: Organizational Behavior Management in Action

Cheerios, Wheaties, Gold Medal Flour, Bisquick, and Betty Crocker cake mixes. Chances are you have not only heard of these products but also purchased, prepared, and/or eaten them. That's no surprise to General Mills, the Minneapolis-based food conglomerate that places products such as these and over 250 others on the shelves of the nation's grocers. General Mills, widely acknowledged as one of the leading marketers in the United States, has invested much time and money in developing programs to ensure that its top brands remain big sellers year after year. One such program, an organizational behavior management system, was first tested in the Grocery Products Sales Division in 1977. The trial went so well that the program was introduced to the rest of the division over the next two and a half years.[1]

General Mills's behavior management program was developed slowly and carefully to account for numerous organizational realities and constraints. The most limiting of these was the physical distance separating managers and sales representatives. As a result of dividing the country into twenty sales regions, each comprising between three and five districts, managers could be responsible for between eighteen and fifty people spread out over thousands of square miles. This made frequent face-to-face interaction with the sales staff virtually impossible. In fact, all direct contact was minimal. Consequently, the behavior management system had to be designed so that desired performance could be both monitored and reinforced via mail and telephone.

Another factor influencing the development of the system was the availability of objective measurement techniques by which to assess sales performance. Because managers couldn't directly observe the behaviors of their sales force, they had to rely on the salespeople's report of their activities. Other, more objective, data were available about market share, sales volume, and distribution—but not on a timely basis (there was a ninety day delay in getting these performance data to managers).

The fact that the sales regions were very different from one another with respect to market conditions and sales management philosophy resulted in the design of a behavior management system that allowed for a great deal of flexibility. This way, the regional managers could develop programs specifically tailored to their needs and circumstances. Additionally, the system was affected by the ability of managers and sales personnel to develop agreed upon criteria for evaluation. Although total amount of sales seemed to be the obvious choice on which to base the system's rewards and punishments, both managers and salespeople realized that many factors outside their control influenced sales volume (e.g., competitor's discounts, store closings). As a result, many different sales activities were included in the operant conditioning program so that salespeople had an opportunity to increase desirable behaviors and be rewarded.

Keeping all these constraints in mind, a five-phase organizational behavior management program was developed and implemented at General Mills. The first step of the program was concerned with information sharing. The headquarters office made available data on the major sales variables of interest, including volume, product distribution, new product sales, incentive earnings, and market share. The purpose of this information was to provide accurate data with which to develop the goals of the program and establish a baseline against which future performance could be compared. Also in this phase, managers were asked how they provided feedback, set goals, and gave reinforcement. By determining who was deficient in these skills, the program's developers could plan training for those who needed it. Finally, managers were asked to provide a list of specific sales activities that they felt needed improvement. The behaviors identified were subsequently used as the basis for program development.

The second phase focused on helping managers understand the behavior management system. They were trained in the principles of operant conditioning. Specifically, they learned about positive and negative reinforcement, extinction, and punishment as well as schedules of reinforcement. In addition, they studied ways to provide feedback. Finally, they practiced setting specific behavioral objectives for their subordinates.

Because of the differences in regional markets, the managers themselves, and the salesforce, managers were given a great deal of leeway in setting their goals. In general, sales objectives such as cases sold per call, number of calls per day, number of advertising features sold, number of open-ended questions asked during presentations, number of promotions sold, and sales of product displays were targeted. Many managers also developed objectives relative to sales administration. These included accuracy of sales forecasts, timeliness of reports, and reduction of expenses. For instance, one manager developed a specific objective about the timeliness of "performance proofs" (these are evidence, usually a newspaper ad, that a store had qualified for a discount offered by General Mills). His stated objective was that all sales personnel in his district would turn in these proofs on time every month. Although ultimately this goal was unmet, the number of late reports declined by 51 percent.

Implementation of the behavior management system was achieved in the third phase of the program. During this time, managers shared the behavioral objectives with their sales staff. In cases where the sales personnel thought the objectives unreasonable or unmeasurable, they were negotiated and changed appropriately. The consequences of meeting, or failing to meet, the established standards were specified. Across all regions it was decided that managers would assess achievement of objectives and provide verbal feedback every six months. However, to ensure that salespeople would not be surprised at the end of the six-month period, they were taught to track their own performance. Contingencies of reinforcement varied across regions as well as within them. Many managers used verbal praise to reward employees. Often, managers would graph sales performance and share the charts with their staff. In many cases, these pictures provided tangible evidence of improved sales performance and served as positive reinforcement in their own right. Because salespeople received a high percentage of their pay from commissions—that is, a percent of sales volume—the most potent reinforcer in the program proved to be the monetary gain salespersons experienced when their sales volume increased. Additionally, most managers made their semi-annual performance evaluations contingent upon meeting the objectives of the behavior management program. In this way future pay raises (which were based on these evaluations) were dependent upon the achievement of the program goals. For example, one manager included on his performance appraisal an evaluation of his staff's effective selling of product displays. These personnel were informed that they would receive a rating of 5 (the highest) if they sold product displays in 80–100 percent of their stores. They would get a rating of 4 if they sold displays in 50–79 percent of their stores, a 3 for sales in 25–49 percent, and a 2 for less than 24 percent. In the case of a twenty-year sales veteran, this system resulted in his increasing the number of product displays sold from 24 percent of his stores to 94 percent. Across the entire district in which this was implemented, displays sold went from 36 percent to 92 percent.[2]

The fourth phase was constructed to provide feedback to the managers running the program. Their managers and the consultants who helped design the program met to determine that they were correctly setting objectives, measuring behavior, and providing reinforcement. Managers who were found to be doing the job properly were given verbal praise. Those who had not yet mastered the required skills were given additional training.

The final element of the program was called "program maintenance." This was designed to further incorporate the program into the management philosophy of the company. Specifically, top managers were trained to provide positive feedback to the managers running the program. In addition, headquarters continued to provide data necessary to evaluate the success of the program in increasing sales volume. Furthermore, managers who continually met sales objectives were identified to top management through letters and reports. It was felt that institutionalizing the program in this way would show the company's commitment to behavior management as a viable system of performance improvement. Although General Mills did not publicly release sales data to show the success of the program, they were so pleased with it that it was introduced throughout the company (e.g., in manufacturing, data processing) and has become a standard organizational management procedure.

Questions for Discussion

1. How does the five-phase organizational behavior management system used by General Mills compare to the six-step model described in this chapter? Identify each of the six steps in the General Mills program.

2. How is positive reinforcement used to keep the managers participating in the OB mod system developed for their staffs?

3. Why is phase two critical to the program's success?

4. Although the managers at General Mills were trained in using punishment, few incorporated this into their program. Why do you think this happened?

Notes

1. Mirman, R. (1982). Performance management in sales organizations. In L. W. Frederiksen (Ed.), *Handbook of organizational behavior management* (pp. 427–476). New York: Wiley.

2. See Note 1, p. 463.

The Reinforcing Value of Social Approval

In this chapter we've shown how the process of reinforcement is responsible for shaping many aspects of behavior in organizations (see pages 44–58). It is important to be aware that social factors such as personal approval may serve as potent *positive reinforcers*, in addition to more formal organizational rewards such as pay. In fact, showing approval—smiling or nodding in agreement—is a particularly effective way of encouraging others to keep talking about a topic. After all, the reward of social approval increases the probability that people will repeat the rewarded behavior. This exercise is designed to demonstrate this phenomenon.

Procedure

1. Members of the class should divide into teams of two (if there's an odd number of students, a team of three may form). One member of each pair will be an *interviewer*, and the other an *observer* (two students may be observers in teams of three). The observer should have access to a digital watch, or one with a sweep-second hand.

2. Each team should go to a nearby location on campus where students congregate socially, such as a lounge or cafeteria. Members of each team should approach a person unknown to either of them, and introduce themselves. (The person approached should be alone and not look busy.) Ask that individual if he or she would mind answering a few questions about his or her preferences for current television shows. Tell the interviewee that it's for a class project in [your professor's name]'s class. If the person approached declines, politely excuse yourself. If the person agrees, thank him or her and explain that the observer will be taking notes. The interviewer begins by asking the interviewee what his or her favorite TV show is.

3. The interviewer should respond positively to some of the interviewee's remarks and neutrally to others. Positive reactions include smiles, head nods, and expressions of agreement. Neutral reactions include showing no emotion, and simply saying "uh huh," or, "yes, I see." (For example, the interviewee may say, "Well, I really like 'The Tonight Show,'" in response to which the interviewer may respond positively, smiling and agreeing. After the interviewee finishes speaking, the interviewer may ask, "Tell me about any other show you like." As the interviewee responds, the interviewer should now act neutrally.) The interviewer continues to act positively to some reactions and neutrally to others for about five to ten minutes (or until the interviewee expresses disinterest).

4. The observer should keep track of the amount of time the interviewee spends talking about specific shows based on whether the interviewer reacted positively or neutrally. Simply note: (a) the show discussed, (b) the interviewer's reaction to the topic (positive or neutral), and (c) the amount of time the interviewee spent talking about that topic.

5. After completing the interview, thank the interviewee and return to class. If the interviewees express any interest or curiosity, explain the project to them.

6. With the instructor recording the data reported by the observers in each team, compute the average length of time (in seconds) the interviewees spoke in response to the interviewers' positive and neutral reactions.

Points to Consider

1. What differences, if any, were observed with respect to the amount of time interviewees spent talking about TV shows for which they received positive social approval compared to those for which no approval was given?

2. Were these findings similar or different for each of the various interviewer-observer pairs? What do you think this means?

3. What do you think would have happened had the interviewers acted negatively with respect to the topic instead of neutrally?

4. What safeguards were incorporated into the procedure to ensure the ethical treatment of the participants in this exercise?

5. Explain specifically how the process of reinforcement operated in the social interactions observed.

6. Do you think social approval serves as a reinforcer of behavior in organizations? Explain why or why not.

CHAPTER THREE

MOTIVATION
IN ORGANIZATIONS

CHAPTER OUTLINE

The Nature of Motivation in Organizations
  Motivation: A Definition
  Motivation and the Work Ethic

Theories of Motivation
  Need Theory
  Equity Theory
  Expectancy Theory

Techniques for Enhancing Motivation
  Motivating by Setting Performance Goals
  Job Design: Creating Motivating Jobs

Special Sections

OB: An International Perspective
  Work Values behind the Great Wall

OB: A Research Perspective
  Procedural Justice: Do the Ends Justify the Means?

OB: A Management Perspective
  The Language of Motivation: It's Not What You Do, But What You Say, That Counts

LEARNING OBJECTIVES

After reading this chapter, you should be able to:
1. Define *motivation* and explain its importance in the field of organizational behavior.
2. Characterize the value placed on work at different periods in history.
3. Describe *need hierarchy theory,* and how it applies to improving behavior in organizations.
4. Explain *equity theory* and some of the research designed to test its basic propositions.
5. Describe the elements of motivation identified by *expectancy theory,* and their interrelationship.
6. Identify and explain the conditions through which goal setting can be used to improve job performance.
7. Distinguish between *job enlargement* and *job enrichment* as techniques of job design.
8. Describe the various components making up the *job characteristics model.*

It just wouldn't stop raining, but that wasn't unusual in the Pacific northwest. Certainly, it didn't dampen the spirits of Peg Hammond, KMEH-TV's top investigative reporter. If anything, the spring showers strengthened her resolve to get to the heart of a story. And what a story she was working on!

Her subject was Jeff Shacklee, a young, second-term senator known to be on the political fast track. During his first term of office Senator Shacklee helped secure funding for a factory making high-tech defense equipment in an economically depressed area of the state. Now, happily employed, his constituents rewarded him by returning him to office with the widest majority of votes in the state's history. He was everyone's "golden boy"—everyone except Peg Hammond, that is. She suspected something was wrong with the deal Shacklee brought to the state and worked hard at digging into it.

"If you ask me, Peg," said Ray Thompson, the station's News Director, "you're wasting your time with this Shacklee thing. It's just not going to pan out. We covered the story when the contracts were signed, and everything looked squeaky clean. Besides, Shacklee's done good things for the state; why make trouble?"

Peg faced the same kind of resistance from her colleagues. Earlier that day, in fact, she was huddled under an umbrella with her colleague from the news department, Renette Benson. They were on their way from the press tent to cover a political rally on the stairs of City Hall when Renette remarked, "Thompson tells me you're trying to dig up some dirt on Shacklee."

"I sure am," answered Peg. "It's got me working day and night. I just know there's more to this deal than meets the eye, and I'm working hard to prove it."

"Why bother?" replied Renette. "Most of us just put in our hours, do our stories, keep out of trouble, and if the station has a good year, we get a raise. You sure won't find me putting in extra hours trying to uncover anyone's misdeeds. Lots of wasted time, if you ask me. What do you get for it? Nothing!"

After taping their respective stories on the rally Renette looked at Peg and wished her good-night. "I'm going home," she said.

"Good-night," Peg replied. "I've got more work to do." Peg couldn't get Renette's words out of her mind as she tirelessly waded through the real estate records in a dark, musty office in City Hall. *Why bother with this*, she asked herself. *I'm not going to win a Pulitzer! No one else is working on it; why should I?*

Renette may have gotten through to her, but just enough to raise some doubts—not enough to stop her.

I'm sure Shacklee's family owns that land where the new manufacturing plant is being built. He must be making a fortune off this deal, Peg thought to herself. *I just know it, and I'm going to keep snooping around until I find something. Let the others rest. I'll show them I'm in this business for keeps! I've got a job to do, and I'll do it as best I can.* And away she worked.

Certainly, Peg and her colleagues expressed some different ideas about working. Peg's interest in pushing forward to get the job done clearly contrasts with Renette's willingness to just get by. Why are these two people so different? What is it about them that makes them respond this way? Just as important, we may ask: what is it about the way managers behave, or the way the job is structured, that creates such crucial differences in the way people act on the job? These are some of the most important questions asked in the field of organizational behavior (see Figure 3.1). In this chapter on **motivation** we will explore several answers to these questions.

FIGURE 3.1   Motivation: A Key Topic in OB
As suggested here, questions about what motivates workers are common. (Source: Reprinted by permission of NEA, Inc.)

As we noted in chapter 1, the field of OB is concerned with both understanding human behavior in organizations and applying that knowledge to improving organizational performance and the quality of life for employees. Nowhere are these goals more clearly realized than in the topic of motivation. Indeed, the study of motivation in organizations has focused on both *what* motivates people and *why,* as well as *how* to use this knowledge to actually motivate them on the job.[1] As such, this chapter will concentrate on both *theories* of motivation and *practical applications* of those theories. In this way, we think you will develop a good understanding of the importance of motivation as a topic of interest to organizational scientists. Before turning to these theories and applications, however, we will begin by taking a closer look at the concept of motivation and its role in organizational behavior.

THE NATURE OF MOTIVATION IN ORGANIZATIONS

On the basis of what we've said so far, you should not be surprised to hear that motivation is one of the most important and widely studied topics in the field of OB.[2] To help us better understand and appreciate what is known in this field, we will explore some very important basic issues about motivation in organizations. First, we need to define the concept of motivation and explain its role in organizational behavior.

Motivation: A Definition

Although motivation is a broad and complex concept, organizational scientists have agreed on its basic characteristics.[3] As such, we define **motivation** as *the set of processes that arouse, direct, and maintain human behavior toward attaining a goal.* Obviously, this definition requires some elaboration. The diagram in Figure 3.2 (on page 76) will help guide our explanation.

The first part of our definition deals with *arousal.* This has to do with the drive behind behavior, the energy behind our actions. A hungry person may be aroused to seek food, and a lonely person may be aroused to seek companionship. People are also concerned about meeting various needs in organizations. Besides being interested in making money, workers are also interested in making a good impression on their supervisors and coworkers. Clearly, the drive to attain these various goals (i.e., the reduction of hunger, the reduction of loneliness, and making a good impression on others) constitutes a major part of the definition of motivation.

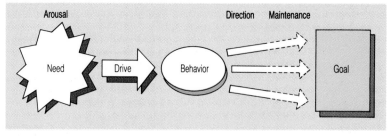

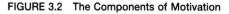

FIGURE 3.2   The Components of Motivation
The process of motivation involves the arousal, direction, and maintenance of behavior
toward a goal.

But, as our definition implies, motivation is more than just the drive behind behavior; it also involves the *direction* behavior takes. People make choices about how to meet their goals. The hungry person, for example, may decide between having a can of soup at home, going out for a fast-food hamburger, or perhaps splurging on a trendy meal at the popular *Chez Yuppie*. Likewise, the lonely person may choose to seek the company of various friends in order to feel less lonely. Even a worker trying to please his or her supervisor may select from among various options: doing the supervisor a special favor, working especially hard on an important project, or complimenting the supervisor on his or her good work. Each of these activities has something in common—they represent some of the possible choices people make to direct their efforts at attaining some goal. These intentional choices are an important part of the concept of motivation.

The final part of our definition deals with *maintaining* behavior directed toward meeting a goal. Certainly, such persistence is important. The hungry or lonely person who gives up on the way to seeking his or her goals will surely not be fulfilled. Workers who do not maintain their actions toward meeting their goals (e.g., writers who type a few pages and then goof off the rest of the day) surely cannot be considered motivated.

To summarize, motivation requires all three components: the arousal, direction, and maintenance of goal-directed behavior. An analogy may help tie these components together. Imagine that you are driving down a road on your way home. The arousal part of motivation is like the energy created by the car's fuel and drive systems (e.g., the engine). The direction component is like the steering wheel, taking you along the chosen road. And finally, the maintenance aspect of the definition is the persistence that keeps you going for the whole trip, until you arrive home—your goal.

Now that we've defined motivation, there are two important points to raise. First, we should make it clear that *motivation and job performance are not synonymous.* In fact, along with an individual's natural skills and the abilities acquired on the job, motivation is just one of several determinants of job performance. Indeed, managers have to be careful about diagnosing a subordinate's sagging performance as a problem of motivation. Although it is all too easy to do so, poor performance can be caused by poor training, inadequate equipment, or many other factors unrelated to motivation. A second key point is that *motivation is multi-faceted.* In other words, employees may have several motives operating at once. This can be problematic when motives conflict. Such a thing might happen, for example, when a worker in a manufacturing plant is motivated to please his or her foreman by being very productive, but is also motivated to avoid antagonizing his or her coworkers by being more productive than they are.

These examples clearly show that motivation is a complex and important concept in the field of OB. This complexity creates challenges for the theories of motivation used in the field. Before turning to these theories, however, we will further set the stage for them by examining the role of motivation in the work ethic.

Motivation and the Work Ethic

Throughout history, views about the meaning and importance of work have shifted dramatically.[4] In ancient Rome, for example, work was considered a curse, a vulgar and degrading activity. Consider the advice of the Roman writer, Cato the Elder, who said, "The best principle of management is to treat both slaves and animals well enough to give them the strength to work hard."[5] As civilization developed, so did more positive feelings about work. By the Middle Ages, a tradition espousing the virtues of hard work was firmly established. Following the teachings of Judeo-Christian philosophers (such as Luther and Calvin), beliefs in the value of work eventually became a cherished tradition in American society. Reflecting this view in modern times, former President Richard M. Nixon once proclaimed, "Labor is good in itself. A man or woman at work . . . becomes a better person by virtue of the act of working."[6]

Despite such inspiring words, many observers of American business trends have attributed problems of sagging production to a general lack of motivation within the workforce.[7] However, it would be misleading to claim that today's employees are poorly motivated. After all, survey findings report that most Americans would continue to work even if they didn't need the money.[8] Although money is certainly important to people, they are motivated to attain many other goals as well. Today's workforce of "baby boomers" (persons born in the years immediately after World War II), raised in a prosperous society, grew up expecting a more comfortable and more leisurely life than their parents, who worked just to survive during the depression of the late 1920s and early 1930s. Because of technological advances which took the drudgery out of many jobs, today's workers are motivated by the prospect of performing jobs that are interesting and challenging—not just jobs that pay well. As a result, it is important to recognize that problems of motivation may be difficult to identify because of the wide variety of rewards that workers may be motivated to achieve. (Although we have been talking here about American work values, the **International Perspective** section below shows how the cultural traditions of various nations are important in influencing the work values of their citizens.)

OB: AN INTERNATIONAL PERSPECTIVE

Work Values behind the Great Wall

Are employees motivated by the same things all over the world? It is an intriguing possibility that the different political and religious traditions of various nations lead people to be motivated by different aspects of their jobs. After all, we cannot avoid being influenced by the cultural values about work that surround us. With this reasoning in mind, Shenkar and Ronen conducted a fascinating study comparing the job-related goals of people in four Chinese-speaking nations—the People's Republic of China, Taiwan, Singapore, and Hong Kong (although it is not a separate nation).[9]

By contrast to Taiwan, Singapore, and Hong Kong, the People's Republic of China is an economically developing nation. Also, because it has only recently been opened up to Western social and economic influence, its people still retain traditional Chinese philosophies, primarily Confucianism. Thus,

individuals from the People's Republic of China may be expected to place different importance on various work goals than workers from neighboring Chinese cultures that have a long history of business interaction with the West.

To test these ideas, a diverse sample of male managers from each of the four countries was asked to complete an extensive questionnaire (in their native language, of course) on which they indicated the personal importance of several job variables. As summarized in Figure 3.3 (on page 78), some interesting similarities and differences emerged.

First, when asked about the *opportunities to be promoted* to a higher-level job, managers from the People's Republic were much less interested than those in the other three Chinese-speaking nations. This was explained in terms of their acceptance of the Maoist tradition promoting equality and

FIGURE 3.3 Comparing Work Goals across Different Chinese Cultures

Research comparing the work goals of managers in the People's Republic of China to those in Taiwan, Singapore, and Hong Kong found those in the People's Republic to be less interested in promotion, more interested in autonomy, and equally interested in doing challenging work. (Source: Based on data in Shenkar & Ronen, 1987; see Note 9.)

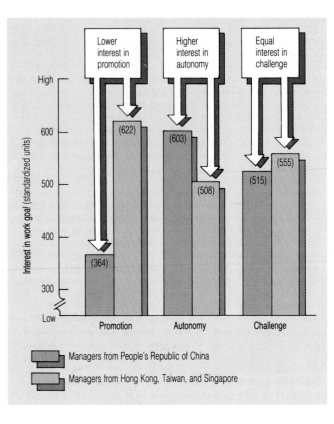

denouncing privileged titles as "remnants of bourgeois ideology." Promotions are not well-rewarded in the People's Republic, and its workers were not motivated to seek them. In contrast, managers from the People's Republic were very highly motivated by *autonomy*—the freedom to do their jobs as they see fit. Chairman Mao's criticism during the Cultural Revolution of those who did not have minds of their own was obviously a message that was clearly heard. Accepting this value, managers from the People's Republic were found to place higher importance on autonomy as a goal than did the managers from the other Chinese-speaking countries. Finally, the managers in all four countries were found to be no different from each other with respect to the value they placed on having *challenging work,* a job that gives a personal sense of achievement. This was due to the fact that people in

all Chinese-speaking countries tend to ignore the distinction between personal goals and collective goals (quite unlike our own, Western culture!).[10]

These findings are of interest for several reasons. First, of course, they nicely demonstrate our point that different values motivate work behavior in different nations. Second, they clearly demonstrate how a nation's religious and political ideologies may be responsible for its people's job goals. Finally, with the opening-up of the People's Republic as a market with which Westerners may conduct business, it may be useful to recognize the unique work values of those with whom they will be dealing. Given how little most Western business persons know about Chinese culture, those who arm themselves with knowledge about it and its work values may be in for fewer surprises, and perhaps gain a competitive advantage over those who do not.

THEORIES OF MOTIVATION

Organizational scientists have studied the topic of motivation using many different theoretical conceptualizations. Our presentation of these theories will be limited to three of the major perspectives—**need theory, equity theory,** and **expectancy theory.** Although all three theories deal with individual motivation, they differ with respect to the scope of their analysis. As we will see, the perspectives range from theories that focus exclusively on individual needs, to theories based on social comparisons, to those that take a broader, organization-wide view. Our presentation of each of these theories will focus not only on what the theory says, but also on how each may be applied to improving organizational functioning and the quality of working life.

Need Theory

The fact that human beings have various needs, some of which may be satisfied on their jobs, has not escaped the attention of organizational researchers and theorists. (In chapter 6 we will discuss workers' needs for achievement and power as important aspects of personality influencing organizational behavior.) Probably the best-known theory of human needs in organizations has been proposed by the psychologist Abraham Maslow.[11]

Maslow's hierarchy of needs. Maslow theorized that people have five types of needs that are activated in a *hierarchical* manner. This means that the needs are aroused in a specific order such that a lower-order need must be satisfied before the next highest-order need is activated. Once a need is met, the next highest need in the hierarchy is triggered, and so on. The five major need categories in Maslow's hierarchy are listed on the left side of Table 3.1.

1. *Physiological needs* are the lowest order, most basic, needs specified by Maslow. These refer to satisfying fundamental biological drives such as the need for food, air, water, and shelter. To satisfy such needs, organizations must provide employees with a salary that allows them to afford adequate living conditions (e.g., food and shelter). Similarly, allowing people sufficient rest breaks is also an important job feature that allows them to meet their physiological needs. More and more frequently, companies are providing exercise and physical fitness programs for their employees—50,000 American and 1,000 Canadian businesses by one recent count.[12] Providing such facilities may also be recognized as an attempt to help employees stay healthy by gratifying their physiological needs. After all, people who are too hungry or too ill to work will hardly be able to make much of a contribution to their companies.

2. *Safety needs,* the second level of needs in Maslow's hierarchy, are activated after physiological needs are met. Safety needs refers to the need for a secure envi-

---

TABLE 3.1 Need Theories: A Comparison

The five needs identified by Maslow's **need hierarchy theory** correspond to the three needs of Alderfer's **ERG theory**. However, while Maslow's theory specifies that needs are activated in order from lowest-level to highest-level, Alderfer's theory specifies that needs may be activated in any order.

Maslow's Need Hierarchy Theory	Alderfer's ERG Theory
Growth Needs:	
5. Self-actualization needs	Growth needs
4. Esteem needs	
Deficiency Needs:	
3. Social needs	Relatedness needs
2. Safety needs	Existence needs
1. Physiological needs	

ronment, free from threats of physical or psychological harm. There are many things organizations do to help satisfy safety needs. For example, they may provide employees with life and health insurance plans, opportunity for payroll savings, and security forces (e.g., police and fire protection staff) that enable work to be performed without fear of harm. Similarly, jobs that provide tenure (such as teachers) and no-layoff agreements enhance psychological security, and may be viewed as promoting the satisfaction of employees' safety needs. To help provide security from variability in business cycles, IBM has, in recent years, changed the way it pays its sales force, shifting away from uncertain commissions in favor of a more secure salary.[13] Such a plan is intended to help satisfy workers' safety needs.

3. *Social needs* represent the third level of needs specified by Maslow. These are theorized to be activated after both physiological and safety needs are met. Social needs refers to the need to be affiliative—to have friends, to be loved and accepted by other people. To help meet social needs, organizations may encourage participation in social events, such as office picnics or parties. Company bowling or softball leagues also provide an opportunity for meeting social needs. Country club memberships provide good opportunities for top executives to engage in valuable "networking" with their fellow executives while meeting their social needs. Earlier, we mentioned that physical fitness programs can help satisfy physiological needs. Of course, they help satisfy social needs, too. Indeed, working out or playing sports with coworkers provides an excellent opportunity to develop friendships (refer to Figure 3.4).

Research has shown that social needs are especially likely to be aroused under conditions in which "organizational uncertainty" exists, such as when the possibility of a merger threatens job security.[14] Under such conditions employees may be likely to seek their coworkers' company to gather information about what's going on. Because the loss of a job surely threatens the satisfaction of workers' physiological and safety needs, it is consistent with Maslow's theory that such conditions arouse security needs.

Taken together as a group, physiological needs, safety needs, and social needs are known as *deficiency needs*. Maslow's idea was that without having these needs met,

FIGURE 3.4   Physical Activity: A Way of Satisfying Several Needs
Companies that provide exercise facilities for their employees may be helping them satisfy their physiological and social needs.

an individual will fail to develop into a healthy person, both physically and psychologically. In contrast, the next two highest-order needs—the ones at the top of the hierarchy— are known as *growth needs*. Gratification of these needs is said to help a person grow and develop to his or her fullest potential.

4. *Esteem needs* are the fourth level of needs. These refer to a person's need to develop self-respect and to gain the approval of others. The desires to achieve success, have prestige, and be recognized by others all fall into this category. Companies do many things to satisfy their employees' esteem needs. They may, for example, have awards banquets to recognize distinguished achievements. Printing articles in company newsletters describing an employee's success, giving keys to the executive washroom, assigning private parking spaces, and posting signs identifying the "employee of the month" are all examples of things that can be done to satisfy esteem needs.

5. *Self-actualization needs* are found at the top of Maslow's hierarchy. These are the needs aroused only after all the lower-order needs have been met. **Self-actualization** refers to the need for self-fulfillment—the desire to become all that one is capable of being, developing one's potential. By working at their maximum creative potential, employees who are self-actualized can be extremely valuable assets to their organizations. Individuals who have self-actualized are working at their peak, and represent the most effective use of an organization's human resources.

Research testing Maslow's theory has supported the distinction between deficiency needs and growth needs. Unfortunately, the research has shown that not all employees are able to satisfy their higher-order needs on the job. For example, Porter found that whereas lower-level managers were only able to satisfy their deficiency needs on the job, managers from the higher echelons of organizations were able to satisfy both their deficiency and growth needs.[15] An interesting study by Betz also examined the extent to which different groups' needs are met—specifically, housewives and women who work outside the home.[16] It was found that full-time homemakers had higher levels of deficiency needs than married women employed outside the home. Presumably, this was because they did not have a job through which these needs could be fulfilled. It was also found that the growth needs of working women were higher than those of full-time homemakers, presumably because their deficiency needs were already satisfied on the job. This evidence is clearly consistent with Maslow's ideas about the satisfaction of deficiency needs prior to growth needs.

Despite such general evidence, Maslow's theory has not received a great deal of support with respect to the specific things it proposes—namely, the exact needs that exist and the order in which they are activated.[17] Many researchers have failed to confirm that there are only five basic categories of needs. Also, these needs haven't been found to be activated in the exact order specified by Maslow.

Alderfer's ERG theory. In response to these criticisms, an alternative formulation has been proposed by Clayton Alderfer.[18] This approach, known as **ERG theory,** is much simpler. Not only does Alderfer specify that there are only three types of needs instead of five, but that these are not necessarily activated in any specific order. In fact, Alderfer postulates that any need may be activated at any time.

The three needs specified by *ERG theory* are the needs for *existence*, *relatedness*, and *growth*. *Existence* needs correspond to Maslow's physiological needs and safety needs. *Relatedness* needs correspond to Maslow's social needs, the need for meaningful social relationships. Finally, *growth* needs correspond to the esteem needs and self-actualization needs in Maslow's theory—the need for developing one's potential. A summary of Maslow's need hierarchy theory and the corresponding needs identified by Alderfer's ERG theory is shown in Table 3.1.

Clearly, ERG theory is much less restrictive than Maslow's need hierarchy theory. Its advantage is that it fits better with research evidence suggesting that although basic categories of need do exist, they are not exactly as specified by Maslow.[19] Despite the fact that need theorists are not in complete agreement about the exact number of needs that exist and the relationships between them, they do agree that satisfying human needs is an important part of motivating behavior on the job.

Equity Theory

In contrast with this focus on individual needs, **equity theory** views motivation from the perspective of the social comparisons workers make among themselves. It proposes that workers are motivated to maintain fair, or "equitable," relationships among themselves and to change those relationships that are unfair, or "inequitable."[20] The ways in which this is done has been a topic of considerable interest in the field of organizational behavior. Equity theory is concerned with people's motivation to escape the negative feelings that result from being treated unfairly on their jobs. Such feelings may result when people engage in the process of *social comparison*—i.e., when they compare themselves to others.

Equity theory proposes that people make social comparisons between themselves and others with respect to two variables—**outcomes** and **inputs. Outcomes** refer to the things workers believe they and others get out of their jobs, including pay, fringe benefits, or prestige. **Inputs** refer to the contributions employees believe they and others make to their jobs, including the amount of time worked, the amount of effort expended, the number of units produced, or the qualifications brought to the job. It is important to note that equity theory is concerned with outcomes and inputs as they are *perceived* by the people involved, *not* necessarily as they actually are. Not surprisingly, therefore, workers may disagree about what constitutes equity and inequity on the job.

Equity theory states that people compare their outcomes and inputs to those of others in the form of a ratio. Specifically, they compare the ratio of their own outcomes/inputs to the ratio of other people's outcomes/inputs. As shown in Figure 3.5, these comparisons can result in any of three states: *overpayment, underpayment,* or *equitable payment.*

- **Overpayment inequity** occurs when someone's outcome/input ratio is *greater than* the corresponding ratio of another person with whom that person compares himself or herself. People who are overpaid are theorized to feel *guilty.*
- **Underpayment inequity** occurs when someone's outcome/input ratio is *less than* the corresponding ratio of another with whom that person compares himself or herself. People who are underpaid are theorized to feel *angry.*
- **Equitable payment** occurs when someone's outcome/input ratio is *equal to* the corresponding ratio of another person with whom that person compares himself or herself. People who are equitably paid are theorized to feel *satisfied.*

To help us understand what equity theory predicts, suppose that Jack and Ray work alongside each other on an assembly line, doing the same job. Both men have the same degree of experience, training, and education (i.e., their inputs are identical). However, while Jack is paid $500/week, Ray is paid only $350/week (i.e., Jack's outcomes are greater than Ray's). How will they feel when they talk to each other one day and learn of this situation? According to equity theory, Jack may be considered overpaid, and would be expected to feel guilty, while Ray may be considered underpaid, and would be expected to feel angry.

According to equity theory, people are motivated to escape these negative emo-

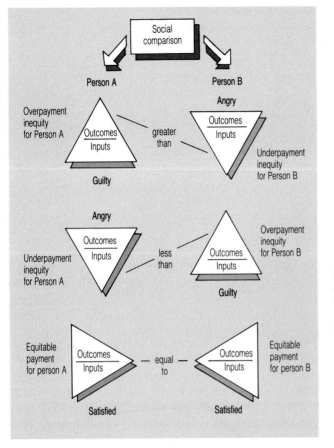

FIGURE 3.5 Equity Theory: An Overview

To judge equity or inequity, people compare the ratios of their own outcomes/inputs to the corresponding ratios of others. The resulting states—overpayment inequity, underpayment inequity, or equitable payment—and their associated emotional responses are summarized here.

tional states of anger and guilt. Equity theory recognizes several ways of resolving inequitable states (see the summary in Table 3.2 on page 84). In our example, there are several things Jack and Ray can do to redress the inequity and feel satisfied. For example, Jack, or any underpaid person, may respond by lowering his inputs. He may not work as hard, arriving at work late, leaving early, taking longer breaks, doing less work, or performing lower quality work. In an extreme case, he may even quit his job. He may also attempt to raise his outcomes, asking the boss for a raise, or even taking home company property (such as tools, or office supplies). All these examples may be considered *behavioral* reactions to inequity because they represent things people can do to change their existing inputs or outcomes.

In addition to these behavioral reactions to underpayment inequity, there are also some likely *psychological* reactions. Given that many people feel uncomfortable stealing from their employers (as they should) or would be unwilling to restrict their productivity or to ask for a raise, they may resort to resolving the inequity by changing the way they think about the situation. Because equity theory deals with perceptions of fairness or unfairness, it is reasonable to expect that inequitable states may be redressed effectively by merely thinking about the circumstances differently. For example, an underpaid person may attempt to rationalize that another's inputs are really higher than his or her own, thereby convincing himself or herself that the other's higher outcomes are justified. One recent study even found that workers who received a 6 percent pay cut rationalized that their pay was still equitable by coming to think of their work

TABLE 3.2   Possible Reactions to Inequity: A Summary

People can respond to overpayment and underpayment inequities in behavioral and/or psychological ways. A few of these are summarized here. These reactions help change the perceived *inequities* into a state of perceived *equity*.

	TYPE OF REACTION	
TYPE OF INEQUITY	BEHAVIORAL (WHAT YOU CAN *DO* IS . . .)	PSYCHOLOGICAL (WHAT YOU CAN *THINK* IS . . .)
Overpayment Inequity	Raise your inputs (e.g., work harder), or lower your outcomes (e.g., work through a paid vacation)	Convince yourself that your outcomes are deserved based on your inputs (e.g., rationalize that you work harder than others and so you deserve more pay)
Underpayment Inequity	Lower your inputs (e.g., reduce effort), or raise your outcomes (e.g., get a raise in pay)	Convince yourself that others' inputs are really higher than your own (e.g., rationalize that the comparison worker is really more qualified, and so deserves higher outcomes)

environments in more favorable terms.[21] So by coming to perceive the situation as equitable, people can effectively reduce their inequity distress.

An analogous set of behavioral and psychological reactions can be identified for overpayment inequity. Specifically, a salaried employee who feels overpaid may raise his or her inputs by working harder, or for longer hours. Similarly, employees who lower their own outcomes by not taking advantage of company-provided fringe benefits may be seen as redressing an overpayment inequity. In addition, overpaid persons may readily convince themselves psychologically that they are really worth their higher outcomes by virtue of their superior inputs. People who receive substantial pay raises may not feel distressed about it at all because they rationalize that the raise is warranted on the basis of their superior inputs, and therefore does not constitute an inequity.

Research has generally supported the theory's claim that people will respond to overpayment and underpayment inequities in the ways just described.[22] In one of the most ambitious tests of equity theory, Pritchard, Dunnette, and Jorgenson hired male clerical workers to work part-time over a two week period.[23] In their simulated company, the experimenters manipulated the equity or inequity of the payment their employees received. *Overpaid* employees were told the pay they received was higher than others doing the same work. *Underpaid* employees were told their pay was lower than that of others doing the same work. *Equitably paid* employees were told the pay they received was equal to that of others doing the same work. The results of the study were consistent with equity theory: people who were overpaid were more productive than those who were equitably paid; and people who were underpaid were less productive than those who were equitably paid. Moreover, both overpaid and underpaid employees reported being more dissatisfied with their jobs than those who were equitably paid. Thus, the people participating in this study behaved precisely as equity theory predicted.

In recent years, conditions of underpayment have been created by **two-tier wage structures**—payment systems in which newer employees are paid less than employees hired at an earlier time to do the same work. Such a wage structure can be considered inequitable because it pays newer employees a lower starting salary than earlier hired, equally-qualified people doing the same job. Not surprisingly, research has shown that employees hired into the lower-wage tier reported their payment to be less fair than those in the upper tier.[24] Lower-paid employees also express great dissatisfaction. One Los Angeles supermarket clerk, paid about half as much as an earlier-hired co-worker, said, "It stinks. They're paying us lower wages for the same work."[25] Not only are they unhappy, but underpaid personnel tend to refuse work assignments, and to quit their jobs. For example, after instituting a two-tier wage structure, two-thirds of the lower-paid employees at the Giant Food supermarket chain quit their jobs during the first three months. Even the proposal of such a two-tier pay structure in the mid-1980s caused United Airline pilots to go on strike. This is not surprising since a two-tier wage system instituted by American Airlines in 1985 virtually cut in half the amount DC–10 pilots would be paid at the top of their careers—a difference of over $64,000 per year![26] Although two-tier wage systems are set up to help companies save money, it's clear that employees' negative reactions to them may make them costlier than ever imagined.

All of our examples of inequity so far have involved pay, but a recent experiment by Greenberg showed that feelings of inequity can be created by factors other than the amount of money received.[27] The definition of outcomes suggests that people may also recognize as rewards the status of the facilities in which they work. Individuals may feel more rewarded by doing their jobs in large, lavishly decorated, private offices connoting their high status in the organization, compared to smaller, undecorated, shared offices connoting their low status in the organization (see Figure 3.6).

The participants in this field experiment were life insurance underwriters of varying degrees of seniority (ranging from underwriter trainees, to associate underwriters, to underwriters). Their job was to evaluate the suitability of applicants for life insurance policies based on various standards. Because these employees' offices were being refurbished, they were temporarily assigned (over a two week period) to the offices of one of their coworkers. Some were assigned to the offices of higher-status persons, and were considered *overpaid* (i.e., they received rewards from their workplaces that were greater than merited by their status). Others were assigned to the offices of lower-status persons, and were considered *underpaid* (i.e., they received rewards from their workplaces that were less than merited by their status). Still others were assigned to the offices of equal-status persons and were considered *equitably paid* (i.e., they

FIGURE 3.6 Office Status: An Important Job Reward
Which office belongs to a top executive and which belongs to a lower-level manager?
Research has shown that office space constitutes an important job reward—a work outcome that can lead to feelings of inequity if it does not match the occupant's organizational status level.

received rewards from their workplaces equivalent to that merited by their status). Finally, there was a *control* group of underwriters who continued working in their own offices throughout the study period. The dependent variable was their "corrected performance score," a measure of how productive they were, taking into account the number of hours they worked and the difficulty of the cases they reviewed. The productivity of the various groups is summarized in Figure 3.7.

As you can see, although all underwriters performed equally well before the office reassignments began, these reassignments had a profound effect on productivity. Overpaid employees (i.e., those assigned to higher-status offices) dramatically improved their performance, exactly as predicted by equity theory. Likewise, underpaid employees (i.e., those assigned to lower-status offices) dramatically lowered their performance, also as predicted by equity theory. Further consistent with equity theory, employees whose workspace rewards were unchanged (i.e., those in the equitably paid group and those in the control group) had performance levels that remained the same during the study. Finally, the figure shows that these changes in performance were temporary. As soon as the underwriters returned to their own offices, their performance returned to its original level. Not only do these findings lend strong support to equity theory, but they show us that people respond to inequities created not only by the money they receive, but by other rewards as well—such as the status value of their workplaces. (The idea that fairness in organizations is determined by more than just money is also central to the work on **procedural justice** described in our **Research Perspective** on page 87.)

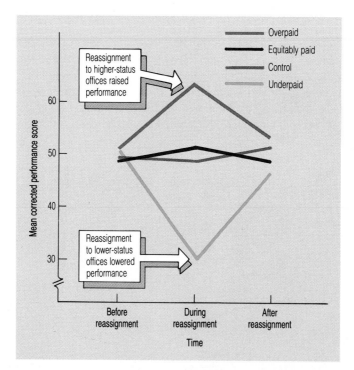

FIGURE 3.7   Responses to Inequities in Office Assignment: An Experimental Demonstration

Supporting equity theory, a recent study found that reassignment to higher-status offices (overpayment) raised job performance, and reassignment to lower-status offices (underpayment) lowered job performance. Employees reassigned to equal-status offices (equitably paid), and those who stayed in their own offices (control), maintained unchanged levels of performance. (Source: Based on data in Greenberg, 1988; see Note 27.)

Procedural Justice: Do the Ends Justify the Means?

Lawyers and judges have long been aware that the fairness of a legal system depends not only on what the verdict of a case may be, but also *how* the case is decided. For a court case to be fair, many rules must be followed: each side must be heard, the jury must be impartial, and so on. These rules reflect a concern for **procedural justice**—the perceived fairness of the rules and procedures used to make decisions.[28]

In recent years, the field of OB has expanded its appreciation for justice in organizations beyond equity theory, and toward consideration of the rules of procedural justice that apply in organizations. The basic idea is that what is fair goes beyond the relative balance of outcomes and inputs, as equity theory says. People believe that what makes their organizations fair also has to do with the fairness of the rules and procedures used—such as how much they are consulted in decisions affecting them (e.g., determining their days off) and how accurately their job performance is evaluated.[29] Apparently, employees are motivated to attain fairness in *how* organizations make decisions as well as in *what* those decisions are.

But can the result of an organizational decision (such as how much to pay someone) be considered fair if it is the result of an unfair procedure? A recent experiment by Greenberg found that the answer depends on how much an employee is paid.[30] Participants in this study performed a clerical task for forty-five minutes in return for which some were paid a low amount ($1), others a moderate amount ($4), and still others a high amount ($7). Also varied was the explanation they were given regarding how their pay was determined. In the *fair procedure* condition they were told that their pay was based on how well they performed relative to others. In the *unfair procedure* condition they were told that their pay was determined in a very arbitrary manner—by their choice of a work room (i.e., people who selected each room received a predetermined amount of pay associated with it). They were then asked to evaluate how fairly they thought they were paid. These ratings are summarized in Figure 3.8.

As Figure 3.8 shows, individuals' perceptions of the fairness of their pay were based on the amount of pay they received in conjunction with the

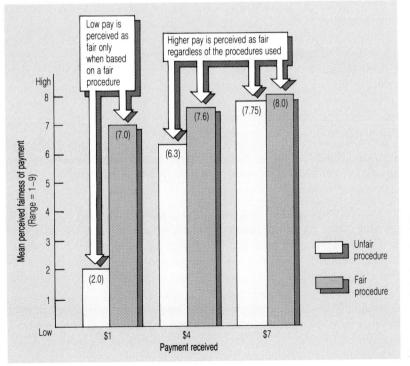

FIGURE 3.8 Fair Pay: It's Not Just What You Get, But How You Get It That Matters

Research has shown that the perceived fairness of payment depends not only on how high or low the pay is, but also the fairness of the procedure used to determine it. Low pay is accepted as fair only if it is based on a fair procedure. Higher pay is accepted as fair regardless. (Source: Based on data in Greenberg, 1987; see Note 30.)

procedure used to determine it. Specifically, people believed that all pay levels—even very low ones—were fair if the pay they received was based on a fair procedure (such as performance level). However, low pay was believed to be very unfair when it was the result of an unfair procedure (such as the arbitrary choice of a work room). Interestingly, though, higher amounts of pay were accepted as fair even when they resulted from unfair procedures! People are apparently very self-serving in their perceptions of fairness. In other words, they are willing to judge as fair any outcome that benefits them. (As we will describe more fully in chapter 4, the self-serving bias takes many different forms, and is a very basic perceptual phenomenon.)

As an analogy, imagine your reactions to different procedures your instructor may use to grade exams. If you receive a high grade, you may think it's fair just because it benefits you. You think of yourself as a good student, and a good student deserves a high grade, so it's fair. However, if you receive a low grade, you might not like it, but accept it as fair if it's clear that the instructor graded it in a careful, unbiased manner. Surely, you'd think your low grade is unfair if your instructor revealed that she graded the paper based on the stair on which it landed when she threw the class's papers down the stairwell.

Findings such as those summarized here represent a growing recognition in the field of OB that employees' concerns about justice go beyond what can be explained by equity theory. Interest in procedural justice is growing all the time.[31]

Expectancy Theory

Expectancy theory is the broadest in scope of the three theories presented in this chapter. Instead of narrowly focusing on individual needs or on social comparisons as the previously described theories have done, expectancy theory looks at the role of motivation in the overall work environment. In essence, the theory asserts that people are motivated to work when they expect they will be able to achieve the things they want from their jobs. Expectancy theory characterizes people as rational beings who think about what they have to do to be rewarded and how much the reward means to them before they perform their jobs. But, as we will see, the theory doesn't just focus on what people think—it also recognizes that these thoughts combine with other aspects of the organizational environment to influence job performance.

Before we describe expectancy theory in more detail, we should note that it has been presented in many different forms—including the important pioneering work of Vroom,[32] and of Porter and Lawler.[33] However, the differences between the various versions of expectancy theory need not concern us; we will describe it in its most general form.

Expectancy theory specifies that motivation is the result of three different types of beliefs that people have. These are known as:

1. **expectancy**—the belief that one's effort will result in performance
2. **instrumentality**—the belief that one's performance will be rewarded
3. **valence**—the perceived value of the rewards to the recipient

Sometimes, workers believe that putting forth a great deal of effort will result in getting a lot accomplished. However, there are other occasions in which hard work will have little effect on how much gets done. For example, an employee operating a faulty piece of equipment may have a very low *expectancy* that his or her efforts will lead to high levels of performance. Someone working under such conditions probably would not continue to exert much effort.

It is also possible that even if an employee works hard and performs at a high level, motivation may falter if that performance is not suitably rewarded by the organization—that is, if the performance was not perceived as *instrumental* in bringing about the rewards. So, for example, a worker who is extremely productive may be poorly motivated to perform if he or she has already reached the top level of pay given by the company.

Finally, even if employees receive rewards based on their performance, they may be poorly motivated if those so-called "rewards" have a low *valence* to them. Someone who doesn't care about the rewards offered by the organization would not be motivated to attempt to attain them. For example, a multi-millionaire would probably be poorly motivated to work for a reward of $100, whereas a person of more modest means would probably perceive that reward as being extremely valuable.

Expectancy theory claims that motivation is a multiplicative function of all three components. This means that higher levels of motivation will result when valence, instrumentality, and expectancy are all high than when they are all low. The multiplicative assumption of the theory also implies that if any one of the components is zero, then the overall level of motivation will be zero. So, even if an employee believes that her effort will result in performance, which will result in reward, motivation may be zero if the valence of the reward she expects to receive is zero. Figure 3.9 summarizes the definitions of expectancy theory components and shows their interrelationships.

Figure 3.9 also shows that expectancy theory assumes that motivation is not equivalent to job performance, but is only one of several determinants of job performance. In particular, the theory assumes that *skills and abilities* also contribute to a person's job performance. It is no secret that some people are better suited to perform their jobs than others by virtue of the unique characteristics and special skills or abilities they bring to their jobs. For example, a tall, strong, well-coordinated person is likely to make a better professional basketball player than a very short, weak, uncoordinated one, even if the shorter person is highly motivated to succeed.

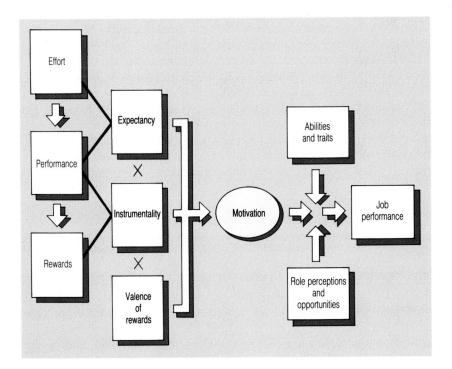

FIGURE 3.9 Expectancy Theory: An Overview
According to *expectancy theory,* motivation is the product of three types of beliefs: expectancy (effort will result in performance) × instrumentality (performance will result in rewards) × valence of rewards (the perceived value of the rewards). It also recognizes that motivation is only one of several factors responsible for job performance.

Expectancy theory also recognizes that job performance will be influenced by people's *role perceptions*. How well workers perform their jobs will depend, in part, on what they believe is expected of them. An assistant manager, for example, may believe her primary job responsibility is to train employees. But if the manager believes the assistant manager should be doing the paperwork instead, she may be seen as performing her job inadequately. Of course, such poor performance results *not* necessarily from poor motivation, but from misunderstandings concerning the role one is expected to play in the organization.

Finally, expectancy theory also recognizes the role of *opportunities to perform* one's job. It is possible that even the best employees will perform at low levels if their opportunities are limited. The work of salespersons provides a good example. Even the most highly motivated salesperson will perform poorly if opportunities are restricted—if the available inventory is very low (as is sometimes the case among certain popular cars), or if the customers are unable to afford the product (as is sometimes the case among salespersons whose territories are heavily populated by unemployed persons).

It is important to recognize that expectancy theory views motivation as just one of several determinants of job performance. Motivation, together with a person's skills and abilities, role perceptions, and opportunities, combine to influence job performance.

Expectancy theory has generated a great deal of research and has been successfully applied to understanding behavior in many different organizational settings.[34] However, although some specific aspects of the theory have been supported (particularly the impact of expectancy and instrumentality on motivation),[35] others have not (such as the contribution of valence to motivation, and the multiplicative assumption).[36] Despite this mixed support, expectancy theory has been a dominant approach to the field of organizational motivation due, in part, to the theory's important implications for organizational practice. Let's consider some of the suggestions made by expectancy theory about how to motivate people on the job (see Table 3.3).

One important suggestion is to *clarify people's expectancies that their effort will lead to performance.* Motivation may be enhanced by training employees to do their jobs more efficiently, thereby achieving higher levels of performance from their efforts. It may also be possible to enhance effort–performance expectancies by following employees' suggestions about ways of changing their jobs. To the extent that employees are aware of problems in their jobs that interfere with their performance, attempting to alleviate these problems may help them perform more efficiently. In essence, what we are saying is: *make the desired performance attainable.* It is important to make it

TABLE 3.3 How to Motivate Employees: Some Suggestions from Expectancy Theory
Expectancy theory makes some specific recommendations for enhancing motivation. Various organizational practices can help implement these recommendations. A few are summarized here.

RECOMMENDATION	CORRESPONDING PRACTICE
Clarify the expectation that working hard will improve job performance	Design jobs so as to make the desired performance more attainable
Clearly link valued rewards to the job performance needed to attain them	Institute *pay-for-performance* plan, paying for meritorious work
Administer rewards that have a high positive valence to workers	Use a *cafeteria-style benefit plan*, allowing workers to select the fringe benefits they most value

clear to people what is expected of them *and* to make it possible for them to attain that level of performance.

A second practical suggestion from expectancy theory is to *clearly link valued rewards and performance*. Using the terminology of expectancy theory, managers should attempt to enhance their subordinates' beliefs about instrumentality—that is, make it clear to them exactly what job behaviors will lead to what rewards. To the extent that it is possible for employees to be paid in ways directly linked to their performance—such as through piece-rate incentive systems, or sales commission plans—expectancy theory specifies that it would be effective to do so because this would enhance beliefs about instrumentality. Indeed, a great deal of research has shown that performance increases can result from carefully implemented merit systems—frequently referred to as **pay-for-performance** systems.[37] One note of caution: not only should employees be led to believe that their performance will be rewarded in a certain way, it is also important to accurately follow up—that is, to actually pay them in the stated way.[38] Enhancing instrumentality beliefs is effective only insofar as these beliefs are borne out in actual practice.

Finally, one of the most obvious practical suggestions from expectancy theory is to *administer rewards that are positively valent to employees*. The carrot at the end of the stick must be a tasty one, according to the theory, for it to have potential as a motivator. These days, when the composition of the workforce is changing with increasing numbers of unmarried parents and single people working, it would be a mistake to assume that all employees care about having the same rewards made available to them by their companies. Some might recognize the incentive value of a pay raise, while others might prefer additional vacation days, improved insurance benefits, or day care facilities for children. With this in mind, more and more companies are instituting **cafeteria-style benefit plans**—incentive systems through which the employees select their fringe benefits from a menu of available alternatives. Given that fringe benefits represent an average of 37 percent of payroll costs, more and more companies are recognizing the value of administering them flexibly.[39] For example, American Can (now known as Primerica) has had a flexible benefit plan since 1978—one which is reportedly very successful. According to one report, almost 95 percent of the company's 8,000 salaried employees believed that the plan allowed them to select benefits that were most valuable to them.[40] The success of these plans suggests that making highly valent rewards available to employees may be an effective motivational technique.

TECHNIQUES FOR ENHANCING MOTIVATION

Having examined the major theories of organizational motivation, we are now prepared to put some of this information to practical use. Our presentation of techniques for improving worker motivation will focus on two different approaches: **goal setting,** an approach in which workers strive to meet specified performance goals, and **job design,** an approach in which jobs are changed or created so as to build in more of what motivates people. As we will see, both approaches have proven to be effective ways of enhancing motivation on the job.

Motivating by Setting Performance Goals

The idea that employees' motivation and performance may be enhanced by setting performance goals is an important part of the dominant management philosophy in contemporary organizations. In view of the vast amount of research applying **goal**

setting procedures to organizational practice, it is possible for us to point out several well-established principles of goal setting.[41] (We will also have more to say about goal setting in chapter 16, when we introduce the topic of *management by objectives.*)

Assign specific goals. Probably the best-established finding of research on goal setting is that people perform at higher levels when asked to meet a specifically high performance goal than when simply asked to "do your best," or when no goal at all is assigned.[42] Employees tend to find specific goals quite challenging, and are motivated to try to meet them—not only to fulfill management's expectations, but also to convince themselves that they have performed well. The quest to attain specific goals has been shown to have beneficial effects on employees' job behaviors in several organizations. Research conducted at Parkdale Mills, Inc. provides a particularly dramatic demonstration of this principle. Before the goal-setting program began, the employees in this organization had an average attendance rate of 86 percent. As part of the goal-setting program, they agreed to raise their average attendance rate to 93 percent. Each day an attendance chart was kept so employees could be kept informed of their progress toward meeting their goal. Within four weeks of setting this goal, they not only met it, but surpassed it—averaging 94.3 percent attendance for the nine weeks following the goal setting.[43]

Similar results were found in another field study, this one involving crews of loggers who hauled logs from a forest to the company's sawmill.[44] Before the study, the loggers tended to load the trucks to only about 60 percent of their legal weight capacity. Then, a specific goal was set, challenging them to load the trucks to 94 percent of their capacity before driving to the plant. Not only was it found that the specific goal was effective in raising performance up to the goal level in just a few weeks, but the effects were long-lasting as well. In fact, the loggers were found to sustain this level of performance as long as seven years later. (Apparently, loading the trucks to 94 percent of their legal weight capacity became an accepted group practice—what we will describe in chapter 8 as a group norm.) Just as impressive were the financial savings the company realized as a result of eliminating wasted trips. Specifically, the company's accountants estimated that $250,000 was saved in the first nine months alone!

Of course, it is not sufficient for performance goals merely to be specific—it is also important to consider the difficulty level of these goals.

Assign difficult, but acceptable, performance goals. The study at Parkdale Mills demonstrated the effectiveness of assigning specific goals. But note also that the goal the organization set was a difficult one. A goal must be difficult and challenging as well as specific for it to raise performance. People work harder to reach higher goals, as long as these are within the limits of their capability. However, as goals become too difficult, performance drops because people reject the goals as unrealistic (see Figure 3.10).[45] For example, you may work much harder in a class that challenges your ability than in one that is very easy, but you would probably tend to give up if the only way of getting an "A" were to get perfect scores on all papers and exams. As Figure 3.10 suggests, the professor who set such an impossible goal would not be motivating students to do their best.

The same thing has been found in industry. At a General Electric manufacturing plant, specific goals were set for productivity and cost reduction. Those goals perceived as challenging, but possible, led to improved performance. However, those goals perceived as unattainable led to decreased performance.[46] Given this, an important question arises as to how to set goals that enhance employees' commitment. After all, as Figure 3.10 shows, the higher the goal workers will accept, the more productive they will be.[47]

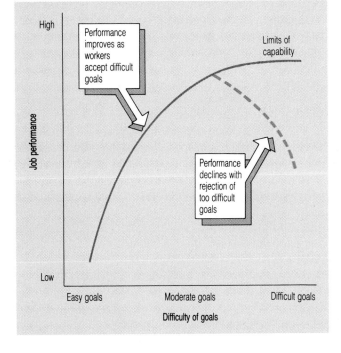

**FIGURE 3.10 Job
Performance: It Depends
on the Acceptance of
Difficult Goals**

Research and theory on
goal setting suggests that
people will accept and
work hard to attain
difficult goals, until they
reach the limits of their
capabilities. However, as
goals become too
difficult, they may be
rejected, and performance
will suffer. (Source:
Adapted from Locke &
Latham, 1984; see Note
45.)

One obvious way of enhancing goal acceptance is to *involve workers in the goal-setting process*. Research on workers' participation in goal setting has been quite extensive and, over the years, has yielded mixed results. Recently, however, it has been agreed that participation in goal setting may enhance job performance more than goals assigned by others.[48] Specifically, it has been found that employees tend to perform at higher levels when they are allowed to participate freely in setting their own performance goals than when their supervisors tell them what goals to meet.[49] Participation in the goal-setting process may be helpful not only because it ensures that employees understand and appreciate the goals, but also because it makes them more committed to attaining these goals. After all, people are unlikely to reject as unreasonable any goals they have had a voice in creating. Also, possibly because workers have more direct knowledge about what it takes to do a job than their supervisors, they are likely to come up with goals that are acceptably high, but not so high as to be rejected as unreasonable.

Sometimes, it is impractical to involve employees in the goal-setting process, so other techniques may be used to enhance goal acceptance. One such approach involves using *psychological contracts* to make people more committed to attaining their goals. By getting employees to publicly commit themselves to attaining a goal, their acceptance of that goal, and their likelihood of attaining it, are increased.

Acceptance of difficult goals can also be enhanced through *supervisory support*. Subordinates can hardly be expected to strive toward attaining goals that their own supervisors don't seem to care about. Research has shown that when a boss gives workers confidence about their abilities, the workers tend to set higher goals, which, of course, leads to higher levels of performance.[50] One form of support is giving workers recognition for meeting their goals. Employees at IBM, in fact, specifically identify the support and personal recognition they receive from their supervisors as an important part of what keeps them working toward their goals.[51]

One very simple and direct technique for enhancing acceptance of goals involves *explaining the logic behind goal setting.* Recognizing that employees may be threatened or intimidated by the imposition of goals, several suggestions for getting them to accept goals have been offered.[52] First, it is necessary to explain how goals were set (such as through past performance), so that people don't feel they are being taken advantage of. Second, the effects of the program on employees' pay should be clearly explained. So, for example, it should be explained to salaried personnel that their pay will not be reduced if they fail to meet the goals. The financial benefits of the program for those paid on a piece-rate basis should also be explained. Finally, involvement in goal-setting programs should be voluntary, and this should be explained to workers. Goal setting will not work if the employees reject the goals and suspect the management of tricking them. With this in mind, a few well-chosen words of reassurance may be useful in getting employees to accept goals. (For more on the beneficial effects of verbal communication on motivation, see the **Management Perspective** section on page 102.)

Provide feedback concerning goal attainment. The final principle of goal setting we will mention is an obvious one (although too often it is not followed in actual practice). Just as golfers need feedback about where their ball is going when they hit it in order to improve their swing, workers need feedback about how closely they are approaching their performance goals in order to meet them.

The importance of combining feedback and goal setting has been shown in a recent field study examining the effects of goal setting on occupational safety.[53] The subjects were employees working in various shops of a manufacturing plant. Before and after safety goals were set, observations were made of various employee behaviors. From these, judgments were made of the percentage of employees performing their jobs in a completely safe manner. During the ten weeks before goal setting began, about 65 percent of the workers performed their jobs safely. Then, after a difficult but attainable goal of 95 percent safe behavior was set, the safety rate rose to over 80 percent—an improvement, but a rate still shy of the goal. Only after the goal setting was accompanied by feedback about safety was the goal met.

A very ambitious recent study of different units in the U.S. Air Force showed that feedback and goal setting together helped improve performance for work groups (as opposed to individuals).[54] The job effectiveness index (a measure of the extent to which expectations were met or exceeded) of five different groups was measured repeatedly over a two year period. During the first nine months, a baseline measure of effectiveness was taken that could be used to compare the relative impact of feedback and goal setting. Then, the groups received feedback for five months (monthly reports explaining how well they performed on various performance measures). After five months of feedback, the groups began the goal-setting phase of the study. During this time, the crew members set goals for themselves with respect to their performance on various measures. Then, for the last five months, in addition to the feedback and goal setting, an incentive (time off from work) was made available to crew members who met their goals. The relative effectiveness of the crews during each phase of the study is shown in Figure 3.11.

As Figure 3.11 clearly shows, feedback and goal setting dramatically increased group effectiveness. Group feedback improved performance approximately 50 percent over the baseline level. The addition of group goal setting improved it 75 percent over baseline. These findings show that the combination of goal setting and feedback helps raise the effectiveness of group performance. Groups that know how well they're doing and have a target goal to shoot for tend to perform very well. Providing incentives, however, improved performance only negligibly. The real incentive seems to be meeting the challenge of performing up to the level of the goal.

In sum, goal setting is a very effective tool managers can use to motivate sub-

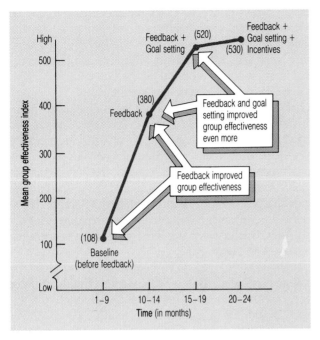

**FIGURE 3.11   Goal Setting
and Feedback: Most Effective
When Combined**

Research on U.S. Air Force
crews over a two year period
showed that feedback
enhanced performance
relative to baseline levels of
group effectiveness, and that
the addition of goal setting
enhanced it even more. After
feedback and goal setting
were used, the introduction
of incentives had negligible
additional impact on
effectiveness. (Based on data
in Pritchard, Jones, Roth,
Stuebing, and Ekeberg, 1988;
see Note 54.)

ordinates. Setting specific, acceptably difficult goals, and providing feedback about progress toward the goal, greatly enhances motivation and job performance.

Job Design: Creating Motivating Jobs

In addition to motivating by setting goals, another method of enhancing motivation is designing jobs so as to make them more appealing to the workers. The roots of this idea can be traced back to the early part of this century when Fredrick W. Taylor attempted to stimulate productivity by analyzing the minute motions involved in work tasks to discover the most efficient ways of performing them. This approach, known as **scientific management,** was intended to make work highly efficient (recall our discussion of scientific management in chapter 1). Unfortunately, however, it also made many jobs highly routine and monotonous. The problem with this, of course, is that people who are bored with their jobs tend to be absent or to quit.[55] As a result, motivational practitioners have sought ways of designing jobs that are simultaneously efficient and pleasant for the workers.

Several contemporary approaches to task design seek to motivate workers in more humane, and effective, ways than scientific management. These approaches tend to motivate workers by designing jobs so they are more involving for the workers performing them. Our discussion will focus on two approaches to job design popular in the 1950s and 1960s—**job enlargement** and **job enrichment**—as well as an approach introduced and studied in the 1970s and 1980s that is still popular today—the **job characteristics model.**

Job enlargement and job enrichment. One of the first modern ways of motivating people in organizations was to redesign jobs according to the principles of **job enlargement.** Job enlargement refers to the practice of expanding the content of a job by increasing the number and variety of tasks performed at the same level. If an employee on an automobile assembly line normally has the job of tightening the lugs on the left rear wheel of the car as it rolls down the assembly line, that job may be enlarged by requiring him to tighten the lugs on all four wheels. Please note that the worker now performs a greater number of specific tasks, but these are all at the same low level of difficulty, and require very little responsibility. Because of this, the enlargement process is said to have increased the *horizontal job loading* of the job. That is, the individual now performs more tasks at the same level of difficulty.

In contrast to job enlargement, **job enrichment** not only gives employees more jobs to do, but gives them more tasks to perform at a higher level. Job enrichment refers to the practice of giving employees the opportunity to have greater responsibility and to take greater control over how to do their jobs. Because people performing enriched jobs have increased opportunities to work at higher levels, the job enrichment process is said to increase the job's *vertical job loading.* (Incidentally, we should note that the idea of job enrichment was developed by Fredrick Herzberg. Because Herzberg's theory focuses heavily on the determinants of job satisfaction, we have reserved discussion of it until chapter 5.) For a summary of the differences between job enlargement and job enrichment, please see Figure 3.12.

Job enlargement and job enrichment programs have been used at some of the largest companies in the United States, including IBM, AT&T, General Foods, Procter & Gamble, and others. However, one of the most extensive and well-known job enrichment programs was developed by the Swedish auto manufacturer, Volvo. In response to serious labor problems in the late 1960s, such as strikes and high rates of absenteeism and turnover, the company's new president, Pehr Gyllenhammar, introduced job enrichment in its assembly plant in the southern Swedish town of Kalmar.[56] Cars were assembled by twenty-five groups of approximately fifteen to twenty-five workers who were each responsible for one part of the car's assembly (e.g., engine assembly, electrical system, etc.). In contrast to the usual assembly line method of manufacturing cars, Volvo's work groups were set up so they could freely plan, organize, and inspect their own work. In time, the workers became more satisfied with their

FIGURE 3.12   Job Enlargement and Job Enrichment: Comparing Two Traditional Approaches to Job Design

Designing jobs by increasing the number of tasks performed at the same level (horizontal job loading) is referred to as *job enlargement.* Designing jobs by increasing workers' responsibility and control over their jobs (vertical job loading) is referred to as *job enrichment.*

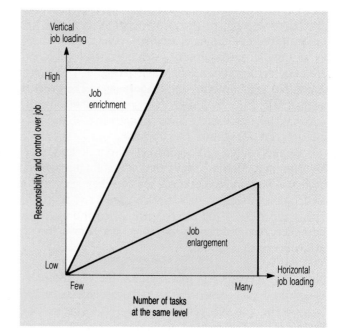

jobs and the plant experienced a significant reduction in turnover and absenteeism. Although it was more costly to manufacture cars this way, the resulting increases in quality and improvements in worker relations enhanced the company's commitment to job enrichment programs.

Although job enrichment was clearly well-received at Volvo, it is important to ask whether job enlargement and enrichment plans succeed generally. The support for job enlargement is mostly anecdotal. There are more case studies than good empirical investigations supporting the effectiveness of job enlargement programs. Job enrichment has been the subject of more rigorous empirical investigations, but here too, critics have found the evidence in support of its effectiveness questionable.[57] In other words, although it is often reported that enlargement and enrichment programs are effective, the scientific evidence is not all that compelling.

Without going into detail about the specific problems with the studies on job enlargement and enrichment programs and their findings, let's review some of the problems that have been identified with putting such programs to use. One obvious problem lies in the *difficulty of implementation.* Clearly, it would be expensive to redesign existing physical plants so as to enrich many jobs. Not only that, but the technology required to perform some jobs makes it difficult, if not impossible, for them to be performed in a different manner. It is perhaps for these reasons that formal job enrichment plans remain quite atypical in the United States. In one survey of 125 industrial firms, only five reported attempts to institute formal job enrichment programs.[58]

In addition to these economic and technical impediments, there's also a human impediment—the problem of *lack of acceptance,* particularly among unionized employees. To quote one AFL-CIO leader, "If you want to enrich the job, enrich the paycheck . . . That's the kind of job enrichment unions believe in."[59] The problem is that not all employees want the added responsibility that goes along with performing enriched jobs. This fact is demonstrated nicely in one study in which six auto workers from Detroit worked in Sweden as engine assemblers in a SAAB plant. In Sweden, enriched jobs are typical, and the auto workers at SAAB exercise a great deal of freedom and responsibility about how to perform their jobs. After a month, five out of the six Americans reported preferring their traditional assembly line jobs. In the words of one of the workers, "If I've got to bust my a— to be meaningful, forget it; I'd rather be monotonous."[60] Clearly, enriched jobs might not be for everyone.

Given this, we may ask: which employees respond most positively to enriched jobs? A recent study found that individuals who were particularly interested in striving to be successful in their lives (a personality trait known as *need for achievement,* which we will discuss more fully in chapter 6) worked harder at enriched jobs because such jobs provided more opportunities to achieve success.[61] However, employees who were less concerned about achieving success found enriched jobs a frustrating, dissatisfying experience. In sum, job enrichment programs may only improve the performance of those who seek enrichment.

One problem with the job enrichment approach as we have presented it thus far is that it fails to specify *how* to enrich a job. In other words, exactly *what* elements of a job need to be enriched for it to be effective? A recent attempt to expand the idea of job enrichment, known as the **job characteristics model,** provides an answer to this important question.

The job characteristics model. This approach assumes that jobs can be redesigned so as to "help individuals regain the chance to experience the kick that comes from doing a job well, and . . . once again *care* about their work and about developing the competence to do it even better."[62] According to Jack Hoffman, an executive at General Electric, this is what his company is trying to do. Specifically,

> What we're all trying to do is get every person feeling important about his or her job, whether they sweep the floor, drive screws in a unit, interact with customers, coordinate in a certain area or are an individual contributor. What we know is that people want more out of a job than that pay check. They want a feeling of input.[63]

This is what the job characteristics model is all about. It helps identify how jobs can be designed to give workers those feelings of importance to which Mr. Hoffman refers. In particular, the job characteristics model specifies that enriching certain elements of jobs is effective in altering people's psychological states in a manner that enhances their work effectiveness.[64]

Specifically, the model identifies five *core job dimensions* that help create three *critical psychological states,* leading, in turn, to several beneficial outcomes for individuals and the organizations employing them (see Figure 3.13). As shown in the diagram, there are three job dimensions—skill variety, task identity, and task significance—that contribute to a task's experienced meaningfulness. Let's take a closer look at these.

- *Skill variety* refers to the extent to which a job requires a number of different activities using several of the worker's skills and talents. For example, a secretary with high

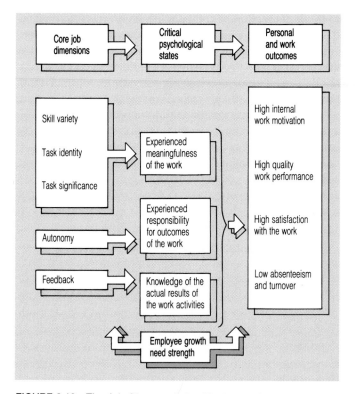

FIGURE 3.13   The Job Characteristics Model: An Overview

The *job characteristics model* stipulates that certain *core job dimensions* create *critical psychological states,* which lead to several beneficial *personal and work outcomes.* The model recognizes that these relationships are strongest among employees who are high in the personality dimension of growth need strength. (Source: Adapted from Hackman & Oldham, 1980; see Note 64.)

skill variety may have to perform many different tasks (i.e., take dictation, do word processing, use both manual and electronic filing systems, answer the telephone, and welcome visitors to the office).

- *Task identity* refers to the extent to which a job requires completing a whole piece of work from beginning to end. For example, tailors will have high task identity if they do everything related to making a whole suit (i.e., measure the client for a suit, select the fabric, cut and sew it, re-fit the customer, and alter it as needed).
- *Task significance* refers to the degree of impact the job is believed to have on other people, either within the organization, or in the world at large. Consider, for example, the high task significance of medical researchers working to find a cure for a serious disease.

These three factors contribute to a task's *experienced meaningfulness*. According to the job characteristics model, a task is considered meaningful if it is experienced as important, valuable, and worthwhile.

The job characteristics model identifies two additional core job dimensions. One of these is autonomy.

- *Autonomy* refers to the extent to which an employee has the freedom and discretion to plan, schedule, and carry out the job as desired. For example, a furniture repair person may act highly autonomously by freely scheduling his or her day's work, and by freely deciding how to tackle each repair job confronted.

Autonomous jobs are said to make workers feel *personally responsible and accountable for the work* they perform. They are free to decide what to do and how to do it, and so they feel more responsible for the results, either good or bad. The fifth core job dimension is feedback.

- *Feedback* refers to the extent to which the job allows people to have information about the effectiveness of their performance. For example, telemarketing representatives regularly receive information about how many calls they made per day and the number and value of the sales made.

Effective feedback gives employees *knowledge of the results of their work*. When a job is designed to provide people with information about the effects of their actions, they will be better able to develop an understanding of how effectively they have performed. Such knowledge helps improve the effectiveness of job performance.

The job characteristics model specifies that the three critical psychological states (experienced meaningfulness, responsibility for outcomes, and knowledge of results) affect various personal and work outcomes—namely: people's feelings of motivation, the quality of work performed, satisfaction with work, and absenteeism and turnover. Specifically, the higher the experienced meaningfulness of work, responsibility for the work performed, and knowledge of results, the more positive the personal and work benefits will be. When they perform jobs that incorporate high levels of the five core job dimensions, employees should feel highly motivated, perform high quality work, be highly satisfied with their jobs, be absent infrequently, and be unlikely to resign from their jobs.

We should also note that the model is theorized to be especially effective in describing the behavior of individuals who are high in *growth need strength*—that is, individuals who have a high need for personal growth and development. Those individuals who are not particularly interested in personal growth and development are not expected to experience the theorized psychological reactions to the core job dimensions, nor consequently, to enjoy the beneficial personal and work outcomes predicted by the model.[65] By including this variable in the model, the job characteristics model recognizes the important limitation of job enrichment noted in the previous section: not everyone wants and benefits from enriched jobs.

Based on the proposed relationship between the core job dimensions and their associated psychological reactions, the model claims that job motivation would be highest when jobs performed are high on the various dimensions. To assess this idea, a questionnaire known as the *Job Diagnostic Survey* (*JDS*) has been developed to measure the degree to which various job characteristics are present in a particular job.[66] Based on responses to the JDS it is possible to make predictions about the degree to which a job motivates the people who perform it. This is done using an index known as the **motivating potential score** (**MPS**). It is computed as follows:

$$MPS = \frac{\text{Skill variety} + \text{Task identity} + \text{Task significance}}{3} \times \text{Autonomy} \times \text{Feedback}$$

The MPS is a summary index of a job's potential for motivating workers. The higher the MPS for any given job, the greater the likelihood of experiencing the beneficial personal and work outcomes specified by the job characteristics model. Knowing a job's MPS helps identify jobs that might benefit by being redesigned.

The job characteristics model has been the focus of many empirical tests, most of which suggest that the model identifies some effective ways of enriching jobs.[67] One study conducted among a group of South African clerical workers found particularly strong support for many aspects of the model.[68] The employees in some of the offices in this organization had their jobs enriched in accord with the suggestions of the job characteristics model. Specifically, they were given the opportunity to: (a) choose what kinds of tasks they would perform (high skill variety), (b) perform the entire job (high task identity), (c) receive instructions regarding how their job fit into the organization as a whole (high task significance), (d) freely set their own schedules and inspect their own work (high autonomy), and (e) keep records of their daily productivity (high feedback). Another group of clerical workers, who were equivalent in all respects except that their jobs were not enriched, served as a control group.

After employees performed the newly designed jobs for six months, comparisons were made between them and their counterparts in the control group who performed the traditional jobs. With respect to most of the outcomes specified by the model, individuals performing the redesigned jobs showed superior results. Questionnaire measures found them feeling more internally motivated and more satisfied with their jobs. Furthermore, objective measures found lower rates of absenteeism and turnover among employees performing the enriched jobs. The only outcome predicted by the model that was not found to differ was actual work performance: performance quality was *not* significantly higher for employees performing the enriched jobs compared to those performing the traditional jobs. This result is typical of those found in many other studies. Enriching jobs appears to have much greater impact on job attitudes and beliefs than on actual job performance—and this is especially true of individuals who are high in growth need strength.[69] Considering the many factors that enter into determining job performance (as discussed in connection with expectancy theory), this finding should not be too surprising. (We will discuss the relationship between job attitudes and performance more thoroughly in chapter 5.)

The job characteristics model specifies several things that can be done to redesign jobs to enhance their motivating potential.[70] We summarize these in the form of general rules in Table 3.4.

TABLE 3.4 Enriching Jobs: Some Suggestions from the Job Characteristics Model
The *job characteristics model* specifies several ways jobs can be designed to incorporate the core job dimensions responsible for enhancing motivation and performance. A few are listed here.

PRINCIPLE OF JOB DESIGN	CORE JOB DIMENSIONS INCORPORATED
1. Combine jobs, enabling workers to perform the entire job	Skill variety Task identity
2. Form natural work units, allowing workers to be identified with their work	Task identity Task significance
3. Establish client relationships, allowing providers of a service to meet the recipients	Skill variety Autonomy Feedback
4. Load jobs vertically, allowing greater responsibility and control over work	Autonomy
5. Open feedback channels, giving workers knowledge of the results of their work	Feedback

(Source: Based on information in Hackman, 1976; see Note 62.)

Principle 1: Combine tasks. Have employees perform an entire job (e.g., manufacturing a product) instead of having several workers perform various parts of the job. Doing so helps provide greater skill variety and task identity.

Principle 2: Form natural work units. Distribute work so that employees are identified with the jobs they've done. For example, a word processing operator can prepare an entire report, instead of having parts of the report completed by several different workers. Designing the job this way enhances skill variety and task significance.

Principle 3: Establish client relationships. Set up jobs so that the person performing a service (such as an auto mechanic) comes into contact with the recipient of the service (such as the car owner). Jobs designed in this manner not only help the worker by providing job feedback, but also provide skill variety (talking to customers in addition to working on cars), and enhance autonomy (by giving workers the freedom to manage their own relationships with clients).

Principle 4: Load jobs vertically. As we described earlier, loading a job vertically involves giving people greater responsibility for their jobs. Taking responsibility and control over job performance away from managers and giving it to their subordinates increases the level of autonomy the jobs offer these lower-level employees.

Principle 5: Open feedback channels. There are many different types of feedback employees may receive, and jobs should be designed to offer as many as possible.[71] Feedback can be provided by customers, supervisors, and coworkers. Cues about job performance can also be provided by the job itself, using various indexes such as the number of words correctly typed per minute, the dollar total of the day's sales, and so on. The more feedback channels used, the more accurate a picture people will have of how well they're doing, and the more motivated they will be to improve.

Despite these specific suggestions, implementing job enrichment programs is not easy. As mentioned earlier, people attempting to enrich jobs face many obstacles related to technical limitations and resistance to change from the workforce. Explaining the reasons for changes and the benefits likely to result from them can help overcome the potentially threatening nature of redesigned jobs. As we will see in the **Management Perspective** section below, such supervisory comments can go a long way toward enhancing employees' motivation.

OB: A MANAGEMENT PERSPECTIVE

The Language of Motivation: It's Not What You Do, But What You Say, That Counts

If you have ever been given a "pep talk," or "chewed out" by your boss, then you know what an important effect a supervisor's words can have on motivation. The idea that a few well-chosen words can work motivational wonders is clearly the common thread running through the various theories and applications reviewed in this chapter. Consider these examples:

- According to *Maslow's need hierarchy theory,* telling people they did a good job may help satisfy their self-esteem needs.
- According to *equity theory,* informing employees about how much their coworkers are paid helps them judge the equity of their own pay.
- According to *expectancy theory,* telling people that they will be paid based on their performance helps establish their instrumentality beliefs.
- According to the concept of *goal setting,* establishing what specific goals individuals and groups should strive for helps improve their performance.
- According to the *job characteristics model,* providing information about the importance of the job and how well it was performed enhances personal and work outcomes.

Recent research has classified the various things supervisors say to enhance motivation into three categories.[72] These include:

1. *perlocutionary language*—things said to reduce people's uncertainty about the effects of their actions (e.g., "If you do it this way, you'll get more done")
2. *locutionary language*—things said to explain what employees should think and do (e.g., "It's your job to complete this task")
3. *illocutionary language*—things said to establish congenial relations between managers and their subordinates by showing concern and empathy for

them (e.g., "I hope you're enjoying working on this project").

The key to *motivational language* is that motivation will be enhanced when people know *what* to do, *how* to do their jobs, and *why* jobs should be done a certain way. With this in mind, here are a few simple guidelines to follow in order to improve your motivational language skills.

Rule 1: Always let others know what you expect of them. Explain your expectations of their performance—not only with respect to what they should do (i.e., *role expectations*), but also how well they should do it (i.e., specific *goals*).

Rule 2: Inform employees of the consequences of their actions. The consequences may be positive (e.g., you will get a 20 percent bonus), or negative (e.g., you will get laid off), but should be made clear whenever possible.

Rule 3: Explain the reasons for your actions. Whatever you do will be much better accepted if it is accompanied by an explanation. Subordinates' insecurities may be alleviated by explanations that provide adequate reassurances. If nothing else, such explanations may help cultivate the impression that the manager's action was the result of considered judgment, and is, therefore, fair and likely to be accepted.[73]

Rule 4: Adopt the employee's own perspective. Show subordinates that you are sincerely aware of their needs, feelings, and concerns. Putting yourself in their place may help you understand their insecurities and suggest the kind of reassurance that reduces their uncertainty.

Following these perlocutionary, locutionary, and illocutionary verbal tactics will, we believe, greatly improve any manager's ability to motivate effectively.

The Nature of Motivation. Motivation is concerned with the set of processes that arouse, direct, and maintain behavior toward a goal. It is not equivalent to job performance, but is one of several determinants of job performance. Today's work ethic motivates people to seek interesting and challenging jobs, although different work values exist in different cultures.

Theories of Motivation. Three major theories of organizational motivation are most popular among researchers and practitioners. Maslow's **need hierarchy theory** postulates that people have five types of needs, activated in a specific order from the most basic, lowest level need (physiological needs) to the highest level need (need for self-actualization). Although this theory has not been supported in rigorous scientific studies, it has been quite useful in suggesting several useful ways of satisfying employees' needs on the job.

    Equity theory claims that people desire to attain an equitable balance between the ratios of their work rewards (outcomes) and their job contributions (inputs) and the corresponding ratios of comparison others. Inequitable states of overpayment and underpayment are undesirable, motivating workers to try to attain equitable conditions. Responses to inequity may be either behavioral or psychological in nature.

    Expectancy theory recognizes that motivation is the product of a person's beliefs about **expectancy** (effort will lead to performance), **instrumentality** (performance will result in reward), and **valence** (the perceived value of the rewards). In conjunction with skills, abilities, role perceptions, and opportunities, motivation contributes to job performance.

Techniques of Motivation. There are several ways of motivating workers. One of the most effective is by **goal setting.** People will improve their performance when specific, acceptably difficult goals are set and feedback about task performance is provided. The task of selecting goals that are acceptable to employees may be facilitated by allowing employees to participate in the goal-setting process.

    Motivation can also be enhanced at the organizational level, by designing or redesigning jobs. **Job design** techniques include **job enlargement** (performing more tasks at the same level) and **job enrichment** (giving workers greater responsibility and control over their jobs). The **job characteristics model,** a currently popular approach to enriching jobs, identifies the specific job dimensions that should be enriched (skill variety, task identity, task significance, autonomy, and feedback), and relates these to the critical psychological states influenced by including these dimensions on a job. These psychological states will, in turn, lead to certain beneficial outcomes for both the worker (e.g., job satisfaction) and the organization (e.g., reduced absenteeism and turnover).

Key Terms

cafeteria-style benefit plans: Incentive systems in which employees have an opportunity to select the fringe benefits they want from a menu of available alternatives.

equitable payment: The state in which one person's outcome/input ratio is equivalent to that of another person with whom this individual compares himself or herself.

equity theory: The theory stating that people strive to maintain ratios of their own outcomes (rewards) to their own inputs (contributions), equal to the outcome/input ratios of others with whom they compare themselves.

ERG theory: An alternative to Maslow's *need hierarchy theory* proposed by Alderfer, which asserts that there are three basic human needs—existence, relatedness, and growth.

expectancy: The beliefs that people hold regarding the extent to which their efforts will influence their performance.

expectancy theory: The theory which asserts that motivation is based on people's beliefs about the probability that effort will lead to performance (*expectancy*), multiplied by the probability that performance will lead to reward (*instrumentality*), multiplied by the perceived value (*valence*) of the reward.

goal setting: The process of determining specific levels of performance for workers to attain.

inequity: The undesirable condition in which someone's outcome/input ratio is not equal to that of another person who is used for comparison. If this inequity favors a person, the result is *overpayment inequity,* which leads to feelings of guilt. If this inequity is to a person's disadvantage, the result is *underpayment inequity,* which leads to feelings of anger.

inputs: Employees' contributions to their jobs, such as their experience, qualifications, or the amount of time worked.

instrumentality: An individual's belief regarding the likelihood of being rewarded in accord with his or her own level of performance.

job characteristics model: An approach taken by organizations toward job enrichment, which specifies that five *core job dimensions* (skill variety, task identity, task significance, autonomy, and job feedback) produce critical psychological states that lead to beneficial outcomes for the worker (e.g., high job satisfaction) and the organization (e.g., high performance).

job design: An approach to motivation suggesting that jobs can be created so as to motivate people. (See *job enlargement, job enrichment,* and the *job characteristics model.*)

job enlargement: The practice of expanding the content of a job so as to include more variety and a greater number of tasks at the same level.

job enrichment: The practice of giving employees a high degree of control over their work, from planning and organization, through implementing the jobs and evaluating the results.

motivating potential score (MPS): A mathematical index describing the degree to which a job is designed so as to motivate people, as suggested by the *job characteristics model.* It is computed on the basis of responses to a questionnaire known as the *job diagnostic survey (JDS).* The higher the *MPS,* the more motivating a job is; the lower the *MPS,* the more the job may stand to benefit from redesign.

motivation: The set of processes that arouse, direct, and maintain human behavior toward attaining a goal.

need hierarchy theory: Maslow's theory that there are five human needs (physiological, safety, social, esteem, and self-actualization) and that these are arranged in such a way that lower, more basic needs must be satisfied before higher-level needs become activated.

outcomes: The rewards employees receive from their jobs, such as salary and recognition.

overpayment inequity: The condition, resulting in feelings of guilt, under which the ratio of one's outcomes/inputs is greater than the corresponding ratio of another person against whom that person compares himself or herself.

pay-for-performance: A payment system in which workers are paid differentially, based on the quantity and quality of their job performance (i.e., *merit pay*). Pay-for-performance plans strengthen *instrumentality* beliefs.

procedural justice: The perceived fairness of the rules and procedures followed in making decisions.

scientific management: An early approach to motivation in which jobs were redesigned to make them simpler and more efficient, although highly routine and monotonous.

self-actualization: The need to discover who we are and to develop ourselves to the fullest potential.

two-tier wage structures: Payment systems in which newer employees are paid less than employees hired at earlier times to do the same work.

underpayment inequity: The condition, resulting in feelings of anger, under which the ratio of one's outcomes/inputs is less than the corresponding ratio of another person against whom that person compares himself or herself.

valence: The value a person places on the rewards he or she expects to receive from an organization.

QUESTIONS FOR DISCUSSION

1. Define the concept of motivation and describe how it is relevant to the field of organizational behavior.

2. Characterize the importance placed on work as a life value at different periods in history. What is the predominant belief about the role of work as a life value in today's society?

3. Maslow's need hierarchy theory specifies several ways to satisfy people's needs on the job. Identify each of the five need categories specified by Maslow and for each one, describe something that can be done on the job to enhance need satisfaction.

4. According to equity theory, how might an individual who is overpaid feel and behave? What might such a person do to alleviate this inequity? How about someone who is underpaid?

5. Imagine a student who performs poorly on an exam and then claims to the instructor, "I tried." According to expectancy theory, what other factors can account for performance besides motivation?

6. Compare and contrast the role of money as a motivator as characterized by need theory, equity theory, and expectancy theory.

7. Imagine that you are establishing a goal-setting program for an organization. Describe the way goals should be set and some of the factors that will make the program effective. What hurdles would have to be overcome?

8. Think of some job with which you are familiar and then describe specific things that can be done to enrich the job using the core job dimensions identified by the job characteristics model. What obstacles would have to be overcome to apply the model to this particular job?

Notes

1. Kanfer, R. L. (in press). Motivation theory and industrial/organizational psychology. In M. D. Dunnette (Ed.), *Handbook of industrial and organizational psychology* (2nd ed.). Palo Alto, CA: Consulting Psychologists Press.

2. Steers, R. M., & Porter, L. W. (Eds.) (1989). *Motivation and work behavior* (5th ed.). New York: McGraw-Hill.

3. Landy, F. J., & Becker, W. S. (1987). Motivation theory reconsidered. In L. L. Cummings & B. M. Staw (Eds.), *Research in organizational behavior,* vol. 9 (pp. 1–38). Greenwich, CT: JAI Press.

4. Furnham, A. (1989). *The Protestant work ethic: The psychology of work beliefs and behaviours.* London: Routledge.

5. Grant, M. (1960). *The world of Rome* (p. 112). London: Weidenfeld and Nocolson.

6. *Newsweek* (1971). October 18, p. 31.

7. Nord, W. R., Brief, A. P., Atieh, J. M., & Doherty, E. M. (1988). Work values and the conduct of organizational behavior. In B. M. Staw & L. L. Cummings (Eds.), *Research in organizational behavior,* vol. 10 (pp. 1–42). Greenwich, CT: JAI Press.

8. *Los Angeles Times* (1981). Work still a labor of love. As reported in *The Columbus Dispatch,* April 20, p. 1.

9. Shenkar, O., & Ronen, S. (1987). Structure and importance of work goals among managers in the People's Republic of China. *Academy of Management Journal, 30,* 564–576.

10. Laaksonen, O. (1984). Management and power structure of Chinese enterprises during and after the Cultural Revolution: With empirical data comparing Chinese and European enterprises. *Organization Studies, 5,* 1–21.

11. Maslow, A. H. (1970). *Motivation and personality* (2nd ed.). New York: Harper & Row.

12. Falkenberg, L. E. (1987). Employee fitness programs: Their impact on the employee and the organization. *Academy of Management Review, 12,* 511–522.

13. Byrne, J. A. (1984, January 30). Motivating Willy Loman. *Forbes,* p. 91.

14. Veroff, J., Reuman, D., & Feld, S. (1984). Motives in American men and women across the life span. *Developmental Psychology, 20,* 1142–1158.

15. Porter, L. W. (1961). A study of perceived need satisfaction in bottom and middle management jobs. *Journal of Applied Psychology, 45,* 1–10.

16. Betz, E. L. (1982). Need fulfillment in the career development of women. *Journal of Vocational Behavior, 20,* 53–66.

17. Wahba, M. A., & Bridwell, L. G. (1976). Maslow reconsidered: A review of research on the need hierarchy theory. *Organizational Behavior and Human Performance, 15,* 212–240.

18. Alderfer, C. P. (1972). *Existence, relatedness, and growth.* New York: Free Press.

19. Salancik, G. R., & Pfeffer, J. (1977). An examination of need-satisfaction models of job satisfaction. *Administrative Science Quarterly, 22,* 427–456.

20. Adams, J. S. (1965). Inequity in social exchange. In L. Berkowitz (Ed.), *Advances in experimental social psychology,* vol. 2 (pp. 267–299). New York: Academic Press.

21. Greenberg, J. (1989). Cognitive re-evaluation of outcomes in response to underpayment inequity. *Academy of Management Journal, 32,* 174–184.

22. Greenberg, J. (1987). A taxonomy of organizational justice theories. *Academy of Management Review, 12,* 9–22.

23. Pritchard, R. D., Dunnette, M. D., & Jorgenson, D. O. (1972). Effects of perceptions of equity and inequity on worker performance and satisfaction. *Journal of Applied Psychology, 57,* 75–94.

24. Martin, J. E., & Peterson, M. M. (1987). Two-tier wage structures: Implications for equity theory. *Academy of Management Journal, 30,* 297–315.

25. Ross, I. (1985, April 29). Employers win big on the move to two-tier contracts. *Fortune, 111*(9), pp. 82–92.

26. See Note 25.

27. Greenberg, J. (1988). Equity and workplace status: A field experiment. *Journal of Applied Psychology, 73,* 606–613.

28. Lind, E. A., & Tyler, T. R. (1988). *The social psychology of procedural justice.* New York: Plenum.

29. Folger, R., & Greenberg, J. (1985). Procedural justice: An interpretive analysis of personnel systems. In K. M. Rowland & G. D. Ferris (Eds.), *Research in personnel and human resource management,* vol. 3 (pp. 141–183). Greenwich, CT: JAI Press.

30. Greenberg, J. (1987). Reactions to procedural injustice in payment allocations: Do the ends justify the means? *Journal of Applied Psychology, 72,* 55–61.

31. See Note 22.

32. Vroom, V. H. (1964). *Work and motivation.* New York: Wiley.

33. Porter, L. W., & Lawler, E. E. (1968). *Managerial attitudes and performance.* Homewood, IL: Irwin.

34. Mitchell, T. R. (1983). Expectancy-value models in organizational psychology. In N. Feather (Ed.), *Expectancy, incentive, and action* (pp. 293–314). Hillsdale, NJ: Lawrence Erlbaum Assocs.

35. Miller, L. E., & Grush, J. E. (1988). Improving predictions in expectancy theory research: Effects of personality, expectancies, and norms. *Academy of Management Journal, 31,* 107–122.

36. Harrell, A., & Stahl, M. (1986). Additive information processing and the relationship between expectancy of success and motivational force. *Academy of Management Journal, 29,* 424–433.

37. Heneman, R. L. (1984). *Pay for performance: Exploring the merit system.* New York: Pergamon Press.

38. Markham, S. E. (1988). Pay-for-performance dilemma revisited: Empirical example of the importance of group effects. *Journal of Applied Psychology, 73,* 172–180.

39. Foegen, J. H. (1982, October 18). Fringe benefits are being diversified too. *Industry Week,* pp. 56–58.

40. Zippo, M. (1982, July–August). Flexible benefits: Just the beginning. *Personnel Journal,* pp. 56–58.

41. Locke, E. & Latham, G. (1990). *A theory of goal setting and task performance.* Englewood Cliffs, NJ: Prentice Hall.

42. Latham, G. P., & Lee, T. W. (1986). Goal setting. In E. A. Locke (Ed.), *Generalizing from laboratory to field settings* (pp. 100–117). Lexington, MA: Lexington Books.

43. Miller, L. (1978). *Behavior management: The new science of managing people at work.* New York: Wiley.

44. Latham, G. P., & Locke, E. (1979). Goal setting—a motivational technique that works. *Organizational Dynamics, 8*(2), 68–80.

45. Locke, E. A., & Latham, G. P. (1984). *Goal Setting for individuals, groups, and organizations.* Chicago: Science Research Assoc.

46. Stedry, A. C., & Kay, E. (1964). *The effects of goal difficulty on performance.* General Electric Company, Behavioral Research Service.

47. See Note 45.

48. Locke, E. A., Latham, G. P., & Erez, M. (1988). The determinants of goal commitment. *Academy of Management Review, 13,* 23–39.

49. Latham, G. P., Erez, M., & Locke, E. A. (1988). Resolving scientific disputes by the joint design of crucial experiments by the antagonists: Application to the Erez–Latham dispute regarding participation in goal setting. *Journal of Applied Psychology, 73,* 753–772.

50. Latham, G. P., & Saari, L. M. (1979). Importance of supportive relationships in goal setting. *Journal of Applied Psychology, 64,* 151–156.

51. Chase, S. (1982, April 8). Life at IBM. *Wall Street Journal,* p. 1.

52. See Note 44.

53. Chhokar, J. S., & Wallin, J. A. (1984). A field study of the effects of feedback frequency on performance. *Journal of Applied Psychology, 69,* 524–530.

54. Pritchard, R. D., Jones, S. D., Roth, P. L., Stuebing, K. K., & Ekeberg, S. E. (1988). Effects of group feedback, goal setting, and incentives on organizational productivity. *Journal of Applied Psychology, 73,* 337–358.

55. Griffin, R. W. (1987). Toward an integrated theory of task design. In L. L. Cummings, & B. M. Staw (Eds.), *Research in organizational behavior,* vol. 9 (pp. 79–120). Greenwich, CT: JAI Press.

56. Gyllenhammar, P. G. (1977). *People at work.* Reading, MA: Addison-Wesley.

57. Fein, M. (1974). Job enrichment: A reevaluation. *Sloan Management Review,* Winter, 69–99.

58. Luthans, F., & Rief, W. E. (1974). Job enrichment: Long on theory, short on practice. *Organizational Dynamics, 2,* 30–43.

59. Winpisinger, W. (1973, February). Job satisfaction: A union response. *AFL–CIO American Federationist,* pp. 8–10.

60. Goldman, R. B. (1976). *A work experiment: Six Americans in a Swedish plant.* New York: Ford Foundation.

61. Steers, R. M., & Spencer, D. G. (1977). The role of achievement motivation in job design. *Journal of Applied Psychology, 62,* 472–479.

62. Hackman, J. R. (1976). Work design. In J. R. Hackman & J. L. Suttle (Eds.), *Improving life at work* (p. 103). Santa Monica, CA: Goodyear.

63. Ropp, K. (1987, October). Candid conversations. *Personnel Administrator,* p. 49.

64. Hackman, J. R., & Oldham, G. R. (1980). *Work redesign.* Reading, MA: Addison-Wesley.

65. Graen, G. B., Scandura, T. A., & Graen, M. R. (1986). A field experimental test of the moderating effects of growth need strength on productivity. *Journal of Applied Psychology, 71,* 484–491.

66. Hackman, J. R., & Oldham, G. R. (1976). Motivation through the design of work: Test of a theory. *Organizational Behavior and Human Performance, 16,* 250–279.

67. Fried, Y., & Ferris, G. R. (1987). The validity of the job characteristics model: A review and meta-analysis. *Personnel Psychology, 40,* 287–322.

68. Orpen, C. (1979). The effects of job enrichment on employee satisfaction, motivation, involvement, and performance: A field experiment. *Human Relations, 32,* 189–217.

69. Loher, B. T., Noe, R. A., Moeller, N. L., & Fitzgerald, M. P. (1985). A meta-analysis of the relation of job characteristics to job satisfaction. *Journal of Applied Psychology, 70,* 280–289.

70. See Note 62.

71. Ilgen, D. R., & Moore, C. F. (1987). Types and choices of performance feedback. *Journal of Applied Psychology, 72,* 401–406.

72. Sullivan, J. J. (1988). Three roles of language in motivation theory. *Academy of Management Review, 13,* 104–115.

73. Greenberg, J. (1990). Looking fair vs. being fair: Managing impressions of organizational justice. In B. M. Staw & L. L. Cummings (Eds.), *Research in organizational behavior,* vol. 12. Greenwich, CT: JAI Press.

**CASE
IN
POINT**

Successful Uses of Job Redesign: Three Organizational Examples

What do JP Industries (an Ann Arbor, Michigan-based conglomerate of hard goods production companies), Deere & Co. (the over-100-year-old manufacturer of farm equipment), and the U.S. Air Force's Tactical Air Command have in common? All have recently learned the value of redesigning the jobs of their personnel. In each of these organizations, performance, productivity, and quality had been much lower than desired. Job redesign was implemented to remedy these unacceptable conditions. The resulting improvements in productivity and motivation were absolutely astounding.[1] Now, let's take a closer look at these success stories.

At JP Industries and at Deere & Co., the bulk of the manufacturing work is completed on assembly lines. Prior to the redesign, individual workers performed one component of the assembly operation, never seeing the finished products or even receiving information about the quality of their work. After the redesign, however, employees were involved in multiple operations, such as checking their own work for defects and quality workmanship. For example, welders at Deere were initially positioned at the far end of the shop floor, welding pieces of equipment to be assembled into machines by others working on the assembly line. If they made a mistake in their welding, they never knew it because the defective parts were discovered days later in another part of the factory. After the redesign, however, welders were teamed with the assembly workers directly responsible for assembling the welded pieces into a finished unit of work. The welders were moved next to the assemblers so they could immediately find out if any of their welding was defective. The results were remarkable. In the redesigned jobs, the number of defectively welded parts decreased from 25 percent to none! Changes like this made it possible to eliminate many inspection jobs as workers take additional responsibility for their own output.[2] According to Jack Lardner, Deere's Vice President for Tractors and Components, "If you know there is somebody to catch your mistakes, you're not nearly as concerned as if you're the only one, and nothing is going to affect the quality downstream except you."[3]

In addition to quality and productivity improvements, enabling employees to take charge of their operations has resulted in vastly improved job attitudes. At JP Industries, for example, one employee who was trained to run a new, more modern piece of equipment and then given full responsibility for its operation and maintenance, soon after began sporting a necktie at work. John Psarouthakis, owner/manager of the company in which this took place, claimed that this represented "A tremendous change in attitude."[4] According to Psarouthakis, redesigning jobs to increase responsibility for quality work results in an individual ". . . really using his or her brains. Because the production process changed, people got upgraded. They learned, so we use brain power along with technology."[5]

Redesigning jobs for increased quality and productivity isn't limited to the production line. In fact, by implementing the principles of work design, the U.S. Air Force's Tactical Air Command saw a drastic turnaround in performance, productivity, and satisfaction. Prior to the change, personnel were assigned in "wings" (i.e., groups) of seventy-two people per unit. Each person in the wing had a particular specialty in working on an aircraft. Because of this specialization, individual members of wings might find themselves assigned to work on as many as ten different planes at once. Additionally, it was necessary to go to a higher ranking officer to have all decisions approved. As a result of these circumstances, only 20 percent of malfunctioning planes were fixed during a regular eight hour shift. Due to the lack of properly functioning aircraft, pilots were often only able to get in about two-thirds of their required flight time. Even then, however, the flights often did not accomplish their missions due to the planes' ineffective functioning.

In redesigning the work flow, personnel were split into twenty-four-person squadrons—each assigned to a specific plane. Squadrons were composed of people qualified in the various forms of aircraft maintenance and repair. Each squadron was positioned at the site of the plane for which they were responsible. Squadron commanders were given full responsibility for overseeing the care and maintenance of a $27 million plane. Additionally, squadrons were given monthly goals for flying specific lengths of time and completing a specified number of missions. If they successfully met or exceeded their goals, the entire squadron would be granted an extra three-day weekend. As a result of this redesign, squadron members took a great deal of pride and ownership in "their" planes. They painted their own names on the aircraft as well as their squadron's logos and names. By assigning full responsibility to the sergeant in charge, decision-making time was cut drastically as squadron members no longer needed to seek approval from their commanding officers. Consequently, within a two-year period the number of hours planes were in the air increased by almost 50 percent. Similarly, there was a 22 percent increase in the number of practice missions flown. Squadrons were meeting their assigned goals as evidenced by the fact that almost all squadrons were averaging ten extra three day weekends per year.[6]

Questions for Discussion

1. Give examples of each of the core job dimensions redesigned at JP Industries, Deere & Co., and the Tactical Air Command.

2. How are the changes in these core job dimensions related to subsequent changes in the critical psychological states of the personnel involved?

3. Discuss the use of goal setting at the Tactical Air Command.

4. At the Tactical Air Command, goal setting and incentives were applied as well as job redesign. Do you think these two motivational programs would have been as effective without the job redesign? Why or why not?

Notes

1. Magnet, M. (1988, August 15). The resurrection of the rust belt. *Fortune,* pp. 40–46.
2. See Note 1.
3. See Note 1, p. 45.
4. See Note 1, p. 44.
5. See Note 1, p. 44.
6. Finegan, J. (1987, January). Four star management. *Inc.,* pp. 42–51.

Problems Implementing Merit Pay Plans:
Two Organizational Examples

Barbara Andrew was pleased to have recently been honored by her employer, Penn Manor School District, in Millersville, Pennsylvania.[1] The $1,000 merit-pay check she received for being in the top 11 percent of Penn Manor's 233 teachers would surely come in handy. Nonetheless, Mrs. Andrew was "horrified" about the potential effect that a merit-pay plan would have on the other teachers. She expressed concern that teachers are "fragile" and that the merit-pay plan could severely damage the egos of the teachers who were not recognized by the plan.

Mrs. Andrew's experience has been repeated around the country as schools increasingly turn to merit-pay plans in attempts to reward the best teachers. The popularity of this approach stems from the belief that these plans will reward good teachers (and hence, hopefully, keep them in the field of education) while setting an example for other teachers. Although such plans have traditionally been popular, critics have noted various problems in their implementation.

At Penn Manor, for example, a science teacher who did not receive a merit award felt personally rejected. Even more problematic is the fact that the criteria for choosing award winners were extremely subjective. As Penn Manor Science Department head, Robert Wyble pointed out, "As department head, I can't tell my teachers, 'This is what you can do to get a merit payment next year.' "[2] Additionally, the fact that there were a limited number of awards created turmoil. For example, at the high school level, there were only ten awards to be distributed among forty-five qualified teachers. A problem also developed from the relatively small dollar amounts of the merit awards. The combination of these issues as well as the lack of any evaluation criteria to determine the success of the program has lead the Penn Manor school board to consider whether perhaps their $25,000 investment in this program has done more harm than good.

As pay-for-performance plans, and merit-pay plans in particular, become increasingly popular, the problems suffered in small school systems may be encountered at the largest of companies. For instance, General Motors recently announced that it would implement a merit-pay plan, not just for the line workers but also for the low level managers, clerical workers, and white-collar staff. A total of 112,000 people will be affected by this change. The motivation for introducing this program at GM is not so very different from that at Penn Manor. Succinctly stated by Roy S. Roberts, GM Vice President of Corporate Personnel, "This business is so competitive, we need everybody pulling their weight."[3]

Although the fundamental rationale for the program may be similar, the implementation of the merit-pay plans at GM and Penn Manor differ substantially. At GM this program also is intended to reduce costs by giving people bonuses that do not become part of their regular salary and so can be distributed in a more flexible manner corresponding to the success of the business.[4] Additionally, because the merit pay will be distributed only once per year, GM has also developed a companion program to provide "spontaneous" rewards. The idea behind this program is that managers can further encourage employees by rewarding particularly good performance with theatre tickets or trips.

Although it is too early to determine if the merit-pay program implemented at GM will be successful, there are some early warning signs. For example, there are those employees who feel that this system is a well-conceived scheme to limit their pay increases. Also, the amount of merit award is determined by individual departments, and therefore may vary from group to group. Nonetheless, Roy S. Roberts, the Vice President of Corporate Personnel, expresses confidence that this new program will be beneficial to GM and its employees. He states, "A merit increase . . . is something you have to earn. To treat people fairly you have to treat people differently."[5]

Questions for Discussion

1. What predictions does equity theory make about the use of merit-pay plans?

2. What predictions does expectancy theory make about the use of merit-pay plans?

3. What predictions do need theories (e.g., Maslow, Alderfer) make about the use of merit-pay plans?

4. How might you integrate goal-setting practices with the use of a merit-pay system?

Notes

1. Schorr, B. (1983, June 16). School's merit-pay program draws gripes from losers—and winners. *Wall Street Journal*, p. 33.

2. See Note 1, p. 33.

3. Schlesinger, J. M. (1988, January 26). GM's new compensation plan reflects general trend tying pay to performance. *Wall Street Journal*, p. 39.

4. Moore, T. (1988, February 15). Make-or-break time for General Motors. *Fortune*, pp. 32–51.

5. See Note 3, p. 39.

**CASE
IN
POINT**

Motivating Mr. Gillett: Mixing Business with Pleasure

Work is drudgery for some, but not for George Gillett, the Chairman of the Gillett Group. Among the companies his large corporate conglomerate has owned are a ski resort in Colorado, the Miami Dolphins football team, and the Harlem Globe Trotters specialty basketball team. The reason behind these acquisitions is simple—Mr. Gillett enjoys skiing, football, and basketball. In short, he likes to have fun, and is attracted to business opportunities that enable him to do so.

As the PINNACLE interview with Mr. Gillett reveals, combining business with having fun has been the driving force behind many of his corporate decisions. This is not to say that Mr. Gillett is adverse to hard work as one might conventionally define it. The many eighteen-hour days he spends managing his business suggest that among the sports he enjoys is deal-making itself. "Work hard, play hard, and combine the two whenever possible" appears to be his business philosophy.

Not only does Mr. Gillett seek to enjoy himself through his various business activities, but he is interested in ensuring that his employees enjoy themselves, too. "This is the employee's company," he says, "not George Gillett's company." He motivates his employees by allowing them to be involved in the business they run. By including his employees in this way, he enables his employees to share in "going for the win."

Questions for Discussion

1. How would you characterize the factors underlying Mr. Gillett's motivation to succeed at business?

2. How can need hierarchy theory, equity theory, and expectancy theory be used to explain Mr. Gillett's actions?

3. Mr. Gillett expressed an interest in involving his employees in his companies' activities. How can he use goal setting and job redesign techniques (e.g., the job characteristics model) to do so?

Goal Setting and Personal Productivity

The effectiveness of goal setting as a motivational technique has been well established. Setting goals that are specific, difficult but acceptable, and providing feedback on their attainment improves job performance (see pages 91–95). As this exercise demonstrates, you can apply these same guidelines to improving your own personal productivity.

Procedure

1. Think of some task you need to perform before the next class meeting. The task should be one for which performance can be measured. Some good examples would be studying a certain subject, writing a term paper, or making improvements in your living quarters.

2. Set specific goals for performing this task, goals that challenge you but are possible to achieve. Make sure the goals are such that progress toward attaining them can be measured. For example, it is appropriate to set the goal of studying two chapters in your history text in the next forty-eight hours. However, the goal of "working harder to improve myself" is much too general.

3. Share your goals with your classmates. Through discussion, help everyone set goals that are specific, measurable, and difficult but acceptable.

4. Once it is clear that everyone has set a specific goal, agree to try to meet these goals and report back to the class on your progress at the next class meeting.

5. During the next class session, take turns reporting on your experiences in meeting your goals. Did you meet your goals? Exactly how well did you do? Do you think setting the goals was helpful? What factors interfered with goal setting?

Points to Consider

1. How many students succeeded in meeting their goals? How many failed? What factors do you believe distinguish between those who succeeded and those who failed?

2. What could have been done to make the unsuccessful students more successful? Did the goals they set for themselves prove too easy or difficult? Was it possible to measure their goal attainment?

3. In what other tasks might you be able to successfully apply goal setting principles?

4. Do you think people are capable of setting their own performance goals, or should they be set with the help of others?

5. Do you think social approval serves as a reinforcer of behavior in organizations? Explain why or why not.

**EXPERIENCING
ORGANIZATIONAL
BEHAVIOR**

CHAPTER FOUR

PERCEPTION: UNDERSTANDING AND EVALUATING OTHERS

CHAPTER OUTLINE

Perception: Some Basic Features
  Attention: Selectivity in Perception
  Organizing Principles in Perception
Social Perception: Understanding Others
  Attribution: Identifying the Causes of Others'
    Behavior
  Cognitive Factors in Social Perception
When Social Perception Fails: Errors in Our Efforts to Understand Others
  Errors in Attribution
  Halo Effects: When Overall Impressions Shape
    Specific Judgments
  Similar-to-Me Effects
  Contrast Effects: The Impact of Prior Events or
    Experiences on Current Perceptions and
    Judgments
  Implicit Personality Theories: Beliefs about How
    Traits Covary

**Stereotypes: Fitting Others into Cognitive Molds
  of Our Own Making**
**Social Perception and Organizational Behavior: Its
Role in Job Interviews and Performance Appraisal**
  Social Perception and Job Interviews
  Social Perception and Performance Appraisal
  Improving the Accuracy of Performance
    Appraisals

Special Sections

OB: An International Perspective
  Nonverbal Communication during Negotiations:
  When Cultural Differences Really Count

OB: A Management Perspective
  Conducting Effective Appraisal Interviews: Some
  "Do's" and "Don'ts"

LEARNING OBJECTIVES

After reading this chapter, you should be able to:
1. Define *perception* and explain why it is an active process.
2. Define *social perception* and indicate its relevance to organizational behavior.
3. Explain how we employ *attribution* to understand the causes of others' behavior.
4. Define *schemas* and explain their role in social perception.
5. Explain such causes of error in social perception as the *self-serving bias, contrast effects, stereotypes,* and *implicit personality theories.*
6. Indicate how social perception can affect *job interviews* and *performance appraisal.*
7. Describe several types of training that can enhance the accuracy of performance appraisal.

It's time, once again, for the semi-annual performance reviews at Franklin Life, and Meg Evans, director of the Claims Department, is about to sit down with Hal Matinko, one of the junior underwriters on her staff. As Hal enters her office, Meg notices that today, for a change, he's clean-shaven and his tie doesn't have the usual assortment of spots and stains. What's more, she catches a whiff of cologne as he walks by her.

Why, he looks practically human! Meg thinks to herself. *I guess he's really up for this review.* To Hal she states, "We both have a busy morning, so let's get started right away. You know the format—we discussed it last week. Here's the evaluation form. Let's take it one category at a time. First, I rated you *Good* on Output and also on Dependability. Your paper flow is fine, and you meet most of your deadlines."

"Thanks," Hal mutters. "I'm glad you feel that way."

"But now," Meg continues somewhat brusquely, "let's turn to a couple of areas where there's room for improvement."

At these words, Hal pulls at his collar, squirms around in his chair, and looks even more nervous than before.

"I gave you a Satisfactory rating on Work Quality. In general, your work's okay, but there have been some problems, too. Just last week Settlement sent back some of your forms with notes about errors. I'm not going to call it sloppy, but there have been more problems than I like to see from this office."

Hal looks upset. "I'm really surprised by that," he blurts out. "I thought my work was at least as good as anyone else's. I'm careful . . . I try my best . . ."

"I'm not questioning that," Meg answers. "I know you work hard. It's just that you need to be more careful."

"Well, I'll sure try, but I don't know how I can do much better. Maybe you just expect too much; I mean, nobody's perfect . . ."

"Let's not argue," Meg answers, a note of irritation in her voice. "*I* think there's room for improvement, and *you* should give it some thought. Let's move on to Initiative. I gave you only a Fair on that."

"What!" Hal exclaims. "I don't understand . . . I've always thought of myself as a self-starter. Didn't I handle that problem with the Granger case? No one told me what to do; I just figured it out for myself."

"True," Meg replies, "but it wasn't all that complicated; and anyway, these ratings aren't supposed to be based on a single incident. They reflect your performance over the entire period."

"But I've been high on initiative other times, too. You just don't seem to notice."

Meg feels her irritation mounting. *What a drag he is*, she thinks to herself. *If only I could get rid of him. He's really not the kind of person I would have hired for my department.* To Hal she remarks, "I *do* notice, Hal. It's my job to be aware of everything that happens here."

"Hmmph!" Hal snorts. "You know what I think? You're biased against me because you didn't hire me, and because I don't come from the same high-class background as you. You made up your mind about me the day you arrived. It doesn't matter what I do, it'll never be good enough . . ."

"That's baloney!" Meg replies heatedly. "I'm as fair with you as anyone else. But if you feel that way, maybe you should start looking for another job. I don't see how we can work together under these conditions."

"Suits me!" Hal says angrily. "I'd rather work someplace where I don't start off with two strikes against me." And with this, he storms out of the office.

After he's gone, Meg sits at her desk thinking. *Imagine—calling me biased! Just who does he think he is! I don't care what his background is, and I'm not against him just because I didn't hire him.* But even as she thinks this, doubt flickers through her mind. *Could there be a grain of truth in Hal's words? Could these factors be affecting her reactions to him?*

It is often said that "everyone sees the world through different eyes," and as the incident described above suggests, this notion—by and large—is true. When exposed to the same information, situations, or events, different persons often report sharply contrasting reactions (refer to Figure 4.1). Further, like the characters in the opening story, each tends to assume that her or his view is correct. Has Hal's work been accurate? Has he shown initiative on the job? He and Meg hold very different ideas on these subjects despite the fact that they have worked together in the same department for many months. The existence of such differences in outlook or perspective under- scores the following point: contrary to what common sense suggests, we do *not* know the world around us in a simple or direct manner. Rather, we actively construct a picture or representation of it through an active and complex process. This process is known as **perception**, and will be the major focus of this chapter. More formally, *perception* can be defined as *the process through which we select, organize, and interpret information brought to us by our senses in order to understand the world around us.*[1]

Why is perception important to the field of OB? Because, quite simply, human behavior in any context—including organizational settings—is largely a function of in- dividuals' current interpretations (perceptions) of the world around them. In other

"There is a perfect example of what is wrong with this country today."   *"There is a perfect example of what is wrong with this country today."*

FIGURE 4.1   Seeing the World through Different Eyes
As suggested by this cartoon, different persons often perceive the world in sharply contrasting ways. (Source: Drawing by Mulligan; © 1978 The New Yorker Magazine, Inc.)

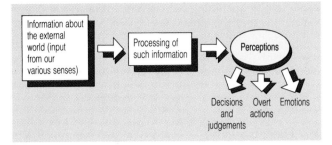

FIGURE 4.2 Perception: A Key Process in Human Behavior

Perceptions—interpretations of information about the external world supplied by our various senses—strongly shape our decisions, judgments, behavior, and feelings.

words, people don't usually respond to input from their eyes, ears, and other sensory receptors in a simple or automatic manner. Instead, they actively *process* such information cognitively, and then react to the interpretations so derived. Perhaps a few concrete examples will help clarify these points and illustrate the relevance of perception to important organizational processes.

First, imagine that during difficult negotiations, one side offers a concession to the other. How will their opponent react? To a large degree, this depends on how they interpret this action: as a sign of weakness, a genuine effort to reach agreement, or some complex type of trap. Next, consider an interviewer who must choose among several job candidates. Clearly, her decision will be strongly affected by her perceptions of the various persons in question—impressions of their appearance, interpersonal skills, and qualifications. Finally, imagine a situation in which an employee has turned in a very poor performance on an important project. Should he be punished or even dismissed? His manager's decision may depend, to a major degree, on whether she perceives this failure as stemming mainly from temporary factors such as family problems that interfered with the subordinate's performance, or from more lasting factors such as a basic lack of ability.

In these and countless other situations, perceptions—interpretations of the external world (and especially of other persons)—shape the feelings, decisions, and behavior of individuals (see Figure 4.2). Since this principle operates just as strongly in work settings as elsewhere, understanding perception can add appreciably to our grasp of many organizational processes. To increase *your* working knowledge of perception, we will first describe several of its basic features—in general, how it operates. Next, we will turn to **social perception**, the process through which we attempt to "make sense" out of other persons by understanding their traits, motives, and intentions. Third, we will consider several common *errors* in perception, biases in this process that sometimes lead us seriously astray with respect to important judgments or decisions. Finally, we will examine the impact of perception on two key organizational processes: one aspect of *employee selection* (job interviews) and evaluation of employees' performance (*performance appraisal*).

PERCEPTION: SOME BASIC FEATURES

At any one moment, we are literally flooded with input from our various senses. Yet, we do not perceive the world as consisting of random collections of colors, sounds, smells, and tastes. On the contrary, we recognize specific objects or people, understand meaningful words and sentences, and notice order and pattern everywhere. These outcomes are due to perception and to the active processing of information it involves. Usually, the construction of a meaningful picture of the world from the raw materials provided by our senses is so automatic that we are hardly aware of its occurrence. Careful study of perception reveals, however, that it actually involves strong tendencies toward *selectivity* and *organization*.

Attention: Selectivity in Perception

If you've ever been to a noisy party, you are already familiar with the fact that perception is (or at least can be) highly selective. In such settings, you can easily decide to screen out all the voices around you except that of the person to whom you are speaking. This individual's words stand out and make sense; those of all the others blend into a single background buzz. If you then decide that you wish to "tune in" on the conversation of other persons standing nearby, you can do so quite readily. In short, you can shift your *attention* from one person and one conversation to others.[2] In such cases, attention is a conscious process; we decide where to direct it and then do so. In others, however, attention seems to follow a course of its own choosing. For example, many persons have great difficulty listening to a dull speaker, no matter how important his or her words. And in other situations, it is all but impossible to turn one's attention away from certain events (e.g., ones that are startling or unexpected, such as the announcement that one's company is about to merge with another business). Why is attention important with respect to perception? Because, in a sense, it acts like a filter or gate: only information to which we pay attention can enter our cognitive systems. And only such information, in turn, can contribute to our understanding of the external world. The next question, then, is obvious: what factors (other than conscious choice) determine the focus of our attention? Many play a role in this regard, but most of them fall into two major categories.

Personal influences on attention: Motives and attitudes. First, attention is often strongly affected by *personal factors*—ones relating to our current motives and attitudes.[3] For example, imagine that you are attending a dull and tedious meeting. What events do you notice? If it's nearly time for lunch and you skipped breakfast that morning, your attention may be riveted on the smell of cooking food from the nearby company cafeteria. If, instead, you strongly like or dislike the person currently speaking, you may concentrate on his or her words and largely ignore everything else. The basic point is this: in any situation, our attention may, potentially, be directed to a wide range of objects or events. The ones that actually become its focus are usually linked, in some manner, to our motives and attitudes.

External influences on attention. Personal factors, however, are only part of the total picture. In addition, the focus of our attention is also affected by external factors—various features of events or objects themselves. One such factor is *salience*—the extent to which a given object or event stands out from the others around it. The greater the salience, the more likely it is to be noticed. For example, if all of the people at a conference are wearing dark clothes, an individual who appears in bright spring colors will be high in salience and stand out from the crowd (see Figure 4.3). In contrast, if the same person is present at a meeting where most others are also dressed in blues, greens, and yellows, he or she will be low in salience, and will not be readily noticed.

Other factors that influence attention include *intensity, size, motion,* and *novelty.* To the extent a given object, person, or event is intense, large in size, shows motion,

FIGURE 4.3 Salience and Attention
Stimuli that stand out from their surroundings are high in *salience*. They often become the focus of our attention. In certain places, like the control room of a nuclear power plant, salience is crucial and the color red is often used to make important controls more visible.

and is unusual or unexpected, it will tend to become the focus of our attention. Advertisers are well aware of these principles, and often apply them to ads, commercials, and roadside signs. When used effectively, such features are highly successful in capturing the attention of potential customers. (Interestingly, though, this by itself does not seem to guarantee that they will purchase the products or services being promoted.[4])

Organizing Principles in Perception

Earlier, we noted that we are rarely aware of single, isolated sensations. Rather, we combine and organize the information supplied by our senses into meaningful patterns. This organization, in turn, tends to occur in accordance with several basic principles.

Figure-ground relationships. Look at Figure 4.4 (on page 120). What do you see? A white cross against a black background? A black cross against a white background? Either interpretation is possible, but one or the other will almost certainly occur. The fact that it does illustrates a basic principle of perceptual organization—our strong tendency to divide the visual world into **figure** and **ground.** In other words, we tend to perceive the world as consisting of *figure,* which has a definite shape and location in space, and *ground,* which has no shape, seems to continue behind the figure, and has no definite location. This tendency has important applications in industrial settings, where it is crucial that controls and information displays be designed so that the patterns employees should notice stand out clearly as figure, and ambiguity is avoided.

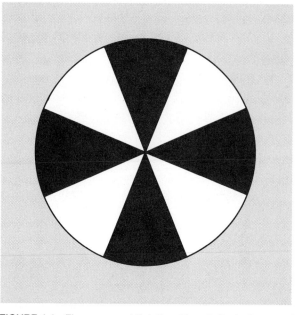

FIGURE 4.4   Figure-ground Relationships: A Basic Aspect of Perception

Do you see a black cross against a white background or a white cross against a black background? Either pattern reflects our tendency to organize the perceptual world into *figure* and *ground.*

FIGURE 4.5   Perceptual Grouping

We seem to possess strong tendencies to group stimuli together in certain ways. Several of these principles of *perceptual grouping* are illustrated here.

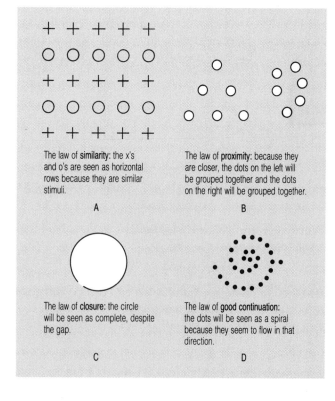

The law of **similarity:** the x's and o's are seen as horizontal rows because they are similar stimuli.

A

The law of **proximity:** because they are closer, the dots on the left will be grouped together and the dots on the right will be grouped together.

B

The law of **closure:** the circle will be seen as complete, despite the gap.

C

The law of **good continuation:** the dots will be seen as a spiral because they seem to flow in that direction.

D

Perceptual grouping. In addition to the figure-ground relationships just described, we also possess strong tendencies to group items or objects together perceptually. Several of these principles are illustrated in Figure 4.5. As you can see, such tendencies are quite powerful. For example, you probably perceive diagram A, which illustrates grouping by *similarity,* as horizontal rows of x's and o's, not as vertical columns of these two letters. Similarly, you probably perceive the item in diagram C as a circle, despite the gap it contains. This illustrates our tendency toward *closure*—perceiving spaces enclosed by a line as simple, complete figures. Please see Figure 4.5 for other principles of perceptual grouping.

One final comment: the principles of perceptual organization described here do not apply only to simple items or patterns. They seem, instead, to be quite general in nature. For example, if several persons work near each other in an office, they may be perceived by their manager as a "unit" because of proximity, even though there is no real reason for viewing them in this manner. Similarly, accomplished persuaders (e.g., successful trial attorneys, salespersons working out of offshore boiler-room operations) often turn the tendency toward closure to their own advantage. Because of courtroom rules or legal restrictions, these persons avoid stating certain conclusions. However, they do provide statements and information which, together, lead their audiences (jurors, potential customers) to generate such conclusions for themselves. In other words, they paint a mental picture with gaps sufficiently small that the temptation to complete them is highly compelling.

SOCIAL PERCEPTION: UNDERSTANDING OTHERS

Other persons are a central part of our lives, both at work and elsewhere. Bosses, coworkers, subordinates, friends, relatives, lovers—all can (and often do) powerfully influence us in many ways. Given this fact, it is not surprising that we often engage in vigorous attempts to understand the people around us—to figure out the reasons behind their actions, to identify their major traits, to recognize their current emotions and their feelings about us. The benefit of attaining accurate information in these respects is obvious: understanding others is essential for interacting with them effectively. To mention just two examples, you certainly wouldn't want to ask your boss for a favor at a time when he or she is angry and irritable. And if an important customer decided to give her business to a competitor, it would be very important for you to know *why* she did so. Clearly, then, **social perception**—the task of combining, integrating, and interpreting information about others to gain an accurate understanding of them—is important.

Several decades of research on social perception leave little doubt that it is a complex process. Among its most important components, however, are **attribution**—efforts to identify the causes behind others' behavior—and **social information processing** (or **social cognition**)—cognitive processes which shape the ways in which we sort, store, and later remember information about other persons.[5,6]

Attribution: Identifying the Causes of Others' Behavior

One question we ask repeatedly about other persons is "Why?" Why did your boss decide to call a meeting at 4:30 P.M. on Friday? Why did one of your suppliers fail to deliver a major order on time? Why does Randi Helson in Accounting always wait at least a day before returning your calls? In short, one thing we frequently want to know about others is *why* they have acted in certain ways. On closer examination, this question breaks down into two major parts: (1) what are others really like—in other words, what major traits or characteristics do they possess, and (2) did their actions stem primarily from internal causes (their own traits, motives, values), or primarily from external causes (factors relating to the situation in which they operate). Research findings suggest that we attempt to answer these two questions in somewhat different ways.[7]

From acts to dispositions: Using others' behavior as a guide to their traits.
Understanding others' major traits can often be very useful. For example, knowing that your opponent in a negotiating session has a reputation for starting with an extreme position, but then backing down and making concessions if her opponent stands firm, can be very helpful in bargaining with her. Similarly, knowing that one of your subordinates is always punctual while another is usually late can be quite useful to you in deciding which to send as your representative to an important meeting. But how, precisely, do we go about identifying others' traits? In general, we do so by observing their behavior and then *inferring* their traits from this information.[8]

At first glance, this might seem to be an easy task. Other people are always doing *something,* so we have a rich source of evidence on which to draw. Unfortunately, there are complications to consider. Perhaps the most important is that others sometimes attempt to conceal their major traits, especially if these are generally viewed as undesirable. Thus, employees who are careless, lazy, and unprincipled do their best to hide these facts from view, and will demonstrate them only under conditions where they feel it is safe to do so, or when their "social guard" is down.

Despite such difficulties, there are several techniques we can use to unveil others' efforts to conceal some of their traits. First, we can focus on actions by these persons that are viewed as unusual or unacceptable in a given situation. (Such actions are low in *social desirability.* In contrast, actions seen as typical or acceptable are high in social desirability.) For example, imagine that during negotiations, another person first offers a concession and then, a few minutes later, withdraws it. This action—bargaining in bad faith—is viewed as highly inappropriate by most persons. The other negotiator's willingness to perform it suggests that he or she is totally lacking in either experience or principle. In either case, you would probably be very reluctant to continue dealing with this person.

Second, we can pay careful attention to actions by others that produce *noncommon effects*—outcomes that would not be produced by other, different actions. Since such behaviors yield highly distinctive effects, they often reveal much about the motives or traits of the persons involved. For instance, following up on the example mentioned above, suppose you learned that the negotiator who reversed his offer during bargaining knew this would make you angry and would probably result in your decision to break off negotiations. Further, you discovered that he had already lined up another party with whom to make a deal. Given this information, you might well conclude that his action was a carefully calculated move, and that he is an unprincipled, manipulative person. Finally, in our efforts to understand others' major traits, we also focus on behaviors that they have freely chosen to perform. Actions forced upon them by role obligations, inflexible company rules, or circumstances beyond their control are relatively uninformative—they tell us little about the individuals' traits.

In sum, by focusing on certain aspects of others' behavior we often *can* attain accurate knowledge of their major traits and characteristics. As we noted earlier, this knowledge is then often useful in planning future interactions with them. (Please see Figure 4.6 for a summary of this aspect of attribution.)

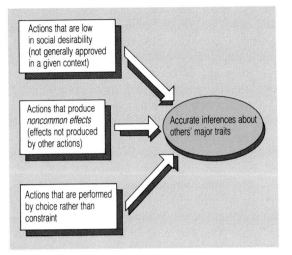

Actions that are low in social desirability (not generally approved in a given context)

Actions that produce *noncommon effects* (effects not produced by other actions)

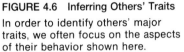

Accurate inferences about others' major traits

Actions that are performed by choice rather than constraint

FIGURE 4.6   Inferring Others' Traits
In order to identify others' major traits, we often focus on the aspects of their behavior shown here.

Causal attribution: Another aspect of the question "Why?" Imagine that you observe the following scene. A manager storms into his subordinate's office and proceeds to rake this person over the coals. He shouts, waves his arms in anger, and threatens the subordinate with dire consequences if his work does not improve. After witnessing this incident, what might you conclude? One possibility is that you would attribute the manager's behavior to internal causes, deciding that he has a bad temper, lacks self-control, and is generally ineffective as a supervisor. In fact, this outcome is likely. We seem to have a strong tendency to attribute others' actions to internal factors when strong evidence to the contrary is lacking.

Another possible interpretation of this scene, though, is markedly different. You might conclude that the manager is simply responding to unbearable behavior on the part of the subordinate. In other words, you might guess that this person has provoked the manager repeatedly by refusing to follow his instructions, by very sloppy work, or by an obvious lack of motivation. In this case you would explain the manager's behavior (and answer the question "Why?") largely in terms of external causes.

In this and many other situations, the conclusions you reach about the relative importance of internal and external causes in shaping others' behavior can have important consequences. If you decide that someone has acted in a specific way because of internal causes (e.g., their own nature or personality), you will expect them to behave in the same manner on future occasions, and may adjust your relations with them accordingly. In contrast, if you decide that someone has acted in a specific way because of external causes (e.g., some event or situation in the world around them), you will realize that their behavior might be very different under other circumstances and you will not expect them to act in the same way at other times. How do we choose between these possibilities? A very large body of research findings suggest the following answer.[9]

In our efforts to determine whether another person has acted in some manner because of internal or external causes, we rely on information about three factors. First, we consider the extent to which other persons also behave in the same manner; this is known as *consensus*. Second, we consider the extent to which this person acts in the same manner at other times; this is known as *consistency*. Finally, we consider the extent to which this person behaves in the same manner in other contexts; this is known as *distinctiveness*. (If he or she acts in the same manner in other contexts or situations, distinctiveness is *low*.) Information about these three factors is then combined and forms the basis for our decisions as to the causes behind another's behavior. More precisely, if consensus, consistency, and distinctiveness are all high, we conclude that this person's actions have probably stemmed from *external* causes. (This means that most other persons act like this one, that this person behaves in the same manner at other times, and that this person does *not* act in the same manner in other situations or contexts.) In contrast, if consensus and distinctiveness are low, but consistency is high, we conclude that this person's actions probably stemmed from *internal* causes. (Here, most other persons do not act like this one, this person acts in the same manner in other situations, and he or she also acts in the same manner at other times.)

Since these comments about causal attribution have been somewhat abstract, let's consider a concrete example to see how the process actually works. Imagine that during an important business lunch, one of the representatives of another company complains about her food, makes critical remarks about the waiter, and indicates strong dislike for the restaurant's decor. Further, imagine that no other member of the group acts in a similar way (consensus is low), you have seen this person act in the same manner at other times (consistency is high), and you have also seen her complain in this fashion in other settings (e.g., during meetings and negotiation sessions; thus, distinctiveness is low). What would you conclude? Probably, that her behavior stems from internal causes: she is a "picky" person, difficult to please.

Now, instead, imagine that several other members of the luncheon group also complain about their food and the service (consensus is high), that you have seen this person complain in the same restaurant at other times (consistency is high), but that you have *not* seen her complain in other settings (e.g., at meetings, in other restaurants). In this case, you would probably conclude that her current behavior stems mainly from external causes: the restaurant really *is* inferior in several respects. (See Figure 4.7 for a summary of these contrasting conclusions.)

Do we really think about others, and the causes behind their actions, in this manner? A large body of evidence suggests that we do.[10] However, there are two additional points that should be noted. First, we don't engage in this type of effortful, cognitive work in every situation. Rather, we are most likely to perform it when faced with unexpected actions by others—ones we can't readily or simply explain.[11] Second, in thinking about the causes behind others' behavior, we also frequently consider another dimension in addition to the internal-external one we have just described: whether these causes are *stable* (lasting) or *unstable* (temporary) in nature.[12] For example, as we will see in more detail in our later discussion of *performance appraisal*, it is important to know whether a given level of performance stems mainly from temporary causes, such as *effort*, or more stable causes, such as *ability* or *experience*. The former can readily be changed; the latter can be altered only slowly, if at all. That managers do, in fact, pay careful attention to this dimension is suggested by a study carried out by Knowlton and Mitchell.[13] In this laboratory simulation, participants had the task of supervising three subordinates, all of whom were assistants of the researchers. Two of these individuals showed an average level of task performance, while the third was either very high or very low in performance. Subjects also received information suggesting that the performance of the stand-out subordinate stemmed mainly from ability or mainly from effort. It was predicted that when later asked to evaluate the performance of all three individuals, subjects would be more extreme in their evaluations of the high or low performing subordinate when his behavior seemed to stem mainly from effort rather than from ability. Results offered clear support for this prediction.

In sum, and to put the process of attribution in context, because other people play such an important role in our lives, we often think about them. When we do, one of

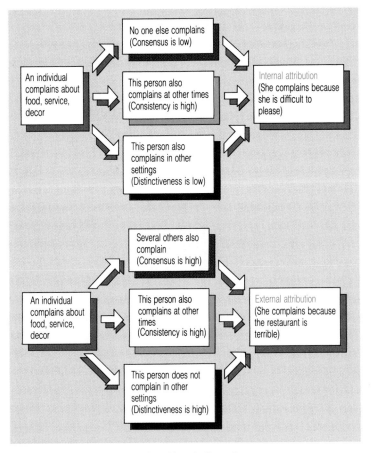

FIGURE 4.7 Causal Attribution: How It Operates

In determining whether others' behavior stems mainly from internal or external causes, we focus on the three types of information shown here.

the key questions we ask is "Why have they acted in certain ways?" To answer this question, we pay careful attention to certain informative aspects of their behavior—what they say and do. Then, from such information, we infer the answers we seek. Finally, we apply such knowledge (our best-guess understanding of others) to our relations with them. In later sections, we'll return to the question of how such attributions (and other aspects of social perception) play an important role in several organizational processes.

Cognitive Factors in Social Perception

There can be little doubt that understanding others requires considerable mental (cognitive) effort. Making sense out of their behavior, understanding their motives, identifying their key traits—all these activities require detailed thought and careful reasoning. Given this fact, it is clear that in order to understand social perception and the ways in which it shapes our evaluations of others, we must comprehend the many cognitive processes on which it is based. In other words, we must understand the ways in which information about others is sorted or categorized, converted to a form that can be entered into memory (*encoded*), actually stored in our memory systems, and later retrieved and used. Together, these processes are known as **social cognition,** and they have been the subject of a very large amount of research.[14,15] In the remainder of this section, we will call your attention to several key aspects of social cognition— ones that have important implications for practical organizational issues such as appraising job performance.

Schemas: Cognitive frameworks for understanding the external world. Have you ever been in a situation where you were literally flooded with new information— unfamiliar facts, terms, and relationships that seemed to whiz by with little meaning? Almost everyone has had this experience, and most find it disconcerting. These experiences are so bewildering because in them, we lack *cognitive frameworks* for handling the incoming information. In other words, we have no existing mental categories or knowledge structures into which such input can be entered. The result: the new information seems to float about freely, with no logical connections to other knowledge already at our disposal. And without such mental "anchors," it is often quickly lost.

Fortunately, of course, this is not typical of our daily lives. In general, we *do* possess the kind of cognitive frameworks referred to above. These are known as **schemas,** and they develop gradually, out of our experience with various facets of the world around us.[16] For example, through a wide range of interactions with others, we form *person schemas*—internal frameworks representing various traits that others can possess. Once such schemas have developed, they play an important part in our comprehension of information about coworkers, friends, and any other individuals we encounter. Similarly, we develop *event schemas* (or *scripts*)—internal knowledge frameworks for various types of situations. For example, most people possess an event schema for business meetings. Such schemas suggest that meetings will begin with a call to order, perhaps followed by reading of the minutes from the last meeting. This will be followed by discussion or presentation of various items on the agenda. Then, at some point, the meeting will be brought to a formal close. Event schemas also exist for many other events or situations as well.

What effects do schemas have once they are formed? This is the key point of our present discussion. Growing evidence suggests that once these cognitive frameworks take shape, they exert powerful effects on how we handle new information, including information about other persons (see Figure 4.8).[17] First, schemas affect *attention*— they determine what events or stimuli we notice. In particular, we tend to notice events or actions by others that are inconsistent with existing schemas. For example, if an individual begins to read poetry or to make off-color remarks at a business meeting, we quickly notice such behaviors even if, up to that point, we were almost falling asleep. The unexpected nature of such actions, and their inconsistency with operative schemas, makes them highly attention-getting.

Second, schemas influence what information is entered into memory (*encoded*). Input that is somehow *relevant* to existing schemas often stands a better chance of being retained than information that is totally irrelevant to these internal knowledge structures. And among such input, information that contradicts or is inconsistent with existing schemas is often easier to retain than information that is consistent.[18] The reason for this is that when confronted with input that contradicts our existing knowledge frameworks, we stop and think about it more carefully than we do when information fits with such schemas.[19] The result is that it has a better chance of being entered into memory. For example, consider the case of a subordinate who suddenly turns in a report that is far better than her previous efforts. Many managers would spend much more time puzzling over this unexpectedly good performance than they would thinking about a more typical, mediocre report by the same person.

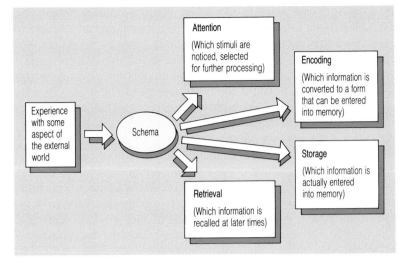

FIGURE 4.8 Schemas: An Overview
Schemas are cognitive frameworks developed through experience with the external world. Once formed, they exert powerful effects on attention and on the encoding, storage, and retrieval of information.

Finally, schemas also shape *retrieval*—they determine what information is recalled from memory in various situations. When, for example, a manager attempts to recall a subordinate's performance in order to rate it on the yearly or semi-yearly evaluation form, she is most likely to remember information consistent with her schema for this person—or for the group to which he or she belongs. Thus, if this schema is one which could be described by the label "arrogant, moody people," the manager will remember information consistent with this framework—she will recall instances in which the subordinate was unpleasant or irritable. If, instead, the schema is one which could be labeled "hard-working, cooperative employees," she is likely to remember incidents and actions by the subordinate that fit *this* cognitive framework.

In sum, schemas strongly affect what information about others we notice, what information about them is entered into memory, and what information is recalled at later times when we evaluate them in various ways. Clearly, then, these cognitive frameworks are a key factor in social perception and in its impact on organizational processes.

Schemas and stereotypes. In several later chapters of this book, we will discuss **stereotypes** and their impact in work settings. For example, in chapter 5 we will consider stereotypes relating to gender and in chapter 9 we will comment on stereotypes relating to age. Here, we merely wish to note that stereotypes can be viewed as a special type of schema. They are schemas which relate membership in a particular category to inferred personal attributes. In short, they are cognitive frameworks suggesting that persons belonging to particular groups (e.g., women, older employees) all share certain traits or characteristics. Like other schemas, stereotypes strongly affect the interpretation and processing of social information. Information relevant to a particular stereotype is more likely to be noticed than information unrelated to such frameworks. And stereotype-consistent information is often more likely to be remembered than information that is inconsistent.[20] Perhaps a concrete example will be helpful.

Consider a male manager who possesses a well-developed stereotype for women. On one occasion, he observes a female member of his department crying. Because of his gender-related schema (his stereotype), his attention is drawn to this event, and he notices it very clearly. Now, six months later, he is asked to evaluate her performance. Again, the stereotype comes into operation. As a result, he remembers this incident vividly—much more vividly than many other actions that are more directly relevant to job performance. Finally, his memory of this event leads him to infer that she is not ready for added responsibility, and he down-rates her for this reason. Other stereotypes operate in a corresponding fashion. Indeed, when such frameworks are strongly established, they have powerful and general effects on our perceptions of others. As we will soon see, this, in turn, can have important implications for key organizational processes. (Another process that often influences social perception is **nonverbal communication**—our ability to infer others' current emotions from information provided by their facial expressions, eye-contact, and body movements.[21] For information on the role of this process in negotiations, see the **International Perspective** section below.)

OB: AN INTERNATIONAL PERSPECTIVE

Nonverbal Communication during Negotiations: When Cultural Differences Really Count

Imagine the following scene: negotiations about a major deal between two large companies (one American, the other Japanese) have reached a crucial stage. In an effort to forge an agreement, the head of the U.S. team places yet another offer on the table. It contains a major concession, so after describing it, she turns her eyes squarely on her Japanese counterpart's face. Much to her dismay, instead of looking back at her with a serious expression, he smiles broadly—in her mind, meaninglessly—and then lowers his eyes, so as to avoid her gaze. *What the heck is he thinking*, she wonders. *Does he find the offer acceptable or not?* And she goes on wondering about it as the seconds tick by and there's absolutely no reply from the Japanese team.

While this incident itself is imaginary, the events described are quite realistic. Careful studies of international negotiations reveal that persons from different cultures use various nonverbal cues in very different ways, and that such differences, in turn, can often be the source of considerable confusion.[22] Returning to the negotiations described above, consider the following: in Japanese culture, a smile is perceived as a means of reducing tension and of averting unpleasantness. Thus, the head of the Japanese team smiled because he sensed, correctly, that this was a very tense moment. Why did he then

lower his eyes? Because in Japan, lowering one's eyes is a sign of respect. Japanese parents expect their children to bow their heads and lower their eyes while being scolded. American parents, in contrast, often demand a precisely opposite pattern. "Look at me when I'm speaking to you!" they remark in similar situations. So when the Japanese negotiator lowered his eyes, it was as a sign of respect for his American counterpart—*not* an indication that he found her offer unacceptable. One additional point: in Japanese culture, it is considered crucial to avoid a direct "no" at almost any cost. As a result, rather than rejecting an offer from an opponent, Japanese negotiators may simply lapse into total silence, or even get up and leave the room. Needless to say, such tactics are totally puzzling to Americans, who expect an immediate response of some kind. (Incidentally, contrary to popular belief, Japanese negotiators, and those from other Oriental nations, are *not* more poker-faced than negotiators from the United States or other Western countries. On the contrary, videotapes made during real or simulated negotiations between Japanese and Americans reveal that the Japanese actually frown and smile more frequently; see Figure 4.9.[23])

Other intriguing differences emerge in negotiations between persons from other cultures. For example, South Koreans show more signs of

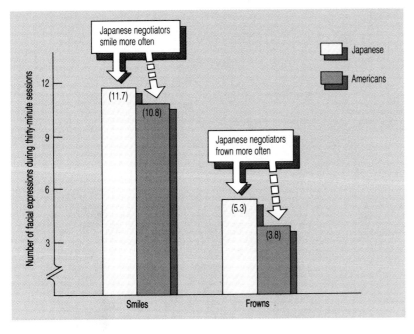

FIGURE 4.9 Facial Expressions during Negotiation

Contrary to popular belief, Japanese executives are not "poker-faced" during negotiations. In fact, they smile and frown more frequently than their American counterparts. (Source: Based on data from Graham, 1988; see Note 23.)

emotion than either Americans or Japanese, and often describe their reactions to various offers more bluntly. Persons from mainland China closely resemble Americans in nonverbal style. Surprisingly though, ones from Taiwan are very different. And Brazilians demonstrate yet another nonverbal style: they often talk without pauses, and touch one another—and their opponents—frequently. Such physical contact is virtually nonexistent in negotiations between persons from many other cultures.

The fact that persons from different cultures use nonverbal cues in contrasting ways points to the following conclusion: in order to prevent such differences from introducing unnecessary "noise" (factors that distort clarity of a message) into delicate international discussions, negotiators and others involved in international business should receive training designed to enhance their awareness of such factors. Only in this way can many needless and potentially costly problems be avoided.

WHEN SOCIAL PERCEPTION FAILS: ERRORS IN OUR EFFORTS TO UNDERSTAND OTHERS

Look at the drawings in Figure 4.10 (on page 130). Do the horizontal lines in (A) appear curved? Do the letters in (B) look as though they are on a slant? In fact, the lines in (A) are straight and the letters in (B) are perfectly vertical. Both drawings illustrate the following point: often, our perceptions of the physical world are misleading. For some reason, we process information brought to us by our senses incorrectly, and so arrive at false conclusions. If perception can encounter such difficulties with respect to relatively simple patterns such as the ones in Figure 4.10, it is not at all surprising that it can fail—and fail badly—with respect to our perceptions of other persons. Actually, there are many ways in which social perception can err and lead us astray in this respect. We will describe several of these errors here, and then indicate their role in important organizational processes in the section that follows.

FIGURE 4.10 Illusions: Errors in Perception of the Physical World

Do you perceive the horizontal lines in (A) as slightly curved and the letters in (B) as leaning away from vertical? If so, you have experienced two powerful visual illusions.

Errors in Attribution

When we described *attribution,* our comments implied that it is a highly rational process—one in which we use all information at our disposal to identify the causes of others' behavior. Usually, this is the case; attribution *is* logical and accurate in many respects. However, it is also subject to several forms of bias that can generate serious errors in our thinking about other persons.

We have already mentioned one of these—our tendency to explain others' actions in terms of internal rather than external causes. In other words, we perceive others as behaving as they do because they possess certain traits or dispositions. The many external factors that may also affect their behavior tend to be ignored, or at least downplayed. This tendency is so strong and general that it has sometimes been termed the **fundamental attribution error.**[24] Its presence seems to derive from the fact that it is easier to explain others' actions in terms of discrete traits than in terms of a complex pattern of situational factors that might also have affected their actions. Unfortunately, this type of attributional error can be quite damaging. It leads us to expect greater consistency in others' behavior than we should; then, we are surprised and chagrined when they act "out of character" in some new situation, and this can contribute to tension and conflict.

A second type of attributional error involves our tendency to attribute success to internal causes (our own sterling qualities!), but failure to external causes (factors beyond our control). This is known as the **self-serving bias,** and is a very common tendency. As a concrete example of this form of bias, consider the case of a salesperson who lands a major account with a very important customer. How will she explain this result? Probably in terms of her own hard work, diligent preparation, and charming personality. In contrast, suppose that she fails to gain this account; how will she explain *this* outcome? The odds are good that she will attribute it to situational factors (e.g., a competitor already had the inside edge, the competition's products were really better for the customer's needs).

What accounts for the occurrence of the self-serving bias? One factor is the motivation to protect or enhance our self-esteem. Obviously, attributing successes to our own qualities but failures to external causes can bolster our own self-image and lessen the negative feelings that might otherwise derive from setbacks. In addition, the self-serving bias seems to derive, at least in part, from largely unconscious tendencies to process information about successes and failures in different ways. These differences are complex, but in general, information about successes is retained more readily, and linked more closely to our own self-concept, than information about failures.[25]

Regardless of its origins, the self-serving bias can have important effects in organizations. It leads each member of a work group to take more credit for success and to blame the others for failure than is actually justified. And it may lead subordinates to view their performance appraisals as unfairly harsh even though managers view them as very lenient. In these ways, it initiates or intensifies interpersonal conflict in many work settings. (See chapter 13 for a further discussion of such effects.) Clearly, then, this is one form of error worth recognizing and avoiding.

Halo Effects: When Overall Impressions Shape Specific Judgments

Have you ever heard the phrase "Love is blind"? It refers to the fact that when individuals are in love, they lose all ability to evaluate the object of their affection in an accurate, impartial manner. Unfortunately, those in love are not the only ones to fall victim to such effects. Once we form an overall impression of another person, this general reaction often has powerful effects on our judgments of his or her specific traits or performances. These tendencies are collectively known as **halo effects,** and can be either positive or negative. If our impression of another person is favorable, we tend to see everything he or she does or says in a positive light (a favorable halo). If, instead, our overall impression is unfavorable, we tend to perceive all of this person's words and actions in a negative manner (a "rusty halo" or "horns" effect).

Another way to think of halo effects in organizational settings is in terms of inflated correlations between various dimensions on which performance is rated. In other words, when the performance of specific employees is rated on several dimensions, halo effects tend to inflate the correlations between these dimensions.[26] Thus, it appears that performance on the various dimensions is more closely linked than is actually the case. In practical terms, this means that persons rated high on some dimensions tend to be rated high on others, even if they don't really deserve these ratings. Conversely, persons rated low on some dimensions tend to be rated low on others, too. We should add that recent evidence indicates that such effects occur only when the dimensions being rated are, in fact, *not* closely related. When they are highly correlated, halo effects do not seem to inflate them any further. Still, regardless of the precise form they take, there is general agreement on one point: when they occur, halo effects reduce accuracy—they interfere with the task of appraising individuals' performance accurately.[27] (Refer to Figure 4.11 on page 132 for an overview of the nature and impact of halo effects.)

An intriguing demonstration of the impact of halo effects on important organizational processes is provided by a study conducted by Binning and his colleagues.[28] In this investigation, male and female subjects were provided with information designed to induce either a favorable or unfavorable impression of a job applicant's suitability for a specific job. After reading this information, they were asked to generate questions they

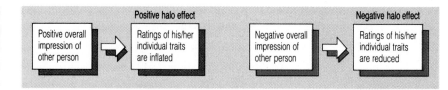

FIGURE 4.11   Halo Effects: Their Basic Nature
Halo effects occur when our overall impression of another person affects our judgments of this person on specific traits or dimensions. Halo effects can be positive or negative in nature.

would ask this person during an interview for the job in question. A new group of subjects then divided these questions into ones designed to seek either positive or negative information about the applicant. It was predicted that subjects given information suggesting that the applicant was well suited for the job would tend to formulate positive questions—ones designed to confirm their favorable initial impression. In contrast, subjects given information suggesting that the applicant was poorly suited for the job would tend to formulate negative questions—ones designed to confirm their negative initial impression. As shown in Figure 4.12, these predictions were generally confirmed. The only exception was that when subjects expected to interview an individual of the opposite sex, they formulated more positive questions for a low-suitability than a high-

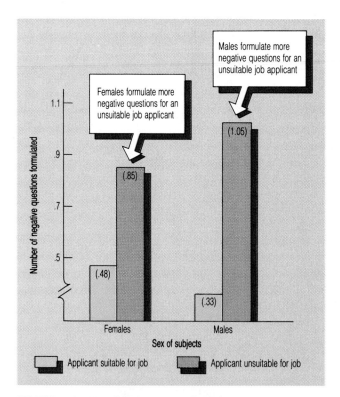

FIGURE 4.12   Halo Effects and Job Interviews
Subjects who received information suggesting that a job applicant was relatively unsuited for a specific job formulated more questions that would yield negative information about him or her in a later interview than did subjects who received information indicating that the applicant was well suited for the job. These findings suggest that subjects' initial impressions of the applicant shaped their strategies for interacting with him or her—a tendency that suggests the impact of halo effects. (Source: Based on Binning, et al., 1988; see Note 28.)

suitability applicant. This unexpected finding might have stemmed from the fact that in such cases, subjects used positive questions as a form of impression management—to enhance their own attractiveness to the opposite sex interviewee.

While the study conducted by Binning et al. was not specifically designed to study the impact of halo effects, its findings can be interpreted as consistent with the impact of this type of bias. In this context, they suggest that halo effects can operate in a disturbing self-fulfilling manner. Once they exist, they shape interactions between the persons involved so that they tend to be confirmed.

Similar-to-Me Effects

It is a well-established principle in the behavioral sciences that individuals tend to like others who are similar to themselves better than others who are dissimilar. Since we tend to evaluate persons we like more favorably than persons we dislike (refer to our discussion of halo effects above), it seems reasonable to expect that perceived similarity might operate as an additional source of perceptual error or bias in organizational settings. In fact, this appears to be the case. The higher the perceived similarity between supervisors and their subordinates, the higher the performance ratings they assign to one another.[29] Thus, similarity, or the **similar-to-me-effect**, as it is often termed, constitutes another potential source of bias with respect to social perception.

Actually, three distinct types of similarity seem to exert such influences, so perhaps a better term would be similar-to-me effect*s*. The first of these, *perceived similarity*, refers to the extent to which persons in a given work setting believe that they share a similar outlook, values, and work habits. The second, termed *perceptual congruence*, focuses more directly on work-related behaviors. It involves the degree to which subordinates and supervisors hold similar views about the factors important in receiving merit pay raises. In other words, such similarity reflects the extent to which subordinates and their supervisors agree about what, precisely, constitutes good performance. A third type of similarity, *demographic similarity*, relates to the extent to which supervisors and subordinates resemble one another in terms of race, age, educational level, and years of service.

That all three types of similarity play an important part in organizations is indicated by a recent study conducted by Turban and Jones.[30] These researchers asked subordinates and supervisors at a large rehabilitation center to provide information on each of the three types of similarity mentioned above. In addition, subordinates reported their level of satisfaction with their jobs and the organization, while supervisors provided overall ratings of their subordinates' performance. When these factors were correlated, it was found that each type of similarity was significantly related to both subordinate job satisfaction and performance.

These findings, and those of related studies, suggest that subordinates who are similar to their supervisors in several respects may have an unfair advantage over those who are not. Correspondingly, supervisors who are perceived as similar by their subordinates may also gain an advantage. We should add, however, that these effects may constitute more than the operation of yet another form of perceptual bias. Additional findings gathered by Turban and Jones indicate that subordinates have greater trust and confidence in supervisors they perceive as similar to themselves than in those they perceive as dissimilar. This suggests that perceived similarity among the persons in a work group may contribute to positive relationships between them. It is possible that this factor, not merely perceptual bias, accounts for the higher evaluations assigned by supervisors to similar subordinates (see Figure 4.13 on page 134). In sum, while it is important to guard against similar-to-me effects when they operate to distort accurate evaluations of performance, increasing perceived similarity between supervisors and their subordinates may yield actual benefits which should not be overlooked.

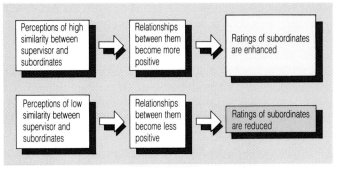

FIGURE 4.13   Potential Benefits of Perceived Similarity

Supervisors often rate subordinates they perceive as similar to themselves more favorably than subordinates they perceive as dissimilar. This may reflect the impact of one form of bias (the *similar-to-me effect*) or, as shown here, the positive effects of perceived similarity on supervisor-subordinate relationships.

Contrast Effects: The Impact of Prior Events or Experiences on Current Perceptions and Judgments

Consider the following situation. A young woman with moderately good qualifications applies for a job with two firms. At the first company, she is interviewed by a personnel director who has just finished speaking with two other applicants. Both were at the top of their college classes, and possess all of the skills and training sought by the company. At the second company, she is interviewed by a personnel director who has just seen two other applicants, neither of whom is at all suitable for the job in question. From which interviewer will she receive higher ratings? The answer seems obvious: from the second. She will be perceived much more favorably by this person because, in contrast to the two other persons he has just seen, she will "shine." Conversely, she will receive lower ratings from the first interviewer because compared to the two persons he has just interviewed, she will appear quite mediocre.

This incident illustrates the potential impact of **contrast effects,** another common source of error in social perception.[31] Such effects refer to the fact that our reaction to a given stimulus (or person) is often influenced by other stimuli (people) we have recently encountered. The impact of contrast effects is, perhaps, most obvious in the context of interviews. However, they can also operate in other organizational contexts as well. For example, in situations where several individuals deliver reports in succession, reactions to each will probably be influenced by the quality of the presentations that preceded it. If the first individual does an outstanding job, the ones who follow may appear quite ordinary; if the first person "bombs," those who follow may benefit from this fact, and appear to be better than they actually are. Many persons are aware of such effects, and attempt to make sure that when they make presentations, they do not immediately follow star performers. Such persons are indeed tough acts to follow, and the costs of doing so with respect to one's own performance evaluations can be high.

Implicit Personality Theories: Beliefs about How Traits Covary

Suppose someone told you that a new member of your department was ambitious, well-organized, and highly motivated. Would you expect this person to be punctual (on time for meetings and other important events)? Almost certainly, you would. Now, in contrast, imagine you were told that a new member of your department was enthusiastic, friendly, and kind. Would you also expect her to be humorous? Again, the answer is yes. Both examples illustrate an important point about social perception. On the basis of our experience with countless people, we formulate **implicit theories of personality**—ideas about which traits or characteristics tend to covary (go together). Then we freely apply these implicit views to other persons, assuming that if they possess certain characteristics they probably possess certain others as well.

Actually, implicit personality theories can be viewed as a special type of *schema*—one which ties various traits together into coherent patterns. To the extent they are indeed schemas, our implicit views about relationships between various traits would be expected to influence our processing of information concerning these traits. The process may unfold as follows. On the basis of observing others' behavior, we conclude that they possess certain traits. Then, we tend to perceive them as possessing other traits which, in our schema, are linked to these observed characteristics. The result: we infer the presence of traits for which, in fact, we have no direct evidence.

That implicit personality theories (or schemas) can operate in precisely this fashion is indicated by a study conducted by Krzystofiak, Cardy, and Newman.[32] They found that subjects' ratings of college instructors were affected by the behaviors of these instructors as described in written vignettes. In addition, however, there was evidence that the ratings were also affected by subjects' inferences about the traits the instructors possessed, and assumed relationships between these characteristics. The practical implication of these findings is clear: in rating others' performance, we may be strongly influenced by schemas suggesting that certain traits tend to covary. In short, once we conclude that individuals we are rating possess certain traits, we may infer that they possess others as well, even in the absence of any strong external evidence for such conclusions.

Stereotypes: Fitting Others into Cognitive Molds of Our Own Making

A final type of error in perceiving others is one we have already described: the operation of **stereotypes.** As you may recall, these are schemas which suggest that membership in a particular group or category is associated with possession of various traits. One result of stereotypes is that persons holding them tend to perceive all members of various groups (especially ones other than their own) as being very much alike (as sharing the same traits and behaviors). And in many cases, these shared traits are seen as largely negative in nature.[33]

You are probably already quite familiar with the nature and impact of some stereotypes—ones relating to race, sex, and age. These have been the subject of a great deal of concern and attention in recent years, as efforts to overcome their negative effects in work settings, and in society generally, have been instituted. However, you may not be as aware of the existence of several other stereotypes that also have powerful effects on key organizational processes. Extremely common are the stereotypes held by individuals trained in various professions or occupations about individuals in other professions or occupations. For example, accountants may be heard to remark, "Oh, you know what those scientist types are like . . . they haven't the slightest idea of keeping track of costs." Conversely, scientists in a research and development unit may state, "Those people in accounting can drive you nuts; all they ever do is worry about those #$%!& forms!" Stereotypes also often exist with respect to departments or work groups. Thus, people in Maintenance may stereotype those in Production; persons in Marketing may stereotype those in Engineering, and so on. Obviously, to the extent various groups in an organization hold stereotypes of one another, communication may suffer and the likelihood of conflict may increase. We'll return to such effects in more detail in chapter 13.

Why do stereotypes exist? Several factors, all relating to the basic ways in which we process information about others, seem to play a part. First, it appears that as human beings, we possess a basic tendency to divide the world into two social categories: *us* and *them*. Moreover, persons we perceive as outside our own group are viewed as being more similar to one another than persons in our own group. In other words, because we have less information about them, we tend to lump them all together, and see them as quite homogeneous.[34] Second, stereotypes seem to derive, in part, from our tendency to do as little cognitive work as possible in thinking about other persons.[35] If, by assigning individuals to particular groups, we can assume that we know much about them (their major traits, how they tend to act), we save the tedious work of understanding them as individuals. Apparently, this shortcut to social perception is too tempting to resist in many cases.

Whatever their origins, stereotypes can exert powerful effects on several aspects of organizational behavior, from performance appraisals to conflict. Thus, they are certainly one potential source of error with important practical consequences.

SOCIAL PERCEPTION AND ORGANIZATIONAL BEHAVIOR: ITS ROLE IN JOB INTERVIEWS AND PERFORMANCE APPRAISAL

In the preceding discussions of social perception, we have repeatedly referred to the impact of this process on important forms of organizational behavior. In this final section, we'll focus directly on this topic. In particular, we'll consider some of the ways in which the processes and errors we have described can, and often do, affect the selection of employees and evaluation of their performance.

Social Perception and Job Interviews

Despite concerns about their fairness and validity, *employment interviews* are still widely used by organizations in the recruitment and selection of employees.[36] Since such interviews involve first meetings between two strangers, it is clear that social perception—efforts by each to understand the other—are an important part of the process. Further, there can be little doubt that the perceptions (*first impressions*) of each applicant formed by interviewers play a major role in the decisions and evaluations they assign to these persons. What factors or aspects of social perception are important in this respect? Recent research has identified several.

Nonverbal cues. One such factor involves the nonverbal cues emitted by job candidates. In general, the more positive the cues transmitted by applicants, the higher the ratings they receive from interviewers.[37] For example, in one study of such effects, male and female subjects conducted simulated interviews with another person, who played the role of an applicant for an entry-level management job.[38] In fact, the applicant was an accomplice, specially trained to behave in one of two ways. In one condition, she emitted many positive nonverbal cues (e.g., she smiled frequently, maintained a high level of eye contact with the interviewer). In another condition, she behaved in a more neutral manner, and did not emit such positive nonverbal cues. After the interview, subjects rated the applicant on several dimensions relating to her qualifications for the job (e.g., her motivation, potential for success) and her personal traits (friendliness, likableness, intelligence). As shown in Figure 4.14, she received higher ratings

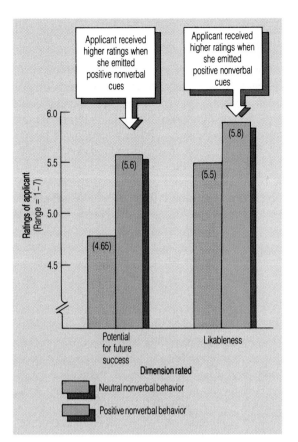

FIGURE 4.14 Nonverbal Cues and
Job Interviews

When an applicant emitted many
positive nonverbal cues during
simulated job interviews, she
received higher ratings from
interviewers than when she emitted
more neutral nonverbal cues.
(Source: Based on data from
Baron, 1986; see Note 38.)

on most of these dimensions when she had previously demonstrated many positive nonverbal cues than when she had shown relatively neutral behavior.

Other findings, however, suggest that emitting a high level of nonverbal cues does not always succeed in generating positive reactions among interviewers. For example, when information about applicants' qualifications is also available, this factor seems predominant.[39] In other words, apparent qualifications exert much stronger effects on the ratings applicants receive than the nature of their nonverbal behavior.[40] Further, when applicants with poor credentials emit many nonverbal cues, they seem to be down-rated relative to ones who do not engage in such behavior.[41] Perhaps this is because interviewers attribute such actions to efforts, by these applicants, to shift attention away from their poor qualifications. Whatever the reason, it is clear that emitting a high level of positive nonverbal cues can sometimes backfire and produce effects opposite the ones intended. The best strategy for applicants to follow, therefore, seems to be this: by all means, practice effective nonverbal behavior, and try to use it to your advantage during an interview. But for best results, combine it with clear evidence of competence and excellent qualifications.

Stereotypes. Earlier, we noted that stereotypes can exert strong effects on our perceptions of others. Do these cognitive frameworks also play a role in job interviews? Again, growing evidence suggests that they do. While several different stereotypes have been studied in this regard, the ones usually viewed as most important, and which have received the most attention, are those relating to sex: *sex role stereotypes.*

Such stereotypes suggest that members of the two sexes possess different characteristics. For example, according to these stereotypes, males tend to be forceful, assertive, and decisive, while females tend to be passive, emotional, and indecisive. We should hasten to note that such stereotypes have, by and large, been proven false: differences between the sexes in such traits are nonexistent, or at least much smaller than sex role stereotypes suggest.[42] This does not prevent them from affecting social perception, however. Several studies have found that under conditions where limited information about job applicants is available, interviewers tend to assign lower ratings to females than to males.[43] The reason does not seem to lie mainly in direct prejudice against females. Rather, it stems from the fact that the characteristics attributed to men by sex role stereotypes seem more appropriate for various jobs (especially managerial ones) than the characteristics attributed to women. In other words, evaluators assign higher ratings to males because they are seen (falsely) as being more suited to various positions than females.

While such results are disturbing, we should note, again, that they have usually been reported in situations where interviewers have little information about applicants. Fortunately, in many real contexts, this is not the case: interviewers receive a considerable amount of information about applicants' previous experience, training, and background. Are the biasing effects of sex role stereotypes weaker under these conditions? A recent study by Graves and Powell suggests that they are.[44]

In this study, corporate recruiters who visited a university were asked to complete a questionnaire about some of the students they interviewed. The questionnaire asked them to rate several factors that might potentially influence their evaluations: each applicant's perceived similarity to the interviewer, interviewers' liking for each applicant, applicants' subjective qualifications (e.g., their ability to express ideas, interest in working for the company, initiative), and applicants' objective qualifications (grades in college). These factors, plus the students' sex, were then examined, to determine whether they were related to the interviewers' ratings. Results were encouraging, at least from the point of view of sex bias or discrimination.

In this realistic context, sex of applicants had little if any effect on such ratings. Rather, the interviewers' decisions were largely a function of the other factors considered (perceived similarity, objective qualifications, and subjective qualifications). In fact, the overall pattern of findings suggested a process such as the one shown in Figure 4.15. Perceived similarity, liking, and objective qualifications all affected interview outcomes through their impact on subjective qualifications; sex of subject had no effect on this factor. In sum, Graves and Powell's results suggest that while the outcome of job interviews may be affected by several forms of bias (e.g., the similar-to-me effect, liking for specific applicants), they are not strongly determined by applicants' sex. Whether this is due to recent changes in society (e.g., growing awareness of sex bias) or to the specific context of the study (interviews on a college campus) cannot be determined at this point. Still, it appears that at least one important type of interview is less subject to this damaging type of bias than might be feared.

Social Perception and Performance Appraisal

One of the most important processes in any organization is the evaluation of performance. Such **performance appraisals** are crucial to effective personnel decisions—determining which employees should receive raises, promotions, bonuses, and other rewards, and which ones, perhaps, should be dismissed. Ideally, performance appraisal should be a totally rational process—one in which completely accurate evaluators use highly valid measures to assign ratings to individual employees. As you can readily guess, however, this ideal is far easier to describe than attain. Many complexities exist

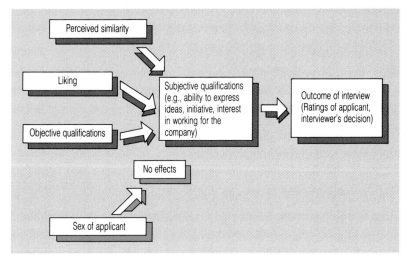

FIGURE 4.15 Factors Affecting the Outcome of Job Interviews

Several factors (perceived similarity, liking, objective qualifications) affected interviewers' ratings of applicants in a college placement center. These factors seemed to influence interviewers' perceptions of the applicants' subjective qualifications. In contrast, applicants' sex had no appreciable effects on these factors or on outcomes of the interview. (Source: Based on data from Graves & Powell, 1988; see Note 44.)

with respect to designing valid measures of performance. For example, if they are to be useful, such measures should reflect *all* important aspects of performance, but should *not* include unrelated or irrelevant behaviors.[45] Similarly, such measures must be presented in a format that raters can easily understand and use.

In addition, human beings are definitely *not* completely accurate in the role of evaluator. They possess a limited capacity to process, store, and retrieve information. Further, their perceptions or interpretations of information relating to performance appear to be subject to many extraneous influences. It is on these factors that we will now focus.

Performance appraisal and expectations. Imagine that you are a manager, faced with the task of evaluating the performance of two of your subordinates. Your expectations for one were quite high; you anticipated that she would do very well. Your expectations for the other were low; you predicted that his work would be average at best. Now, looking at the records, and searching your own memory, you conclude that both have been average. Do you assign different ratings to each? A completely rational rater would not. Since the two persons show similar levels of performance, they should receive similar ratings. In fact, however, this does not seem to be the way most evaluators operate. Because the first employee has disconfirmed your predictions while the second has not, you might actually assign lower ratings to the former. No one likes to be wrong, and the negative feelings generated by discovering that your predictions failed might well spill over to influence your perceptions, and evaluations, of the first individual. That such effects actually occur with respect to real performance appraisals is indicated in a study carried out by Hogan.[46]

In this investigation, supervisors in a large bank were asked to indicate how well they expected their two newest tellers to do on the job. Then, four months later, they rated the actual performance of these individuals. Results indicated that when their expectations were disconfirmed, the supervisors rated the tellers lower than when these expectations were confirmed. In other words, these managers assigned lower ratings to tellers who performed either better or worse than they predicted than to tellers whose performance matched their earlier predictions. (These comparisons were made with actual level of performance held constant through statistical means.)

These findings have unsettling implications, especially for persons who expend extra effort on the job and do better than their supervisors expect. Apparently, such unanticipated increments in performance may sometimes result in *lower* rather than higher performance appraisals. Does this mean that employees are locked into whatever level of performance their managers expect? Not necessarily. Perhaps effects such as the ones noted by Hogan can be avoided if managers realize that their predictions failed simply because a new element entered the equation—increased motivation on the part of a subordinate. In any case, the effect of prior expectations on performance ratings emphasizes the fact noted earlier: human beings are definitely *not* totally rational or accurate evaluators. On the contrary, their behavior in this role can be strongly affected by many factors that shape their perceptions of others but which, presumably, should not be part of the process.

Performance appraisal and attributions. Now, imagine once again that you are a manager faced with the task of evaluating two subordinates. As before, these persons demonstrate similar, average levels of performance. However, you also know that one is a very talented individual, with a great deal of experience, who is coasting along, putting a minimum of effort into her work. The other is a new and inexperienced person with less obvious talent, but a penchant for hard work: he does his very best every day. Would you assign equal ratings to the two people? Perhaps; but it is also quite possible that you will give higher ratings to the latter person. The reason is clear: hard work and effort seem more deserving of credit (and reward) than underutilized talent. In other words, you might assign different ratings to these two persons because although their actual levels of performance are similar, the *reasons behind* their performance are sharply different. In short, as we noted on page 121, *attributions* often play an important role in performance appraisal. Do practicing managers actually behave in this fashion? Research findings suggest that they do. In some cases, at least, they assign higher ratings to subordinates whose performance seems to stem from high motivation and effort than to subordinates whose similar performance stems mainly from talent or past experience.[47]

One more point: attribution also enters performance appraisal in another manner. Few persons enjoy giving negative feedback to others, even if it is deserved. Yet, it may be their job to deliver it. How can they avoid the unpleasantness associated with this task? One technique involves attributing a subordinate's poor performance to external factors beyond his or her control (e.g., bad luck, work overload, actions by other persons that interfered with good performance). Evidence for these effects, too, exists. In the study by Hogan described above, it was also noted that the lower the ratings assigned by the bank supervisors to their tellers, the greater the supervisors' tendencies to attribute such performance to external causes. In sum, attributions not only shape performance ratings; they may also provide raters with a means of softening the blow when delivering negative feedback.

Performance appraisal and escalation of commitment. After making decisions, individuals often feel compelled to stick to them, even if they turn out to be bad ones. As the phrase "throwing good money after bad" suggests, the results of this tendency—often described as **escalation of commitment**—can be costly. Why do decision-makers get caught in this trap of ever-growing costs? We'll return to this process in more detail in our discussion of decision making (chapter 14), but one explanation is this: decision-makers feel compelled to continue because (1) admitting they were wrong will result in considerable loss of face, and (2) they experience pressure to justify the costs they've already incurred.[48] But why do we introduce this process here? Because, unfortunately, it seems to constitute another potential source of bias with respect to performance appraisals. This has been convincingly demonstrated by Schoorman.[49]

Schoorman reasoned that escalation of commitment would cause managers to evaluate persons whom they had previously hired (or had recommended be hired) more favorably than persons in whose hiring they had not been directly involved. This would be the case because by evaluating such persons positively, the managers could justify their earlier decisions. Similarly, he predicted that managers would evaluate persons they had previously recommended *not* be hired less favorably than ones in whose hiring they had not been involved.

To test these predictions, he asked managers in a large company to evaluate the performance of clerical workers. Information on whether the managers had been involved in the hiring of each person, and whether they had agreed or disagreed with the decision to hire this person, was also obtained. As you can see from Figure 4.16, results supported both hypotheses. Managers evaluated employees they had hired or recommended more favorably than ones in whose hiring they had not been involved. And they evaluated employees they had recommended *not* be hired less favorably than ones in whose hiring they had not been involved. In short, their previous decisions seemed to bias their later evaluations.

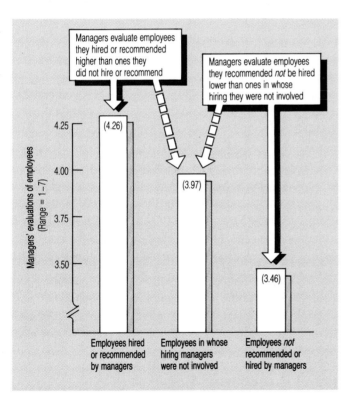

FIGURE 4.16   Escalation of Commitment and Performance Appraisal
Managers rated employees they had hired or recommended more favorably than ones in whose hiring they had not been directly involved. Similarly, they rated employees they recommended *not* be hired less favorably than those in whose hiring they had not been involved. These findings illustrate the impact of escalation of commitment on performance appraisal. (Source: Based on data from Schoorman, 1988; see Note 49.)

These findings suggest that managers should be on guard against yet another potential source of bias in their performance appraisals—the tendency to give an important edge to "their people"—ones they personally have hired. (Sources of bias aside, how should performance appraisal interviews be handled? For some concrete tips, please see the **Management Perspective** section below.)

OB: A MANAGEMENT PERSPECTIVE

Conducting Effective Appraisal Interviews: Some "Do's" and "Don'ts"

Many managers report that providing feedback to subordinates in the context of a formal appraisal interview is one of the most difficult tasks they must perform. Unless such sessions turn into a "love feast," they include at least a dollop of negative feedback, and this is something most people are reluctant to deliver.[50] How can the potential unpleasantness of such sessions be minimized, and their value in improving employee motivation and performance enhanced? There are no simple answers, but observing the following guidelines can help.

Do the Following:

1. Agree, in advance, on the content of the interview—exactly what issues will be discussed.
2. Agree on the process—how the interview will be conducted, what materials will be considered, and the sequence of these events.
3. During the interview, try to give feedback that is specific in nature and considerate in tone. General statements (e.g., "You need to improve") aren't nearly as helpful as ones that focus on specific actions employees should take (e.g., "You should file all R-20 reports on time").
4. Focus on the subordinate's behavior, not on your inferences about the traits or characteristics it suggests. (This will help minimize the impact of such cognitive factors as implicit personality theories and stereotypes.)
5. Develop a concrete plan for improvement—one

that outlines specific actions the subordinate can take to obtain higher evaluations next time.

6. Emphasize the fact that you are trying to help. Your goal is to help the subordinate improve, *not* to wreck her or his ego.
7. End by summarizing the major points, and with as much encouragement as you can muster. Employees should leave feeling hopeful and capable of implementing the plan that has been developed.

Don't Do the Following:

1. Don't schedule the interview at a very busy time, or the end of the day; if you do, it will be hard to give it the attention it deserves.
2. Don't use threats (e.g., "If you don't improve, you're through"). These usually generate negative, counterproductive reactions on the part of subordinates.
3. Don't compare the individual negatively to others ("If only you had handled it like Sue . . .").
4. Don't attribute poor performance to stable internal causes (e.g., the employee's personality or lack of ability); if you can't attribute poor performance to temporary, external factors, leave this issue open.
5. Don't establish barriers to open communication (e.g., don't hold the interview in the supervisor's office if this is the only time the employee ever comes there; don't place physical barriers such as a desk between yourself and the person being appraised).

Improving the Accuracy of Performance Appraisals

Performance appraisal, as we noted earlier, is a serious business. Errors in this process can have important effects on both individuals and organizations. Promising careers can be shattered by unfair or inaccurate assessments. And organizations can experience major costs if undeserving persons *are* rewarded and rise to positions they can't handle. Given these facts, efforts to make appraisals as accurate as possible seem well worthwhile. How can this goal be reached? One approach involves providing raters with special training—experiences designed to help them overcome serious sources of error. A number of different procedures have been developed for this purpose. The most promising of these, however, appear to be those based largely on an *information-processing* approach to performance appraisal.[51,52] According to this perspective, appraisal is a complex cognitive process in which raters must notice, encode, store, and later recall information about ratees. Then, they must use this information to evaluate ratees in some manner. In order to improve appraisal accuracy, therefore, raters' ability to perform these tasks must be enhanced. Two techniques seem especially helpful in this regard.

The first of these is known as **frame of reference training.**[53] As its name suggests, such training is designed primarily to establish a common frame of reference raters can use in evaluating performance. In this training, the work or tasks to be evaluated are described in detail, and raters are given practice with using the rating instruments and scales they will employ. Detailed feedback on their accuracy in using these scales is also provided. Next, they are given clear explanations for the ratings assigned to various behaviors or levels of performance by expert raters. In sum, raters receive information on key dimensions of performance they are to evaluate, get practice in evaluating specific examples of performance, and receive feedback on their practice ratings. In this manner, the links between performance dimensions and actual behavior are clarified.

Growing evidence suggests that frame of reference training is quite successful. Individuals who receive it demonstrate less tendency toward halo effects and other forms of rating errors and greater accuracy than individuals who receive no training, or those who are simply informed about the nature of such errors.[54] Frame of reference training seems to succeed, at least in part, because it induces raters to engage in what has been termed *deeper levels of processing*—careful, detailed thought about ratees' behavior. Such processing has been found to enhance memory for various forms of information.[55]

Two other techniques that are successful in improving the accuracy of performance appraisal are *training in observational skills*—efforts to help raters become better observers of subordinates' behavior (e.g., learning to take careful notes on their actions)—and *decision training*—helping raters understand the kind of inferential errors decision-makers often make when combining information about others. This training involves familiarizing raters with such potential errors as assigning inappropriate weights to various behaviors by subordinates, jumping to false conclusions about them, and ignoring the perils of biased data (e.g., inadequate samples of subordinates' behavior).[56] Both training in observational skills and decision training appear to reduce several types of errors while enhancing overall accuracy. Fortunately, these gains are attained after only a few hours of training. In view of this fact, we can conclude on a fairly optimistic note. Evaluating others' performance is indeed a complex and difficult task, subject to several forms of error. Yet, armed with appropriate training and practice, managers *can* learn to perform it accurately. Organizations concerned with the fairness of this process, therefore, should make certain that such training is provided to all persons who assume a supervisory role.

Summary and Review

Basic Aspects of Perception. Perception is the process through which we select, organize, and interpret information brought to us by our senses. Perception is *selective:* we tend to notice some stimuli while largely ignoring others. Perception is also *organized;* we tend to combine sensory information into meaningful patterns.

Social Perception: Perceiving Other Persons. Because other persons play a central role in our lives, we frequently attempt to understand them. This often involves **attribution**—efforts to understand the causes of others' actions. We accomplish this task by focusing on certain aspects of their behavior (e.g., actions which are not socially desirable or which produce *noncommon effects*). In order to determine whether others' actions have stemmed mainly from internal or external causes, we consider three types of information about their behavior: *consensus* (whether others act in the same way), *consistency* (whether they behave in the same manner across time), and *distinctiveness* (whether they behave in the same manner in other situations).

Social perception can also be viewed as a *cognitive process* in which individuals notice, encode, store, and later retrieve information about others. Such information processing is often strongly affected by **schemas**—cognitive frameworks for understanding the world around us developed through experience. Once established, schemas may determine which information we notice, which information is entered into memory, and which is later remembered. Schemas play a role in **stereotypes**—cognitive frameworks that relate membership in specific groups to the possession of various traits or characteristics.

Errors in Social Perception. Social perception is subject to several sources of error. The **self-serving bias** involves our tendency to attribute successes to internal causes (our own traits), but failures to external factors. **Halo effects** occur when our overall impression of another person affects perceptions of this person's individual traits or behaviors. We also tend to like, and evaluate more positively, persons who are similar to ourselves (the **similar-to-me effect**). Other potential sources of error include **stereotypes, implicit personality theories,** and **contrast effects.**

Social Perception and Organizational Behavior. Social perception plays an important role in several forms of organizational behavior. It affects the outcomes of job interviews, where the ratings assigned to applicants are often influenced by such factors as the nonverbal cues they emit and by various stereotypes (e.g., sex role stereotypes). It also influences **performance appraisal.** Here, evaluations of others' performance can be affected by expectations about them, perceived similarity between raters and ratees, and even whether the rater was involved in hiring the persons being evaluated. Fortunately, the accuracy of performance appraisal can be enhanced by providing raters with special types of training (e.g., frame of reference training, training in observational skills, and training designed to clarify the nature of potential sources of bias in decision making).

KEY TERMS

attribution: The process through which individuals attempt to determine the causes behind others' behavior.

contrast effects: Refers to the fact that evaluations of a given person on some dimension may be affected by prior contact with others who are considerably higher or lower than this individual on the same dimension.

escalation of commitment: The tendency to stick to prior decisions, even if growing evidence indicates that they are faulty or inadequate.

figure and ground: The tendency to divide the visual world, perceptually, into two major categories—*figure*

(that which has shape and a location in space) and *ground* (that which has no shape and no definite location).

frame of reference training: A technique for enhancing accuracy in performance appraisals, in which raters receive training designed to clarify the links between behavior and rating dimensions.

fundamental attribution error: Refers to the tendency to attribute others' actions to internal causes (e.g., their traits) while largely ignoring external factors that may have also influenced such behavior.

halo effects: The tendency for the overall impressions of others to affect objective evaluations of their specific traits. (Alternatively, the perception of spuriously elevated correlations between various traits being rated or evaluated.)

implicit theories of personality: Beliefs suggesting that certain traits or characteristics tend to occur together. Such beliefs lead us to conclude that if other persons possess certain traits, they are likely to possess others as well.

nonverbal communication: The process through which individuals acquire information about others' current emotions or feelings from cues provided by such sources as facial expressions, eye contact, and body language.

perception: The process through which we select, organize, and interpret information gathered by our senses in order to understand the world around us.

performance appraisal: The process of evaluating employee performance on various work-relevant dimensions.

schemas: Cognitive frameworks developed through experience which affect the way in which information about

the external world is noticed, encoded, stored, and remembered.

self-serving bias: A form of attributional error in which individuals attribute successes to internal causes (their own traits), but attribute failure to external factors beyond their control.

similar-to-me effect: The tendency of raters to assign higher evaluations to ratees who are similar to themselves in various respects (e.g., in terms of attitudes, demographic factors).

social information processing (or social cognition): The process through which social information is sorted, stored, and retrieved from memory.

social perception: The process through which individuals attempt to combine, integrate, and interpret information about others.

stereotype: The belief that all members of a specific group share similar negative traits and behaviors.

QUESTIONS FOR DISCUSSION

1. What do various visual illusions tell us about the nature of perception?

2. In what work-related contexts is it important to be able to determine whether others' behavior stems primarily from internal or external causes?

3. Schemas can't be seen or measured directly. Given this fact, how can we obtain evidence for the existence of such cognitive frameworks?

4. How can the self-serving bias serve as a potential cause of friction and conflict in organizations?

5. It is often said that all stereotypes contain a grain of truth. Do you think this is correct? If so, why?

6. On the basis of information provided in this chapter, how should individuals prepare for important job interviews?

7. Are nonverbal cues useful in determining whether another person is trying to deceive you? If so, which ones are helpful in this respect? Why?

8. Since we can only evaluate people in terms of available information, what steps might raters take to improve their memory for pertinent information?

9. If you could undergo any type of special training you desired in order to improve your own accuracy as a rater of others' performance, what type would you choose? Why?

NOTES

1. Sekuler, R., & Blake, R. (1985). *Perception.* New York: Random House.

2. Solso, R. L. (1988). *Cognitive psychology* (2nd ed.). Boston: Allyn & Bacon.

3. See Note 2.

4. Fiske, S. E., & Taylor, S. E. (1984). *Social cognition.* Reading, MA: Addison-Wesley.

5. Ross, M., & Fletcher, G. J. O. (1985). *Attribution and social perception.* In G. Lindzey & E. Aronson (Eds.), *Handbook of social psychology* (2nd ed.). New York: Random House.

6. Kleinke, C. L. (1986). *Meeting and understanding people.* New York: Freeman.

7. See Note 5.

8. See Note 5.

9. Kelley, H. H., & Michela, J. L. (1980). Attribution theory and research. *Annual Review of Psychology, 31,* 457–501.

10. Harvey, J. H., & Wewary, G. H. (1981). *Perspectives on attributional processes.* Dubuque, IA: Wm. C. Brown.

11. Hansen, R. D. (1980). Common sense attribution. *Journal of Personality and Social Psychology, 39,* 996–1009.

12. Weiner, B. (1985). An attributional theory of achievement motivation and emotion. *Psychological Review, 82,* 548–573.

13. Knowlton, W. A., Jr., & Mitchell, T. R. (1980).

Effects of causal attributions on a supervisor's evaluation of subordinate performance. *Journal of Applied Psychology, 65,* 459–466.

14. Fiske, S. T., & Taylor, S. E. (1984). *Social cognition.* Reading, MA: Addison-Wesley.

15. Wyer, R. S., Jr., & Srull, T. K. (1986). Human cognition in its social context. *Psychological Review, 93,* 322–359.

16. Wyer, R. S., & Srull, T. K. (Eds.) (1988). *Advances in social cognition,* vol. 1. Hillsdale, NJ: Erlbaum.

17. Taylor, S. E., & Crocker, J. (1981). Schematic bases of social information processing. In E. T. Higgins, C. P. Herman, & M. P. Zanna (Eds.), *Social cognition: The Ontario symposium.* Hillsdale, NJ: Erlbaum.

18. See Note 14.

19. O'Sullivan, C., & Durso, F. T. (1984). Effects of schema-incongruent information on memory for stereotypical attributes. *Journal of Personality and Social Psychology, 47,* 55–70.

20. Dovidio, J. H., Evans, N., & Tyler, R. B. (1986). Racial stereotypes: The contents of their cognitive representations. *Journal of Experimental Social Psychology, 22,* 22–37.

21. Siegman, A. W., & Feldstein, S. (Eds.) (1988). *Nonverbal behavior and communication* (2nd ed.). Hillsdale, NJ: Erlbaum.

22. Pfeiffer, J. (1988). How not to lose the trade wars by cultural gaffes. *Smithsonian, 18,* 145–156.

23. Graham, J. (1988). Cited in Pfeiffer, J. (1988); see Note 22.

24. Johnson, J. T., Jemmott, J. B., III, & Pettigrew, T. F. (1984). Causal attribution and dispositional inference: Evidence of inconsistent judgments. *Journal of Experimental Social Psychology, 20,* 567–585.

25. Mullen, B., & Riordan, C. A. (1988). Self-serving attributions for performance in naturalistic settings: A meta-analytic review. *Journal of Applied Social Psychology, 18,* 3–22.

26. Murphy, K. R., & Reynolds, D. H. (1988). Does true halo affect observed halo? *Journal of Applied Psychology, 73,* 235–238.

27. Fisicaro, S. A. (1988). A reexamination of the relation between halo error and accuracy. *Journal of Applied Social Psychology, 73,* 239–244.

28. Binning, J. F., Goldstein, M. A., Garcia, M. F., & Scattaregia, J. H. (1988). Effects of preinterview impressions on questioning strategies in same- and opposite-sex employment interviews. *Journal of Applied Psychology, 73,* 30–37.

29. Pulakos, E. D., & Wexley, K. N. (1983). The relationship among perceptual similarity, sex, and performance ratings in manager-subordinate dyads. *Academy of Management Journal, 26,* 129–139.

30. Turban, D. B., & Jones, A. P. (1988). Supervisor-subordinate similarity: Types, effects, and mechanisms. *Journal of Applied Psychology, 73,* 228–234.

31. See Note 4.

32. Ainlay, S. C., Becker, G., & Coleman, L. (Eds.) (1986). *The dilemma of difference.* New York: Plenum.

33. Krzystofiak, F., Cardy, R., & Newman, J. (1988). Implicit personality and performance appraisal: The influence of trait inferences on evaluations of behavior. *Journal of Applied Psychology, 73,* 515–521.

34. Linville, P. W. (1982). The complexity-extremity effect and age-based stereotyping. *Journal of Personality and Social Psychology, 42,* 183–211.

35. See Note 4.

36. Arvey, R. D., & Campion, J. E. (1982). The employment interview: A summary and review of recent research. *Personnel Psychology, 35,* 281–322.

37. Imada, A. S., & Hakel, M. D. (1977). Influence of nonverbal communication and rater proximity on impressions and decisions in simulated employment interviews. *Journal of Applied Psychology, 62,* 295–300.

38. Baron, R. A. (1986). Self-presentation in job interviews: When there can be "too much of a good thing." *Journal of Applied Social Psychology, 16,* 16–28.

39. Rasmussen, K. G., Jr. (1984). Nonverbal behavior, verbal behavior, résumé credentials, and selection interview outcomes. *Journal of Applied Psychology, 69,* 551–556.

40. Riggio, R. E., & Throckmorton, B. (1988). The relative effects of verbal and nonverbal behavior, appearance, and social skills on evaluations made in hiring interviews. *Journal of Applied Social Psychology, 18,* 331–348.

41. See Note 39.

42. Parsons, J. E., Adler, T., & Meece, J. L. (1984). Sex differences in achievement: A test of alternate theories. *Journal of Personality and Social Psychology, 46,* 26–43.

43. Tosi, H. L., & Einbender, S. W. (1985). The effects of type and amount of information in sex discrimination research: A meta-analysis. *Academy of Management Journal, 28,* 712–723.

44. Graves, L. M., & Powell, G. N. (1988). An investigation of sex discrimination in recruiters' evaluations of actual applicants. *Journal of Applied Psychology, 72,* 20–29.

45. Saal, F. E., & Knight, P. A. (1988). *Industrial/organizational psychology: Science and practice.* Pacific Grove, CA: Brooks/Cole.

46. Hogan, E. A. (1987). Effects of prior expectations on performance ratings: A longitudinal study. *Academy of Management Journal, 30,* 354–368.

47. Mitchell, T. R., Green, S. G., & Wood, R. S. (1982). An attributional model of leadership and the poor performing subordinate: Development and validation. In B. M. Staw & L. L. Cummings (Eds.), *Research in organizational behavior,* vol. 3. Greenwich, CT: JAI Press.

48. Staw, B. M., & Ross, J. (1978). Commitment to a policy decision: A multitheoretical perspective. *Administrative Science Quarterly, 23,* 40–64.

49. Schoorman, F. D. (1988). Escalation bias in performance appraisals: An unintended consequence of supervisor participation in hiring decisions. *Journal of Applied Psychology, 73,* 58–62.

50. Baron, R. A. Negative effects of destructive criticism: Impact on conflict, self-efficacy, and task performance. *Journal of Applied Psychology, 73,* 199–207.

51. DeNisi, A. S., Cafferty, T. P., & Meglino, B. M. (1984). A cognitive view of the appraisal process: A model and research propositions. *Organizational Behavior and Human Performance, 33,* 360–396.

52. Feldman, J. M. (1981). Beyond attribution theory: Cognitive processes in performance appraisal. *Journal of Applied Psychology, 66,* 127–142.

53. McIntyre, R., Smith, D., & Hassett, C. (1984). Accuracy of performance ratings as affected by rater training and perceived purpose of rating. *Journal of Applied Psychology, 69,* 147–156.

54. Athey, T. R., & McIntyre, R. M. (1987). Effect of rater training on rater accuracy: Levels-of-processing theory and social facilitation theory perspectives. *Journal of Applied Psychology, 72,* 567–572.

55. Craik, F. I., & Lockhart, R. S. (1972). Levels of processing: a framework for memory research. *Journal of Verbal Learning and Verbal Behavior, 11,* 671–684.

56. Hedge, J. W., & Kavanagh, M. J. (1988). Improving the accuracy of performance evaluations: Comparison of three methods of performance appraiser training. *Journal of Applied Psychology, 73,* 68–73.

Hidden Traps in Performance Appraisal

Ann B. Hopkins believed she would get promoted to a partnership at Price Waterhouse, one of the "Big Eight" public accounting firms.[1] *After all*, she thought, *I brought in some $34 million in consulting contracts, more than anyone else applying for partnership, and billed more hours in the preceding year than any other candidate.* So, when her application for partner was first deferred for a year and then denied, she was very disturbed. *How could this happen,* she thought.

The answer to this question isn't entirely clear, and it probably never will be. What is clear, however, is that Ann Hopkins believed she was the victim of sexual stereotyping and discrimination in the performance evaluation process. She believed this discrimination was responsible for the denial of her promotion—an allegation she has claimed in a lawsuit. According to records introduced in court, the partners who decided her fate (all of whom are males) described Ann as arrogant, abrasive, overbearing, insensitive, impatient, and hard-nosed. Of course, all of these characteristics might be legitimate reasons to deny someone promotion. However, the partners also described Ann as "macho," and needing to go to "charm school." These latter assertions, as well as one partner's advice for her to "walk more femininely, talk more femininely, dress more femininely, . . . wear make-up, have [her] hair styled, and wear jewelry"[2] contributed to her belief that she had been the victim of sexual stereotyping. Because she did not conform to the typical partner's stereotype of a female partner, she alleges, she was denied promotion.

Two lower courts have found in favor of Ann Hopkins. They have said that Price Waterhouse's "evident sexism" in the evaluation process came into play in their decision to deny her partnership. The case will be heard before the U.S. Supreme Court.

Of course, women are not the only group about whom stereotypes may lead to discriminatory treatment. The growing internationalization of the economy has resulted in many people from other countries living and working in the United States. Unfortunately, it seems that stereotypes of these groups are prevalent. In particular, Asian-Americans feel that stereotypes of them often result in their being denied promotions to management positions. Interestingly, these promotions are denied despite the fact that the prevailing stereotype of Asian-Americans is generally quite positive.[3]

They are viewed as the "model minority." Asian-Americans often graduate at or near the top of their college classes and are heavily recruited for entry level technical and professional jobs. Often, they perform exceptionally well in these positions. However, suggests Jim Tso, president of the Organization of Chinese Americans, their high level of competence makes companies reluctant to promote them. The rationale for this seems to be that because they have demonstrated such expertise at lower levels, it would be a shame to lose them by promoting them to management.

David Lam, an engineer at Hewlett-Packard, suspected this happened to him. After three years in his job he was passed over for promotion to a management position that he had requested. Instead, a Caucasian with two years of experience—hired by Lam—was given the promotion. Lam believes that the problem of discrimination has two components. He says, "Part of it is because there's strong prejudice prevailing in the corporate world. The other half is that Asians don't try hard enough to integrate."[4]

Lam's assertions are echoed by others. One vice president of a large Midwestern company (he requested anonymity) said he would like to employ many more people of Asian descent because they are "loyal and hard working." He doesn't consider promoting them, however, because they "have to have pats on the back constantly."[5] A manager at Westinghouse, Kenneth Chang, recognizes that his career opportunities may be limited if he doesn't go to cocktail parties and learn how to play golf.

Stereotypes of Asian-Americans as passive and quiet seem to present the biggest obstacle to their filling management roles. If they are, in fact, quiet, management uses this as proof of their inability to handle managerial responsibilities. On the other hand, if they are aggressive, this is taken as evidence that they don't fit in! Although promotion wasn't at issue, when Terry Koroda worked at Merrill, Lynch, Pierce, Fenner & Smith Inc. he experienced these mixed expectations when he took an aggressive stance in the negotiation for a new computer system. The people in the purchasing department were wary of his behavior and attempted to bypass his suggestions. Nonetheless, he prevailed upon them to let him manage the negotiations. This resulted in the purchase of a system that saved the company $30,000 a month in computer costs.

Kung Lee Wang, who started the Organization of Chinese Americans, believes that the discrimination resulting from stereotyping can be ended. His suggestion is that Asian-Americans find mentors within their organizations. He claims that sponsors can be instrumental in teaching valued social and political skills as well as exerting influence to help get their protegees into management positions.

Whatever the reasons for stereotyping, some actions will have to be taken to eliminate the discrimination that follows. This results from the simple fact that the number of Asian-American managers is a very small percentage of the total number employed in technical and professional jobs. Without visible opportunities for promotion, those in lower level ranks who desire positions will go elsewhere—either to companies in the United States that ban discrimination, or to other countries entirely—thus creating a shortage of experienced and valued employees to fill important positions in organizations.

Questions for Discussion

1. What stereotypes did the Price Waterhouse partners appear to hold of women?

2. How did these stereotypes affect the partners' judgment of Ann Hopkins' suitability for promotion?

3. What might a company do to ensure that it does not fall victim to making performance appraisals on the basis of sex role stereotypes?

4. Why does the prevailing stereotype of Asian-Americans result in their being denied management positions?

5. Why are stereotypes particularly unfair to individuals who are members of a minority?

6. Do you think Kung Lee Wang's idea about mentors is a good one? Why or why not?

Notes

1. McCarthy, M. J. (1988, June 14). Supreme court to rule on sex-bias case. *Wall Street Journal*, p. 37.

2. See Note 1, p. 37.

3. Yu, W. (1985, September 11). Asian-Americans charge prejudice slows climb to management ranks. *Wall Street Journal*, p. 35.

4. See Note 3, p. 35.

5. See Note 3, p. 35.

**EXPERIENCING
ORGANIZATIONAL
BEHAVIOR**

The All Too Powerful Impact of Stereotypes

Most people are well aware of the existence of stereotypes. They realize that in the past, negative stereotypes were responsible for unfair treatment of women and minority group members in many work settings. At the same time, though, most persons do not recognize the existence and potentially powerful impact of a wide range of other stereotypes. This exercise is designed to demonstrate the fact that your own thinking (enlightened as it may be) can be affected by various stereotypes, even if you think you are an eminently fair-minded and unbiased person. Follow the directions below for some first-hand insights into such effects.

Procedure

Rate the members of the following groups on each of the following dimensions. (Circle one number for each characteristic.)

Investment Bankers

Liberal						Conservative
1	2	3	4	5	6	7

Intelligent						Unintelligent
1	2	3	4	5	6	7

Greedy						Generous
1	2	3	4	5	6	7

Dull						Interesting
1	2	3	4	5	6	7

Advertising Executives

Liberal						Conservative
1	2	3	4	5	6	7

Intelligent						Unintelligent
1	2	3	4	5	6	7

Greedy						Generous
1	2	3	4	5	6	7

Dull						Interesting
1	2	3	4	5	6	7

Engineers

Liberal						Conservative
1	2	3	4	5	6	7

Intelligent						Unintelligent
1	2	3	4	5	6	7

Greedy						Generous
1	2	3	4	5	6	7

Dull						Interesting
1	2	3	4	5	6	7

Professors

Liberal						Conservative
1	2	3	4	5	6	7

Intelligent						Unintelligent
1	2	3	4	5	6	7

151
**Experiencing
Organizational
Behavior**

Greedy						Generous
1	2	3	4	5	6	7

Dull						Interesting
1	2	3	4	5	6	7

Belly Dancers

Liberal						Conservative
1	2	3	4	5	6	7

Intelligent						Unintelligent
1	2	3	4	5	6	7

Greedy						Generous
1	2	3	4	5	6	7

Dull						Interesting
1	2	3	4	5	6	7

Points to Consider

Did your ratings of the various groups differ? If you are like most people, they probably did. For example, you probably rated investment bankers as more conservative and less interesting than belly dancers (and, we hope, professors!). Similarly, you probably rated engineers, investment bankers, and professors as more intelligent than dancers. Moreover—and this is an important point—your ratings may well have differed *even if you do not know members of these various professions personally.*

The point of this exercise is straightforward. We hold stereotypes concerning the supposed traits or characteristics of many different groups. Further, such beliefs are so pervasive that we are often unaware of their existence until, as in this demonstration, they are called into action. Given the widespread existence of stereotypes and their potential effects on important organizational processes, it is important to be aware of them and to try to resist their influence. If you choose, instead, to ignore them, you may well fall victim to serious errors in perceiving others.

CHAPTER FIVE

WORK-RELATED ATTITUDES: THEIR NATURE AND IMPACT

CHAPTER OUTLINE

Attitudes: Their Basic Nature and How They Can Be Changed
Changing Attitudes: The Process of Persuasion
Changing Our Own Attitudes: The Role of Cognitive Dissonance

Job Satisfaction: Attitudes toward One's Work
Measuring Job Satisfaction: Assessing Reactions to Work
Job Satisfaction: Some Major Causes
The Prevalence of Job Satisfaction: Do Most People Like Their Work?
Job Satisfaction: Its Major Effects

Organizational Commitment: Attitudes toward Organizations
Factors Affecting Organizational Commitment
Major Effects of Organizational Commitment

Prejudice: Negative Attitudes toward Other Organization Members
Prejudice Based on Sex
Sexism in Work Settings: An Optimistic Conclusion

Special Sections

OB: A Research Perspective
When Professionals Perform Non-Professional Jobs: Loss of Work-Related Status and Job Satisfaction

OB: A Research Perspective
Employee Stock Ownership Plans: Their Positive Impact on Organizational Commitment

LEARNING OBJECTIVES

After reading this chapter, you should be able to:
1. Define *attitudes* and describe their relevance to the field of OB.
2. List several factors that affect the process of *persuasion*.
3. Explain the process of *cognitive dissonance* and indicate how it often leads individuals to change their own attitudes.
4. Define *job satisfaction* and explain how it is measured.
5. Describe several factors that affect job satisfaction, and indicate how job satisfaction influences key aspects of organizational behavior.
6. Define *organizational commitment* and explain both its causes and effects.
7. Define *prejudice* and describe evidence suggesting that one important form of prejudice (sexism) is decreasing.

"Boy, does he have nerve," Ross Holcomb remarks with obvious disgust as he pulls up a chair and joins Kate Bergan and Frank Stoll in the company cafeteria.

"What's up?" Kate asks, fork poised in mid-air. "You look like you've had a rough morning."

"I'll say!" Ross replies. "It's that Glenn Vargas again. What a supervisor! *This* time he wants to send me out west the week before my vacation. And with a killer schedule—three plant visits in four days. I'll come back totally exhausted. What a drag!"

"Yeah, that's rough," Frank chimes in. "But after all, when you get back to the office you'll have three weeks to recover, and *someone* has to get out there for those checks."

"That doesn't cut it with me," Ross answers. "What the heck do I care? I've been looking forward to this vacation for months. I don't want it ruined by some dumb routine."

"Hold on, Ross," Kate interrupts. "Those checks aren't just routine. If they're not done, and done right, it can cost the company big money. You know what happens when there's a major problem and we get down-time on one of the lines."

"Big deal!" Ross answers, waving his arm in the air. "So it'll cost some bucks. This company can afford it. And besides, that's not really part of my job anyway. Lois Heilbrun is supposed to take care of it."

"I know," Kate agrees, "but her group is really short-handed right now. You remember—Dick Weinberg left with just a couple weeks' notice, and they haven't been able to replace him yet."

Shaking his head, Ross waves off Kate's objections. "Let me say it again as clear as I know how: *I really don't care.* I'm going to enjoy my vacation, no matter what."

"Well, it's that kind of attitude that makes it hard for everyone," Kate answers, color rising to her cheeks. "We're all in this together, and if we aren't willing to pitch in and help out once in a while, it's a real shame. Besides, this company's been good to you. Don't you have any loyalty to it?"

"Not me," Ross answers with annoyance. "My main concern is taking care of 'Yours Truly.' The company can look out for itself."

"Hey you two, calm down," Frank interjects. "This is lunch, not a meeting of the local debating society. Leave this stuff for some other time."

"Yeah, sure," Kate agrees. "It's just that I can't help getting upset when I hear people say they're not willing to put one extra ounce of effort into their work. Maybe I'm nuts, but I really think that's the main reason we're having so much trouble staying competitive these days."

Human beings are seldom totally neutral about almost any aspect of the world around them. On the contrary, they have likes and dislikes, aversions and preferences for people, events, objects, and activities. Since work occupies such a major role in most persons' lives, it is hardly surprising that it is the object of such positive and negative reactions, and that these **work-related attitudes** can be quite intense. While some people like their jobs and have positive feelings about the organizations in which they work, others dislike their jobs, and—like Ross, the character in our opening incident—feel little commitment to or identification with their organization. These **attitudes** are important, for they often influence key aspects of organizational behavior—

"And please don't hesitate to call on us. Our dedicated staff will be delighted to serve you."

FIGURE 5.1   Work-related Attitudes: An Important Topic for OB
Work-related attitudes often strongly affect important aspects of organizational behavior.
(Source: Drawing by Koren; © 1983 The New Yorker Magazine, Inc.)

task performance, absenteeism, and turnover, to mention just a few (see Figure 5.1 on page 154).

Since work-related attitudes are important for both the persons who hold them and the organizations in which they work, we'll consider them in detail in this chapter. First, we'll provide some background information about *attitudes* in general, describing their basic nature and how they can be changed. Second, we'll examine **job satisfac-tion**—individuals' positive or negative feelings about their jobs.[1] In this context, we'll describe several factors that contribute to feelings of satisfaction or dissatisfaction with one's work, and the effects of such reactions on key forms of organizational behavior. Next, we'll turn to **organizational commitment**—attitudes relating to an entire organization rather than to specific jobs, and which reflect individuals' levels of iden-tification with the organizations that employ them.[2] Finally, we'll turn to a special type of work-related attitude—**prejudice.**[3] This involves negative views about other or-ganization members (or potential members) belonging to specific groups or categories (e.g., women, older persons, members of various minorities). As we will see, such attitudes can be very disruptive to effective organizational functioning and also have great significance for society as a whole.

ATTITUDES: THEIR BASIC NATURE AND HOW THEY CAN BE CHANGED

Earlier, we stated that attitudes involve our reactions to various aspects of the external world—reactions to people, objects, activities, or ideas, to name just a few major categories. On closer examination, such reactions seem to involve three major com-ponents. First, they include an *evaluative* aspect, reflecting various degrees of liking or disliking for specific items or events. Second, they involve a *cognitive component*— beliefs about the object, person, or event with which the attitude is concerned. Finally, they include a behavioral component—intentions to act in certain ways toward the

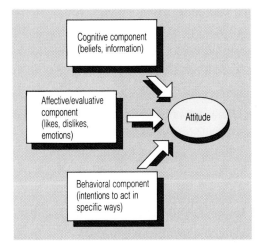

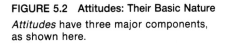

FIGURE 5.2 Attitudes: Their Basic Nature
Attitudes have three major components, as shown here.

attitude object. For example, consider your boss. You may like her very much (an evaluative reaction), believe that she is fair in her treatment of subordinates (a cognitive component), and intend to continue working with her for the foreseeable future (an intention). Attitudes, then, consist of stable combinations of these three components. More precisely, attitudes can be defined as *relatively stable clusters of feelings, beliefs, and behavior tendencies (intentions directed toward some aspect of the external world).* (See Figure 5.2.)[4] Please note the phrase *relatively stable.* This refers to the fact that once formed, attitudes tend to persist. Indeed, as we'll soon see, changing them usually requires considerable effort.

Work-related attitudes, then, involve lasting feelings, beliefs, and behavior tendencies toward various aspects of work, work settings, or the people in them. Such attitudes may focus on supervisors, subordinates, customers, competitors, specific tasks, company policies, new equipment, reward systems, the entire organization, or virtually any other aspect of work you can imagine. In fact, individuals can—and often do—hold well-developed attitudes toward all of these and countless other objects or events.

Why are such attitudes important for the field of OB? Because in many cases, they affect key aspects of organizational behavior. Work-related attitudes are one of the many factors influencing important outcomes such as task performance, absence from work, and voluntary turnover. Since they are only *one* such factor, however, it is misleading to assume that work-related attitudes will always (or even usually) produce such effects in a direct and straightforward manner. This point is clearly illustrated by the following example. At first glance, it seems reasonable to assume that if employees in a large organization hold negative attitudes about their jobs and their company, the rate of voluntary turnover will be high. This will probably *not* be the case, however, if the job market is very soft, and these persons realize that if they quit, the probability of obtaining another position is quite low. In this and many other situations, a link between work-related attitudes and important aspects of either individual behavior or organizational functioning may exist, but other factors may moderate it, or make it difficult to observe.

In view of this fact, it is important to keep the following basic principle in mind as you read this chapter: work-related attitudes certainly exist, are held by most persons in work settings, and are related to several aspects of organizational behavior. However, their impact varies greatly across situations, and is not apparent to the same degree in all contexts at all times.

Changing Attitudes: The Process of Persuasion

If, as we have just suggested, work-related attitudes play an important role in many forms of organizational behavior, an intriguing possibility follows: perhaps change in certain of these attitudes will be followed by desirable changes in behavior. Perhaps, for instance, increments in employees' satisfaction with their current jobs will result in enhanced task performance or in reduced rates of absence from work. Such possibilities have stimulated a great deal of research in OB, much of it directed toward improving organizational functioning through planned change in employees' attitudes and behavior. Since we will consider *organizational development* in chapter 16, we won't describe it in detail here. Instead, we'll focus primarily on the basic nature of attitude change—how it occurs and the factors that affect it.

Factors affecting persuasion. As you probably know from personal experience, attempts to alter attitudes are very common. Each day, we are exposed to many attempts to alter our reactions to a wide range of issues or objects. These range from multi-million dollar advertising campaigns for various products, to direct attempts at influence from family, friends, bosses, and coworkers. The form of such appeals varies greatly, but in work settings, most attempts to alter attitudes involve the process of **persuasion** (see Figure 5.3).[5]

In this process, target persons are exposed to written or spoken messages designed to change their views through the presentation of "logical" arguments and convincing "facts." As the quotation marks suggest, the arguments presented are often far from logical and the facts anything but authoritative. Usually, though, efforts are made to conceal these flaws, and the message received retains an outward appearance of reason and logic.

Because it is a powerful process in organizations and many other settings, persuasion has been the focus of a great deal of research attention. This work has revealed that while many different factors determine whether, and to what extent, the process succeeds, among the most important of these are certain characteristics of the *communicator* (the person doing the persuading), and certain aspects of the *communication* itself (its specific content).

FIGURE 5.3   Persuasion: Changing Attitudes in Organizations

Persuasion—efforts to change attitudes and hence behavior—is a common process in organizations.

Characteristics of communicators: Who is most effective? With respect to communicator characteristics, three seem to be most central: *attractiveness, style,* and *credibility*. All things being equal, attractive communicators—ones we like—are more effective in altering attitudes than unattractive ones. Similarly, persons who present their message in a fluent, convincing style tend to be more persuasive than those who stumble over their words or seem lacking in self-confidence. Interestingly—and contrary to what common sense suggests—people who speak at a faster-than-average rate are often more persuasive than ones who speak more slowly.[6] Thus, fast talkers seem more likely to be trusted (or at least believed) than people who speak at an average rate.

The single most important characteristic determining a communicator's success at persuasion, however, appears to be this person's *credibility*—the extent to which he or she seems trustworthy or believable. The higher a communicator is on this dimension, the more attitude change she or he will produce. What determines credibility? A communicator's apparent *expertise* for one thing; we tend to accept the statements of persons who seem to know what they are talking about more readily than the statements of those who seem less certain of their views or positions. In addition, a communicator's apparent *motives* play an important role. Persons who have little to gain from changing our views are usually more influential than ones who will indeed gain from efforts at persuasion. For example, if Lee Iacocca (CEO of Chrysler Corp.) severely criticizes management practices in U.S. auto companies, and states that these must drastically improve if the companies are to survive, we are likely to take what he says seriously and, perhaps, to be influenced by his words. After all, he is a top manager in this industry and is, in a sense, criticizing himself and many of his friends and subordinates. In contrast, if a similar scathing attack on management were issued by the head of a powerful labor union, we might discount these comments, for in this case, the person making them has much to gain from influencing public opinion.

Aspects of persuasive communications. The *content* of a persuasive message, too, is important in determining its success in changing attitudes. First, the material it contains should be presented in a manner, and at a level, that is intelligible to the recipients. The reason for this is obvious: messages people cannot understand have little chance of affecting their views. Failure to take account of this basic fact is all too common in business settings, where persons with technical knowledge overlook the fact that others don't share this expertise and "talk over their heads" during meetings or presentations. The result: their audience is annoyed, and little if any attitude change results.

Second, it is often useful to take the current attitudes of recipients into account. Research findings indicate that persuasive messages presenting views very different from those held by persons who receive them tend to be rejected out of hand. They are viewed as extreme and unreasonable, and have little chance of changing attitudes. In contrast, messages that present views only moderately divergent from those held by recipients are seen as more reasonable, and at least have a *chance* of altering attitudes.[7]

We could readily continue with this discussion, for many different factors seem to influence the process of persuasion. Instead, though, we'd like to note that recently, research on this process has taken a somewhat different path. Instead of asking "What kinds of messages produce the most attitude change?" recent studies have focused on the following issue: "What cognitive processes determine whether someone will or will not be persuaded?" In other words, efforts have been made to tie the process of persuasion more closely to current knowledge about human cognition generally, and *social cognition*—the manner in which we process, store, and remember social information.[8] Since we have already considered social cognition in our discussion of perception, we won't return to it here. However, we should note that research conducted within this perspective suggests that persons exposed to persuasive messages actively attempt to process the information these contain. They extract the key points, and relate these to information already at their disposal. They remember facts and information that agree or disagree with the persuasive message, and formulate these into arguments for and against its accuracy.[9] Whether, and to what extent, they then alter their attitudes depends on the relative weight of these self-generated arguments and the extent to which information in the persuasive message is consistent with their existing cognitive frameworks (*schemas*). (See Figure 5.4 for an overview of this process.) In short, persuasion appears to be an *active* process involving a great deal of cognitive effort, not one in which target persons are passively changed by convincing external messages.

Changing Our Own Attitudes: The Role of Cognitive Dissonance

Suppose that as graduation approaches, a college student receives two job offers. After much agonizing, she selects one. Will her attitudes toward the two companies now change? If she is like most people, they may. After the student accepts one of the two jobs, she may find that her evaluation of this position, and the company that offered it, has improved: it now seems better than it did initially, before the decision was reached. Conversely, she may find that her attitude toward the rejected firm has become less favorable. The same process occurs after other kinds of decisions, too. Whether individuals choose among cars, schools, lovers, or courses of action, they often experience a positive shift in attitudes toward the chosen alternative, and a negative shift in attitudes toward the others. Why? The answer seems to lie in a process known as **cognitive dissonance.**[10]

In simplest terms, dissonance refers to the fact that human beings dislike inconsistency. When we say one thing but do another, or discover that one attitude we hold is inconsistent with another that we also accept, an unpleasant state of *dissonance* arises. We notice the inconsistency between our words and deeds, or between our various

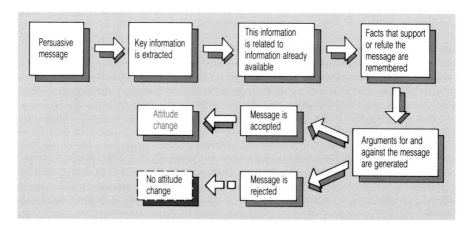

FIGURE 5.4 Persuasion: A Cognitive Perspective
The *cognitive approach* to persuasion suggests that it is an *active* process in which individuals process information contained in persuasive messages.

attitudes, and react negatively to it. As the above example suggests, dissonance is also generated by many decisions. When we choose one alternative, we must necessarily forego the benefits of the others. As a result, *post-decision dissonance* arises.

Many factors determine the magnitude of dissonance and the precise ways in which we seek to reduce it. Since it is usually easier to change our attitudes than our behavior, cognitive dissonance often leads to attitude change. We've already noted how this occurs following decisions: chosen alternatives are enhanced while rejected ones are derogated. In other cases, we may change our attitudes to bring them into line with our overt actions, or alter one attitude to make it more consistent with others.

For example, suppose that you believe quite strongly in affirmative action (special efforts to hire and promote members of minority groups who have previously been the victims of discrimination). At the same time, you also believe in promotion on the basis of merit. No problems arise until, one day, a person from a minority group is promoted over one of your close friends at work, despite the fact that your friend has more experience and is better qualified in several ways. Confronted with this situation, you experience dissonance: your two attitudes are inconsistent. What happens next? The chances are good that one or the other of these views will change. You may become less favorable toward affirmative action or less supportive of promotions-by-merit (please see Figure 5.5).

Because it is an unpleasant state most persons wish to reduce, dissonance can be used as an important entering wedge for persuasion.[11] If would-be persuaders can place individuals in a situation where they will experience dissonance unless they alter their attitudes in desired directions, considerable success is possible. In organizations, tactics based on dissonance are applied in many contexts. One of the most important of these

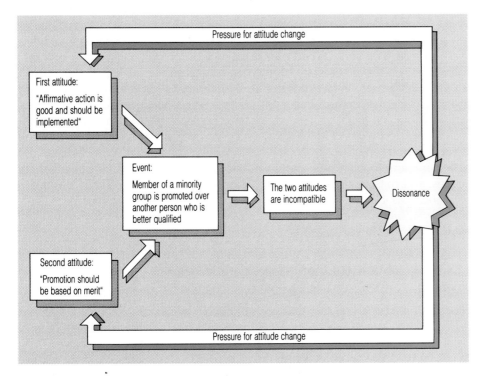

FIGURE 5.5 Cognitive Dissonance as a Source of Attitude Change

When individuals notice that two of their attitudes are inconsistent, an unpleasant state of *dissonance* occurs. This generates pressures to change one, or perhaps both, of the attitudes.

is their use by persons favoring the adoption of some plan or course of action. Such individuals often concentrate their efforts on getting decision-makers in their organization to make an initial, tentative commitment to the plan. They realize that once this is done, the decision-makers may become quite reluctant to pull out and reverse their choices, even if initial results are negative. Dissonance appears to be one of several factors involved in the reluctance to cut one's losses. In situations where an initial investment in some course of action has been made, but outcomes are negative, the persons involved realize that they chose this plan voluntarily, and hold at least mildly positive attitudes about it. Yet, such views are inconsistent with the knowledge that the plan is not succeeding. This results in dissonance, which can be reduced in either of two ways: pulling out and cutting their losses, or concluding that the plan *will* work if given enough time, or if more resources are invested in it. Since it is easier to change one's beliefs than one's behavior, the latter tendency often prevails, with the result that what started out as a very tentative commitment grows stronger and stronger over time—just as the persuaders originally intended. (As you may recall, we considered such effects, sometimes known as **escalation of commitment,** in chapter 4. We'll return to them in more detail in chapter 14, which deals with decision making.)

In sum, the induction of dissonance can be a powerful tactic of persuasion. In fact, as noted in the heading of this section, under the right conditions, persons experiencing this unpleasant cognitive state become virtual allies of those who wish to persuade them by generating internal pressures to change their own attitudes!

JOB SATISFACTION: ATTITUDES TOWARD ONE'S WORK

Like it or not, work plays a dominant role in our lives. It occupies more of our time than any other single activity. It provides the economic basis for our necessities, luxuries, and chosen lifestyle. For most persons, it is central to the self-concept: we define ourselves, at least in part, through our careers, jobs, or professions. It seems reasonable to expect that any activity of such central importance will serve as the object of strong attitudes and, in fact, this is true. Most persons can readily report positive and negative feelings toward their jobs, various beliefs about them, and behavioral intentions relating to them. In short, they report holding various attitudes toward their work and specific aspects of it. These attitudes are generally summarized by the term **job satisfaction,** and it is on this topic that we will focus next. More formally, *job satisfaction* refers to individuals' cognitive, affective, and evaluative reactions toward their jobs.[12] In considering this topic, we'll address four related questions: How is job satisfaction measured? What factors affect it? How satisfied (or dissatisfied), generally, are people with their jobs? And what effects do such attitudes have on organizational behavior?

Measuring Job Satisfaction: Assessing Reactions to Work

Attitudes are certainly real, but they are not directly visible. People do not go about proclaiming their views to everyone they meet. On the contrary, they usually keep their attitudes about politics, religion, and other matters largely to themselves. Attitudes about work are no exception to this general rule. Most persons express these views openly only to a small group of friends or relatives—certainly *not* to all of their supervisors or subordinates. For this reason, measuring job satisfaction is a more difficult task than you might initially guess. Several techniques for assessing this important aspect of work environments do exist, however. Among the most useful of these are *rating scales* or *questionnaires, critical incidents,* and *interviews.*

Rating scales and questionnaires: Measuring job satisfaction through self-report. The most common approach to measuring job satisfaction involves the use of special rating scales or questionnaires. In this method, employees are asked to complete special forms on which they report their current reactions to their jobs. A number of scales have been developed for this purpose, and they vary greatly in form and scope. For example, one that is very popular, the **Job Descriptive Index (JDI)**, presents individuals with lists of adjectives and asks them to indicate whether each does or does not describe a particular aspect of their work.[13] They do so by placing a *Y* for "yes," an *N* for "no," or a *?* for "undecided" next to each adjective. One interesting feature of this scale is that it measures reactions to five distinct aspects of jobs: the work itself, pay, promotional opportunities, supervision, and people (coworkers).

Another widely used measure of job satisfaction is the **Minnesota Satisfaction Questionnaire (MSQ)**. On this scale, individuals rate the extent to which they are satisfied with various aspects of their present job (e.g., their degree of responsibility, opportunities for advancement, pay).[14] Such ratings range from "not at all satisfied" through "extremely satisfied." Obviously, the higher the ratings individuals report, the greater their degree of satisfaction with various aspects of their job.

Other scales focus in more detail on specific facets of job satisfaction. For example, as its name suggests, the **Pay Satisfaction Questionnaire (PSQ)** is primarily concerned with attitudes about various aspects of pay. A recent study by Scarpello, Huber, and Vandenberg indicates that this scale measures individuals' reactions to *pay level* (how much they actually receive), *raises, pay structure and administration* (how pay is allocated by rank, and how it is actually distributed to employees—weekly, monthly, and so on), and *benefits* (sick leave, vacations, insurance, etc.).[15] Items similar to those used on the JDI, MSQ, and PSQ are shown in Table 5.1.

An important advantage of rating scales such as the JDI, MSQ, or PSQ is that they can be completed quickly and efficiently by large numbers of people. Another is that because they have already been administered to many thousands of individuals, average scores for persons in many kinds of jobs and many types of organizations are available. Thus, it is possible to compare the scores of persons in a given company with these,

TABLE 5.1 Items Similar to Those on Popular Measures of Job Satisfaction

The items shown here are similar to those used on three popular measures of job satisfaction. (Please note: the items shown are *not* identical to ones on the actual scales.)

Job Description Index (JDI)	Minnesota Satisfaction Questionnaire (MSQ)	Pay Satisfaction Questionnaire — Item	Pay Satisfaction Questionnaire — Aspect of Pay
Enter "Yes," "No," or "?" for each description or word below.	Indicate the extent to which you are satisfied with each aspect of your present job. Enter one number next to each aspect.	My current pay	Pay Level
Work itself: ___ Routine		Size of my salary	Pay Level
___ Satisfactory	1 = Not At All Satisfied	Typical raises	Raises
___ Good	2 = Not Satisfied	How raises are determined	Raises
Promotions: ___ Dead-end job	3 = Neither Satisfied Nor Dissatisfied	Number of benefits	Benefits
___ Few Promotions	4 = Satisfied		
___ Good Opportunity for Promotion	5 = Extremely Satisfied		
	___ Utilization of Your Abilities		
	___ Authority		
	___ Company Polices and Practices		
	___ Independence		
	___ Supervision–Human Relations		

(Source: Based on items from the JDI, MSQ, and PSQ; see Notes 13, 14, & 15)

and obtain a measure of *relative* satisfaction—very useful information in many cases. However, there is a key problem with such scales. As is true with all self-report measures, the usefulness of the results obtained depends on the respondents' honesty, as well as their ability to report accurately on their feelings. (Since these are sometimes unclear, a certain degree of error can be introduced into the measurement process.) To the extent cooperation from respondents is lacking, and they are unable to identify and describe their own reactions, the findings obtained with such questionnaires can be misleading.

Critical incidents and job satisfaction. A second technique for assessing job satisfaction is the **critical incident procedure.** Here, individuals describe incidents relating to their work that they found especially satisfying or dissatisfying. Their replies are then carefully examined to uncover underlying themes and reactions.[16] For example, if many employees mention situations in which they felt physically uncomfortable on the job as especially upsetting, an important role of this factor (physical comfort) in work-related attitudes would be suggested.

Interviews and other face-to-face meetings. Additional techniques for assessing job satisfaction involve interviews with employees, and what have sometimes been termed *confrontation meetings*. Interviews permit a more detailed exploration of employees' attitudes than questionnaires, and are sometimes useful for this reason. In addition, they may sometimes provide revealing insights into the causes of job satisfaction and work-related attitudes. For example, in one recent study, Sutton and Callahan used interviews to study the effects on employees of their organizations' filing for protection under Chapter 11 of the Federal Bankruptcy Code.[17] These interviews provided intriguing information on how this event affected participants' attitudes toward their jobs and toward their organization. In confrontation meetings, employees are invited to "lay it on the line," and discuss their major complaints and concerns with management. If such sessions are conducted skillfully, problems that adversely affect job satisfaction, but which might otherwise remain hidden, can be brought out into the open. Then steps to correct or eliminate them can be developed.

Job Satisfaction: Some Major Causes

If you were to administer one of the questionnaires described earlier to several hundred people working in a given organization, you would probably note large differences in their responses. Some would report mainly positive attitudes toward their jobs, others would report mainly negative ones, while most would fall somewhere in between. What accounts for these differences? In short, what factors contribute to varying degrees of job satisfaction or dissatisfaction? Attempts to answer this question have taken two basic forms. First, some scholars have sought to develop comprehensive *theories of job satisfaction*—frameworks for understanding not only which factors influence such attitudes, but also *why* they exert such effects. We will examine several of these theories here. Second, other researchers have adopted a more empirical approach, focusing primarily on the task of identifying variables responsible for positive or negative reactions toward work. Key findings of this line of research, too, will be summarized below.

Theories of job satisfaction: Herzberg's two-factor theory and Locke's value theory. One well-known theory of job satisfaction, Herzberg's **two-factor theory** (sometimes known as **motivator-hygiene theory**) focuses on the following issue: do job satisfaction and dissatisfaction stem from the same conditions, or are they actually the result of different sets of factors?[18] Common sense suggests that both reactions derive from common causes. Certain factors produce job satisfaction when they are present, but feelings of dissatisfaction when they are absent. According to Frederick Herzberg, however, this is not the case. His *two-factor theory* contends that job satisfaction and dissatisfaction actually derive from contrasting sources. You may find it interesting to learn how Herzberg first reached this surprising conclusion.

He began by conducting a study in which more than two hundred engineers and accountants were asked to describe times when they felt especially satisfied or dissatisfied with their jobs.[19] Thus, he used the *critical incident* technique described above. Careful analysis of their answers yielded the following pattern of results. When describing incidents in which they felt dissatisfied, many persons mentioned conditions surrounding their jobs rather than the work itself. For instance, they commented on such factors as physical working conditions, pay, security, the quality of supervision they received, company policies, and their social relations with others at work. To the extent these conditions were positive, feelings of dissatisfaction were prevented. Because such factors prevented negative reactions, Herzberg termed them *hygienes* or *maintenance factors*. In contrast, when describing incidents in which they felt especially satisfied or happy with their jobs, respondents often mentioned factors relating more directly to the work they performed or to outcomes deriving from it. They commented on the nature of their jobs and daily tasks, achievement in them, promotion opportunities, recognition from management, increased responsibility, and the chance for personal growth. Because such factors contributed to positive attitudes (i.e., job satisfaction), Herzberg labeled them *motivators*. (Please see Figure 5.6 for a summary of the factors he identified as motivators and hygienes.) As you can see, these factors are closely related to the *growth needs* specified by Maslow's theory of motivation (refer to chapter 3). Thus, Herzberg's theory suggests that job satisfaction stems from the satisfaction of higher-level needs. Similarly, job dissatisfaction is related to conditions that fail to satisfy lower-level needs (social needs, physiological needs).

Has research supported the accuracy of the two-factor theory? Unfortunately, results have been mixed. Some studies have yielded results consistent with the theory's central claim that job satisfaction and dissatisfaction stem from different factors. For example, in one study, conducted by Machungwa and Schmitt, several hundred employees in a developing nation (Zambia) described times when they worked exceptionally hard or when they put little effort into their work.[20] Careful analysis of these incidents indicated that positive attitudes and high effort were related to factors similar to Herzberg's motivators (e.g., opportunities for advancement or personal growth). Con-

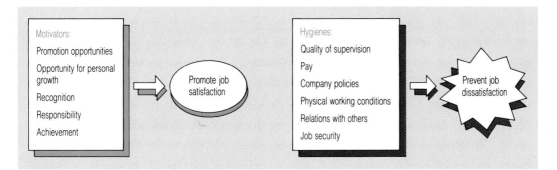

FIGURE 5.6 Herzberg's Two-Factor Theory
Herzberg's *two-factor theory* suggests that job satisfaction and job dissatisfaction stem from different sets of factors. These are labeled *motivators* and *hygienes,* respectively.

versely, negative attitudes and low effort were linked to factors similar to hygienes (e.g., perceived fairness in organizational practices, physical work conditions).

In several other studies, however, it was found that factors labeled as hygienes and motivators exerted strong effects on *both* satisfaction and dissatisfaction.[21] Such findings are contrary to the theory's basic assertion that these positive and negative attitudes stem from distinct clusters of variables.

In view of such evidence, Herzberg's theory should be viewed as an intriguing, but unverified, framework for understanding job satisfaction. This is not to say, however, that it has been of little value. First, as noted by Landy, although the theory does not seem useful in predicting employee satisfaction and motivation, it does seem to provide a useful framework for describing the conditions people find satisfying and dissatisfying. Second, the theory has called attention to the important role in job satisfaction of such factors as the opportunity for personal growth, recognition, and increased responsibility. Attention to such factors, in turn, has stimulated much work on *job enlargement* and *job enrichment*—discussed in chapter 3. In this way, Herzberg's theory has contributed much to the field of organizational behavior, despite the lack of clear support for some of its key predictions.

A second important theory of job satisfaction is Locke's **value theory**.[22] According to this theory, job satisfaction derives primarily from the extent to which the rewards or outcomes provided by jobs match those desired or valued by individuals. The closer this match—the more jobs provide what people want or value—the higher people's satisfaction. Note that the rewards or outcomes people value and desire are not necessarily *needs,* as described by Maslow's theory, or as reflected in Herzberg's two-factor theory. For example, among a group of highly paid executives, the need for money might be minimal. Their investments, holdings in the stock option plan, and other financial resources guarantee that this basic need is well met. However, these executives might still desire money, and value it highly.

Locke's theory suggests that if we know the value individuals place on particular work-related outcomes, we can use this information to predict the impact of such factors on their job satisfaction. The greater the value or importance of each factor, the larger the shifts in satisfaction changes in it will produce. Thus, if employees in a particular organization greatly value *autonomy* (freedom to set their own tasks or alter their own work schedules), changes in this variable will greatly affect their satisfaction. In contrast, if they place a high value on money, shifts in compensation will alter satisfaction. Locke's theory has not been the subject of extensive research, but its emphasis on *values* suggests that job satisfaction may stem from many factors, not simply from the extent to which a small number of basic needs are, or are not, met. In this respect, it is fully consistent with the findings of research on the causes of job satisfaction—the topic to which we turn next.

Causes of job satisfaction: An overview. While efforts to formulate comprehensive theories of job satisfaction have met with mixed success, research designed simply to identify those factors which influence such attitudes has made great progress. Many of the conditions that lead individuals to hold positive or negative views of their jobs have been identified. These are highly varied in nature, and cannot be easily summarized. However, most seem to fall into three major categories: (1) factors relating to *organizational policies or procedures,* (2) factors relating to *specific aspects of jobs* or the *settings* in which they are performed, and (3) factors relating to *personal characteristics of employees.*

Organizational factors and job satisfaction: As you can probably guess, one of the most important factors determining job satisfaction is the type of *reward system* an organization uses—how rewards such as pay and promotions are distributed. Satisfaction is enhanced by reward systems employees view as fair and reasonable, but reduced by systems they consider unfair or unreasonable. The importance of this factor is suggested by the findings of a study conducted by Berkowitz, Fraser, Treasure, and Cochran.[23] These investigators phoned a random sample of several hundred employed persons and conducted interviews in which these persons answered a number of questions about their current jobs and satisfaction with their pay. Results indicated that the single best predictor of such satisfaction was subjects' perceptions that they were receiving the amount of compensation they deserved—that they were being treated fairly. (As you may recall, perceptions of *equity* also play an important role in work motivation; refer to our discussion of this topic in chapter 3.)

A second factor that exerts a strong impact on job satisfaction involves specific organizational policies. In particular, satisfaction is enhanced by policies that permit employees to participate in decisions that involve them[24] and by policies that spread responsibility and authority throughout an organization rather than concentrating it in a few hands.

A third factor that should be mentioned is *perceived quality of supervision.* When employees perceive their supervisors as fair and competent and believe that supervisors have their best interests at heart, satisfaction tends to be high. In contrast, when employees view their supervisors as unfair, incompetent, or as pursuing selfish motives, satisfaction tends to be low.[25]

Jobs, work settings, and job satisfaction: If you've ever wondered how people who perform certain jobs can bear them you are aware of the fact that characteristics of jobs themselves also play an important part in determining job satisfaction. Since jobs differ in countless ways and involve an incredibly wide range of activities, research concerned with this issue has attempted to uncover common themes—factors that, to the extent they are present or absent in almost any job, affect attitudes toward it. Several such factors have been identified.

The first of these is *overall work load.* Most persons tend to prefer jobs that are somewhat challenging—ones that keep them busy but are not overly exhausting. In short, there appears to be a happy medium where the work load is neither so high as to be stressful nor so low as to be boring. A second, and somewhat related factor, is *variety.* In general, jobs that provide at least some variation in activities yield higher levels of satisfaction than those that are dull and totally repetitive.[26] Finally, jobs that permit pleasant social interactions (friendly contact with others) usually yield higher levels of satisfaction than jobs that leave little room for such contact.

At this point, we should note that not all of these findings apply equally well to all individuals. While most people tend to prefer work that is moderately challenging and varied, some would rather work at repetitive tasks demanding low levels of effort. Similarly, while most employees prefer social contact with others, some strongly prefer to work alone, and perceive contacts with others as an annoying waste of time (see our discussion of the *Type A behavior pattern* in chapter 6).

Other aspects of jobs that affect satisfaction (or dissatisfaction) with them are included in the *job characteristics model* proposed by Hackman and Oldham, which we reviewed in detail in chapter 3.[27] As you may recall, that model suggests that such characteristics of jobs as skill variety, task identity (completing a whole piece of work), task significance, autonomy, and feedback affect critical psychological states (e.g., experienced meaningfulness of work, experienced responsibility for outcomes, knowledge of actual results). These states, in turn, affect important work-related outcomes, including job satisfaction.

Turning to the impact of work settings, considerable evidence points to the conclusion that several physical aspects of workspaces play an important role in reported job satisfaction.[28] Useful evidence on such effects has been reported recently by Oldham and Fried.[29] These researchers investigated the impact of four aspects of work settings on job satisfaction among full-time clerical employees at a large university. The four variables they considered were: (1) *social density*—the number of persons working in each office, (2) *darkness*—the level of illumination in each of these work settings, (3) *number of enclosures*—the number of walls or partitions surrounding each person's desk, and (4) *interpersonal distance*—the distance between each desk (see Figure 5.7). Results indicated that all four factors affected participants' job satisfaction. As expected, job satisfaction was lower when social density was high, illumination level was low, there were relatively few enclosures, and interpersonal distance was small than when the opposite conditions prevailed. Moreover, these four factors combined so that the lowest level of satisfaction occurred when all four negative conditions were present simultaneously.

Other physical aspects of work settings, too, have been found to affect work-related attitudes. Among these are temperature, noise, and air quality. As you might expect, job satisfaction is higher in the presence of comfortable temperatures, when noise is relatively low, and when air quality is good, than under conditions of excessive heat or cold, high levels of noise, and poor air quality.[30]

Finally, the *social environment* in which individuals work can also affect job satisfaction. To the extent that employees like their coworkers, believe that they can count on them for help, and feel that they are part of a cohesive, friendly group, satisfaction is high. To the extent such conditions are lacking, it is often considerably lower.[31]

Personal characteristics and job satisfaction: People differ in countless ways. Further, as we will see in chapter 6, many of these differences have important implications for organizational behavior. Here, we simply wish to note that several *personal character-istics* have been found to affect job satisfaction. For example, people high in self-esteem tend to report higher levels of satisfaction with their jobs than persons low in self-esteem.[32] Similarly, persons who are high in the ability to withstand stress tend to report higher job satisfaction than persons low in this ability.[33] Also, individuals who believe they can influence or control their own outcomes tend to report higher job satisfaction than those who feel that such outcomes are outside their personal influence.[34] Persons who are high in status and seniority often report higher levels of

FIGURE 5.7   The Nature of Work Settings and Job Satisfaction
Job satisfaction is often strongly affected by physical aspects of work settings (e.g., crowding, privacy, lighting).

satisfaction than those who are low in status or seniority.[35] Such findings probably stem, at least in part, from the fact that persons in the former group actually enjoy better working conditions than those in the latter. However, they may also reflect the fact that persons happy in a given job or organization tend to remain in it, and thus are higher in status and seniority as a result of their positive attitudes. Finally, job satisfaction appears to be influenced, at least in some cases, by *general life satisfaction*— satisfaction in all aspects of life, including work and non-work settings. While findings on this relationship have not been entirely consistent, several studies suggest that high levels of life satisfaction may spill over into high levels of job satisfaction, and vice versa.[36]

In sum, a wide range of factors, from the functioning and policies of organizations, to the requirements of specific jobs and the personal characteristics of individuals, contribute to varying levels of job satisfaction and dissatisfaction. The list is long, but since establishing conditions that foster job satisfaction is one important step toward enhancing both individual welfare and organizational effectiveness, determining the factors on it appears to be a very worthwhile enterprise. (For information on another factor that can strongly affect job satisfaction, please see the **Research Perspective** section below.)

OB: A RESEARCH PERSPECTIVE

When Professionals Perform Non-Professional Jobs: Loss of Work-Related Status and Job Satisfaction

Suppose that at some time in the future, you are a top executive at a large company. Because of a down-turn in the business cycle, it is necessary to make cuts in the number of employees in your organization. Many of these persons are professionals in various field, and you are very reluctant to let them go. You realize that finding and hiring such talented individuals when economic conditions improve will be a difficult and time-consuming chore. What should do you do? One possibility would be to retain as many of these professionals as possible, but to reassign them to non-professional jobs. Suppose you opted for this course of action; what would its impact be on the persons involved? Would they be so grateful at having retained their jobs (and salaries) that their job satisfaction would remain unchanged? Or would they experience strong negative reactions to their change in duties and work-related status? A study carried out by Schlenker and Gutek suggests that the latter outcome would be more likely.[37]

These researchers investigated employee reactions in a large government agency that actually adopted the strategy described above. Faced with cuts in staff necessitated by a reduced budget, the agency reassigned many professional employees (social workers) to non-professional jobs. These jobs involved such tasks as interviewing applicants, verifying required documentations for cases, and filling out forms. Schlenker and Gutek asked these reassigned professionals, and a comparable group who were not reassigned, to complete questionnaires dealing with several issues. These included their professional role identification (how strongly they identified with their chosen profession), their role involvement (how important their work was in shaping their self-image), their self-esteem, their current job satisfaction, and their intentions of remaining on the job. (Participants completed the questionnaire nine months after the reassignment took place.)

Results indicated that contrary to initial predictions, the reassigned employees did *not* demonstrate a drop in professional role identity or involvement. In other words, they remained committed to and identified with their chosen profession. However, consistent with other hypotheses, the reassigned employees did report lower job satisfaction, lower self-esteem, and lower intention of remaining on the job than those who had not been reassigned (see Figure 5.8 on page 168). In short, the loss of job-related status they experienced exerted widespread, negative effects on their self-esteem and work-related attitudes.

In sum, the results obtained by Schlenker and Gutek suggest that sudden reassignment to a lower

FIGURE 5.8 Loss of Status and Job Satisfaction

Social workers who were reassigned to non-professional jobs did not show reduced professional role identification or involvement. However, they did demonstrate lower job satisfaction and self-esteem than other social workers who were not reassigned to non-professional jobs. (Source: Based on data from Schlenker & Gutek, 1987; see Note 37.)

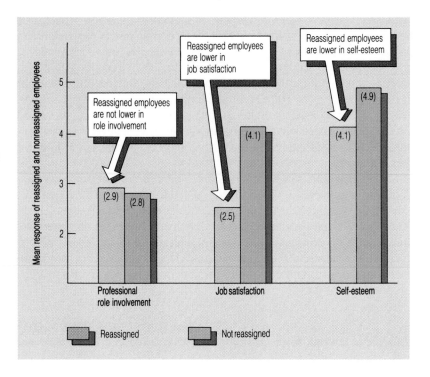

status job can produce a personal "crisis" for the individuals involved that is quite similar, in several respects, to that generated by unemployment—by losing one's job altogether. Given the negative effects produced by such events, it seems clear that organizations contemplating this strategy should weigh the relative costs and benefits it provides very carefully before proceeding.

The Prevalence of Job Satisfaction: Do Most People Like Their Work?

Imagine that you approached a large sample of persons working in many different organizations at many different jobs, and asked them to complete one of the standard measures of job satisfaction described earlier. What would you find? Would most report positive or negative attitudes? Many popular films and television shows suggest that you would uncover large reservoirs of dissatisfaction—that most people would report being bored or worse by their jobs. In fact, however, large-scale surveys of job satisfaction do not support this gloomy picture. On the contrary, most suggest that a large majority of persons are relatively satisfied with their current jobs. Surveys that have continued for several decades indicate that eighty to ninety percent of employees are relatively satisfied with their jobs.[38]

These results paint a fairly comforting picture of prevailing work-related attitudes. But how does this picture square with recent trends toward rising absenteeism and turnover in many businesses, and with declines in productivity in the United States and other countries that have only been reversed in the past few years? If most persons are so happy with their jobs, what accounts for these trends? The answer, it appears, is that the actual situation is far more complex than might initially be suspected.

First, while job satisfaction *is* generally high, these positive attitudes are by no means uniformly distributed across all aspects of work and work settings. Satisfaction with pay is generally lower than satisfaction with quality of supervision or with such factors as having sufficient help from others, or the proper equipment for doing one's job. Thus, when we ask "How satisfied are employees generally?" we may overlook important facets of this issue.

Second, job satisfaction varies greatly across different groups of employees. Managers, technical and professional workers, and self-employed persons generally report higher satisfaction than blue-collar personnel.[39] Similarly, older workers and those who have held their jobs for longer periods of time report greater satisfaction than younger ones or those lacking the benefits of seniority. Members of minority groups tend to indicate lower overall levels of satisfaction, and until recently, females reported lower levels of satisfaction than males. These latter differences appear to be declining, as barriers to advancement by minority group members and women have decreased. However, they have not entirely vanished even at present.

A third point to keep in mind concerning the high levels of job satisfaction uncovered in many surveys is this: in one sense, such findings are more apparent than real. In fact, they may stem as much from the way in which job satisfaction is measured as from high levels of positive attitudes among employees. That this is so is suggested by the fact that when asked if they would choose the same work again (assuming they could start their careers over) many persons answer "No." More than half of white-collar employees indicate that they would select some other job or career. Among blue-collar persons the figure is even higher, with fully three-quarters reporting they would prefer other jobs.[40] Clearly, then, many people are not as happy with their work as standard surveys of job satisfaction seem to suggest.

If this is so, why do so many persons report relatively high levels of job satisfaction? One possibility involves the operation of *cognitive dissonance*. Most persons realize that they will probably have to stay in the job they now hold, or one quite similar to it; economic conditions and family obligations rarely permit people the luxury of a high degree of job mobility. Thus, if they report being dissatisfied with their present work, most persons will experience considerable dissonance. After all, stating that they dislike their jobs is clearly inconsistent with the knowledge that remaining in them is a necessity. In order to avoid such inconsistency (and the unpleasant dissonance it generates), many persons may choose both to report and to perceive their work in relatively favorable terms. At present, no direct evidence for the operation of this process exists. However, a large body of research findings supports the impact of dissonance on many other types of attitudes, and there is no reason to assume that work-related attitudes are not strongly affected by this powerful process as well.

Job Satisfaction: Its Major Effects

In discussing the success or failure of specific organizations, practicing managers (and many others) often refer to the important influence of *employee morale*. They suggest that successful organizations are ones in which morale is high, while those which fail are ones in which morale is low. Is this actually the case? In other words, does job satisfaction really exert strong effects on important aspects of organizational behavior? In general, the answer appears to be "yes." As we will soon note, job satisfaction among employees does affect many aspects of organizational behavior (e.g., task performance, voluntary turnover). It is also important to note, however, that this relationship is far from simple or direct. As we stated earlier, attitudes *do* affect behavior in many instances, but this is not always the case. Sometimes their impact is blocked by external factors or conditions. And attitudes are most likely to shape overt actions when they are specific and strong; they are far less likely to produce such effects when they are general or weak. Thus, it would be naive to expect the impact of job satisfaction to be readily visible in all situations and contexts. Having offered this cautionary note, we will now summarize current evidence concerning the ways in which these work-related attitudes do often influence behavior in work settings.

Job satisfaction, absenteeism, and turnover. Consider two employees. Both hate to get up early in the morning, and dislike commuting very much. However, one likes her job, while the other dislikes it. Which person is more likely to call in sick or miss work for other reasons? The answer is obvious: the one who dislikes her job. That job satisfaction does affect absence from work in this manner is indicated by the findings of many different studies. In general, the lower individuals' satisfaction with their jobs, the more likely they are to be absent from work.[41] As you might well guess, though, the strength of this relationship is modest rather than strong. This is because job satisfaction is just one of many different factors influencing employees' decisions to report or not report to work.

Similar findings have also been obtained with respect to voluntary turnover. The lower individuals' level of satisfaction with their jobs, the more likely they are to resign and seek other opportunities. Again, the strength of this relationship is modest, and for similar reasons.[42] Many factors relating to individuals, their jobs, and economic conditions shape decisions to move from one job to another. Several of the factors affecting voluntary turnover are described in a model of this process proposed by Mobley.[43] According to this model, job dissatisfaction leads employees to think about the possibility of quitting. This, in turn, leads to the decision to begin searching for another job. If this search is successful, the individual next develops definite intentions to either quit or remain on the job. These intentions are then reflected in concrete actions (actually quitting or remaining in the organization; see Figure 5.9 for a summary of this process).

The suggestion that economic conditions, and hence the success of an initial search for alternative jobs, exerts a strong impact on voluntary turnover is supported by the

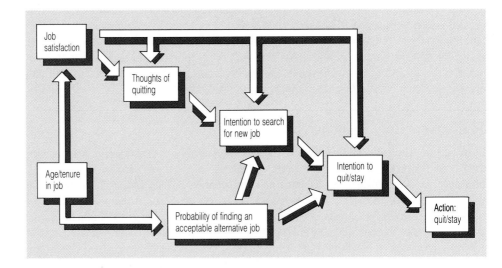

FIGURE 5.9 Voluntary Withdrawal: An Overview
According to a model proposed by Mobley, voluntary turnover involves a complex process: low levels of job satisfaction begin a process in which individuals first think about quitting, then search for another job, and finally form intentions to quit or stay in their present job. At several steps in this process the probability of finding an acceptable alternative job plays a key role. (Source: Based on suggestions by Mobley, 1978; see Note 43.)

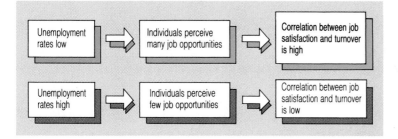

FIGURE 5.10 Job Satisfaction, Economic Conditions, and Turnover
When unemployment rates are low, individuals perceive many opportunities for other jobs. Thus, their level of job satisfaction is a good predictor of turnover (whether they will remain in their current jobs or seek others). In contrast, when unemployment rates are high, individuals perceive few opportunities for other jobs. Under these conditions, job satisfaction is not a good predictor of turnover. (Source: Based on suggestions by Carsten & Spector, 1987; see Note 44.)

findings of a study by Carsten and Spector.[44] These researchers examined the results of a large number of previous studies concerned with turnover. For each, they contacted the persons who had conducted the study, and determined the precise dates during which data had been collected. Then, Carsten and Spector obtained data on the unemployment rates prevailing at those times. They predicted that the relationship between job satisfaction and turnover would be stronger at times when unemployment was low than at times when it was high. When unemployment was low, they reasoned, individuals would perceive many opportunities for other jobs. Thus, the lower their satisfaction, the more likely they would be to leave their current positions. In contrast, when unemployment was high, individuals would realize that they could not readily find another position. As a result, they would tend to remain in their current job regardless of their satisfaction with it. In short, poor economic conditions would serve as an external factor preventing job satisfaction from affecting overt, work-related behavior (see Figure 5.10). Results confirmed these predictions. The higher unemployment rates were, the lower the correlation between job satisfaction and turnover.

We should add that factors known to affect job satisfaction have also been found to affect voluntary turnover. For example, in their study of the impact of physical aspects of work settings on job satisfaction, Oldham and Fried also measured turnover among participants.[45] They found that poor physical conditions (e.g., few office enclosures, low levels of illumination) were related to increased turnover. These and other findings suggest that factors that reduce job satisfaction often increase turnover as well. While this finding does not, by itself, indicate that low job satisfaction is a direct cause of turnover, it is consistent with other evidence suggesting that this is the case.

Job satisfaction and task performance. Many managers seem to operate according to the belief that "happy workers are productive workers." Is this really the case? Is job satisfaction directly linked to task performance or productivity? Some evidence suggests that this is so. In a recent review of studies concerned with the impact of participation in decision making on both job satisfaction and productivity, Miller and Monge found evidence for the view that the opportunity to participate in decision making increases job satisfaction and that such positive attitudes, in turn, facilitate productivity.[46] However, other findings suggest that the overall picture is more complex. In many studies, job satisfaction has been found to have little, if any, effect on task performance. Why is this the case? Several possibilities exist.

First, it should be noted that in many work settings, there is little room for large

FIGURE 5.11 Why, Sometimes, Job Satisfaction Cannot Affect Performance

Many jobs are structured so that the persons holding them can neither exceed nor fall below certain levels of performance. In such cases, job satisfaction has little opportunity to influence performance.

changes in performance. Jobs are structured so that the persons holding them *must* maintain at least some minimum level of performance. If they do not, they cannot retain their jobs (see Figure 5.11). Further, there is often little leeway for *exceeding* these minimum standards. Even if an individual increases his or her own output, this may have no impact because needed input from other employees, who have not increased their effort, is lacking. The result: an individual who, because of high job satisfaction, increases his or her output may soon find that he or she has little to do! In such cases, even very high levels of job satisfaction have little effect on overall productivity.

Second, it may actually be the case that job satisfaction and productivity are not directly linked. Rather, any apparent relationship between them may stem from the fact that both are related to a third factor—receipt of various rewards. As suggested by Porter and Lawler, the situation may be as follows.[47] Past levels of performance lead to the receipt of both extrinsic rewards (e.g., pay, promotions) and intrinsic rewards (e.g., feelings of accomplishment). If employees judge these rewards to be fair, they may come to perceive a link between their performance and these outcomes. This, in turn, may have two effects. First, it may encourage high levels of effort, and so good performance. Second, it may lead to high levels of job satisfaction. In short, high productivity and high job satisfaction may both stem from the same conditions. These two factors themselves, however, may not be directly linked.

For these and other reasons, job satisfaction may not be directly related to performance in many contexts. We should note, however, that this conclusion may hold true only with respect to "standard" measures of performance. That is, job satisfaction does not, by itself, strongly affect the quantity or quality of employees' output. However, it may well influence other aspects of their on-the-job behavior. For example, it may affect **citizenship behaviors** (or *good citizen* behaviors).[48] These are actions by

FIGURE 5.12 One Type of Citizenship Behavior

Although she may not realize it, Cathy's willingness to help others in her organization may contribute to its overall effectiveness. (Source: Universal Press Syndicate.)

individuals that enhance social relationships and cooperation within an organization (e.g., offering help to coworkers when it is requested, demonstrating a cheerful, cooperative attitude, protecting or conserving the organization's resources, tolerating temporary inconveniences without complaint). Such actions may contribute to the smooth and effective functioning of organizations without showing up directly in monthly summaries of output or sales. Presumably, the higher individuals' satisfaction with their jobs, the more likely they will be to engage in such actions (see Figure 5.12).

Evidence for precisely such a relationship has been reported by Bateman and Organ.[49] These investigators asked supervisors at a large university to rate their subordinates in terms of their tendency to engage in the type of citizenship behaviors described above. At the same time, the employees reported on their own level of job satisfaction by completing the Job Descriptive Index. Results indicated that there was indeed a positive relationship between reported satisfaction and rated citizenship behaviors. The higher subjects' job satisfaction, the higher the citizenship ratings they received from their supervisors.

These findings suggest that in answer to the question "Are job satisfaction and performance linked?" we should first respond, "What kind of performance do you have in mind?" For many traditional indices of job performance, a link between positive work attitudes and performance may exist, but is difficult to demonstrate. For other aspects of performance such as citizenship behaviors, it may be somewhat stronger, or at least easier to observe.

ORGANIZATIONAL COMMITMENT:
ATTITUDES TOWARD ORGANIZATIONS

Have you ever known someone who loved his work but hated the company that employed him? Conversely, have you ever known anyone who hated her job, but felt strong loyalty toward her company? If you have encountered individuals of either type, you are already aware of an important fact: positive or negative feelings about one's job are only part of the total picture where work-related attitudes are concerned. In addition to holding such views, individuals often also possess positive or negative attitudes toward their entire organization. Such attitudes are usually termed **organizational commitment** and reflect the extent to which an individual identifies with and is involved with his or her organization.[50] Specifically, a high degree of organizational commitment implies: (1) strong acceptance of the organization's goals and values,

(2) willingness to exert effort on its behalf, and (3) a strong desire to remain within the organization.[51]

That job satisfaction and organizational commitment are indeed distinct types of work-related attitudes is supported by the findings of Brooke, Russell, and Price.[52] They asked full-time employees of a large hospital to complete questionnaires designed to measure job satisfaction, organizational commitment, routinization (the extent to which their jobs were repetitive in nature), and work-related stress. When they analyzed participants' responses, they found that a single factor could not account for their replies; rather, job satisfaction and organizational commitment appeared to represent separate and distinct factors. Further, these two work-related attitudes were related in different ways to the other variables measured. For example, routinization was strongly (and negatively) related to job satisfaction: the more routine their jobs were, the less employees liked them. In contrast, routinization was only weakly related to reported organizational commitment. Together, these findings support the view that job satisfaction and organizational commitment should in fact be distinguished.

While there is agreement that job satisfaction and organizational commitment are distinct types of work-related attitudes, the relationship between them remains uncertain. Common sense seems to suggest that high levels of job satisfaction, maintained over time, should tend to generate feelings of organizational commitment. In short, if people are pleased with and like their jobs, these feelings should ultimately generalize to their entire organization. However, research designed to assess the accuracy of this prediction has yielded mixed results. One study, conducted by Bateman and Strasser, has reported evidence pointing to precisely the opposite conclusion—that high levels of job satisfaction *stem from* rather than produce high levels of organizational commitment.[53] On the other hand, an investigation conducted by Curry, Wakefield, Price, and Mueller found no direct causal link between these two types of attitudes.[54]

In view of these latter findings, it seems premature to conclude that organizational commitment causes high levels of job satisfaction, or vice versa. Instead, it seems most appropriate to suggest that both are distinct types of work-related attitudes and that both affect important aspects of organizational functioning. However, they do not appear to be direct causes of one another, as has often been assumed.

Factors Affecting Organizational Commitment

As we have already noted, organizational commitment derives from many different sources. First, it is affected by several aspects of jobs themselves. The higher the level of responsibility and autonomy connected with a given job, the less repetitive and more interesting it is, the higher the level of commitment expressed by the persons who fill it. On the other hand, the fewer promotional opportunities, and the greater the tension and ambiguity associated with a job, the lower the level of commitment it tends to generate.[55]

Second, organizational commitment is affected by the existence of other employment opportunities. The greater the perceived chances of finding another job and the greater the desirability of such alternatives, the lower an individual's commitment tends to be.[56]

Third, organizational commitment is also affected by several personal characteristics. Older employees, those with tenure or seniority, and those who are satisfied with their own level of work performance tend to report higher levels of organizational commitment than others. In the past, it was often suggested that women demonstrate lower levels of commitment than men. Then, this difference was used as justification for providing female employees with lower compensation. ("They aren't really committed to this company, so why reward them?") Recent findings, however, indicate that such differences in overall organizational commitment probably don't exist, and that the two sexes actually show roughly equal levels of commitment to their organizations.[57]

Finally, organizational commitment is strongly affected by several factors relating to work settings generally. The more satisfied individuals are with their supervisors, with the fairness of performance appraisals, and the more they feel that their organization cares about their welfare, the higher their level of commitment. (For evidence concerning another factor that also contributes to high levels of organizational commitment—employee ownership of their company—see the **Research Perspective** section below.)

OB: A RESEARCH PERSPECTIVE

Employee Stock Ownership Plans: Their Positive Impact on Organizational Commitment

In recent years, several thousand organizations in the United States alone have adopted **Employee Stock Ownership Plans** (ESOPs). Indeed, while fewer than 1,000 had such plans in 1976, more than 8,000 have them in place at the present time. Within the context of such plans, employees receive stock in their organization on an annual basis. The cumulative effects of such benefits can be substantial. In the average ESOP, employees own from twenty to forty percent of the company's stock.

Such plans are established for many different reasons (e.g., to gain tax advantages, to finance capital acquisition, to purchase the shares of a retiring owner). Perhaps the most important single reason, though, is that of enhancing effort and commitment among employees. It seems only reasonable to expect that individuals who actually own a portion of their company will feel more committed to it, with all that this implies in terms of enhanced effort, reduced turnover, and so on. Is this actually the case? Growing evidence suggests that it is.[58] Employees in organizations that operate ESOPs do often report higher levels of organizational commitment than ones in comparable organizations without such plans. Why is this so? The results of an investigation conducted by Klein suggest that two factors are most important: (1) partial ownership of a company enhances employees' influence in important decisions and this, in turn, increases their feelings of commitment; (2) the financial benefits provided enhance positive attitudes toward the organization in a direct (and readily understandable) manner.[59]

In order to gather evidence on the impact of

ESOPs, Klein enlisted the cooperation of thirty-seven companies which had adopted such plans. In each, she obtained information on the nature of the plan (e.g., the size of the annual company contribution, management's reasons for establishing it, the extent to which management attempted to inform employees about the ESOP and its operation). In addition, she asked several hundred employees at these companies to report on their satisfaction with the plans, their level of organizational commitment, and the extent to which they influenced important company decisions.

When these data were examined, several intriguing findings emerged. First, as expected, the larger the financial benefits provided, the greater employees' satisfaction with the plans and the stronger their organizational commitment. Second, the greater employees' reported role in decision making, the higher their organizational commitment. In addition, organizational commitment was also fostered by strong commitment to the ESOP by top management and by extensive communications about the plan to employees (please see Figure 5.13 on page 176). In sum, both the financial benefits provided, and the approach of top management in establishing and running the plan, were important in determining whether, and to what extent, it enhanced positive attitudes among employees.

In conclusion, ESOPs do seem to offer one effective means for increasing organizational commitment among employees. However, to be successful, such plans must be more than mere "window-dressing." They must reflect genuine

FIGURE 5.13 ESOPs and Organizational Commitment

Employee Stock Ownership Plans (ESOPs) are most likely to generate high levels of organizational commitment among employees when they provide substantial financial benefits, when they afford employees a considerable voice in decision making, when the plans have the full support of management, and when information about the plans is communicated clearly and fully to employees. (Source: Based on findings reported by Klein, 1987; see Note 59.)

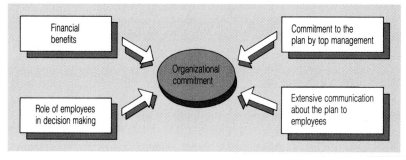

commitment to shared ownership on the part of management, they must be explained clearly and fully to employees, and they must provide significant financial benefits to participants. When these conditions are met, the benefits both to individuals and to their organization can be substantial.

Major Effects of Organizational Commitment

It seems reasonable to predict that persons who feel deeply committed to their organization will behave differently at work than persons who do not. In fact, growing evidence supports this suggestion. Organizational commitment appears to greatly affect several aspects of work behavior.

First, the higher individuals' feelings of commitment, the lower their rates of absenteeism and turnover. Second, the higher such commitment, the less likely they are to engage in an active search for another position. Organizational commitment also appears to be linked to both effort and performance.[60] The higher employees' commitment toward their company, the greater the effort they are willing to invest on its behalf and so, in many cases, the better their performance.

Taking all these findings into account, it seems clear that steps designed to generate high levels of organizational commitment among employees are well worthwhile. A committed workforce, it appears, is indeed a stable and productive one. This is not to suggest that organizational commitment cannot have potential costs, however. While highly committed employees may work hard and remain on the job, they may also be resistant to change. Such persons may be strongly committed to existing ways of handling various tasks, and to existing organizational culture. Such commitment may prove costly in the face of shifting conditions which dictate the need for major change. Such possibilities aside, however, high levels of organizational commitment are often beneficial, and should be fostered in most situations.

PREJUDICE: NEGATIVE ATTITUDES TOWARD OTHER ORGANIZATION MEMBERS

Most people would agree that the warning "Don't jump to conclusions" is good advice. Yet, where reactions to other persons are concerned, this advice is often ignored. Individuals often *do* jump to conclusions about others. They often base important judgments about the people they meet on their ethnic background, race, sex, or age. Even worse, such judgments are usually negative in nature. It is assumed that another person possesses undesirable traits simply because he or she fits within a specific social cat-

176

egory. These reactions are termed **prejudice.** More precisely, prejudice can be defined as *negative attitudes toward the members of specific groups based solely on their membership in those groups.* [61]

Prejudice has serious implications for society as a whole. Indeed, recent decades have been marked by vigorous efforts in many nations to eliminate the harmful effects of such attitudes. In addition, prejudice can, and does, play a role in organizations and organizational behavior. First, where such reactions exist, they may be the cause of friction or conflict. If specific persons hold negative attitudes toward others simply because of differences in their personal background, training, or professional identification, it may be difficult for them to work together. This can have truly devastating effects on cooperation and efficiency.

Second, prejudice may have adverse effects on the careers of persons who are the target of such attitudes. These individuals may encounter various forms of discrimination—some overt, some quite subtle—with respect to hiring, promotion, pay, and appraisal of their work. Third, organizations themselves may suffer greatly from such practices. If talented individuals are overlooked or passed over simply because of their membership in certain groups, the organizations involved may suffer a loss of precious human resources—a loss few can afford.

Most research on the impact of prejudice in work settings has focused on *racism,* prejudice based on race, and *sexism,* prejudice based on sex. [62] We should note, however, that other forms are also relevant to organizational behavior. For example, prejudice based on *age* is all too common. Laws in the United States and elsewhere have done much to counter the negative impact of such attitudes on older employees, but in more subtle forms, such reactions continue to exist. For example, within a given organization, there are often clear beliefs about the appropriate age-range for individuals occupying various positions. Thus, it may be implicitly assumed that first-line managers should be in the late twenties or early thirties, that department heads should be in the mid thirties to mid forties, and that vice presidents should be at least age forty. [63] Then, individuals who attain a given position sooner than expected may benefit from an age-related halo, while those who attain it later than anticipated, or who remain in a position longer than expected, may be evaluated negatively.

Many other forms of prejudice exist as well. As we noted in chapter 4, individuals in various departments or occupational groups often perceive persons in other departments or occupations as "all alike," mainly in negative ways. ("You know how engineers are!" "All those design people are a little flaky.") While all of these reactions are worthy of attention, the form of prejudice that has received the most attention in OB in recent years is sexism. Since prejudice based on sex continues to be the focus of legislative, political, and research interest, we will now examine it in more detail.

Prejudice Based on Sex

Change—and at an increasingly rapid pace—has certainly been the slogan of the 1970s and 1980s. Organizations have been no exception to this trend, and they, too, have altered in many ways. One of the most dramatic shifts they have experienced involves the entry (or re-entry) into the workforce of vast numbers of women. A large majority of adult females now work full-time in the United States and other Western nations. And they do not occupy only relatively low-level jobs: growing numbers have moved into responsible managerial positions. Currently, more than thirty percent of managers in the United States are females, compared to less than ten percent twenty years ago. Despite such change, however, disparities in average salary remain, and as Steinberg and Shapiro have noted, "Women populate corporations but they rarely run them." [64] They are not, as yet, fully represented in higher managerial ranks. Why is this the case? Given the existence of legislation banning discrimination based on sex, this factor no longer seems central. Another possiblity is that sufficient time has not yet passed for women to move into senior management-level positions. To some extent, this is probably true: overt barriers against female advancement have disappeared (or at least decreased) only quite recently. Careful research on this question, however, also points to other potential causes—subtle, but often powerful forces, that continue to operate against women in many work settings.

The role of sex role stereotypes. One such force involves the persistence of traditional views about the characteristics supposedly possessed by men and women. Such views (often known as *sex role stereotypes*) suggest that males tend to be aggressive, forceful, persistent, and decisive, while females tend to be passive, submissive, dependent, and emotional. Growing evidence indicates that such differences are largely false: males and females do not differ as consistently or to as large a degree in these ways as sex role stereotypes suggest.[65] Yet, such beliefs persist, and continue to play a role in organizational settings. One reason for this is that the traits attributed to males by these stereotypes are ones which seem consistent with managerial success, while the traits attributed to females are ones which seem inconsistent with such success. The result: females are perceived as less suited for managerial positions, even when they possess appropriate credentials for them.

Evidence for the operation of such sex role stereotypes has been obtained by Heilman and her colleagues in a series of related studies.[66] In these experiments, it has been repeatedly found that females are perceived as less suited for jobs traditionally filled by males, and that any characteristics which serve to emphasize or activate female sex role stereotypes tend to intensify such negative effects. For example, females who are physically attractive are perceived as being more feminine and therefore less suited for managerial roles than females who are less physically attractive. Interestingly, the impact of sex role stereotypes can be countered if clear evidence for a woman's ability or competence is provided. In such cases, females applying for traditionally male-dominated jobs (e.g., sports photographer) actually receive *higher* ratings than males.[67] Apparently, this is so because they are perceived as a special subgroup—one that is even more competent than males for such jobs. In general, though, traditional sex role stereotypes tend to operate against success and advancement by women in work settings.

The role of expectations. Another factor impeding advancement by females in at least some work settings involves their expectations. In general, women seem to hold lower expectations about their careers than men. For example, among recent business graduates, females expect to receive lower starting and peak salaries than males. Several factors probably contribute to such differences (e.g., the fact that females specialize in lower-paying areas than do males; their observation that on average, females do, in fact, tend to earn less than males in most organizations). Whatever the basis, it is a general rule in life that people tend to get what they expect. Thus, the lower expectations held by females may be one factor operating against them in many instances.

The role of self-confidence. Confidence, it is often said, is the single best predictor of success. People who expect to succeed often do; those who expect to fail find that these predictions, too, are confirmed. Unfortunately, women tend to express lower self-confidence than men in many achievement situations. Thus, the fact that they have not as yet attained full equality with men in many work settings may stem, at least in part, from this factor. Evidence suggesting that this is indeed the case has been reported by McCarty.[68]

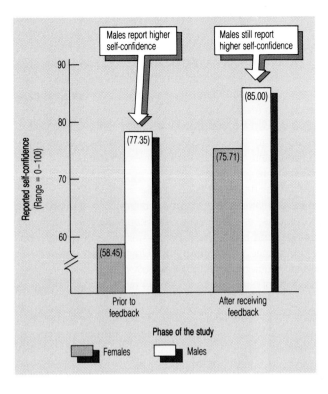

FIGURE 5.14 Feedback and Self-Confidence among Males and Females

Females reported lower self-confidence than males before receiving feedback about their performance. After receiving positive feedback, their self-confidence increased but it was still lower than that of males. (Only data for the positive feedback condition are shown.) (Source: Based on data from McCarty, 1986; see Note 68.)

In a laboratory study on this issue, she asked male and female students to work on tasks involving creativity. Subjects performed three such tasks (devising unique uses for ordinary objects such as a pencil or wire hanger), and received feedback about their performance on each one. Some learned that they had done very well (positive feedback), others that they had done quite poorly (negative feedback), while still others received no feedback whatsoever. Subjects were asked to rate their self-confidence both before working on the tasks and again after receiving feedback. As you can see from Figure 15.14, women reported lower levels of self-confidence before working on the tasks. More importantly, while positive feedback did increase their self-confidence, it did not eliminate the difference in favor of men; women continued to report lower self-confidence throughout the study. Finally, men who received no feedback during the study reported self-confidence as high as that of women who had received positive feedback.

Together, these findings suggest that positive feedback about task performance may be especially important for women. Even in its absence, men express relatively high degrees of self-confidence. However, women report similar levels of confidence only in the context of encouraging feedback. This is a point managers who wish to foster advancement among women would do well to consider.

Sexism in Work Settings: An Optimistic Conclusion

There is no doubt that in the past, the aspirations and careers of large numbers of women were adversely affected by sexism. The costs, in terms of both wasted potential and personal disappointments, were certainly great. Fortunately, the situation has altered considerably in recent years, permitting us to conclude on a more optimistic note. As we have already indicated, increasing numbers of women are moving into managerial positions; and growing numbers are rising to the very top positions in large organizations. Perhaps even more encouraging, several recent studies have reported evidence suggesting that sexist attitudes, too, are on the wane. For example, in one large-scale study involving evaluations of the performance of more than six hundred male and female store managers by their male and female supervisors, Peters and his colleagues found no indication of discrimination against females.[69] Indeed, both male and female supervisors actually assigned *higher* ratings to female managers than to male ones. Similarly, in a study we described in chapter 4, Graves and Powell recently found little, if any, evidence for discrimination based on sex in the evaluation of job applicants in a university employment center.[70] Finally, Grams and Schwab found that experts in employment compensation did not rate jobs filled predominantly by females as less compensable (i.e., less deserving of various rewards) than jobs filled mainly by males.[71]

Together, these findings point to major shifts toward reduced sex discrimination in the world of work. Females, it seems, are receiving more equitable treatment now than in the past. Of course, this does not imply that sexism—or other forms of prejudice—are no longer of major importance in organizations. On the contrary, women and other groups still face serious problems that must be overcome (e.g., women constitute the overwhelming majority of the victims of sexual harassment).[72] It does appear, however, that at least some types of prejudice are on the wane, and are less influential than in the past. It is our hope, of course, that such trends will continue, and that at some point in the future the impact of sexism and other forms of work-related prejudice will indeed be negligible.

SUMMARY AND REVIEW

The Nature of Attitudes. Attitudes are stable clusters of feelings, beliefs, and behavior tendencies directed toward some aspect of the external world. **Work-related attitudes** involve such reactions toward various aspects of work settings or the people in them. Attitudes are most likely to affect behavior when they are specific and intense, and when external factors do not block their impact.

Changing Attitudes. Efforts to change attitudes often involve **persuasion,** a process in which one individual attempts to change the attitudes of one or more others through written, spoken, or taped messages. The success of persuasion in altering attitudes depends on several characteristics of the person who delivers such messages and the content and form of the messages delivered.

When individuals discover that two attitudes they hold are inconsistent, or that their attitudes and their behavior are inconsistent, an unpleasant state of **cognitive dissonance** results. This produces pressure to alter either the attitudes or behaviors involved.

Job Satisfaction. Job satisfaction involves positive or negative attitudes toward one's work. Such attitudes can be measured by rating scales and questionnaires such as the JDI or MSQ, or by asking individuals to describe instances relating to their work that they found especially satisfying or dissatisfying (the *critical incident technique*).

According to Herzberg's **two-factor theory,** job satisfaction and dissatisfaction stem from different factors. Evidence for the accuracy of this theory has been mixed at best. Locke's **value theory** suggests that job satisfaction reflects the apparent match between the outcomes individuals desire from their jobs (what they *value*), and what they believe they are actually receiving.

Job satisfaction is affected by many factors relating to organizational policies and procedures, specific aspects of jobs and work settings, and personal characteristics of employees. Most persons report being at least moderately satisfied with their current jobs. However, these high levels of satisfaction may be more apparent than real. Job satisfaction affects important aspects of organizational behavior, such as absenteeism and voluntary turnover. Its impact on task performance is less certain, but some evidence indicates that it may have an effect on **citizenship behaviors.**

Organizational Commitment. Organizational commitment involves attitudes on the part of individuals toward their organization. High levels of organizational commitment are associated with strong acceptance of the organizations' goals and values and willingness to exert efforts on its behalf. Organizational commitment stems from many different factors (e.g., the level of responsibility or autonomy connected with a given job, employee ownership of the company). It affects several aspects of organizational behavior (e.g., absenteeism, turnover).

Prejudice in Work Settings. Prejudice refers to negative attitudes toward the members of specific groups. Forms of prejudice especially relevant to work settings involve those based on *age, race,* or *sex.*

Large numbers of women have entered the work force in recent decades, yet they have not attained full equality with men in terms of pay or levels of responsibility. Such differences may stem, in part, from overt discrimination against females. However, they seem to result primarily from several forces operating against women in organizations. These include *sex role stereotypes,* and lower *expectations* and *self-confidence* among women. Growing evidence suggests that such forces are on the wane, and that sexism, as well as other forms of prejudice, may exert decreasing effects in organizations in the future.

KEY TERMS

attitudes: Stable clusters of feelings, beliefs, and behavioral intentions directed toward specific aspects of the external world.

citizenship behaviors: Actions by employees that contribute to the smooth functioning of their organization, but which are not part of their formal job description.

cognitive dissonance: An unpleasant state that occurs when individuals notice inconsistencies between various attitudes they hold, or between such attitudes and their behavior.

critical incident procedure: A technique for measuring job satisfaction in which emloyees describe incidents relating to their work which they found especially satisfying or dissatisfying.

escalation of commitment: A process in which individuals experience growing pressure to continue with a chosen course of action, despite the fact that it is yielding negative (or at least disappointing) outcomes.

Employee Stock Ownership Plans (ESOPs): Plans whereby emloyees of an organization receive shares of stock in it on an annual basis. Thus, they become part owners of the company for which they work.

Job Descriptive Index (JDI): A rating scale for assessing job satisfaction. Individuals respond to this questionnaire by indicating whether various adjectives describe aspects of their work.

job satisfaction: Positive or negative attitudes held by individuals toward their jobs.

Minnesota Satisfaction Questionnaire (MSQ): A rating scale for assessing job satisfaction. Individuals completing this scale indicate the extent to which they are satisfied with various aspects of their jobs.

motivator-hygiene theory: see *two-factor theory.*

organizational commitment: Attitudes held by individuals toward the entire organization. High levels of organizational commitment are associated with acceptance of the organization's values and willingness to expend effort on its behalf.

Pay Satisfaction Questionnaire: A questionnaire designed to assess employees' level of satisfaction with various aspects of their pay (e.g., its overall level, raises, benefits).

persuasion: A process in which one or more individuals attempt to alter the attitudes of others.

prejudice: Negative attitudes toward the members of specific groups, based solely on the fact that they are a member of that group. Prejudice can be based on age, sex, race, and even occupation or profession.

two-factor theory (of job satisfaction): A theory, devised by Herzberg, suggesting that satisfaction and dissatisfaction stem from different groups of variables (*motivators* and *hygienes,* respectively).

value theory (of job satisfaction): A theory, devised by Locke, suggesting that job satisfaction depends primarily on the match between the outcomes individuals value in their jobs and their perceptions about the availability of such outcomes.

work-related attitudes: Attitudes relating to any aspect of work or work settings.

Questions for Discussion

1. How is *persuasion* used in organizations? Does using this process contribute to career success?

2. After making decisions, individuals often come up with many reasons supporting their choice. How does cognitive dissonance explain this common tendency?

3. Suppose that as a manager, you wanted to enhance job satisfaction among your subordinates. What concrete steps might you take to accomplish this goal?

4. Most people indicate that they are reasonably satisfied with their jobs. Why? How might we go about determining whether such satisfaction is real or only apparent?

5. Voluntary withdrawal is a costly problem for many companies. What steps might be taken to reduce the incidence of such decisions by valued employees?

6. In what ways can high levels of organizational commitment among employees actually lead to negative outcomes for their company?

7. Do you think we will ever reach the point at which the proportion of top executives who are female equals the proportion of females in the general population? Why or why not?

Notes

1. Locke, E. A. (1988). The nature and causes of job satisfaction. In M. Dunnette (Ed.), *Handbook of industrial and organizational psychology* (2nd ed.). Palo Alto, CA: Consulting Psychologists Press.

2. Mowday, R. T., Steers, R. M., & Porter, L. W. (1979). The measurement of organizational commitment. *Journal of Vocational Behavior, 14,* 224–247.

3. Baron, R. A., Byrne, D., & Suls, J. (1989). *Exploring social psychology* (3rd ed.). Boston: Allyn & Bacon.

4. Petty, R. E., & Cacioppo, J. T. (1986). *Attitude change: Central and peripheral routes to persuasion.* New York: Springer-Verlag.

5. See Note 3.

6. Miller, N., Maruyama, G., Beaber, R. J., & Valone, K. (1976). Speed of speech and persuasion. *Journal of Personality and Social Psychology, 34,* 615–624.

7. See Note 3.

8. Wyer, R. S., & Srull, T. K. (1984). *Handbook of social cognition.* Hillsdale, NJ: Erlbaum.

9. See Note 4.

10. Festinger, L. (1957). *A theory of cognitive dissonance.* Evanston, IL: Row, Peterson.

11. Petty, R. E., & Cacioppo, J. T. (1986). *Attitude change: Central and peripheral routes to persuasion.* New York: Springer-Verlag.

12. See Note 1.

13. Smith, P. C., Kendall, L. M., & Hulin, C. L. (1969). *The measurement of satisfaction in work and retirement.* Chicago: Rand McNally.

14. Weiss, D. J., Dawis, R. V., England, G. W., & Lofquist, L. H. (1967). *Manual for the Minnesota Satisfaction Questionnaire* (Minnesota Studies on Vocational Rehabilitation, vol. 22). Minneapolis, MN: Industrial Relations Center, Work Adjustment Project, University of Minnesota.

15. Scarpello., V., Huber, V., & Vandenberg, R. J. (1988). Compensation satisfaction: Its measurement and dimensionality. *Journal of Applied Psychology, 73,* 163–171.

16. Sutton, R. I., & Callahan, A. L. (1987). The stigma of bankruptcy: Spoiled organizational image and its management. *Academy of Management Journal, 30,* 405–436.

17. Herzberg, F., Mausner, B., & Snyderman, B. (1959). *The motivation to work.* New York: Wiley.

18. Herzberg, E. (1966). *Work and the nature of man.* Cleveland, OH: World.

19. Herzberg, E. (1964). The motivation-hygiene concept and problems of manpower. *Personnel Administrator, 27,* 3–7.

20. Machungawa, P. D., & Schmitt, N. (1983). Work motivation in a developing country. *Journal of Appied Psychology, 68,* 31–42.

21. Landy, F. J. (1985). *Psychology of work behavior* (3rd ed.). Homewood, IL: Dorsey Press.

22. Locke, E. A. (1976). The nature and causes of job satisfaction. In M. D. Dunnette (Ed.), *Handbook of industrial*

and organizational psychology. Palo Alto, CA: Consulting Psychologists Press.

23. Berkowitz, L., Fraser, C., Treasure, F. P., & Cochran, S. (1987). Pay equity, job gratifications, and comparisons in pay satisfaction. *Journal of Applied Psychology, 27,* 544–551.

24. Locke, E. A., & Schweiger, D. M. (1979). Participation in decision-making: One more look. *Research in Organizational Behavior, 1,* 265–339.

25. Trempe, J., Rigny, A. J., & Haccoun, R. R. (1985). Subordinate satisfaction with male and female managers: Role of perceived supervisory influence. *Journal of Applied Psychology, 70,* 44–47.

26. Curry, J. P., Wakefield, D. S., Price, J. L., & Mueller, C. W. (1986). *Academy of Management Journal, 29,* 847–858.

27. Hackman, J. R., & Oldham, G. R. (1976). Motivation through the design of work: Test of a theory. *Organizational Behavior and Human Performance, 16,* 250–279.

28. Sundstrom, E. (1986). *Workplaces.* Cambridge, England: Cambridge Univ. Press.

29. Oldham, G. R., & Fried, Y. (1987). Employee reactions to workspace characteristics. *Journal of Applied Psychology, 72,* 75–80.

30. See Note 22.

31. See Note 1.

32. See Note 1.

33. Scheier, M. F., Weintraub, J. K., & Carver, C. S. (1986). Coping with stress: Divergent strategies of optimists and pessimists. *Journal of Personality and Social Psychology, 51,* 1257–1264.

34. Andrisani, P. J., & Nestel, C. (1976). Internal-external control as a contributor to and outcome of work experience. *Journal of Applied Psychology, 61,* 156–165.

35. Near, J. P., Smith, C. A., Rice, R. W., & Hunt, R. G. (1984). A comparison of work and non-work predictors of life satisfaction. *Academy of Management Journal, 27,* 33–42.

36. See Note 1.

37. Schlenker, J. A., & Gutek, B. A. (1987). Effects of role loss on work-related attitudes. *Journal of Applied Psychology, 72,* 287–293.

38. Quinn, R. P., & Staines, G. L. (1979). *The 1977 quality of employment survey.* Ann Arbor: Institute for Social Research.

39. Weaver, C. N. (1980). Job satisfaction in the United States in the 1970s. *Journal of Applied Psychology, 65,* 364–367.

40. Kahn, R. L. (1972). The meaning of work: Interpretations and proposals for measurement. In A. A. Campbell and P. E. Converseg (Eds.), *The human meaning of social change.* New York: Basic Books.

41. Porter, L. W., & Steers, R. M. (1973). Organizational work and personal factors in employee turnover and absenteeism. *Psychological Bulletin, 80,* 151–176.

42. Mowday, R. T., Koberg, C. S., & McArthur, A. W. (1984). The psychology of the withdrawal process: A cross-validational test of Mobley's intermediate linkages model of turnover in two samples. *Academy of Management Journal, 27,* 79–94.

43. Mobley, W. H., Horner, S. O., & Hollingsworth, A. T. (1978). An evaluation of precursors of hospital employee turnover. *Journal of Applied Psychology, 63,* 408–414.

44. Carsten, J. M., & Spector, P. E. (1987). Unemployment, job satisfaction, and employee turnover: A meta-analytic test of the Muchinsky model. *Journal of Applied Psychology, 72,* 374–381.

45. Oldham, G. R., & Fried, Y. (1987). Employee reactions to workspace characteristics. *Journal of Applied Psychology, 72,* 75–80.

46. Miller, K. I., & Monge, P. R. (1986). Participation, satisfaction, and productivity: A meta-analytic review. *Academy of Management Journal, 29,* 727–753.

47. Porter, L. W., & Lawler, E. E., III (1968). *Managerial attitudes and performance.* Homewood, IL: Dorsey Press.

48. Organ, D. W. (1988). *Organizational citizenship behavior.* Lexington, MA: Lexington Books.

49. Bateman, T. S., & Organ, D. W. (1983). Job satisfaction and the Good Soldier: The relationships between affect and employee "citizenship." *Academy of Management Journal, 26,* 587–595.

50. Mowday, R. T., Porter, L. W., & Steers, R. M. (1979). The measurement of organizational commitment. *Journal of Vocational Behavior, 14,* 224–247.

51. Reichers, A. E. (1985). A review and reconceptualization of organizational commitment. *Academy of Management Review, 10,* 465–476.

52. Brooke, P. B., Jr., Russell, D. W., & Price, J. L. (1988). Discriminant validation of measures of job satisfaction, job involvement, and organizational commitment. *Journal of Applied Psychology, 73,* 139–145.

53. Bateman, T. S., & Strasser, S. (1984). A longitudinal analysis of the antecedents of organizational commitment. *Academy of Management Journal, 27,* 95–112.

54. Curry, J. P., Wakefield, D. S., Price, J. L., & Mueller, C. W. (1986). On the causal ordering of job satisfaction and organizational commitment. *Academy of Management Journal, 29,* 847–858.

55. See Note 54.

56. See Note 53.

57. Bruning, N. A., & Snyder, R. A. (1983). Sex and position as predictors of organizational commitment. *Academy of Management Journal, 26,* 485–491.

58. Rosen, C., Klein, K. J., & Young, K. M. (1986). *Employee ownership in the United States: The equity solution.* Lexington, MA: Lexington Books.

59. Klein, K. J. (1987). Employee stock ownership and employee attitudes: A test of three models. *Journal of Applied Psychology, 72,* 319–332.

60. Saal, F. E., & Knight, P. A. (1987). *Industrial/organizational psychology: Science and practice.* Pacific Grove, CA: Brooks/Cole.

61. Stephan, W. G. (1985). Intergroup relations. In G.

Lindzey & E. Aronson (Eds.), *Handbook of social psychology* (3rd ed.). New York: Random House.

62. Hess, B. B., & Feree, M. M. (eds.) (1988). *Analyzing gender: A handbook of social science research.* Newbury Park, CA: Sage.

63. Lawrence, B. S. (1988). New wrinkles in the theory of age: Demography, norms, and performance ratings. *Academy of Management Journal, 31,* 309–337.

64. Steinberg, R., & Shapiro, S. (1982). Sex differences in personality traits of female and male master of business administration students. *Journal of Applied Psychology, 67,* 306–310.

65. Heilman, M. E., & Martell, R. F. (1986). Exposure to successful women: Antidote to sex discrimination in applicant screening decisions? *Organizational Behavior and Human Decision Processes, 37,* 376–390.

66. Heilman, M. E., Martell, R. F., & Simon, M. C. (1988). The vagaries of sex bias: Conditions regulating the undervaluation, equivaluation, and overvaluation of female job applicants. *Organizational Behavior and Human Decision Processes, 41,* 98–110.

67. Major, B., & Konar, E. (1984). An investigation of sex differences in pay expectations and their possible causes. *Academy of Management Journal, 27,* 777–792.

68. McCarty, P. A. (1986). Effects of feedback on the self-confidence of men and women. *Academy of Management Journal, 29,* 840–847.

69. Peters, L. H., O'Connor, E. J., Weekley, J., Pooylan, A., Frank, B., & Erenkrantz, B. (1984). Sex bias and managerial evaluations: A replication and extention. *Journal of Applied Psychology, 69,* 349–352.

70. Graves, L. M., & Powell, G. N. (1988). An investigation of sex discrimination in recruiters' evaluations of actual applicants. *Journal of Applied Psychology, 73,* 20–29.

71. Grams, R., & Schwab, D. P. (1985). An investigation of systematic gender-related error in job evaluation. *Academy of Management Journal, 28,* 279–290.

72. Terpstra, D. E., & Baker, D. D. (1988). Outcomes of sexual harassment charges. *Academy of Management Journal, 31,* 185–194.

Walt Disney World: A Magical Place to Work

Walt Disney World—The Magic Kingdom. Did you ever wonder how a business that employs over 25,000 people in 1,100 different jobs serving over 25 million customers a year maintains that magic?[1] Although Disney managers will tell you that the answer is "pixie dust," it takes much more than a sorcerer's potion to attain the level of success and profitability achieved by Disney. It takes people who are dedicated to their jobs and committed to the organization. Disney goes to great lengths to ensure that their employees have such positive work attitudes.

At Disney World, managers begin to express their concern about employee attitudes even before anyone is hired. Because work at Disney is very fast paced and demanding, all potential employees undergo an eight to ten minute interview during which they are told about the joys and drawbacks of working at Disney. As a result of this screening, many potential hirees decide not to pursue employment. Those who are still interested are then given a forty-five minute interview during which they learn some of the policies and procedures of working in the Magic Kingdom.

Once hired, personnel are trained at length about the way Disney operates. The purpose of this orientation is to get the new people excited about their jobs and committed to Disney's way of doing things. Training begins with a two day course in "traditions." During this time employees learn that they are called "cast members;" that they haven't been hired for a job, but "cast" in a show. Carrying the theatrical analogy further, they are taught that they don't wear uniforms but rather, costumes. Similarly, they learn that the people who visit Disney World are Guests (capital G), not customers. In addition, during the first day of class they are given an overview of the Disney history, achievements, and philosophy. On the second day of class they get additional information about policies, procedures, and benefits as well as a tour of the workplace.

Management's concern for employee satisfaction and commitment doesn't end with the training. It is incorporated into everyday interaction between managers and cast members. Specifically, management has four goals when communicating with the cast: (1) to share company goals; (2) to reinforce Disney values and traditions; (3) to share information; and (4) to create a legacy for the employees. Senior manager Doug Cody explains the purpose of this: "Relevant information in an effective medium on a timely basis gives employees pride, morale, and a sense of belonging."[2]

Not surprisingly, Disney engages in various other actions to try and generate employee satisfaction and commitment. For example, between 60 percent and 80 percent of internal promotions for salaried positions are filled from within the company. In addition, the cast and managers share responsibility for employee safety, guest relations, and providing high quality entertainment. Employee achievements are recognized with various awards such as Cast Member of the Month/Quarter/Year. Furthermore, picnics, Christmas parties, and the availability of a recreation facility and an on-site day care program contribute to the positive attitudes of Disney personnel.

Management uses numerous means of gathering information to determine the extent to which employees are satisfied and committed as well as whether corporate actions impact on these attitudes. Employees are regularly given a written opinion survey with both multiple choice and essay questions that asks them to comment on various topics. Focus groups, in which a small number of managers and employees meet to share ideas, are also used to determine how things are going. Even employees who leave Disney are given an exit interview to find out why they are quitting and if they were satisfied. Finally, there is the "I Have an Idea" program that rewards employees with up to $10,000 for submitting an original idea to management.

All this attention to employee attitudes has a big payoff for Disney. The organization has repeatedly received praise as being one of the best service companies in America.[3] In fact, so much acclaim has been directed at the success of Disney's management, they have developed a program to train managers of other companies in their techniques and philosophies. In addition, Disney was selected as one of the hundred best companies to work for in the United States.[4] Of course, all this attention to employee needs results in many people wanting to work at Disney, so they have no trouble recruiting talented and dedicated personnel.

The outcome of all this is the world's most successful theme park. Guests flock from everywhere to Disney World. At $28 per daily pass plus monies spent on hotels and lodging, Disney World does business of close to $1 billion per year. If that isn't a testimony to the value of satisfied and committed employees, nothing is!

Questions for Discussion

1. What company policies contribute to the job satisfaction of Disney employees?

2. Identify two motivators and two hygiene factors present at Disney World.

3. How does Disney try to increase employee commitment?

4. Could Disney's management policies work in organizations in other industries? Why or why not?

5. Would you like to work at Disney World? Why or Why not?

Notes

1. Blocklyn, P. L. (1988, December). Making magic: The Disney approach to people management. *Personnel, 65,* pp. 28–35.

2. See Note 1, p. 32.

3. Peters, T. J., & Waterman, R. H., Jr. (1982). *In search of excellence.* New York: Harper & Row.

4. Levering, R., Moskowitz, M., & Katz, M. (1984). *The 100 best companies to work for in America.* Reading, MA: Addison-Wesley.

Getting What You Expect: Anticipated Compensation of Women and Men

Despite efforts to eliminate differences in pay for women and men, a gender gap persists in this respect. As we enter the 1990s, women's average salaries are still considerably lower than men's. Many factors probably contribute to this state of affairs. Because of past sexual discrimination, women have filled many jobs—especially higher-level ones—for shorter periods than their male counterparts. Further, women have often been encouraged to enter lower-paying fields or occupations. Yet another factor that contributes to the present gender gap, however, is this: women hold lower expectations with respect to both starting and highest career salaries than men. You can demonstrate this difference for yourself by following the instructions below.

Procedure

Ask five to ten classmates of each sex to answer the following questions. (It would be best to work only with individuals who have *not* yet had a course in OB.)

1. What *starting salary* do you expect to receive on your first full-time job?
2. What will be the *highest* salary you will receive during your career? (Estimate in terms of current prices and salaries.)
3. How long will it be (in years and months) before you receive your first major promotion?
4. What field or occupation do you plan to enter after graduation?

Points to Consider

After you have collected data from all respondents, add the figures for males and females separately, and compare the means (averages) on each question. In all likelihood, you will find that females report somewhat lower expectations than males. Why? One possibility is that many females plan to enter fields offering relatively lower pay. Another possibility is that these expectations simply reflect current conditions: females recognize that they actually receive lower pay, on average, than males. Can you think of other reasons for these differences in expectations? Will they disappear in the future as efforts to eliminate sexism continue?

CHAPTER SIX

PERSONALITY: INDIVIDUAL DIFFERENCES AND ORGANIZATIONAL BEHAVIOR

CHAPTER OUTLINE

Personality: Its Basic Nature
  Personality: A Note on Its Origins
  Personality and Organizational Behavior

Work-Related Aspects of Personality
  The Type A Behavior Pattern: Its Effects on Health, Task Performance, and Interpersonal Relations
  Machiavellianism: Using Others on the Way to Success
  Locus of Control: Perceived Control over One's Outcomes and Fate
  Social Skills: Individual Differences in the Ability to Get Along with Others
  Self-Monitoring: Public Image versus Private Reality
  Self-Efficacy: Beliefs in One's Ability to Perform Various Tasks
  Self-Esteem: The Importance of Self-Evaluations
  Work-Related Motives: Achievement, Power, and Affiliation

Measuring Personality: Some Basic Methods
  Inventories and Questionnaires: Assessing Personality through Self-Report
  Projective Techniques: Ambiguous Stimuli and Personality Assessment
  Using Information about Personality: Some Words of Caution

Special Sections

OB: An International Perspective
  Type A's and Type B's on the Job: Evidence from Two Different Cultures

OB: A Research Perspective
  Personal Motives and Presidential Politics: Does Having the Right Motives Make a Leader Great?

OB: A Management Perspective
  Putting Personality Measures to Practical Use: Assessment Centers and the Identification of Managerial Talent

LEARNING OBJECTIVES

After reading this chapter, you should be able to:
  1. Define personality and indicate why it is relevant to OB.
    2. Describe the following personality characteristics and indicate their relationship to important forms of organizational behavior: Type A Behavior Pattern, Machiavellianism, Social Skills, Locus of Control, Self-Monitoring, Self-Efficacy, Self-Esteem.
      3. Explain how achievement, power, and affiliation motivation influence organizational behavior.
        4. Explain how personality is measured.
          5. Describe the nature of assessment centers and their usefulness in identifying managerial talent.

"Well, how are Doug and Fran getting along?" Mark Peters asks Nancy DeFalco. (Both are members of Grammex Inc.'s Commercial Products Division.)

"How do you *think?*" Nancy replies.

Mark chuckles. "Like oil and water, of course. What else?"

"You got it," Nancy says, shaking her head. "I never *could* figure out why Phil made them co-directors of the Tennessee project. Talk about people with different styles!"

"I'll say," Mark agrees. "They seem to be on totally different wavelengths."

"Right. Doug is always in such a hurry—you'd think he was just about to run out of time. And Fran; talk about relaxed. Sometimes I wonder if there's *anything* that can get her excited."

"Yep; she's a cool one, all right," Mark agrees. "But that's not the only way they're opposites. Doug's such a worrier; he *never* seems confident about anything. Always talking about the downside and the risks."

"And Fran's the eternal optimist—she's always so surprised if things don't turn out perfectly, the way she's planned."

"But you know, that may be one reason she's so much better with people. No one likes a pessimist. Everyone who works with Fran really gets a kick out of her style."

"They *do,* and I'm sure that's part of it," Nancy remarks. "But they also like the fact that she's so expressive—you know, open with her feelings. You can always tell what she's thinking. Doug's such a poker-face. If he's got any emotions, you'd never know it. Another thing: Fran reads people so well. That's probably why she never gets on anyone's nerves the way Doug does."

"You're right!" Mark replies, continuing where Nancy left off. "Sometimes it's like he's not aware at all. Just plows ahead, no matter how people are reacting. That's really cost him a time or two."

"Yeah, if he didn't get so much done, I doubt that he'd have made it to Grade Four. But anyway, I wouldn't want to be part of *that* project. From what I've heard, the tension is so thick at their meetings you can practically cut it with a knife."

"I know," Mark agrees. "That old saying about 'Opposites attracting' is bull. It's *hard* for people as different as those two to work together." After a brief pause, he continues, "You know, I really think that's something Phil should have considered when he made up the assignments."

"Variety," it is often said, "is the spice of life." If this is true, then other people certainly provide us with lots of spice! They differ from one another in a seemingly endless number of ways. Further, as our opening story suggests, such differences often count—and count heavily—in work settings. To mention just a few examples, differences between individuals often play a key role in determining who is best suited for a given job, who will be chosen for it, and how she or he actually performs once assigned to the position.

Many differences between individuals are related to organizational behavior. Among the most important, though, are those involving **personality**—differences in terms of lasting *traits* or characteristics. It is on these differences that we will focus in the present chapter. To clarify their nature and their relevance to the field of OB, we'll proceed as follows. First we'll define personality more precisely, and comment on the origins of the differences it involves. Second, we'll examine several specific traits that have been shown, in recent research, to have important implications for organizational behavior. Third, we'll consider various methods for measuring personality, techniques that are necessary if we wish to compare individuals in this regard and then put such knowledge to practical use.

PERSONALITY: ITS BASIC NATURE

If our experience with other people tells us anything, it is this: First, they are all *unique*—each possesses a pattern of traits and characteristics not fully duplicated in any other individual. Second, these traits or characteristics are fairly *stable* over time. Thus, if someone you know is bright, conscientious, and arrogant today, the chances are good that she will demonstrate the same characteristics a month, a year, or even ten years in the future. These two facts form the basis for a definition of **personality** that is currently accepted by most experts on this topic: it is *the unique but stable set of characteristics and behavior that sets each individual apart from others.*[1] In short, it refers to the lasting ways in which a given person is different from all others.

Do you find this definition reasonable? Probably so. Most people accept the view that human beings possess specific traits (tendencies to think and act in certain ways) and that these traits are fairly constant over time. You may be surprised to learn, therefore, that until quite recently, a heated controversy existed in the behavioral sciences over the accuracy of these beliefs.

On one side of this debate were scientists who contended that people do *not* possess lasting traits.[2] According to these researchers (whom we might term the "anti-personality" camp), behavior is shaped largely by external factors or conditions. Thus, we should not expect people to behave consistently at different times or in different settings. Indeed, our belief that they do is largely an illusion stemming from the fact that we *want* to perceive such consistency—it makes our task of predicting others' actions easier.

On the other side of the controversy were scientists who held, equally strongly, that stable traits *do* exist, and that these lead individuals to behave consistently at different times and in many settings. Which of these views has prevailed? As you can guess from the presence of this chapter, the latter one. The weight of scientific opinion has swung strongly toward the view that individual behavior *does* often stem, at least in part, from stable traits or characteristics. Several lines of evidence offer support for this conclusion.

First, in a number of recent studies, the behavior of individuals has been studied for extended periods of time (months or even years). The result: a great deal of consistency with respect to basic aspects of personality has been observed.[3,4]

Second, other research indicates that individuals' behavior does indeed reflect their stable traits whenever this is feasible—in situations where these personal tendencies are not overwhelmed by powerful situational factors.[5] As an illustration of this point, consider the following incidents. A young woman known to her coworkers as hot tempered is "chewed out" by an important customer for failing to deliver a large order on time. She shows no anger; in fact, she apologizes and promises to get the problem straightened out. At another time, the same person receives a bill from a local garage for service on her car. Upon opening it, she immediately phones the garage and shouts angrily at the owner, accusing him of trying to cheat her. What accounts for her sharply contrasting behavior in the two situations? One possible answer involves situational pressures. In the first, these were high: the young woman could not lose her temper because, quite simply, the costs of doing so were too high. In the latter, in contrast, such costs were much lower, and her underlying trait (a violent temper) could emerge

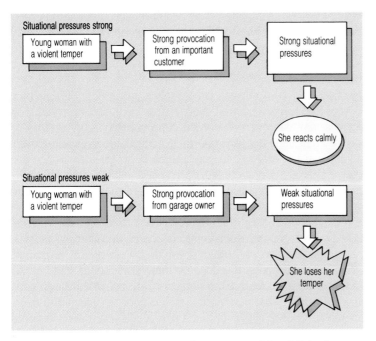

FIGURE 6.1 Personality, Situational Pressures, and Overt Behavior

Individuals' behavior may fail to reflect their underlying traits or characteristics when situational pressures are strong (upper panel). However, various traits may greatly affect individuals' actions when such pressures are weak (lower panel).

(see Figure 6.1). In sum, personality *is* important in determining individuals' behavior, but only in contexts where external pressures do not overwhelm such differences and prevent them from appearing.

Third, and perhaps most revealing of all, people seem to differ in the extent to which they are consistent. In other words, the tendency to behave in the same (or at least similar) manner across situations is itself an aspect of personality.[6] At one extreme are persons whose actions stem largely from their underlying traits or preferences. As you can probably guess, they show a high degree of consistency across situations and over time. At the other extreme are individuals whose behavior is shaped mainly by external factors; they often behave differently in different contexts and show less consistency.[7] Thus, the fact that specific persons do not show similar patterns of behavior in all settings does not, by itself, argue against the existence of lasting traits. On the contrary, individual differences in degree of consistency may actually reflect the impact of one such trait or characteristic. We'll return to such differences in a later section of this chapter, where we consider an aspect of personality known as **self-monitoring.**[8]

Personality: A Note on Its Origins

To recapitulate: at present, there is little disagreement over the facts that people differ from one another in important ways, and some of these differences, at least, are stable over time. Considerably greater controversy persists, however, over another issue: what are the origins of such differences? In other words, to what extent is personality learned, and to what extent does it reflect the operation of genetic factors? A few years ago, most behavioral scientists would have offered a reply strongly favoring the impact of learning. The prevailing view was that differences between individuals with respect to various traits stem mainly from exposure to different experiences and life histories.[9] Now, however, a somewhat different view has emerged. Growing evidence suggests that while learning is certainly important in shaping personality, genetic factors seem to play a role as well.

Much of the support for this view derives from studies performed with identical twins who, for various reasons, were separated shortly after birth. Because such persons share the same genes, any differences between them in behavior or personality must reflect the impact of environmental factors—their contrasting lives and experiences following separation. On the other hand, similarities between such twins must stem from genetic factors; after all, they were separated early in life and did not share the same experiences. How much resemblance exists between these twins in terms of personality? Surprisingly, a considerable amount. In fact, careful studies reveal that these twins resemble one another in their traits and behavior to an amazing degree, despite having been raised in sharply contrasting environments.[10] Such findings suggest that personality, like height, eye color, and other physical characteristics, is shaped, in part, by genetic factors. But please note: this does *not* imply that various traits cannot be modified. People can, and often do, alter many aspects of their physical appearance. Thus, there is no reason to assume that personality, too, cannot be changed. Indeed, as noted below, considerable evidence suggests that it *can* be altered, and that various traits are definitely not "set in stone," immutable throughout life.

Personality and Organizational Behavior

Most people find personality an intriguing topic. They are aware of the fact that human beings differ in many ways and that these differences are important in everyday life. But how relevant is knowledge about personality to the field of OB? In other words, does knowing something about this topic really contribute to our understanding of behavior in organizational settings, and to the goals we described in chapter 1—enhancing both productivity *and* the quality of working life? We feel that it does. Further, this view is not simply a reflection of our personal opinions. On the contrary, recent studies suggest that personality affects a wide range of organizational processes—from task performance and absenteeism,[11] to personnel selection and hiring decisions.[12] For example, consider a recent study by Paunonen, Jackson, and Oberman.[13]

These researchers reasoned that in deciding whether various applicants are suited for a specific job, raters consider the extent to which the personalities of applicants match those required by the job. The closer this match, the higher the ratings they assign. To determine if this was indeed the case, Paunonen and his colleagues asked subjects to rate the suitability of applicants for two positions—engineer and accountant. Subjects based their ratings, in part, on audiotapes in which applicants made comments suggesting that they possessed various traits. In one condition, these traits matched those actually found among accountants (e.g., applicants indicated that they were high in the need for cognitive structure and order, low in need for change, and low in impulsivity). In another condition, the applicants indicated that they possessed the traits found among engineers (e.g., a high need for achievement, high endurance). As predicted, subjects rated the applicants higher when the traits they seemed to possess matched those required by the job they were seeking to fill (see Figure 6.2). Of course, other factors, too, influenced their decisions (e.g., the applicant's apparent level of competence, as revealed by letters of recommendation). Still, personality—and subjects' views about the traits needed for success in a given field—strongly affected their ratings. As we will see, this is only one of many ways in which personality is linked to important aspects of organizational behavior and key processes occurring within organizations.

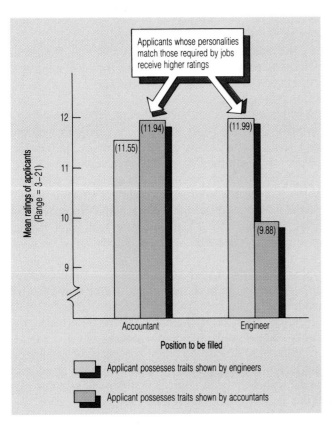

FIGURE 6.2 Personality and Personnel Selection

Subjects rated job applicants higher when they seemed to possess the traits required for a particular job than when they did not. This was true for two different positions: accountant and engineer. (Source: Based on data from Paunonen, Jackson, & Oberman, 1987; see Note 13.)

WORK-RELATED ASPECTS OF PERSONALITY

Basic research on personality has often focused on the task of understanding its essential nature—identifying the key dimensions along which people differ and the complex interrelations between them. From the perspective of OB, however, the most valuable studies have been those concerned with traits or characteristics that have direct bearing on behavior in work settings. Several of these are described below.

The Type A Behavior Pattern: Its Effects on Health, Task Performance, and Interpersonal Relations

Think about all the persons you know. Can you name one who always seems to be in a hurry, is extremely competitive, and is often irritable? Now, in contrast, try to name one who shows the opposite pattern—someone who is relaxed, not very competitive, and easy-going in relations with others. The persons you now have in mind represent extremes on one key dimension of personality. The first individual would be labeled **Type A,** while the second would be labeled **Type B.**[14] Persons classified as Type A show high levels of competitiveness, irritability, and time urgency (they are always in a hurry). In addition, they demonstrate certain stylistic patterns, such as loud and accelerated speech, and a tendency to respond very quickly in many contexts (e.g., during conversations they often begin speaking before others are through). Persons classified as Type B show an opposite pattern. Individuals are classified as Type A or Type B on the basis of their responses to the Jenkins Activity Survey, a personality test designed to measure these patterns, or on the basis of their reactions during a special type of structured interview.[15]

As you can probably guess, the differences between Type A and Type B persons have important implications for their behavior in work settings. The most central of these involves differences in their personal health, their performance on many tasks, and their relations with others.

The Type A pattern and health. Common sense suggests that persons who frequently push themselves to their limits may adversely affect their own health. For this reason, friends and relatives often plead with them to slow down and enjoy life more. In this case, common sense seems to be correct. Research findings indicate that Type A's are more than twice as likely as Type B's to experience serious heart disease.[16] Further, they are more likely to suffer a second heart attack if the first one is not fatal. In this respect, Type A persons certainly pay a high price for their hard-driving, overstimulated lifestyle. (Please see the discussion of stress in chapter 7 for more information on this topic.)

Recent evidence helps explain why Type A's are so much more at risk than Type B's in this regard. First, from a subjective point of view, Type A's tend to perceive themselves as being more overloaded or stressed by their jobs than Type B's.[17] As we'll note in chapter 7, such *cognitive appraisals* play a crucial role in determining the level of stress actually experienced by individuals in many situations.

Second, Type A's seem to respond to stress with more pronounced physiological reactions than Type B's.[18] This fact is illustrated clearly in an investigation by Hill and her colleagues.[19] These researchers studied the behavior of first-year medical students at three times: during a vacation period, during a stressful examination period, and again during a second vacation period. They found that several of the stylistic components of Type A behavior described above (e.g., loud, explosive speech, short response latency) increased among Type A's during the high stress exam period (see Figure 6.3). In addition, and perhaps even more important, Type A's showed larger increases than Type B's in resting heart rate during the examination period. These findings suggest that during periods of stress, Type A's subject their cardiovascular systems to greater "wear and tear." And since the competitive, hard-driving style of Type A's often leads them to *seek* stress-inducing challenge, it is not surprising that their health then suffers.

The Type A pattern and task performance. Given their high level of competitiveness, it seems reasonable to expect that Type A's will work harder at various tasks than other persons, and will perform at higher levels. In fact, however, the situation turns out to be more complex than this. On the one hand, Type A's *do* tend to work faster on many tasks than Type B's, even when no pressure or deadline is involved. Similarly, they are able to get more done in the presence of distractions.[20] And Type A's often seek more challenge in their work and daily lives than Type B's. For example, when given a choice, they select more difficult tasks than Type B's.[21]

Surprisingly, though, Type A's do not *always* perform better than Type B's. For example, Type A's frequently do poorly on tasks requiring patience or careful, considered judgment. They are simply in too much of a hurry to complete such work in an effective manner.[22] More important, surveys reveal that most members of *top* management are Type B, not Type A. Several factors probably contribute to this pattern. First, it is possible that Type A's simply don't last long enough to rise to the highest management levels—the health risks outlined above tend to remove them from contention at a relatively early age! Second, the impatient, always-in-a-hurry style of Type A's is generally incompatible with the decision-making role of top-level executives.

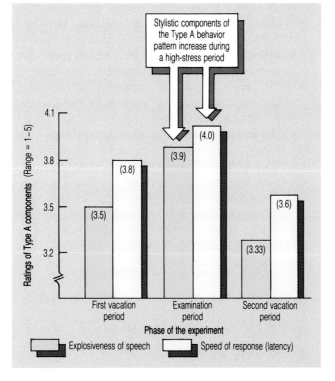

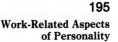
FIGURE 6.3 Type A Behavior under Stress

First year medical students classified as being Type A showed more components of the Type A behavior pattern during a high-stress examination period than during vacation periods that preceded and followed such stress. (Source: Based on data from Hill et al., 1987; see Note 19.)

Finally, the impatient, hostile style of Type A's may irritate the persons around them—a factor that can adversely affect their chances for promotion.

In sum, available evidence suggests that Type A's tend to do better than Type B's on some tasks—especially ones involving time pressure or solitary work. However, they may actually do *worse* than Type B's on tasks involving complex judgment, accuracy rather than speed, and working as part of a team. Thus, neither pattern appears to have an overall edge. Rather, it is the nature of the tasks being performed that will usually determine whether Type A's or Type B's tend to excel. (Is the Type A–Type B dimension relevant to task performance in various cultures, or is it restricted in its impact to Western nations such as the United States? For evidence on this issue, please see the **International Perspective** below.)

OB: AN INTERNATIONAL PERSPECTIVE

Type A's and Type B's on the Job: Evidence from Two Different Cultures

Do persons classified as Type A or Type B behave in similar ways around the world? And are such differences visible in their on-the-job behavior? Evidence reported by Evans, Palsane, and Carrere suggests that the answer to both questions is "yes."[23] These researchers studied the performance of urban bus drivers in two sharply contrasting cultures—the United States and India. They chose this particular occupation because it is known to be

quite stressful, and they reasoned that differences between Type A's and Type B's would be readily visible in this context.

To compare the Type A and Type B drivers, Evans and his associates examined three sources of data. First, they asked drivers in both categories (Type A's and Type B's) to rate the stressfulness of their work on a specific day. Second, they obtained records of each driver's prior accidents, absences, and official reprimands. Finally, they had trained raters ride on the drivers' buses, and record the frequency with which they blew their horns, passed other vehicles, and stepped on their brakes. (The drivers were classified as being Type A or Type B on the basis of their responses to the Jenkins Activity Survey.)

Results revealed consistent differences between Type A and Type B drivers on most measures in both countries. As expected, Type A drivers reported higher levels of job stress than Type B drivers. Similarly, Type A drivers had more accidents than Type B drivers in both India and the United States (see Figure 6.4). Finally, direct observations revealed that in India, but not in the United States, Type A drivers engaged in braking, passing, and horn-blowing at a higher rate than Type B drivers. Evans and his colleagues suggested that

the failure to observe corresponding differences in the United States may have stemmed from the fact that driving conditions there were much less congested. As a result, the overall rate of such actions was so low that differences between Type A's and Type B's could not emerge.

Considered as a whole, the findings reported by Evans, Palsane, and Carrere suggest that the Type A–Type B dimension is an important aspect of personality in different cultures, and is not restricted in its impact to the United States where it was first described and studied. Moreover, their results indicate that this aspect of personality can affect several forms of on-the-job behavior. In view of this evidence, it seems clear that the Type A–Type B dimension has important implications for both organizations and the field of OB.

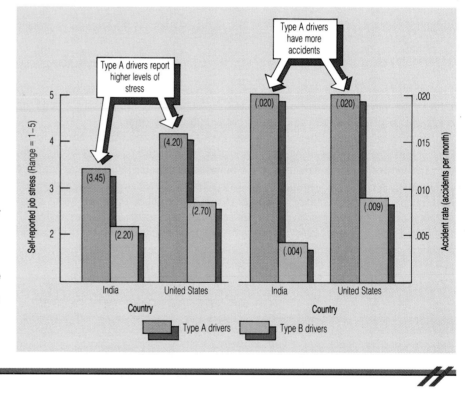

FIGURE 6.4 Type A Behavior and Job Performance in the United States and India

Type A bus drivers reported higher levels of job stress and became involved in more accidents than Type B bus drivers. This was true both in the United States and India. (Source: Based on data from Evans, Palsane, & Carrere, 1987; see Note 23.)

The Type A pattern and interpersonal relations. In addition to differences in personal health and task performance, Type A and Type B persons also demonstrate contrasting styles of interpersonal behavior. First, because they are always in a hurry, Type A's tend to become impatient with other persons, and frequently grow angry if someone delays them in any way. Second, when given a choice, Type A's prefer to work by themselves rather than with others. They are definitely loners—not team

TABLE 6.1 Conflict and the Type A Behavior Pattern

Type A managers report a higher incidence of conflict than Type B managers (or managers who are not clearly Type A or Type B) with subordinates and peers. Type A managers also report a slightly higher incidence of conflict with supervisors.

	TYPE B	INDETERMINATE	TYPE A
Subordinates	2.45	3.21	3.49
Peers	2.45	3.19	3.00
Supervisors	2.75	2.41	2.77

(Source: Based on data from Baron, 1989; see Note 25.)

players. Third, Type A's are more irritable and aggressive than Type B's. They lose their tempers more frequently, and are more likely to lash out at others for even slight provocations.[24] As a result of these tendencies, Type A's report becoming involved in more conflicts at work than Type B's. In one recent study on this issue, Baron asked managers at a large food-processing company to indicate the frequency with which they experience conflict with subordinates, peers, and supervisors.[25] As you can see from Table 6.1, those classified as Type A reported a significantly higher frequency of conflict than those classified as Type B or those who did not fall clearly into one or the other of these two categories. In sum, several characteristics of Type A's seem to get them into more than their share of interpersonal difficulties at work.

Machiavellianism: Using Others on the Way to Success

In 1513 the Italian philosopher Niccolo Machiavelli published a book entitled *The Prince*. In it, he outlined a ruthless strategy for seizing and holding political power. The main thrust of his approach was simple: other persons can be readily used or manipulated by sticking to a few basic rules. Among the guiding principles he recommended were: (1) never show humility—arrogance is far more effective when dealing with others; (2) morality and ethics are for the weak—powerful persons feel free to lie, cheat, and deceive whenever this suits their purpose; (3) it is much better to be feared than loved. In general, Machiavelli urged those who desired power to adopt a totally pragmatic approach to life. Let others be swayed by considerations of friendship, loyalty, or fair play, he suggested; a truly successful leader should always be above such factors. In short, he or she should be willing to do *whatever it takes to get his or her way.*

Unsettlingly, the ideas Machiavelli proposed are still very much with us. In fact, they are readily visible in many books that have made their way onto the best-seller lists in recent years—books that describe similar self-centered strategies for gaining power and success (see Figure 6.5 on page 198). The popularity of such books suggests that people today are as fascinated by the tactics Machiavelli described as they were more than four centuries ago. But are these strategies really put to actual use? Are there individuals who choose to live by the ruthless, self-serving creed Machiavelli proposed? The answer appears to be "yes." When large numbers of persons complete a test designed to measure acceptance of Machiavelli's suggestions (the *Mach scale*), many receive very high scores.[26] Thus, persons with a Machiavellian orientation (often called *High Machs*) are quite common. Indeed, you are almost certain to encounter them during your own career. Since this is so, it is useful to know two things about them: (1) how they operate—how, precisely, they manage to manipulate others for their own gain, and (2) how you can defend yourself against them.

FIGURE 6.5 Modern Recommendations for Gaining Power

Many best-selling books recommend tactics for gaining power that are similar to those suggested by Machiavelli.

High Machs: Their preferred strategies. Influence, as noted in chapter 12, is a central fact of life in modern organizations. Many persons direct a great deal of time and effort to persuading others to accept their views or recommendations.[27] Yet few are as effective in accomplishing this task as High Machs. What accounts for their success in this respect? Several factors seem to play a role. First, High Machs follow Machiavelli's advice about being *pragmatic*. As far as they are concerned, any means is justified so long as it helps them toward their goals. Thus, they are perfectly willing to lie, cheat, play "dirty tricks," or engage in virtually any actions that succeed. Second, High Machs often possess characteristics associated with successful persuasion, including confidence, eloquence, and competence. These traits, combined with their pure pragmatism, can be quite devastating. Third, High Machs are often very adept at choosing situations in which their preferred tactics are most likely to work. Such situations include those in which they can interact with the persons they intend to manipulate face-to-face, in which there are few clear rules, and in which others' emotions are running high. Since High Machs never let their "hearts rule their heads," they can take full advantage of the fact that others' emotions make them especially vulnerable to manipulation.[28] Finally, High Machs are skilled at various political maneuvers, such as forming coalitions with others. And as you might expect, in these coalitions, most of the advantages are theirs.

High Machs: How to protect yourself against them. Given their lack of concern with the welfare of other persons, and their seeming lack of conscience, High Machs are wily adversaries indeed. Yet, there *are* strategies for protecting yourself against them. Here are several that may prove useful.

    1. Expose them to others. One reason High Machs often get away with breaking promises, lying, and using "dirty tricks" is that in many cases, their victims choose to remain silent. This is hardly surprising; few people wish to call attention to the fact that they have been cheated or manipulated. Unfortunately, this understandable desire to protect one's ego plays directly into the High Mach's hands, leaving them free to repeat the process. One effective means of dealing with them involves exposing their unprincipled behavior. Once their actions are made public within an organization, High Machs may find it much harder to pursue their manipulative tactics on future occasions.

2. Pay attention to what others do, not what they say. High Machs are often masters at deception. They frequently succeed in convincing other people that they have their best interests at heart, just when they (the High Machs) are busy cutting the ground out from under them. While it is often difficult to see through such maneuvers, focusing on what others *do* rather than on what they *say* may help. If their actions suggest that they are cold-bloodedly manipulating the persons around them, even while loudly proclaiming commitment to such principles as loyalty and fair play, chances are good that they are Machiavellian in orientation and should be carefully avoided.

3. Avoid situations that give High Machs an edge. In order to assure their success, High Machs prefer to operate in certain types of situations—ones in which others' emotions run high and in which others are uncertain about how to proceed. The reason for this preference is simple: High Machs realize that under such conditions, many persons will be distracted and less likely to recognize the fact that they are being manipulated for someone else's gain. It is usually wise, therefore, to avoid such situations. And if this is not possible, at least refrain from making important decisions or commitments at that time. Such restraint may make it harder for High Machs to use you for their own benefit.

Together, these points may help you avoid falling under the spell—and into the clutches—of unprincipled, pragmatic High Machs. Given the presence of at least some High Machs in most organizations, and the dangers they pose to the unwary, it is worth keeping these suggestions, and the existence of this unsettling aspect of personality, firmly in mind.

Locus of Control: Perceived Control over One's Outcomes and Fate

Before going any further, please answer the questions in Table 6.2 below.

TABLE 6.2 Measuring Locus of Control
These items are similar to ones appearing on an inventory designed to measure one important aspect of personality—*locus of control.*

For each item below, indicate whether you feel that choice (a) or choice (b) is closer to your own beliefs.

1. (a) I am the master of my fate.
   (b) A great deal of what happens to me is probably a matter of choice.

2. (a) Promotions are earned through hard work and persistence.
   (b) Making a lot of money is largely a matter of getting the right breaks.

3. (a) People like me can change the course of world affairs if we make ourselves heard.
   (b) It is only wishful thinking to believe that we can really influence what happens in society at large.

4. (a) In my experience, I have noticed that there is usually a direct connection between how hard I study and the grades I get.
   (b) Many times the reactions of professors seem haphazard to me.

5. (a) Getting along with people is a skill that must be practiced.
   (b) It is almost impossible to figure out how to please some people.

How did you respond to these items? If you chose (a) for most, you probably believe that there is a direct link between your own actions and the kind of outcomes you experience. You feel that, by and large, you can influence your own fate: what you do in most situations really matters. If, instead, you selected (b) for most items, you probably feel that there is a weaker or less direct relationship between your own actions and the outcomes you obtain. You believe that often, forces beyond your direct control (e.g., luck, fate, others' actions), have strong effects on your life.[29]

The items in Table 6.2 are similar to ones on a test designed to measure this dimension—generally known as **locus of control**.[30] At one extreme are *Internals,* persons who believe that their outcomes stem mainly from their own actions. At the other are *Externals,* individuals who believe that much of what happens to them is the result of external causes beyond their direct control. As you can probably guess, most people fall somewhere in between, and are neither very high nor very low on this characteristic.

Locus of control is related to several important aspects of organizational behavior. First, and perhaps most important, the stronger individuals' beliefs in internal control, the stronger their tendencies to perceive direct links between their effort and their performance, and their performance and various rewards.[31] As we noted in chapter 3, such expectancies often play a key role in motivation, so differences with respect to locus of control can be reflected in differences in work motivation and task performance (see Figure 6.6). Perhaps as a result of these tendencies, Internals tend to be more successful in their careers than Externals. They hold higher level jobs, are promoted more quickly, and earn more money.[32] In addition, Internals report higher satisfaction with their jobs, and seem to cope better with high levels of stress than Externals.[33,34] Taking all these findings into account, it seems clear that from the point of view of organizations, Internals often make better employees than Externals. Thus, this may be one factor worth considering when making decisions relating to hiring or promotions.

One final point: locus of control, like many other personality characteristics or dimensions, is definitely open to change. When individuals find themselves in situations where good performance is both recognized and rewarded, even persons initially holding strong beliefs in external locus of control tend to shift toward a more internal orientation.

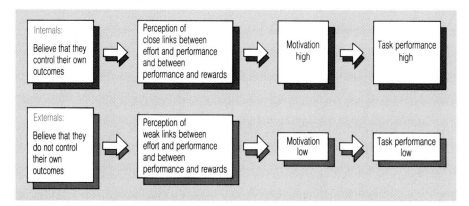

FIGURE 6.6 Locus of Control, Motivation, and Task Performance
Internals believe that they largely determine their own outcomes. As a result, they generally perceive clear links between effort and performance and between performance and rewards. High levels of motivation and task performance then follow. In contrast, *externals* believe that their outcomes are determined largely by forces beyond their control. As a result, their motivation and task performance tend to be lower in many situations.

This is one more reason why careful attention to establishing effective reward systems is an important task for all organizations and managers.

Social Skills: Individual Differences in the Ability to Get Along with Others

Consider two individuals. One is viewed as brilliant and hard-working by most other members of her organization. However, she is also widely disliked and perceived as difficult to get along with. The other is viewed as merely competent in job skills and average in effort, but is extremely popular with peers, subordinates, and supervisors. Which individual is likely to get the next promotion? While this will depend heavily on the evaluation and promotion procedures within the organization, the odds are quite good that it is the second individual, the more popular one, who will get the nod. A considerable body of evidence points to the conclusion that being liked by others is often a much better predictor of success than intellectual brilliance, high motivation, or other desirable qualities.[35]

While this state of affairs may strike you as somewhat unfair, it appears to be a fact of life in most work settings, and given this, a very practical question arises: what determines whether, and to what extent, someone is liked or disliked by others? As you can probably guess, many factors are involved. Research findings suggest, however, that one of the most important of these is the possession of various *social skills*.[36] Such skills, in turn, seem to center primarily around personal characteristics that enable individuals to communicate effectively with others. People possessing a high level of social skills communicate well and clearly, are perceived as honest and credible, and make very good first impressions. In contrast, persons lacking in social skills are relatively poor at interpersonal communication and are perceived negatively by the people around them.

In recent years, efforts have been made to identify the basic or most important components of social skills. The results of this research suggest six that are most important:

1. **emotional expressivity**—the ability to express emotions nonverbally (e.g., through gestures)
2. **emotional sensitivity**—the ability to "read" the emotional and nonverbal communications of others
3. **emotional control**—skill in stifling spontaneous expressions when this is necessary or feigning emotions that are not really experienced
4. **social expressivity**—the ability to speak fluently and engage others in social interaction
5. **social sensitivity**—the ability to understand others' verbal statements, plus general knowledge of social norms (knowing what's considered appropriate in various situations)
6. **social control**—skill at self-presentation (presenting oneself to others in a favorable light) and at playing various social roles (e.g., the respectful subordinate, the caring supervisor).

A questionnaire designed to measure individual differences in such skills (the *Social Skills Inventory*) has been devised by Riggio; sample items from it are presented in Table 6.3 (on page 202).[37]

Are individuals high in such skills actually more likable than those who are relatively low? A study by Friedman, Riggio, and Casella indicates that this is indeed the case.[38] In this investigation, male and female students first completed several tests designed to measure their social skills (e.g., emotional expressivity, ability to present themselves

TABLE 6.3 Measuring Social Skills
Items similar to the ones presented here are used to measure individual differences in social skills.

ASPECT OF SOCIAL SKILLS	SAMPLE ITEM
Emotional Expressivity	I have been told that I have an expressive face.
Emotional Sensitivity	I can always tell how people feel about me.
Emotional Control	I can hide my real feelings from just about anyone.
Social Expressivity	I usually take the first step and introduce myself to strangers.
Social Sensitivity	I often worry about making a good impression on others.
Social Control	I find it easy to play different roles in different situations.

(Source: Based on items by Riggio, 1986; see Note 35.)

favorably, social sensitivity). Then, they were videotaped as they entered a room and interacted briefly with two strangers (accomplices of the researchers). Finally, a group of twelve raters watched these tapes, and evaluated the likability of each subject. Results indicated that the higher these individuals were on social skills, the higher the ratings they received. Further, social skills exerted a stronger effect on their rated likability than did their physical attractiveness.

Other findings indicate that persons high in social skills are viewed as more honest and believable both when telling the truth and when lying than persons low in social skills.[39] These results suggest that one reason socially skilled individuals are often successful in their careers is that they are trusted more by others, and so are more effective at persuasion. Whatever the precise mechanisms involved, though, one fact is clear: expressive, articulate, tactful persons have a definite edge in many situations. Fortunately, training programs designed to enhance various social skills exist and some, at least, appear to be quite effective.[40] Several of these programs are highly popular, and are completed by thousands of persons each year. Participation in them may well prove worthwhile for individuals who suspect that their careers, and personal adjustment, are being hampered by deficits in this important dimension.

Self-Monitoring: Public Image versus Private Reality

Consider the following question: to what extent do you behave differently with different groups of people or in different situations? Answering may be difficult, for most individuals do adjust their behavior in this respect to some degree. For example, most behave somewhat differently when interacting with subordinates than when interacting with their bosses. Yet considerable individual differences in this tendency also seem to exist. At one extreme are persons who readily adjust their own behavior so as to produce positive reactions in others. They are known as *high self-monitors,* and their actions are usually guided by the requirements of a given situation. As high self-monitors themselves report, they are indeed "different with different persons and in different situations."[41] At the other end of this dimension of **self-monitoring** are persons who seem less aware of or concerned with their impact on others. Their actions usually reflect their inner feelings and attitudes, and they are less likely to change or adjust in each new context.

At this point, we should note that self-monitoring actually involves three major, and somewhat distinct, tendencies. One is the willingness to be the center of attention—a tendency to behave in outgoing, extraverted ways. (This is closely related to the social skill of emotional expressiveness.) A second tendency reflects individuals' sensitivity to the reactions of others. Finally, a third involves individuals' ability (and willingness) to adjust their behavior so as to induce positive reactions in others.[42]

Whatever the precise components or skills involved in self-monitoring, individual differences along this dimension (which can be measured by any of several tests) are related to important aspects of organizational behavior. First, high self-monitors are often more effective than low self-monitors in jobs that require *boundary-spanning*—communicating and interacting with different groups of persons who, because of contrasting goals, training, or skills, "speak different languages."[43] Since they can readily adjust their actions to the norms, expectations, and styles of each group, high self-monitors are more successful in dealing with them, and this enhances their performance. Boundary-spanning roles are very important in most organizations, so assigning persons high in self-monitoring to such positions can yield substantial benefits.

Second, self-monitoring appears to be related to performance in other tasks or roles, especially ones requiring clear communication. In one recent study concerned with this relationship, Larkin asked college students to think of the best or worst instructor they had ever had.[44] When they rated these individuals in terms of self-monitoring, clear differences emerged: the best teachers were rated much higher (see Figure 6.7). In a follow-up study, Larkin asked participants to imagine that they were

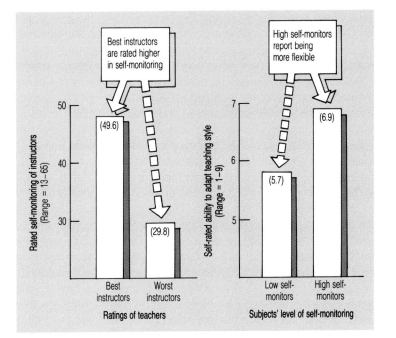

FIGURE 6.7 Self-monitoring and Task Performance
Subjects rated the best instructors they had in college as higher in self-monitoring than the worst instructors. Also, subjects high in self-monitoring reported being better able than subjects low in self-monitoring to match their own teaching style to the needs of persons they might tutor. (Source: Based on data from Larkin, 1987; see Note 44.)

going to tutor two students, one who was very tense and nervous, and one who was overconfident. Subjects then rated the extent to which they felt they could change their teaching style to fit the needs of each individual. As predicted, persons who were high in self-monitoring reported greater flexibility than those who were low in self-monitoring (see Figure 6.7 on page 203).

Finally, self-monitoring is also related to certain aspects of organizational conflict. Persons high in self-monitoring report stronger tendencies to resolve conflicts through collaboration or compromise, and weaker tendencies to resolve conflicts through avoidance or competition than persons low in self-monitoring. In short, they seem to approach conflicts in a more conciliatory manner, and with greater concern for long-range solutions than low self-monitors.[45] (We'll consider organizational conflict in detail in chapter 13.)

In light of all these findings, it seems clear that self-monitoring is an aspect of personality with important implications for understanding organizational behavior.

Self-Efficacy: Beliefs in One's Ability to Perform Various Tasks

Suppose that two individuals are assigned the same task by their supervisor, and that each must work on it alone. One is confident of her ability to carry it out successfully, while the other has serious doubts on this score. Which person is more likely to succeed? Assuming that all other factors (e.g., differences in their ability or motivation) are held constant, it is reasonable to predict that the first will do better. She is higher in what has been termed **self-efficacy**—belief in one's capability to perform a specific task.[46]

When considered in the context of a given task, self-efficacy is not, strictly speaking, an aspect of personality. However, individuals seem to acquire general expectations concerning their ability to perform a wide range of tasks in many different contexts. Such generalized beliefs about self-efficacy are stable over time, and can reasonably be viewed as another important dimension along which individuals differ in a consistent, stable manner.

How do feelings of self-efficacy develop? According to Bandura, the leading expert on this factor, partly through direct experiences, in which individuals perform various tasks and receive feedback on their success, and partly through *vicarious experiences,* in which they observe others performing various tasks and attaining varying levels of success at them.[47] Whatever their precise source, beliefs about self-efficacy appear to exert strong effects on task performance. The stronger individuals' beliefs that they can perform successfully, the higher their performance actually tends to be.

Not surprisingly, research on self-efficacy suggests that it is closely related to work motivation in many settings (see chapter 3). First, feelings of self-efficacy influence the difficulty of goals chosen by individuals. The higher self-efficacy, the more difficult and challenging such goals tend to be.[48] Second, self-efficacy may moderate reactions to various types of feedback. Individuals high in self-efficacy may respond to negative feedback (information suggesting that they are not reaching their goals or meeting established standards of performance) with increased effort and motivation. In contrast, persons low in self-efficacy may give up and reduce their motivation in the face of such feedback.[49] (See Figure 6.8.) Interestingly, a recent study by Baron suggests that feedback that is *destructive* in nature (e.g., it is inconsiderate in tone, general rather than specific, contains threats) reduces both feelings of self-efficacy and self-set goals.[50] Thus, such feedback—which is often delivered by managers when they become angry with subordinates and lose their tempers—may have lasting, negative effects on motivation.

Self-efficacy is a relatively new topic of study in OB, but has already been identified

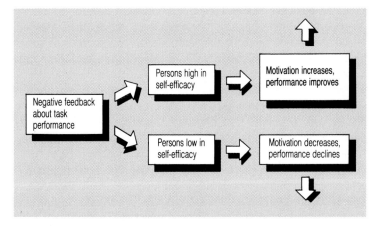

FIGURE 6.8   Effects of Negative Feedback on Persons Low and High in Self-efficacy
Following the receipt of negative feedback on their performance, individuals low in self-efficacy experience reductions in motivation. As a result, their performance may decline still further. In contrast, persons high in self-efficacy react to such feedback with increased motivation and improved performance.

as having important implications for several processes.[51] First, given its role in motivation, it may affect performance on many different tasks. Second, it may play a role in training of employees and in career counseling with them (see chapter 9). Low self-efficacy with respect to specific tasks may help pinpoint areas in which additional skills or training are needed. And more general performance problems may be traced, ultimately, to generalized, low levels of this factor. Third, self-efficacy may be related to reactions to performance appraisals. As noted above, individuals high in self-efficacy may respond to negative feedback in more constructive ways than those low in self-efficacy. Finally, low self-efficacy may pose an internal barrier to advancement by some members of previously disadvantaged minority groups. Such persons may doubt their own ability to perform certain tasks. This, in turn, may actually reduce their performance in these areas. To the extent that this is so, self-efficacy may be an important factor to consider in efforts to overcome the harmful effects of prejudice and discrimination.

Self-Esteem: The Importance of Self-Evaluations

Beliefs about one's ability to perform specific tasks are an important part of the *self-concept*—individuals' conceptions of their own abilities, traits, and skills. Yet, they are only a small portion of this concept. Another important aspect concerns **self-esteem**—the extent to which people hold positive or negative views about themselves. Persons high in self-esteem evaluate themselves favorably—they believe that they possess many desirable traits and qualities. In contrast, persons low in self-esteem evaluate themselves unfavorably—they conclude that they are lacking in important respects, and that they possess characteristics others find unappealing. Do such feelings affect behavior in organizational settings? Considerable evidence indicates that they do.[52]

First, persons high in self-esteem often report higher levels of job satisfaction and motivation than persons low in self-esteem. Second, they actually perform at higher levels on some tasks and in some settings. Third, and perhaps even more unsettling, persons high in self-esteem are more successful in identifying, and then obtaining, appropriate jobs. Evidence pointing to such conclusions is provided by a study conducted by Ellis and Taylor.[53]

These researchers asked business school seniors to complete several questionnaires. Some of these provided measures of subjects' self-esteem, while others yielded evidence on the nature and success of subjects' job search (e.g., the sources of information they used, the number of job offers they actually received). In addition, ratings of participants by organizational recruiters who had interviewed them were also obtained. Ellis and Taylor predicted that persons low in self-esteem would generally conduct less adequate job searches and attain less favorable results than persons high in self-esteem. Specifically, they expected that the lower subjects' self-esteem, the less likely they would be to use informal sources of information (e.g., friends, relatives), the fewer offers they would receive, and the lower the ratings they would get from interviewers. Results supported all of these hypotheses. Thus, low self-esteem appeared to be quite costly for these young individuals about to launch their careers.

Although our comments so far sound somewhat discouraging, we can conclude on a more positive note. Low self-esteem can indeed be damaging to individuals' careers, but it *can* be changed. Several practical techniques for enhancing self-esteem, and thereby countering its negative effects, exist. For example, it has been found that one serious problem faced by low self-esteem persons is their tendency to show a pattern of attributions opposite to that of most others. Instead of demonstrating the kind of *self-serving bias* we described in chapter 4, in which successes are attributed largely to internal causes (their own sterling qualities), but failures are attributed to external ones, low self-esteem people show opposite tendencies. They often blame themselves for failures, and refuse to take credit for success (see Figure 6.9). Training designed to reverse these tendencies can help boost both the confidence and later performance of low self-esteem persons.[54] Other techniques include exposing low self-esteem persons to positive feedback or success, and helping them overcome the feelings of depression and hopelessness from which they often suffer. Through such procedures, the harmful effects of a negative self-image can be reduced. Then, both individuals and the organizations in which they work can reap important benefits.

Work-Related Motives: Achievement, Power, and Affiliation

Some people, such as the young woman shown in Figure 6.10, seem to yearn for success. Others concentrate on status; they want to be admired and respected by others. And some individuals seem primarily concerned with friendship or love; pleas-

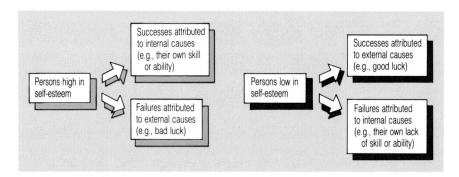

FIGURE 6.9 Self-esteem and Attributions for Successes and Failures
Persons low in self-esteem often demonstrate a pattern of attributions for successes and failures opposite to that of persons high in self-esteem. They blame themselves for negative outcomes and refuse to take credit for positive ones.

"Please, sir, I want it all."

FIGURE 6.10   Achievement Motivation: An Extreme Case
The person shown here is certainly high in at least one personal motive—the desire for success or achievement. (Source: Drawing by W. Miller; © 1986 The New Yorker Magazine, Inc.)

ant, satisfying relations with others are what they crave most. Do such differences in motivation play a role in organizational behavior? They certainly do. Differences with respect to several basic motives can affect performance on many tasks, success in leadership roles, and a wide range of other outcomes. We will now examine the impact of three such motives—**achievement, power,** and **affiliation motivation.** (Recall that we considered several theories of motivation concerned with individual needs in chapter 3.)

Achievement motivation: The quest for excellence. As its name suggests, **achievement motivation** (sometimes termed the *need for achievement*) relates to the strength of individuals' desire to excel—to succeed at difficult tasks and do them better than anyone else. Persons high in such motivation show several consistent tendencies.[55] First, they are task-oriented in outlook. Their major concern is getting things done and accomplishing concrete goals. Additional considerations, such as good relations with others, are of less concern to them. Second, they tend to prefer situations involving moderate levels of risk or difficulty. In contrast, persons low in achievement motivation tend to prefer situations involving either very low or very high levels of risk. Why this preference for moderate risk among persons high in the achievement motive? Because situations involving moderate risk are ones in which the odds of success are good, but are still sufficiently challenging to make the effort worthwhile. Persons low in achievement motivation, in contrast, prefer very low or high levels of risk because in the former they are almost certain to succeed, while in the latter they can attribute failure to external causes (e.g., the extreme difficulty of the task). Third, persons high in achievement motivation strongly desire feedback on their performance. This allows them to adjust their goals in terms of current conditions and to know when, and to what degree, they have succeeded.

Given their strong desire to excel, it seems reasonable to predict that persons high in achievement motivation will attain greater success in their careers than others. To some extent, this is true. Persons high in achievement motivation gain promotions more rapidly than persons low in such motivation, at least early in their careers.[56] However, persons high in achievement motivation do not always make superior managers. In fact, sometimes they are worse in this role than those who are lower in this motive. This is due to two factors. First, persons high in achievement motivation want to do everything themselves—they are reluctant to delegate. This gets them into serious trouble in many organizations. Second, they desire immediate feedback on their work. Often, this is unavailable, and its absence can interfere with their efficiency.

Affiliation and power motivation: Two sides of the same coin? At first glance, the desire to be in charge (**power motivation**) and the desire to have close, friendly relations with others (**affiliation motivation**) appear to be unrelated. It is possible to imagine people high on both dimensions, people who are low on both, and people who are high on one and low on the other. Research findings suggest, however, that where organizational behavior is concerned, the two are often linked.

First, consider the question of managerial success. What kind of individuals are most successful in this role? One possibility, suggested by McClelland and Boyatzis, is as follows: persons *high* in power motivation but *low* in affiliation motivation. Such persons will focus on gaining influence over others while at the same time avoiding the trap of being unduly concerned about being liked by them. In other words, they will seek power and influence, but won't shy away from the tough decisions (and actions) often required by this quest. (According to McClelland and Boyatzis, another characteristic—a high degree of *self-control*, is also important for managerial success. Persons who easily lose their temper or show a low degree of self-discipline won't succeed as managers even if they possess a high need for power and a low need for affiliation.) Are individuals who possess this combination of traits—known as the **leadership motivation pattern** (or **LMP**) actually more effective managers than those who don't? A study by McClelland and Boyatzis suggests that this is so.[57]

In this investigation, managers' levels of power motivation, affiliation motivation, and self-control were assessed by means of appropriate tests. On the basis of this information, the managers were then divided into two groups: those who demonstrated the LMP and those who did not. Next, the researchers obtained information about subjects' job level eight and sixteen years after they joined their organizations. Results offered clear support for the role of the leadership motive pattern in managerial success, at least for managers who held non-technical positions. For this group, persons who possessed the LMP were much more likely to be promoted to higher-level jobs than those who did not. (These findings did not hold true for managers holding technical jobs because for them, promotion depended mainly on technical competence, not the ability to deal effectively with others.)

These findings, and those of several other studies, suggest that individual differences with respect to several motives are closely linked to important aspects of organizational behavior. The nature of this relationship, however, is far from simple. To understand how individuals' motives influence their job performance or careers, we must take into account not only the motives themselves, but also the combinations or patterns in which they occur, the specific jobs being performed, and the organizational context in which these motives operate. Only when the complex interplay of such factors is given full consideration can knowledge about individuals' motives yield valuable insights into their behavior at work and in work settings. (Do individual differences in achievement, affiliation, and power motivation play a role in the success of political leaders as well as business managers? For intriguing evidence that they do, see the **Research Perspective** on page 209.)

Personal Motives and Presidential Politics: Does Having the Right Motives Make a Leader Great?

In the two hundred years since it emerged as an independent nation, the United States has had thirty-five different presidents. Some have been acclaimed as "great" while others have been viewed as merely adequate—or worse! What accounts for such differences? Many possibilities exist, but one is directly linked to the present discussion of work-related motives. Perhaps popular or great political leaders are ones whose motives match those of their society. In other words, perhaps the closer the fit between a leader's own pattern of motives and those present among his or her followers, the more popular the leader will be and therefore, the more successful at accomplishing major goals. Evidence suggesting that this is actually the case has recently been provided by Winter.[58]

In an ingenious study, he examined the inaugural addresses of the first thirty-four American presidents, and scored these speeches for the presence of three key motives: achievement, affiliation, and power. As shown by Table 6.4, large differences along these dimensions existed. Winter then estimated the level of each of these motives prevailing in American society at the time each president was elected. This information was derived from careful analysis of popular novels, children's

books, and even hymns. (Systematic techniques for assessing the level of each of these motivations from popular literature have been developed.) Obviously, there are many complexities with respect to such data. Modern presidents don't usually write their own speeches, so the content of their speeches may reflect the motives of members of their staffs rather than their own. Since most politicians do approve and modify their important speeches, however, it seems likely that the themes present in these documents do reflect their own underlying motives.

Putting such potential problems aside, Winter then correlated the scores of each president on achievement, affiliation, and power with an index of their popularity (the percent of the vote they received), and with ratings of their "greatness" provided by more than five hundred historians. Results were intriguing, to say the least. First, as Winter predicted, the closer the match between a president's apparent motives and those of society, the greater his popularity. Second, and perhaps more surprising, the closer this match, the *lower* the presidents' ratings of greatness. In sum, it appeared that while popularity was indeed a function of the closeness of leader-society match, greatness was linked to the presidents' being different—holding a

TABLE 6.4   The Personal Motives of American Presidents

Careful analysis of the inaugural speeches of U.S. presidents indicates that they have differed greatly in terms of achievement, affiliation, and power motivation. (Scores are the number of images relating to each motive per 1,000 words in each president's inaugural speech.)

President	SCORE ON EACH MOTIVE		
	Achievement	Affiliation	Power
George Washington	3.85	3.86	4.62
Thomas Jefferson	5.65	3.30	6.59
Andrew Jackson	4.48	2.69	5.38
Abraham Lincoln	3.34	2.23	6.97
Theodore Roosevelt	8.14	1.02	4.02
Franklin Roosevelt	6.37	2.12	8.50
John Kennedy	5.90	9.59	11.81
Richard Nixon	8.94	8.00	7.06
Jimmy Carter	10.60	4.89	8.16
Ronald Reagan	7.78	3.28	9.01

(Source: Based on data from Winter, 1987; see Note 58.)

pattern of motives that contrasted somewhat with those of society at large. (Among the leaders who were most discrepant from society at the time of their election were Washington, Lincoln, Truman, and Kennedy.) These findings suggest that there may be at least a grain of truth in the popular notion that in order to be considered "great," a leader must truly lead—he or she must change society in important ways, not merely reflect its current views. Regardless of whether this interpretation is accepted, one point seems clear: the pattern of achievement, affiliation, and power motivation shown by political candidates may play an important role in determining whether they are elected, and how successfully they perform once they are in office.

Measuring Personality: Some Basic Methods

Physical traits such as height and weight can be measured directly. Various aspects of personality, however, cannot be assessed this way. There are no rulers for measuring ambition, no thermometers for assessing self-esteem, and no scales for "weighing" social skills. How can differences among individuals on these important dimensions be quantified? Several methods exist for accomplishing this task. Among the most important of these are *inventories* or *questionnaires,* and **projective techniques.**

Inventories and Questionnaires: Assessing Personality through Self-Report

By far the most widely used method for assessing personality involves the administration of *inventories* or *questionnaires.* These consist of a series of questions or statements to which individuals respond in various ways. Persons completing such tests may be asked to indicate whether various statements are true or false about themselves, or to report on whether and how often they experience certain feelings. Their answers to these items are then scored by means of special forms and compared with those obtained from hundreds or even thousands of other persons who have also taken the test. In this way, an individual's relative standing on the trait or traits being measured can be determined. For example, it might be found that an individual applying for a job as a loan officer at a bank has scored higher than 90 percent of recent college graduates on a test that measures willingness to take risks. Obviously, this information could have a direct bearing on the decision to hire or not hire this person. (He would not appear to be well suited for this position!) Similarly, it might be found that an individual seeking a job in customer relations, in which she must soothe angry people, scores very high on a test of social skills. Again, this could be useful in deciding whether she is suited for the job in question. (On this basis, at least, she would seem to be an appropriate choice.) Because a great deal is known about constructing inventories or questionnaires, such measures of personality are viewed as very useful. In fact, this is the method used to assess most of the traits or characteristics discussed earlier in this chapter. (One notable exception: Type A behavior is often assessed by means of a structured interview, in which the interviewer focuses on various stylistic components that reveal an individual's standing on this dimension.)

Projective Techniques: Ambiguous Stimuli and Personality Assessment

Look at the drawing in the photo in Figure 6.11. What is happening? Now, consider these questions: Would your interpretation differ from those of other persons? And

FIGURE 6.11 Projective Techniques: An Example
Drawings similar to the one in this photo are used in a popular projective technique for measuring personality (the TAT).

would this reveal anything about differences between your personality and others'? Another means for measuring personality assumes that the answer to both questions is "yes." Briefly, such **projective techniques** assume that if different persons are exposed to ambiguous stimuli, each will report something different. The pattern of these differences, in turn, will reveal much about important aspects of personality.

Actually, the illustration in Figure 6.12 is similar to the ones contained in a widely used test designed to measure individual differences in achievement and power motivation, the *Thematic Apperception Test* or *TAT*.[59] This test consists of a series of ambiguous drawings, and people taking it are asked to make up a story about each. These are carefully analyzed for certain basic themes, in accordance with highly specific scoring procedures. Considerable evidence suggests that the TAT provides valuable information about individual differences with respect to several personal motives. However, such evidence is lacking for several other projective techniques (e.g., the famous *Rorschach Ink Blot Test*). Thus, scores derived from such tests should be interpreted with a great deal of caution. Please note, by the way, that the task of scoring and interpreting projectives tests is complex. It should only be performed by individuals who have had extensive training in such procedures. (How can organizations put measures of personality and other individual differences to practical use? For information on this topic, please see the **Management Perspective** below.)

OB: A MANAGEMENT PERSPECTIVE

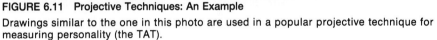

Putting Personality Measures to Practical Use: Assessment Centers and the Identification of Managerial Talent

A key task organizations face is identifying talented persons—ones suited for management or leadership roles. Many techniques for accomplishing this task have been developed, but one of the most successful has been the conduction of **assessment centers**.[60] The rationale behind these procedures is as follows:

it is assumed that certain traits or characteristics are closely related to success as a manager. To the extent this is so, careful assessment of these characteristics should prove useful in predicting individuals' potential for this role.

Assessment centers are much more elaborate in

scope than the techniques for measuring personality (or other individual differences) we have considered so far. Typically, they require two or three days rather than one or two hours of individuals' time. During this period, the persons being assessed are asked to perform a wide range of tasks designed to simulate conditions and activities they might encounter in their current (or future) jobs (see Figure 6.12). For example, one assessment center, run for many years by AT&T, requires two days of testing and includes an "in-basket" exercise (in which individuals must deal with a number of memos, letters, and other items that might normally appear on a manager's desk each day), leaderless group discussions, simulated interviews, paper-and-pencil tests, and various management games or simulations.

Another key aspect of assessment centers is their emphasis on a number of different characteristics. Information relating to administrative skills, work motivation, social skills, creativity, maturity, independence, and many other traits is gathered. In some cases, the individuals who conduct such assessments are specially trained professionals. In other cases, they are people highly experienced in the tasks and jobs involved (practicing managers). In many assessment centers, several raters assess each participant and then discuss their reactions until they reach a consensus. In others, individual ratings by each assessor are maintained, and no consensus is sought. Regardless of such differences, all assessment centers involve efforts to measure a number of work-related characteristics through a wide range of tasks and careful observations by several different raters.

While assessment centers often focus on identifying management potential or talent, they have also been used for several other purposes as well. These include selection of employees, placement, promotion, and career management or development (see chapter 9). That they are useful in all these respects is suggested by a recent review of published literature on this topic by Gaugler and her colleagues.[61] This review employed a technique known as **meta-analysis,** which statistically combines the results of many different studies to determine the strength and consistency of the findings they report. Results indicated that in general, assessment centers are indeed useful: the information they provide is helpful in predicting management potential, future performance, and other important outcomes. However, assessment centers

FIGURE 6.12 Assessment Centers: One Technique for Measuring Managerial Talent
Assessment centers are used to measure and predict managerial success. Persons participating in them perform a wide range of tasks assumed to be related to activities required by managerial jobs.

were not found equally valid for all purposes. They appeared to be most successful when used for early identification of managerial talent, but least successful when used to determine which individuals should be promoted. Further, they were more successful in predicting future potential than in predicting ratings of current job performance. Finally, assessment centers seemed to be most successful when trained professionals (e.g., experts on personality or individual differences) rather than coworkers or supervisors served as assessors, and when several evaluation devices were used.

The findings reported by Gaugler et al., and those in related research, suggest that assessment centers can be a useful tool, yielding important practical benefits.[62] We should add, however, that assessment centers are certainly not an unmixed blessing. They are very costly to conduct, and negative ratings, if revealed to participants, can undermine their confidence, and hence their value to their organizations. Still, assessment centers appear to represent a potentially valuable technique for measuring important differences between individuals and for choosing those persons most suited for increased management responsibility.

Using Information about Personality: Some Words of Caution

Personality is a fascinating topic. Almost everyone is interested in other people, and insights into the characteristics that make them unique are intriguing, to say the least. Further, as we have already seen, many aspects of personality appear to be related to important forms of organizational behavior. Given these facts, it is hardly surprising that many organizations have sought to gather such information and put it to use in several ways (e.g., in selecting employees, conducting performance appraisals). While we fully understand the temptation do so, there are several reasons for exercising a healthy degree of caution in this regard.

First, some measures of personality are of doubtful *reliability* and *validity*. They do not yield the same scores when applied to the same persons on different occasions (i.e., they are unreliable). And they may not actually measure what they claim to measure (they are invalid). To the extent this is so, it is unwise to base important decisions on them, for they will not serve as useful predictors of future job performance.

Second, even when measures of personality are both reliable and valid, relationships between the traits they assess and organizational behavior are often complex. For example, as we noted earlier, Type A persons do *not* always perform better than Type B persons; the nature of the tasks in question and several other factors determine which of these groups has an edge. For this reason, information about this and many other aspects of personality must be interpreted with care.

Third, when using information about personality, it is all too easy to fall into the trap of allowing the labels we assign to specific persons to influence our perceptions of them. In other words, once we have labeled someone as being Type A, a high self-monitor, or low in social skills, these labels may color our perceptions of everything they say or do. The result: they (and we) are locked into these categories, even if they are false.

For all these reasons, it is important to exercise caution in the use of information about others' personalities. Such information can indeed be revealing, but should only be employed when three conditions are met: (1) the information itself is accurate (it is reliable and valid); (2) it has direct bearing on performance or other key aspects of organizational behavior; and (3) the persons who interpret and use it have sufficient training and experience to do so adequately. If uncertainty exists with respect to any of these conditions, the best course of action is a conservative one: refrain from using such information for organizational purposes until these concerns have been eliminated.

SUMMARY AND REVIEW

The Nature of Personality. **Personality** refers to the unique but stable set of characteristics and behaviors that set each individual apart from others. It is influenced by genetic factors as well as by experience, and plays an important role in several aspects of organizational behavior (e.g., task performance, organizational conflict).

Work-Related Aspects of Personality. Several aspects of personality are especially relevant to organizational behavior. Persons demonstrating the **Type A** behavior pattern show a high level of competitiveness, time urgency, and hostility or irritability. They are more likely than Type B persons to experience heart attacks. Type A persons perform better than Type B persons on some tasks (e.g., ones requiring speed), but are worse on others (e.g., tasks requiring considered judgment). Differences in the performance of Type A and Type B persons appear to exist in many different cultures.

Type A persons lose their tempers more often than Type B persons and report being involved in organizational conflict with greater frequency.

Individuals who adopt a manipulative approach to their relations with others are sometimes described as being high in **Machiavellianism.** Such persons are not influenced by considerations of loyalty, friendship, or ethics. Rather, they do whatever is necessary to get their way and to win in a wide range of contexts.

Individuals who possess effective *social skills* often advance in their careers more quickly than persons lacking such skills. They are better able to express and manage their own emotions, better able to read the emotions of others, and better at interpersonal communication. Persons high in social skills are generally liked more by others. Several different programs exist for enhancing individuals' social skills.

Persons high in **self-monitoring** are expressive, concerned with making good impressions on others, and can adapt their behavior to match requirements of a given situation. High self-monitors make more effective boundary-spanners than low self-monitors, and are rated as being better teachers by many students.

Individuals who believe that they possess the capability of performing various tasks (those high in **self-efficacy**) often attain higher levels of performance than persons lacking in such confidence (those low in self-efficacy). Persons high in self-efficacy react to negative feedback by increasing their effort and motivation. In contrast, those low in self-efficacy show reductions in motivation and subsequent performance. Self-efficacy is related to a wide range of organizational processes (e.g., personnel selection, performance appraisal).

Several personal motives (**achievement, power,** and **affiliation motivation**) are relevant to organizational behavior. Persons high in the need for achievement advance in their careers more quickly than persons low in the need for achievement. Individuals showing the **leadership motivation pattern** (high need for power, low need for affiliation, high self-control) are more successful as managers than persons not demonstrating this pattern. Careful analysis of the inaugural addresses of American presidents indicates that these persons have differed sharply in terms of achievement, power, and affiliation motivation. Those most similar to their societies in this respect during their terms in office have been most popular.

Measuring Personality. Personality is often assessed by means of *inventories* and *questionnaires* in which individuals answer various questions about themselves. It is sometimes also measured by means of **projective techniques.** Here, individuals respond to ambiguous stimuli. The responses they give are assumed to reflect their underlying traits or motives. Finally, personality (and many other individual differences) can be measured in **assessment centers**—complex procedures in which individuals perform a wide range of tasks assumed to be related to their current or future jobs. Recent evidence suggests that assessment centers are effective in measuring managerial potential.

Key Terms

achievement motivation: The desire to meet standards of excellence and accomplish tasks more successfully than others.

affiliation motivation: The desire to establish and maintain positive relations with others.

assessment centers: An approach to measuring personality based on the ratings of individuals' behavior in a wide range of tasks performed over a two or three day period.

leadership motivation pattern (LMP): A pattern consisting of high need for power, low need for affiliation, and high degree of self-control. This pattern of motives appears to be related to managerial success.

locus of control: The extent to which individuals believe that their outcomes are determined by their own actions (*Internals*) or by factors beyond their direct control (*Externals*).

Machiavellianism: A personality trait involving willingness to manipulate or use others for one's own purposes.

meta-analysis: A statistical technique for assessing the strength and consistency of research findings across a number of different studies.

personality: The unique but stable pattern of characteristics that sets each individual apart from others.

power motivation: Motivation to exert influence over others.

projective techniques: Methods for measuring personality, in which individuals respond to ambiguous stimuli (e.g., drawings, inkblots). Their responses, presumably, provide insights into their major personality traits.

self-efficacy: Individuals' beliefs concerning their ability to perform specific tasks successfully.

self-esteem: Individuals' evaluations of their own traits and behavior.

self-monitoring: An aspect of personality involving the extent to which an individual's behavior reflects his or her underlying attitudes and values, or efforts to adjust actions to current, situational conditions. Self-monitoring also involves expressiveness and willingness to be the center of attention.

Type A behavior pattern: A pattern of behavior involving a high level of competitiveness, time urgency, and irritability. This pattern is related to several aspects of health, performance on many tasks, and interpersonal relations.

Type B behavior pattern: A pattern of behavior opposite to that shown by Type A individuals.

QUESTIONS FOR DISCUSSION

1. Why do individuals with contrasting personalities often act in similar ways in similar situations?

2. Suppose you had to choose one of two individuals for a middle management position. One of these persons is Type A and the other is Type B. Which would you select? Why?

3. Describe three useful personality characteristics for an individual whose job requires frequent negotiations with others.

4. Imagine that one of your subordinates was a "fatalist"—he believed everything that happened to him was beyond his control. What might you do to change such views?

5. On the basis of the information contained in this chapter, do you believe that some individuals are truly "born to lead" while others are "born to follow"? Why or why not?

6. Suppose that you were given the task of identifying talented young people in your organization who should be groomed for the "fast track" to upper management. How would you identify such persons?

7. Do you think that all human beings, even those living in very different cultures, differ in terms of the same set of personality traits? If so, what might these basic traits be?

NOTES

1. Carver, C. S., & Scheier, M. F. (1988). *Perspectives on personality.* Boston: Allyn & Bacon.

2. Mischel, W. (1985). *Personality: Lost or found? Identifying when individual differences make a difference.* Paper presented at the meetings of the American Psychological Association, Los Angeles.

3. Larsen, R. J. (1987). The stability of mood variability: A special analytic approach to daily mood assessments. *Journal of Personality and Social Psychology, 52,* 1195–1204.

4. Costa, P. T., Jr., & McCrae, R. R. (1988). Personality in adulthood: A six-year longitudinal study of self-reports and spouse ratings on the NEO personality inventory. *Journal of Personality and Social Psychology, 54,* 853–865.

5. See Note 1.

6. Kenrick, D. T., & Stringfield, D. O. (1980). Personality traits and the eye of the beholder: Crossing some traditional philosophical boundaries in the search for consistency in all people. *Psychological Review, 87,* 88–104.

7. Snyder, M. (1987). *Public appearances/Private realities: The psychology of self-monitoring.* New York: Freeman.

8. See Note 7.

9. Aronoff, J., & Wilson, J. P. (1985). *Personality in the social process.* Hillsdale, NJ: Erlbaum.

10. Bouchard, T. J., Jr. (1984). Twins reared together and apart: What they tell us about human diversity. In S.W. Fox (Ed.), *Individuality and determinism.* New York: Plenum.

11. Ferris, G. R., Bergin, T. G., & Wayne, J. (1988). Personal characteristics, job performance, and absenteeism of public school teachers. *Journal of Applied Social Psychology, 18,* 552–563.

12. Tenopyr, M. L., & Oeltjen, P. D. (1982). Personnel selection and classification. *Annual Review of Psychology, 33,* 581–618.

13. Paunonen, S. V., Jackson, D. N., & Oberman, S. M. (1987). Personnel selection decisions: Effects of applicant personality and the letter of reference. *Organizational Behavior and Human Decision Processes, 40,* 96–114.

14. Friedman, M., & Rosenman, R. H. (1974). *Type A behavior and your heart.* New York: Knopf.

15. Glass, D. C. (1977). *Behavior patterns, stress, and coronary disease.* Hillsdale, NJ: Erlbaum.

16. See Note 14.

17. Kirmeyer, S. L. (1988). Coping with competing demands: Interruption and the Type A pattern. *Journal of Applied Psychology, 73,* 621–629.

18. Holmes, D. S., McGilley, B. M., & Houston, B. K. (1984). Task-related arousal of Type A and Type B persons: Level of challenge and response specificity. *Journal of Personality and Social Psychology, 46,* 1322–1327.

19. Hill, D. R., Krantz, D. S., Contrada, R. J., Hedges, S. M., & Ratliff-Crain, J. A. (1987). Stability and change in Type A components and cardiovascular reactivity in medical students during periods of academic stress. *Journal of Applied Social Psychology, 17,* 679–698.

20. Fazio, R. H., Cooper, M., Dayson, K., & Johnson, M. (1981). Control and the coronary-prone behavior pattern: Responses to multiple situational demands. *Personality and Social Psychology Bulletin, 7,* 97–102.

21. Ortega, D. F., & Pipal, J. E. (1984). Challenge seeking and the Type A-coronary prone behavior pattern. *Journal of Personality and Social Psychology, 46,* 1328–1334.

22. Glass, D. C., Snyder, M. L., & Hollis, J. (1974). Time urgency and the Type A coronary-prone behavior pattern. *Journal of Applied Social Psychology, 4,* 125–140.

23. Evans, G. W., Palsane, M. N., & Carrere, S. (1987). Type A behavior and occupational stress: A cross-cultural study of blue collar workers. *Journal of Personality and Social Psychology, 52,* 1002–1007.

24. Holmes, D. S., & Will, M. J. (1985). Expression of interpersonal aggression by angered and nonangered persons with the Type A and Type B behavior patterns. *Journal of Personality and Social Psychology, 48,* 723–727.

25. Baron, R. A. (1989). Personality and organizational conflict: Effects of the Type A behavior pattern and self-monitoring. *Organizational Behavior and Human Decision Processes* (in press).

26. Christie, R., & Geis, F. L. (Eds.) (1970). *Studies in Machiavellianism.* New York: Academic Press.

27. See Note 24.

28. Christie, R., & Geis, F. L. (1970). The ten dollar game. In R. Christie & F. L. Geis (Eds.), *Studies in Machiavellianism.* New York: Academic Press.

29. Baron, R. A., Byrne, D., & Suls, J. M. (1989). *Exploring social psychology* (3rd ed.). Boston: Allyn & Bacon.

30. Rotter, J. B. (1975). Some problems and misconceptions related to the construct of internal versus external control of reinforcement. *Journal of Consulting and Clinical Psychology, 43,* 56–67.

31. Szilagyi, A. D., Jr., & Sims, H. P., Jr. (1975). Locus of control and expectancies across multiple organizational levels. *Journal of Applied Psychology, 61,* 156–165.

32. Andrisani, P. J., & Nestel, C. (1976). Internal-external control as a contributor to and outcome of work experience. *Journal of Applied Psychology, 61,* 156–165.

33. Anderson, C. R. (1977). Locus of control, coping behaviors, and performance in a stress setting: A longitudinal study. *Journal of Applied Psychology, 62,* 446–451.

34. Lefcourt, H. M., Martin, R. A., & Saleh, W. E. (1984). Locus of control and social support: Interactive moderators of stress. *Journal of Personality and Social Psychology, 47,* 378–389.

35. Riggio, R. E. (1986). Assessment of basic social skills. *Journal of Personality and Social Psychology, 51,* 649–660.

36. Friedman, H. S., Riggio, R. E., & Casella, D. F. (1988). Nonverbal skill, personal charisma, and initial attraction. *Personality and Social Psychology Bulletin, 14,* 203–211.

37. See Note 35.

38. See Note 36.

39. Riggio, R. E., Tucker, J., & Throckmorton, B. (1987). Social skills and deception ability. *Personality and Social Psychology Bulletin, 13,* 568–577.

40. Friedman, H. S. (1979). The concept of skill in nonverbal communication: Implications for understanding social interactions. In R. Rosenthal (Ed.), *Skill in nonverbal communication.* Cambridge, MA: Oelgeschlager, Gunn & Hain.

41. See Note 7.

42. Briggs, S. R., & Cheek, J. M. (1988). On the nature of self-monitoring: Problems with assessment, problems with validity. *Journal of Personality and Social Psychology, 54,* 663–678.

43. Caldwell, D. F., & O'Reilly, C. A., III. (1982). Boundary spanning and individual performance: The impact of self-monitoring. *Journal of Applied Psychology, 67,* 124–127.

44. Larkin, J. E. (1987). Are good teachers perceived as high self-monitors? *Personality and Social Psychology Bulletin, 23,* 64–72.

45. See Note 27.

46. Bandura, A. (1977). *Social learning theory.* Englewood Cliffs, NJ: Prentice-Hall.

47. Bandura, A. (1986). *Social cognitive theory.* Englewood Cliffs, NJ: Prentice-Hall.

48. Locke, E. A., Frederick, E., Lee, C., & Bobko, P. (1984). The effect of self-efficacy, goals, and task strategies on task performance. *Journal of Applied Psychology, 69,* 241–251.

49. Bandura, A., & Cervone, D. (1986). Differential engagement of self-reactive influences in cognitively-based motivation. *Organizational Behavior and Human Decision Processes, 38,* 92–113.

50. Baron, R. A. (1988). Negative effects of destructive criticism: Impact on conflict, self-efficacy, and task performance. *Journal of Applied Psychology, 73,* 199–207.

51. Gist, M. E. (1987). Self-efficacy: Implications for organizational behavior and human resource management. *Academy of Management Review, 12,* 472–485.

52. Brockner, J. (1988). *Self-esteem at work.* New York: Lexington Books.

53. Ellis, R. A., & Taylor, M. S. (1983). Role of self-esteem within the job search process. *Journal of Applied Psychology, 68,* 632–640.

54. Brockner, J., & Guare, J. (1983). Improving the performance of low self-esteem individuals: An attributional approach. *Academy of Management Journal, 36,* 642–656.

55. McClelland, D. C. (1961). *The achieving society*. Princeton, NJ: Van Nostrand.

56. McClelland, D. C. (1977). Entrepreneurship and management in the years ahead. In C. A. Bramlette, Jr. (Ed.), *The individual and the future of organizations*. Atlanta: Georgia State Univ., College of Business Administration.

57. McClelland, D. C., & Boyatzis, R. E. (1982). Leadership motive pattern and long-term success in management. *Journal of Applied Psychology, 67,* 737–743.

58. Winter, D. G. (1987). Leader appeal, leader performance, and the motive profiles of leaders and followers: A study of American presidents and elections. *Journal of Personality and Social Psychology, 52,* 196–202.

59. See Note 55.

60. Thornton, G. C., III, & Byham, W. C. (1982). *Assessment centers and managerial performance*. New York: Academic Press.

61. Gaugler, B. B., Rosenthal, D. B., Thornton, G. C., III, & Bentson, C. (1988). Meta-analysis of assessment center validity. *Journal of Applied Psychology, 72,* 493–511.

62. Ritchie, R. J., & Moses, J. L. (1983). Assessment center correlates of women's advancement into middle management: A 7-year longitudinal analysis. *Journal of Applied Psychology, 68,* 227–231.

David and Debbi: Two Very Different Cookies

Have you ever purchased freshly baked cookies at a store specializing in cookies? Do you prefer cool and crunchy cookies or warm and soft ones? Do you purchase cookies because you are hungry and want a snack or because you want to be reminded of the cookies your mother baked for you in your childhood? The founders and owners of two of the largest and most successful cookie stores in the country, David Liederman of David's Cookies and Debbi Fields of Mrs. Fields' Cookies, are betting that there are enough people with each preference to keep their empires growing in size and profitability. This hope, however, is about the only thing David and Debbi share. In fact, the entire business philosophy and organization as well as the types of products sold at each company differ as a result of David and Debbi's very different personalities, personal beliefs, and approaches to life.

David is a fast talker. He is generally engaged in several activities at once. He believes that the purchase of cookies is an impulse decision based on one's current level of hunger. He views the cookie industry as cut-throat competition where there will be one winner and many losers. To ensure his winning, he has built what he believes to be a no-fault system for cookie management. This system evolved out of his beliefs that people (1) are not to be trusted because they are lazy and irresponsible, (2) need to be managed at close range, and (3) will make mistakes if you give them an opportunity. As a result, he has franchised his operations so that local owner/managers will be able to closely supervise their staffs. He also has developed machinery and equipment that takes the guesswork out of baking cookies. Dough is mixed in centralized locations and then sent to the stores where employees scoop it out onto baking sheets. Next, the ovens are programmed so that the cookies will automatically cook at the right temperature for the correct amount of time. By serving cool and crunchy cookies, David's Cookies also eliminates the need for monitoring the cookies' temperature after they are removed from the ovens. After all, a cool cookie won't change temperature while waiting to be purchased.[1]

Debbi runs a very different shop. She loves posting cute quips around her stores and offices, such as, "Good enough never is" and "We're a people company." She believes strongly in the ability and desire of her employees to do a good job and to please customers. She feels that people come to her store not to purchase a cookie to satisfy their hunger, but to have a "feel good" experience. She assumes that with trust, caring, and the sharing of the proper corporate values, all of her employees will do their best. As a result, her stores are operated very differently from David's. For instance, all of her stores are company owned. This way, she can set the agenda throughout the company and serve as a role model to all her employees. Cookies are made on the premises of her various stores. The employees not only make the dough and place it on the baking sheets, they monitor the ovens for the finished product and then keep track of the time the cookies are on the shelf awaiting purchase. No cookie at Mrs. Fields' is to be sold if it is more than two hours old![2]

David and Debbi are also different with respect to the way they organize their businesses. David oversees his empire from New York City. On a typical day he takes numerous phone calls—none lasting more than a few minutes—makes visits to the locally co-owned stores, plans business strategy and marketing maneuvers, and in general leads a busy, hectic lifestyle. Debbi, on the other hand, runs her business from Park City, Utah. Although her days are kept busy overseeing the various operations of her approximately 500 stores—a task she handles through the use of a highly complex computer program as well as electronic and voice mail—she doesn't handle the business planning, marketing, and finance by herself. Rather, she has delegated that part of running the business to her husband, Randy Fields.[3] This frees her to concentrate on the employees, ensuring that they all recognize and operate according to the principles she has established. As she says, "I'm there to teach [the employees]. I'm their support system. We do it together, and we start feeling good about what we're doing. . . . I do understand one thing, and that is feelings, and emotion, and caring. You know, everybody likes to be made to feel special and important. They like to be acknowledged. That's my real role. To make people feel important and to create an opportunity for them. That's really my role as the cookie president, the cookie person."[4]

In contrast to Mrs. Fields' approach, David Liederman's philosophy about how to run a business is evidenced in his words about the trouble he is having introducing a new brownie into his stores. "I can't introduce them, because I can't get the formula to a state yet so that all the employee has to do, like with the cookies, is open up a container, put the brownies in something, and bake them. With my brownies, you have to add eggs, and I am terrified of sending anything out there where an employee has to do anything to the food. . . . You have to think at the lowest common denominator. One of the reasons we do so well in the cookie business is that a chimpanzee could take cookies out of the bag and, more often than not, put them on the tray properly."[5]

Questions for Discussion

1. Is David a Type A or Type B? Debbi? Give examples to support your answer.

2. Do David and Debbi differ in their degree of Machiavellianism?

3. How do David and Debbi differ in their respective needs for achievement, power, and affiliation?

4. What do you believe is the end result of Debbi's trying to increase the self-efficacy perceptions of her employees? What do you think are the effects of David's beliefs about the self-efficacy of his employees?

5. Would you rather work for David or Debbi? Why?

Notes

1. Richman, T. (1984, July). A tale of two companies. *Inc.*, pp. 38–43.
2. See Note 1.
3. Richman, T. (1987, October). Mrs. Fields' secret ingredient. *Inc.*, pp. 65–72.
4. See Note 1, p. 42.
5. See Note 1, p. 40.

**EXPERIENCING
ORGANIZATIONAL
BEHAVIOR**

Are You High or Low in Self-Monitoring?

One dimension of personality that is closely related to several aspects of OB is *self-monitoring*. Persons high and low on this dimension differ in several respects that can strongly affect their behavior and performance in organizational settings. Where do you fall in terms of self-monitoring? To find out, follow the directions below.

Procedure

Please indicate whether each of the statements below is true (or mostly true) or false (or mostly false) about yourself. If a statement is true (or mostly true) enter the letter *T* in the blank space. If it is false (or mostly false) enter the letter *F*.

——— 1. It is difficult for me to imitate the actions of other people.
——— 2. My behavior usually reflects my true feelings, attitudes, or beliefs.
——— 3. At parties and social gatherings, I always try to say and do things others will like.
——— 4. I can give a speech on almost any topic—even ones about which I know very little.
——— 5. I would probably make a very poor actor.
——— 6. Sometimes I put on a show to impress or entertain people.
——— 7. I find it difficult to argue for ideas which I don't believe.
——— 8. In different situations and with different people I often act in very different ways.
——— 9. I would not change my attitudes or my actions in order to please other people or win their approval.
——— 10. Sometimes other people think I am experiencing stronger emotions than I really am.
——— 11. I am not especially good at making other people like me.
——— 12. If I have a strong reason for doing so, I can look others in the eye and lie with a straight face.
——— 13. I make up my own mind about movies, books, or music; I don't rely on the advice of my friends in these respects.
——— 14. At a party, I usually let others keep the jokes and stories going.
——— 15. I'm not always the person I seem to be.

To obtain your score, use the following key:

1. F, 2. F, 3. T, 4. T, 5. F, 6. T, 7. F, 8. T, 9. F, 10. T, 11. F, 12. T, 13. F, 14. F, 15. T

(Note: These items are similar to ones on a scale developed by M. Snyder to measure self-monitoring, 1987; see Note 7.)

Add one point to your total for each answer that matches this key.

Points to Consider

How did you score? If your total was eight or higher, you are probably high in self-monitoring. If it was four or lower, you are relatively low on this dimension. Persons high in self-monitoring are more willing than those low in self-monitoring to change their actions or statements in order to win the approval of others. They are also somewhat more sensitive to the reactions of others and more outgoing or expressive. Can you think of jobs or tasks in which such characteristics would be helpful? Research findings suggest that they are especially valuable in sales and in jobs involving *boundary spanning*—communication with several different groups.

Can you think of jobs or task in which being low in self-monitoring would be advantageous? For what kinds of positions would you prefer to hire persons high or low on this dimension?

CHAPTER SEVEN

STRESS:
ITS CAUSES, IMPACT, AND MANAGEMENT

CHAPTER OUTLINE

Stress: Its Basic Nature

Stress: Its Major Causes
  Work-Related Causes of Stress
  Personal (Life-Related) Causes of Stress

Stress: Some Major Effects
  Stress and Health: The Silent Killer
  Stress and Task Performance
  Burnout: Stress and Psychological Adjustment

Individual Differences in Resistance to Stress:
Optimism, Pessimism, and Hardiness
  Optimism: A Buffer against Stress
  Hardiness: Viewing Stress as Challenge
  The Type A Behavior Pattern Revisited
  Tension Discharge Rate

Managing Stress: Some Useful Tactics
  Personal Tactics for Managing Stress
  Organization-Based Strategies for Managing
    Stress

Special Sections

OB: A Management Perspective
  Sexual Harassment: An Especially Objectionable
  Source of Stress at Work

OB: A Research Perspective
  Stress and Decision Making: Poor Choices, Bad
  Strategies

OB: An International Perspective
  Managerial Stress in Different Cultures: Evidence
  from the United Kingdom and Singapore

LEARNING OBJECTIVES

After reading this chapter, you should be able to:
  1. Define stress in terms of its physiological, psychological, and cognitive components.
  2. Describe several major work-related causes of stress.
  3. Describe the impact of stress on personal health, task performance, and decision making.
  4. Define burnout and indicate why it occurs.
  5. Explain how reactions to stress are affected by several personal characteristics (e.g., optimism, hardiness).
  6. Describe several personal and organizational techniques for managing stress.

"Okay, that wraps it up for today," Blair Peterson remarks, bringing the meeting to an end. "Sue—you'll be presenting next week on the status of the 6250 project; and Ken will give us a progress report on the Blairton deal. See you all then."

As she gathers up her things, Sue Benson feels a growing sense of panic. *How am I ever going to get all that stuff together by next week*, she wonders. *And how will I ever be able to cover it all in thirty minutes? I've got so much else to do this week. And I hate making presentations . . . That Blair Peterson . . . ugh . . . what a cold fish . . . No, I can't do it!* Thinking this, she shudders visibly.

Noticing her look of despair, Ken Burke walks over and asks, "What's wrong, Sue? You look as though someone just put a dent in your dream-mobile."

Despite her mounting panic, Sue smiles. Everyone knows how much she loves her new convertible, and she realizes that she probably does have a tragic expression on her face. "No, it's not that," she murmurs to Ken as they leave the meeting room together. "It's just that I've been so loaded down lately—so much to do and so little time. I just don't see how I'll be ready by next week. And to tell you the truth, the thought of speaking to this group scares me stiff . . ." Sue breaks off, and a look of total panic re-enters her eyes.

"Hey, calm down," Ken says. "It's not that bad. Really, it's all in how you look at it. For me, presenting is an opportunity—a chance to show 'em what good work I've been doing lately—you know, knock 'em dead with my incredible competence!"

Ken's charm and good humor bring a brief smile to Sue's lips.

"That's okay for *you*," she answers. "But for me, it's different. I don't see it that way at all. What if I get up there and forget what I'm going to say? I'll make a total fool of myself, and that'll be the end once and for all . . ." As she visualizes this scene, Sue's eyes begin to water. "Oh, Ken, what am I going to do?" she blurts out.

Ken, too, looks upset, but his words are comforting. "The first thing is, *stop worrying!* You can do it if you try. Next, talk to Brad; I'm sure he'll be a big help."

"That's just it; he's out of town on a two week trip. I haven't seen him since Monday. I wish he were here!"

"Isn't it always like that? Just when you need your spouse most, he's unavailable. Happens to me and Gwen all the time. Well, don't just wait around for him to get back. Call him! What are telephones for? I'm sure he'll be a big help. And then, prepare like you've never prepared before. Go over that stuff until it's coming out of your ears. That'll build your confidence and if you believe you can do it, you really can."

At these words, Sue's brow clears a little. *Maybe there is hope*, she thinks to herself. *Ken's right—the main thing is to stay calm and really prepare*. Out loud she says, "There's a lot to what you say. If I give up or panic, I really *am* in for it. I'm going to follow your advice. First, I'll call Brad; just hearing his voice will make me feel better. Then, I'm going to start preparing. I'll show 'em! I'll put on a good show next week or get wiped out in the attempt!"

"Now you're talking," Ken says. "I know it'll turn out fine." With these words, he turns down the hall toward his own office, stopping briefly after a few steps to flash the high sign and a big smile.

Have you ever felt like Sue—that you were right on the edge of being overwhelmed by events in your life that you could not control and with which you might be unable to cope? If so, you are already quite familiar with **stress**—the main focus of this chapter.

Unfortunately, stress is an all too common part of life in the late twentieth century, something few individuals can avoid. Moreover, stress is costly for both organizations and individuals. Growing evidence suggests that high levels of stress adversely affect physical health, psychological well-being, and task performance.[1]

Given such effects, it is clear that stress is a topic of considerable importance to the field of OB. So in this chapter, we will consider it in detail. First, we'll consider the *basic nature* of stress—what it is and the kind of reactions it involves. Next, we'll turn to its *major causes,* factors in work settings and life in general that tend to induce high levels of stress. Third, we'll examine the *impact of stress*—its effects on health, task performance, and the course of personal careers. Fourth, we'll also consider several *personal factors* that either moderate or intensify the impact of stress. Finally, we'll describe several techniques for *coping with* or *managing stress*—procedures that help reduce or counter its harmful effects (see Figure 7.1).

STRESS: ITS BASIC NATURE

When asked to describe their own experiences with stress, many persons emphasize its emotional nature. They refer to stress largely as an unpleasant subjective state accompanied by high levels of arousal. To a degree, such descriptions are accurate: stress does indeed involve a subjective, emotional component. However, experts on this subject now agree that this is only part of the total picture. Full understanding of stress and its many effects must involve attention to three related issues.

First, consider the *physiological aspects* of stress. According to Selye, a leading expert on this topic, these can be divided into several distinct stages.[2] When confronted with any threat to our safety or well-being, we experience an immediate and vigorous *alarm reaction.* Arousal rises quickly to high levels, and many physiological changes that prepare our bodies for strenuous activity (either flight or combat) take place. This initial reaction is soon replaced by a second stage known as *resistance.* Here, activation remains relatively high, but drops to levels that are more sustainable over relatively long periods of time. If stress persists, the body's resources may become depleted

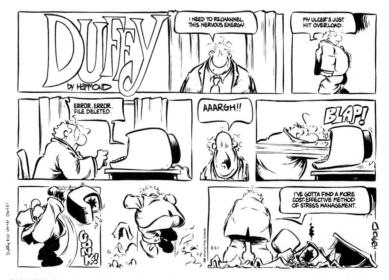

FIGURE 7.1 How *Not* to Manage Stress
Managing stress effectively is an important goal for most individuals. (Source: DUFFY copyright 1988 Universal Press Syndicate. Reprinted with permission. All rights reserved.)

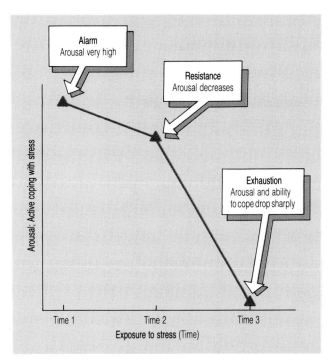

FIGURE 7.2 Physiological Reactions to Stress

When we are exposed to stress, several physiological changes occur. First, we experience a vigorous *alarm reaction*. This is followed by a stage of *resistance* in which we actively seek to cope with the source of stress. If stress persists, a final stage of *exhaustion* may occur, in which our ability to cope with stress drops to low levels. (Source: Based on suggestions by Selye; see Note 2.)

and a final stage known as *exhaustion* occurs. At this point, the ability to cope (at least physically) decreases sharply, and severe biological damage may result if stress persists (see Figure 7.2 for a summary of these physiological reactions.)

Second, in order to fully understand stress it is necessary to consider the external events or stimuli that induce it—the nature of various **stressors.** What is it about these stimuli that produces stress? What do they have in common? No final answers to such questions currently exist, but it appears that many stressful events share the following properties: (1) they are so intense, in some respect, that they produce a state of *overload*—we can no longer adapt to them; (2) they evoke simultaneous incompatible tendencies (e.g., urges to both approach and avoid some object or activity); and (3) they are uncontrollable—outside our ability to change or influence.

Finally, and perhaps most important of all, stress involves the operation of several cognitive factors. Perhaps the most central of these is individuals' *cognitive appraisal* of a given situation or potential stressor. In simple terms, stress occurs only to the extent that the persons involved perceive (1) that the situation is somehow threatening to their important goals, and (2) that they will be unable to cope with these potential dangers or demands.[3] In short, stress does not simply shape our thoughts; in many cases, it derives from and is strongly affected by them.

A clear example of the operation of such cognitive factors was provided by our chapter-opening story. Sue perceived the task of making a formal presentation to other members of her company as very threatening. Indeed, when confronted with it, she experienced strong feelings of panic and despair. In contrast, one of her friends, Ken, viewed such presentations as an opportunity to make a favorable impression on important persons within the organization. The result: he did not experience high levels of stress in this context. In sum, the contrasting perceptions of these two persons with respect to the same situation led them to experience very different reactions and levels of stress. (See Figure 7.3 on page 226).

To understand the nature of stress, therefore, it is necessary to consider the

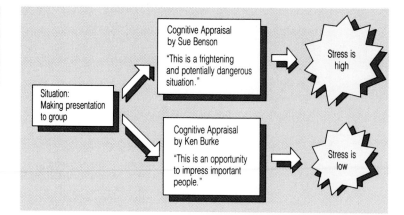

FIGURE 7.3 Cognitive Appraisals and Stress

Whether, and to what extent, a given situation induces stress among individuals depends upon their *cognitive appraisals* (i.e., perceptions) of it. Because she views making a formal presentation as frightening and potentially harmful, Sue Benson experiences a high level of stress when confronted with this task. In contrast, because he views making a presentation in positive terms, Ken Burke experiences a much lower level of stress.

emotional and physiological reactions it involves, the external conditions that produce it, and the cognitive processes that play a role in its occurrence.[4] Taking all these factors into account, we can define **stress** as *a pattern of emotional states and physiological reactions occurring in situations where individuals perceive threats to their important goals which they may be unable to meet.*[5] In short, stress occurs where individuals feel, rightly or wrongly, that they may soon be overwhelmed by events or circumstances that exceed their personal resources.[6]

STRESS: ITS MAJOR CAUSES

What factors contribute to stress in work settings? Unfortunately, the list is a long one. As we will soon see, many different conditions play a role in this regard. Moreover, these factors are not independent in their effects. For example, the presence of one stressor may intensify reactions to one or more others. For purposes of this discussion, however, we will consider each major cause of work-related stress separately. In addition, for purposes of clarity, we will divide these factors into two major categories: those relating directly to organizations or jobs, and those relating to other aspects of individuals' lives.

Work-Related Causes of Stress

As anyone who has been employed well knows, work settings are often highly stressful environments. Yet it is also clear that they vary greatly in this respect. Some jobs and organizations expose individuals to high levels of stress on a regular basis. In contrast, others involve much lower levels and frequency of stress. What factors account for these differences? What are the major causes of stress in organizational contexts? A complete answer to this question is beyond the scope of this chapter. However, several of the most important sources of stress in the workplace are described below.

Occupational demands: Some jobs are more stressful than others. Consider the following jobs: production manager, librarian, emergency room physician, janitor, firefighter, college professor, airline pilot. Do they differ in degree of stressfulness? Obviously, they do. Some, such as emergency room physician, firefighter, and airline pilot, expose the persons who hold them to high levels of stress. Others, such as college professor, janitor, and librarian, do not. This basic fact—that some jobs are much more stressful than others—has been confirmed by the results of a careful survey involving more than 130 different occupations.[7] Results of this survey indicate that several jobs (e.g., physician, office manager, foreman, waitress or waiter) are quite high in stress. In contrast, others (e.g., maid, craft workers, farm laborer) are much lower in this regard. But what, precisely, makes some jobs more stressful than others? A partial answer is provided by a study conducted by Shaw and Riskind.[8]

These researchers reviewed information about the levels of stress experienced by persons holding a very wide range of jobs—from executive and architect on the one hand to secretary and factory worker on the other. Then, they related this information about stressfulness to various aspects of the jobs themselves. Results indicated that several features of jobs are indeed related to the levels of stress they generate. For example, the greater the extent to which a given job requires (1) making decisions, (2) constant monitoring of devices or materials, (3) repeated exchange of information with others, (4) unpleasant physical conditions, and (5) performing unstructured rather than structured tasks, the more stressful it tends to be (see Figure 7.4). Moreover—and this is the most important point—such relationships were found to be quite general in nature. Thus, the greater the extent to which virtually *any* job possesses these characteristics, the higher the level of stress it produces among persons holding it, regardless of the specific tasks being performed. This is certainly a point worth considering when planning a career, or choosing between potential jobs (see the discussion of these topics in chapter 9).

Role conflict: Stress from conflicting demands. Consider the following situation. Because she has done excellent work for several years, a young chemist is promoted to the position of Assistant Director for Research. In her new role, she must oversee numerous projects being carried out in her company's laboratories. As a member of

FIGURE 7.4   Stress and Occupational Demands

Jobs that require certain types of activities (e.g., making decisions, dangerous physical conditions, repeated exchange of information with others) are higher in stress than jobs that do not require these activities.

her organization's management team, she must try to assure that these projects are completed in a timely and cost-efficient manner, and that they contribute to the company's stated goals (e.g., to the development of new products). Now, however, one of the scientists in her department informs her that he has uncovered an interesting new phenomenon. It is not directly related to the work he is doing, but he feels it is exciting, scientifically, and should be pursued. What does the Assistant Director do? Her job seems to require that she discourage the scientist from going off on a tangent, spending company time and money on topics not directly related to his work. Yet as a chemist, she fully appreciates the potential scientific value of his discovery.

As you can see, this may be an unpleasant and potentially stressful situation for the young woman in question. She is experiencing **role conflict**—conflicting demands from her obligations as Assistant Director for Research and her professional identity as a chemist. Unfortunately, role conflict is common in many work settings. Most people fulfill several roles in their lives, and as a result, frequently find that the demands of one role conflict with the demands of another. Should an individual stay late at the office and so miss his child's recital or Little League game (a conflict between the roles of parent and employee)? Should an employee report a theft of company property by a coworker to her supervisor (a conflict between being a good organizational citizen and being loyal to one's own work group)? These are just a few examples of the many ways in which role conflict can arise. When it does, it often serves as an important source of work-related stress.

Interestingly, recent evidence gathered by Newton and Keenan indicates that the adverse effects of role conflict are less pronounced in work settings characterized by warmth and support than in those where such factors are lacking.[9] These findings suggest that while a degree of role conflict is probably unavoidable in many contexts, its contribution to overall levels of stress can be reduced by other, positive conditions.

Role ambiguity: Stress from uncertainty. Even if individuals avoid the stress associated with role conflict, however, they may still encounter an even more common source of job-related stress: **role ambiguity.** This occurs when individuals are uncertain about several matters relating to their jobs: the scope of their responsibilities, what's expected of them, how to divide their time between various duties. Most persons dislike such uncertainty and find it quite stressful, but it is often unavoidable. Thus, role ambiguity is quite common. In fact, 35 to 60 percent of employees surveyed report experiencing it to some degree.[10] Clearly, then, it is one major cause of stress in many work settings.

Overload and underload: Doing too much or too little. When the phrase "work-related stress" is mentioned, most people envision scenes in which employees are asked to do too much—more work than they can handle in a given period of time. In fact, this image is often correct, for such *overload* is one important cause of stress in many work settings. A distinction should be made, however, between **quantitative overload**—situations in which individuals are asked to do more work than they can complete in a specific period of time—and **qualitative overload**—employees' belief that they lack the required skills or abilities to perform a given job. Both types of overload are unpleasant, and research findings suggest that both can lead to high levels of stress.[11]

Yet, overload is only part of the total picture. While being asked to do too much can be stressful, so can being asked to do too little. In fact, there seems to be considerable truth in the following statement: "The hardest job in the world is doing nothing—you can't take a break." *Underload* leads to boredom and monotony. Since these reactions are quite unpleasant, underload, too, can be stressful. Again, there is a distinction between **quantitative underload** and **qualitative underload.** Quantitative underload refers to the boredom that results when employees have so little to do that they find themselves sitting around much of the time. In contrast, qualitative underload refers to the lack of mental stimulation that accompanies many routine, repetitive jobs. (See Figure 7.5 for an overview of the nature of these various types of overload and underload.)

Responsibility for others: A heavy burden. In any organization, there is a division of responsibility. Some persons deal primarily with the physical side of the business (e.g., obtaining supplies, directing production, maintaining equipment), others focus mainly on financial matters (e.g., budgets, taxes, accounting), and still others—usually supervisors or managers—deal primarily with people. Are there any differences in the level of stress associated with these contrasting roles? Research suggests that there are. In general, individuals who are responsible for other people—who must motivate them, reward or punish them, communicate with them—experience higher levels of stress than persons who handle other organizational functions.[12] Such persons are more likely to report feelings of tension and anxiety, and are actually more likely to show overt symptoms of stress such as ulcers or hypertension than their counterparts in finance or supply. The reasons behind this difference are complex, so only two are

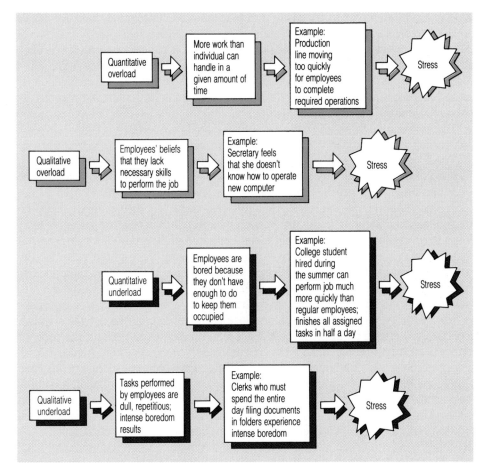

FIGURE 7.5   Overload and Underload: Contrasting Patterns
Both *overload* and *underload* can be sources of stress at work. Two distinct patterns (quantitative and qualitative) exist for each.

mentioned here. First, it is managers who must, ultimately, confront the human costs of organizational policies and decisions. For example, it is they who must deliver negative feedback and then witness the distress it often generates. Second, it is their task to deal with the many frictions that are a normal part of human relations at work. This involves listening to endless complaints, mediating disputes, promoting cooperation, and exercising leadership. All of these tasks are demanding, and can contribute to the total burden of stress experienced by managers.

Lack of social support: The costs of isolation. According to one old saying, "Misery loves company." In the context of stress, this statement implies that if we have to face stressful conditions, it's better to do so along with others (and with their support) rather than alone. Many people accept this view as correct. When confronted with stress, they seek support and comfort from others. Does this strategy actually work? In general, the answer seems to be "yes." When individuals believe they have the friendship and support of others at work, their ability to resist the adverse effects of stress seems to increase. For example, in one investigation on this topic, Oullette-Kobasa and Pucetti studied managers at a large public utility who were experiencing high levels of stress.[13] They found that among such persons, those who felt they had the support of their immediate supervisors reported fewer physical symptoms associated with stress than managers who did not feel that they enjoyed such support.

How does social support help individuals deal with stress? Several mechanisms may play a role. First, having friends to turn to in times of difficulty may help individuals perceive stressful events as less threatening and more under their control than would otherwise be the case. Second, friends can often suggest useful strategies for dealing with sources of stress. Third, they can help reduce the negative feelings which often accompany exposure to stressful events. Direct evidence that this latter function is, perhaps, the most important is provided by an ingenious study completed recently by Costanza, Derlega, and Winstead.[14]

These researchers asked participants in the study to perform a highly stressful task: guiding a live tarantula through a maze after watching one of the researchers do so. (The tarantula was inside a fishing net from which it could not escape, but through which it could extend its legs.) Individuals took part in the study with a friend and before performing this stressful task, some were given an opportunity to have a brief conversation with this person. One group was told to discuss their feelings about the situation, another was told to discuss how they expected to handle the guidance task, while a third was told to talk only about topics unrelated to the study. A fourth (control) group was not given any opportunity to talk with a friend; they waited alone for the start of the task. Costanza and his colleagues predicted that talking about their feelings might actually intensify subjects' fears; after all, such activities would cause them to dwell on their concerns and anxieties. In contrast, talking about how they would perform the task or topics unrelated to it would reduce such feelings. These activities would, respectively, increase participants' confidence in their abilities to perform the task, or distract them from thinking about what lay ahead. As you can see from Figure 7.6, all these predictions were confirmed. When individuals completed a questionnaire designed to measure their anxiety, those permitted to discuss unrelated topics or how they would handle the task reported lower fear than those who waited alone or those who discussed their feelings. These results suggest that social support helps individuals deal with (and reduce) the negative feelings often generated by stressful conditions.

Lack of participation in decisions: Helplessness strikes again. As we have noted on several occasions, most persons want to feel that they have at least some control over their own fate. The opposite belief—that we are helpless pawns tossed

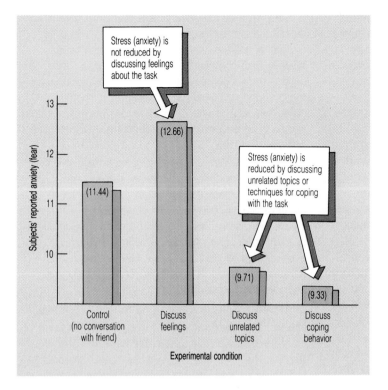

FIGURE 7.6   Social Support and Coping with Stress
Subjects given an opportunity to discuss with a friend either (1) how they would handle a forthcoming stressful task, or (2) topics unrelated to the task reported lower fear (i.e., stress) than subjects who discussed their feelings about the task or those given no opportunity to converse with a friend. These findings suggest that *social support* often reduces negative feelings associated with stress. (Source: Based on data from Costanza, Derlega, and Winstead, 1988; see Note 14.)

about by forces beyond our control—is quite disturbing. Unfortunately, one factor contributing to such feelings is common in work settings: lack of participation by employees in decisions affecting their jobs. Most persons feel that they know a good deal about their work. Thus, when they are prevented from offering input into decisions concerning them, they feel left out and unable to control their own outcomes. The result: they experience considerable stress. In general, then, permitting employees to participate in decisions that affect their jobs seems to be a wise strategy. Not only does it enhance their work-related attitudes, it helps counter an important source of work-related stress as well. (For information on another, and highly unsettling, cause of stress in work settings, please see the **Management Perspective** section below.)

OB: A MANAGEMENT PERSPECTIVE

Sexual Harassment: An Especially Objectionable Source of Stress at Work

In recent decades, millions of women have joined the workforce in the United States and many other nations. Indeed, at present, a large majority of females—both married and single—are working full

time. As the sexual composition of work settings has shifted, a disturbing problem has increased in frequency: **sexual harassment.**[15] This term refers to unwanted contact or communication of a sexual nature, and can range from forced physical contact and sexual propositions linked to threats or promises of changes in job status, to offensive remarks or unwanted nonverbal attention (e.g., stares, gestures, whistles), and repeated requests for dates. Women are the overwhelming victims of such actions, but men are also subject to sexual harassment on some occasions.

The incidence of sexual harassment appears to have increased in recent decades. Surveys reveal that more than 25 percent of female employees of the U.S. federal government have experienced sexual harassment at least once during their careers. Similarly, the number of complaints of harassment filed with the Equal Employment Opportunity Commission rose from 4,272 in 1981 to 7,273 in 1985. Of course, it is difficult to know whether these figures indicate an actual rise in the incidence of sexual harassment or merely greater willingness of employees to report its occurrence. Whichever interpretation is more accurate, however, it is clear that being subjected to sexual harassment is a highly unpleasant and stressful experience for the persons involved.

Can organizations, and individual managers, do anything to reduce the frequency of such objectionable behavior? Growing evidence suggests that they can.[16] In fact, taking a number of recent studies on this topic into account, the following recommendations seem useful:

1. Develop formal policies concerning sexual harassment—ones that clearly specify the types of behavior that will constitute such harassment. These policies, and potential penalties, should then be communicated in a clear manner to all employees.

2. An in-house mechanism for complaints about sexual harassment should be established. In other words, employees should have some means of voicing such complaints without turning, at once, to legal action. This mechanism should be more than a mere sounding board for complaints; it should be clear that appropriate disciplinary action will be taken should it be determined that sexual harassment has actually occurred.

3. Third, employees should be informed that it is their duty to serve as witnesses to instances of sexual harassment if they are in a position to observe their occurrence. In other words, efforts should be made to overcome the natural reluctance of many persons to become involved in such proceedings by explaining that eliminating sexual harassment is in the best interest of all employees and the entire organization.

Recent findings obtained by Terpstra and Baker indicate that courts are most likely to rule in favor of employees complaining of sexual harassment under the following conditions: (1) when they have been subjected to serious forms of harassment (e.g., forced physical contact, sexual propositions linked to job outcomes), (2) when they have witnesses to such harassment, and (3) when they informed management of the problem prior to taking legal action, but no steps were then taken to correct the situation.[17] In view of these results, it certainly seems wise for all organizations to implement the recommendations listed above. Doing so will help reduce the incidence and severity of sexual harassment. And this, in turn, will contribute to the welfare of both individual employees and their organizations.

Other work-related sources of stress: Appraisals, working conditions, and change. While the factors described above appear to be among the most important sources of stress in organizations, several others are also worthy of mention. Perhaps the most important of these is the process of **performance appraisal** (refer to our discussion of this topic in chapter 4). Being evaluated by their supervisors is a highly stressful experience for many persons; after all, the stakes are high (their future career is on the line), and the possibility of negative feedback is real. For this reason, it is important that such appraisals be conducted in as calm, rational, and fair a manner as possible. This often involves considerable preparation on the part of the manager *and* the persons being evaluated (e.g., it should be decided, in advance, exactly what aspects of performance will be considered, and what form evaluations will take). The effort invested in such tasks is well worthwhile, though, for the annual or semi-annual performance appraisal can be a major source of stress in most organizations.

A second potential source of stress in many work settings is the *physical conditions* prevailing in them. Unpleasant environmental conditions such as extreme heat or cold, loud noise, crowding, and poor lighting can all act as stressors and exert negative effects upon employees exposed to them.[18] Third, stress often derives from *change* within an organization. Shifts in company policies, reorganizations, mergers, and major changes in top management can all generate high levels of uncertainty, and, therefore, high levels of stress. Evidence for the stress-inducing nature of mergers has recently been collected by Baron and Bingley.[19] These investigators asked employees in two organizations that were about to merge to report on their current levels of job-related stress at several points in time: two months prior to the merger, one month after the merger took place, and six months after it was completed. Consistent with initial predictions, results revealed that reported stress rose immediately after the merger, but then decreased with the passage of time, presumably because necessary adjustments were completed.

Personal (Life-Related) Causes of Stress

While work is clearly one of the most important activities in many people's lives, it is far from the only activity. Most individuals have a full and varied life outside the workplace as well as within it. Given this fact, it is not surprising that events outside work settings often generate stress that persists, and is carried back to work the next day. Many events or experiences contribute to life-related stress—everything from family squabbles to leaking rooves to cars that won't start on cold mornings. Most, however, seem to fit under two broad categories: *major stressful life events,* and *daily hassles.*[20]

Stressful life events. Death of a spouse, divorce, injury to one's child, a stock market crash, failure in school, unwanted pregnancy; unless an individual leads a truly charmed life, he or she is likely to experience traumatic events or changes like these at some point in time. What are the effects of such events? This question was first studied by Holmes and Rahe, who asked large groups of persons to assign arbitrary points (from one to one hundred) to various life events according to how much readjustment each had required.[21] Holmes and Rahe reasoned that the greater the number of points assigned to a given event, the more stressful it was for the persons experiencing it.

Some of the values assigned by subjects to various stressful life events are shown in Table 7.1 (on page 234). As you can see, the highest numbers were assigned to such serious events as death of a spouse, divorce, or marital separation. In contrast, smaller numbers of points were assigned to such events as change in residence, vacation, or minor violations of the law (e.g., receiving a speeding ticket).

Going further, Holmes and Rahe then related the total number of points accumulated by individuals during a single year to changes in their personal health. The dramatic results obtained did much to stir interest in the effects of stress among scientists in several different fields. The greater the number of "stress points" people accumulated, the greater their likelihood of becoming seriously ill. For example, in one study on this topic, Holmes and Masuda asked patients at a university medical center to report all significant life changes (events) during the past eighteen months.[22] Persons who experienced events totaling 300 points or more showed a much higher incidence of illness during the next nine months than those with 200 points or less (49 percent versus 9 percent).

At this point, we should note that this seemingly simple relationship between stress and health is complicated by the existence of large individual differences in the ability to withstand the impact of stress.[23] While some persons suffer ill effects after exposure to a few mildly stressful events, others remain healthy even after prolonged exposure

TABLE 7.1 Life Events as a Source of Stress

When asked to assign arbitrary points (1–100) to various life events according to the degree of readjustment they required, a large group of individuals provided these values. The higher the numbers shown, the more stressful the events listed.

EVENT	RELATIVE STRESSFULNESS
Death of a Spouse	100
Divorce	73
Marital Separation	65
Jail Term	63
Death of a Close Family Member	63
Personal Injury or Illness	53
Marriage	50
Fired from Job	47
Retirement	45
Pregnancy	40
Death of a Close Friend	37
Son or Daughter Leaving Home	29
Trouble with In-Laws	28
Trouble with Boss	23
Change in Residence	20
Vacation	13
Christmas	12
Minor Violations of the Law	11

(Source: Based on data from Holmes & Masuda, 1974; see Note 22.)

to high levels of stress; they are described as being *stress-resistant* or *hardy*. We'll return to such differences below. For the moment, we merely wish to emphasize that in general, the greater the number of stressful life events experienced by individuals, the greater the likelihood that their subsequent health will suffer in some manner.

The hassles of daily life. While traumatic life events such as the ones studied by Holmes and Rahe are clearly very stressful, they are relatively rare. Many persons live for years, or even decades, without experiencing any of them. Does this mean that such individuals live their lives in a serene lake of tranquility? Hardly. Daily life is filled with countless minor sources of stress that seem to make up for their relatively low intensity by their high frequency of occurrence. That such *daily hassles* are an important cause of stress is suggested by the findings of several studies by Lazarus and his colleagues.[24] These researchers have developed a *Hassles Scale* on which individuals indicate the extent to which they have been "hassled" by common events during the past month. As shown in Table 7.2, items included in this scale deal with a wide range of everyday events (e.g., having too many things to do at once, shopping, concerns over money). When scores on the Hassles Scale are related to reports of psychological symptoms, strong positive correlations are obtained.[25] In short, the more stress people report as a result of such daily hassles, the poorer their psychological well-being. Similarly, scores on this scale are also linked to physical health. The more stress of this sort reported by individuals, the poorer their health tends to be. Indeed, some findings suggest that stress induced by daily hassles has stronger effects on health than that resulting from traumatic life events.[26]

TABLE 7.2   Daily Hassles as a Source of Stress
The everyday events and concerns shown here are ones many persons describe as common sources of stress.

Household Hassles	Preparing Meals
	Shopping
Time Pressure Hassles	Too Many Things to Do
	Too Many Responsibilities
Inner Concern Hassles	Being Lonely
	Fear of Confrontation
Environmental Hassles	Neighborhood Deterioration
	Noise
	Crime
Financial Responsibility	Concerns about Owing Money
	Financial Responsibility for Someone Who Doesn't Live with You

(Source: Based on information in Lazarus et al., 1985; see Note 24.)

In sum, while traumatic life events such as the death of loved ones or the loss of one's job are stressful and have adverse effects on health, the minor hassles of daily life—perhaps because of their frequent, repetitive nature—may sometimes prove even more crucial in this respect. Whatever their relative importance, both traumatic life events and daily hassles are important sources of stress for many persons. And since the stress generated is often carried into their jobs by the persons involved, they are certainly worth noting in this discussion of stress and its impact in work settings.

STRESS: SOME MAJOR EFFECTS

By now, we're sure you are convinced of two facts: (1) stress stems from many sources, and (2) it exerts important effects on the persons who experience it. What may not yet be apparent, though, is just how powerful and far-reaching such effects can be. As we will now note, systematic research on the impact of stress suggests that it can influence physical and psychological well-being, performance on many tasks, and even the course of individual careers. We will now describe several of these effects in more detail.

Stress and Health: The Silent Killer

How strong is the link between stress and personal health? According to medical experts, very strong indeed. In fact, some authorities estimate that stress plays some role in anywhere from 50 to 70 percent of all forms of physical illness.[27] Moreover, included in these figures are some of the most serious and life-threatening ailments known to medical science. To list just a few, stress has been implicated in the occurrence of heart disease, high blood pressure, hardening of the arteries, ulcers, and even diabetes. How does it produce such effects? The mechanisms involved have yet to be determined, but a good first guess is as follows: by draining our resources and keeping us off balance physiologically, stress upsets our complex internal chemistry. In particular, it may interfere with the efficient operation of our *immune system*—the mechanism through which our bodies recognize and destroy potentially harmful substances and intruders (e.g., bacteria, viruses, cancer cells).

Foreign substances that enter our bodies are known as *antigens*. When they appear, certain types of white blood cells begin to multiply. These attack the antigens, often destroying them. Other white blood cells produce *antibodies,* chemical substances which combine with antigens and so neutralize them. When functioning normally, the immune system is nothing short of amazing: each day it removes or destroys many potential threats to our health and well-being. Unfortunately, prolonged exposure to stress seems to disrupt this system. In studies with animals, those exposed to inescapable shock (a very stressful condition) demonstrate reduced production of white blood cells relative to those exposed to shocks from which they can escape (a less stressful condition).[28] Among human beings, persons experiencing high levels of stress (e.g., individuals taking an examination, mourning the loss of a spouse) show similar disruptions in their immune systems.[29] Together, such findings suggest that high levels of stress may indeed undermine the operation of the immune system, and so reduce our ability to resist many serious illnesses.

We should add that at present, evidence linking stress to impairment of the immune system is far from conclusive. Still, given the high stakes involved—personal health and well-being—many persons may choose to act on these preliminary findings even before a final scientific verdict is reached. In short, they may attempt to reduce the levels of stress in their daily lives in order to protect themselves against the harmful effects described above.

Stress and Task Performance

Look at the cartoon in Figure 7.7. Is Cathy correct? Does stress improve performance on a wide range of tasks? At one time, it was generally believed that this was so. Specifically, the relationship between stress and performance on many tasks was assumed to be curvilinear in nature, so that at first, increments in stress (from none to low or moderate levels), were energizing, and so led to improved performance. Beyond some point, however, additional increments in stress were assumed to be distracting or to interfere with performance in other ways. Thus, at high or very high levels of stress, performance would actually fall.

While this relationship may hold true under some conditions, growing evidence suggests that stress exerts mainly negative effects on task performance. In other

FIGURE 7.7 Stress and Task Performance: An Inaccurate View
Contrary to what Cathy believes, high levels of stress generally tend to interfere with task performance, not enhance it. (Source: CATHY copyright 1984 Universal Press Syndicate. Reprinted with permission. All rights reserved.)

words, performance can be disrupted even by relatively low levels of stress. Evidence pointing to this conclusion is provided in a study conducted by Motowidlo, Packard, and Manning.[30] These researchers asked a large group of nurses to describe their own levels of work-related stress. Ratings of their actual job performance were then obtained from supervisors or coworkers. Results indicated that the higher the nurses' feelings of stress, the lower their job performance. In other words, there was no evidence for initial increments in performance, as the curvilinear hypothesis suggests.

These findings, and those of several other studies, indicate that in many real-life settings, performance may be reduced even by low or moderate levels of stress. Why is this the case? Shouldn't the activation produced by moderate levels of stress facilitate performance in many situations? Although this possibility remains, and may apply in some situations (see below), there are several reasons why even moderate levels of stress might be expected to interfere with task performance. First, even relatively mild stress can be distracting. Individuals experiencing it may focus on the unpleasant feelings and emotions stress involves rather than on the task at hand. The result: their performance suffers. Second, prolonged or repeated exposure to even mild levels of stress may have harmful effects on health, and this may interfere with effective performance. Finally, a large body of research indicates that as arousal increases, task performance may at first rise, but at some point, begins to fall.[31] The precise location of this *inflection point* (the point at which the direction of the function reverses) seems to depend, to an important extent, on the complexity of the task being performed. The greater the complexity, the lower the levels of arousal at which a downturn in performance occurs. Are the tasks performed by today's employees more complex than those in the past? Many observers contend that they are. For this reason, too, even relatively mild levels of stress may interfere with performance in today's complex world of work.

Having said all this, we must note that there are exceptions to the general rule that stress interferes with task performance. First, some individuals, at least, do seem to "rise to the occasion," and turn in exceptional performances at times of high stress. This may result from the fact that they are truly expert in the tasks being performed, so that the inflection point in the arousal-performance function described previously is very high (see Figure 7.8). Alternatively, it may be the case that for persons who are

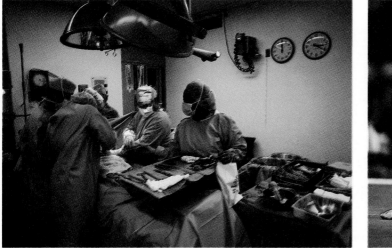 

FIGURE 7.8 Exceptional Performance in the Presence of Extreme Stress
Sometimes, individuals perform exceptionally well in the face of high levels of stress. Such outcomes may stem from the fact that they are expert in the tasks in question, or from their tendency to perceive such situations as challenging rather than merely stressful.

exceptionally skilled at a given task, even very high levels of stress are cognitively appraised as a *challenge* rather than a *threat*. As we noted earlier, stress exerts adverse effects primarily when it is viewed in the latter terms.

Second, large individual differences seem to exist with respect to the impact of stress on task performance. As your own experience may suggest, some individuals do indeed seem to thrive on stress: they actively seek arousal and high levels of sensation or stimulation. For such persons, stress is exhilirating, and may enhance their performance. In contrast, other persons react in an opposite manner. They seek to avoid arousal and high levels of sensation. Such individuals find stress upsetting, and it may interfere with their performance on many tasks. Direct evidence for such differences in reactions to stress has been reported by Martin and his colleagues.[32]

They asked college students to complete a questionnaire designed to distinguish between the two types of persons described above (labeled *paratelic dominant* and *telic dominant* by Martin and his colleagues). Then, they had these two groups of persons play a videogame under either non-stressful or moderately stressful conditions. In the non-stressful condition, subjects' scores were not displayed and they were told to relax and enjoy the game. In the moderately stressful condition, in contrast, subjects were shown a very high score and were instructed to attempt to beat it. In addition, their own scores were visible throughout the game, and were recorded by the experimenter. Martin and his associates predicted that stress would enhance performance by the sensation-seeking, arousal-enjoying (paratelic) subjects, but would interfere with per-

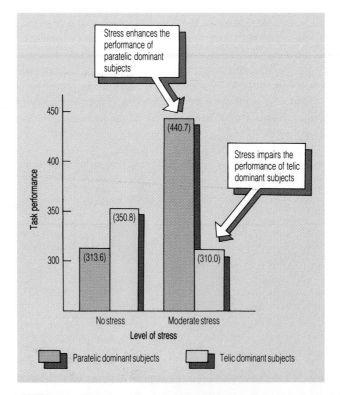

FIGURE 7.9 Stress and Task Performance: The Role of Individual Differences
Moderate levels of stress enhanced the performance of individuals who seek and enjoy arousal (those who are *paratelic dominant*). In contrast, stress reduced the performance of individuals who seek to avoid arousal and high levels of sensation (those who are *telic dominant*). (Source: Based on data from Martin et al., 1988; see Note 32.)

formance among the sensation- and arousal-avoidant (telic) subjects. As you can see from Figure 7.9, results supported these predictions. Paratelic dominant subjects scored higher under stressful conditions, while telic dominant subjects scored lower.

Taking the findings reported by Martin et al. and other evidence into account, the most reasonable conclusion we can offer concerning stress and task performance is as follows: in many situations, stress can indeed interfere with performance. However, its precise effects depend on several different factors (e.g., complexity of the task being performed, personal characteristics of the individuals involved, their previous experience with this task). In view of such complexities, generalizations about the impact of stress on task performance should be made with considerable caution. (Does stress play a role in *decision making,* one very important type of task most managers frequently perform? For evidence on this issue, please see the **Research Perspective** below.)

OB: A RESEARCH PERSPECTIVE

Stress and Decision Making: Poor Choices, Bad Strategies

As we'll note in more detail in chapter 14, making decisions is one of the most important activities managers perform. And the higher their status or responsibility within an organization, the more crucial this process becomes. Unfortunately, as individuals rise to higher and higher positions, the level of stress they encounter often increases. As a result, many decisions are made under highly stressful conditions. Does this affect the quality of the decisions reached or the process by which they are formed? An experiment performed by Keinan indicates that this is so.[33]

In his study, Keinan asked subjects to make decisions with respect to a series of analogies. For example, one read as follows: "Butter is to margarine as sugar is to . . ." The choices were: beets, saccharine, honey, lemon, candy, chocolate. [The correct answer is saccharine.] For each analogy, subjects could examine any of the six choices by pressing the appropriate key on a computer keyboard. The keys could be pressed in any order subjects wished, as often as they desired. After making their decision, subjects indicated their choice by pressing another key. Stress was introduced into the situation by informing two-thirds of the subjects that they might receive painful electric shocks during the session. One-third were told that these shocks would be delivered at random and were uncontrollable in any manner. Another third were told that the shocks would occur whenever they made errors; presumably these shocks *were* controllable. Subjects in a final (control) group were never threatened with the shocks. Please note: no shocks were ever delivered to participants. Stress

was introduced into the situation merely by mentioning that they might occur.

Keinan predicted that subjects exposed to stress (the threat of painful shocks) would perform more poorly than those for whom stress was absent. To test this hypothesis, he examined several aspects of decision making: the *quality* of subjects' performance (did they choose the right answers?), *premature closure* (did they make decisions before examining all of the possible choices?), and *non-systematic scanning* (did they examine the choices in a systematic way or in a disorganized manner?). As you can see from Figure 7.10 (on page 240), Keinan's hypothesis was confirmed: on all three measures, subjects exposed to stress did indeed do more poorly. The process through which they attempted to reach their decisions was ineffective (e.g., they failed to examine all alternatives), and the decisions themselves tended to be wrong.

Interestingly, the two stress groups (controllable and uncontrollable shocks) did not differ. Apparently, this stemmed from the fact that subjects in the controllable group doubted their ability to avoid the shocks. Thus, in a sense, they were perceived as unavoidable by both groups. This issue aside, the major implications of Keinan's results seem clear. Individuals who must make decisions in the presence of high levels of stress should take special care to guard against shooting from the hip—making decisions without carefully considering all possible choices. If they don't, the decisions they make are likely to be wrong and to prove costly to both themselves and their organizations.

FIGURE 7.10 Stress: Its Impact on Decisions

Individuals exposed to stress were less effective in making decisions than those not exposed to stress. They tended to make decisions before examining all possible choices (they demonstrated premature closure), and the decisions they made tended to be wrong (they showed low decision quality). (Source: Based on data from Keinan, 1987; see Note 33.)

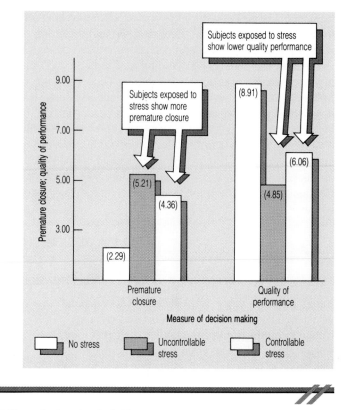

Burnout: Stress and Psychological Adjustment

Most jobs involve some degree of stress. Yet somehow, the persons performing them manage to cope; they continue to function despite their daily encounters with various stressors. Some individuals, though, are not so fortunate. Over time, they seem to be worn down (or out) by repeated exposure to stress. Such persons are often described as suffering from **burnout,** and they demonstrate several distinct characteristics.[34]

First, victims of burnout suffer from *physical exhaustion.* They have low energy and feel tired much of the time. In addition, they report many symptoms of physical strain such as frequent headaches, nausea, poor sleep, and changes in eating habits (e.g., loss of appetite). Second, they experience *emotional exhaustion.* Depression, feelings of helplessness, and feelings of being trapped in one's job are all part of the picture. Third, persons suffering from burnout often demonstrate *mental* or *attitudinal exhaustion.* They become cynical about others, hold negative attitudes toward them, and tend to derogate themselves, their jobs, their organizations, and even life in general. To put it simply, they come to view the world around them through dark gray rather than rose-colored glasses. Finally, they often report feelings of *low personal accomplishment.*[35] Persons suffering from burnout conclude that they haven't been able to accomplish much in the past, and assume that they probably won't succeed in this respect in the future, either. In sum, burnout can be defined as a syndrome of emotional, physical, and mental exhaustion coupled with feelings of low self-esteem or low self-efficacy, resulting from prolonged exposure to intense stress.[36] Please see Figure 7.11 for a summary of the major components of the burnout syndrome.

Burnout: Some major causes. What are the causes of burnout? As we have already noted, the primary factor appears to be prolonged exposure to stress. However, other variables also play a role. In particular, a number of conditions within an organization

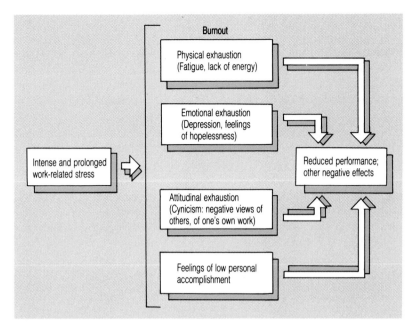

FIGURE 7.11 Burnout: Its Major Components
When individuals are exposed to high levels of stress over prolonged periods of time, they may experience *burnout*. This is a syndrome involving physical, mental, and attitudinal exhaustion, plus feelings of low personal accomplishment.

plus several personal characteristics seem to determine whether, and to what degree, specific individuals experience burnout.[37] For example, job conditions implying that one's efforts are useless, ineffective, or unappreciated seem to contribute to burnout.[38] Under such conditions, individuals develop the feelings of low personal accomplishment which are an important part of burnout. Similarly, poor opportunities for promotion and the presence of inflexible rules and procedures lead employees to feel that they are trapped in an unfair system and contribute to the development of negative views about their jobs.[39] One of the most important factors contributing to burnout, however, is the *leadership style* adopted by employees' supervisors.

Evidence concerning this relationship has been reported by Seltzer and Numerof.[40] These researchers asked over 800 M.B.A. students to report on their own levels of burnout, the leadership style of their supervisors, and several other factors (e.g., their position within their organization, their age, marital status). Results indicated that the lower the amount of consideration demonstrated by their supervisors (i.e., the lower their concern with employees' welfare or with maintaining friendly relations with them), the higher employees' reported levels of burnout. Among the other variables studied, only marital status exerted significant effects: married individuals reported lower levels of burnout than those who were single. (We'll return to the impact of various styles of leadership in chapter 11.)

Burnout: Its major effects. Whatever the precise causes of burnout, once it develops, it has important consequences. First, it may lead individuals to seek new jobs or careers. In one study concerned with the impact of burnout, Jackson, Schwab, and Schuler asked several hundred teachers to complete a questionnaire designed to measure burnout and to report on the extent to which they would prefer to be in another job or career.[41] As expected, the greater the teachers' degree of burnout, the more likely they were to prefer another job and to be actively considering a change of occupation.

Second, persons suffering from burnout may seek administrative roles where they can hide from jobs they have grown to hate behind huge piles of forms. While this pattern certainly occurs, it appears to be relatively rare. Most victims of burnout seem either to change jobs or to withdraw psychologically and mark time until retirement.

Burnout: Can it be reversed? Before concluding, we should comment briefly on one final question: can burnout be reversed? Fortunately, growing evidence suggests that it can. With appropriate help, victims of burnout can recover from their physical and psychological exhaustion. If ongoing stress is reduced, if individuals gain added support from friends and co-workers, and if they cultivate hobbies and other outside interests, at least some persons, it appears, can return to positive attitudes and renewed productivity. Such results can only be attained, however, through active efforts designed to overcome burnout and to change the conditions from which it develops. (Are the causes and effects of stress similar in different cultures? For some revealing information on this question, refer to the **International Perspective** section below.)

OB: AN INTERNATIONAL PERSPECTIVE

Managerial Stress in Different Cultures: Evidence from the United Kingdom and Singapore

In the modern world economy, managers in different nations perform highly similar tasks. It might be assumed, therefore, that the factors contributing to stress, too, are similar. Somewhat surprisingly, efforts to examine the causes and effects of stress in organizations operating in different cultures suggest that this is not so. Perhaps the clearest evidence pointing to this conclusion has been reported by Richardson and Tang, in a study designed to compare the causes and effects of managerial stress in two very different nations: the United Kingdom and Singapore.[42]

In this investigation, the researchers asked a sample of 142 managers in Singapore to complete questionnaires designed to measure the causes of stress in their jobs, the impact of such stress on their personal health, and various aspects of personality that might, potentially, mediate the impact of stress. The results obtained were then compared with those from a very similar study conducted in the United Kingdom by Cooper and Marshall.[43]

Results indicated that in its impact, stress was quite similar in both nations. The higher the levels of stress reported by individuals, the more symptoms of poor health they experienced. However, as shown in Table 7.3, the causes of stress appeared to be quite

different in the two cultures. Among the Singapore sample, accountability (responsibility), office politics, and role conflict were the most important factors. In contrast, in the U.K. sample, overload, bureaucracy, and job security were the factors most closely related to reported stress. What accounts for these differences? Richardson and Tang suggest that they stem directly from cultural factors. In Singapore, managers express a desire to avoid responsibility—they simply don't want to be in charge. This is consistent with traditional values in many oriental cultures, which make many persons reluctant to accept roles that set them apart from others in their group. In Western nations, in contrast, responsibility is often viewed as a sign of status, and is eagerly sought by many persons. Similarly, the importance of office politics in generating stress among the Singapore managers is understandable in view of the fact that Singapore is composed of highly diverse language, cultural, and racial groups (Chinese, Malay, Indian). This leads to strong concerns over the impact of such factors on their careers and their role in office politics. In the United Kingdom, which is more homogenous in these respects, such factors are of less concern to managers and less important as potential sources of stress.

In sum, cross-cultural research suggests that the

TABLE 7.3 Reported Causes of Managerial Stress in Two Cultures

Male managers in Singapore and the United Kingdom reported different (but somewhat overlapping) causes of stress in their jobs. Factors are listed in order of descending importance.

RELATIVE RANK (IMPORTANCE)	NATION	
	SINGAPORE	UNITED KINGDOM
1	Accountability	Overload
2	Office Conflict	Bureaucracy
3	Role Conflict	Job Security
4	Quantitative Overload	Career Development
5	Bureaucracy	Uncertainty
6	Responsibility for People	Lack of Autonomy
7	Managing People	Underload
8	Qualitative Overload	Job Challenges

(Source: Richardson & Tang, 1986; see Note 43.)

causes of stress may vary in different nations and, moreover, that such differences are closely linked to contrasting cultural values. Efforts to understand the nature of stress and its impact in work settings, therefore, must take careful account of such differences and their potential effects.

INDIVIDUAL DIFFERENCES IN RESISTANCE TO STRESS:
OPTIMISM, PESSIMISM, AND HARDINESS

There can be little doubt that individuals differ greatly in their resistance to stress. Some suffer ill effects after exposure to brief periods of relatively mild stress, while others are able to function effectively even after prolonged exposure to much higher levels of stress. How do such persons differ? Research on this topic suggests that several personal tendencies or dispositions are crucial.

Optimism: A Buffer against Stress

One personal factor that seems to play an important role in determining resistance to stress is the familiar dimension of *optimism-pessimism*. Optimists, of course, are people who see the glass as half full; they are hopeful in their outlook on life, interpret a wide range of situations in a positive light, and tend to expect favorable outcomes and results. Pessimists, in contrast, are individuals who see the glass as half empty; they interpret many situations negatively, and expect unfavorable outcomes and results. Recent studies indicate that, as you might well guess, optimists are much more stress resistant than pessimists. For example, optimists are much less likely than pessimists to report physical illness and symptoms during highly stressful periods such as final exams.[44]

Additional findings help explain why. Optimists and pessimists seem to adopt sharply contrasting tactics for coping with stress. Optimists concentrate on *problem-focused coping*—making and enacting specific plans for dealing with sources of stress. In addition, they seek *social support*—the advice and help of friends and others, and refrain from engaging in other activities until current problems are solved and stress is reduced. In contrast, pessimists tend to adopt different strategies, such as giving

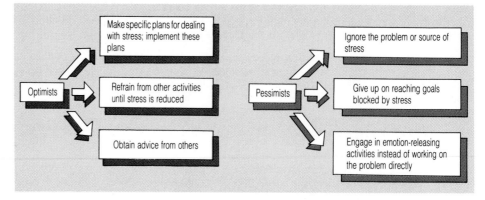

FIGURE 7.12 Optimists and Pessimists: Contrasting Strategies for Coping with Stress

Optimists and pessimists adopt different strategies for coping with stress. In general, those chosen by optimists are more effective. (Source: Based on suggestions by Scheier, Weintraub, & Carver, 1986; see Note 45.)

up in their efforts to reach goals with which stress is interfering, and denying that the stressful events have even occurred.[45] (See Figure 7.12.) Obviously, the former strategies are often more effective than the latter.

Hardiness: Viewing Stress as Challenge

A second characteristic that seems to distinguish stress-resistant people from those who are more susceptible to its harmful effects is known as **hardiness.**[46] Actually, this term refers to a cluster of characteristics rather than just one. Hardy persons seem to differ from others in three respects. First, they show higher levels of *commitment*—deeper involvement in their jobs and other life activities; *control*—the belief that they can, in fact, influence important events in their lives and the outcomes they experience; and *challenge*—they perceive change as a challenge and an opportunity to grow rather than as a threat to their security.

Together, these characteristics tend to arm hardy persons with high resistance to stress. For example, in one study on this topic, Oullette-Kobaska and Pucetti asked executives at a larger public utility to complete questionnaires designed to measure their level of hardiness, the number of stressful life events they had recently experienced, and their current health.[47] Results indicated that persons classified as high in hardiness did indeed report better health than those low in hardiness, even when they had recently encountered major stressful life changes. Similar results have been reported in several other studies with persons from different occupations (e.g., nurses, lawyers, police officers).[48] Together, such findings suggest that hardiness is a useful concept for understanding the impact of stress. However, we should also note that recent evidence suggests that commitment and a sense of control are the most important components of hardiness.[49] Thus, further research concerned with this personal dimension and its role in resistance to stress should focus primarily on these aspects.

The Type A Behavior Pattern Revisited

In chapter 6, we noted that persons who demonstrate the Type A behavior pattern seem to respond more strongly than others to various forms of stress. Specifically, they show higher levels of arousal in the presence of stress than Type B's. Here, we wish to note that not only do Type A's react more strongly to stress, they seem to actually invite it. Specifically, they tend to behave in ways that increase their work load and generate conditions most persons would describe as stressful. Direct evidence for such effects has recently been reported by Kirmeyer and Biggers, in a study of civilian radio dispatchers in police departments.[50] These researchers had seventy-two dispatchers complete a standard measure of Type A behavior (the Jenkins Activity Survey). Then, they observed their behavior on the job during several work shifts. As predicted, these observations revealed that the higher the dispatchers scored on the Type A dimension, the more likely they were to initiate work, to engage in and complete more work, and to divide their attention between two or more simultaneous tasks. As Kirmeyer and Biggers put it (1988, p. 1003): "By their actions Type A's not only constructed for themselves a highly demanding work environment but also created conditions likely to evoke a driven, time-urgent, and impatient behavioral style." Clearly, this is one more reason why individuals who demonstrate the Type A pattern should take steps to modify their behavior: doing so may be extremely beneficial to their health!

Tension Discharge Rate

Nearly everyone experiences some degree of pressure or stress at work—this is a basic fact of life in modern organizations. However, individuals differ greatly in terms of how they handle such feelings at the end of the day. Some seem capable of leaving tension behind when they head for home. In contrast, others take it with them as excess psychological baggage. Which group is more likely to suffer harmful effects from exposure to stress? Obviously, those in the latter. That this is indeed the case, and that individual differences in **tension discharge rate** really matter, is indicated by a study conducted by Matteson and Ivancevich.[51] These researchers had several hundred medical technologists complete two questionnaires. One measured tension discharge rate—the rate at which individuals dissipated their job-related tensions at the end of the day. The second measured several aspects of personal health (e.g., the total number of health problems the technologists had experienced during the past six months). When responses to these two questionnaires were compared, it was found that that persons low in tension discharge rate (those who carried stress home with them at the end of the day) did indeed report poorer health than persons high in tension discharge rate. These findings suggest that the ability to leave one's worries behind at the end of the day can be very beneficial where resisting the harmful impact of stress is concerned. Thus, this is an additional determining factor in the ultimate impact of work-related stress.

MANAGING STRESS: SOME USEFUL TACTICS

Stress stems from so many different factors and conditions that it is probably impossible to eliminate it entirely from our lives. What both individuals and organizations *can* do, however, is take steps to reduce its intensity and minimize its harmful effects—to *cope* with stress when it occurs. Several strategies for attaining these goals exist. Here, we'll consider these under two major headings: techniques individuals can apply themselves and techniques requiring interventions by organizations.

Personal Tactics for Managing Stress

What steps can individuals take to protect themselves against the adverse effects of stress? Several exist and can be readily put to use.

Improved diet and exercise. First, and perhaps foremost, persons concerned with enhancing their own "stress tolerance" can try to increase their *physical fitness*. This involves two major actions: enhancing nutrition and exercise. With respect to nutrition, reduced intake of salt and saturated fats, coupled with increased consumption of fiber and vitamin-rich fruits and vegetables, are steps in the right (adaptive) direction. Such shifts in eating habits enhance the body's ability to cope with the physiological effects of stress, and so to resist its harmful health-related effects.[52]

Exercise, too, can be very helpful in this respect. Growing evidence suggests that persons who exercise regularly show considerably lower rates of various stress-related diseases than those who do not.[53,54] Finally, exercise can reduce both the unpleasant feelings that accompany stress and the physiological strain often associated with it.[55]

Relaxation training and meditation. Two other techniques that often prove useful in the battle against stress are **relaxation training,** and **meditation.** Both are designed to help individuals replace feelings of strain and tension with ones of relaxation.

In *relaxation training,* individuals are first taught to induce relaxation in their own muscles.[56] This involves alternate tensing and relaxing of various muscles in order to become very familiar with the different feelings associated with these two states. As a result of such training, individuals gradually become capable of inducing muscle relaxation at will. Next, persons undergoing relaxation training are asked to think about situations in which they typically experience stress. As they do, they practice relaxation in the presence of such thoughts. If this training is successful, persons who have undergone it can then transfer the ability to generate feelings of relaxation to situations in which they actually experience stress. As a result, they are better able to cope with such feelings than they had been previously. (See Figure 7.13 for a summary of these procedures.)

A related tactic is **meditation.** Persons using meditation adopt a comfortable position, close their eyes, and clear all disturbing thoughts from their minds. Then they silently repeat a single syllable or *mantra* over and over again. In some forms of meditation, a specific position or posture is required (e.g., the Lotus position in Zen meditation); in others, it is assumed that any posture users find comfortable will do. Meditation remains somewhat controversial, but many persons report that it helps them feel relaxed. Further, some studies report that meditation induces brain-wave patterns indicative of a calm mental state.[57]

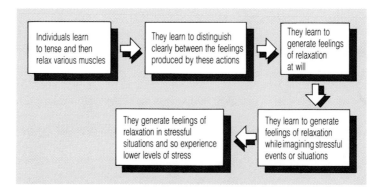

FIGURE 7.13 Relaxation Training: An Overview
Through *relaxation training,* individuals learn to generate feelings of relaxation at times when they are exposed to stress. Such feelings help to counter both the tension associated with stress and its harmful effects on personal health.

Changing behavioral and cognitive reactions to stress. The tactics for coping with stress mentioned so far focus primarily on modifying *physiological* reactions to stress—reducing the arousal it produces and enhancing our ability to withstand its harmful biological effects. Other tactics for managing stress focus, instead, on modifying our *behavioral* and *cognitive* reactions in stressful situations.[58] These techniques are based on the following assertion: While we can't always change the world around us, we *can* often change our reactions to it. In this way, we can enhance our ability to handle stress.

With respect to *behavioral reactions* to stress, several procedures can be useful. First, when faced with events they find very stressful, individuals can often help themselves to stem the rising tide of anxiety by adopting actions that are incompatible with such feelings. For example, instead of allowing their speech to become increasingly rapid and intense as they become upset, they can consciously modulate this aspect of their behavior. The result may be a reduction in arousal and tension. This technique is especially helpful for Type A's, whose always-in-a-hurry style tends to magnify reactions to stress in many situations.

Similarly, when confronted with rising tension, individuals can consciously choose to insert a brief period of delay (sometimes known as *time-out*). This can involve taking a short break, going to the nearest restroom to splash cold water on one's face, or any other action that yields a few moments of "breathing space." Such actions interrupt the cycle of ever-rising tension that accompanies stress, and can help to restore equilibrium and the feeling of being at least partly in control of ongoing events.

Turning to *cognitive reactions*, we have already discussed the importance of cognitive appraisals in determining reactions to stress. Put simply, when individuals perceive situations as threatening, dangerous, or out of control, the stress they experience rises, and may soon reach extreme levels. Even worse, when exposed to stress, many persons engage in what some researchers describe as inappropriate "self-talk."[59] They tell themselves over and over again how horrible and unbearable it will be if they fail, if they are not perfect, or if they can't convince others to agree with them. Obviously, such reactions serve as an added source of stress, and also intensify stress that is already present as a result of other factors. Fortunately, such reactions *can* be modified. Indeed, for many persons merely recognizing that they have implicitly accepted such an irrational and self-defeating quest for perfection is sufficient to produce beneficial change and heightened resistance to stress. Please note: this in no way implies tendencies to ignore real threats or dangers, or to surrender all efforts to improve. On the contrary, it merely suggests that where managing stress is concerned, efforts to assess situations *rationally* and to choose goals one can *reasonably* hope to achieve, can be very helpful.

Additional tactics for managing stress that can be used by individuals include developing hobbies that distract them from the pressures of their jobs, taking short vacations in order to "unwind," and learning to structure their work and personal lives so that these do not consist of a perpetual struggle to meet important deadlines. Through such steps, many persons can enhance their ability to meet—and cope with—the unavoidable stress connected with their work.

Organization-Based Strategies for Managing Stress

While individuals can increase their own resistance to stress, they cannot, by themselves, eliminate many of its causes from their work environments. For this reason, organizations, too, can play a key role in stress management. They can adopt changes in their internal structure and procedures, or alter the nature of jobs to reduce stress among employees.

Changes in organizational structure and function. Several changes in organizational policy and function are useful in reducing job-related stress. First, such benefits can sometimes be gained by *decentralization*—a process in which authority is spread more widely throughout an organization. This reduces feelings of helplessness among employees, and so reduces their overall level of stress. Second, employees can be afforded greater participation in decisions, especially ones involving their jobs. As we noted earlier, the lack of opportunities for such input can be a major source of stress. Third, steps can be taken to assure that performance appraisals and the distribution of organizational rewards are as fair as possible. To the extent individuals perceive that these matters are being handled in a reasonable manner, the stress relating to them can be significantly reduced.

Changes in the nature of specific jobs. In addition to the changes described above, stress can also be reduced through careful attention to the nature of specific jobs. For example, the stress resulting from boring, repetitive tasks can be lessened through *job enlargement*—efforts to broaden the scope of the activities they involve. Second, stress deriving from feelings of lack of control can be reduced by *job enrichment*— procedures in which employees are provided with more responsibility for planning and directing their own work. Third, the stressfulness of specific jobs can be reduced through such steps as limiting unnecessary travel or geographic relocations. Finally, important causes of stress can be removed through eliminating hazardous or unpleasant working conditions.

Employee fitness programs. Before concluding, we should mention one additional procedure for enhancing employees' ability to resist stress—**employee fitness programs.** These are programs, run and funded by organizations, to improve the physical fitness of their employees.[60] Such programs are based, in part, on the evidence reviewed above, suggesting that improved physical fitness increases individuals' resistance to the adverse effects of stress. However, their growing popularity also derives from findings suggesting that physical fitness reduces absenteeism and enhances productivity,[61] plus other evidence suggesting that employee fitness programs contribute to commitment and other positive attitudes among employees.[62] (These latter benefits stem from the fact that employees perceive company-sponsored fitness programs as a sign that the organization is truly concerned about their welfare.) Given these important benefits, it is not at all surprising that such programs have grown in popularity and are now widespread throughout many different industries; indeed more than 50,000 are in operation at the present time.[63]

Summary and Review

The Nature of Stress. Stress is a pattern of emotional states and physiological reactions occurring in situations where individuals perceive threats to their important goals, which they may be unable to meet. To fully understand stress, we must consider the external factors that produce individuals' *cognitive appraisal* of stressors, and the internal reactions (e.g., physiological arousal) that accompany it.

Major Causes of Stress. Stress in work settings stems from many different factors. Several of these are directly related to jobs and organizations themselves (e.g., occupational demands, role conflict and ambiguity, responsibility for others, underload and overload, lack of social support). One especially unsettling cause of work-related stress is **sexual harassment,** unwanted sexual contact or communication. Other sources of work-related stress include performance appraisals and physical working conditions.

Stress also stems from events and situations outside work settings. *Stressful life events* such as divorce or death of a close relative are an important source of stress. When individuals experience several of these events within a relatively short period of time, their health may suffer greatly. Stress also stems from the *hassles of daily life*— milder but frequent events that strain individuals' resources.

Effects of Stress. Stress often has an adverse impact on health. Indeed, it has been implicated in such serious illnesses as heart disease and high blood pressure. Even relatively moderate levels of stress appear to interfere with the effective performance of many tasks. However, large individual differences exist in this respect. Stress actually seems to enhance the performance of those who enjoy and seek arousal or high levels of stimulation (*paratelic dominant* persons). However, it interferes with the performance of those who dislike arousal or stimulation (*telic dominant* persons).

Prolonged exposure to intense stress may result in **burnout,** a syndrome consisting of physical, emotional, and mental exhaustion, plus intense feelings of low personal accomplishment. Burnout is affected by several different factors, but one of the most important of these appears to be the *leadership style* adopted by supervisors. Burnout is more common among the subordinates of leaders who are low in showing consideration than among leaders who are high in such behavior.

Stress stems from somewhat different factors in different cultures. Its effects on health, though, seem to be quite similar around the world.

Individual Differences in Resistance to Stress. Large individual differences exist in the ability to resist stress. *Optimists* are better able to cope with stress than pessimists. Persons high in **hardiness** (a combination of high commitment, feelings of personal control, and the tendency to perceive change as a challenge rather than a threat) are better able to resist the adverse effects of stress than persons low in hardiness. Type A persons are more susceptible to the impact of stress than others because they behave in ways that expose them to high levels of stress and because they react more strongly to it when it occurs. Persons who are able to leave stress at the office (those high in **tension discharge rate**) are less affected by stress than those who carry it home with them at the end of the day (those who are low in tension discharge rate).

Techniques for Managing Stress. Several techniques are useful in managing stress. Individuals can improve their physical fitness through changes in diet or exercise. Alternatively, they can adopt techniques designed to help them relax following exposure to stress (**relaxation training, meditation**). Modifying both *behavioral* and *cognitive* reactions to stress is also very helpful. Organizations can act to reduce stress among employees by changes in their internal structure (e.g., decentralization of authority) and by adjusting the requirements of specific jobs. In recent years, many companies have sponsored **employee fitness programs.** Such programs enhance the physical fitness of employees, and also encourage positive work-related attitudes such as organizational commitment.

KEY TERMS

burnout: A syndrome resulting from prolonged exposure to stress. It consists of physical, emotional, and mental exhaustion, plus feelings of a lack of personal accomplishment.

employee fitness programs: Organization-sponsored programs designed to enhance the physical fitness of employees.

hardiness: A combination of traits (commitment to one's work, a sense of personal control, the ability to view change as a challenge rather than as a threat) which enables individuals to resist the harmful effects of stress.

meditation: A technique for inducing relaxation in which individuals clear disturbing thoughts from their minds by repeating a single syllable (*mantra*).

performance appraisal: The process through which individuals' job performance is evaluated and feedback about this is provided to them.

qualitative overload: The belief, among employees, that they lack the skills or abilities needed to perform their jobs.

qualitative underload: The lack of mental stimulation that accompanies many routine, repetitive jobs.

quantitative overload: Occurs when individuals are required to do more work than they can actually accomplish in a given period of time.

quantitative underload: Occurs when individuals have so little to do that they spend much of their time doing nothing.

relaxation training: Procedures through which individuals learn to relax in order to reduce anxiety or stress.

role ambiguity: Uncertainty among employees about the key requirements of their jobs and how they should divide their time between various tasks.

role conflict: Occurs when different groups or persons make incompatible demands on an individual.

sexual harassment: Unwanted contact or communication of a sexual nature.

stress: A pattern of emotional states and physiological reactions occurring in situations where individuals perceive threats to their important goals that they feel unable to meet.

stressors: Various factors in the external environment that induce stress among persons exposed to them.

tension discharge rate: The rate at which individuals rid themselves of work-related tension at the end of the day. Persons high in *tension discharge rate* leave such tensions at the office, while those low in this characteristic tend to bring them home.

QUESTIONS FOR DISCUSSION

1. Two individuals exposed to the same situation may experience widely different levels of stress. Why?

2. Suppose you were considering a new job. What factors would you examine closely in order to determine how stressful the new position might be?

3. It has long been widely believed that stress enhances performance on many tasks, at least up to a point. Is this really the case? If not, why?

4. Imagine that you were choosing employees for a high-stress job. What personal characteristics would you seek in the persons you hired? What characteristics would you try to avoid?

5. Some individuals seem to thrive on high levels of stress; indeed, they actively choose work settings that provide such excitement. Will such persons suffer harmful effects from their chosen lifestyles, or are they relatively immune to such effects?

6. Suppose you found that you were suffering harmful effects (both physical and psychological) as a result of high levels of stress. What steps might you take to manage stress or cope with it?

7. Stress-related illnesses often prove very costly to organizations in terms of employee absence. What steps can companies take to reduce such effects and their associated costs?

NOTES

1. Kahn, R. (1989). Stress and behavior in work settings. In M. D. Dunnette (Ed.), *Handbook of industrial and organizational psychology* (2nd ed.). Palo Alto, CA: Consulting Psychologists Press.

2. Selye, H. (1976). *Stress in health and disease.* Boston: Butterworths.

3. Lazarus, R. S., & Folkman, S. (1984). *Stress, appraisal, and coping.* New York: Springer.

4. Lazarus, R. S., Delongis, A., Folkman, S., & Gruen, R. (1985). Stress and adaptational outcomes: The problem of confounded measures. *American Psychologist, 40,* 770–779.

5. See Note 1.

6. McGrath, J. E. (1976). Stress and behavior in organizations. In M. D. Dunnette (Ed.), *Handbook of industrial and organizational psychology.* Palo Alto, CA: Consulting Psychologists Press.

7. National Institute for Occupational Safety and Health, Department of Health, Education, and Welfare (1978). Washington, D.C.: Government Printing Office.

8. Shaw, J. B., & Riskind, J. H. (1983). Predicting job stress using data from the position analysis questionnaire. *Journal of Applied Psychology, 68,* 253–261.

9. Newton, T. J., & Keenan, A. (1987). Role stress reexamined: An investigation of role stress predictors. *Organizational Behavior and Human Decision Processes, 40,* 346–368.

10. See Note 6.

11. French, J. R. P., & Caplan, R. D. (1972). Organizational stress and individual strain. In A. J. Morrow (Ed.), *The failure of success.* New York: Amacom.

12. McClean, A. A. (1980). *Work stress.* Reading, MA: Addison-Wesley.

13. Oullette-Kobasa, S. C., & Pucetti, M. C. (1983). Personality and social resources in stress resistance. *Journal of Personality and Social Psychology, 45,* 839–850.

14. Costanza, R. S., Derlega, V. J., & Winstead, B. A. (1988). Positive and negative forms of social support: Effects of conversational topics on coping with stress among same-sex friends. *Journal of Experimental Social Psychology, 24,* 182–193.

15. Gutek, B., Nakamura, C. Y., Gahart, M., Handschumacher, J. W., & Russell, D. (1980). Sexuality and the workplace. *Basic and Applied Social Psychology, 1,* 255–265.

16. Ewing, D. W. (1983). Your right to fire. *Harvard Business Review, 61*(2), 32–42.

17. Terpstra, D. E., & Baker, D. D. (1988). Outcomes of sexual harassment charges. *Academy of Management Journal, 31,* 185–194.

18. Oldham, G. R., & Fried, Y. (1987). Employee reactions to workspace characteristics. *Journal of Applied Psychology, 72,* 75–80.

19. Baron, R. A., & Bingley, J. (1988). *Effects of a merger on work-related attitudes, stereotyping, and conflict.* Paper presented at the meetings of the Eastern Psychological Association, Boston.

20. See Note 4.

21. Holmes, T. H., & Rahe, R. H. (1967). Social readjustment rating scale. *Journal of Psychosomatic Research, 11,* 213–218.

22. Holmes, T. H., & Masuda, M. (1974). Life change and illness susceptibility. In B. S. Dohrenwend & B. P. Dohrenwend (Eds.), *Stressful life events: Their nature and effects* (pp. 45–72). New York: Wiley.

23. See Note 13.

24. See Note 4.

25. See Note 4.

26. Weinberger, M., Hiner, S. L., & Tierney, W. M. (1987). In support of hassles as a measure of stress in predicting health outcomes. *Journal of Biological Medicine, 10,* 19–31.

27. Frese, M. (1985). Stress at work and psychosomatic complaints: A causal interpretation. *Journal of Applied Psychology, 70,* 314–328.

28. Ader, R., & Cohen, N. (1984). Behavior and the immune system. In W. D. Gentry (Ed.), *Handbook of behavioral medicine.* New York: Guilford.

29. Locke, S. E. (1982). Stress, adaptation, and immunity: Studies in humans. *General Hospital Psychiatry, 4,* 16–25.

30. Motowidlo, S. J., Packard, J. S., & Manning, M. R. (1986). Occupational stress: Its causes and consequences for job performance. *Journal of Applied Psychology, 71,* 618–629.

31. Berlyne, D. E. (1967). Arousal and reinforcement. In D. Levine (Ed.), *Nebraska Symposium on Motivation,* vol. 15 (pp. 279–286). Lincoln, NE: Univ. of Nebraska Press.

32. Martin, R. A., Kuiper, N. A., Olinger, L. J., & Dobbin, J. (1988). Is stress always bad? Telic versus paratelic dominance as a stress-mediating variable. *Journal of Personality and Social Psychology, 53,* 970–982.

33. Keinan, G. (1987). Decision making under stress: Scanning of alternatives under controllable and uncontrollable threats. *Journal of Personality and Social Psychology, 52,* 638–644.

34. Maslach, C. (1982). Understanding burnout: Definitional issues in analyzing a complex phenomenon. In W. S. Paine (Ed.), *Job stress and burnout: Research, theory, and intervention perspectives.* Beverly Hills: Sage.

35. Maslach, C., & Jackson, S. E. (1984). Burnout in organizational settings. In S. Oskamp (Ed.), *Applied social psychology annual,* vol. 5 (pp. 135–154). Beverly Hills: Sage.

36. See Note 34.

37. Golombiewski, R. T., Nunzenrider, R. F., & Stevenson, J. G. (1986). *Stress in organizations: Toward a phase model of burnout.* New York: Praeger Publishers.

38. Pines, A. M., Aronson, E., & Kafry, D. (1981). *Burnout: From tedium to personal growth.* New York: Freeman.

39. Gaines, J., & Jermier, J. M. (1983). Emotional exhaustion in high stress organizations. *Academy of Management Journal, 26,* 567–586.

40. Seltzer, J., & Numerof, R. E. (1988). Supervisory leadership and subordinate burnout. *Academy of Management Journal, 31,* 439–446.

41. Jackson, S. E., Schwab, R. L., & Schuler, R. S. (1986). Toward an understanding of the burnout phenomenon. *Journal of Applied Psychology, 71,* 630–640.

42. Marshall, J., & Cooper, C. L. (1979). *Executives under pressure.* London: Macmillan.

43. Richardson, S., & Tang, E. (1986). Male managers under stress in Singapore. *International Journal of Industrial Ergonomics, 1,* 115–126.

44. Scheier, M. F., & Carver, C. S. (1985). Optimism, coping, and health: Assessment and implications of generalized outcome expectancies. *Health Psychology, 4,* 219–247.

45. Scheier, M. F., Weintraub, J. K., & Carver, C. S. (1986). Coping with stress: Divergent strategies of optimists and pessimists. *Journal of Personality and Social Psychology, 51,* 1257–1264.

46. Kobasa, S. C. (1979). Stressful life events, personality, and health: An inquiry into hardiness. *Journal of Personality and Social Psychology, 37,* 1–11.

47. See Note 13.

48. Rich, V. L., & Rich, A. R. (1985). *Personality hardiness and burnout in female staff nurses.* Paper presented at the annual convention of the American Psychological Association, Los Angeles.

49. Hull, J. G., Van Treuren, R. R., & Virnelli, S. (1987). Hardiness and health: A critique and alternative ap-

proach. *Journal of Personality and Social Psychology, 53,* 518–530.

50. Kirmeyer, S. L., & Biggers, K. (1988). Environmental demand and demand engendering behavior: An observational analysis of the Type A pattern. *Journal of Personality and Social Psychology, 54,* 997–1005.

51. Matteson, M. T., & Ivancevich, J. M. (1983). Note on tension discharge rate as an employee health status predictor. *Academy of Management Journal, 26,* 540–545.

52. Davis, M., Eshelman, E. R., & McKay, M. (1982). *The relaxation and stress reduction workbook.* Oakland, CA: New Harbinger Publications.

53. See Note 12.

54. Girdana, D., & Everly, G. (1979). *Controlling stress and tension: A holistic approach.* Englewood Cliffs, NJ: Prentice-Hall.

55. Falkenberg, L. E. (1987). Employee fitness programs: Their impact on the employee and the organization. *Academy of Management Review, 12,* 511–522.

56. Wallace, B., & Fisher, L. E. (1987). *Consciousness and behavior* (2nd ed.). Boston: Allyn & Bacon.

57. Wallace, R. K., & Benson, H. (1972). The physiology of meditation. *Scientific American, 226,* pp. 84–90.

58. Roskies, E. (1987). *Stress management for the healthy Type A.* New York: Guilford Press.

59. Meichenbaum. *Stress inoculation training.* New York: Pergamon.

60. Shepherd, R. J., Cox, M., & Corey, P. (1981). Fitness program participation: Its effects on workers' performance. *Journal of Occupational Medicine, 23,* 359–363.

61. Shephard, R. J., Cox, M., & Corey, P. (1981). Fitness program: Its effect on workers' performance. *Journal of Occupational Medicine, 23,* 359–363.

62. Cox, M., Shephard, R., & Corey, P. (1981). Influence of an employee fitness programme upon fitness, productivity and absenteeism. *Ergonomics, 24,* 795–806.

63. See Note 55.

The Unexpected Stress of Success

Wes Creel, co-founder of Creel Morrell Inc., a graphic design firm, had not been feeling well. In fact, he had been feeling so badly that he decided to go to the world-famous Cooper Clinic in Dallas to check into what he might do to improve the physical symptoms that were resulting from the stress associated with the fast growth of his company. Although Creel may have been the most visible employee to seek medical attention, he was hardly the only one feeling the stresses of the company's success.[1] Employees joked, a little too seriously, that C.M.I.—the company's initials—stood for Crisis Management Inc. The jokes turned sour, though, as employees, chronically stressed from the huge workload, suddenly quit when they could no longer tolerate the excessive pressure. This, of course, only made it worse for the remaining employees. Although Creel understood that everyone in the company was experiencing stress in a harmful way, he didn't understand why. After all, the graphic design firm that he co-founded with his wife, Nancy, and graphic designer, Eric Morrell—Creel Morrell Inc. (of Austin Texas)—was amazingly successful! The company had grown from $0 to $4 million in revenues in less than seven years, making the *Inc.* list of the 500 fastest growing small businesses three years in a row. C.M.I. had more business than it could handle!

Of course, it was this great volume as well as the *way* they tried to handle it that led to the stresses experienced by Creel and his employees. Creel was so delighted that businesses wanted his company's services (for designing brochures, annual reports, signs, training materials, and business cards, among other projects) that no job was ever turned down—no matter how small. Because small jobs, such as business cards, were generally added on to an already busy designer's work load, the designers were constantly struggling to keep up with their work. Additionally, because Creel Morrell had prided itself on doing top-of-the-line projects such as annual reports, small projects like business cards were held in low esteem. Consequently, the designers who found themselves having to work on these low-level projects became irritated as well as overworked.

The heavy work load was not the only problem underlying the stress experienced by the Creel Morrell staff. Creel believed in hands-on management to the extreme. After all, he reasoned, it was his job to ensure the growth and development of the company. As a result, he got involved in nearly all decision making—even such day to day decisions as selecting the types of soda for the drink machine! No one could make a decision without having his prior approval. In addition, he tended to hoard information resulting in his employees' beliefs that "You [Creel] are the only one who knows what is going on."[2] Related to this, employees felt that they didn't get to participate in discussions about decision making. Ironically, Creel himself felt irritated by the fact that the employees didn't make more of their own decisions and didn't participate in the decision-making process.

When Creel checked into the Cooper Clinic he received quite a shock. His physician informed him that if he didn't change his lifestyle, reduce the stress in his life, and improve his physical health, he wouldn't live another fifteen years (at the time he was only thirty-three!). Creel recognized that something drastic had to be done in order to save not only his life but the life of his company. After much searching for answers, a consultant was called on to help identify the company's problems and to develop some solutions.

After seven monthly meetings during which problems and potential solutions were identified, things began to improve at Creel Morrell. An internship program was implemented that brought in local college students to help work on the small projects. This freed the senior designers from the routine projects and let them concentrate on the more complicated and prestigious design work. It also resulted in a supply of well-trained individuals who could easily fit into the company after graduation. Additionally, employees developed their own job descriptions. This resulted in two major benefits. First, each employee now clearly understood his or her own particular job responsibilities. Second, doing this helped identify areas where work was not getting done— thus prompting the hiring of someone to fill these needs. Furthermore, decision making was pushed down to lower levels. No longer was Creel's approval necessary for mundane decisions. This was further helped by the fact that Creel and his wife moved to a satellite office near their home in Houston. As a result they weren't around much to be contacted about decisions. Also, they reduced their tremendous commuting time, enabling them to spend more time with their family.

Although no individual stress-reduction program was implemented at Creel Morrell, corporate changes allowed for individuals to reduce their stress at work significantly enough so they could achieve a more comfortable existence at work as well as in their non-work pursuits. By doing so, the company continued to grow—revenues were expected to rise to $6 million after the change. Meanwhile, Creel's personal health and lifestyle also improved—he took vacations, began jogging, and shed fifty excess pounds.

Questions for Discussion

1. What types of work-related stress did Wes Creel experience? Give examples.

2. What types of work-related stress did the employees of Creel Morrell experience? Give examples.

3. What organizational change strategies were implemented to reduce stress at Creel Morrell? Give examples.

4. Although it is clear that stress affected the physical health of Creel and his employees, did it also affect the corporate health of C.M.I.? What do you think would have happened if nothing had changed?

Notes

1. Brown, P. (1987, May). Stop the treadmill, I want to get off. *Inc.,* pp. 92–98.
2. See Note 1, p. 94.

Burnout Blues

As the police officer approached the side of his new BMW, Bob Weiss realized he was in trouble. On this evening, typical in all ways, Bob had been entertaining clients, drinking too much, and had almost flipped his car over while trying to merge onto the highway. This would have been his fourth accident in less than three years. Luckily, he gained control of the car and kept it right-side-up, injuring no one. An officer witnessed the entire event. Although Bob did not get a ticket (the officer knew Bob from his former job as a journalist), he did get an inspiration: he realized that he was burned out.[1]

Bob's story starts innocently enough. At age twenty-four, he quit his job as a newspaper reporter and began his own public relations company. In Denver, where he lived, there were many new small companies in need of publicity and promotion. Bob's own new small company, Alyn-Weiss & Associates, began to grow by leaps and bounds. Although seven additional employees were hired, Bob believed there was no business without him. As a result, he involved himself in all of the business's affairs. Not only did he oversee all aspects of work at the office, he also constantly courted clients, entertaining them at private country clubs and posh restaurants. He came to believe he needed to be on call all day, everyday. His undivided focus on his business resulted in the break-up of his marriage, the loss of all his friendships, and neglect of all the leisure activities he once enjoyed. In addition, his health suffered. He regularly came down with the flu for three days every three months.

After the near-accident, Weiss developed a new approach to doing business. He decided to work smarter and not harder. His first step in this approach was to reduce the size of the business by dropping all low-revenue accounts and letting the number of employees shrink through attrition. That done, he found the following year that he worked less hard, yet realized a 25 percent increase in net revenues. He next installed a computerized billing system and sought the services of attorneys to urge clients to pay their bills on time. He also moved his office closer to his home, reducing his commuting time. Now he takes off every Wednesday afternoon to spend time with his new wife. Now, Bob works less hard, while his business prospers. Weiss describes his new philosophy, "Let's face it, a business that's half the business and twice as well run is the same business—probably better."[2]

Questions for Discussion

1. Why does it so frequently take an emergency to alert people who are suffering from burnout to their condition?

2. What stages of burnout did Bob Weiss experience?

3. Do you think Bob Weiss is a Type A or Type B? How might this have contributed to his mental attitude?

Notes

1. Grossmann, J. (1987, September), Burnout. *Inc.*, pp. 89–96.
2. See Note 1, p. 93.

Personal Characteristics and Resistance to Stress

Individuals differ greatly in their ability to withstand the effects of stress. While some literally crumble in the face of high levels of stress, others survive—or even thrive—in its presence. Where do you stand on this dimension? For some insight into this issue, follow the instructions below.

Procedure

Please indicate the extent to which you agree or disagree with each of the statements listed below. (Circle one answer for each.)

LIFE ORIENTATION TEST

1. I hardly ever expect things to go my way.

Strongly Disagree	Disagree	Uncertain	Agree	Strongly Agree
1	2	3	4	5

2. In unusual times, I generally expect the best.

Strongly Disagree	Disagree	Uncertain	Agree	Strongly Agree
1	2	3	4	5

3. I tend to worry about the possibility of failure.

Strongly Disagree	Disagree	Uncertain	Agree	Strongly Agree
1	2	3	4	5

4. I'm usually pretty certain that things will turn out well in the end.

Strongly Disagree	Disagree	Uncertain	Agree	Strongly Agree
1	2	3	4	5

5. Most difficulties can be overcome by hard work.

Strongly Disagree	Disagree	Uncertain	Agree	Strongly Agree
1	2	3	4	5

6. Very few people can be relied on or trusted.

Strongly Disagree	Disagree	Uncertain	Agree	Strongly Agree
1	2	3	4	5

7. When I face a difficult problem, I often try to avoid thinking about it.

Strongly Disagree	Disagree	Uncertain	Agree	Strongly Agree
1	2	3	4	5

8. Painful life experiences often help us to grow as individuals.

Strongly Disagree	Disagree	Uncertain	Agree	Strongly Agree
1	2	3	4	5

To obtain your score:

Add numbers for items 2, 4, 5, and 8.
From this, subtract numbers for items 1, 3, 6, and 7.

Your Score: _____

Points to Consider

The questions you have just answered are similar to ones on a widely-used test designed to measure individual differences in *optimism-pessimism*. If you scored twelve or above, you are quite high on this dimension (i.e., you are an optimist). If you scored four or below, you are low on this dimension. Research findings suggest that optimists are generally better able to resist the adverse effects of stress than pessimists. Does your own position on the optimism-pessimism dimension reflect your own ability to cope with stress?

If you are something of a pessimist, don't despair. In contrast to many other personal characteristics, your standing on the optimism-pessimism dimension can be readily modified. All that's necessary, in many cases, is a shift in personal perceptions— from viewing many situations as potentially threatening and filled with hidden (or obvious) pitfalls, to ones filled with challenge and opportunity. If you are relatively pessimistic, you might find it worthwhile to pursue this type of shift. The health you improve may well be your own!

CHAPTER EIGHT

GROUP DYNAMICS: UNDERSTANDING GROUPS AT WORK

CHAPTER OUTLINE

Groups at Work: Some Basic Issues
What Is a Group?
Types of Groups within Organizations
The Development of Groups

The Structure of Work Groups
Roles: The Many Hats We Wear
Norms: A Group's Unspoken Rules
Status: The Prestige of Group Membership
Cohesiveness: Getting the "Team Spirit"

Task Performance: Working with and around Others
Social Facilitation: Individual Performance in the Presence of Others

Social Loafing: "Free Riding" When Working with Others
Performance on Other Types of Group Tasks

Special Sections

OB: A Management Perspective
Guidelines for Creating Effective Work Teams

OB: A Research Perspective
Social Loafing on a Judgmental Task: The Importance of Feeling Dispensable

LEARNING OBJECTIVES

After reading this chapter, you should be able to:
1. Define what a group is, and distinguish a group from other collections of people.
2. Identify different types of groups operating within organizations and understand how they develop.
3. Describe the different roles played by individuals within organizations.
4. Understand what norms are and how they develop within groups.
5. Distinguish between different forms of status and explain how they influence organizational behavior.
6. Identify the causes and consequences of group cohesiveness within organizations.
7. Describe the phenomenon of social facilitation and explain why it occurs.
8. Identify and describe the social loafing effect and some ways of overcoming it.
9. Distinguish between additive, compensatory, disjunctive, and conjunctive group tasks, and summarize how well these different groups perform relative to individuals.

For three years Eddie Appleton worked alone in the dispatcher's office at Cramer Enterprises, an importer and wholesaler of Asian manufactured goods. Now, however, the company had grown so large that Eddie couldn't do the job by himself anymore. There were just too many shipments coming in and too many delivery trucks going out to keep track of. Mr. Cramer, the owner, knew it, and hired Ben Fong and Andy Chapman to assist Eddie. But Eddie wasn't used to help and couldn't quite get the hang of working with his new assistants.

"Hey, you guys, keep it down," Eddie said, "I'm trying to get some work done here."

"Keep cool, man," replied Andy, "Ben and I were just checking with the loading dock for spaces to unload the next trailer. We gotta talk to do our jobs!"

"Yeah," Ben chimed in, "you want us to talk in sign language or something?" They all laughed.

"No problem, guys. You know, I can help you with where to put that trailer. There's usually space over in D-22 around this time. Give me the phone, I'll call down to the loading dock and make sure."

Ben and Andy just looked at each other, but then Ben spoke up. "Hey Eddie, you gonna let us do our jobs or what?"

Before Eddie could answer, Andy spoke up too. "He's right, Eddie, what's the matter with you? You don't let us talk, you don't give us a chance to work. We're not much of a team around here."

"Sorry, you're right," replied Eddie. "I guess I'm just used to doing this job alone. For three years I did everything, I had no distractions, no one to share the work with. I just kinda got used to taking care of everything myself."

"No way you can do that anymore," Ben replied. "Old man Cramer told us you were getting swamped. Now, we're here to help."

"That's right," added Andy, "we're supposed to work as a team now, the 'Dispatching Department,' that's what it says on the door."

"I suppose you're right," said Eddie. "I always wanted some help around here, but when Cramer gave it to me, I just wasn't ready for it. After working by myself for so long, I forgot how to work as part of a team."

"No problem," said Ben.

"That's right," Andy chimed in, "we'll all have to learn to work together if we're gonna get anything done around here."

"Okay, okay, I'm convinced," apologized Eddie. "Thanks for putting up with me. You guys are okay. I think we'll have a pretty good Dispatching Department after all— if you guys keep me in line."

"You can count on that," Ben replied.

Keeping this conversation in mind, a few weeks later Eddie came to work with something to show everyone he was ready to be part of a group—windbreakers in the company's colors with each guy's name on the back. On the front was a patch identifying the wearer as member of the "Dispatching Department."

"Gentlemen," Eddie proudly proclaimed as he handed the jackets to Andy and Ben, "our team jackets."

Only time will tell, of course, whether or not Cramer Enterprises' Dispatching Department eventually will function as an effective work team. There are clearly some obstacles to overcome as Eddie makes the transition from working alone to working as part of a group. He will have to learn to work in the presence of others, and he will have to learn to coordinate his efforts with Ben and Andy. How will the group grow and develop? Will a team spirit develop as the group evolves? Would the company have been better off keeping Eddie working alone, or will the group help the company be more productive? These questions are all basic to the field of **group dynamics**—an important topic in organizational behavior, and the focus of this chapter.

Group dynamics focuses on the nature of groups—the factors governing their formation and development, their structural elements, and their interrelations with individuals, other groups, and the organizations within which they exist.[1] Given the prevalence of groups in organizations, group dynamics is a very important topic in the field of organizational behavior. Moreover, it has a very long history of study in the social sciences. In fact, it has been said that the study of social groups "does not 'belong' to any one of the recognized social sciences alone. It is the common property of all."[2] As such, our presentation of group dynamics will be derived from work in the fields of psychology, sociology, communication, and anthropology, and applied to the domain of work organizations.

There are many key aspects of group dynamics of interest to social scientists studying organizational behavior. Specifically, we will focus on how groups are structured, the dynamics of their operation, and the forces that keep them together. We will then examine group performance, first exploring how individuals are influenced by the presence of groups, and finally reviewing the performance of different types of work groups. Before proceeding with these topics, however, we will begin by considering some very basic issues about the nature of groups themselves.

GROUPS AT WORK: SOME BASIC ISSUES

In order to understand the dynamics of groups and their influence on individual and organizational functioning, we must begin by addressing some very basic questions—namely, what is a group, what types of groups exist, and how do groups form?

What Is a Group?

Imagine three people waiting in line at the cashier's desk at a department store. Now, compare them to Eddie, Ben and Andy, the three characters in our opening story. Which collection of people would you consider a "group"? Although in our everyday language we may refer to the people waiting in line as a "group," they are clearly not a group in the same sense as our three characters at Cramer Enterprises. Obviously, a group is more than just a collection of people, but what exactly makes a group a group?

Social scientists have formally defined a **group** as *a collection of two or more interacting individuals with a stable pattern of relationships between them who share common goals and who perceive themselves as being a group.*[3] Obviously, this definition needs to be examined more closely. For this reason, we have summarized the various parts of the definition in Figure 8.1.

One of the most obvious characteristics of a group is that it is composed of *two or more people in social interaction.* In other words, the members of a group have to have some influence on each other. The interaction between the parties may be either verbal (such as sharing strategies for a corporate takeover), or nonverbal (such as exchanging smiles in the hallway), but the parties must have some impact on each other to be considered a group.

In addition to having social interaction, a group must also possess a *stable structure.*

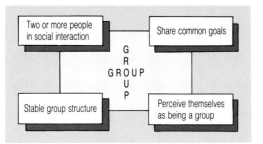

FIGURE 8.1 A Group: Its Defining Characteristics

The four major defining characteristics of a group are summarized here. As shown, to be a group, there must be two or more people in social interaction who share common goals, have a stable group structure, and perceive themselves as being in a group.

Although groups can and often do change, there must be some stable relationships between the members that keep a group together and functioning as a unit. A collection of people that constantly changes (e.g., the collection of people inside an office waiting room at any one time) cannot be thought of as a group. For it to be a group, some greater stability would be required.

A third characteristic of a group is that its members *share common goals.* Groups often form because of some common interest or goal that individuals could not realize alone. For example, a sports team is a group that may be sustained by the mutual interests of its members in winning a championship. The members share this dream and work together to bring it to reality.

Finally, to be a group, the *individual members must perceive themselves as a group.* Groups are composed of people who recognize each other as a member of their group and can distinguish these individuals from nonmembers. The members of a Board of Governors or a bowling team, for example, know who is in their group and who is not. By contrast, shoppers in a checkout line probably don't recognize each other as members of a group. Although they stand physically close to each other and may interact, they may have little in common (except, perhaps, a shared interest in reaching the end of the line) and fail to identify themselves with the others in the line.

By defining groups in terms of these four characteristics, we have identified a group as a very special collection of individuals. As we shall see, these characteristics are responsible for the very important effects groups have on organizational behavior. In order to better understand these effects, we will now review the wide variety of groups that operate within organizations.

Types of Groups within Organizations

What do the following have in common: a company bowling team, four guys getting together for their Thursday night poker game, the board of directors of a large corporation, and the three-person crew of a commercial airliner? As you probably guessed, the answer is that they are all groups. (See the photos in Figure 8.2 on page 261.) Despite this common characteristic, it should be clear from these examples that there are many types of groups in organizations.

Formal groups. Perhaps the most basic way of identifying types of groups is by distinguishing between *formal groups* and *informal groups* (see the summary in Figure 8.3 on page 261). **Formal groups** are created by the organization, intentionally designed to direct its members toward some important organizational goal. One type of formal group is referred to as a *command group,* a group determined by the connections between individuals on an organizational chart. For example, a command group may be formed by the vice president of marketing for a large organization who gathers

FIGURE 8.2 Two Types of Groups
Despite the differences between the collections of individuals shown in these photos, both have something in common: each is a group.

together his or her regional marketing directors from around the country to develop a new national advertising campaign. The point is that command groups are determined by the organization's rules regarding who reports to whom, and are usually composed of a supervisor and his or her subordinates.

It is also possible for formal organizational groups to be formed around some specific task, referred to as a *task group*. Unlike command groups, a task group may be composed of individuals with some special interest or expertise in some specific area regardless of their positions in the organizational hierarchy. For example, a company may have a committee on equal employment opportunities whose members monitor the fair hiring practices of the organization. It may be composed of personnel specialists, corporate vice presidents, and workers from the shop floor. Whether they are permanent committees, known as *standing committees,* or temporary ones formed for special purposes (such as a committee formed to recommend solutions to a parking problem), known as *ad hoc committees,* or *task forces,* task groups represent a commonly occurring type of group in organizations.

Two very special types of formal organizational groups are *boards* and *commissions.* Boards consist of people who are either elected or appointed to manage some entity. Typically, they are responsible for taking into account the interests of those who se-

FIGURE 8.3 Varieties of Formal and Informal Groups

In organizations, distinctions may be made between formal groups (such as *command groups* and *task groups*), and informal groups (such as *interest groups* and *friendship groups*).

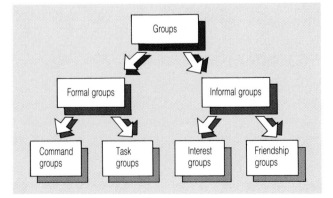

lected them (i.e., their constituents). For example, a board of directors is chosen by the stockholders of a corporation to manage its operations. Similarly, school boards are selected to direct the educational activities of a community's schools in a manner consistent with the community's goals and values.

Although similar to boards in their operation, *commissions* tend to operate in the government sector. You may be familiar with the Securities and Exchange Commission, the body that oversees the operations of the stock market, or the Federal Communications Commission, the body that regulates the activities of television and radio stations. Both these boards are entrusted with responsibility for assuring that the general public's interests are protected, each within its own sphere of influence.

All of the formal groups we've described thus far must take direction from some outside person or group. Committees and task forces must answer to management, and boards and commissions are responsible to their constituencies. However, some groups, known as *self-regulating work groups,* are relatively free to control their own work. Members of such groups are allowed to control their own work assignments, are encouraged to perform a variety of different tasks, have the authority to do the job as they wish (purchase necessary supplies and equipment, train workers, etc.), and are even responsible for controlling the quality of their work. Self-regulated work groups function best when they are given nonroutine, creative tasks to perform and have cordial relations between members. Under such conditions, self-regulated work groups have proven very successful. Specifically, compared to groups that are not allowed to regulate their own work, recent research has found that self-regulated groups tend to have higher job satisfaction among their members, reduced turnover, increased productivity, and reduced production costs (largely as a result of implementing the innovations recommended by the groups).[4] Such findings—based on recent research in work groups as diverse as coal miners, aviation workers, scientists and engineers, garment workers, school teachers, and others—suggest that self-regulated work groups may hold a promising future in many organizations.

Informal groups. Of course, not all groups found in organizations are as formal as those we've identified thus far. It is also quite common for informal groups to develop. **Informal groups** are groups that develop naturally among an organization's personnel without any direction from the management of the organization within which they operate. One key factor in the formation of informal groups is a common interest shared by its members. People who get together to satisfy a common interest may be said to have formed an *interest group.* For example, a group of employees who band together to seek union representation, or to march together to protest their company's pollution of the environment, may be called an interest group. The common goal sought by members of an interest group may unite workers at many different organizational levels. The key thing to keep in mind is that membership in an interest group is voluntary— it is not forced by the organization, but encouraged by the expression of common interests.

Of course, sometimes the interests that bind individuals together are far more diffuse. Groups may develop out of a common interest in participating in sports, or going to the movies, or just getting together to talk. These kinds of informal groups are known as *friendship groups.* A group of coworkers who hang out together during lunch may also bowl or play cards together after work. Friendship groups extend beyond the workplace because they provide opportunities for satisfying the social needs of workers that are so important to their well-being (as you may recall from our discussion of Maslow's need hierarchy theory in chapter 3).

It is important to keep in mind that informal work groups are an important part of life in organizations. Although they develop without the direct encouragement of management, it is often the case that friendships originate out of formal organizational contact. For example, three employees working along side each other on the assembly line may get to talking and discover their mutual interest in basketball, and may decide to shoot baskets, or perhaps go to games together after work. Interestingly, such informal friendship groups can have very beneficial effects on organizational functioning.

In fact, one of the oldest established findings in the field of group dynamics is that being part of a desirable work group can help promote job satisfaction. This was demonstrated forty years ago by Van Zelst's study of carpenters and bricklayers working on a housing development.[5] During the first five months of the job, the men got to learn all about each other by being assigned many different coworkers by their supervisors. Then, they were allowed to work in groups of those they liked best. This new arrangement resulted in a greatly reduced rate of turnover and a drop in the cost of building the housing development. Among the greatest benefits were the personal gains experienced by the workers themselves. To quote one of the workers, "The work is a lot more interesting when you've got a buddy working with you. You certainly like it a lot better anyway."[6]

As this study shows, both formal and informal group contact are important determinants of behavior in organizations. Having established this, we can now consider another very important basic issue—how groups develop.

The Development of Groups

Whether they are the result of formal, organizationally-directed pressures, or more informal social processes, groups go through several stages of development. Just as infants develop in certain ways during their first months of life, groups also show relatively stable signs of maturation and development.[7] One popular theory identifies five distinct stages through which groups develop.[8] As we describe these below, it may help to note our summary of the five stages shown in Table 8.1.

The first stage of group development is known as *forming*. It is during this stage of group development that the members get acquainted with each other. They establish the ground rules by trying to find out what behaviors are acceptable, both with respect to the job (how productive they are expected to be) and interpersonal relations (who's

TABLE 8.1   The Five Stages of Group Development
As outlined in this model, groups go through several stages of development.

STAGE	PRIMARY CHARACTERISTIC
1. Forming	Members get to know each other and seek to establish ground rules
2. Storming	Members come to resist control of group leaders and show hostility
3. Norming	Members work together, developing close relationships and feelings of camaraderie
4. Performing	Group members work toward getting their job done
5. Adjourning	Groups may disband after either meeting their goals, or because members leave

(Source: Based on information in Tuckman & Jensen, 1977; see Note 8.)

really in charge). During the forming stage people tend to be a bit confused and uncertain about how to act in the group and how beneficial it will be to become a member of the group. Once the individuals come to think of themselves as members of a group, the forming stage is complete.

The second stage of group development is referred to as *storming*. As the name implies, this stage is characterized by a high degree of conflict within the group. Members of the group come to resist the control of the group's leaders and show hostility toward each other. If these conflicts are not resolved and group members withdraw, the group may disband. However, as conflicts are resolved and the group's leadership is accepted, the storming stage is complete.

The third stage of group development is known as *norming*. It is during this stage that the group becomes most cohesive and identification as a member of the group becomes greatest. Close relationships develop, shared feelings become common, and a keen interest in finding mutually agreeable solutions develops. Feelings of camaraderie and shared responsibility for the group's activities are heightened. The norming stage is complete when the members of the group come to accept a common set of expectations that constitutes an acceptable way of doing things.

The fourth stage is known as *performing*, the stage during which questions about group relationships and leadership have been resolved and the group is ready to work. Having fully developed, energy may now be devoted to getting the job done—the group's good relations and acceptance of the leadership helps the group perform well.

Recognizing that not all groups last forever, the final stage is known as *adjourning*. Groups may cease to exist because they have met their goals and are no longer needed (such as an ad hoc group created to raise money for a charity project), in which case the end is abrupt. In other cases, groups may adjourn gradually, as the group disintegrates, either because members leave, or because the norms that have developed are no longer effective for the group.

To help illustrate these various stages, imagine that you have just joined your university's football team. At first, you and the other rookies feel each other out. You watch and see who plays best, who helps the team most, who seems to take charge, and the like (the forming stage). Then, you may see a battle over choice of first-string positions, and the offensive and defensive captains slots (the storming stage). Soon, this will be resolved, and the various first-stringers and captains will be established. At this stage, the group members will become most cooperative, working together as a team, hanging out together, and wearing their team jackets on campus (the norming stage). Now it becomes possible for the team members to work together to play their best (the performing stage). Once the season is over, players graduate, and so on, the team may be disbanded (the adjourning stage).

It is important to keep in mind that groups can be in any one stage of development at any given time. Moreover, the amount of time a group may spend in any given stage is highly variable. In fact, some groups may fail long before they have had a chance to work together. Recent research has revealed that the boundaries between the various stages may not be clearly distinct, and that several stages may be combined, especially as deadline pressures force groups to take action.[9] As such, it is best to think of this five-stage model as a general framework of group formation. Although many of the stages may be followed, the dynamic nature of groups makes it unlikely that they will always progress through the various stages in a set, predictable order.

The stages of group development discussed thus far are part of a natural progression. However, groups are sometimes intentionally created by management for the purpose of doing certain jobs. In such cases, it is important to construct work groups that can be made maximally effective. The **Management Perspective** section below provides some guidelines on how to best construct effective work teams.

Guidelines for Creating Effective Work Teams

Because groups of employees—often called *work teams*—are so commonly found in organizations, it is useful to consider how such teams may be created so as to maximize their effectiveness. Managers who want a work group to perform properly cannot hope for success just by collecting some people and giving them a job to do. A model recently proposed by J. Richard Hackman provides some useful guidance regarding how to effectively design work teams.[10] As we present this model, you may find it useful to refer to the summary in Figure 8.4.

The first stage of creating an effective work team is known as *prework*. One of the most important objectives of this phase is to determine whether or not a group should be created. A manager may decide to have several individuals working alone answer to him, or a group may be created if it is believed that groups may form the most creative and insightful ways of getting things done. In considering this, it is important to note exactly what work needs to be done. The group's objectives must be established, and an inventory of the skills needed to do the job should be made. In addition, decisions should be made in advance about what authority the group should have. They may just be advisory to the manager, or they may be given full responsibility and authority for executing their task (i.e., self-regulating). Such very basic decisions comprise the prework stage of team formation.

Building upon this, stage two involves *creating performance conditions*. In this stage, managers are to ensure that the group has the proper conditions in which to operate in order to get its job done. Resources should be provided that are necessary for the group's success. This involves both material resources (e.g., tools, equipment, and money), as well as human resources (e.g., the appropriate blend of skilled professionals). Unless managers help create the proper conditions for group success, they are passively allowing the possibility of failure.

Stage three involves *forming and building the team*. There are three things that can be done to help a work team get off to a good start. First, it is important to *form boundaries*—i.e., to clearly establish who is and who is not a member of the group. As strange as it may seem, membership in many work groups is often left very unclear. Reducing such ambiguity can help avoid confusion and frustration. Second, members must *accept the task to perform*. Sometimes, group members have different ideas about what their group is expected to do. It is necessary for all the group members to agree on

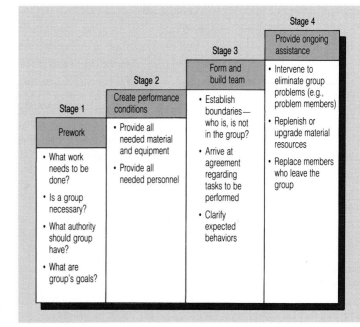

FIGURE 8.4 Stages of Creating Effective Work Teams

Rather than just throwing groups together and allowing them to perform, managers can take several steps to ensure the success of work teams. Four important steps are outlined here. (Source: Based on information in Hackman, 1987; see Note 10.)

Stage 1	Stage 2	Stage 3	Stage 4
Prework	Create performance conditions	Form and build team	Provide ongoing assistance
• What work needs to be done? • Is a group necessary? • What authority should group have? • What are group's goals?	• Provide all needed material and equipment • Provide all needed personnel	• Establish boundaries—who is, is not in the group? • Arrive at agreement regarding tasks to be performed • Clarify expected behaviors	• Intervene to eliminate group problems (e.g., problem members) • Replenish or upgrade material resources • Replace members who leave the group

what should be done and how the various duties will be subdivided in order for the group to function most effectively. Third, explicit attention should be given to *clarifying expected behaviors.* Managers should make perfectly clear those tasks for which their subordinates will be responsible. Will they be responsible for monitoring and planning their own work? If so, such expectations should be spelled out explicitly.

Finally, once a group is functioning, it is considered useful to *provide ongoing assistance.* Although once groups start operating they often guide themselves, managers may be able to help by providing opportunities for the group to eliminate problems and perform even better. For example, disruptive group members may be either counseled or replaced. Similarly, material resources may have to be replenished or upgraded. Although it may be unwise for a manager to intervene in the successful affairs of a group that has taken on its own life, it also may be unwise to neglect opportunities to help a group improve and learn from its experiences.

Most likely, as you ponder these suggestions, you will recognize the considerable managerial skill and hard work it takes to create and manage work teams. However, as managers learn these skills, and as group members have successful experiences as members of effective work teams, the deliberate steps outlined above may become second nature to all concerned. As Hackman concludes, "When that stage is reached, the considerable investment required to learn how to use work teams well can pay substantial dividends—in work effectiveness and in the quality of the experience of both managers and group members."[11]

THE STRUCTURE OF WORK GROUPS

As noted earlier, one of the key characteristics of a group is its stable structure. When social scientists use the term **group structure,** they are referring to the interrelationships between the individuals comprising a group, the guidelines to group behavior that make group functioning orderly and predictable. The structure of a group has been likened to the interrelationship between the planets in our solar system.[12] Just as we may learn about the solar system by studying the interrelationship between the planets, we may learn about groups by studying the relationships between the people comprising them. In this section we will describe four different aspects of group structure: the various parts played by group members (*roles*), the rules and expectations that develop within groups (*norms*), the prestige of group membership (*status*), and the members' sense of belonging (*cohesiveness*).

Roles: The Many Hats We Wear

One of the primary structural elements of groups is the fact that members tend to play specific roles in group interaction. Social scientists use the term *role* in much the same way as a director of a play would refer to the character who plays a part. Indeed, the part one plays in the overall group structure is what we mean by a role. More formally, we may define a **role** as the typical behaviors that characterize a person in a social context.[13]

In organizations, many roles are assigned by virtue of an individual's position within the organization. For example, a boss may be expected to give orders, and a teacher may be expected to lecture and to give exams. Typically, these are formally prescribed in the person's job description or the company's policy manual. For example, the president of the United States (whose role assignments largely come from the U.S. Constitution) makes foreign policy decisions, attempts to improve the American economy, and so on—all behaviors expected of the person occupying that office. These are behaviors expected of the person playing that role, the person referred to as the *role incumbent.* When a new president takes office that person assumes the same role and has the same powers as the previous president. The same behaviors are expected of whomever is occupying the role. Although the specific behaviors of individual presidents may vary, the fact remains that certain behaviors are expected of role incumbents (referred to as *role expectations*).

The fact that the role incumbent recognizes the expectations of his or her role helps avoid the social disorganization that would surely result if clear role expectations did not exist. Sometimes, however, workers may be confused about the things that are expected of them on the job, such as their level of authority or their responsibility. Such *role ambiguity,* as it is called, is typically experienced by new members of organizations who have not had much of a chance to "learn the ropes," and often results in job dissatisfaction, a lack of commitment to the organization, and an interest in leaving the job.[14]

Role differentiation: Specialized functions of group members. As work groups and social groups develop, the various group members come to play different roles in the social structure—a process referred to as **role differentiation.** The emergence of different roles in groups is a naturally occurring process. Think of committees to which you may have belonged. Was there one member who joked and made people feel better, and another member who worked hard to get the group to focus on the issue at hand? These examples of differentiated roles are, in fact, typical of role behaviors that emerge in groups. Organizations, for example, often have their "office comedian" who makes everyone laugh, or the "company gossip," who shares others' secrets, or the "grand old man" who tells newcomers the stories about the company's "good old days." Group researchers long ago found that there emerges in groups one person who more than anyone else helps the group reach its goal.[15] Such a person is said to play the *task-oriented* role. In addition, another group member may emerge who is quite supportive and nurturant, someone who makes everyone else feel good. Such a person is said to play a *socio-emotional* (or *relations-oriented*) role. Still others may be recognized for the things they do for themselves, often at the expense of the group—individuals recognized for playing a *self-oriented* role.

There are many specific role behaviors that can fall into either of these categories. Some of these more specific subroles are listed in Table 8.2. Although this simple distinction will help us understand some of the roles found in work groups, we should

TABLE 8.2 Some Roles Commonly Played by Group Members

Organizational roles may be differentiated into *task-oriented, relations-oriented* (or *socio-emotional*), and *self-oriented* roles—each of which has several subroles. A number of these are shown here.

TASK-ORIENTED ROLES	RELATIONS-ORIENTED ROLES	SELF-ORIENTED ROLES
Initiator-contributors: Recommend new solutions to group problems	*Harmonizers:* Mediate group conflicts	*Blockers:* Act stubborn and resistant to the group
Information seekers: Attempt to obtain the necessary facts	*Compromisers:* Shift own opinions to create group harmony	*Recognition seekers:* Call attention to their own achievements
Opinion givers: Share own opinions with others	*Encouragers:* Praise and encourage others	*Dominators:* Assert authority by manipulating the group
Energizers: Stimulate the group into action whenever interest drops	*Expediters:* Suggest ways the groups can operate more smoothly	*Avoiders:* Maintain distance, isolate themselves from fellow group members

(Source: Based on Benne & Sheats, 1948; see Note 15.)

note that more complex conceptualizations have been proposed, including one that identifies as many as twenty-six different roles.[16] These efforts at understanding role differentiation, regardless of how simple or complex the distinctions may be, help make the point that similarities between groups may be recognized by the common roles members play.

Role conflict: Competing demands from the roles we play. Researchers in the field of OB have expressed a great deal of interest in the concept of **role conflict**— the idea that the appropriate behaviors for enacting one role may be inconsistent with the appropriate behaviors for enacting another role or other requirements of the same role. It shouldn't be too surprising that a person's various role requirements may conflict given the many roles people play—employee, friend, and family member, to name just a few (see chapter 7).

Although there are many types of role conflicts, the two most common varieties are *interrole* conflict and *intrarole* conflict.[17] These are summarized in Figure 8.5. **Interrole conflict** refers to the incompatible demands made on someone playing two or more roles. A common example is when a friendship develops between a supervisor and his or her subordinates. What a supervisor may be expected to do as a boss (e.g., be tough) may conflict with the behaviors expected as a friend (e.g., be sympathetic). As a result, it may be difficult to fulfill the demands of both roles simultaneously. Another common interrole conflict is created by the simultaneous demands of fulfilling work role obligations and family role obligations. Such conflicts can have a variety of serious consequences on both work life and family life.[18]

Employees also may experience **intrarole conflict,** in which there are contradictory demands within a single role as viewed by different members of the group (referred to as *role senders*). A good example is the dual set of expectations faced by foremen. As members of their work groups, foremen are expected to be loyal to their fellow group members, which may be difficult given that upper management may expect them to support corporate interests as well. Intrarole conflict can also stem from ambiguities inherent in the positions held by role incumbents.[19] If it isn't clear what a person occupying a given role is expected to do, it is not surprising to find that different people expect different things of a role incumbent, thereby creating intrarole conflict.

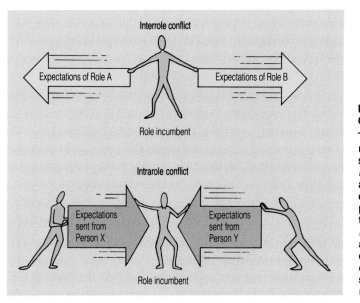

FIGURE 8.5   Role Conflict: Two Sources

Two major sources of role conflict are summarized here. In *interrole conflict*, there are different sets of expectations on a person playing more than one role. In *intrarole conflict*, there are different sets of expectations sent from different persons to someone playing one role.

Research has revealed a variety of negative consequences resulting from role conflict, including job dissatisfaction, poor group performance, and the rejection of other group members.[20] One study of interrole conflict has found that the more managers and their subordinates disagreed about the subordinate's role expectations, the more the subordinate experienced work-related stress and uncertainty about the possibility of promotion (see chapter 7).[21] A particularly important focus of recent research on role conflict has been the contradictory demands made on workers by their jobs and their families, a common problem faced by members of today's dual-career families. For example, in one study, Cooke and Rousseau examined the role conflicts experienced by 200 teachers.[22] The researchers found that the more teachers experienced conflicts between their roles as teachers and family members (such as taking home extra work to do), the more they reported feeling work overload (difficulty having enough time to get their work done) and high role conflict (interference between job demands and free-time activities), and the more they showed symptoms of physical and psychological strain. These findings clearly demonstrate how role conflicts can have a severe negative impact on workers' job performance as well as their personal well-being.

Norms: A Group's Unspoken Rules

One feature of groups that enhances their orderly functioning is the existence of group *norms*. **Norms** may be defined as generally agreed upon informal rules that guide group members' behavior.[23] They represent shared ways of viewing the world. Norms differ from organizational rules in that they are *not* formal and written. In fact, group members may not even be aware of the subtle group norms that exist and regulate their behavior. Yet these norms may have very profound effects on behavior. Norms tend to regulate the behavior of groups in important ways, by fostering workers' honesty and loyalty to the company, establishing the appropriate ways to dress, and dictating when it is appropriate to be late or absent from work, among others.

Normative influences on behavior. If you recall the pressures placed on you by your peers as you grew up to dress or wear your hair in certain styles, you are well aware of the profound normative pressures exerted by groups. Norms can be either *prescriptive*—dictating the behaviors that should be performed—or *proscriptive*—dictating the behaviors that should be avoided. For example, work groups may develop prescriptive norms to follow their leader, or to pitch in and help a group member who needs assistance. They may also develop proscriptive norms to avoid arriving at work late, or to refrain from blowing the whistle on each other.

Sometimes the pressure to conform to norms is subtle, as in the dirty looks given a manager by his peers for having gone to lunch with one of the assembly line workers. Other times, normative pressures may be quite severe, as when one production worker strikes another because he is performing at too high a level and making his coworkers look bad. In fact, as shown in Figure 8.6, employees may receive approval for behaving within a normatively acceptable range, but receive displays of disapproval for exceeding these limits in either direction.[24] Although curves of this type may take different shapes for different organizational behaviors (such as norms regarding absenteeism and attempts to exert influence on group members), it is important to realize the potent pressures created by group norms to behave in whatever way the group deems acceptable.

A good illustration of the impact of normative pressures on work performance may be seen in an experiment by Mitchell, Rothman, and Liden.[25] These investigators hired college students to place lids on ice cream containers. The employees in one condition faced a wall chart revealing the alleged productivity of others doing the same job. Employees in another condition were provided with the same productivity information,

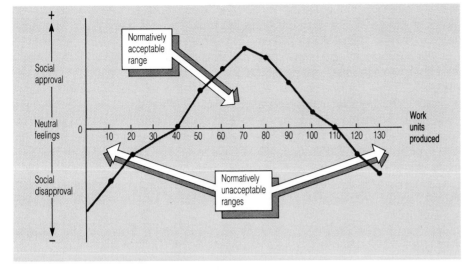

FIGURE 8.6 Norms: Defining Socially Acceptable Work Behavior
Employees often experience normative pressures to perform within a socially acceptable
range. Performance higher than or lower than this range is socially disapproved. (Source:
Based on Nadler, Hackman, & Lawler, 1979; see Note 24.)

but in the form of actually seeing the work performed by another. It was found that
the participants in the study were more likely to match the production levels of other
workers (i.e., to conform to the observed performance norm set by others) than to
match summary data presented in chart form. People apparently felt the pressure to
match the demonstrated performance level of others, thereby providing an excellent
illustration of the impact of social norms on job performance.

The development of norms. The question of how group norms develop has been
of considerable interest to organizational researchers.[26] An insightful analysis of the
way norms develop in work groups has been presented by Feldman.[27] Table 8.3 summarizes the four steps in this model.

TABLE 8.3 How Norms Develop
This table summarizes four ways in which group norms can
develop.

BASIS OF NORM DEVELOPMENT	EXAMPLE
1. Precedents set over time	Seating location of each group member around a table
2. Carryovers from other situations	Professional standards of conduct
3. Explicit statements from others	Working a certain way because you are told "that's how we do it around here"
4. Critical events in group history	After the organization suffers a loss due to one person's divulging company secrets, a norm develops to maintain secrecy

(Source: Based on Feldman, 1984; see Note 27.)

First, it may be said that norms develop due to *precedents set over time*. Whatever behaviors emerge at a first group meeting will usually set the standard for how that group is to operate. Initial group patterns of behavior frequently become normative, such as where people sit, and how formal or informal the meeting will be. Such routines help establish a predictable, orderly interaction pattern.

Similarly, norms develop because of *carryovers from other situations*. Group members usually draw from their previous experiences in other situations to guide their behaviors in new situations. The norms governing professional behavior apply here. For example, the norm for a physician to behave ethically and to exercise a pleasant bedside manner is generalizable from one hospital to another. Thus, a doctor changing hospitals can expect the same norms of professionalism to preside in the new setting. Such carryover norms can assist in making interaction easier in new social situations. Carryover norms mean that there may be fewer new norms to learn, thereby enhancing the ease of social interaction.

Sometimes norms also develop in response to an *explicit statement by a superior or a coworker*. Newcomers to groups quickly "learn the ropes" when one of their coworkers tells them, "that's the way we do it around here." The explanation is an explicit statement of the norms, it describes what one should do or avoid doing to be accepted by the group. Sometimes the explicit statement of group norms represents the accepted desires of a powerful group member, such as a supervisor. If a supervisor wants reports to be prepared in a certain way, or expects a certain degree of formality or informality in addressing others, norms may develop to adapt these standards. The socialization of new group members frequently requires learning group norms by listening to more experienced group members.[28]

Finally, group norms may develop out of *critical events in the group's history*. If an employee releases an important organizational secret to a competitor, causing a loss to the company, a norm to maintain secrecy may develop out of this incident. In a similar manner, a professional group that decides to censure the inappropriate behavior of one of its members (e.g., a member of congress who accepts a bribe, or a physician who uses poor medical judgment) may be seen as acting to reaffirm its commitment to the violated norm. Both incidents represent critical events that helped either establish or reaffirm a group norm.

Status: The Prestige of Group Membership

Have you ever been attracted to a group because of the prestige accorded its members? You may have wanted to join a certain fraternity or sorority on your campus because it is highly regarded by the students. Aspiring members of street gangs long for the day they can wear their gang's "colors" in the streets. No doubt, members of Superbowl-winning football teams proudly sport their superbowl rings to identify themselves as a member of a championship team. Clearly, one of the potential rewards of group membership is the status associated with being in that group. Even within social groups, different members are accorded different levels of prestige. Fraternity and sorority officers, gang leaders, and team captains, for example, may well be recognized as more important members of their respective groups. This is the idea behind **status**—the relative social position or rank given to groups or group members by others.[29]

Formal and informal status. Within most organizations, status may be recognized as both formal and informal in nature. *Formal status* refers to attempts to differentiate between the degrees of formal authority given employees by an organization. This is typically accomplished through the use of *status symbols*—objects reflecting the position of an individual within an organization's hierarchy. Some examples of status symbols

FIGURE 8.7 Desk Size: One Sign of Status in Many Organizations

As shown here, status symbols such as desk size help reflect the level of influence a person has within an organization. (Source: Reprinted with special permission of NAS, Inc.)

include job titles (e.g., "Director"), perquisites, or "perks," (e.g., a reserved parking space), the opportunity to do desirable and highly regarded work (e.g., serving on important committees), and luxurious working conditions (e.g., a large, private office that is lavishly decorated).[30] (For an example, see Figure 8.7.)

Status symbols help groups in many ways.[31] For one, such symbols serve to remind organizational members of their relative roles, thereby reducing uncertainty and providing stability to the social order (e.g., your small desk reminds you that you are an indian, not a chief). In addition, they provide assurance of the various rewards that are available to those who perform at a superior level (e.g., maybe one day I'll have the key to the executive wash room). They also provide a sense of identification by reminding members of the group's values (e.g., a gang's jacket may remind its wearer of his expected loyalty and boldness). It is, therefore, not surprising that organizations do much to reinforce formal status through the use of status symbols.

It is also important to recognize the widespread use of systems of *informal status* operating within organizations. These refer to the prestige accorded individuals with certain characteristics that are not formally dictated by the organization. For example, employees who are older and more experienced may be perceived as higher in status by their coworkers. Those who have certain special skills (such as the home-run hitters on a baseball team) also may be regarded as having higher status than others. The lower value generally placed on the work of women and members of minority groups, however unfortunate, can also be considered an example of informal status in operation.[32]

It is important to remember that status is not something that is fixed or tangible. Status, like beauty, is in the eyes of the beholder. It is conferred on those who hold it in the case of both formal and informal status. If members of an organization fail to recognize certain positions or certain jobs as being more important than others, then those who hold them are unlikely to receive different amounts of status because of this. Similarly, informal status is also in the eyes of the beholder. For example, employees who do not value the greater experience of a coworker with seniority would probably not show that person any special deference. Our point is simple: status differences exist only when status dimensions are recognized and valued by others.

The influence of status on organizational behavior. One of the best established findings in the study of group dynamics is that higher status persons tend to be more influential than lower status persons. This phenomenon may be seen in a classic study of decision making in three-man bomber crews.[33] After the crews had difficulty solving a problem, the experimenter planted clues to the solution with either a low-status group member (the tail gunner) or a high-status group member (the pilot). It was found that the solutions offered by the pilots were far more likely to be adopted than the same solutions presented by the tail gunners. Apparently, the greater status accorded the pilots (by virtue of the fact that they tended to be more experienced and hold higher military ranks) was responsible for the greater influence they wielded. Similar findings have been obtained in analyses of jury deliberations. Research in this area has shown that members of juries having high-status jobs (such as professional persons) tend to exert greater influence over their fellow jurors than others holding lower occupational status.[34]

Status differences are also largely responsible for the way people communicate with each other. For example, persons of lower status are likely to address those of higher status by their titles, such as "General," or "Mr. President," or "Doctor," whereas less formality—using only first names—is commonly found in addressing persons of lower status.[35] Similarly, it has been found that people prefer communicating with others of equal status, and are uncomfortable communicating with others of much higher or much lower status levels.[36] However, when persons of unequal status do communicate, it is usually considered more acceptable for the higher status person to initiate the conversation. This phenomenon is demonstrated clearly in a classic study by Whyte.[37] Observing the interaction between waitresses (considered lower status) and chefs (considered higher status), Whyte found that conflicts emerged when the waitresses passed their orders directly to the chefs. The chefs resented the initiation of action from the lower status waitresses. Then, after an "order wheel" was installed, the waitresses simply attached their orders to it, thereby allowing the chefs to take the orders whenever they were ready. In so doing, higher status persons no longer had to respond to the actions of lower status persons, and a considerable amount of conflict was eliminated. Such findings are typical of the tendency for persons of higher status to expect to influence others rather than to be influenced by them.

Cohesiveness: Getting the "Team Spirit"

One very obvious determinant of any group's structure is its *cohesiveness*. We may define **cohesiveness** as the pressures group members face to remain part of their groups. Highly cohesive work groups are ones in which the members are attracted to each other, accept the group's goals, and help work toward meeting them. In very uncohesive groups, the members dislike each other and may even work at cross-purposes.[38] In essence, cohesiveness refers to a "we" feeling, an "espirit de corps," a sense of "belonging" to a group.

What makes a group cohesive? Several important factors have been shown to influence the extent to which group members tend to "stick together." One such factor involves the *severity of initiation into the group*. Research has shown that the greater the difficulty people overcome to become a member of a group, the more cohesive the group will be.[39] To understand this, consider how highly cohesive certain groups may be that you have worked hard to join. Was it particularly difficult to "make the cut" in your sports team? Were you accepted into an extremely competitive school? Indeed, the rigorous requirements for gaining entry into such elite groups as the most prestigious medical schools and military training schools may well be responsible for the high degree of camaraderie found in such groups. Having "passed the test" tends to keep individuals together, and separates them from those who are unwilling or unable to "pay the price" of admission.

Group cohesion also tends to be strengthened under conditions of *high external threat or competition*. When workers face a "common enemy," they tend to be drawn

FIGURE 8.8 External Threat: A Source of Group Cohesion

As demonstrated in these photographs, the presence of a common enemy can help foster group cohesiveness.

together. Such cohesion not only makes workers feel safer and better protected, but also aids them by encouraging them to work closely together and coordinate their efforts toward the common enemy (see the photos in Figure 8.8). Under such conditions, petty disagreements that may have caused dissention within groups tend to be put aside so that a coordinated attack on the enemy can be mobilized.

The dynamics of such a situation have been clearly demonstrated in a classic study of 11- and 12-year-old boys attending camp by Sherif and his associates.[40] When they first arrived at camp, the boys were divided into two groups living in separate cottages. During the first few weeks, the members of each group worked together on projects that required high degrees of cooperation within the groups (e.g., preparing dinner required one boy to get firewood, another to mix soft drinks, another to make hamburgers, etc.). Soon, feelings of cohesiveness developed, and the groups gave themselves names to establish their identities—the "Rattlers" and the "Eagles." Next, a meeting was arranged between the two groups, and they soon challenged each other to various competitive events. Rapidly, they became enemies, not only fighting each other on the playing field, but raiding each others' cottages, and having food fights.

At this point, an interesting observation was made: the more the Rattlers and the Eagles fought each other, the more cooperative the members of each group became toward each other, and the greater degree of cohesiveness they experienced. Reasoning that the imposition of an enemy strengthened the animosity between the groups and the cohesiveness within them, Sherif attempted to bring the two groups together by presenting them with a common enemy. Various catastrophes were staged that forced the two groups to work together. For example, a breakdown in the camp's plumbing system required the boys to form a bucket brigade. On another occasion, the breakdown of a truck forced them to band together, pulling to help start it. In both cases the boys from both groups worked together to oppose their common threats and felt cohesive as a single unit—now, they were operating as members of the same camp, not as opposing subgroups within that camp. However, as soon as the problems were solved and the common enemy disappeared, the groups reverted to the much lower levels of cohesiveness that existed before the common external threat. This fascinating study provides solid evidence of the extent to which a common external threat can help high degrees of cohesiveness develop within groups.

Research has also shown that the cohesiveness of groups is established by several additional factors.[41] For one, cohesiveness generally tends to be greater the more time group members spend together. Obviously, limited interaction cannot help but interfere with opportunities to develop bonds between group members. Similarly, it is known that cohesiveness tends to be greater in smaller groups. Generally speaking, groups that are too large make it difficult for members to interact, and therefore, for cohesiveness to reach a high level. Finally, because "nothing succeeds like success," groups with a history of success tend to be highly cohesive. It is often said that "everyone loves a winner," and the success of a group tends to help unite its members as they rally around their success. It is for this reason that employees tend to be loyal to successful companies, and members of winning athletic teams tend to be so interested in not being traded away from them. As summarized on the left side of Figure 8.9, these are among many factors that contribute to the cohesiveness of a group.

The benefits and costs of cohesive groups. Although we often hear about the benefits of highly cohesive groups, the consequences of cohesiveness are not always positive. In fact, research has shown both positive and negative effects of cohesiveness (see the summary on the right side of Figure 8.9).

On the positive side, it is known that people enjoy belonging to highly cohesive groups. Members of closely-knit work groups participate more fully in their groups' activities, more readily accept their group's goals, and are absent from their jobs less often than members of less cohesive groups.[42] Not surprisingly, cohesive groups tend to work together quite well and are often exceptionally productive. Their willingness to work together and conform to the group's norms is often considered responsible for their success.[43]

However, the tendency for members of highly cohesive groups to go along with their fellow members' wishes sometimes has negative consequences for the ultimate group product. Consider, for example, the actions of the highly cohesive Committee to Re-elect President Nixon preceding the 1972 presidential election. The Watergate conspirators were a highly cohesive group—so cohesive, in fact, that they were blinded to the possibility that they were committing illegal and unethical acts. Poor decisions

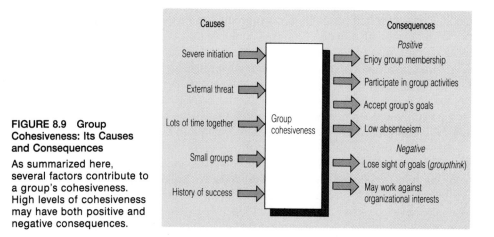

FIGURE 8.9 Group Cohesiveness: Its Causes and Consequences

As summarized here, several factors contribute to a group's cohesiveness. High levels of cohesiveness may have both positive and negative consequences.

resulting from too high a level of cohesiveness reflect a phenomenon known as *groupthink*.[44] Groupthink occurs when a group is so cohesive that its members potentially lose sight of its ultimate goals for fear of disrupting the group itself. (Because of the negative impact of groupthink on the quality of group decisions, we will discuss this phenomenon in greater detail in the context of decision making in chapter 14.)

Group cohesion can influence productivity in many other ways. It makes sense that after a group experiences success its members will feel more committed to each other. Similarly, we might expect a cohesive group to work well together and to achieve a high level of success. However, just because members of a work group are strongly committed to each other does not mean that the group will perform well within their organization.[45] For example, if a group's goals are contrary to the organization's goals, a highly cohesive group may actually do a great deal of harm to an organization. Highly cohesive workers who conspire to sabotage their employers are a good example. Apparently, group cohesiveness can have either positive or negative effects on performance.

One of the first studies to look at the relationship between group cohesion and organizational productivity was conducted almost forty years ago by Stanley Seashore.[46] The participants in this experiment were employees of a manufacturing plant who formed over 200 small work groups. These persons completed questionnaires measuring the degree of cohesiveness of their work groups, which were then compared with job performance over a three month period. It was found that high cohesiveness was associated with high productivity when group members felt that management supported them, but low productivity when management threatened them. This implies that a cohesive work group may only be successful if what they are doing goes along with management's wishes.

More recently, in a study conducted at a public utility it was found that in highly cohesive groups a supportive managerial style was related to higher performance, but not in weakly cohesive groups.[47] A similar tendency for high performance levels to be associated with highly cohesive groups operating under a supportive managerial atmosphere has also been found in a study of soldiers in the Israeli army.[48] It appears then, that there is no simple relationship between group cohesion and job performance. Our summary of these studies in Figure 8.10 shows that a cohesive group *can* enhance

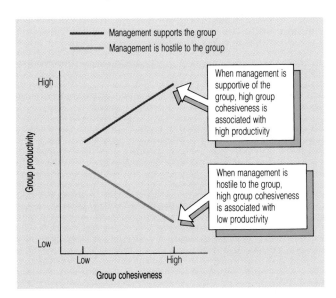

FIGURE 8.10 Group Cohesion and Productivity: Mediating Effects of Management

Several studies have shown that the relationship between group performance and group cohesiveness depends on management's support for and acceptance of the group. Greater cohesion is associated with greater productivity when management is supportive of the group, and less productivity when management is hostile to the group.

productivity, but *only* when the manager's style supports the group's efforts. If a group of workers bands together but finds that its efforts are not supported by the company's management, then it will perform poorly. Cohesion can aid productivity as long as superiors and subordinates are not operating in opposition to each other. Organizations may well benefit by the existence of cohesive groups, but only when the groups and the organizations are working together.

TASK PERFORMANCE: WORKING WITH AND AROUND OTHERS

Now that we have reviewed the basic elements of group structure, we are prepared to examine an aspect of group dynamics most relevant to the field of organizational behavior—the effects of groups on performance. We will consider this issue from two different perspectives. First, we will look at the influence of the presence of a group on individual performance. Then, we will consider how well different types of groups perform as a whole.

Social Facilitation: Individual Performance in the Presence of Others

Imagine that you have been studying drama for five years and you are now ready for your first acting audition in front of some Hollywood producers. You have been rehearsing diligently for several months, getting ready for the part. Now, you are no longer alone at home with your script in front of you. Your name is announced and silence fills the auditorium as you walk to the front of the stage. How will you perform now that you are in front of an audience? Will you freeze, forgetting the lines you studied so intensely when you practiced alone? Or will the audience spur you on to your best performance yet? In other words, what impact would the presence of the audience have on your behavior?

Almost a century ago this same question was asked by a bicycling enthusiast named Norman Triplett who put his skills as a social scientist to work to find an answer.[49] Triplett noticed that cyclists invariably achieved faster times when they raced against others than when they raced alone, against the clock. Intrigued by these observations, he conducted a laboratory experiment requiring children, either alone or in pairs, to play a game in which they were required to turn a fishing reel as fast as possible. Just as he had observed at the bicycle track, Triplett found that the children performed the task better when they were in the presence of another person than when they were alone.

As other scientists began studying the effects of the presence of an audience or of *coactors* (people working on the same task at the same time) on individual performance, it was not always found that performance improved, as Triplett noted. In fact, sometimes it was found that people did worse when performing a task in the presence of others than when alone. This tendency for the presence of others to enhance an individual's performance at times and to impair it at times became known as **social facilitation.** (Although the word "facilitation" implies improvements in task performance, it is important to note that scientists use the term *social facilitation* to refer to both performance improvements and decrements stemming from the presence of others.) For many years, scientists were confused about the seemingly contradictory effects of others' presence on task performance. Then, in the mid 1960s, Robert Zajonc proposed a model that accounted for the apparent inconsistency in the findings regarding social facilitation.[50] Zajonc's model offered a simple, yet elegant explanation of when others' presence would help and when it would hinder performance.

A model of social facilitation. Zajonc reasoned that social facilitation was the result of the heightened emotional arousal (e.g., feelings of tension and excitement) people experience when in the presence of others. (Wouldn't you feel more tension playing the piano in front of an audience than alone?) When people are aroused, they tend to perform the most *dominant response*—their most likely behavior in that setting. (It may be considered an example of a dominant act to return the smile of a smiling coworker; it is a very well-learned act to smile at another who smiles at you.) If someone is performing a very well-learned act, the dominant response would be a correct one (such as speaking the right lines in an acting audition). However, if the behavior in question is relatively novel, newly learned, the dominant response would be expected to be incorrect (such as speaking the incorrect lines during an audition). Together, these ideas are known as Zajonc's **drive theory of social facilitation.** According to this theory, the presence of others increases arousal, which increases the tendency to perform the most dominant responses. If these responses are correct, the resulting performance will be enhanced; if they are incorrect, the performance will be impaired. (For a summary, see Figure 8.11.) A considerable amount of research has shown support for this theory: people (and lower animals too) perform better on a task in the presence of others if that task is very well learned, but poorer if it is not well learned.[51]

Why are others arousing? Some possible explanations. Although it is well established that dominant responses—whether correct or incorrect—are enhanced by the presence of others, there is considerable disagreement about exactly *why* these effects occur. Several perspectives have been offered (for a summary, see Figure 8.12 on page 280).

As we have already explained, Zajonc proposed that the presence of others makes

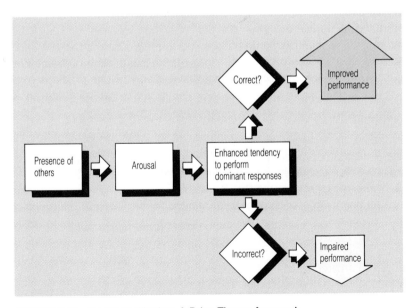

FIGURE 8.11   Social Facilitation: A Drive Theory Approach

The *drive theory of social facilitation* states that the presence of others is arousing. Such increased arousal enhances the tendency to perform the most dominant (i.e., strongest) responses. If these are correct, performance will be improved, but if these are incorrect, performance will be impaired.

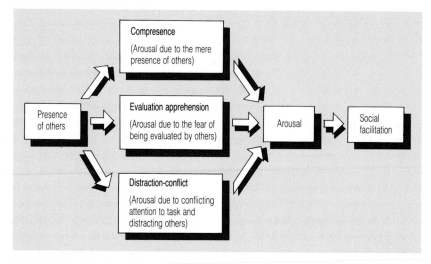

FIGURE 8.12   Why Are Others Arousing? Three Explanations for Social Facilitation
Theorists studying social facilitation have identified three different explanations for the arousing effects of the presence of others. The *compresence* explanation says that arousal is a natural reaction to the mere presence of others. The *evaluation apprehension* explanation says that arousal follows from the fear of being evaluated by others. Finally, the *distraction-conflict model* says that arousal is due to the conflict between paying attention to the task and to the distracting others.

people feel aroused. According to Zajonc, this arousal results simply because the others are there, what he calls their "mere presence." He uses the term *compresence* to refer to the presence of others and the innately arousing effect that it has.[52]

Other scientists have modified Zajonc's approach, claiming that the arousal resulting from others' presence is not due to the fact that others are simply there, but that these others can potentially evaluate the person.[53] Their major idea is that social facilitation results from **evaluation apprehension**—the fear of being evaluated, or judged by another person. Indeed, people may be aroused by performing a task in the presence of others because of their concern over what those others might think of them. For example, a concert pianist may suffer evaluation apprehension when he or she is concerned about the reactions of music critics seated in the audience. Likewise, industrial workers may suffer evaluation apprehension when they are worried about what their boss thinks about their work.

Does social facilitation occur simply because other people are present, or because those others can evaluate our performance? Although both of these factors may be involved, a third possibility is suggested by the **distraction-conflict model** proposed by R. S. Baron.[54] This model recognizes that the presence of others creates a conflict between paying attention to others and paying attention to the task at hand. The conflict created by these tendencies leads to increased arousal (which, in turn, leads to social facilitation, as shown in Figure 8.12). If you've ever tried doing a homework assignment while your friends or family watch TV nearby, then you're probably already aware of the conflict that can be created by competing demands for your attention. Such conflicts tend to be arousing, and lead to social facilitation. There is growing evidence to suggest that the distraction-conflict model accounts for social facilitation within work groups.[55]

However promising the distraction-conflict model may be in explaining social facilitation, it is certainly true that all the explanations noted provide some important insight into the social facilitation process. It is important to keep in mind that although an explanation for the processes underlying social facilitation are somewhat unclear, the effect itself may have a profound influence on organizational behavior.

Social Loafing: "Free Riding" When Working with Others

Thus far, our discussion has focused on tasks in which people work in the presence of others to produce an individual result. Although there are many such tasks performed in organizations (e.g., typists working in a typing pool), not all tasks fall into this category. There are many other jobs done in organizations in which group members work together to produce a group product. On many group tasks, the individual contributions of the group members are added together to form the group's product. Such tasks are considered **additive tasks,** and include activities like several persons combining their efforts to stuff envelopes for a political campaign, or several persons working together to mow a lawn or shovel snow off a driveway.

The phenomenon of social loafing. When people know that their work will be combined with that of others, an interesting thing often happens: they stop working as hard as they did as individuals, appearing to let others do their work for them, going on a "free ride." As suggested by the old saying, "Many hands make light the work," a group of people would be expected to be more productive than any one individual. (See Figure 8.13.) Five people raking leaves would get more work done than only one person, as you might expect, but generally *not* five times more! This effect was first noted over fifty years ago by a German scientist named Ringlemann, who compared the amount of force exerted by different size groups of people pulling on a rope. Specifically, he found that one person pulling on a rope alone exerted an average of 63 kilograms of force. However, in groups of three, the per-person force dropped to 53 kilograms, and in groups of eight it was reduced to only 31 kilograms per person— less than half the effort exerted by people working alone! In short, the greater the number of people working together on the task, the less effort each one put forth— an effect known as **social loafing.**

The phenomenon of social loafing has been studied extensively in recent years by Latané and his associates. In one of their earliest experiments, groups of students were asked to perform a very simple additive task—to clap and cheer as loudly as they

THE FAR SIDE   By GARY LARSON

How social animals work together.

FIGURE 8.13 Many Hands Make Light the Work

According to the phenomenon of *social loafing*, the more people involved in a group task, the less each individual will contribute to its outcome. (Source: THE FAR SIDE cartoon by Gary Larson is reprinted by permission of Chronicle Features, San Francisco, CA.)

could.[56] The participants were told that the experimenter was interested in seeing how much noise people could make in social settings. Comparisons were made between the amount of noise produced by one person relative to groups of two and six persons. Although more people made more noise, the amount of noise made per person dropped dramatically as the group size increased. Pairs of people made 82 percent as much noise as individuals working alone, and groups of six produced only 74 percent as much noise. Such findings clearly demonstrate the social loafing effect.

The phenomena of social loafing may be explained by **social impact theory.**[57] According to this theory, the impact of any social force acting on a group is divided equally among its members. The larger the size of the group, the less is the impact of the force on any one member. In the study noted above, the participants faced external pressure to make as much noise as possible. With more people present, the less pressure each person faced to perform well. That is, the responsibility for doing the job was diffused over more people when the size of the group increased. As a result, each group member felt less responsible for behaving appropriately, and social loafing occurred. (Although feeling less responsible for an outcome is clearly one factor responsible for the social loafing phenomenon, the effect may also result from other experiences likely to arise among people performing their jobs. As described in the **Research Perspective** section below, people may also engage in social loafing because they feel that the presence of others makes their contributions less needed—that is, more dispensable.)

OB: A RESEARCH PERSPECTIVE

Social Loafing on a Judgmental Task: The Importance of Feeling Dispensable

Imagine that you are working for a vocational research center, helping to evaluate part-time jobs for college students. Specifically, you are responsible for reading descriptions of various jobs on several key dimensions (e.g., flexibility of hours, friendliness of coworkers, etc.) and giving each one a numerical rating reflecting your judgment of how good or bad it is. Your judgments are used as the means of informing other college students about prospective part-time positions. How much effort will you put into the job? Will you carefully consider all the dimensions for all the jobs, or will you make your judgments more hastily?

Recent research by Weldon and Mustari suggests that the answer to these questions depends on the number of other people whose judgments you believe will be combined with yours.[58] In their laboratory experiment, these investigators had college students perform a judgment task like the one just described. The participants were told either that they were the only one responsible for making these judgments, or that their judgments would be one of two, or one of sixteen that would be combined to make the final job evaluations. How complex were the students' judgments; how thoroughly did they

perform the judgment task? As shown in Figure 8.14, the findings demonstrate the social loafing phenomenon: students exerted less cognitive effort (i.e., they made less complex judgments) when they believed that other judgments would be taken into account. (The complexity of the judgments was determined using complex mathematical formulas, which we will not go into here.)

These findings are valuable because they show that the social loafing phenomenon occurs when people perform cognitive-judgmental tasks (as opposed to physical tasks, such as pulling a rope or making noise, where the effect has already been demonstrated). Beyond generalizing the phenomenon to mental tasks, the findings of the Weldon and Mustari study are also important because of the insight they provide as to why the social loafing effect occurred. A series of questions answered by the research participants regarding how dispensable (i.e., unnecessary) they felt were extremely helpful in this regard. When the participants believed they were one of sixteen to make judgments, they felt their judgments were more dispensable than either those who made the only judgment, or those whose judgments would be combined with the judgments of

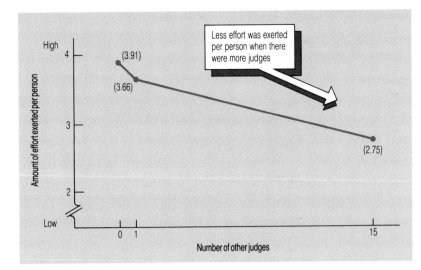

FIGURE 8.14 Social Loafing: An Experimental Demonstration

Research on Weldon and Mustari demonstrates the effects of *social loafing* on a judgment task: the greater the number of others with whom people believed their judgments would be combined, the less effort each individual exerted. (Source: Based on data reported by Weldon & Mustari, 1988; see Note 58.)

only one other person. Specifically, such persons reported feeling that their judgments were more of a waste of time, and that they more likely duplicated the judgments of others. As a result, they put less effort into their own work.

These findings suggest that social loafing may occur because people believe that their contributions to a joint effort involving many others are needed less than they would be if the same task was performed without the input of others. Although we tend to think of people engaging in social loafing as "free riders" who believe they can get away with reducing their efforts in a large group, the Weldon and Mustari findings suggest that there may be more to social loafing than merely hoping to use others for

a free ride. Reduced effort also may be the result of believing that one's contributions are unnecessary and not very important. Given that many employees perform their jobs in large groups, it is important to realize that they may reduce their efforts simply because the size of the group makes them feel dispensable. Accordingly, supervisors should be sensitive to this possibility and consider it carefully before assuming that a poorly performing employee is lazy—especially one working in a large group. Reduced effort on the part of some employees simply may be the result of their feeling that the size of their work group renders their contributions less necessary.

Overcoming social loafing: Some strategies. Obviously, the tendency for people to reduce their effort when working with others could be a serious problem in organizations. Fortunately, some research has shown that the tendency for social loafing to occur can be overcome. Some suggestions for attaining this goal are summarized in Table 8.4 (on page 284).

One possible antidote to social loafing seems to be: *make each performer identifiable.* It may be reasoned that social loafing occurs when people feel they can get away with "taking it easy"—namely, under conditions in which each worker's inputs are not identified. Identifying each person's performance has proven an effective way of countering social loafing in an experiment by Williams and his associates.[59] In this study it was found that male swimmers swam 100 meters faster alone than as members of a relay team— a social loafing effect—but only when their names and times were *not* announced. However, this decrement was completely eliminated when each swimmer's name and time were called out. Apparently, with some attempt at identifying the contributions of individual performers to an additive task, social loafing can be overcome. Potential social loafers are not likely to loaf if they believe they may get caught.

TABLE 8.4 Overcoming Social Loafing: Some Recommendations

Because of the potentially detrimental effects of social loafing on organizational productivity, several tactics for minimizing or eliminating its impact have been noted. Some of the best established techniques are summarized here.

RECOMMENDATION	DESCRIPTION/RATIONALE
Make workers identifiable	By pointing out individuals' contributions to their groups' performance, people would be unlikely to get away with taking a free ride.
Make work more involving	Jobs that are involving are not likely to induce social loafing; the fact that they are so interesting keeps people performing at a high level.
Reward individuals for their contributions to their group	Instead of rewarding only individual contributions, employees should be rewarded for helping others, for enhancing their groups' overall performance level.

Another potential way of overcoming social loafing is by *making work tasks more involving.* Recent research has revealed that persons are unlikely to go along for a free ride when the task they are performing is believed to be highly involving and important.[60] To help in this regard, it has been suggested that managers should *reward individuals for contributing to their group's performance.*[61] Instead of the usual practice of rewarding employees for their individual performance, rewarding them for their contributions to a group effort (e.g., providing all salespersons in a territory a bonus if they jointly exceed their sales goal) may help them focus more on collective concerns and less on individualistic concerns. In doing so, people would be expected to become more sensitive to the overall performance of their work groups. This is important, of course, in that the success of an organization is more likely to be influenced by the collective efforts of groups than by the individual contributions of any one member.

Performance on Other Types of Group Tasks

The phenomenon of social loafing has been demonstrated to occur on additive tasks—as described earlier, those in which the individual contributions of group members are added together. However, there are other types of tasks that groups may perform, each of which has its own unique characteristics.

Compensatory tasks: The benefits of compromise. On some tasks the inputs of various group members are averaged together to create a single group outcome. These are known as **compensatory tasks.** The resulting compromise solution is referred to as *compensatory* because one person's judgments may compensate for another's. Imagine that a group of people are attempting to judge the temperature of the room they are in. As you might expect, the judgments made by some group members that are incorrect in one direction (e.g., too high) may be offset by the judgments of others that are incorrect in the other direction (e.g., too low). As a result, more accurate decisions would be made by averaging the decisions of everyone in the group than by most individual members. Several studies have found that on compensatory tasks groups *do* tend to make more accurate judgments than many individual group members.[62]

Disjunctive tasks: When "the truth" wins out. On a **disjunctive task** the members of a group cannot compromise; they must select a solution offered by one of the members of the group. A group of executives meeting to determine whether or not to merge with another company cannot compromise; they either do or do not merge. A disjunctive task is of the "either-or" variety.

Suppose a group of people are given the following car-trading problem to solve:

> A used car salesman bought a car from one customer for $3,000 and then sold it to another customer for $4,000. He then bought it back for $5,000 and resold it for $6,000. How much money did the salesman make?

Each group member comes up with his or her own answer, but only one solution can be accepted. Whether or not the group will perform better on such a task than any single individual will depend, of course, on whether or not anyone in the group comes up with the right answer, *and* whether or not the group accepts that answer.

Because the odds of any one person coming up with the right answer are higher in larger groups, it is not surprising to find that larger groups out-perform smaller groups on disjunctive tasks.[63] However, just because someone in the group has the right answer does not always mean that it will be recognized as correct by the other members of the group. On some tasks with obvious correct answers (referred to as *Eureka* tasks), as soon as the correct answer is given, it is immediately recognized and accepted by the group (Eureka, that's it!). On other tasks, however, such as our car-trading problem, the correct answer is not immediately obvious and needs to be explained before the group is likely to accept it. This is known as the *truth supported wins rule.* For the correct answer to be taken as the group's answer, that answer not only has to be obtained, but it then has to be supported by the group. On a Eureka task the truth usually wins out, giving the advantage to the group over most individuals. However, on the other, less obvious tasks, any potential group advantage is less certain.

(Oh yes, the answer to our car-trading problem: the salesman made $2,000.)

Conjunctive tasks: Slowed down by the "weakest link." A **conjunctive task** is one in which a group's performance is limited by the performance of the worst-performing member. For example, a group of mountain climbers can move no faster than the speed of the slowest-moving member of the expedition. Similarly, the effectiveness of a pit crew of an auto racing team is limited by the time it takes to perform the most time-consuming task (e.g., changing the tires or filling the gas tank). (See Figure 8.15.)

FIGURE 8.15 Conjunctive Group Tasks: Some Examples
As shown in these examples, groups performing *conjunctive tasks* are necessarily held back by the slowest member. The mountain climbers can go no faster than the slowest member of the expedition. Neither can the race car driver leave the pit until the slowest service operation is performed.

It should be readily apparent that most individuals will do better than a group on a conjunctive task. Imagine a group of people filling sandbags and passing them to each other in a line, attempting to secure a crumbling retaining wall. If any one person consistently drops the bags or otherwise falters, the group will be probably far *less* effective with than without this person. In such a situation, the group is forced to adjust its performance downward to the level of the poorest performer.

In some cases, such as an expedition of mountain climbers whose safety is ensured by slowing the pace to accommodate the slowest climber, the lower performance of conjunctive groups is not problematic. However, most work organizations can hardly afford to be slowed down by an ineffective team member. If any one individual proves so inept that his or her group suffers, that person may be fired, or face so much social pressure from group members that he or she may resign. As an analogy, the final assembly of an automobile can be no faster than the speed at which the various subassemblies are manufactured. It is therefore not surprising to find that some auto manufacturing plants are closed when they are plagued by technical problems or labor stoppages. Similarly, it is often found that the construction of an entire building must come to a standstill when just one of the construction unions goes on strike.

Some final considerations. In Figure 8.16 we have summarized the likely effects of task type on group performance. On some tasks (e.g., additive tasks) groups may be expected to outperform individual group members, although on others (e.g., conjunctive tasks), the average individual would outperform the group. Accordingly, answers to questions about the relative productivity of individuals and groups would depend to a great extent on the nature of the task the group is performing.

Of course, the picture is far more complex than suggested by this diagram. For example, although the social loafing effect makes individuals inefficient on additive tasks, groups performing additive tasks tend to do better than individuals at an overall level because there are several people contributing to the overall outcome. Also, whether

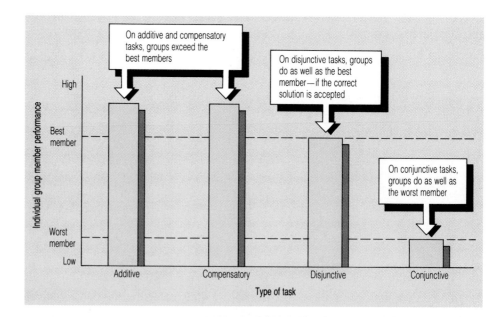

FIGURE 8.16   Group versus Individual Productivity: The Influence of Task Type
As summarized here, how effectively groups perform relative to individuals depends on the type of task performed. (Source: Based on suggestions by Steiner, 1976; see Note 62.)

or not the group's decision on a disjunctive task is as good as the best individual judgment depends on the group's willingness to accept that answer. Obviously, the topic of group performance is very complex, and we have only begun to scratch its surface in this chapter. You will find issues of group productivity appearing elsewhere in this book, particularly in our discussions of communication (chapter 10), power (chapter 12), and decision making (chapter 14).

Summary and Review

The Nature of Groups. Groups are defined as a collection of two or more interacting individuals with a stable pattern of relationships between them who share common goals and who perceive themselves as being a group. Within organizations, there are two major classes of groups—*formal groups* and *informal groups.* Groups often develop by going through five principle stages—*forming, storming, norming, performing,* and *adjourning.*

Group Structure. The structure of work groups (i.e., the pattern of interrelationships between the individuals comprising a group; the guidelines of group behavior that make group functioning orderly and predictable) is determined by four key factors. **Roles** represent the typical pattern of behavior in a specific social context. Roles are often differentiated into *task-oriented* roles (concerned about getting the job done), *socio-emotional* roles (concerned about the social climate of the group), and *self-oriented* roles (concerned about one's own well-being). Roles often place conflicting demands on people, such as between the competing demands placed on someone playing different roles (i.e., **interrole conflict**), or the contradictory demands placed on someone within a certain role (i.e., **intrarole conflict**).

Norms, a set of generally agreed upon informal rules, have profound effects on dictating the variety and quantity of organizational behaviors performed. **Status,** a person's prestige ranking within a group, represents another structural element of groups. It may be either formal or informal in nature, and in either case dictates the nature of communication and social influence within groups.

A final element of group structure is **cohesiveness,** the pressures faced by group members to remain in their groups. Group cohesiveness is created by several factors, including severe group initiations and the presence of external threats. Although highly cohesive groups may perform better than noncohesive groups, this is not always the case. Cohesiveness aids performance if the group's goals are consistent with management's interests.

Task Performance. Individual productivity is influenced by the presence of other group members. Sometimes, a person's performance improves in the presence of others (when the job they do is well-learned), and sometimes performance declines in the presence of others (when the job is novel). This phenomenon is known as **social facilitation.** These effects have been attributed to the *mere presence* of others, the **evaluation apprehension** caused by others, and the conflicting tendencies to pay attention to others vs. the task at hand (i.e., the **distraction-conflict model**).

Group productivity is affected by the type of task performed. On **additive tasks,** where each member's individual contributions are combined, **social loafing** occurs. According to this phenomenon, the more people who work on a task, the less each group member contributes to it. On **compensatory tasks,** the judgments made by the group members are averaged together, and groups tend to do better than the average individual group member. On **disjunctive tasks,** one solution to a problem must be accepted. So long as one group member comes up with the answer and convinces others of its correctness, the group will do as well as the best individual. On **conjunctive tasks** the group can do no better than the poorest group member. As a result, groups tend to perform worse than the average individual group member.

KEY TERMS

additive tasks: Types of group tasks in which the coordinated efforts of several persons are added together to form the group's product.

cohesiveness: The pressures on group members to remain a part of the group.

compensatory tasks: Particular group tasks in which the average of all members' contributions is taken as the group's product.

conjunctive tasks: Types of group tasks in which the performance of the poorest member is taken as the group's product.

disjunctive tasks: Types of group tasks in which only one member's judgment is taken as the group's product.

distraction-conflict model: A conceptualization defining social facilitation in terms of the tendency for others' presence to cause a conflict between directing attention to others versus directing attention to the task at hand.

drive theory of social facilitation: The theory according to which the presence of others increases arousal, which increases people's tendencies to perform the dominant response. If that response is well learned, performance will improve, but if it is novel, performance will be impaired.

evaluation apprehension: The fear of being evaluated or judged by another person, which accounts for the arousing effect of others' presence.

formal groups: Groups that are dictated by the organization, intentionally designed to direct its members toward some organizational goal.

group: A collection of two or more interacting individuals who maintain stable patterns of relationships, share common goals, and perceive themselves as being a group.

group dynamics: The social science field focusing on the nature of groups—the factors governing their formation and development, the elements of their structure, and their interrelationships with individuals, other groups, and organizations.

group structure: The pattern of interrelationships between the individuals comprising a group; the guidelines of group behavior that make group functioning orderly and predictable.

informal groups: Groups that develop naturally among workers, without any direction from the organization within which they operate.

interrole conflict: The incompatible demands made on someone playing two or more different roles.

intrarole conflict: The contradictory demands made on one person, by virtue of the different sets of expectations imposed on that person by others.

norms: Generally agreed upon informal rules that guide group members' behavior.

role: The typical behaviors that characterize a person in a specific social context.

role conflict: A condition that results when the appropriate behaviors for enacting one role are inconsistent with the appropriate behaviors for enacting another role (see *interrole conflict*) or other requirements of the same role (see *intrarole conflict*).

role differentiation: The tendency for various specialized roles to emerge as groups develop.

social facilitation: The tendency for the presence of others, sometimes, to enhance an individual's performance and, at other times, to impair it.

social impact theory: The theory that explains *social loafing* in terms of the diffused responsibility for doing what is expected of each member of a group. The larger the size of a group, the less each member is influenced by the social forces acting on the group.

social loafing: The tendency for group members to exert less individual effort on an additive task as the size of the group increases.

status: The relative prestige, social position, or rank given to groups or individuals by others.

QUESTIONS FOR DISCUSSION

1. Define what a *group* is. Would you say that a collection of people waiting in line at a movie theater constitutes a group? Why or why not?

2. Within organizations, some groups are *formal* and others are *informal*. Distinguish between these two types of groups and give an example of each within any organization with which you are familiar.

3. Identify the stages of *group development* noted in the

text, and apply them to any group to which you belong. Do all the stages apply?

4. Distinguish between *task-oriented, relations-oriented,* and *self-oriented* roles within groups. Give an account of someone playing each of these roles within any groups with which you are familiar.

5. Four factors are responsible for *norm development.* Identify these and give an example of each one.

6. How do differences in formal or informal *status* influence the way people behave in organizations?

7. Argue for or against the following statement: *Group cohesiveness* aids the attainment of organizational goals.

8. Imagine that you are about to go on stage to give a solo piano recital. How would the phenomenon of *social facilitation* explain your likely performance?

9. Describe some conditions existing within organizations that may lead to the *social loafing effect,* and some steps that can be taken to overcome it.

10. Compare and contrast how well groups may be expected to perform tasks that are *additive, compensatory, disjunctive,* and *conjunctive.* Give an example of each kind of group task.

NOTES

1. Cartwright, D., & Zander, A. (1968). Origins of group dynamics. In D. Cartwright, & A. Zander (Eds.), *Group dynamics: Research and theory* (pp. 3–21). New York: Harper & Row.

2. Hare, A. P., Borgatta, E. F., & Bales, R. F. (1955). *Small groups: Studies in social interaction* (p. vi). New York: Knopf.

3. Forsyth, D. L. (1983). *An introduction to group dynamics.* Monterey, CA: Brooks/Cole.

4. Pearce, J. A., II, & Ravlin, E. C. (1987). The design and activation of self-regulating work groups. *Human Relations, 40,* 751–782.

5. Van Zelst, R. H. (1952). Sociometrically selected work teams increase production. *Personnel Psychology, 5,* 175–185.

6. See Note 4, p. 183.

7. Long, S. (1984). Early integration in groups: "A group to join and a group to create." *Human Relations, 37,* 311–332.

8. Tuckman, B. W., & Jensen, M. A. (1977). Stages of small group development revisited. *Group and Organization Studies, 2,* 419–427.

9. Gersick, C. J. G. (1988). Time and transition in work teams: Toward a new model of group development. *Academy of Management Journal, 31,* 9–41.

10. Hackman, J. R. (1987). The design of work teams. In J. W. Lorsch (Ed.), *Handbook of organizational behavior* (pp. 315–342). Englewood Cliffs, NJ: Prentice-Hall.

11. See Note 9, p. 338.

12. See Note 3.

13. Biddle, B. J. (1979). *Role theory: Expectations, identities, and behavior.* New York: Academic Press.

14. Jackson, S. E., & Schuler, R. S. (1985). A meta-analysis and conceptual critique of research on role ambiguity and role conflict in work settings. *Organizational Behavior and Human Decision Processes, 36,* 16–78.

15. Benne, K. D., & Sheats, P. (1948). Functional roles of group members. *Journal of Social Issues, 4,* 41–49.

16. Bales, R. F. (1980). *SYMLOG case study kit.* New York: Free Press.

17. Katz, D., & Kahn, R. L. (1978). *The social psychology of organizations* (2nd ed.). New York: Wiley.

18. Greenhaus, J. H., & Beutell, N. J. (1985). Sources of conflict between work and family roles. *Academy of Management Review, 10,* 76–88.

19. Pearce, J. L. (1981). Bringing some clarity to role ambiguity research. *Academy of Management Review, 6,* 665–674.

20. Van Sell, M., Brief, A. P., & Schuler, R. S. (1981). Role conflict and role ambiguity: Integration of the literature and directions for future research. *Human Relations, 34,* 43–71.

21. Berger-Gross, V., & Kraut, A. I. (1984). "Great expectations": A no-conflict explanation of role conflict. *Journal of Applied Psychology, 69,* 261–271.

22. Cooke, R. A., & Rousseau, D. M. (1984). Stress and strain from family roles and work-role expectations. *Journal of Applied Psychology, 69,* 252–260.

23. Hackman, J. R. (in press). Group influences on individuals in organizations. In M. D. Dunnette (Ed.), *Handbook of industrial/organizational psychology* (2nd ed.). Palo Alto, CA: Consulting Psychologists Press.

24. Nadler, D., Hackman, J. R., & Lawler, E. E., III. (1979). *Managing organizational behavior.* Boston: Little, Brown.

25. Mitchell, T. R., Rothman, M., & Liden, R. C. (1985). Effects of normative information on task performance. *Journal of Applied Psychology, 70,* 48–55.

26. Bettenhause, K., & Murnighan, J. K. (1985). The emergence of norms in competitive decision-making groups. *Administrative Science Quarterly, 30,* 350–372.

27. Feldman, D. C. (1984). The development and enforcement of group norms. *Academy of Management Review, 9,* 47–53.

28. Wanous, J. P., Reichers, A. E., & Malik, S. D. (1984). Organizational socialization and group development: Toward an integrative perspective. *Academy of Management Review, 9,* 670–683.

29. Wilson, S. (1978). *Informal groups: An introduction.* Englewood Cliffs, NJ: Prentice-Hall.

30. Greenberg, J. (1988). Equity and workplace status: A field experiment. *Journal of Applied Psychology, 73,* 606–613.

31. Stryker, S., & Macke, A. S. (1978). Status inconsistency and role conflict. In R. H. Turner, J. Coleman, & R. C. Fox (Eds.), *Annual review of sociology,* vol. 4 (pp. 57–90). Palo Alto, CA: Annual Reviews.

32. Jackson, L. A., & Grabski, S. V. (1988). Perceptions of fair pay and the gender wage gap. *Journal of Applied Social Psychology, 18,* 606–625.

33. Torrance, E. P. (1954). Some consequences of power differences on decision making in permanent and temporary three-man groups. *Research Studies, Washington State College, 22,* 130–140.

34. Greenberg, J. (1976). The role of seating position in group interaction: A review, with applications for group trainers. *Group and Organization Studies, 1,* 310–327.

35. McLaughlin, M. L., Cody, M. J., & Rosenstein, N. E. (1983). Account sequences in conversations between strangers. *Communication Monographs, 50,* 102–125.

36. Luft, J. (1984). *Group processes* (3rd ed.). Palo Alto, CA: Mayfield Publishing.

37. Whyte, W. F. (1948). *Human relations in the restaurant industry.* New York: McGraw-Hill.

38. Hare, A. P. (1976). *Handbook of small group research* (2nd ed.). New York: Free Press.

39. Aronson, E., & Mills, J. (1959). The effects of severity of initiation on liking for a group. *Journal of Abnormal and Social Psychology, 59,* 177–181.

40. Sherif, M., Harvey, O. J., White, B. J., Hood, W. R., & Sherif, C. W. (1961). *Intergroup cooperation and competition: The Robber's Cave experiment.* Norman, OK: University Book Exchange.

41. See Note 3.

42. Cartwright, D. (1968). The nature of group cohesiveness. In D. Cartwright & A. Zander (Eds.), *Group dynamics: Research and theory* (3rd ed.). (pp. 91–109). New York: Harper & Row.

43. Shaw, M. E. (1981). *Group dynamics: The dynamics of small group behavior* (3rd ed.). New York: McGraw-Hill.

44. Janis, I. L. (1982). *Groupthink: Psychological studies of policy decisions and fiascos* (2nd ed.). Boston: Houghton, Mifflin.

45. Douglas, T. (1983). *Groups: Understanding people gathered together.* New York: Tavistock.

46. Seashore, S. E. (1954). *Group cohesiveness in the industrial work group.* Ann Arbor, MI: Institute for Social Research.

47. Schreischeim, J. F. (1980). The social context of leader-subordinate relations: An investigation of the effects of group cohesiveness. *Journal of Applied Psychology, 65,* 183–194.

48. Tziner, A., & Vardi, Y. (1982). Effects of command style and group cohesiveness on the performance effectiveness of self-selected tank crews. *Journal of Applied Psychology, 67,* 769–775.

49. Triplett, N. (1898). The dynamogenic factor in pacemaking and competition. *American Journal of Psychology, 9,* 507–533.

50. Zajonc, R. B. (1965). Social facilitation. *Science, 149,* 269–274.

51. Bond, C. F., Jr., & Titus, L. J. (1983). Social facilitation: A meta-analysis of 241 studies. *Psychological Bulletin, 94,* 265–292.

52. Zajonc, R. B. (1980). Compresence. In P. B. Paulus (Ed.), *Psychology of group influence* (pp. 35–60). Hillsdale, NJ: Erlbaum.

53. Cottrell, N. B. (1972). Social facilitation. In C. G. McClintock (Ed.), *Experimental social psychology* (pp. 214–241). New York: Holt, Rinehart, & Winston.

54. Baron, R. S. (1986). Distraction-conflict theory: Progress and problems. In L. Berkowitz (Ed.), *Advances in experimental social psychology,* vol. 19 (pp. 1–40). New York: Academic Press.

55. Ferris, G., & Rowland, K. (1983). Social facilitation effects on behavioral and perceptual task performance measures. *Group and Organization Studies, 8,* 421–438.

56. Latané, B., Williams, K., & Harkins, S. (1979). Many hands make light the work: The causes and consequences of social loafing. *Journal of Personality and Social Psychology, 37,* 822–832.

57. Latané, B., & Nida, S. (1980). Social impact theory and group influence: A social engineering perspective. In P. B. Paulus (Ed.), *Psychology of group influence* (pp. 3–34). Hillsdale, NJ: Erlbaum.

58. Weldon, E., & Mustari, E. L. (1988). Felt dispensability in groups of coactors: The effects of shared responsibility and explicit anonymity on cognitive effort. *Organizational Behavior and Human Decision Processes, 41,* 330–351.

59. Williams, K. D., Nida, S. A., Baca, L. D., & Latané, B. (1989). Social loafing and swimming: Effects of identifiablility on individual and relay performance of intercollegiate swimmers. *Basic and Applied Social Psychology, 10,* 73–82.

60. Brickner, M. A., Harkins, S. G., & Ostrom, T. M. (1986). Effects of personal involvement: Thought-provoking implications for social loafing. *Journal of Personality and Social Psychology, 51,* 763–769.

61. Albanese, R. & Van Fleet, D. D. (1985). Rational behavior in groups: The free-riding tendency. *Academy of Management Review, 10,* 244–255.

62. Steiner, I. D. (1976). Task-performing groups. In J. W. Thibaut, J. T., Spence, & R. C. Carson (Eds.), *Contemporary topics in social psychology* (pp. 393–422). Morristown, NJ: General Learning Press.

63. Steiner, I. D. (1972). *Group processes and productivity.* New York: Academic Press.

The Rogers Commission: An Insider's View

When he was first approached by William Graham, the head of NASA, to participate in the Presidential task force that was to investigate the *Challenger* disaster, Richard Feynman's initial thought was, "how am I gonna get out of this?"[1] Feynman, a Nobel laureate in physics, greatly disliked working with groups. He wanted to do things his own way and believed a thirteen-member task force wouldn't be able to determine conclusively the reason for the explosion. Nonetheless, Feynman's wife convinced him to join the investigation—an action he referred to as "committing suicide."

As Feynman discovered upon his arrival in Washington, D.C., the Rogers Commission was not to be just another Presidential task force. This group, after all, was assembled to investigate a major American tragedy—the fatal launch of the space shuttle *Challenger* on January 28, 1986. The commission consisted of twelve members in addition to Feynman: two government attorneys, one manager from the Office of Management and Budget, one Pentagon official, the editor of *Aviation Week,* four aeronautical engineers, and four physicists. Included among these were Neil Armstrong, the first astronaut to walk on the moon and Sally Ride, the first female astronaut in space.

Few of the team members knew one another prior to their first meeting. After introductions were made, Chairman Rogers read the following executive order:

> The Commission shall: (1) Review the circumstances surrounding the accident and establish the probable cause or causes of the accident; and (2) Develop recommendations for corrective or other action based upon the Commission's findings and determinations.[2]

It was decided that the committee would complete its investigation in no longer than 120 days. Further, some general outline of the plan of attack was identified. Feynman felt that the first meeting had run smoothly. Although he would have liked more details about the group's plan of attack, he was delighted the commission would only take 120 days of his time.

The second meeting of the Commission was a public forum in which the group was given a general presentation by NASA officials. This was followed by a brief question-and-answer period. Again, Feynman was concerned about the lack of detailed planning. He also wondered why it was necessary to hold public meetings repeating everything that had happened in private discussions.

The third meeting occurred a few days later. At this gathering much discussion took place. As a result of this, the nature and form of the investigation became clear. Rogers wanted the investigation to be run in a tightly controlled, orderly fashion. He believed all the members of the task force should have access to the same information at the same time. In order to orchestrate this outcome, he arranged for the entire group to travel to the Kennedy Space Center in Florida to interact with NASA employees and get a close-up inspection of the facility. Feynman, predictably, didn't like this approach. He believed he could be more useful to the team if he was left to investigate on his own. Because of his background in physics, he felt certain he could extract important and complex information from the various scientists involved. Nonetheless, after three days of arguing this point with Rogers, it became clear to Feynman that for the time being he would have to abide by the plan Rogers had made.

Basically, Rogers had decided that preliminary closed-door meetings would be followed by public meetings. The purpose of this was to discourage the appearance of any type of cover-up by the Commission members. Nasty rumors had been circulating that the Commission wouldn't be effective—especially if fault was found with NASA. To avoid this criticism, Rogers deemed it necessary to automatically keep the public informed about the progress of the Commission and its findings.

The task force continued to meet as a whole unit for one month, after which time four subgroups were formed to investigate different activities. These groups explored pre-launch activities; design, development, and production; accident analysis; and mission and operations planning. At this time (during which the bulk of the investigation took place), each subcommittee went its own way and Commission members mostly interacted only with members of their subteams. Trying to communicate with the others, Feynman wrote an interim report on his portion of the investigation (accident analysis) and sent it to be distributed to all Commission members. Interestingly, however, Rogers kept this report from being distributed to the others because he didn't want it to interfere with their work.

After two months of investigating NASA, the various contractors, and the government, the Commission members were called back to Washington, D. C. to write their final report. Feynman hoped that in writing the report the group members would hold lengthy discussions to analyze their findings. Instead, one person would write a section of the report and another would edit. When a discussion developed it was usually about wording as opposed to ideas of substance.

When the report was mostly completed, the Commission met as an entire unit once again. In one of their final meetings they began to develop a list of recommendations. According to Feynman, the discussion would proceed something like this: "Somebody would say, 'maybe one of the things we should discuss is the establishment of a safety board.' I'm thinking, At last! We're going to have a discussion! But it turns out that this tentative list of topics becomes the recommendations."[3] This "discussion" yielded nine recommendations. Following the final meeting, Rogers tried to add a tenth recommendation, one strongly urging the government to continue supporting NASA. After protests from various committee members, this recommendation was reworded and relabeled a concluding thought.

The Rogers Commission's final report did provide an explanation for the cause of the shuttle disaster. (The O-rings that were to seal exhaust fumes inside the rocket did not create the necessary seal because of the low temperature at launch time.) It also provided a list of recommendations. This information was presented to President Reagan in a ceremony held in the Rose Garden in June 1986. Feynman, who felt the Commission report neglected some technical details, issued his own report days later.[4] Just over two years later, NASA successfully resumed the Shuttle program with the launch of *Discovery*.

Questions for Discussion

1. Was the Rogers Commission a formal or informal group? Why?

2. Using the stages of group development outlined in Figure 8.1, trace the development of the Commission.

3. Did the Commission fulfill the guidelines for effective work teams as outlined by Hackman (see Figure 8.4)?

4. Was this a cohesive group? Why or why not?

5. The members of this Commission were all of high status relative to office/rank/accomplishment. Might this have made any difference to the groups functioning?

6. What role did Feynman play in this group?

Notes

1. Feynman, R. P. (1988). *What do you care what other people think?* (p. 116). New York: W. W. Norton.

2. See Note 1, p. 124.

3. See Note 1, p. 199.

4. Marshall, E. (1986, June 27). Feynman issues his own shuttle report, attacking NASA's risk estimates. *Science, 232,* p. 1596.

The Social Loafing Effect: A Classroom Demonstration

The greater the number of people contributing to your group's task output, the less your individual productivity is likely to be. This phenomenon, known as *social loafing,* can have serious adverse influences on group performance (see pages 281–284). The following exercise is designed to demonstrate this effect.

Procedure

1. Select an additive task that may be conveniently performed in class. For example, you may form groups whose members combine their individual contributions to any of the following tasks: (a) copying entries from a telephone book onto index cards, (b) counting the number of sheets in a large stack of paper, or (c) folding letters and inserting them into envelopes.

2. Perform the task for a period of ten minutes, in groups of different sizes. Try to do your best. Select one person at random to perform the task alone. Combine the remaining students into groups of two, three, four, and so on until the largest possible group is formed (remaining students can simply be included in the largest group). Make random selections by drawing names written on folded slips of paper.

3. After ten minutes, count the number of units you have produced (be it entries copied, sheets counted, letters folded and inserted, or whatever output results from the task performed).

4. Each group computes the average number of units produced by its individual members.

5. At the board, the instructor will record this information in graph form, plotting the average number of units produced per individual (on the vertical axis) as a function of the size of the individuals' work group (on the horizontal axis).

Points to Consider

1. Did the general pattern of performance obtained reveal the social loafing effect? What basis is there for this conclusion?

2. If you did not find evidence for the social loafing effect, why do you think this happened? Might it have been because you expected it to occur and refrained from the natural tendency to lower your individual performance in groups? To test this possibility, repeat the exercise using participants who do not know about this phenomenon. Compare the results.

3. How did members of different size groups feel about the contributions they were making to the task they performed? Specifically, did members of larger groups feel more dispensable, or that they could easily get away with doing less?

4. What could have been done to counteract any "free riding" that may have occurred in this demonstration?

**EXPERIENCING
ORGANIZATIONAL
BEHAVIOR**

CHAPTER NINE

THE COURSE OF WORKING LIFE: ORGANIZATIONAL CULTURE, ORGANIZATIONAL SOCIALIZATION, AND CAREER DEVELOPMENT

CHAPTER OUTLINE

Organizational Culture: Its Origins, Nature, and Effects
Organizational Culture: Its Origins
Organizational Culture: Why and How It Changes
Organizational Culture: Its Major Effects

Organizational Socialization: The Process of Joining Up
Major Stages in the Socialization Process
Organizational Socialization: How It Occurs
Mentors and Socialization

Careers: How Work and Work Experiences Change throughout Life
Career Changes: Basic Dimensions
Career Development and Life Stages
Career Issues: Early, Middle, and Late

Career Systems: Organizational Strategies for Managing Careers
Career Management Programs: Fostering Career Development

Special Sections

OB: A Management Perspective
Imposing a Corporate Culture: When Saying Isn't Doing

OB: A Research Perspective
Realistic Job Previews: What Type Works Best?

OB: A Management Perspective
Effective Socialization Programs: Some Basic Guidelines

LEARNING OBJECTIVES

After reading this chapter, you should be able to:
1. Define the term *organizational culture* and indicate how such culture develops.
2. Describe some of the ways in which organizational culture affects both individual employees and organizational effectiveness.
3. Define the term *organizational socialization* and indicate how this process takes place in functioning organizations.
4. Summarize the potential advantages and disadvantages to both parties of *mentor-protege relationships*.
5. Define the term *career* and explain how changes in individuals' jobs and work-related experiences reflect different stages in their lives.
6. Describe important issues individuals must confront in the early, middle, and later stages of their careers.
7. Describe the nature and purpose of the *career systems* developed by most organizations and explain how these are related to strategic plans and policies.

Melissa Pliser is upset; and well she should be, given the intense look of displeasure on the face of her boss, Jackie Martin. The two (who work for a manufacturer of high-tech testing equipment) have just completed a call on a medium-sized customer, and for the first time, Jackie let Melissa carry the ball and handle most of the discussions. From Jackie's expression, Melissa knows that she must have done something wrong. But since they closed the order, she can't for the life of her figure out what it is.

"Well, come on, let me have it," Melissa remarks. "I can tell that you're unhappy about something, but I don't know what it is. I thought it all went pretty well."

"It did, until you made that promise about March delivery of our new 5036 line. You know that it probably won't be ready by then."

"Well we closed the order, didn't we? Isn't that our top priority? Once we get the business, we can handle the delays somehow."

"Maybe that's what they did at Tri-Co," Jackie answers, referring to Melissa's last job, "but that's not *our* style. When we promise delivery, we stand behind it, no *ifs, buts,* or *maybes.*"

"Isn't that a little rigid?" Melissa asks, a look of puzzlement in her eyes. "And won't it cost us some business?"

"If it does, that's the breaks," Jackie answers with a shrug of her shoulders. "The way we look at it, you can get away with that 'promise 'em anything' routine once or maybe twice at the outside. After that, you've blown your credibility and no one will even listen to you when you come around. Good will and long-term service, that's what we believe in. We're a class act, and we behave like one. If we had a kind of Company Ten Commandments, the one on top of the list would probably be: 'Only promise what you can definitely, positively deliver.' That goes for everyone, and especially for people like us in Sales."

"Well, I'm really sorry . . . I didn't mean to do anything out of line. But no one ever told me *that* during my orientation. In fact, I got the opposite impression—this is a red-hot outfit on a roll, and we're going to continue that 22 percent growth curve right into the future, no matter what."

"We are and this *is* an aggressive company. But like I just said: we don't promise what we can't deliver. It's one of our basic principles."

"I'll sure remember that from now on," Melissa states with conviction. Then, after a brief pause, she continues. "You know, it's really great working with you like this, Jackie. I'm learning so much. No one ever took such an interest in me at my last job."

Smiling now, Jackie pats her young subordinate on the arm. "I only do it because I figure you're worth it. You've got a great future with us once you get some experience and figure out what's what. And, hey, it's working with people like you that keeps me feeling young!"

If you live a full, normal lifespan, you will spend forty, fifty, or even more years at work. In the past, most persons spent the majority, if not all, of these years, within a single organization. They entered a company after finishing their formal education, and remained with it for several decades (see Figure 9.1 on page 296). Recently, however, this pattern has altered significantly. Most individuals now work for several different companies during the course of their careers; and growing numbers even shift from one type of job or occupation to another.[1] Because of these trends, millions of persons have experiences similar to those encountered by Melissa, the young character mentioned above. When persons move from one organization to another, they discover

FIGURE 9.1 Careers: The Traditional Model
In the past, many individuals spent most, if not all, of their working lives with a single organization.

subtle (as well as relatively obvious) differences between their new work environments and their old ones. Adjusting to these differences can involve acquiring new job skills, new information, and even new attitudes or values. Further, such adjustments are crucial: only to the extent they are completed successfully do the persons involved become accepted, fully functioning members of their new organizations.[2]

Compounding the difficulties produced by frequent job changes, geographic transfers and the like, are other aspects of life in the late twentieth century. Many of these relate to growing complexity in the competing demands of work and family life (e.g., how to manage two-career families). Others reflect changing attitudes about the relative importance of careers and personal fulfillment.[3] Taking note of such trends, researchers in OB have focused increasing attention on what might be termed *the course of working life*—changes individuals encounter during their forty to fifty years of work. In this chapter, we'll consider some of the most important of these. As we'll soon note, many of these changes center around the task of adjusting to life in a new organization— "learning the ropes" in a new work setting. Such adjustments, in turn, involve two important issues: **organizational culture**—the shared beliefs, expectations, and values held by members of a given organization, and to which newcomers must adjust— and **organizational socialization**—the process through which new employees actually make such adjustments and become fully functioning members of their organizations. Finally, we'll turn to **careers,** the sequence of jobs, roles, and positions held by individuals during their working lives.[4] Here, we'll consider both *personal factors* in career development (e.g., career choice, the complex interplay between personal development and careers), and efforts by organizations to assist employees with their careers and to manage their human resources through **career systems.**[5]

ORGANIZATIONAL CULTURE: ITS ORIGINS, NATURE, AND EFFECTS

Anyone who has worked in several different organizations is familiar with the fact that each is unique. Even organizations concerned with the same activities or that provide similar products or services can be very different places in which to work. One reason for this is obvious: different organizations are composed of different persons. Since these individuals are unique in many respects, it is not at all surprising that this uniqueness is mirrored in the organizations themselves. This is only part of the total picture, however. In many organizations, employees are a constantly changing cast of characters—old ones leave and new ones join with considerable frequency. Despite such shifts, however, the organizations themselves alter slowly, if at all. In fact, it is often the new employees who change rather than the organization. In a sense, then, organizations have an existence of their own, quite apart from the persons of which they are composed. They may remain relatively stable in many respects even in the face of high rates of turnover.

What accounts for such stability? One answer involves the impact of **organizational culture**—beliefs, attitudes, values, and expectations shared by most organization members.[6] Once established, such beliefs and values tend to persist, unless relatively dramatic events (e.g., radical shifts in the external environment) necessitate change. And collectively, they affect many activities and processes within the organization. To mention a single example, have you ever met or done business with a representative of "Big Blue" (IBM)? If so, you probably noticed that this individual was dressed very conservatively. This is not an accident: employees of IBM are expected to dress and behave in certain ways—ones consistent with its well-established corporate culture.

Countless other examples exist, for organizational culture is often readily apparent in the actions of individuals and groups, in *norms* governing behavior in various situations, in formal corporate philosophy, in informal rules concerning such matters as who communicates with whom or how various rewards will be distributed, and even in business strategies or values (e.g., views about the importance of price leadership or product quality). In short, an organization's culture is often a powerful force determining how it operates and how it performs.[7]

At this point, we should pause briefly to clarify an important issue. Our comments so far seem to suggest that each organization has only one culture—a single shared set of attitudes, values, and beliefs that impinge on all of its members. In fact, this is rarely the case. Research findings suggest that several *subcultures*, based upon occupational, professional, or functional divisions, usually exist within a single organization.[8] In short, persons belonging to different fields or who work in departments with different functions, often share more attitudes and beliefs with others in their own fields or work units than they do with persons in other portions of the company. It is important to keep the existence of these subcultures in mind when considering organizational culture and its effects. Having commented on this issue, we can now turn to several basic questions about organizational culture: How and why does it originate? What causes it to change or to remain stable? What are its major effects?

Organizational Culture: Its Origins

Why do many individuals within an organization (or, at least, within its major divisions) share basic attitudes, values, and expectations? Several factors contribute to this state of affairs, and hence to the emergence of organizational culture.

First, organizational culture may be traced, at least in part, to the founders of the company. These persons often possess dynamic personalities, strong values, and a clear vision of how the organization should be. Since they are on the scene first, and play a key role in hiring initial staff, their attitudes and values are readily transmitted to new employees. The result: these views become the accepted ones in the organization, and persist as long as the founders are on the scene, or even longer. For example, Debbi Fields, the founder of Mrs. Fields' Cookies (a chain of cookie stores found in many shopping malls), believes strongly in the motivation and ability of employees to do a good job. As a result, she has designed the operations of her stores to provide employees with a considerable amount of autonomy, and with opportunities to use their own initiative to generate goodwill among customers. These attitudes permeate the entire company, and are a part of its basic culture.

Second, organizational culture often develops out of an organization's experience with the external environment.[9] Every organization must find a niche for itself in its industry and in the marketplace. As it struggles to do so in its early days, it may find that some values and practices work better for it than others. For example, one company may determine that delivering defect-free products is its strong point; by doing so, it can build up a core of solid customers who prefer it to other competing businesses. As a result, the organization may gradually acquire a deep, shared commitment to high quality. In contrast, another company may find that selling products of moderate quality, but at attractive prices, works best for it. The result: a dominant value centering around *price leadership* takes shape. In these and countless other ways, an organization's culture is shaped by its interaction with the external environment.

Third, culture also develops from the need to maintain effective working relationships among organization members. Depending on the nature of its business, and the characteristics of the persons it must hire, different expectations and values may develop. Thus, consider a young, high-tech firm, operating in an environment where innovation is the key ingredient in success. Because such a company needs rapid and open communication between its employees, informal working relationships and open expression of views may come to be valued within it. In contrast, very different values and styles of communication may develop in other organizations working in other industries and with different types of personnel. (See Figure 9.2 for a summary of factors affecting the emergence and form of organizational culture.)

In sum, an organization's culture is often shaped by influential persons present in its early days, by the external environment in which it operates, and by the nature of

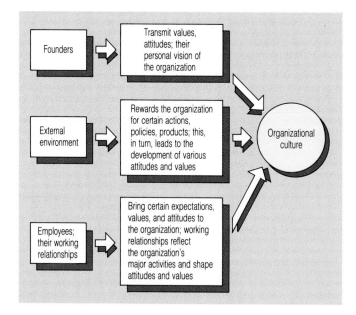

FIGURE 9.2 Sources of Organizational Culture
An organization's culture generally springs from several factors. These include the influence of founders, various features of the external environment, and the attitudes or values of employees.

its business and its employees. In a large, mature organization, links between current culture and these contributing factors may be difficult to discern. Nonetheless, it is likely that they played a role in its emergence and early form.

Organizational Culture: Why and How It Changes

Our earlier comments about the relative stability of organizational culture may have left you wondering about the following questions: if culture tends to be so stable, why, and how, does it ever change? Why, in short, isn't it simply passed from one generation of organization members to the next in a fixed and relatively static manner? The basic answer, of course, is that the world in which an organization operates changes. External events (e.g., shifting market conditions, arrival of new competitors, altered government policies) may necessitate shifts in an organization's mode of doing business and thus in its internal culture. (Refer to chapter 16 for a detailed discussion of the many factors that contribute to organizational change.)

Similarly, over time, the persons entering an organization may differ in important ways from those already in it. As a function of demographic and related shifts in society at large, they may be younger or older, more varied in ethnic or racial backgrounds, and have more (or perhaps less) formal education. Because of these differences, they may interpret and react to an organization's culture in new ways. These shifting reactions, in turn, may alter the organization's culture in various respects—shifts that may increase in magnitude as the new employees move up the corporate hierarchy and acquire growing influence and power. Such change is more likely to take place when organizations do not purposely screen applicants to ensure that they already possess views and orientations consistent with the organization's culture.[10]

Yet another factor contributing to change in an organization's culture relates to the culture itself. As noted recently by Wilkins and Dyer, cultures may be classified as change-oriented (morphogenetic) or stability-oriented (homeostatic) in nature.[11] In other words, some view change as a desirable outcome to be actively encouraged, while others perceive it as a threat or necessary evil to be avoided. Obviously, those oriented toward change are much more likely to shift over time than those that are not.

Finally, cultural change may result from conscious decisions to alter the internal structure or basic operation of an organization. Once such decisions are reached, many practices in the company that both reflect and contribute to its culture may be altered. For example, different criteria for recruiting new members or promoting current ones may be adopted. Similarly, managers may be directed to focus their attention on different aspects of subordinates' behavior than was true in the past. As these shifts are implemented, new norms governing preferred or acceptable behavior emerge, and attitudes and beliefs supporting such norms tend to develop. The result may be a considerable shift in existing culture.

In sum, operating together, several factors make it highly unlikely that the culture of a given organization will remain entirely constant over long periods of time. Changes in people, the external environment, and a host of other external influences virtually assure that over the long haul, some degree of change, not total stability, will be the likely outcome in most organizations. (Refer to Figure 9.3 on page 300 for a summary of the factors that influence such change.)

Organizational Culture: Its Major Effects

Because it involves shared expectations, values, and attitudes, organizational culture exerts many important effects both on individuals and organizational processes. With respect to organization members, culture generates strong, if often subtle, pressures

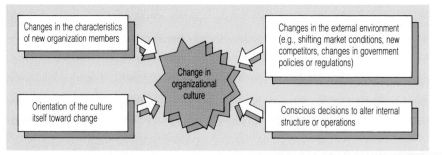

Changes in the characteristics of new organization members

Changes in the external environment (e.g., shifting market conditions, new competitors, changes in government policies or regulations)

Change in organizational culture

Orientation of the culture itself toward change

Conscious decisions to alter internal structure or operations

FIGURE 9.3   Organizational Culture: Some Sources of Change
As shown here, several factors contribute to change in organizational culture.

to *go along*—to think and act in ways that are consistent with the existing culture. Thus, if an organization's culture stresses such values as service to customers, participative decision making, and a paternalistic attitude toward employees, individuals within the company will tend to adopt these values in their own behavior. If, in contrast, an organization's culture involves maximizing output, centralized decision making, and "going by the book," individuals' actions will often reflect *these* attitudes and values.[12]

Turning to the impact of culture on organizational processes, much research has focused on the possibility of a link between culture and performance.[13] One view is that in order to influence performance, organizational culture must be *strong* (basic aspects of the culture are strongly accepted by most employees), and must also possess certain key traits (e.g., humanistic values, concern about quality and innovativeness of products).[14] Some findings appear to support this contention. For example, Dennison reported that corporations with cultural values favoring participation by employees (in decision making and other processes) generate a return on investment twice as great as corporations lacking this value.[15] Similarly, in their best-selling book, *In Search of Excellence,* Peters and Waterman reported that possession of a "strong" culture characterized eighty highly successful firms in the United States. While such studies are intriguing and make for stimulating reading, recent reviews by Saffold, and Siehl and Martin, suggest that they do not as yet provide compelling evidence for a clear link between culture and performance.[16,17]

First, much of the research on this issue has assumed that organizations possess a single, unitary culture. As noted previously, this is not always the case. Therefore, the findings reported may apply only to some groups of employees—perhaps, especially, top management in the companies studied. Second, serious questions remain about the measures of cultural *strength* used in these projects. Different researchers have adopted different definitions; thus, it is not clear that the same variable was being assessed in all cases. Third, none of the studies conducted to date have included appropriate comparison groups. To demonstrate that possession of certain types of culture contributes to corporate success, it is necessary to show that such cultures are indeed characteristic of highly productive organizations, but not of less successful ones. To date, no clear data have been reported on this issue.

In view of these problems, it seems safest to conclude that a link between organizational culture and performance remains a reasonable, but as yet unverified, possibility. Further evidence is needed before development of a strong, appropriate culture can be added to the list of recommended procedures for enhancing corporate performance. (In fact, some evidence suggests that steps to develop and impose such a success-oriented culture on an organization may backfire and lead to disaster rather than excellence. For a summary of this evidence, please see the **Management Perspective** on page 301.)

Imposing a Corporate Culture: When Saying Isn't Doing

If, as we have contended, an organization's culture often exerts strong effects on its members, an intriguing possibility is suggested: why not create a culture that will enhance positive outcomes for the organization? In other words, why not intentionally establish a culture that will encourage desirable goals such as innovation, product quality, and open communication? Just such a strategy was attempted recently by a growing young company in California's Silicon Valley—an organization widely touted, at the time, as the next Apple Computer.[18] Top management, meeting in a series of closed sessions, devised a document designed to express what they hoped to establish as the central values of the company. These included "Attention to detail," "Doing it right the first time," "Delivering defect-free products," and "Open communication throughout the company." This document was circulated to middle managers who also met in closed session to discuss and refine it. After that, it was presented to rank-and-file employees as the guiding set of principles for all of the firm's operations.

What happened? Peter Reynolds, a trained anthropologist, was present on the scene, working as a software trainer. His description of the events that followed highlights the pitfalls of trying to dictate a corporate culture.[19] The first point Reynolds addresses is the sizable gap that quickly developed between the management-stated "culture" and actual conditions within the company. At the same time that product quality was being touted as a key aspect of the firm's basic culture, defective units (computers) were being regularly and knowingly shipped to many customers. Similarly, while the stated "culture" paid lip service to an open style of communication and employee participation in decisions, top management actually enforced a strict chain of command and offered employees little opportunity for providing input. Under these circumstances, employees generally viewed management's attempt to dictate a favorable corporate culture with a mixture of cynicism and resentment (see Figure 9.4). For example, one response to the obvious gap between statements about commitment to product quality and the actual low quality standards that prevailed was the following statement, made by employees in manufacturing: "We do have a zero-defect program: don't test the product and you'll find zero defects." When asked for their views about the artificial

FIGURE 9.4 Culture Gaps: One Source of Cynicism among Employees

When top management pays lip service to specific values, but then takes actions that are clearly inconsistent with these values, high levels of employee cynicism may result.

corporate culture, many employees described it as being useless, silly, or even worse.

Not surprisingly, morale dropped sharply, turnover increased, and the company's financial situation deteriorated rapidly as it became infamous for delivering shoddy products at a much later date than promised. Ultimately, it went bankrupt, closing its doors in the face of an unpayable multi-million dollar debt.

Do these events contain any message for practicing managers? We feel they do. First, they suggest that in actuality, there is no way to dictate or proclaim a corporate culture in an already existing company. While intentional efforts to establish a specific culture may succeed when an organization is brand new, once it has been operating for several years, efforts to dictate a "new" or "improved" culture are unlikely to succeed.

Second, efforts to impose a new or altered

culture will probably be greeted by employees with skepticism and resistance. As one employee of the computer company noted: "You can't create values." Third, such reactions are likely to be maximized when noticeable gaps between the stated culture and actual conditions exist. Indeed, clear disparity between officially stated values or policies and those demonstrated by top management can prove disastrous. In the short run they are confusing; in the long run they may convert initial enthusiasm among employees into cynicism and apathy. In sum, organizational culture is indeed an important aspect of many work settings, and is well worth considering. However, claims that it can be created on the spot, or readily converted into a dazzling force for excellence should be greeted with skepticism. The odds are strong that they are grossly overstated.

Organizational Socialization: The Process of Joining Up

Think back over the jobs you have held in recent years. Can you recall your feelings and reactions during the first few days (or weeks) on each? If you can, you probably remember that these were uncomfortable periods. As a new employee, you were suddenly confronted with a work environment that was different in many respects from ones you had previously encountered. All the people around you were unfamiliar, and you had to begin the process of getting to know them—and their many personal quirks! Unless your job was identical to one you had performed before, you also found it necessary to learn several new procedures, skills, and operations relating to it. You had to identify and try to understand the policies, practices, and procedures in force in your new organization, so that you would know how to carry out your work assignments in accordance with them. And of course, you had to begin forming an image of the organization's culture—its unique style, approach to doing business, and central values.

Given the complexity of these tasks, it is obvious that successfully completing them is important to the future performance of virtually *any* new employee. In other words, the speed and ease with which individuals "learn the ropes" in organizations they have recently joined are crucial issues from both the individual's and organization's point of view. The process through which this task is accomplished is known as **organizational socialization.** More formally, it can be defined as *the process through which individuals are transformed from outsiders to participating, effective members of organizations.*[20] In a sense, **careers** can be viewed as consisting of a series of socialization experiences, as individuals move into new organizations or new positions in their present one. Thus, understanding organizational socialization is important to understanding several aspects of careers and career development.

In this section, therefore, we'll consider several key aspects of such socialization. First, we'll describe the basic stages of socialization—steps through which most persons pass en route to becoming full members of their organization and work group. Next, we'll consider various techniques used by organizations to help smooth new employees' passage through this difficult process. Finally, we'll consider the role of **mentors**—older and more experienced coworkers—in the socialization process.

Major Stages in the Socialization Process

In one sense, organizational socialization is a continuous process—one that begins before individuals actually arrive on the scene and proceeds for weeks or months after their entry. Despite this fact, it makes sense to divide it into three basic periods which are often marked by discrete events signifying their beginning and their end. These have been described by Feldman as the stages of *getting in, breaking in,* and *settling in.*[21]

Getting in: Anticipatory socialization. Before individuals actually join an organization, they usually know quite a bit about it. Such information, which is the basis for expectations concerning what the organization and their specific jobs will be like, is obtained from several sources. In many cases, it is provided by friends or relatives already working for the organization. These individuals provide a wealth of information (not all of it accurate!) which strongly colors the perceptions and expectations of new recruits.

Second, individuals often acquire information about an organization from professional journals, from magazine and newspaper articles, from its annual reports, and other formal sources.

Third, and perhaps most important, potential employees gain such information from the organization's *recruitment procedures.* Since competition for top-notch employees is always intense, successful recruitment of such persons usually involves a skilled combination of salesmanship and diplomacy. Recruiters tend to describe their companies in glowing terms, glossing over internal problems and emphasizing positive features. The result is that potential employees receive an unrealistically positive impression about what working in it will be like. When they actually arrive on the job and find that their expectations are not met, disappointment, dissatisfaction, and even resentment about being misled can follow. Such reactions, in turn, can contribute to high rates of turnover, low organizational commitment and other negative outcomes.[22]

In extreme cases, the reactions experienced by employees upon discovering that conditions in the organization are not what they expected can take the form of **entry shock**—strong feelings of dismay, confusion, and disillusionment.[23] For example, consider the reactions of a new college graduate who enters an organization with high hopes and positive expectations. Much to her chagrin, she finds that conditions are not at all what she expected. Her supervisor seems to have little interest in her; contrary to expectations formed during her interview, she discovers that her input is rarely invited and that she has little role in decision making. The work she is asked to perform is far less stimulating than she anticipated, and in contrast to conditions in college, where she received feedback from her professors on a regular basis, she now receives such input only on relatively rare occasions. Finally, she is disillusioned to learn that promotions, raises, and other rewards are distributed largely on the basis of organizational politics—not strictly on the basis of merit as she assumed. Hit with this unsettling combination of disappointments, she rapidly loses interest in her work and decides to begin another job search as soon as possible.

Can such reactions be avoided, or at least reduced? One technique that seems quite useful in this respect is **realistic job previews**—providing job applicants with accurate descriptions of the jobs they will perform and the organizations they will enter.[24] Growing evidence suggests that persons exposed to such previews later report higher satisfaction and show lower turnover than those who receive standard, glowing—but often misleading—information about the companies in question. Such benefits are greater when individuals can afford to be selective about accepting a given position than when the job market is tight, but they do seem to be helpful in a wide range of contexts.[25] (What type of realistic job previews are best? Ones that reduce overly optimistic expectations, ones that counter overly pessimistic expectations, or ones that do both? And why, precisely, do such previews work? For information on these issues, please see the **Research Perspective** on page 304.)

Realistic Job Previews: What Type Works Best?

According to one old saying "To be forewarned is to be forearmed." In other words, knowing what to expect in a situation may help us prepare for it in some way and so, perhaps, increase our ability to handle it when it actually occurs. As we have already noted, this seems to be true with respect to **realistic job previews.**[26] When individuals are given accurate information about negative aspects of a job or organization, they often react more favorably (or, at least, less negatively) to such conditions when later confronted with them than when they were not provided with realistic previews. But what form should such previews take? On the one hand, they might concentrate on reducing overly optimistic expectations. On the other, they might focus on reducing overly pessimistic expectations. Is either of these approaches superior? Or should they be combined for maximum effect? A recent study by Meglino, Denisi, Youngblood, and Williams provides relatively clear-cut answers to these questions.[27]

Participants in this investigation were army recruits about to undergo basic training. Prior to the first day of training, persons in three different groups were exposed to one of the following types of realistic previews: (1) *reduction* previews, designed to reduce overly optimistic expectations by focusing on a number of problems faced by new recruits; (2) *enhancement* previews, designed to reduce overly pessimistic expectations by indicating that various activities were not as difficult as recruits anticipated, or (3) *combination* previews, which made use of both techniques. These previews were presented in the form of professionally produced videotapes, designed to provide an overview of basic training. The content of the tapes was varied in appropriate ways so as to generate the different types of realistic previews. (Individuals in a fourth group, a control condition, received no realistic previews.)

The effects of these various treatments on participants' later reactions were assessed in several ways. First, their rate of voluntary turnover was assessed over the course of basic training. Second,

FIGURE 9.5   Positive Effects of Realistic Job Previews

Army recruits who received realistic previews designed to reduce both overly optimistic and overly pessimistic expectations (combination previews) showed lower rates of voluntary turnover than recruits who received other types of previews or no realistic previews at all. Similar findings were also obtained with respect to trust in the army and recruits' job satisfaction. (Source: Based on data from Meglino et al., 1988; see Note 27.)

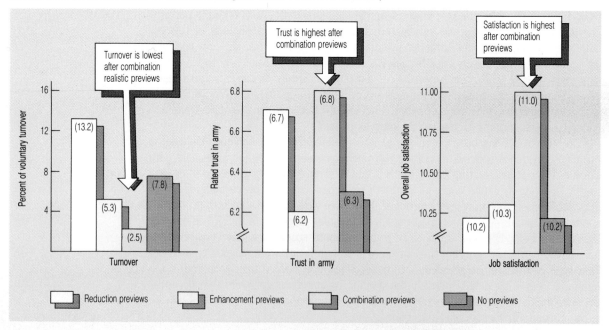

participants reported on their reactions to the army along several dimensions (e.g., they rated the extent to which it was honest in its dealing with soldiers and could be trusted, the extent to which it cared about them as individuals, their commitment to the army, and their level of satisfaction with various aspects of their new jobs as soldiers). It was predicted that on all these measures, the most favorable results would be obtained with the combination previews. As shown in Figure 9.5, this hypothesis was generally confirmed. Voluntary turnover was indeed lowest in the combination preview group. Similarly, trust in the army, commitment to it, and reported job satisfaction were highest in this condition as well. Interestingly, the reduction previews generated the highest level of turnover, perhaps because this tape contained a great deal of negative information about army life (e.g., it stressed the problems involved in living and working with strangers, having no privacy, homesickness), but provided little information about coping with such difficulties. Finally, it was also found that the realistic previews were more effective with individuals who were above average in intelligence

than those who were below average. This latter finding seemed to stem from the fact that more intelligent persons directed more attention to the realistic previews when they were shown and understood their content somewhat better.

The results reported by Meglino and his colleagues support the view that realistic previews are indeed effective from the standpoint of reducing voluntary turnover and enhancing positive reactions to a new job. In addition, they suggest that the benefits of such previews may stem, at least in part, from feelings on the part of new employees that the organization is honest in its dealings with them, and also from greater degrees of commitment to it. Finally, the findings of this project indicate that a combined approach, designed to both reduce overly optimistic expectations and lessen overly pessimistic ones, may often be best. Such previews give potential employees a balanced picture of the conditions they will face when actually on the job and this, in turn, may be highly effective in avoiding *entry shock* and other negative reactions when they actually come on board.

Breaking in: The encounter stage. The second major stage in organizational socialization begins when individuals actually assume their new duties. During this stage, they face several key tasks. First, they must master the skills required by their new jobs. Second, they must become oriented to the practices and procedures of the organization. This often involves unlearning old habits or behaviors and acquiring new ones, for coworkers quickly become tired of hearing a new recruit say, "That's not how we did it where I worked before." Third, new members of an organization must establish good social relations with other members of their work group. They must get to know these people and gain their acceptance. Only when they do, can they become full members of the team.

It is during the encounter stage, of course, that formal *training* and *orientation programs* are conducted. These are designed to help individuals accomplish the tasks described above. We will comment further on the nature of such programs below.

Settling in: The metamorphosis stage. Some time after an individual enters an organization, he or she attains full member status. Depending on the type and length of the training program used, this entry may be marked by a formal ceremony or may be quite informal. In the former case, individuals may attend a dinner, reception, or graduation exercise at which they exchange their temporary, provisional title (e.g., trainee, apprentice) for a more permanent one. Alternatively, they may receive a concrete sign of their new status (e.g., the key to the executive washroom, a pass to the executive dining room, a permanent identity badge). In other cases, especially when training has been shorter or informal in nature, full acceptance into the work group may not be marked by any specific ceremony. Instead, it may be acknowledged by informal actions, such as being invited to lunch by coworkers or being assigned a seat at their table in the dining room.

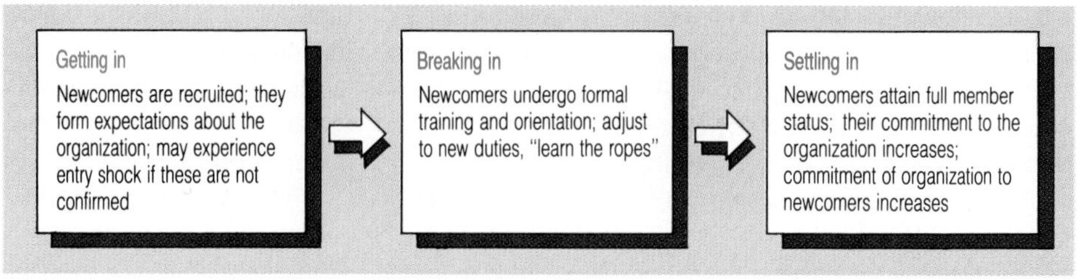

Getting in	Breaking in	Settling in
Newcomers are recruited; they form expectations about the organization; may experience entry shock if these are not confirmed	Newcomers undergo formal training and orientation; adjust to new duties, "learn the ropes"	Newcomers attain full member status; their commitment to the organization increases; commitment of organization to newcomers increases

FIGURE 9.6   Organizational Socialization: Its Major Phases
The process of *organizational socialization* is complex and involves many different activities. In general, however, it can be divided into the three major stages or phases illustrated here.

Whatever form it takes, the settling in phase of socialization marks important shifts for both individuals and organizations. Employees now make permanent adjustments to their jobs (e.g., they resolve conflicting demands between their jobs and their personal lives). And organizations now treat them as if they will be long-term members of the work team rather than temporary fill-ins. (Refer to Figure 9.6 for a summary of events and activities occurring during the three major stages of organizational socialization.)

Organizational Socialization: How It Occurs

Most organizations have some type of program or procedure designed to help new employees orient and adjust to their new jobs. However, as you might expect, these programs differ in many respects. According to Van Maanen, a researcher who has studied this process in great detail, most of these differences involve the dimensions shown in Table 9.1.[28]

First, socialization programs differ in terms of whether newcomers are socialized individually or in groups. The former approach is often adopted by organizations that hire people all through the year at different times. The latter is adopted by organizations that hire groups of persons at specific times. For example, one of the authors underwent a collective socialization program when he entered a large federal agency. He and other

TABLE 9.1   Strategies for People-processing
Programs of organizational socialization can vary along each of the dimensions listed here.

DIMENSION	EXPLANATION
Individual–Group	Are newcomers socialized individually or as part of groups of trainees?
Informal–Formal	Is training formal or on-the-job?
Sequential–Nonsequential	Do newcomers progress toward full-member status one step at a time, or do they become members as soon as orientation is over?
Serial–Disjunctive	Is training conducted by members of the organization or by others?
Investiture–Divestiture	Does training seek to affirm the self-confidence of newcomers or reduce it?
Fixed–Variable	Do newcomers know or not know when their probationary period will end?

(Source: Based on suggestions by Van Maanen, 1978; see Note 28.)

new recruits were sent to a resort where they participated in a five day long formal program designed to orient them to their new positions and responsibilities.

Second, socialization can be *formal,* as in the program just mentioned, or *informal,* involving on-the-job experiences. Formal programs are generally used when new employees are quite unfamiliar with their new roles or in connection with complex jobs. Informal ones are often used when employees already know much about their positions, or when their jobs are simple.

Third, socialization can be *sequential,* involving a process in which recruits obtain full membership in the organization by passing through a series of concrete steps or stages (e.g., they may be designated as trainees, apprentices, assistants, and so on, as they complete specific periods of time with the organization). In contrast, socialization can be *nonsequential.* Here, newcomers receive full member status as soon as orientation and training are completed.

A fourth dimension involves the question of whether newcomers are trained by experienced members of the group (*serial* training) or by persons who do not belong to the organization itself (*disjunctive*). In the latter type of training, professionals with special expertise are hired for this specific purpose.

Fifth, socialization programs often differ with respect to whether they are designed to affirm the ability and self-confidence of recruits (*investiture programs*) or to strip away their feelings of self-confidence so that they will be in a better state to accept new roles and patterns of behavior (*divestiture programs*). The former process is often used with high-level recruits. Since these persons were hired on the basis of their credentials and expertise, their new organizations don't want to change them. On the contrary, their entry is meant to be as smooth and pleasant as possible.

In contrast, divestiture programs are designed to strip away certain characteristics or attitudes that new recruits bring with them to the new organization. Such tactics are often applied to persons entering military service, professional or graduate school, or college-level sports. The goal is to "shake them up," so they more readily surrender any current attitudes and behaviors they brought with them which are counter-productive from their new organization's point of view. For example, medical and professional schools, faced with newcomers who have experienced a great deal of previous academic success, load these new students with extremely heavy programs to make them painfully aware of their own limitations and of the demands of their new roles.

Finally, socialization programs differ in terms of whether newcomers know in advance when their probationary period will end (*fixed programs*), or do not know when they will gain full acceptance (*variable programs*).

In sum, the procedures employed by organizations to socialize their new recruits differ in many ways. As you might suspect, no single pattern or combination of these techniques is best. Rather, their relative effectiveness varies in different situations, in different organizations, and with contrasting groups of employees. (Are there any guidelines organizations can follow in order to conduct effective socialization programs? Research findings and practical experience suggest that there are. For an overview of some of these, please see the **Management Perspective** below.)

OB: A MANAGEMENT PERSPECTIVE

Effective Socialization Programs: Some Basic Guidelines

While organizational socialization is a complex process with many interacting facets, it essentially involves the successful attainment of three major goals: (1) providing employees with the basic work skills and information needed for their jobs, (2) orienting them to the practices, policies, and procedures of the organization, (3) helping them adjust to membership in their new work groups. Below are some general guidelines that often prove useful in reaching each of these goals.

Training: As noted in chapter 2, several techniques exist for providing new skills and information.[29] Here, we'll mention a few we did not previously consider in detail.

In the *sink-or-swim* approach, recruits are simply placed in their new jobs, and learn what they need from practical experience. In *job rotation,* they work at several different jobs in succession, thus acquiring a broad range of skills useful in different contexts. Finally, in full-time *training,* they participate in training programs ranging from classroom instruction to detailed on-the-job training. Whatever form they take, training programs should adopt the following principles in order to succeed:

1. Determine precisely what skills and information individuals need for their jobs; do *not* assume that their previous experience or professional training has armed them with these skills or information.
2. Provide individuals with feedback on their work, and a sense of accomplishment about their growing expertise.
3. Tailor training programs to the needs of specific jobs; general or generic training cannot be readily applied or transferred in many cases.
4. Evaluate the success of training programs on a regular basis; do not assume that they are succeeding.

Orientation: Orientation programs focus on helping individuals understand current organization practices, policies and procedures. Most are fairly short-term in scope, occupying a few hours or a single day. In order for such programs to succeed, they should take account of the following principles:

1. Avoid information overload. New employees cannot possibly absorb everything they need to know about the organization in a single day; this should be spread out over a longer period of time.
2. Don't overemphasize paperwork; it is impossible for individuals to gain an accurate overview of an organization and how it operates from a day spent filling out one form after another.
3. Orientation sessions should avoid scare tactics in which new employees are warned that their chances of success are quite low or which focus

too heavily on praising the organization and its current practices.
4. Be certain that the information provided is relevant; it should also be provided on a need-to-know basis.
5. Build in two-way communication so that new recruits do not merely receive information in a passive manner; they should have opportunities to raise questions and seek clarification.

Adjustment to work groups: Work groups are a primary source of help for new employees. The persons around them are doing similar jobs, and are often happy to share their knowledge and expertise with newcomers. In addition, they can provide much needed social support and encouragement in those trying early days. It is crucial, therefore, that socialization programs assist individuals in becoming integrated into their new work units. The following principles are often helpful in this respect.

1. Socialization should occur, as much as possible, within the work group; disjunctive procedures conducted by persons from outside the organization are often less effective.
2. Be careful to expose new recruits primarily to talented, supportive coworkers with positive attitudes toward the organization; avoid exposure to employees with less favorable attitudes or work habits.
3. Avoid segregating newcomers into their own work unit; this can amount to "the blind leading the blind," and can foster the development of faulty perceptions and beliefs about the organization.
4. Tell new recruits how long they will be on probationary status, and when they will become full-fledged members of the organization; this helps eliminate one important and unnecessary source of ambiguity and worry.

By following these principles, organizations can help their new employees navigate successfully through the many pitfalls of organizational entry and socialization. The result will be recruits who are able to assume full responsibility and membership more quickly than might otherwise be the case, and who will hold more positive attitudes toward the organization, its procedures, and their coworkers.

Mentors and Socialization

In many fields, young and inexperienced individuals learn much from older, more experienced ones. Thus, in medicine and law, interns learn from established physicians and attorneys; and in science, graduate students acquire a broad range of knowledge and skills from the researchers under whose guidance they work. Does the same process of *mentorship* operate in work settings? A growing body of evidence suggests that it does.[30] Young and relatively inexperienced employees often report that they have learned a great deal from a **mentor**—an older and more experienced employee who advises, counsels, and otherwise enhances their personal development.

Research on the nature of such relationships suggests that mentors do many things for their proteges. They provide much needed emotional support and confidence. They advance the protege's career by nominating him or her for promotions, and by providing opportunities for the protege to demonstrate his or her competence. They suggest useful strategies for achieving work objectives, ones proteges might not generate for themselves. They bring the protege to the attention of top management—a necessary first step for advancement. Finally, they protect proteges from the repercussions of errors, and help them avoid situations that may be risky for their careers.

Of course, these potential gains are offset by possible risks or hazards. Proteges who hitch their wagon to a falling rather than a rising star may find their own careers in danger when their mentors suffer setbacks. Indeed, in some cases they may find themselves without a job if a purge follows defeat in a political struggle (see chapter 12). In addition, mentors are only human, so not all the advice they supply is helpful. And there is always the danger that proteges will become so dependent upon their mentors that their development as self-reliant individuals able to accept authority and responsibility is slowed.

While our comments so far might suggest that mentors are totally selfless persons—benefactors who want little or nothing in return—this is not actually the case.[31] On the contrary, they expect several things from proteges. First, they expect their proteges to turn in hard work and effort on assigned tasks. Second, they expect them to be loyal supporters within the organization; after all, they are now members of the mentor's team! Third, mentors may gain recognition from others in the company for helping to nurture young talent, and can bask in the reflected glory of any success gained by their proteges. Finally, they may reap psychological benefits from feeling needed, and from a sense of accomplishment in helping the younger generation. (Please see Figure 9.7 on page 310 for an overview of the potential benefits and dangers to both parties of mentor-protege relationships.)

Other findings suggest that mentor-protege pairs do not form at random. Mentors are usually older than their proteges (by about eight to fifteen years). They tend to be persons with considerable power and status within their companies. As a result, they are able to assist rising young stars without feeling threatened. How do mentors select their proteges? Existing evidence suggests that they are impressed with a young employee's initial performance, or find interacting with them easy and pleasant.[32] This may be because mentor and protege share similar attitudes and backgrounds, or because proteges are socially skilled and clearly transmit their desire for an experienced tutor. In still other cases, would-be proteges approach potential mentors and actively ask for help or attempt to initiate a relationship in other ways.

Most human relationships develop over time and mentorship is no exception to this general rule. In fact, most mentor-protege relationships seem to pass through several distinct phases.[33] The first, known as *initiation,* lasts from six months to a year and represents the period during which the relationship gets started and takes on importance for both parties. The second phase, known as *cultivation,* may last from

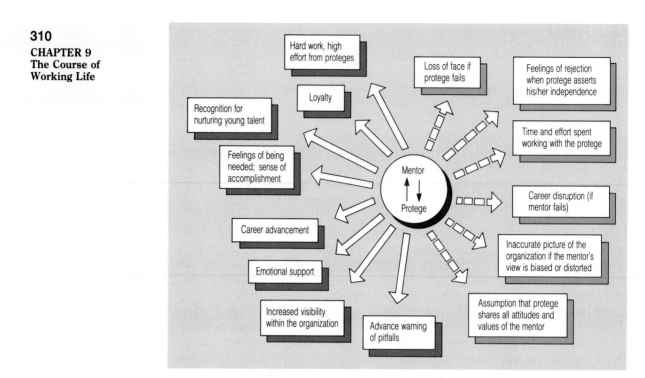

FIGURE 9.7   Mentoring: Potential Gains, Potential Losses
Mentor-protege relationships yield important benefits to both participants. However, as indicated here, such relationships also contain elements of risk on both sides.

two to five years. During this time, the bond between mentor and protege deepens, and the young individual may make rapid career strides because of the skilled assistance he or she is receiving. The third stage, *separation*, begins when the protege feels it is time to assert independence and strike out on his or her own, or when there is some externally produced change in the role relationships (e.g., the protege is promoted; the mentor is transferred). Separation can also occur if the mentor feels unable to continue providing support and guidance to the protege (e.g., if the mentor is experiencing physical illness or psychological problems). This phase can be quite stressful in cases where the mentor resents the protege's growing independence, or in instances where the protege feels that the mentor has withdrawn support and guidance prematurely. If separation is successful, the relationship may enter a final stage termed *redefinition*. Here, both persons perceive their bond primarily as one of friendship. They come to treat one another as equals, and the roles of mentor and protege may fade away completely. However, the mentor may continue to take pride in the accomplishments of the former protege, while this person may continue to feel a debt of gratitude toward the former mentor. (Please see Figure 9.8 for a summary of these stages.)

Recent evidence suggests that some of the early claims for the powerful benefits of mentorship were probably overstated.[34] Nevertheless, having an experienced, powerful mentor does seem helpful in many situations, and gives at least some young persons an important edge. Unfortunately, this conclusion has unsettling implications for women, who often seem to have less access to suitable mentors than men. As noted recently by Noe, several factors contribute to this state of affairs.[35] First, there are simply fewer senior female executives available to serve as mentors for young

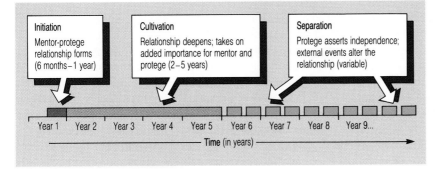

FIGURE 9.8 Development of Mentor-Protege Relationships

Mentor–protege relationships change over time and seem to pass through several distinct stages. (Source: Based on suggestions by Kram, 1985; see Note 30.)

female employees. Second, women have fewer interactions with persons in positions of power in many organizations. As a result, they are less plugged in to informal networks, and less likely to obtain a mentor. Third, because of recent affirmative action efforts, women are highly visible in many organizations. This may cause at least some potential mentors to feel reluctant to adopt this role; after all, if a female protege is unsuccessful, her failure will receive more attention and reflect on the mentor to a greater extent than might be the case with a male protege. Fourth, many potential male mentors are reluctant to adopt this role because of concern over misinterpretation of the relationship. They realize that their interest in and concern with a younger female employee may well be misinterpreted by others, and this may pose a danger to their own careers.

For these and other reasons, women are less likely to obtain mentors than men. This, in turn, may reduce their opportunities to acquire new skills and may slow the progress of their careers. Clearly, this is a possibility organizations should examine with care.

CAREERS: HOW WORK AND WORK EXPERIENCES
CHANGE THROUGHOUT LIFE

"Change," it is often said, "is the only constant." Where the course of working life is concerned, this comment certainly seems accurate. During their working years (which typically fill from forty to fifty years), most individuals experience major shifts with respect to their work. The tasks they perform, the status they enjoy, the roles they play, their geographic location, the compensation they receive—all these features of working life, plus many others, can alter radically as the decades slip by. Together, such changes constitute an individual's **career.** More formally, careers can be defined as *the sequence of attitudes and behaviors associated with work-related activities experienced by individuals over the span of their working lives.*[36]

While work-related changes are certainly important, it is crucial to note that they are only part of the total picture. As individuals move through various stages or portions of their careers, they are also moving from one stage of life to another. Youth is replaced by maturity, which gives way to middle age, and so on. This inexorable movement through the lifespan, and the changes in family obligations and personal relationships it brings, is often closely linked to changes in individuals' careers. Thus, it is impossible to isolate one of these topics (careers) from the other (development during adult life).

Recognizing this fact, we will call attention to the links between careers and life events and change at several points. Such an approach is consistent with recent research on the course of individual careers (**career development**), and also with the major theme of this entire chapter: change throughout the course of working life.[37]

A second guiding principle of our discussion is recognition of the fact that as is true of many other topics in this text, careers can (and should) be considered from both a *micro* and a *macro* perspective.[38] The micro perspective involves such issues as how individuals make their career decisions, how they balance work (career) and non-work activities and obligations, and how they cope with successive transitions requiring socialization into new groups. In contrast, the macro perspective focuses on how organizations can develop and implement effective **career systems**—programs that are part of their overall efforts to manage human resources, and which enable them to recruit, train, and retain employees with the background and skills they require.[39] Information relating to both perspectives (micro and macro) will be presented.

Career Changes: Basic Dimensions

All careers are unique, but viewed from the perspective of an outside observer, most seem to develop along three basic dimensions.[40] First, careers often involve *vertical movement*—promotions up the hierarchy within an organization. Of course, different individuals working in different settings experience vertical movement at tremendously different rates.

Second, careers often involve *horizontal movement*. This reflects changes in specific job functions or, more rarely, in major fields or specialties. For example, persons trained in engineering often shift from working as practicing engineers into management or administrative roles. Similarly, individuals who start out in marketing may move into sales or vice versa. In recent years, growing numbers of persons have been willing to make such horizontal moves, despite the fact that this may involve a considerable amount of retraining.[41] Presumably, this trend reflects society's growing interest in self-fulfillment through one's work.

Finally, careers also involve what Schein terms *radial movement,* toward the inner circle of management in an organization. Such movement often follows vertical movement (i.e., promotion), but this is not always the case. For example, an individual may receive a promotion which moves her out of the central office, where real power resides, and into a branch or subsidiary operation. The promotion is real, but the individual is now further away from the corporation's inner circle than before. (See Figure 9.9 for a summary of these three dimensions of career change.)

Career Development and Life Stages

At the same time that careers develop along the dimensions noted above, they also seem to move through repeated cycles of stability and change.[42] Soon after an individual has been hired or promoted to a new position, there is a stage of *career growth*. During these periods, individuals consolidate their recent gains by acquiring the new skills and information needed to perform their current job effectively. As this process is completed, they enter a stage of *stabilization*—one in which they are performing their job to their fullest capacity, and things are on a (temporary) even keel. This is followed by a period of *transition,* in which individuals prepare themselves, psychologically, for their next move upward. During this period they anticipate the demands of their next career stage, and get ready to meet them. When the expected promotion arrives, the cycle starts over again. In short, the careers of many individuals are marked by a process in which they grow into each new position, become acclimated to it, and then begin preparations for the next step on the ladder (see Figure 9.10).

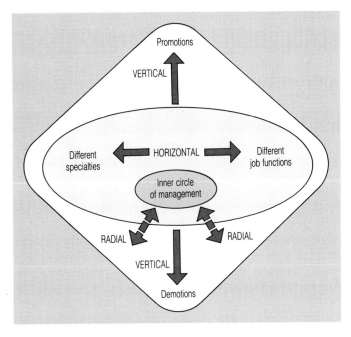

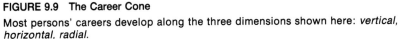

FIGURE 9.9 The Career Cone

Most persons' careers develop along the three dimensions shown here: *vertical, horizontal, radial.*

Crosscutting this cycle are important critical choice points most persons face in their career planning. These are age-related and occur for different individuals at different points on the cycle of growth, stabilization, and transition noted above.[42]

The first of these critical age-related choice points arises at about age thirty. At this time, many persons confront a number of decisions that are either irreversible or difficult to change. Should they marry? Start a family? Stick with their present careers or seek another one? Make career or family central in their lives? Such issues must be faced and resolved, and the decisions individuals make with respect to each will strongly affect the remainder of their lives.

The second occurs during the early forties. At this time, individuals must decide whether to have a last child—or any—before, biologically, it is too late. Perhaps even more important, this is the period during which most persons first come face to face with their own mortality. Signs of age become more obvious, and many individuals undergo a subtle shift in perceptions of their own lifespan. Prior to age forty, most think in terms of how long they have lived—their current age. After forty, an increasing proportion begin to think in terms of how many years they have left until retirement, or until death. Adding to the stress of this mid-life period is the fact that many persons must now confront the limits of their careers. They can see with increasing clarity just

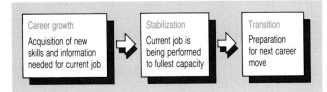

FIGURE 9.10 The Career Change Cycle

Careers often move through repeated cycles of *career growth, stabilization,* and *transition.*

how far they can realistically expect to go, and by what margin they will fall short of attaining cherished dreams and hopes of glory. In the light of such conclusions, they must decide to remain with the same organization or strike out on new career paths different from the ones they originally charted. Time, it seems, is running out, and this may be the last opportunity for initiating radical change.

The final critical choice point occurs as individuals move into their late fifties. The key question here is, how should they spend the rest of their lives? Become deeply involved in the lives of children and grandchildren? Remain focused on their own lives and activities? Should they remain active at work or begin a gradual process of withdrawal? Should they move out of their current home (which may be far too large now that their children are grown)? What kind of retirement do they want, and how should they plan for it? Questions such as these must be answered as individuals begin seriously contemplating the end of their own careers and their coming *retirement.* (Please see Figure 9.11 for a summary of these key life choice points.)

Clearly, age-related factors in individuals' lives have an important bearing on their careers. The proverbial *biological clock* is indeed always running, and individuals must take it carefully into account as they map the course of their careers, and weigh the responsibilities of families and other interests against the demands of their jobs and professions.

Career Issues: Early, Middle, and Late

At different points in life, we face different issues or problems. The twenties are a time of getting started—choosing a career, getting established in it, selecting a mate. For many persons, the thirties bring rising family responsibilities, as they start or add to their families. The forties bring a mid-life crisis for at least some individuals, as they realize that they are now as close to the end as to the beginning, and come to terms with the fact that they will never achieve many of their youthful dreams. And so the process continues: different concerns and problems during different decades of life.

In a corresponding manner, different stages of our careers are also marked by contrasting issues. Because these are often divided into issues relating to *early, middle,* and *late* career stages, we'll consider them in this way here.

FIGURE 9.11 Critical Periods of Adult Life

Change occurs throughout life. However, research findings suggest that there are several critical choice points that are especially stressful for many persons. These occur at about age thirty, in the early forties, and again in the late fifties.

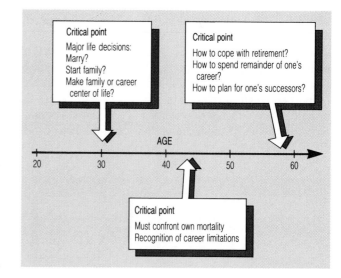

Early career issues. Perhaps the key task faced by individuals during their early careers is *career planning*. This is when most of us must map the course of our future careers, deciding what types of jobs and activities we will pursue in the decades that follow. How do we make such decisions? What factors lead us to select one path over all the others? One intriguing answer is provided by the concept of **career anchors,** first proposed by Schein.[43] According to Schein, an expert on careers and career development, by the time individuals enter their early thirties, most have fairly clear ideas or *self-perceptions* of their talents and abilities, needs and motives, and attitudes and values. Together, these self-perceptions come to guide and stabilize a person's career, as they attempt to choose jobs and goals that are consistent with these basic characteristics. Schein terms these self-perceptions **career anchors,** since they tend to firmly attach individuals' careers to their underlying abilities, needs, and values. While everyone has such anchors, they may take several distinct forms.

For some persons, career anchors are *technical* or *functional* in nature. Their primary concern in making job decisions and mapping their future careers involves the *content* of work. They want to do certain things, and plan their careers accordingly. For a second group, career anchors emphasize *managerial competence*. Persons in this category want to attain high-level management positions. They like to analyze and solve difficult business problems, enjoy influencing others, and like exercising power. Thus, they choose career paths that will lead them to such goals.

A third group is primarily concerned with *security* and *stability*. Their search for security often leads them to enter large, stable companies, and long-term employment with a single firm. A fourth group, in contrast, emphasizes *creativity* or *entrepreneurship* in career plans. Such persons want to build or create a product which is unique and of their own devising. They are good at starting and running small companies but, like Mitch Kapor of Lotus Development fame, they may choose to leave when these organizations become too large and bureaucratic in nature. Finally, some individuals emphasize *autonomy* and *independence*. They want to be free of external constraints, and prefer to work at their own pace and set their own goals. Such persons often select careers in academia and professional writing, or prefer to run their own small businesses. (See Figure 9.12 for a summary of these different career anchors.)

While the task of identifying their abilities, motives, and values is important, it is hardly the only issue individuals face during the early portion of their careers. In addition,

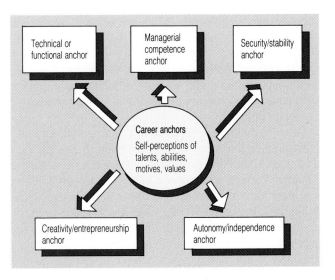

FIGURE 9.12 Contrasting Types of Career Anchors

Individuals' perceptions of their own abilities, motives, and values often serve as *career anchors*. Individuals then attempt to choose jobs and goals consistent with these characteristics. Such career anchors often emphasize one or more of the factors shown here. (Based on suggestions by Schein, 1978; see Note 41.)

they must confront relatively frequent *job changes*—ones stemming from transfers and promotions. While such changes can be beneficial to individuals' careers, they involve considerable costs, both for organizations and the persons involved. Individuals who are transferred or promoted are expected to "hit the floor running"—to demonstrate high performance from the very start. Further, such demands occur just when they must establish new networks of social support, learn new skills, and eliminate old patterns of behavior and attitudes no longer appropriate to their new position. Clearly, this is an unsettling combination of events, but one that must be handled successfully if individuals are to stay on track with respect to their own career plans.

One hazard faced by at least some persons early in their careers is also worth noting—a danger described by Lewicki as **organizational seduction.**[44] This refers to situations in which the promise of rapid promotions and raises encourages young employees to make career moves that are actually against their best long-term interests. How do organizations "seduce" talented individuals into making such decisions? According to Lewicki, through a combination of challenging, stimulating work, extremely pleasant work environments, and many opportunities to fulfill rising status needs (e.g., they are provided with memberships in prestigious clubs, invited to meetings with top management). If they succumb to such inducement, the persons involved become deeply committed to the organization—so much so that they are willing to sacrifice virtually all other aspects of their lives to their work, and experience intense guilt if they even think about leaving. The costs of allowing oneself to fall into this trap can be high, so young and ambitious persons should be on guard against doing so unless they have carefully considered all the costs and ramifications.

Middle career issues. As we noted earlier, age forty marks the end of the dream for many persons. It is at this point they realize they will never go as far as they had hoped and will never fulfill many of their fondest dreams.[45] At the same time, persons in this age group find that because they have already risen to fairly high-level positions within their organizations, there are fewer and fewer promotions available for them. As if this were not enough, when they glance back over their shoulders they see hordes of ambitious younger persons, more energetic and better trained (technically) than themselves, pushing up from behind. No wonder many persons find turning forty an unsettling experience! (See Figure 9.13).

In sum, a key issue facing individuals in the middle part of their careers is: since I can't get where I really hoped to be, what can I do instead? Some persons, of course, answer this question by retreating into cynicism and apathy. As we saw in chapter 7, they experience *burnout* and become liabilities to themselves and to their companies. Fortunately, however, there are other, more constructive ways of handling this dilemma.

First, individuals can choose to become *mentors*. In fact, it is at this stage in their careers that they are expected to assume such a role in many organizations. Since we have already described the satisfactions and benefits of serving as a mentor, there's no need to elaborate on this career path here.

Second, individuals at this stage of their careers can remain active in their work, but expand their interests so that they no longer focus exclusively on their jobs. This can involve a conscious decision to spend more time with their families, the development of new hobbies, and related actions. Persons who choose this route forego some of the potential that may remain in their careers. However, they derive adequate satisfaction from other sources, and so remain personally happy and emotionally secure.

Another, and related, issue faced by many persons in mid-career is the discovery that they have reached a **career plateau.**[46] In short, they find that they have arrived at a point from which they are unlikely to gain further promotions or be given increased

"Nothing serious, Bob—just a case of the forties."

FIGURE 9.13   Careers in Mid Life
In their forties, most persons must come to terms with the fact that they will probably never realize some of their fondest hopes and dreams. This can be the source of a *mid-life crisis* for at least some individuals. (Source: Drawing by Mankoff; ©1988 The New Yorker Magazine, Inc.)

responsibility and authority. They are at a virtual dead end in their careers. What leads to this state of affairs? Potentially, several factors. First, as noted earlier, some individuals consciously choose to put a brake on their own careers. They may not wish to take on added responsibility, or they don't want to leave a particular geographic region. Others find themselves part of a two-career family, and wish to maximize joint outcomes for both members. Persons in these categories can retain a high level of performance, despite the fact that they have little chance of advancement. For others, however, entry into a career plateau is less voluntary. They may have failed to keep up with developments in their fields, and so no longer possess the skills and knowledge required for further promotions. Alternatively, they may find themselves in a company suffering from slow growth or no growth at all. Such a pattern severely restricts the number of promotions available, and traps at least some organization members in their present jobs.

Fortunately, involuntary career plateaus do not have to be permanent. By recognizing the need for change and taking such steps as seeking retraining, developing alternate roles within the organization (e.g., serving as a mentor), or actually moving to another job, some persons, at least, can escape from such dead ends and the malaise that often accompanies them. In order to help employees cope with such problems and plan effectively for the development of their own careers, many organizations have established **career management programs.** (We'll comment further on these below.)

Late career issues. Studs Terkel once suggested, somewhat tongue-in-cheek, that there are five distinct stages to careers.[47] He summarized these by the following statements:

"Who is this guy, John Fortune?"
"Gee, it would be great if we could get that guy, what's his name?"
"If we could only get John Fortune."
"I'd like to get a young John Fortune."
"Who's John Fortune?"

What these statements suggest is that with careers, as with almost anything else, what goes up usually, at some point, also comes down. This is the key issue most individuals face in the later years of their careers. Many find that they have indeed gone as far as they can go, and have either accomplished key goals or will never be able to achieve them. They must also come to terms with the fact that, like their physical energies, their power and influence within the organization are beginning to wane.

Yet another, related, problem faced by older employees is the fact that they increasingly become the subject of negative stereotypes. Typically, they are viewed as being less productive, efficient, motivated, and capable of working under pressure than younger persons.[48] And such stereotypes persist despite strong evidence that they are inaccurate. Indeed, one recent review of previous research on the relationship between age and job performance suggests that older workers (perhaps because of their greater experience) are actually *more* productive than younger ones![49] Still, the stereotypes remain and are a fact of life for many individuals as they approach the end of their careers.

Another late career issue for many persons is *job succession*—who will take over when they retire? Few persons who have spent years building up a business or department take this matter lightly. They want someone to follow in their footsteps who shares their values and will maintain the standards they have established. What sort of successors should they seek in order to attain these goals? The results of an intriguing study by McCall and Lombardo (1983) offer some tentative answers.[50]

These researchers interviewed top executives and human resource managers in several large corporations. The goal of the project was uncovering differences between managers who made it to the top and were perceived as highly successful and those whose careers were somehow derailed along the way. Table 9.2 summarizes the major findings. As you can see, highly successful persons—ones most of us would choose as current leaders or as future successors—possess a mixed bag of desirable characteristics. They are bright, analytical thinkers who are highly motivated for success, but maintain a good sense of humor and are skilled in dealing with others. They work hard and expect high commitment and effort from others, but are also diplomatic and avoid confrontations whenever possible. Obviously, identifying such persons is an im-

TABLE 9.2 Characteristics Related to Managerial Success
Highly successful managers demonstrate several traits or characteristics that set them apart from less successful managers.

CHARACTERISTICS OF HIGHLY SUCCESSFUL MANAGERS
High intellectual ability
Analytic thinkers
Highly motivated
Encourage hard work among subordinates
Work hard themselves
High quality standards for own and others' work
Sense of humor; able to laugh at selves
Good control of own tempers
Many contacts rather than a single, powerul mentor
Appear consistent and predictable to subordinates

(Source: Based on data reported by McCall & Lombardo, 1983; see Note 50.)

portant goal for all organizations, and is especially crucial for top managers as they begin the search for an excellent successor.

Another issue individuals face late in their careers is coming to terms with their own retirement. This involves a gradual re-orientation away from their careers and work, toward the leisure-time activities that will become dominant during retirement. In addition, it should involve careful planning to meet the special challenges faced by retired workers—a loss of social contact with many friends, reduced feelings of accomplishment, reduced earnings. Fortunately, growing evidence suggests that if individuals take the time to prepare for such factors, the end of their working years can be a new beginning. It can mark entry into a period of renewed personal growth and fulfillment, rather than merely signalling inevitable decline.

Career Systems: Organizational Strategies for Managing Careers

In order to succeed, most organizations need a continuous flow of talented, skilled individuals to fill existing or newly created positions. Meeting such requirements involves the establishment of an effective system for *recruiting* promising employees, for *promoting* them if they are successful, and for eliminating them if they prove unsuccessful or nonessential.[51] To be fully effective, such a system must take account of employees' needs and expectations as well as future company requirements, for individuals who feel that their personal plans and aspirations are blocked will not stay on the job if they have any other options available. In short, most, if not all, organizations need an effective **career system** designed to accomplish the goals outlined above.

How should such systems be designed? Research on this issue suggests that there is no single answer. Rather, the career system adopted by a particular organization should reflect its strategic policies and intentions.[52] In other words, depending on their general business strategies, different organizations may find different systems more or less effective.

While career systems can vary in many respects, two dimensions seem to underlie many of these differences.[53] The first of these, labeled *supply flow,* refers to the extent to which organizations seek to fill non-entry level positions from the external labor market or from their own internal resources. IBM represents the high end of this dimension; airline companies, who recruit primarily from the outside, fall at the low end.

The second dimension, labeled *assignment flow,* refers to the degree to which assignment of individuals to particular tasks is based on their contribution to the entire group or their individual performance. At one end of this dimension are companies that base assignments on individual contributions (e.g., investment banks, law firms), while at the other end are ones that base assignments primarily on contributions to the group (e.g., government agencies). Together, these two dimensions yield the four patterns shown in Figure 9.14 (on page 320). Sonnenfeld and Peiperl describe these, respectively, by the colorful terms *fortress, baseball team, club,* and *academy.*[54] As you examine Figure 9.14, you will see why these terms seem to fit each of the four patterns shown.

What factors lead specific organizations to choose one or the other of these contrasting career systems? Sonnenberg and Peiperl suggest that the answer lies, at least in part, in their strategic policies and intentions. Companies that focus primarily on product innovation and need highly talented employees (*prospectors*), adopt systems that involve assignment or promotion on the basis of individual contributions, and that recruit from the outside. Obviously, such a system fits with the needs and strategies of this type of company. In contrast, companies that have a narrow range of products and a relatively narrow market, and which rarely adopt innovations (*defenders*), often

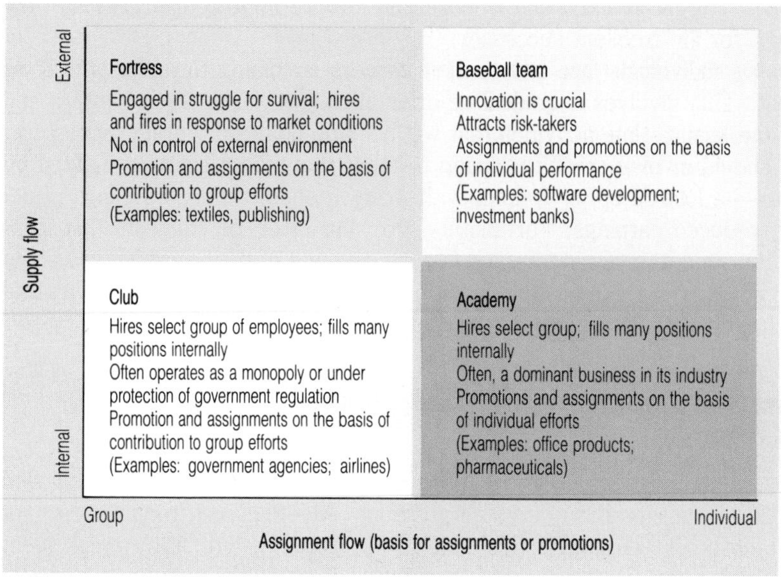

Supply flow (vertical axis, External / Internal)

External

Fortress

Engaged in struggle for survival; hires
and fires in response to market conditions
Not in control of external environment
Promotion and assignments on the basis of
contribution to group efforts
(Examples: textiles, publishing)

Baseball team

Innovation is crucial
Attracts risk-takers
Assignments and promotions on the basis
of individual performance
(Examples: software development;
investment banks)

Internal

Club

Hires select group of employees; fills many
positions internally
Often operates as a monopoly or under
protection of government regulation
Promotion and assignments on the basis of
contribution to group efforts
(Examples: government agencies; airlines)

Academy

Hires select group; fills many positions
internally
Often, a dominant business in its industry
Promotions and assignments on the basis
of individual efforts
(Examples: office products;
pharmaceuticals)

Group — **Individual**

Assignment flow (basis for assignments or promotions)

FIGURE 9.14   Major Types of Career Systems
According to Sonnenfeld and Peiperl, *career systems* can be divided into four major types,
depending on the extent to which they involve recruitment of non-entry level employees from
the external labor market (*supply flow*) and the extent to which promotions are made on the
basis of individual performance or contributions to group efforts (*assignment flow*).
Organizations adopt these systems in response to the environments in which they operate
and their strategic policies and intentions. (Source: Based on suggestions by Sonnenfeld &
Peiperl, 1988; see Note 52.)

develop career systems that promote or assign individuals to tasks on the basis of group
contribution, and that fill non-entry level positions primarily from internal sources. This
is appropriate, since they want to produce loyal, long-term employees.

In sum, most organizations need an effective and well-developed career system
to assure fulfillment of their human resource needs. The precise form of such systems,
however, often reflects the strategic intentions and policies they are pursuing.

Career Management Programs: Fostering Career Development

Earlier, we noted that in order to be effective, career systems must consider the
expectations and goals of employees as well as the needs of organizations. Recognizing
this fact, growing numbers of organizations have recently developed formal **career
management programs** as part of their larger human resources systems.[55] These
programs vary greatly in scope and content, but most involve efforts to (1) help employees assess their own career strengths and weaknesses, (2) set priorities and specific
career goals, (3) provide information on various career paths and alternatives within
the organization, and (4) offer employees yearly reviews of their progress toward these
goals by managers who have received training in conducting such assessments. In
addition, special workshops and technical training opportunities are often part of such
programs.

Three major goals are generally sought by such career management programs.
First, they are designed to help individuals improve their performance, partly by getting
them involved in setting their own goals and recognizing their own strengths and weak-

nesses. Second, they are designed to clarify options available within the organization and so reduce uncertainty and anxiety among employees. Third, they seek to focus employees' career plans upon the organization and so, perhaps, enhance their commitment to it.[56]

A concrete example of such a program is provided by the Wane Division of the American Instruments Corporation.[57] In order to assist employees with career development, Wane established the following resources:

1. A Developmental Lab—a two day workshop conducted at the company's Center for Managerial Development. It provides employees with personal assessments of their managerial styles, plus training in several managerial skills.
2. A Career Development and Self-Exploration Guide—a paper-and-pencil self-assessment exercise designed to help employees understand their strengths and weaknesses, and to set career priorities.
3. A Career Review Discussion and Career Action Planning Guide—a guide which describes how managers can be helpful to employees at different career stages, plus recommendations to managers for conducting career discussions with subordinates.
4. Several training options, including training in corporate management development and in technical subjects relating to individuals' jobs.
5. Career Counseling Workshops for Managers—workshops designed to help managers develop skills necessary to assist employees in their career development. This takes the form of intensive one day sessions.

Programs like this one are expensive to operate, so a key question about them is: do they yield positive results? For example, do they enhance employees' commitment and satisfaction with their jobs and organization? Research findings suggest that this is indeed the case, but only when employees perceive a close *match* between their own plans for their careers and those held by their organization.[58] For example, in one study on this issue, Granrose and Portwood asked several hundred employed persons a series of questions dealing with the availability of career information in their organizations, career planning activities, and the match between their own career plans and those expressed by their companies. Results indicated that the closer the match between participants' own career plans and those reported by their companies, the greater their expressed satisfaction with their organizations, and the less likely they were to be searching for other jobs.

Other findings suggested that a useful model of the impact of career management programs is as follows: perceptions of organizational planning activities and the perceived availability of career information increase employees' participation in career assistance programs. In addition, such planning activities increase their awareness of the organization's plans for their own careers. If their own plans and those of the organization match, satisfaction is increased. If they do not match, satisfaction is reduced, and individuals search for alternatives outside their current organization (see Figure 9.15 on page 322).

These findings, and those reported in related projects, suggest that career planning programs are indeed useful in several respects, and can yield important benefits for individuals and organizations alike. In order to succeed, however, they must strive to attain a match between actual career opportunities and employees' aspirations. When individuals perceive that their own plans and goals are shared by their organization, satisfaction and commitment may follow. When, instead, they discover that the path they would like to pursue is *not* the one envisioned for them by their company, they may conclude—and rightly so—that their best interests lie elsewhere. This can be an advantage if the persons who recognize such mismatches and choose to leave are the ones an organization would prefer to see go. It can pose a serious problem, however,

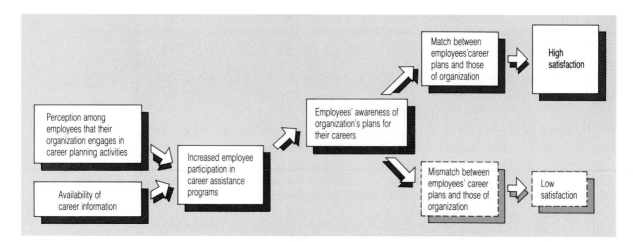

FIGURE 9.15   Career Assistance Programs: One Model of Their Effects

According to one model of *career assistance programs,* employees' perceptions of career planning activities and the availability of career information within their organization increase their participation in such programs. This, in turn, enhances their awareness of the organization's plans for their careers. If these match with employees' own plans, high job satisfaction and commitment result. If these do not match, low job satisfaction and commitment may follow. (Source: Based on suggestions by Granrose & Portwood, 1987; see Note 58.)

if those who depart are the very people the organization would dearly love to retain. To the extent this is so, strenuous efforts to enhance career opportunities for talented persons would seem to be essential.

SUMMARY AND REVIEW

Organizational Culture. The shared beliefs, attitudes, values, and expectations held by individuals in a given organization constitute its **organizational culture.** Organizational culture stems from the impact of influential founders and develops out of shared experiences. It changes when external conditions (e.g., important characteristics of individuals entering an organization) alter. Organizational culture exerts strong pressure on individuals to think and act like others in the organization. Certain types of organizational culture may be related to high levels of performance, but this link has not been clearly established. Efforts by management to impose an artificial culture on an organization are generally unwise.

Organizational Socialization. The process through which newcomers learn the ropes in their organizations and become full-fledged members is known as **organizational socialization.** This process involves three distinct stages known, respectively, as *getting in, breaking in,* and *settling in.* When individuals have unrealistically optimistic expectations about an organization, they may react negatively when actual conditions do not match these expectations. Such reactions can be avoided or reduced through **realistic job previews.** Recent evidence suggests that previews designed to both reduce overly optimistic and overly pessimistic expectations are more effective than ones designed to accomplish only one or the other of these goals. Various techniques for socializing new employees into an organization exist. The most useful of these tend to provide individuals with the skills they need for performing their jobs and with adequate orientation to the organization's policies and procedures. **Mentors** can play an important beneficial role in socialization.

Careers, Career Systems, and Career Development. The sequence of occupations and jobs individuals hold during their working lives constitutes their **careers.** Most careers develop *vertically,* through promotions, *horizontally,* through different jobs or functions, and *radially,* toward inner circles of power within an organization. Crucial points in career planning occur at key times during individual's lives—for example at about age thirty, during the early forties, and again in the late fifties. Each career stage involves somewhat different issues. Important early career issues involve the establishment of **career anchors, job changes,** and **organizational seduction.** Middle career issues involve coming to terms with the fact that all of one's hopes and dreams will not be realized, and the possibility of **career plateaus.** Late career issues involve accepting reduced power and influence, choosing one's successors, and preparing for retirement. Most organizations establish **career systems,** designed to fill current and projected needs for human resources. The nature of these systems often reflects the strategic plans and intentions of these organizations. Many organizations attempt to assist employees in their career planning through **career management programs.** Research findings suggest that these are successful to the extent that employees perceive a match between their own career plans and those proposed for them by their organization.

KEY TERMS

career anchors: Individuals' self-perceptions of their own abilities, motives, and values, and their efforts to choose jobs or careers consistent with these self-perceptions.

career development: The pattern of changes that occur during an individual's career.

career management (assistance) programs: Organization-sponsored programs designed to assist individuals in planning their careers.

career plateaus: Points in careers from which individuals are unlikely to gain further promotions or receive increased responsibility.

career systems: Organizational programs designed to help recruit, train, and retain employees possessing the training and skills required by specific organizations.

careers: The sequence of attitudes and behaviors associated with work-related activities experienced by individuals over the span of their working lives.

entry shock: The confusion and disorientation experienced by many newcomers to an organization.

mentor: An older and more experienced employee who offers advice, assistance, and protection to a younger and less experienced one.

organizational culture: The shared attitudes, values, and expectations held by members of a given organization.

organizational seduction: A process through which an organization obtains extremely high levels of effort and commitment from young employees by providing them with highly attractive benefits (e.g., pleasant working conditions, opportunities to enhance their status).

organizational socialization: The process through which newcomers to an organization are converted to full-fledged members who share its major values and understand its policies and procedures.

realistic job previews: Accurate information concerning conditions within an organization, provided to potential employees prior to their decision to join the organization.

QUESTIONS FOR DISCUSSION

1. It is often said that the founders of a company continue to influence it long after they have retired or departed for other reasons. Is this true? Why or why not?

2. Suppose that a relatively small company is acquired by a larger one. Further, assume that the attitudes, values, and policies in the two organizations differ substantially. Will the culture of the smaller company change? Will the culture of the larger company change?

3. Imagine that you were planning an orientation program for new employees of your company. What major points would you try to incorporate?

4. Most successful executives report that they had one

or more mentors during their careers. Do you think having a mentor is necessary for success? If so, why? If not, why?

5. What are your major values at present? Do you think you will hold the same values ten years from now? Twenty years? Thirty years?

6. Do you think there is a relationship between *burnout*

and the mid-life crisis that many persons experience during their forties? If so, what is the nature of this relationship?

7. Consider a company that has a secure market niche. It has few competitors and the external environment in which it operates is quite stable. What type of *career system* for recruiting, training, and retaining appropriate employees would such a company be likely to develop?

NOTES

1. Feldman, D. C. (1988). *Managing careers in organizations.* Glenview, IL: Scott, Foresman.

2. Wanous, J. P., Reichers, A. E., & Malik, S. D. (1984). Organizational socialization and group development: Toward an integrative perspective. *Academy of Management Review, 9,* 670–683.

3. Hall, D. T. (1976). *Careers in organizations.* Pacific Palisades, CA: Goodyear Publishing.

4. Hall, D. T. (1987). Careers and socialization. *Journal of Management, 13,* 301–321.

5. Sonnenfeld, J. (1984). *Career management: An introduction to self-assessment, career development, and career systems.* Chicago: SRA.

6. Schein, E. H. (1985). How culture forms, develops, and changes. In R. H. Kilmann, M. J. Saxton, & R. Serpa (Eds.), *Gaining control of the corporate culture* (pp. 17–43). San Francisco: Jossey-Bass.

7. Dennison, D. (1984). Bringing corporate culture to the bottom line. *Organizational Dynamics, 13,* 5–22.

8. Nahavandi, A., & Malekzadeh, A. R. (1988). Acculturation in mergers and acquisitions. *Academy of Management Review, 13,* 79–90.

9. See Note 6.

10. See Note 1.

11. Wilkins, A. L., & Dyer, W. G., Jr. (1988). Toward culturally sensitive theories of culture change. *Academy of Management Review, 13,* 522–533.

12. Wiener, Y. (1988). Forms of value systems: A focus on organizational effectiveness and cultural change and maintenance. *Academy of Management Review, 13,* 534–545.

13. Saffold, G. S., III. (1988). Culture traits, strength, and organizational performance: Moving beyond "strong" culture. *Academy of Management Review, 13,* 546–558.

14. Akin, G., & Hopelain, D. (1986). Finding the culture of productivity. *Organizational Dynamics, 7,* 19–32.

15. See Note 7.

16. See Note 13.

17. Siehl, C., & Martin, J. (1988). Organizational culture: A key to financial performance? *Research Paper Series,* Graduate School of Business, Stanford Univ. (Paper No. 998)

18. Reynolds, P. C. (1987). Imposing a corporate culture. *Psychology Today, 21*(3), 33–38.

19. See Note 18.

20. Feldman, J. C. (1976). A contingency theory of socialization. *Administrative Science Quarterly, 21,* 433–452.

21. Feldman, D. C. (1980). A socialization process that helps new recruits succeed. *Personnel, 57,* 11–23.

22. Wanous, J. P. (1981). *Organizational entry.* Reading, MA: Addison-Wesley.

23. Louis, M. R. (1980). Surprise and sense making: What newcomers experience in entering unfamiliar organizational settings. *Administrative Science Quarterly, 25,* 226–251.

24. Wanous, J. P. (1983). The entry of newcomers into organizations. In J. R. Hackman, E. E. Lawler, & L. W. Porter (Eds.), *Perspectives on behavior in organizations* (2nd ed., pp. 126–135). New York: McGraw-Hill.

25. McEvoy, G. M., & Cascio, W. F. (1985). Strategies for reducing employee turnover: A meta analysis. *Journal of Applied Psychology, 70,* 342–353.

26. See Note 22.

27. Meglino, B. M., DeNisi, A. S., Youngblood, S. A., & Williams, K. J. (1988). Effects of realistic job previews: A comparison using an enhancement and a reduction preview. *Journal of Applied Psychology, 73,* 259–266.

28. Van Maanen, J. (1978). People processing: Strategies of organizational socialization. *Organizational Dynamics, 7,* 18–36.

29. See Note 1.

30. Kram, K. E. (1985). *Mentoring at work: Developmental relationships in organizational life.* Glenview, IL: Scott, Foresman.

31. Burke, R. J. (1984). Mentors in organizations. *Group and Organization Studies, 9,* 353–472.

32. See Note 30.

33. Kram, K. E. (1983). Phases of the mentor relationship. *Academy of Management Journal, 26,* 608–625.

34. Hurley, D. (1988). The mentor mystique. *Psychology Today, 22*(5), 38–43.

35. Noe, R. A. (1988). Women and mentoring: A review and research agenda. *Academy of Management Review, 13,* 65–78.

36. See Note 3.

37. Hall, D. T. (1986). Career development in organizations: Where do we go from here? In D. T. Hall & Assocs. (Eds.), *Career development in organizations* (pp. 332–351). San Francisco: Jossey-Bass.

38. See Note 4.

39. Sonnenfeld, J. (1984). *Managing career systems: Channeling the flow of executive careers.* Homewood, IL: Irwin.

40. Schein, E. H. (1971). The individual, the organization, and the career: A conceptual scheme. *Journal of Applied Behavioral Science, 7,* 401–426.

41. Schein, E. H. (1978). *Career dynamics: Matching individual and organizational needs*. Reading, MA: Addison-Wesley.

42. Levinson, D. J. (1986). A conception of adult development. *American Psychologist, 41,* 3–13.

43. See Note 41.

44. Lewicki, R. J. (1981). Organizational seduction: Building commitment to organizations. *Organizational Dynamics, 10,* 5–22.

45. Dalton, G. W., Thompson, P. H., & Price, R. (1977, Summer). Career stages: A model of professional careers in organizations. *Organizational Dynamics,* pp. 19–42.

46. Ference, T. P., Stoner, J. A. F., & Warren, E. K. (1977). Managing the career plateau. *Academy of Management Review, 2,* 602–612.

47. Terkel, S. (1974). *Working*. New York: Pantheon.

48. Rosen, B., & Jerdee, T. H. (1976). The nature of job-related age stereotypes. *Journal of Applied Psychology, 61,* 180–183.

49. Waldman, D. A., & Avolio, B. J. (1986). A meta-analysis of age differences in job performance. *Journal of Applied Psychology, 71,* 33–38.

50. McCall, M. W., Jr., & Lombardo, M. M. (1983). What makes a top executive? *Psychology Today, 16*(2), 26–31.

51. Hall, D. T., & Hall, F. S. (1976). What's new in career management. *Organizational Dynamics, 5,* 17–33.

52. Sonnenfeld, J. A., & Peiperl, M. A. (1988). Staffing policy as a strategic response: A typology of career systems. *Academy of Management Review, 13,* 588–600.

53. Miller, E. J., & Rice, A. K. (1967). *Systems of organization: The control of task and sentient boundaries*. London: Tavistock.

54. See Note 52.

55. See Note 39.

56. Gutteridge, T. G. (1986). Organizational career development systems: The state of the practice. In D. T. Hall & Assocs. (Eds.), *Career development in organizations* (pp. 50–94). San Francisco: Jossey-Bass.

57. Sonnenfeld, J., & Blanck, P. (1983). *Case: The Wane Division of the American Instruments Corporation*. Harvard Business School, Case 9-483-094.

58. Granrose, C. S., & Portwood, J. D. (1987). Matching individual career plans and organizational career management. *Academy of Management Journal, 30,* 699–720.

326

CHAPTER 9
The Course of
Working Life

CASE
IN
POINT

Corporate Culture at Ben & Jerry's Ice Cream: Tutti Fruitti?

On May 5, 1978, a small experimental business began to take form at a renovated gas station in Burlington, Vermont.[1] Here, Ben Cohen and Jerry Greenfield opened their first Ben & Jerry's ice cream parlor. At the beginning, they believed that they would simply produce and sell their ice cream products at this parlor and then someday sell their small business to pursue other activities. With this in mind, they decided that running this business should provide something more than simply money. They determined that the parlor should be fun, provide opportunities for creativity, adventure, self-expression, and above all be socially responsible.

Although Ben and Jerry may have had modest aspirations for the growth of their company, their ice cream products proved so popular that growth was inevitable. From their beginning as a single parlor, Ben & Jerry's Homemade, Inc. doubled in size in each of their first eight years of operation and continued growing so that by their tenth anniversary, sales topped $31.8 million. After ten years in business the company had grown to over 150 employees, fifty company-owned parlors, sixty franchises, a production facility, national grocery and chain store distribution of their products, internationally located parlors, joint business ventures, and the operation of a charitable foundation.

The path from single ice cream parlor to multi-million dollar, publicly owned company has been a rocky one filled with crisis, turmoil, and ever-present growth. Remaining stable throughout, however, has been Ben's insistence on maintaining the company philosophy of acting as a force for social change. This belief has driven almost all company decisions made within the first ten years. For example, as demand for the product put pressure on the company to increase production, thereby necessitating an influx of capital, it was decided to take the company public—but only within the immediate community served by Ben & Jerry's. This, it was felt, would make the company more community oriented. As a result, the initial stock offering was limited to residents of Vermont. Furthermore, so that people who might not ordinarily find themselves investors could participate, the price of the initial offering was kept low enough so that people occupying all levels of the economic spectrum could purchase the stock. Another example of company philosophy driving business decisions was the plan to open a store in Moscow. The business plan for this store specified that all the profits from this store be devoted to fostering East-West exchange programs. Also in keeping with the belief in social change and responsibility, a charitable operation was set up—the Ben & Jerry's Foundation—funded by 7.5 percent of the company's pre-tax profits.

The corporate philosophy does not apply only to decisions that are external to the firm, but also to internal decisions. For example, the company actively recruits and hires the handicapped. They provide free therapy sessions (with guaranteed anonymity) to all who wish to take advantage of them. The pay system, built on a principle of "5 to 1" incorporates the philosophy of social change. This means that the highest paid employee at Ben & Jerry's may earn only five times the salary of the lowest paid employee. (As of July, 1988, the highest possible salary was $84,240.) The rationale behind this is two-fold. First, this suggests that if top managers want a raise, then they will first have to increase the salaries of the lowest paid employees—the people whose hard work contributes to the company's success. Second, by de-emphasizing financial compensation, it is hoped that Ben & Jerry's will attract employees who recognize the value of the Ben & Jerry's culture and who are not looking to make a fast buck.

In addition to the pay system, the committee structure and organizational chart reflects the corporate philosophy of encouraging fun, goodwill, and charitable activity. Jerry, Undersecretary of the Joy Committee, sees to it that joy and fun are reinforced and encouraged in the workplace to help alleviate stress and tension. His position on the organizational chart is colored blue to reflect his personal mission.

At Ben & Jerry's, rituals and symbols abound. One of the most pervasive symbols is the company logo—the name of the firm over which is a small herd of cows and under which is one large cow. This logo is silk-screened on T-shirts frequently worn by employees. In one particularly popular ceremony, Ben and an individual from the sales, finance, or production department dress in sumo wrestlers' costumes and do a belly bounce to determine who has the "baddest belly" in the company. This ceremony not only provides bragging rights for the winner, it acts as an opportunity for everyone to get in on the fun and games and be reminded about the corporate mission. Another ceremony involves the presentation of the "first year hat." Every employee with the company for one year is presented a baseball cap at a company-wide ceremony. Additionally, entire company outings to Montreal baseball and hockey games are arranged. Even the "enemy" is ritualized and celebrated. At Ben & Jerry's the enemy isn't other premium ice cream makers (such as Steve's Homemade or Haagen-Dazs), but rather, a focus on traditional corporate values such as bottom line profits. Thus, when employees engage in activities that may save the company money they are said to be doing something "Fredlike"—in honor of Fred Lager the company's first MBA and financial manager. Employees who suggest a cost saving idea may be nominated for the "Fred-of-the Month" award.

Despite of all this goodwill, fun, and what Ben likes to call "weirdness," there are some problems lurking on Ben & Jerry's horizon. As the company has grown there has been, by necessity, a move toward departmentalization. This has resulted in less of a family feeling between employees as well as overlapping responsibilities and decreasing communication. There have been continued crises like the one in the summer of 1987. Two new machines designed to help pack and seal ice cream containers were delivered late and proved too complex to operate immediately, as hoped. As a result, production did not keep up with demand, and one week the company found itself short 300 pallets of ice cream. All hands were called in and the production facilities operated around the clock until the orders were filled. The management committee and many employees complain that there is no sense of direction. They want to develop plans for growth, while Ben and the board of directors steadfastly refuse the plans. Ben wants to continue reinforcing the company mission without regard to planning for and accommodating continued growth. In addition, some top managers of the company are irritated by the "5 to 1" pay plan. They feel that they are professionals who deserve a higher salary than is currently available to them. Meanwhile, the premium ice cream market is maturing and sales are plateauing, and new companies (e.g., Steve's Homemade) have been actively cutting into Ben & Jerry's market.

In the summer of their tenth year, Jerry—who left the company after five years and came back three years later—was resigned to the possibility of some change. He said, "The idea, I think, is to maintain the values of your culture and yet bring it along with you. I mean, you don't want to stay stuck in the past."[2] Ben, however, believes that the worst thing that could happen to the company he helped found would be for it to be just like a regular business.

Questions for Discussion

1. Describe the culture at Ben & Jerry's.

2. How is the culture transmitted to new employees?

3. How can Schein's work on the influence of the founder on culture be applied to what has happened at Ben & Jerry's?

4. Would you want to begin, continue, or end your career in a company like this? Why or why not?

Notes

1. Larson, E. (1988, July). Forever young. *Inc.*, pp. 50–62.
2. See Note 1, p. 62.

Corporate Culture at SAS

Persons belonging to a specific organization often come to share a wide range of attitudes, beliefs, and values. Together, these constitute the organization's *culture*. Organizational culture, in turn, can exert strong effects on efficiency, work-related attitudes, and many other important processes.

A clear example of one organization's culture is provided by the PINNACLE interview with Jan Carlzon, President and Chief Executive of Scandinavian Airlines. In his comments, Mr. Carlzon notes that at SAS (as his company is widely known), *service* is the most important product. In short, satisfying customers is central to the organization's success, and is a basic aspect of its culture. Another value is maintaining close and friendly relations with each of the thirty-three separate unions with which the company must deal. Mr. Carlzon sees this is a cornerstone of SAS's success and a basic feature of its way of doing business.

Now, to complicate the picture, SAS has entered into an agreement to coordinate flights with Continental Airlines—a company owned by Texas Air. Frank Lorenzo, the head of Texas Air, is known for having a very different philosophy of dealing with employees. His approach is decidedly confrontational, and bitter disputes have marked previous takeovers of several airlines by Texas Air (for example, Eastern Airlines).

How will these two different corporate cultures mesh in the new joint venture? Only time will tell. However, as the interview suggests, Mr. Carlzon is well aware of the potential problems, and has already taken steps to minimize their impact. Stay tuned for further developments!

Questions for Discussion

1. In what ways do you think the cultures of SAS and Continental Airlines differ?

2. Does the existing corporate culture at SAS reflect the fact that it is based in Scandinavia, a particular region of Europe with a unique history?

3. Why do you think Mr. Carlzon has been so successful in dealing with so many different unions?

**EXPERIENCING
ORGANIZATIONAL
BEHAVIOR**

Personal Values throughout Life

Many people believe that once they are adults, they undergo little change aside from physical aging. They assume, often without question, that their goals and values will remain largely unaltered as the decades come and go. Is this really so? To gather some first-hand evidence on this issue, please perform the exercise described below.

Procedure

First, list the three personal goals you are currently seeking that are most important to you. Think carefully, and list only the ones you value most.

1.
2.
3.

Now, try to remember the personal goals that were most important to you five years ago. List them below.

1.
2.
3.

Finally, imagine yourself ten years from now. What personal goals will be most important to you then? List these below.

1.
2.
3.

Points to Consider

Did you notice any shifts in your major personal goals? If you are like most people, you probably did. Studies of how people change and develop over time suggest that many undergo major shifts in their goals, values, and beliefs during the fifty, sixty, or more years they spend as adults. Shifts in goals and values, in turn, often have profound effects on their careers. For example, individuals who highly value such goals as status and wealth early in their careers often find that these goals lose much of their appeal as they grow older. Later in life, these persons report that other goals, such as happiness, good health, or peace of mind have replaced their earlier ones.

Will you, too, change in these ways? Only time, and your own experience, can reveal the answer. But being aware of the fact that most people continue to change during their adult years is an important insight for planning your own career and for managing the careers of persons who will work under your supervision.

CHAPTER TEN

COMMUNICATION IN ORGANIZATIONS

CHAPTER OUTLINE

Communication: Its Basic Nature
  Communication: A Working Definition and a
    Model
  Forms of Communication: Verbal and Nonverbal

Major Influences on Organizational Communication
  Organizational Structure: Directing the Flow of
    Messages
  Communication Networks: Formal Channels of
    Information
  Informal Communication Networks: Organizations'
    Hidden Pathways
  Communication and the Work Environment:
    Technology and Office Design

**Overcoming Communication Barriers: Enhancing the
Flow of Information**

Becoming a Better Communicator: Individual
  Strategies
Improving Communication on the Job:
  Organizational Strategies

Special Sections

OB: A Research Perspective
  Written or Spoken Communication? Matching the
  Medium to the Message

OB: A Management Perspective
  Managing the Hidden Messages behind Corporate
  Relocations

LEARNING OBJECTIVES

After reading this chapter, you should be able to:
  1. Define the process of communication and describe its major forms.
  2. Identify and describe the most prevalent nonverbal communication cues operating in organizations.
  3. Distinguish between messages that are best communicated in written and in spoken forms.
  4. Describe how the formal structure of an organization influences the nature of the communication that occurs within it.
  5. Distinguish between centralized and decentralized communication networks with respect to their relative superiority in performing different tasks.
  6. Describe how informal patterns of communication operate within organizations.
  7. Understand the impact of technology and of the physical layout of offices on communication between people in offices.
  8. Identify and describe measures that can be taken by individuals and by organizations to improve communication effectiveness.

". . . And so, with your help, I'm sure we can make our state the best place in the nation to live, work, and raise a family!"

With these words, Marty Wilkins, candidate for state senator, stepped down from the podium amidst enthusiastic applause from his hard-working staff and the audience of fifty or so loyal followers gathered for the occasion. This campaign speech over, candidate Wilkins was ushered into his waiting limousine and rushed off to the next town for a repeat performance at another gathering.

At the hall, it was clear from the look on campaign manager Paul Curtis's face that something was wrong. His assistant, Bud Sherrod, had just handed him the results of the *Gazette's* latest poll and he didn't like what he saw.

"You gotta be kidding, Bud," Paul said in shock. "Fourteen percentage points behind Smelmann overall!"

"Look," Bud was quick to point out, "it's even worse among those most likely to vote—twenty-one points."

"With only two weeks to election day," Paul added, "it doesn't look good for us."

Bud nodded in agreement as both men tried to hide their disappointment from the rest of the campaign staff and the crowd of admirers that was still breaking up. They knew something had to be done and walked to Paul's nearby office to plan how best to pick up the pieces.

"Okay, Bud," Paul instructed, "the first thing we have to do is keep this information from Marty. If he finds out, he'll really be devastated. Any hint that he's weakening and the Smelmann gang will surely come in to finish the job. So, we have to protect him."

"You're right, Paul," Bud quickly agreed.

"Not only that, but we have to keep the campaign staff's spirits up, too. When they get hold of those figures, a lot of them will surely quit. They'll give up hope and not want to work in vain—besides, they won't want to be associated with a loser."

"Of course, Paul," Bud interrupted, "we'll just tell them our own polls show we're catching up and that with their continued support, we can pull ahead."

"Know what really got us?" Paul asked. "That darn nuclear power plant issue. It just won't die."

"You're right. Marty opposed it on safety and ecology grounds, and Smelmann picked up on it saying that Wilkins didn't want to help bring jobs to the state. Did he ever twist that around!"

Paul nodded in agreement. "Somehow, it was as if that were the only issue involved. That whole ordeal left Marty with the image of someone who didn't care about unemployment, instead of someone who cares about the health and safety of people and the environment."

"We've got to keep on setting the record straight, getting our point across. It just isn't easy, especially if we lose staffers."

"Our first order of business, then, should be to undo the damage caused by that *Gazette* poll. In fact, you may want to act now before it's released!"

"Fine," Bud concurred, "I'll issue a memo to all campaign staffers. Or, maybe I'll hold a meeting. Something this important should be said in person."

"You're right. We've got to get our message across to all our campaign workers."

Bud nodded and said, "Yeah, I only hope we do a better job of getting our message across to our staffers than Marty does of getting *his* message across to the voters."

It is tempting to feel sorry for Marty Wilkins. His important campaign message was intentionally misrepresented to the public by his opponent. Now, it looks like he is about to lose an election. On top of this, his closest aides won't even tell him the truth about how he stands in the polls. As unfortunate as this situation may be, it is not unusual. Indeed, there are many similar situations in other groups and organizations where important information is distorted and withheld, with undesirable consequences.

If there is any one lesson to be learned from this story about the Wilkins senatorial campaign, it is that effective **communication** is crucial to success. The candidate's popularity appeared to suffer because he was unable to get his message across to the public. Issues of communication played a part in two other ways in this story. For one, the decision to shelter Marty and his staffers from the negative results of the poll involved limiting and misrepresenting the information that reached them. In addition, the decision to help minimize the poll's potentially damaging effects by an in-person meeting rather than by a written memo represents yet another important aspect of the communication process. Clearly, the communication—or miscommunication—of information is an essential part of this story.

As all of this suggests, communication is a critical and complex phenomenon. Many management scholars have recognized the importance of communication as an organizational process. Typical of such thinking, one current management theorist described organizational communication as "the social glue used to found an organization in the first place, and the glue that continues to keep the organization tied together."[1] Writing much earlier, former New Jersey Bell Telephone President Chester Barnard said, "In any exhaustive theory of organization, communication would occupy a central place, because the structure, extensiveness, and scope of the organization are almost entirely determined by communication techniques."[2] Such statements are not surprising in view of the fact that practicing managers spend more time communicating than they spend in any other activity. Indeed, it has been found that supervisors spend as much as 80 percent of their work days engaging in some form of communication, such as speaking or listening to others, or writing to and reading material from others.[3] So it appears that the process of communication is crucial to organizations and forms its very "lifeblood" (see Figure 10.1).

FIGURE 10.1 Communication: A Common Managerial Activity
What do all the people shown here have in common? They are all engaging in the most common managerial activity—the process of communication.

Given the importance of communication in organizations, we will examine this process very closely in this chapter. First, we will carefully define communication and describe a basic *model of communication,* a framework for describing its fundamental steps. We will also review some of the most basic forms the communication process takes in organizations. Second, we will examine several of the major *influences on communication,* aspects of the social and work environments that shape the nature and direction of the flow of information. Finally, we will turn to several *barriers to effective communication* and consider techniques for overcoming them.

COMMUNICATION: ITS BASIC NATURE

Before we can fully appreciate the process of organizational communication, there are some very basic issues we need to address. To begin, we will formally define what we mean by communication and then elaborate on the process by which it occurs. Following this, we will describe the various forms organizational communication may take.

Communication: A Working Definition and a Model

What do the following situations have in common? Your boss issues a memo limiting all employees' coffee breaks to ten minutes. A junior executive prepares and submits a report about the financial status of a potential corporate takeover prospect. The dispatcher of a taxi company directs Cab 706 to pick up a fare at 74 Cherry Drive. A foreman smiles at one of his men and gives him a pat on the back in exchange for a job well done. You probably realize that each of these incidents involves some form of communication. Although most of us already have a good idea of what communication entails, we could better understand communication in organizations by more closely examining the meaning of the term.

With this in mind, we may define **communication** as *the process by which a person, group, or organization (the sender) transmits some type of information (the message) to another person, group, or organization (the receiver).* To clarify this definition, and to further elaborate on how the process works, we have summarized the communication process in the model shown in Figure 10.2. Please refer to this diagram as we describe the various components of the model.

The process begins when one party has an idea that it wishes to transmit to another (either party may be an individual, a group, or an entire organization). It is the sender's mission to transform the idea into a form that can be sent to and understood by the intended *receiver.* This is what happens in the process of **encoding**—translating the idea into a form that may be recognized by the receiver, such as written or spoken language. We encode information when we select the words we use to write a letter or speak to someone in person. This process is critical if we hope to adequately communicate our ideas. Yet the difficulty we all sometimes have thinking about the best way to say something suggests that our capacity to encode messages is far from perfect. As we will see later in this chapter, limitations in people's abilities to accurately encode their ideas is a serious weakness in the communication process, but fortunately, one that can be corrected.

After a message is encoded, it is ready to be transmitted over one or more *channels of communication* to reach the intended receiver. These may be understood as pathways along which encoded information is transmitted. Telephone lines, radio and television signals, fiber-optic cables, mail routes, and even the air waves that carry the vibrations of our voices all represent potential channels of communication. Of course, the form of encoding largely determines the way information may be transmitted. Visual information—such as pictures and written words—may be mailed, delivered in person by

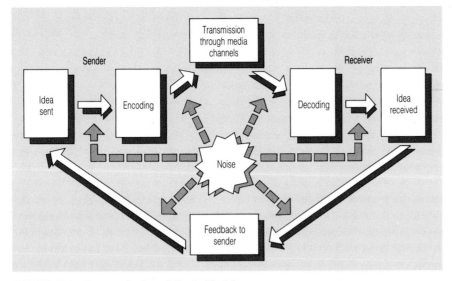

FIGURE 10.2   Communication: A Basic Model

In its most basic form, communication consists of the distinct steps shown here. First, a *sender* desires to make an idea known to a *receiver* (either party may be an individual, a group, or an organization). The idea must be *encoded,* converted into a form that can be transmitted (e.g., the written or spoken word). This message is then sent via one of several communication channels (e.g., telephone, and/or letter) to the receiver. This receiver must then *decode* the message—convert it back into an understandable idea. This idea may then be returned to the sender in the form of *feedback.* The model also recognizes that *noise,* factors distorting or limiting the flow of information, may enter into the process at any of several points.

a courier, shipped by an express delivery service, or, with increasing popularity, sent by "fax" machines (see Figure 10.3). Oral information may be transmitted over the telephone, via radio and television waves, and of course, the old fashioned way—in person. (As we will see in the next section, the choice of a communication media depends not only on the type of encoding used, but also on the nature of the message itself.) Whatever channel is used, the goal is to send the encoded message accurately to the desired receiver.

FIGURE 10.3   Channels of Communication: Some Common Varieties

As shown here, messages can be transmitted in many ways. These range from the old fashioned methods of messengers and face-to-face verbal communication, to newer, high-tech devices such as fax machines and satellite dishes.

You will recall that the *receiver* is the desired target of a message, be it another person, group, organization, or even a computer. Once the message is received, the recipient must begin the process of **decoding**—that is, converting the message back into ideas. This can involve many different subprocesses, such as comprehending spoken and written words, interpreting facial expressions, and the like. To the extent that the sender's message is accurately decoded by the receiver, the ideas understood will be the ones intended. Of course, our ability to accurately comprehend and interpret information received from others may be imperfect (e.g., restricted by unclear messages, or by the language skills of the receiver, etc.). Thus, as in the case of encoding, limitations in our ability to decode information represents another potential weakness in the communication process. Fortunately, as we will describe later in this chapter, the necessary skills may be improved.

Finally, once a message has been decoded, the process can be reversed such that the receiver transmits a message back to the original sender. This is known as *feedback*—that is, knowledge about the impact of messages on receivers. Receiving feedback allows senders to determine whether or not their messages have been understood and had the desired effects. At the same time, giving feedback can help convince receivers that the sender (e.g., a manager) really cares about what he or she has to say. Once received, feedback can trigger another idea from the sender, and another cycle of transferring information may begin. For this reason we have characterized the process of communication summarized in Figure 10.2 as continuous.

Despite the apparent simplicity of the communication process, the phenomenon rarely operates as flawlessly as we have described it here. As we will see, there are many potential barriers to effective communication. The name given to factors that distort the clarity of a message is **noise.** As we have shown in Figure 10.2, noise can occur at any point along the communication process. For example, messages that are poorly encoded (e.g., written in an unclear way), or decoded (e.g., not comprehended), or channels of communication that are too noisy or full static all may reduce communication's effectiveness. These factors, and others (e.g., time pressure, organizational politics), may contribute to the distortion of information transmitted from one party to another.

In concluding, it is important to note that organizational communication is really much more complex than we have described it here. In any organization, the process of encoding, transmitting, decoding, and sending feedback is likely to be taking place simultaneously among many people and groups at once. Furthermore, other considerations such as differences in communicators' authority levels, the purpose of the communication, management philosophy, limitations imposed by marketing considerations, and legal constraints are just a few of the many factors that make the process of communication so complicated. Clearly, a great deal more is involved than just the simple transfer of information. As you continue reading this chapter, you will come to appreciate many of the factors that make the process of organizational communication so complex and so important.

Forms of Communication: Verbal and Nonverbal

As we have been suggesting all along, organizational communication can take several forms. It is obvious that we transfer information when we write to others and when we speak to them. Although sometimes less obvious, we also communicate *nonverbally,* through our gestures, our posture, the clothes we wear, the way we use time, the physical distances we keep from others, and so on.

Verbal communication: Speaking with words. Because you are reading this book, we know you are familiar with verbal communication—transmitting and receiving ideas using words. Verbal communication can be either *oral,* using spoken language in forms such as face-to-face talks, telephone conversations, tape recordings, and the like, or *written,* in forms such as memos, letters, order blanks, and electronic mail, to name just a few. Because both oral and written communications involve the use of words, they fall under the heading of verbal communications.

What types of verbal communications are most effective? Research has shown that supervisors believe communication is most effective when oral messages are followed by written ones.[4] This combination is especially preferred under several conditions: when immediate action is required, an important policy change is being made, a praise-worthy employee is identified, and a company directive or order is announced. When the information to be communicated is of a general nature, or requires only future action, written forms are judged to be most effective.

Apparently, the oral message is useful in getting others' immediate attention, and the follow-up written portion helps make the message more permanent, something that can be referred to in the future. Oral messages also have the benefit of allowing for immediate two-way communication between parties, whereas written communiques are frequently only one-way (or take too long for a response if they are two-way). Not surprisingly, researchers have found that two-way communications (e.g., face-to-face discussions, or telephone conversations) are more commonly used in organizations than one-way communications (e.g., memos). For example, Klauss and Bass found that approximately 83 percent of the communications taking place among civilian employees of a U.S. Naval agency used two-way media.[5] In fact, 55 percent of all communications were individual face-to-face interactions. One-way, written communications tended to be reserved for more formal, official messages that needed to be referred to in the future at the receiver's convenience (e.g., official announcements about position openings). Apparently, both written and spoken communications have their place in organizational communication. (What factors determine when each of these forms of communication will be used? As we will describe in the **Research Perspective** section on page 340, managers tend to base their media choices on the degree of clarity or ambiguity of the messages they are trying to send.)

It would be misleading to conclude this section with the idea that managerial communication occurs only at the verbal level. Although words are a very important part of communication, of course, they represent only one way of transmitting messages. A great deal of what is communicated in organizations is also done in the absence of words—that is, nonverbally.

Nonverbal communication: Speaking without words. As we have already noted in chapter 4, nonverbal cues represent an important source of information influencing our impressions of people. Others' smiles and eye contact tend to enhance our positive feelings about them. Here, we will describe how other nonverbal cues may provide useful vehicles of communication. Simply put, **nonverbal communication** refers to the transmission of messages without the use of words. Some of the most prevalent nonverbal communication cues in organizations have to do with manners of dress and the uses of time and space. (For a whimsical example of nonverbal communication in action in one organizational setting, see Figure 10.4 on page 338.)

Style of Dress. If you have ever heard the expression "clothes make the man," you are probably already aware of the importance of mode of dress as a vehicle of communication. This is especially the case in organizations where, as self-styled "wardrobe engineer" John T. Malloy reminds us, what we wear communicates a great deal about our competence as employees.[6] Organizational researchers are becoming increasingly aware of the importance of style of dress as a communication vehicle. Consider, for example, a recent study by Forsythe, Drake, and Cox, who showed videotapes of

FRANK AND ERNEST ©**by Bob Thaves**

FIGURE 10.4   Nonverbal Cues: An Important Form of Communication
As shown here, nonverbal cues (such as facial expression) can communicate a great deal about what someone is thinking. (Source: Reprinted by permission of NEA, Inc.)

women dressed in one of four costumes to a group of personnel administrators.[7] The costumes differed with respect to how masculine they were perceived to be by a panel of judges (the clothes ranged from a very masculine navy tailored business suit, to a more feminine beige dress in a soft fabric). The personnel administrators were asked to view the applicants in their various costumes and rank how likely they would be to hire each one. It was found that the least likely hired candidate was the woman dressed in the most feminine costume. However, the most likely hired candidate was *not* the one wearing the most masculine costume, but something in between—namely, a beige tailored suit with a blazer jacket and a rust blouse with a narrow bow at the neck.

Although these findings are interesting, we should note that it would be unwise to generalize them to other situations. In other words, women, please don't automatically rush out and buy this outfit thinking it might be your key to success! As you might imagine, what we communicate by the clothing we wear is not a simple matter. It is important to keep in mind that we cannot make up for the absence of critical job skills by simply putting on the right clothes. People who are qualified for jobs, however, may communicate certain things about themselves by the way they dress. Clearly, one of the key messages sent by the clothes people wear is their understanding of the appropriate way of presenting themselves for the job. Generally speaking, the most positive images are communicated when someone is dressed appropriately for the occasion. An important reason for this appears to be that people who are dressed just right for an occasion tend to feel better about themselves; they have higher levels of self-confidence. For example, in one study, student job candidates appeared for an interview wearing either their informal street clothes (e.g., t-shirts and jeans), or more formal garb (e.g., suits with shirts and ties). Those who wore the more formal clothing not only felt they made a more positive impression than those dressed less appropriately, but also tended to express this more positive self image by requesting a starting annual salary that was, on average, $4,000 higher.[8] Apparently, then, clothing may be a powerful vehicle of communication not only because of what it connotes about the wearer, but also because it changes the feelings of the wearer.

Time: the waiting game. As we have noted, another important mechanism of nonverbal communication in organizations is the use of time. Indeed, the way we use time says a great deal about us. Have you ever waited for hours in the outer office of a doctor or dentist? Surely you have—after all, they have special "waiting rooms" just for this purpose! Why do you have to wait for such persons? Mainly because these people have special skills that put high demands on their services. Their time is organized in a manner that is most efficient for them—by keeping others lined up to see them.

Medical professionals are not the only ones who make people wait to see them. In fact, individuals in high status positions often communicate the idea that their time is more valuable than others' (and therefore, that they hold higher status positions) by making others wait to see them. This is a very subtle, but important form of nonverbal communication. Typically, the longer you have to wait to see someone, the higher the organizational status that person has attained. This has been shown in a recent study by Greenberg.[9] Participants in this investigation were applicants for a job as office manager at various companies who awaited interviews with people of higher status (vice presidents), lower status (assistant office managers), or equal status (another office manager). As summarized in Figure 10.5, the higher the status of the person job candidates waited to see, the longer they had to wait.

The vice president interviewers communicated their higher status to the candidates by making them wait to see them. In contrast, assistant office manager interviewers communicated their lower status to candidates by being prompt—an act conveying deference and respect. It is interesting to note that interviewers also communicated their liking for prospective employees (whose application files they studied in advance) by not making them wait. Specifically, candidates who were subsequently hired had to wait less time to see their future bosses than those who were not hired. Apparently, interviewers wanted to communicate their liking for the most desirable candidates by treating them politely and *not* making them wait. If time is viewed as a resource, it is not surprising that it may be used as a symbol of organizational status. Important people can communicate their status nonverbally by making others wait for them. Hence, the use of time is an important mechanism of nonverbal communication in organizations.

The use of space: what does it say about you? Like time, space is another important communication vehicle. Research has shown that one's organizational status is communicated by the amount of space at one's disposal. The more space one commands, the more powerful one is likely to be in an organization. For example, research has

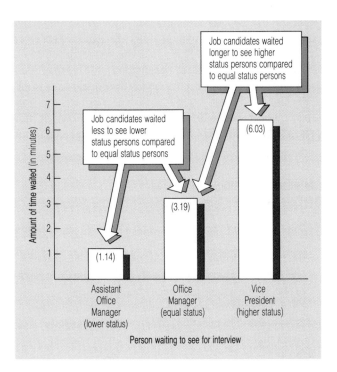

FIGURE 10.5 Communicating Status through Time Delays: The Organizational Waiting Game

Research has shown that the higher another's status relative to oneself, the more one has to wait to see that person. These findings suggest that the use of time is a nonverbal mechanism for communicating one's organizational status. (Source: Based on data reported in Greenberg, 1989; see Note 9.)

shown that higher status life insurance underwriters have larger desks and larger offices than lower status underwriter trainees.[10] It is not only the amount of space that communicates organizational status, but also the way that space is arranged. For example, among faculty members at a small college, it was found that senior professors were more likely to arrange their offices so as to separate themselves from visitors with their desks, whereas junior professors were less likely to impose such physical barriers.[11] These various office arrangements systematically communicated different things about the occupants. Specifically, professors who did not distance themselves from their students by use of their desks were seen as more open and unbiased in their dealing with students than those who used their desks as a physical barrier.

The use of space appears to have symbolic value in communicating something about group interaction. Consider who usually sits at the heads of rectangular tables. In most cases, it is the group leader. It is, in fact, traditional for leaders to do so. But at the same time, studies have shown that people emerging as the leaders of groups tend to be ones who just happened to be sitting at the heads of a table.[12] Apparently, where a person sits influences the available communication possibilities. Sitting at the head of a rectangular table enables a person to see everyone else and to be seen by them. It is, therefore, not surprising that leaders tend to emerge from such positions.

Finally, it is interesting to note that it is not only individuals who communicate something about themselves by the use of space, but organizations as well. Consider, for example, that the former President of Pepsico, John Scully, notes that his company's world headquarters were designed to communicate the idea to visitors that they were seeing "the most important company in the world."[13] Similarly, by adding a second office tower to it's company headquarters in Cincinnati, Procter & Gamble was said to be attempting to create a gateway-like complex that communicated the company's connection to the community.[14] As these examples suggest, space is used by organizations as well as by individuals to communicate their identities.

In concluding this section, it is important to note that the variables of nonverbal communication presented here—style of dress, and the use of time and space—represent only some of the important mechanisms of nonverbal communication. In chapter 4 we noted that facial expressions and eye contact are important cues to our emotional states. Indeed, they are also useful sources of information about someone's perceived suitability for employment.[15] It is important to note that whatever nonverbal channels of communication are employed, they are also used in conjunction with verbal information. Neither is isolated; both work together as vehicles of communication in organizations. What we do, how we look, and what we say all matter. (In fact, the *form* in which we say things also matters. As detailed in the **Research Perspective** section below, our choice of written and spoken communication can have a great impact on organizational behavior.)

OB: A RESEARCH PERSPECTIVE

Written or Spoken Communication? Matching the Medium to the Message

Have you ever found it so difficult to write a letter trying to explain something that you just gave up and opted for a phone call or an in-person visit instead? In contrast, haven't there also been times when you preferred writing a letter to confronting someone in person? If you answered "yes" to either of these questions, then you are already aware of the idea that people prefer to communicate some messages in writing and others using speech. However, you have probably not given too much thought to the conditions under which people prefer each of these forms of communication. When do people prefer communicating their ideas in written or spoken forms?

Recent research has shown that the choice of a communication media greatly depends on a very important factor—the degree of clarity or ambiguity of the message being sent. Specifically, studying this factor, Daft, Lengel, and Trevino reasoned that oral media (e.g., telephone conversations and face-to-face meetings) are preferable to written media (e.g., notes and memos) when messages are ambiguous (requiring a great deal of assistance in interpreting them), whereas written media are preferable when messages are clear.[16] The researchers surveyed a sample of managers about the media they preferred using to communicate messages that differed with respect to how clear or ambiguous they were. (For example, "giving a subordinate a set of cost figures" was prejudged to be a very unambiguous type of message, whereas, "getting an explanation about a complicated technical matter" was prejudged to be a very ambiguous type of message.) The results, summarized in Figure 10.6, show that the choice of medium was related to the clarity or ambiguity of the messages.

These data reveal two interesting trends. First, the more ambiguous the message, the more managers preferred using oral media (such as telephones or face-to-face contact). Second, the clearer the message, the more managers preferred using written media (such as letters or memos). Apparently, most managers were sensitive to the need to use communications media that allowed them to take advantage of the rich avenues for two-way oral communications when necessary, and to use the more efficient one-way, written communications when these were adequate.

We should note, however, that whereas many managers selected media based on the pattern described here (those identified as being "media sensitive"), others did not. They made their media choices almost randomly (this group was identified as being "media insensitive"). Further analyses of the data revealed that these differences were related to the managers' job performance. It was expected that those who were media sensitive would be more effective than those who were media insensitive. After all, effective communication is an important part of a manager's activities, and using the appropriate medium could enhance their effectiveness. Comparisons of the performance ratings of managers

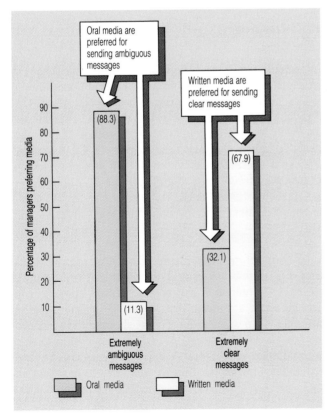

FIGURE 10.6 Oral or Written Communication? Matching the Medium to the Message

What type of communications medium do managers prefer using? The research findings reviewed here show that it depends on the degree of clarity or ambiguity of the message. Oral media (e.g., telephones or face-to-face contact) were preferred for ambiguous messages; written media (e.g., letters or memos) were preferred for clear messages. (Source: Based on data in Daft, Lengel, & Trevino, 1987; see Note 16.)

in the media sensitive and media insensitive groups supported this hypothesis. Specifically, whereas most of the media sensitive managers (87 percent) received their company's highest performance ratings, only about half of the media insensitive managers (47 percent) received equally high evaluations.

Apparently, the skill of selecting the appropriate communications medium is an important aspect of a manager's success. Although it is difficult to say whether the managers' choices of communications media was directly responsible for their success, or whether their media sensitivity was part of an overall set of managerial skills that together led to their success, these findings highlight the importance of making appropriate media choices in successful managerial communication.

MAJOR INFLUENCES ON ORGANIZATIONAL COMMUNICATION

It is a basic fact of life on the job that almost everyone engages in communication. Yet, just as basic is the idea that who we communicate with and how we do so varies considerably from person to person, from job to job, and from organization to organization. The communication process is influenced by many factors. For example, formal organizational rules require some persons to communicate with others, although informal patterns of communication also tend to develop in organizations. The way we communicate is also affected by such external factors as the kinds of technology used on the job, and the way offices are laid out. Given how important such factors may be, we will now describe some of these key influences on organizational communication.

Organizational Structure: Directing the Flow of Messages

Although the basic process of communication as we have described it thus far is similar in many different social contexts, a unique feature of organizations has a profound impact on the communication process—namely, the structure of the organization itself. Organizations are often designed in ways that dictate who may and may not communicate with whom. Given this, we may ask: how is the communication process affected by the structure of an organization? To begin, we must first specify what is meant by **organizational structure.** We use this term to refer to the *formally prescribed pattern of interrelationships existing between the various units of an organization.* Although we will have a great deal more to say about organizational structure in chapter 15, organizational structure influences communication in many important ways that we can describe here.

Organizational structure: Its impact on communication. An organization's structure may be described using a diagram referred to as an **organizational chart.** Such a diagram provides a graphic representation of an organization's structure. It may be likened to an x-ray of an organization, a drawing that shows the planned, formal connections between its various units.[17] An organizational chart showing the structure of part of a fictitious organization is shown in Figure 10.7. (Please keep in mind that this diagram represents only one possible way of structuring an organization. Several other possibilities are described in detail in chapter 15.) We will refer to this diagram to make several important points about the impact of an organization's structure on the flow of information.

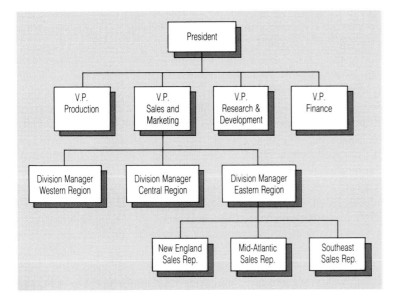

FIGURE 10.7   An Organizational Chart: A Map of an Organization's Formal Communication Networks

An *organizational chart* indicates the formally prescribed patterns of communication in an organization. Shown here is part of an organizational chart for one branch of a hypothetical manufacturing company.

Note the various boxes in the diagram and the lines connecting them. Each box represents an organizational unit—a person performing a specific job. The diagram shows the titles of the persons performing the various jobs and the formally prescribed pattern of communication between them. These are relatively fixed and defined. Each individual is responsible for performing a certain job, playing a certain role. Should the persons working in the organization leave their jobs, they must be replaced if their jobs are to be done. The key point is that the formal structure of an organization does not change just because the personnel changes. This is what keeps organizations stable and predictable. (For example, the structure of the U.S. government does not change whenever a new president is elected. It remains the same even though new persons may occupy the various positions.)

The lines connecting the boxes in an organizational chart are lines of authority showing who must answer to whom within an organization. Each person is responsible to (or answers to) the person at the next higher level to which he or she is connected. At the same time, people are also responsible for (or give orders to) those who are immediately below them. The boxes and lines form a sort of blueprint of an organization showing not only what people have to do, but with whom they have to communicate in order for it to operate properly.

As you look at the organizational chart in Figure 10.7, it is clear that people may be differentiated with respect to their level in the organization's *hierarchy*. In other words, not all persons are at the same level; some are higher up in terms of the formal organizational power they wield (e.g., the company president), and others are lower down (e.g., department managers). Such differences in one's level in an organizational hierarchy may be communicated in various ways. For example, persons at higher levels tend to be called by their titles (e.g., "Mr. Chairman"), and are usually addressed in a formal manner. Such individuals may also communicate their higher positions by virtue of the way they dress (e.g., formal as opposed to informal attire) and by the size and location of their offices in the corporate complex. Indeed, differences in organizational level are communicated in many different ways.

Communicating up, down, and across the organizational chart. As you might imagine, the nature and form of communication varies greatly as a function of people's relative positions within an organization. Even a quick look at an organizational chart reveals that information may flow up (from lower to higher levels), down (from higher to lower levels), or horizontally (between people at the same level). However, as summarized in Figure 10.8, different types of information typically travel in different directions within a hierarchy.

Imagine that you are a supervisor. What type of messages do you think would characterize communication between you and your subordinates? Typically, *downward communication* consists of instructions, directions, and orders—messages telling subordinates what they should be doing.[18] We would also expect to find feedback on past performance flowing in a downward direction (such as when managers tell subordinates how well they have been working). A vice president of sales, for example, might direct members of her sales force to promote a certain product among their customers, and she may then congratulate them for being successful in doing so.

Downward communication flows from one level to the next lowest one, slowly trickling down to the bottom. As a message passes through to the next lower level on its way to the bottom, it often becomes less and less accurate (especially if the information is spoken as opposed to written). Based on this, it is not surprising to find that the most effective downward communication techniques are ones directly aimed at those who are most affected by the messages—namely, small group meetings and organizational publications targeting specific groups.[19] Importantly, there are signs that such methods are being used—and successfully at that! For example, executives at Tandem Computers hold monthly teleconferences with their employees (600 hours' worth in 1985 alone), and in-person discussions and a monthly newsletter are used to keep employees up-to-date on General Motors' activities in its Packard Electric plant in

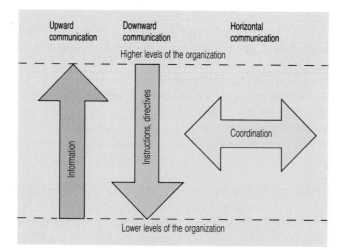

FIGURE 10.8   Upward, Downward, and Horizontal Communication: An Overview
The types of messages communicated within organizations tend to differ according to whether they are traveling upward (from lower to higher levels), downward (from higher to lower levels), or horizontally (across the same levels).

Mississippi. Such efforts at improving downward communication have been credited with improving productivity and reducing turnover in both companies.[20]

Upward communication flows from lower levels to higher levels within an organization, such as from a subordinate to her supervisor. As you might imagine, messages flowing in this direction tend to contain the information managers need to do their jobs, such as data required for decision making, and the status of various projects. In short, upward communication is designed to keep managers aware of what is going on. Among the various types of information flowing upward are suggestions for improvement, status reports, reactions to work-related issues, new ideas, and so on.

It is important to note that upward communication is not simply the reverse of downward communication. The difference in status between the communicating parties makes for some important distinctions. For example, it has been established that upward communication occurs much less frequently than downward communication. In fact, one classic study found that 70 percent of assembly-line workers initiated communication with their supervisors less than once a month.[21] Among managers, a recent study revealed that less than 15 percent of their total communication was directed at their superiors.[22] Research has also shown that when people do communicate upward, their conversations tend to be shorter than discussions with their peers.[23]

Perhaps more importantly, we should note that upward communication often tends to suffer from serious inaccuracies. One aspect of this problem is due to the fact that subordinates frequently feel they must highlight their accomplishments and downplay their mistakes if they are to be looked upon favorably.[24] Another factor that limits upward communication is the tendency for some individuals to fear that they will be rebuked by their supervisors if they speak to them, especially when they fear their outspokenness will threaten their superiors and lessen their own chances for promotion.[25] As a result of such dynamics, it is not unusual to find that upward communication tends to be quite limited. This feature of upward communication can cause serious problems in jobs requiring a high degree of coordination between persons. The dynamics between pilots and copilots of commercial airliners are a perfect example of this problem. Too many times copilots are reluctant to clearly assert themselves to pilots when they fear an error is being made. Norms in the cockpit dictate that a senior person should not be contradicted, and so copilots are frequently much too polite to do so. Unfortunately, some fatal accidents have been directly attributed to such failures of upward communication in the cockpit. One well-known case is the 1982 Air Florida accident in which cockpit voice recordings revealed that the copilot's warnings to the pilot were too subtle to avoid the crash in which seventy-eight persons lost their lives after the plane struck a bridge in Washington, D.C.[26] (Fortunately, there is preliminary evidence that members of cockpit crews who are being trained to avoid such problems—in what is referred to as Cockpit Resource Management programs—are less subject to such failures, although it is too soon to gauge the programs' effectiveness.[27])

Finally, we note the nature of *horizontal communication* within organizations. Messages that flow laterally (at the same organizational level) are characterized by efforts at coordination (attempts to work together). Consider, for example, how a Vice President of Marketing would have to coordinate her efforts at initiating an advertising campaign for a new product with information from the Vice President of Production about when the first products will be coming off the assembly line. Unlike vertical communication, in which the parties are at different status levels, horizontal communication involves persons at the same level, and therefore tends to be easier and friendlier. Communication between peers also tends to be more casual and occurs more quickly because fewer social barriers exist between the parties. We should note, however, that even horizontal communication can be problematic. For example, people in different departments may feel that they are competing against each other for valued organizational resources and may show resentment toward each other, thereby substituting an antagonistic, competitive orientation for the friendlier, cooperative one needed to get things done.[28]

Communication Networks: Formal Channels of Information

Imagine two different work groups in the Sales and Marketing Division of a large corporation. One is comprised of a team of creative writers, artists, and market researchers sitting around a table working together on developing the company's new advertising campaign. Another is comprised of field representatives in various territories who report to regional sales managers throughout the country about consumers' preferences for various products. These people, in turn, analyze this information and report it to the Vice President of Sales and Marketing. If you think about how these two groups differ, one key variable becomes obvious: the *pattern* of communication within them is not the same. Whereas members of the creative team working on the advertising campaign can all communicate with each other at once, people in the sales force speak only to those who are immediately above or below them. The patterns determining which organizational units (either people or groups) communicate to which other units are referred to as **communication networks.**

As you might imagine, there are many different possible communication networks within organizations. Do such arrangements matter? Do they make any difference with respect to how well groups do their jobs and how satisfied groups members feel? A considerable amount of research has shown that the nature of the communication linkages between group members can greatly influence group functioning.[29] So that we can appreciate these research findings, let's first consider some of the possible configurations of connections between people. Some of the most commonly studied possibilities are shown in Figure 10.9. (These various diagrams depict communication networks that have five members, although they can have any number of members from three or more.) In each diagram, the circles represent individual people and the lines connecting them represent two-way lines of communication between them. (While some communication may flow only in one direction, for simplicity's sake only two-way, mutual communication flows will be used in our examples.)

As Figure 10.9 highlights, communication networks may differ with respect to a key feature: their degree of **centralization.** Briefly, this refers to the degree to which information must flow through a specific member of the network. As you can see from Figure 10.9, communication networks such as the *Y, Wheel,* and *Chain* are identified as **centralized networks.** For members within them to communicate with each other, they must go through a central person who is at the "crossroads" of the information flow. In contrast, the *Circle* and *Comcon* are referred to as **decentralized networks** because information can freely flow between members without going through a central person. People in decentralized networks have equal access to information, whereas those in centralized networks are unequal because the individuals at the centers have access to more information than others.

Research has shown that these differences in communication networks are largely responsible for determining how effectively groups will perform various jobs. Generally speaking, it has been found that when the tasks being performed are simple, centralized networks perform better, but when the tasks are more complex, decentralized networks perform better.[30] Specifically, comparing these two types of networks: *centralized networks are faster and more accurate on simple tasks, whereas decentralized networks are faster and more accurate on complex tasks.*

Why is this so? The answer has to do with the pressures put on the central member

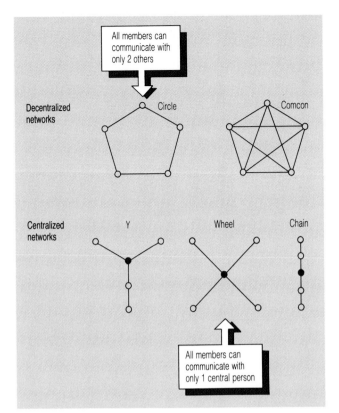

**FIGURE
10.9 Communication
Networks: Some Basic
Types**

Some examples of five-person communication networks are shown here. Networks such as the *Circle* and *Comcon* give all members equal opportunities to communicate with each other, and are known as *decentralized networks.* In contrast, networks such as the *Y, Wheel,* and *Chain* contain members (marked by a filled-in circle) through whom messages must pass to reach others.

of a centralized network. The more information any one member of a group has to deal with, the greater the degree of **saturation** that person experiences. If you've ever tried working on several homework assignments at the same time, then you probably already know how information saturation can cause performance to suffer. This is what happens when a centralized network performs a complex task. The central person becomes so overloaded with information that the group is slowed down and many errors are made. However, when the problem is simple, the central person can easily solve it alone after she receives all the information from the other members. In decentralized networks, there is no one central person, so information and work demands are more evenly distributed. As a result, on simple tasks the information needed to solve the problem may be spread out over all the group members, causing delays in coming to a solution. This same feature represents an advantage, however, when tasks are highly complex because it prevents any single member from becoming saturated and lowering the group's performance. (Please see our summary of these processes in Figure 10.10 on page 348.) In short, centralization is a double-edged sword. When tasks are simple, centralization facilitates getting the job done. However, when tasks are complex, it may cause saturation, bringing performance to a halt.

Research also shows that centralized and decentralized networks differ in terms of the satisfaction of their members. Would you be more satisfied as a member of a centralized or decentralized group? Most people enjoy the greater equality in decision making that occurs in decentralized networks. Such groups give everyone involved an equal status. In contrast, as a peripheral member of a centralized network, you would be less powerful than the central member and left out of the decision-making process. The central member controls more of the flow of information and is clearly more im-

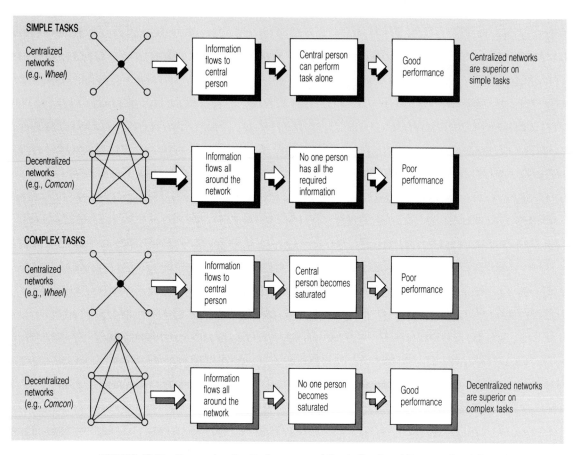

FIGURE 10.10 Comparing the Performance of Centralized and Decentralized Communication Networks: The Influence of Task Complexity

As shown here, centralized networks are superior on *simple* tasks (top), and decentralized networks are superior on *complex* tasks (bottom).

portant, leading many peripheral members to feel that their contributions are not fully appreciated. Together, these factors combine to cause lower overall levels of satisfaction among members of centralized networks compared to those in decentralized networks.

In sum, formal communication networks clearly play an important role in organizations. However, formal communication networks may be only one of several factors responsible for organizational communication. One important consideration is that although the lines of communication between people can greatly influence their job performance and satisfaction, the various advantages and limitations of different communication networks tend to disappear the longer the groups are in operation.[31] As group members gain more experience interacting with each other, they may learn to overcome the limitations imposed by their communication networks. (For example, they may learn to send messages to specific individuals who have proven themselves in the past to be particularly competent at solving certain kinds of problems.) In other words, although the differences between various communication networks may be quite powerful, they may be only temporary, accounting for the behavior of newly-formed groups.

Another important point is that any formal lines of communication operate in organizations in conjunction with widespread informal networks that also may help groups accomplish their goals. Even if formal channels impede the communication of information, informal connections between people—such as friendships, or contacts in other departments—may help the communication process. (Consider, for example, the widespread use of informal channels of communication by the character "Radar" O'Reilly on the TV show *M*A*S*H*. Using his contacts to trade his unit's hypodermic syringes for another unit's toilet paper represents the operation of informal as opposed to formal channels of communication.) As we will describe next, the informal connections between people are extremely important in organizational communications.

Informal Communication Networks: Organizations' Hidden Pathways

For a moment, think about the persons with whom you communicate during the course of an average day. Friends, family members, classmates, and colleagues at work are among those with whom you may have *informal communication*—information shared without any formally imposed obligations or restrictions. When you begin thinking about it carefully, it is quite surprising to see how widespread our informal networks can be. You know someone who knows someone else, who knows your best friend—and before long, your informal networks become very far-reaching. In fact, we often use the phrase "it's a small world" to describe our connections to others through an intricate network of informal connections.

It is easy to imagine how important the flow of informal information may be within organizations. People transmit information to those with whom they come into contact, thereby providing conduits through which messages can travel. The idea that people are connected in this way has been used to explain a very important organizational phenomenon—turnover. Do people resign from their jobs in ways that are random and unrelated to each other? A recent study by Krackhardt and Porter suggests that they do not, but rather, that they do so because of the informal communication patterns between them.[32] These investigators theorized that voluntary turnover (i.e., employees freely electing to resign their jobs) occurs as a result of a *snowball effect*. A snowball does not accumulate snowflakes randomly, but rather, collects those snowflakes that are in its path. Analogously, it was reasoned, patterns of voluntary turnover may not be independently distributed within a work group, but may be the result of people's influences on each other. Thus, predicting which people will resign from their jobs may be based, in large part, on knowledge of the communication patterns within groups. Someone who leaves her job for a better one in another organization may know someone who has already done so. Krackhardt and Porter found support for this snowball effect among teenagers working in fast-food restaurants. Specifically, turnover tended to be concentrated among groups of people who communicated informally with each other a great deal before they resigned. (For a suggestion regarding how this may operate, please see Figure 10.11 on page 350.) This study provides an excellent example of the importance of informal patterns of communication in organizations.

Informal communication networks are characterized by the fact that they are often comprised of individuals at different organizational levels. People can tell anyone in the network whatever informal information they wish. For example, one investigator found that jokes and funny stories tended to cross organizational boundaries, and were freely shared by those in both the managerial and nonmanagerial ranks of organizations.[33] On the other hand, it would be quite unlikely—and considered "out of line"—for one of the lower-level employees to communicate something about how to do the job to an upper-level employee. What flows within the pathways of informal communication is informal information, messages not necessarily related to individuals' work.

It is this feature of anyone telling something informal to anyone else that makes

FIGURE 10.11 Informal Communication Networks: A Predictor of Turnover Patterns

The informal networks of communication between people (shown in dotted lines) provide channels through which messages about better job opportunities may be communicated. Patterns of voluntary turnover have been linked to the existence of such informal networks. (Source: Based on suggestions by Krackhardt & Porter, 1986; see Note 32.)

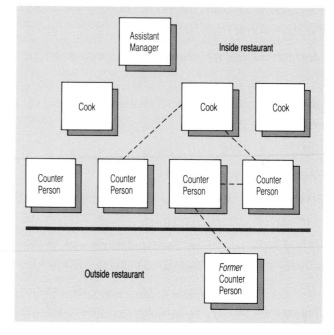

for the usually very rapid flow of information along the organizational **grapevine.** You are probably aware of the fact that the grapevine refers to the pathways through which unofficial, informal information travels. However, you may be unaware of the interesting fact that the term is believed to have originated during the U.S. Civil War when makeshift telegraph lines hastily strung up among trees hung loosely, resembling grapevines.[34] (The messages traveling along these lines were often garbled, thereby associating the grapevine with messages that are incomplete, distorted, or inaccurate.) In contrast to a formal organizational message, which might take several days to reach its desired audience, information traveling along the organizational grapevine tends to flow very rapidly, often within hours. This is not only because informal communication can cross formal organizational boundaries (e.g., you might be able to tell a good joke to almost anyone, not just your boss or subordinates with whom you are required to communicate), but also because informal information tends to be communicated orally. As we noted earlier, oral messages are communicated faster than written ones, but may become increasingly inaccurate as they flow from person to person in oral form. (As we will note later, this can be a serious organizational problem, but one that can be corrected.) Because of the confusion they may cause, some have sought to eliminate grapevines, but they are not necessarily bad. Informally socializing with our coworkers can help make work groups more cohesive (as you may recall from chapter 8), and may also provide excellent opportunities for desired human contact, keeping the work environment stimulating. Grapevines must be considered an inevitable fact of life in organizations.[35] Where there are people, there will be informal communication along the grapevine.

It is interesting to note that most of the information communicated along the grapevine is accurate. In fact, one study found that 82 percent of the information communicated along a particular company's organizational grapevine was accurate.[36] The problem with interpreting this figure is that the inaccurate portions of some messages may be likely to alter their overall meaning. If, for example, a story is going around that someone got passed up for promotion over a lower-ranking employee, there may be quite a bit of dissension caused in the workplace. However, if everything is true except the fact that the person turned down the promotion because it involved relocating, then this important fact completely alters the nature of the situation. Only one fact needs to be inaccurate before the accuracy of communication suffers.

This problem of inaccuracy is clearly responsible for giving the grapevine such a bad reputation. In extreme cases, information may be transmitted that is almost totally without any basis in fact and usually unverifiable, messages known as **rumors.** Typically, rumors are based on speculation, an overactive imagination, and wishful thinking, rather than facts. Rumors flow like wildfire throughout organizations because the information they present is so interesting and ambiguous. As such, it is open to embellishment as it passes orally from one person to the next. Before you know it, almost everyone in the organization has heard the rumor, and its inaccurate message becomes taken as fact ("it must be true, everyone knows it"). Hence, even if there was, at one point, some truth to a rumor, the message quickly becomes untrue.

If you've ever been the victim of a rumor, you know how difficult it can be to negate and undo their effects. This is especially the case among organizations, which can also be the victims of rumors, such as commonly heard rumors about the possibility of corporate takeovers. Such rumors not only influence the value of the company's stock, but also threaten employees' feelings of job security. As one example of the negative effects of rumors, a rumor about the use of worms in McDonald's hamburgers circulated in the Chicago area in the late 1970s. Despite the fact that the rumor was completely untrue, sales dropped as much as 30 percent in some restaurants.[37] Although McDonald's survived the rumor, such a cut in business volume no doubt hurt.

What, then, can be done to counter the effects of rumors? Although this is a difficult question to answer, there is some research evidence available suggesting that directly refuting a rumor may *not* help counter its effects.[38] Directly refuting a rumor only serves to help spread it among those who have not already heard about it ("oh, I didn't know people thought that") and strengthen it among those who already heard it ("if it weren't true, they wouldn't be protesting so much"). Instead, it helps to direct people's attention away from the rumor, instead focusing on other things they know about the target of the rumor. In research studying the McDonald's rumor, for example, it was found that reminding people about other things they thought about McDonald's (e.g., that it is a clean, family-oriented place) helped counter the negative effects of the rumor. Keep in mind that the rumored information that someone has about any target may be just part of the set of beliefs held. If you should ever become the victim of a rumor (vicious or otherwise), remember: directing people's attention to other positive things they already believe about you may be a helpful way of countering the effects of the rumor. Although rumors may be impossible to stop, their effects can, with some effort, be effectively managed.

It would be misleading to emphasize only the negative effects of informal communication networks. It is also true that the informal flow of information from person to person can be quite beneficial. For example, research has shown that the more involved people are in their organizations' communication networks, the more powerful and influential they become on the job.[39] Informal connections apparently help people attain formal power (we will have more to say about the attainment of power in chapter 12). It has also been shown that the informal connections between scientists is an important mechanism through which they share ideas, what has been referred to as an *invisible college.*[40] The transmittal of scientific knowledge is affected by the patterns of communication through which that knowledge is directed. It is important to note that the communication here is strictly informal; it did not have to be shared, but it was, informally. Still, it was quite influential. Indeed, as we have shown, information that is communicated informally can have potent effects on organizational functioning.

Communication and the Work Environment: Technology and Office Design

Management theorists have long been aware of the importance of the work environment as a determinant of organizational communication. For example, in his book on office management written over sixty years ago, William Henry Leffingwell noted that clerks could be more productive if they did not have to leave their desks in order to communicate with each other.[41] To avoid making clerks waste time by walking around, he recommended using such devices as pneumatic tubes, elevators, conveyor belts, and a variety of buzzers and bells to make communication more efficient for office workers. Such devices may seem primitive by today's modern technological standards (in which complex computer and telephone networks are commonly used to transmit messages), but the basic idea is the same: technology can enhance the flow of information, and hence, the quality of organizational functioning. (For a whimsical look at this process, please see Figure 10.12.)

It would be incorrect, however, to assume that modern technological advances have made the organizational communication process any more pleasant for today's office workers than it was for those Leffingwell studied in the 1920s. One of the key culprits seems to be the ever-present video display terminals that have replaced the paper-cluttered desks of office workers in the past. Clerical employees forced to do their work in the shadow of a green or amber screen all day may miss human contact, especially when they are encased in cubicles separated from others by tall partitions. In an attempt to escape such isolation, the employees in one office studied by Zuboff mischievously pried open the seam of a metal partition that separated them from their coworkers.[42] People reported feeling isolated and solitary, and longed for the kind of informal contact denied them by the design of their surroundings.

Generally speaking, although the use of "on-line" technology can improve office productivity, there is a hidden cost in using these methods. The problem, Zuboff notes,

"I still miss the days when we just read the letters and made a list."

FIGURE 10.12 Modern Technology: A Major Influence on Communication

Although this example may be a bit extreme, modern advances in technology have changed many of the ways people communicate with each other. (Source: From *The Wall Street Journal*—Permission, Cartoon Features Syndicate.)

FIGURE 10.13   Computer Terminals: Communication Help or Hindrance?
Although computer terminals can make communicating vast quantities of information faster
and more accurate than ever before, they may reduce important forms of interpersonal
contact.

is that such automation minimizes important contact between managers and their subordinates. Technology that takes away decision-making powers may preclude the need
for some management supervision. We are not saying that computers may make supervisors obsolete, but that they may diminish subordinates' need to interact with their
supervisors during the course of their jobs. Thus, critical opportunities to help identify
and solve organizational problems may be lost (or at least, temporarily misplaced) in
the process. Machinery that makes interpersonal collaboration unnecessary may add
to feelings of social isolation. This idea applies to the shop floor too, where research
has shown that the use of robots is recognized as a potential threat to communication
between supervisors and their subordinates.[43] Obviously, organizational scientists are
just beginning to recognize the challenges to effective communication posed by the use
of modern technology in the workplace (see Figure 10.13).

In addition to the effects of high technology, another element of the work environment—and a much more basic one—may also have profound influences on communication—namely, the design of offices. During the 1960s it was very popular for
offices to be designed without interior walls or partitions, using one large open space,
what was referred to as the *open-plan office*. (Because many schools were designed in
this way, it is possible that you may have attended classes in a similar "open-plan
classroom.") The idea behind such designs was to encourage open communication
between people by eliminating the walls that served as barriers to communication in
conventional, walled offices. Basically, the idea makes sense, especially if you consider
the fact that people tend to avoid communicating with others who are located more
than twenty-five feet away from them.[44] However, open-plan offices have their problems too. Notably, they have been found to be noisier, and to offer much less privacy
than traditional offices.[45]

In a recent study, Oldham surveyed the reactions of insurance company claims
adjusters at two different times—once while they were working in an open office, and
again after they moved to an office of the same size that had partitions (4–6 feet high)
separating them from each other.[46] As shown in Figure 10.14 (on page 354), the new
offices with partitions brought about improvements in several areas. The employees

FIGURE 10.14 Open versus Closed Offices: Which Are Preferred?

Research has shown that clerical employees were more satisfied working in partitioned offices than open-plan offices. Partitioned offices were also recognized as providing greater possibilities for focusing on the task at hand, and for communicating in private. (Source: Based on data in Oldham, 1988; see Note 46.)

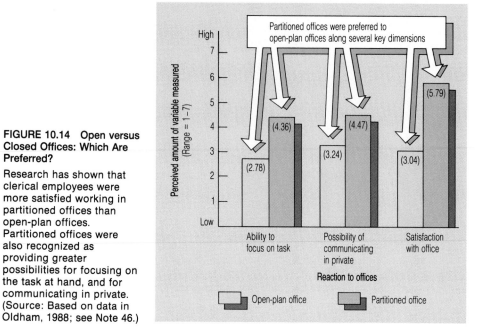

studied believed they were better able to focus on the work at hand, and that they could more effectively communicate privately with others. They were also more satisfied with the office itself. Such research findings suggest that office design may have a complex effect on communication. Although open-plan offices may make it easier for clerical workers to interact with each other, the lack of privacy may actually make communication less effective than in traditional, closed-plan offices.

As we have noted here, the work environment can profoundly influence communication. Office machinery can make it easier than ever to communicate vast quantities of information to others. But such equipment may isolate employees, keeping them from the kinds of social interaction they seek and the formal interaction with their supervisors that may be most helpful to organizations. Research on the layout of open offices leads to similarly complex conclusions. While open-plan offices may make it easier to gain access to others, their characteristically high levels of background noise and their lack of privacy may actually make communication more difficult. In sum, there is no one best way to use machinery or to design an environment for effective communication. There are clearly tradeoffs involved. Effective communication in today's high tech world demands the use of impersonal machines, but using them more than ever creates the need for informal social contact that is so vital to organizational communication.

OVERCOMING COMMUNICATION BARRIERS: ENHANCING THE FLOW OF INFORMATION

Throughout this chapter we have noted the central role of communication in organizational functioning. Given this, it is easy to understand how any efforts at improving the communication process in organizations may have highly desirable payoffs for organizations, as well as the individuals and groups working in them. There are several steps that can be taken to obtain the benefits of effective communication. In this final section we will describe some of these techniques, including measures that can be taken by individuals, as well as tactics for improving communication that involve entire organizations.

Becoming a Better Communicator: Individual Strategies

Imagine that someone is talking to you, but you cannot understand what the speaker is saying. Now, imagine reading a letter so clearly written that you know exactly what ideas the writer had in mind. If you've ever experienced any situations like these, you can appreciate the importance of communicating clearly and effectively. Bad communication is easy to recognize; you usually know it when someone isn't coming across to you. However, good communication isn't a skill we can take for granted, and it isn't easily acquired. Top executives often work long and hard at honing their communication skills. So, while we don't expect you will become an expert communicator just by taking the tips we describe here, we think you will find them a useful head start at understanding some of the necessary elements of effective interpersonal communication.

Keep language simple. Have you ever pulled your "previously-owned motor vehicle" up to a gas pump and found yourself greeted by a "petroleum transfer engineer" who filled your "fuel containment module"? Or, perhaps, you've gone to a "home improvement center" looking to purchase a "manually powered impact device"? In either case, we wouldn't blame you if you went to another "operating entity" that had a better "customer interface capacity." Certainly, you've already encountered enough business double-talk without getting any more from us. Our point is that using such seemingly formal language may impose a serious barrier on communication.

It is important to keep in mind that all organizations, fields, social groups, and professions have their **jargon**—that is, their own specialized language. Your own college or university may have a "quad," or, as a student, you may have a "roomie" who wants to go "Greek," and is interested in "rushing." These terms are examples of a college student's jargon. No doubt, you've encountered a lot of language in this book that may at first sound strange to you. Our point is that the use of jargon is inevitable when people within the same field or social groups communicate with each other. Some degree of highly specialized language may help communication by providing an easy way for people in the same fields to share complex ideas. Jargon also allows professionals to identify unknown others as persons in their field because they "speak the same language." For example, management professors would describe this book as dealing with the field of *OB*, a term that would have a very different meaning to medical doctors (for whom it refers to the field of obstetrics). Obviously, within professions jargon helps communication, but it can lead to confusion when it is used outside of the groups within which it has meaning (please refer to Table 10.1 on page 356).

Studying the use of jargon in one large organization, Kanter noted that a *COMVOC*—itself a jargon term for "common vocabulary"—developed among its members.[47] For example, within some divisions there were "fast trackers" who "shot from the hip" to go for "the big win." Unfortunately people in other departments of the corporation who didn't understand this jargon often felt out of place, creating a barrier to clear communication. This happened not only between various departments of the large organization studied by Kanter, but also between various employees and their family members, who, as a result, often had great difficulty understanding what their spouses or parents did on the job. In fact, the wives of male executives identified over 100 unfamiliar work-related terms and phrases that they could not understand. Ac-

TABLE 10.1   Can You Pass the Business Jargon Test?
The world of business is full of words and phrases that seem strange to the uninitiated. Using a field's specialized terms (known as *jargon*) may hinder communication with persons who are outside the field. See how many of the business-related terms on the left you can correctly match with the meanings shown on the right. Compare your answers to the correct pairings shown below.

Term	Definition
1. greenmail	a. testing others' reactions to an idea
2. churn	b. a bigshot, a very important person
3. sysop	c. to operate smoothly and effectively
4. stand the gaff	d. a location where important decisions are made
5. grunt	e. to be in a confused, turbulant state
6. puzzle palace	f. purchasing another's stock holdings to stop them from taking over a company
7. run it up the flagpole	
8. galley-west	g. to increase a firm's business activity, so as to appear to be productive
9. poo-bah	
10. hit on all six	h. a low-ranking person
	i. person who manages a computer bulletin board
	j. to persist, endure against rigorous odds

(Source: Based on definitions appearing in Chapman, R. L., *New dictionary of American slang*, New York: Harper & Row, 1986.)
The correct pairings are as follows: 1 = f, 2 = g, 3 = i, 4 = j, 5 = h, 6 = d, 7 = a, 8 = e, 9 = b, and 10 = c.

cordingly, we can safely say that jargon may be an effective communication device between people within one's social or professional group, but should be avoided when attempting to communicate with outsiders. *You* might know what you mean, but using jargon others don't understand will not help you get your point across to others. And, of course, that is what communication is all about.

In addition to avoiding jargon, verbal communication between people should also tend to use language that is short, simple, and to the point. Hence, it is often wise to adopt the **K.I.S.S. principle** when communicating with others—that is, *K*eep *I*t *S*hort and *S*imple.[48] People are better able to understand messages that do not overwhelm them with too much information at once than those that present more than they can absorb. A wise communicator is sensitive to this and knows how to monitor her audience for signs of overloading audience members' circuits with too much information. Again, it is important to keep in mind that just because you may know what you are talking about, you may not be able to get your ideas across to others unless you package them in doses small and simple enough to be understood. When this is done effectively, even the most complex ideas can be clearly communicated.

Be an active, attentive listener. Just as it is important to present your ideas in ways that make them understandable to others (i.e., sending messages), it is equally important to work at being a good listener (i.e., receiving messages). Although listening to others comprises a large percentage of the time spent communicating, it has been established that people tend to actually pay attention to and comprehend only a small percentage of the information directed at them in the course of doing their jobs.[49]

Most of us usually think of listening as a passive process of taking in information sent by others, but when done correctly the process of listening should be much more active. For example, it is important to ask questions if you don't understand something, and to nod or otherwise signal if you do understand. Such cues provide critical feedback to the communicator about the extent to which he or she is getting across to you. As a listener, you can do your share to help the communication process by letting the message-sender know if and how his messages are coming across to you. Asking questions and putting the speaker's ideas into your own words are helpful ways of staying alert and taking in all the information being presented.

It is also very useful to avoid distractions in the environment and concentrate on what the other person is saying. (As you may recall from chapter 4, attention is a critical part of the perception process.) When listening to others, also try to avoid immediately jumping to conclusions or evaluating their remarks. It is important to completely take in what is being said before you reach your own conclusions about it. Certainly, it is much too easy to simply dismiss someone because you don't like what is being said. Doing so, of course, poses a formidable barrier to effective communication. Being a good listener also involves making sure you are aware of others' main points. What is the speaker trying to say? Be sure you understand another's ideas before you formulate your reply. Too many of us interrupt speakers with our own ideas before we have fully heard theirs. If this sounds like something you do, rest assured that it is not only quite common, but correctable. Although it requires some effort, incorporating these suggestions into your own listening habits cannot help but make you a better listener. Indeed, many organizations have sought to help their employees in this way. For example, the corporate giant Unisys has for some time (since it was known as the Sperry Corporation) systematically trained thousands of its employees in effective listening skills (using seminars and self-training cassettes). Clearly, Unisys is among those companies acknowledging the importance of good listening skills in promoting effective organizational communication.

Improving Communication on the Job: Organizational Strategies

Thus far, we have described ways individuals can improve their communication abilities by being a better sender and receiver of messages. In addition to these important skills, there are also ways to enhance the communication process at the organizational level. Given the importance of information to the survival of organizations, it is essential that communication be as effective as possible. We will now consider some things organizations can do to improve the quality of the communications that take place within them.

Obtaining feedback. To operate most effectively, organizations must be able to communicate accurately with those who keep them running—their employees. Unfortunately, for many of the reasons reviewed in this chapter, people are often unwilling or unable to communicate their ideas to top management. Part of the problem is the lack of available channels for upward communication and people's reluctance to use whatever ones exist. How, then, can organizations obtain information from their employees?

There are several techniques for effectively soliciting feedback. *Employee surveys* can be used to gather information about employees' attitudes and opinions about key areas of organizational operations. Questionnaires administered at regular intervals may be useful for spotting changes in attitudes as they occur. Such surveys tend to be quite effective when their results are shared with employees, especially when the feedback is used as the basis for changing the way things are done.

A second means of facilitating upward communication in organizations is using *suggestion systems*. Too many times, employees' good ideas about how to improve organizational functioning fail to work their way up the organizational chart because the people with the ideas do not know how to reach the people who can implement them.

Even worse, they may feel they will not be listened to even if they can reach the right person. *Suggestion boxes* are designed to help avoid these problems, to help provide a conduit for employees' ideas. Recent research has found that about 15 percent of employees use their companies' suggestion boxes, and that about 25 percent of the suggestions made are implemented.[50] Employees are usually rewarded for their successful suggestions, either with a flat monetary reward or some percentage of the money saved by implementing the suggestion. The oldest continuously operating suggestion system has been in operation at the Eastman Kodak Company since 1898. At that time, a worker was awarded $2 for pointing out the advantages of washing the windows in the company's production department. Since then, almost two million suggestions have been made at Kodak, including one that yielded an award of $47,800 to the man who suggested mounting film boxes on cards for display racks at retail stores.[51]

A third method of providing important information is through *corporate hotlines,* telephone lines staffed by corporate personnel ready to answer employees' questions, listen to their comments, and the like.[52] A good example of this is the "Let's Talk" program that AT&T developed to answer its employees' questions at the time of the company's antitrust divestiture. By providing personnel with easy access to information, companies benefit in several ways. It not only shows employees that the company cares about them, but also encourages them to address their concerns before the issues become more serious. In addition, by keeping track of the kinds of questions and concerns voiced, top management is given a good source of feedback about the things that are on employees' minds. Such information can be invaluable when attempting to improve organizational conditions.

Together, the three methods we have referred to here (see summary in Table 10.2) can effectively break down the barriers that too frequently restrict the flow of information from lower-level personnel to upper-level managers. They represent ways of improving the upward flow of communication in organizations. Effective communication not only requires obtaining enough feedback, but also appropriately accessing it. In other words, it is important to control the amount of information being communicated at any one time so as to avoid being inundated.

Gauging the flow of information. Imagine a busy manager surrounded by a tall stack of papers, with a telephone receiver in each ear and a crowd of people gathered around, waiting to talk to her. Obviously, the many demands put on this person can slow down the system and make its operation less accurate. When any part of a com-

TABLE 10.2 Obtaining Employee Feedback: Some Useful Techniques
The techniques summarized here are designed to improve organizational functioning by providing top management with information about the attitudes and ideas of the workforce. They are used to promote the upward flow of information.

Technique	Description
Employee Surveys	Questionnaires assessing workers' attitudes and opinions about key areas of organizational functioning, especially when results are shared with the workforce
Suggestion Systems	Formal mechanisms through which employees can submit ideas for improving things in organizations (often by putting a note in a *suggestion box*); good ideas are implemented and the persons who submitted them are rewarded
Corporate Hotlines	Telephone numbers employees may call to ask questions about important organizational matters; useful in addressing workers' concerns before they become too serious

munication network (be it an individual, a committee, etc.) becomes bogged down with more information than it can handle effectively, a condition of **overload** is said to exist. Consider, for example, the bottleneck in the flow of routine financial information that might result when the members of the accounting department of an organization are tied up preparing corporate tax returns. (Such an overloaded condition experienced by the organization is analogous to the experience of saturation encountered by central members of a centralized communication network.) Naturally, such a state poses a serious threat to effective organizational communication. Fortunately, however, several steps can be taken to manage information more effectively.

For one, organizations may employ *gatekeepers,* persons whose jobs require them to control the flow of information to potentially overloaded units. For example, executive assistants are responsible for making sure that busy executives are not overloaded by the demands of other persons or groups. Newspaper editors and television news directors may also be thought of as gatekeepers, since such individuals decide what news will and will not be shared with the public. It is an essential part of these individuals' jobs to avoid overloading others by gauging the flow of information to them.

Overload can also be avoided through *queuing.* This term refers to lining up incoming information so that it can be managed in an orderly fashion. The practices of "stacking" jets as they approach a busy airport or making customers take a number (i.e., defining their position in the line) at a busy deli counter are both designed to avoid the chaos that may otherwise result when too many demands are made on the system at once. For a summary of these techniques, please see Figure 10.15.

When systems are overloaded, problems of *distortion* and *omission* are likely to result. That is, messages may be either changed or left out when they are passed on

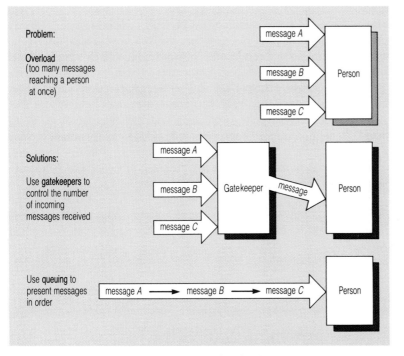

FIGURE 10.15 Overload: A Problem That Can Be Solved
Overload, receiving too many messages at once, can seriously interfere with organizational functioning. It can be minimized using *gatekeepers* and *queuing*.

from one organizational unit to the next. If you've ever played the parlor game "telephone" (in which one person whispers a message to another, who passes it on to another, and so on until it reaches the last person) you have likely experienced—or contributed to—the ways messages get distorted and omitted. When you consider the important messages that are often communicated in organizations, these problems can be extremely serious. They also tend to be quite extreme. A dramatic demonstration of this was reported in a study tracing the flow of downward communication in over one hundred organizations. It was found that messages communicated downward over five levels lost approximately 80 percent of their original information by the time they reached their destination at the lowest level of the organizational hierarchy.[53] Obviously, something needs to be done.

One strategy that has proven effective in avoiding the problems of distortion and omission is *redundancy*. Making messages redundant involves transmitting them again, often in another form or via another channel. For example, in attempting to communicate an important message to her subordinates, a manager may tell them the message and then follow it up with a written memo. In fact, one study has found that managers frequently encourage this practice.[54] Another thing that can be done to avoid distortion and omission is the practice of *verification*. This refers to making sure messages have been received accurately. Pilots use verification when they repeat the messages given them by air traffic controllers. Doing so assures both parties that the messages the pilots heard were the actual messages the controllers sent. Given how busy pilots may be during takeoffs and landings and the interference inherent in radio transmissions, coupled with the importance of the messages themselves, the practice of verifying messages is a wise safety measure. The practice is not only used in airline communication systems, but may be used by individual communicators as well. Active listeners may wish to verify that they correctly understood a speaker, and do so by paraphrasing the speaker's remarks within a question, asking "If I heard you correctly, you were saying. . . ."

As we have noted here, for the communication process to operate as effectively as it can, a concerted effort is required of everyone involved in it. Those who send messages should make them clear and redundant, those who receive messages should listen actively and verify what they have heard, and the system within which communication occurs should provide gatekeepers and/or mechanisms for queuing that guard against the possibility of overload. Together, these measures help ensure that communication occurs effectively, avoiding confusion and misunderstandings at all stages of the process. (Indeed, efforts to improve communication in organizations may require reducing employees' uncertainties about what is happening in the company, minimizing the chances that they misinterpret what they see or hear. The **Management Perspective** section below explains how such miscommunications are likely to occur at an important time—when organizations relocate. We will not only illustrate how moving a company to a new location can trigger miscommunications between corporate officers and employees, but also offer some specific recommendations about how to avoid them.)

OB: A MANAGEMENT PERSPECTIVE

Managing the Hidden Messages behind Corporate Relocations

It is often said that actions speak louder than words, and this old adage applies especially well to the actions of organizations. A particular action to which employees pay close attention is one that has been happening in record numbers in recent years—corporate relocation. As Isabella and Ornstein caution us, such relocations involve more than just physical changes.[55] The act of moving a company to a new location sends messages to its employees. Unless corporate officials take steps to carefully manage these messages, they run the risk of unintentionally communicating potentially disruptive ideas about the organization and the role of the employees working within it.

Although companies move for various reasons, employees may not accept these explanations at face value. A major reason for this stems from the inevitable psychological trauma resulting from leaving a safe, familiar environment full of memories for a new one. Employees may suffer not only a fear of the unknown and the uncertainties of a new environment, but even a loss of identity with their old communities—especially when a company has long been associated with a particular city. (This was the case, for example, when the Firestone Tire and Rubber Company left its longtime home in Akron for a new one in Chicago.) In response to such upheaval, people tend to seek information that helps them cope with their new situation. How will the move affect their lives?

In the process of searching for such information, employees are likely to find hidden messages in their companies' relocation decisions. Companies move for many different reasons (e.g., the need for more or less space, to reduce costs, to improve a corporate image, and so on). Although these reasons may be clearly explained to the employees, the trauma of moving may lead them to misinterpret or reinterpret these reasons. Consider the examples reviewed in Table 10.3. Each one presents a way that companies may unintentionally communicate an unwanted message to their employees.

Unfortunately, such interpretations may result in potentially disruptive forms of organizational behavior. For example, employees who fear a loss of job security, or simply no longer fitting in, may be expected to resign in favor of new, more secure, jobs. Isabella and Ornstein suggest several ways in which corporations can avoid sending such hidden messages.

1. *Bring certainty to the situation.* Employees will inevitably have many questions about the new location. What is the community like? What will the new facility look like? Where will various offices be located? The less employers tell their employees, the more likely employees are to become overly concerned with such matters, leading to stress and lowered performance. It is advisable for management to do everything it can to reduce uncertainty for its workforce, such as arranging pre-move visits, providing assistance in finding employment for spouses, and so on. In short, helping to make the unknown better known is likely to reduce dissatisfaction. What is *not* communicated to employees may be more unsettling than what is!

2. *Keep an eye on employees' feelings about relocation.* It is important to monitor concerns about

TABLE 10.3 Corporate Relocations: Their Official versus Hidden Meanings

As summarized here, although the reasons for the relocation of several large companies were formally explained to the employees, workers were likely to interpret the relocations in different ways. Such discrepancies between messages sent by organizations and their interpretation by employees can have serious detrimental effects on both organizations and employees alike.

COMPANY	OFFICIAL EXPLANATION FOR MOVE	POSSIBLE HIDDEN MESSAGE COMMUNICATED BY MOVE
Fuqua Industries	Some of the conglomerate's companies were sold, so less space is needed	The company is downsizing and/or going out of business, thereby threatening job security
Bell & Howell Co.	Company was deleting its core business (cameras), and diversifying	The company's goals are changing, creating uncertainty and a fear of the unknown
RJR Nabisco, Inc.	R. J. Reynolds Industries acquired Nabisco Brands and moved its headquarters from Winston-Salem, NC to Atlanta (Nabisco's headquarters)	Nabisco really won the takeover battle, causing resentment toward the new parent company among former R. J. Reynolds employees

(Source: Adapted from Isabella & Ornstein, 1988; see Note 55.)

the move at various points in the process. Some factors may bother people at different times. At first, employees may be most concerned about the personal aspects of the move (giving up their homes, finding new ones, and so on). Later, they may think about how well they will fit with the company's new plans. Key executives will have to constantly gather feedback from employees about their concerns, and address these concerns with honest, thorough information. Not doing so may undermine the success of the relocation efforts.

3. *Make messages consistent.* Employees may seek information from several sources, and for the answers to be accepted, they must be the same each time. Hearing one thing from one manager and something completely different from another (which can easily happen given the confusion likely to occur during a relocation) only serves to fuel, rather than reduce, workers' uncertainties, even further lowering morale.

4. *Retain some of the old while establishing the new.* Too many changes at once can be overwhelming. Therefore, managers are urged to keep many aspects of the old workplace intact while

introducing new ones. It would be unwise, for example, to teach secretaries a new electronic filing system immediately upon their move to new offices. Uncertainty, fear of the unknown, and insecurity may be greatly reduced by introducing one change at a time.

Corporate relocations may represent a tremendous opportunity for new growth and prosperity, both at the organizational and individual levels. But for these benefits to be realized, managers must first sensitize themselves to the human side of the logistical project, recognizing that moving people is not like moving machines. The suggestions outlined here represent some useful steps toward eliminating some of the inherent hidden messages triggered by the corporate relocation process. Companies that have followed them, such as the Montgomery Ward Life Insurance Company, have noted ready acceptance of their relocations among most employees. Clearly, effective communication can be an important part of what it takes to minimize the inevitable human costs of corporate relocation.

SUMMARY AND REVIEW

The Nature of Communication. The process of **communication** occurs when a sender of information *encodes* a message and transmits it over communication channels to a receiver, who *decodes* it, and then sends feedback. Factors interfering with these processes are known as **noise.** Communication may be either verbal or nonverbal. Verbal messages may be either written (which are more enduring) or spoken (which are quicker). Messages are also communicated *nonverbally,* through manner of dress, and the use of time and space—all of which reflect an individual's organizational status.

Factors Affecting Communication. Communication is influenced by **organizational structure,** the formally prescribed pattern of interrelationships between people within organizations. Structure dictates who must communicate with whom (as reflected in an **organizational chart,** a diagram outlining these reporting relationships), and the form that communication takes. Orders flow down an organizational hierarchy, and information flows upward. However, the upward flow of information is often distorted. Attempts at coordination characterize horizontal communication, messages between organizational members at the same level.

Formally imposed patterns of communication, called **communication networks,** influence job performance and satisfaction over brief periods of time. **Centralized networks** have members through whom messages must travel. In **decentralized networks,** though, all members play an equal role in transmitting information. On simple tasks, centralized networks perform faster and more accurately; on complex tasks, decentralized networks do better. Members of decentralized networks tend to be more satisfied than members of centralized networks.

Information also flows along *informal communication networks.* These informal connections between people are responsible for spreading information very quickly because they transcend formal organizational boundaries. Informal pathways known as the **grapevine** are often responsible for the rapid transmission of partially inaccurate information.

Elements of the work environment also influence organizational communication. The use of computer terminals may help transmit large amounts of information quickly and accurately, but this technology tends to minimize desired human contact. It also reduces opportunities for potentially useful interaction with supervisors. Offices designed without walls or partitions separating workers, *open-plan offices,* may make communication easier than closed offices. Because these are also noisier and provide fewer opportunities for private communication, they may not effectively facilitate communication.

Improving the Communication Process. Individuals can learn to become better communicators by keeping their messages brief and by avoiding the use of **jargon** when communicating with those who are not familiar with such specialized terms. They may also improve their listening skills, learning to listen actively (thinking about and questioning the speaker) and attentively (without distraction).

At the organizational level, communication may be improved by using techniques that provide for employee feedback (e.g., *employee surveys, suggestion systems,* and *corporate hotlines*). The problem of **overload** can be reduced by using gatekeepers (individuals who control the flow of information to others), or by *queuing* (the orderly lining up of incoming information). The *distortion and omission* of messages can be minimized by making messages *redundant* and by encouraging their *verification*.

KEY TERMS

centralization: The degree to which information must flow through a specific central member of the communication network.

centralized networks: Communication networks that have central members through which all information must pass to reach other members (e.g., the *Y,* the *Wheel,* and the *Chain*).

communication: The process by which a person, group, or organization (the sender) transmits some type of information (the message) to another person, group, or organization (the receiver).

communication networks: Pre-established patterns dictating who may communicate with whom (see *centralized networks* and *decentralized networks*).

decentralized networks: Communication networks in which all members play an equal role in the transmittal of information (e.g., the *Circle,* and the *Comcon*).

decoding: The process by which a receiver of messages transforms them back into the sender's ideas.

encoding: The process by which an idea is transformed so that it can be transmitted to, and recognized by, a receiver (e.g., a written or spoken message).

grapevine: An organization's informal channels of communication, based mainly on friendship or acquaintance.

jargon: The specialized language used by a particular group (e.g., people within a profession).

K.I.S.S. principle: A basic principle of communication advising that messages should be as short and simple as possible. (An abbreviation for Keep It Short and Simple.)

noise: Factors capable of distorting the clarity of messages at any point during the communication process.

nonverbal communication: The transmission of messages without the use of words (e.g., by gestures, the use of space, etc.).

organizational chart: A diagram showing the formal structure of an organization, indicating who is to communicate with whom.

organizational structure: The formally prescribed pattern of interrelationships existing between the various units of an organization.

overload: The condition in which a unit of an organization becomes overburdened with too much incoming information.

rumors: Information with little basis in fact, often transmitted through informal channels (see *grapevine*).

saturation: The amount of information a single member of a communication network must handle.

363
Key Terms

QUESTIONS FOR DISCUSSION

1. Identify and describe the various elements comprising the model of communication effectiveness described in the text.

2. Describe how any three types of nonverbal cues influence communication within organizations.

3. Imagine that you are a manager attempting to explain the use of a certain new computer software package to a subordinate. Should this be accomplished using written communication, oral communication, or both? Explain.

4. What is an *organizational chart?* What does it reveal about the nature of communication within organizations?

5. Imagine that you are putting together groups of five employees to evaluate proposed methods for disposing of nuclear waste. What type of communication network would be most appropriate? Why?

6. Argue for or against the following statement: "Rumors pose a threat to the effective operation of organizations."

7. Suppose you were designing a new office. What considerations of technology and physical design should enter into your plan if you are trying to make it as effective as possible for communication?

8. In Shakespeare's *Hamlet*, Polonius said, "Give every man thine ear, but few thy voice." Discuss the implications of this advice for being an effective listener. What other suggestions should be followed for enhancing the effectiveness of listening?

9. Identify any two problems of organizational communication, and measures that can be taken to overcome them.

NOTES

1. Roberts, K. H. (1984). *Communicating in organizations* (p. 4). Chicago: Science Research Assoc.
2. Barnard, C. I. (1938). *The functions of the executive.* Cambridge, MA: Harvard Univ. Press.
3. Mintzberg, H. (1973). *The nature of managerial work.* New York: Harper & Row.
4. Level, D. A. (1972). Communication effectiveness: Methods and situation. *Journal of Business Communication, 10,* 19–25.
5. Klauss, R., & Bass, B. M. (1982). *International communication in organizations.* New York: Academic Press.
6. Malloy, J. T. (1975). *Dress for success.* New York: Warner Books.
7. Forsythe, S., Drake, M. F., & Cox, C. E. (1985). Influence of applicant's dress on interviewer's selection decisions. *Journal of Applied Psychology, 70,* 374–378.
8. Solomon, M. R. (1986, April). Dress for effect. *Psychology Today,* pp. 20–28.
9. Greenberg, J. (1989). The organizational waiting game: Status as a status-asserting or status neutralizing tactic. *Basic and Applied Social Psychology, 10,* 13–26.
10. Greenberg, J. (1988). Equity and workplace status: A field experiment. *Journal of Applied Psychology, 73,* 606–613.
11. Zweigenhaft, R. L. (1976). Personal space in the faculty office: Desk placement and student-faculty interaction. *Journal of Applied Psychology, 61,* 529–532.
12. Greenberg, J. (1976). The role of seating position in group interaction: A review, with applications for group trainers. *Group and Organization Studies, 1,* 310–327.
13. Scully, J. (1987). *Odyssey: Pepsi to Apple . . . a journey of adventure, ideas, and the future.* New York: Harper & Row.
14. Carstairs, E. (1986, February). No ivory tower for Procter & Gamble. *Corporate Design and Reality,* pp. 24–30.
15. Rasmussen, K. G., Jr. (1984). Nonverbal behavior, verbal behavior, résumé credentials, and selection interview outcomes. *Journal of Applied Psychology, 69,* 551–556.
16. Daft, R. L., Lengel, R. H., & Trevino, L. K. (1987). Message equivocality, media selection, and manager performance: Implications for information systems. *MIS Quarterly, 11,* 355–366.
17. Argyris, C. (1974). *Behind the front page: Organizational self-renewal in a metropolitan newspaper.* San Francisco: Jossey-Bass.
18. Hawkins, B. L., & Preston, P. (1981). *Managerial communication.* Santa Monica, CA: Goodyear.
19. Szilagyi, A. (1981). *Management and performance.* Glenview, IL: Scott, Foresman.
20. Kiechell, W., III. (1986, January 6). No word from on high. *Fortune,* pp. 19, 26.
21. Walker, C. R., & Guest, R. H. (1952). *The man on the assembly line.* Cambridge, MA: Harvard University Press.
22. Luthans, F., & Larsen, J. K. (1986). How managers really communicate. *Human Relations, 39,* 161–178.
23. Kirmeyer, S. L., & Lin, T. (1987). Social support: Its relationship to observed communication with peers and superiors. *Academy of Management Journal, 30,* 138–151.
24. Read, W. (1962). Upward communication in industrial hierarchies. *Human Relations, 15,* 3–16.
25. Glauser, M. J. (1984). Upward information flow in organizations: Review and conceptual analysis. *Human Relations, 37,* 613–643.
26. Foushee, H. C. (1984). Dyads and triads at 35,000 feet: Factors affecting group processes and aircrew performance. *American Psychologist, 39,* 885–893.
27. Stark, E. (1988, October). Wild blue blunders. *Psychology Today,* pp. 30–32.
28. Rogers, E. M., & Rogers, A. (1976). *Communication in organizations.* New York: Free Press.

29. Shaw, M. E. (1978). Communication networks fourteen years later. In L. Berkowitz (Ed.), *Group processes* (pp. 351–361). New York: Academic Press.

30. Forsyth, D. R. (1983). *An introduction to group dynamics*. Monterey, CA: Brooks/Cole.

31. Burgess, R. L. (1968). Communication networks: An experimental reevaluation. *Journal of Experimental Social Psychology, 4*, 324–327.

32. Krackhardt, D., & Porter, L. W. (1986). The snowball effect: Turnover embedded in communication networks. *Journal of Applied Psychology, 71*, 50–55.

33. Duncan, J. W. (1984). Perceived humor and social network patterns in a sample of task-oriented groups: A reexamination of prior research. *Human Relations, 37*, 895–907.

34. Flexner, S. B. (1982). *Listening to America*. New York: Simon and Schuster.

35. Baskin, O. W., & Aronoff, C. E. (1989). *Interpersonal communication in organizations*. Santa Monica, CA: Goodyear.

36. Walton, E. (1961). How efficient is the grapevine? *Personnel, 28*, 45–49.

37. Thibaut, A. M., Calder, B. J., & Sternthal, B. (1981). Using information processing theory to design marketing strategies. *Journal of Marketing Research, 18*, 73–79.

38. See Note 37.

39. Brass, D. J. (1985). Men's and women's networks: A study of interaction patterns and influence in an organization. *Academy of Management Journal, 28*, 327–343.

40. West, C. K., & Hoerr, W. A. (1985). Communication and work patterns among productive scholars in psycho-educational research: The invisible college hypothesis. *Human Relations, 18*, 127–137.

41. Leffingwell, W. H. (1925). *Office management*. Chicago: A. W. Shaw.

42. Zuboff, S. (1988). *In the age of the smart machine*. New York: Basic Books.

43. Chao, G. T., & Kozlowski, S. W. J. (1986). Employee perceptions on the implementation of robotic manufacturing technology. *Journal of Applied Psychology, 71*, 70–76.

44. Allen, T. J. (1966). Performance information channels in the transfer of technology. *Industrial Management, 8*, 87–98.

45. Zalesny, M. D., & Farce, R. V. (1987). Traditional versus open offices: A comparison of sociotechnical, social relations, and symbolic meaning perspectives. *Academy of Management Journal, 30*, 240–259.

46. Oldham, G. R. (1988). Effects of changes in workspace partitions and spatial density on employee reactions: A quasi-experiment. *Journal of Applied Psychology, 73*, 253–258.

47. Kanter, R. M. (1977). *Men and women of the corporation*. New York: Basic Books.

48. Borman, E. (1982). *Interpersonal communication in the modern organization* (2nd ed.). Englewood Cliffs, NJ: Prentice-Hall.

49. Rowe, M. P., & Baker, M. (1984, May–June). Are you hearing enough employee concerns? *Harvard Business Review*, pp. 127–135.

50. Vernyi, B. (1987, April 26). Institute aims to boost quality of company suggestion boxes. *Toledo Blade*, Section B, p. 2.

51. Bergerson, A. W. (1977, May). Employee suggestion plan still going strong at Kodak. *Supervisory Management, 22*, 32–36.

52. Taft, W. F. (1985). Bulletin boards, exhibits, hotlines. In C. Reuss & D. Silvis (Eds.), *Inside organizational communication* (2nd ed., pp. 183–189). New York: Longman.

53. Nichols, R. G. (1962, Winter). Listening is good business. *Management of Personnel Quarterly*, p. 4.

54. See Note 4.

55. Isabella, L. A., & Ornstein, S. (1988, May). Getting and giving the hidden message on relocation. *Personnel*, pp. 30–39.

How Communication Saved Lives, a Popular Product, and a Company

> We believe our first responsibility is to the doctors, nurses and patients, to mothers and all others who use our products and services. In meeting their needs everything we do must be of high quality. We must constantly strive to reduce our costs in order to maintain reasonable prices. Customer orders must be serviced promptly and accurately. Our suppliers and distributors must have an opportunity to make a fair profit.
>
> We are responsible to our employees . . .
>
> We are responsible to the communities in which we live and work and the world community as well . . .
>
> Our final responsibility is to our stockholders . . . (Excerpted from the Johnson & Johnson Credo).[1]

Although numerous companies have mottos, slogans, and credos, few take them as seriously as the Johnson & Johnson Company of New Brunswick, New Jersey. Johnson & Johnson has not only demonstrated adherence to their ideals in good times, but more remarkably, in bad times as well. In late 1982 Johnson & Johnson had an unfortunate opportunity to show how committed to their values they really were when one of their most profitable and widely distributed products—Extra-Strength Tylenol capsules—was linked to seven deaths in the greater Chicago area.

To this day, it is uncertain who was responsible for tampering with Tylenol capsules by placing highly toxic cyanide in them and then placing the bottles back on the shelves of various stores. At the time of the deaths it was even more uncertain how the cyanide had gotten into the capsules. Initially, two people died of cyanide poisoning; however, the preliminary medical reports suggested that one person had died of a stroke and the other a massive heart attack. Doctors did not even begin to suspect that poison was involved until three relatives of one of the initial victims came down with the same symptoms and subsequently died. They had taken the same Tylenol that had poisoned the first family member. At about this time, two firefighters who were involved in the investigation realized that the only thing the victims had in common was that they all had taken Tylenol prior to their deaths. After this discovery was made, the possibility was considered that the tampering had been done at a Johnson & Johnson plant. However, the fact that there were different lot numbers on the bottles, and that these lot numbers signified that the Tylenol had been packaged in different parts of the country, eliminated that initial hypothesis. At about this time, the medical specialists confirmed that all the deaths were due to cyanide poisoning. Thus began the search for more tainted bottles of the drug.[2,3]

It would have been impossible for Johnson & Johnson, or any other company, to prepare a contingency disaster plan that would have helped deal with a catastrophe of this kind. Instead, what they did was follow their credo to the letter and take actions designed first and foremost to prevent any more deaths. Johnson & Johnson did this by communicating in a large number of ways with their distributors, medical professionals, and the American public. One of the most significant steps was to recall all 31 million bottles of Extra-Strength Tylenol capsules then currently on the shelves of stores throughout the nation. Although it was clear that no one at the company had perpetrated this crime, Johnson & Johnson nonetheless felt that it should recall all of the drug to ensure that no more deaths would occur.

This action immediately communicated to everyone that Johnson & Johnson was acting responsibly and in a trustworthy manner. At the same time, the company sent half a million mailgrams to doctors and hospitals, advising them of the tamperings and asking them to stop recommending Extra-Strength Tylenol capsules to their patients. The company also contacted 15,000 retailers and distributors requesting their help in withdrawing bottles of Tylenol from the shelves. To reach the general public, Johnson & Johnson established a special public relations team that held press conferences daily and fielded all queries from the media. In addition, James E. Burke, the CEO, agreed to go on the extremely popular *Donahue* and *60 Minutes* TV shows to publicize the tragedy and to urge consumers not to take Extra-Strength Tylenol capsules. The company also set up toll-free phone lines to answer consumers' calls. To deal with the concerns of their 79,000 employees worldwide, Johnson & Johnson sent letters to all of them, as well as retirees, explaining their understanding of what had happened in Chicago.[4]

To deal with the fast breaking information as it happened within the company, Johnson & Johnson set up a key decision-making and strategy team including Burke; David R. Clare, President; Wayne K. Nelson, Company Group Chairman; Arthur M. Quilty, Executive Committee member; George S. Frazza, General Counsel; David E. Collins, Chairman of the McNeil subsidiary that manufactured the Extra-Strength Tylenol; and Lawrence G. Foster, Corporate Vice President of Public Relations. This group met twice a day for the duration of the crisis "to make decisions on rapidly developing events and to coordinate companywide efforts."[5]

Because Johnson & Johnson dealt so effectively with the tragedy of the poisonings, they were able to reintroduce Extra-Strength Tylenol capsules to the marketplace just six weeks after the crisis. Just as it had been during the crisis, the communication of the reintroduction was very clear, timely, and forthright. Johnson & Johnson officials announced the reintroduction during a teleconference held on November 11, 1982. This teleconference was beamed by satellite to twenty-two cities.[6] As a result, evening news programs all over the country carried the announcement that Extra-Strength Tylenol capsules would be sold in tamper-resistant packaging. Of course, Johnson & Johnson also developed an advertising campaign to accompany their product's reappearance.[7] As physicians and hospitals had been the primary mechanism through which Tylenol was recommended to patients, Johnson & Johnson embarked on a campaign to inform them about the changes in packaging. By the end of the year, a salesforce of 2,250 people had made over 1 million presentations to doctors and others in the medical community.[8] Finally, Johnson & Johnson provided coupons to consumers to encourage their purchase of the newly-packaged Extra-Strength Tylenol capsules.

It is clear that the extensive communications Johnson & Johnson engaged in both during and after the crisis were effective in maintaining the company's image and their ability to reintroduce a popular product. Although the financial costs of their actions were significant ($.27 per share),[9] they did gain back 95 percent of the market they had lost when they pulled their product from the shelves.[10] They also managed to keep consumer, doctor, and retailer confidence in the company's products and their ability to manage under the most extreme conditions.

Questions for Discussion

1. What types of verbal and nonverbal (action) communications did Johnson & Johnson use in dealing with the Tylenol poisonings?

2. What symbolic messages did Johnson & Johnson send to their various constituents? How did they communicate these messages?

3. Describe the communication networks established by Johnson & Johnson to handle the crisis.

4. How did Johnson & Johnson's handling of this tragedy help minimize the number of rumors circulating?

5. What communication strategies did Johnson & Johnson use to most effectively share their message with the general and medical public?

Notes

1. Levering, R., Moskowitz, M., & Katz, M. (1984). *The 100 best companies to work for in America.* Reading, MA: Addison-Wesley.

2. The Tylenol scare (1982, October 11). *Newsweek,* pp. 32–36.

3. Buchholz, R. (1989). *Fundamental concepts and problems in business ethics.* Englewood Cliffs, NJ: Prentice-Hall.

4. The Tylenol comeback (1982, December). Reprinted from *Johnson & Johnson Worldwide 17,* no. 5, pp. 5–6.

5. See Note 3, p. 222.

6. See Note 3.

7. See Note 3.

8. See Note 4.

9. *Johnson & Johnson Annual Report* (1982). p. 37.

10. Tylenol's miracle comeback (1983, October 17). *Time,* p. 62.

Becoming an Active Listener

369
**Experiencing
Organizational
Behavior**

**EXPERIENCING
ORGANIZATIONAL
BEHAVIOR**

What makes an effective communicator? Most people would probably say it's his or her ability to express ideas—to speak and write clearly. Of course these skills are important, but listening is, too. Being a good communicator requires listening carefully, picking up others' ideas. But doesn't listening come naturally? Although we might hear others, most of us tend to be very inefficient listeners. That is, we fail to pay attention and understand most of what others are saying. When it comes to communication in organizations, this can be quite problematic. Recognizing this, many people in organizations are trained in becoming more *active listeners* (see pages 356–357).

Procedure

1. Review the following "do's and don'ts" of active listening.

Do	*Don't*
Show empathy; support the speaker.	Judge and draw conclusions.
Explain what you think was said.	Evaluate the ideas expressed.

2. As a class, consider how an active listener would respond to someone saying, "I worked for hours on that stupid project, and the boss didn't like it. That'll be the last time I work so hard for him."

Listening actively, it would be correct to say, "You seem disappointed that your boss didn't approve of your work." Such a response shows that you understand the speaker and encourages him or her to give more thought to the problem at hand. In contrast, it would be incorrect to say either "You should have started that project long ago" (too judgmental) or "At least you have a good job" (no empathy).

3. The instructor should now read each of the following statements out loud. Listen actively to each one and respond to it in a way that shows you've listened actively. Discuss several students' responses relative to the guidelines for active listening noted above.

a. I just found out my boss only gave me a 2 percent raise. If that's the kind of appreciation they show for hard work around here, they can get themselves another sucker!
b. Why did you take Barbara's side on that budget vote? I thought you agreed with me, but apparently not. Sometimes it's tough to tell your friends from your enemies.
c. It really sounds like a good offer. The pay is competitive, and I've always wanted to live in Crowdville.
d. I'm really tired of those staff meetings. All we ever do is gripe. If you ask me, it's just a waste of time.
e. Try as I might, I just can't get the hang of that new computer system. Yesterday, I messed with it for hours and got nowhere.
f. Being part of the Rafstone Products team is a dream come true. I just hope I can cut it around here with all those big shots.
g. Everybody's gone on vacation this week, but I have to hang around to get caught up on my work. At least that's what Mr. Nasty wanted. Sure wish I could be getting a tan like everyone else!

Points to Consider

1. Did it become easier for you to think of appropriate responses as you practiced more?

2. Had you not been attempting to listen actively, how would you have tended to respond? More judgmentally?

3. What mistakes were made most commonly by your classmates in responding to these statements?

4. Do you think you will be able to apply your active listening skills to your own interactions with others? Explain.

5. What personal benefits do you imagine will result for both speakers and listeners from using active listening techniques?

6. When do you think it would be most appropriate to use and to not use active listening skills in organizations?

7. How would you feel as the speaker if you heard the responses of your classmates?

CHAPTER ELEVEN

LEADERSHIP: ITS NATURE AND IMPACT IN ORGANIZATIONS

CHAPTER OUTLINE

Leadership: Its Basic Nature
  Leadership: A Working Definition
  Leaders and Managers: Why the Two Are Not
    Identical
Leader Traits and Leader Behaviors
  The Trait Approach: Leadership and Personal
    Characteristics
  Leader Behavior: Some Key Dimensions
  Organizational Constraints on Leader Behavior
**Major Theories of Leadership: The Contingency
Model, Normative Theory, and Path-Goal Theory**
  Fiedler's Contingency Theory: Matching Leaders
    and Tasks
  Normative Theory: Decision Making and Leader
    Effectiveness
  Path-Goal Theory: Leaders as Guides to Valued
    Goals

**Additional Perspectives on Leadership: The Vertical
Dyad Linkage Model, Substitutes for Leadership, and
Situational Leadership Theory**
  The VDL Model: The Importance of Leader-
    Follower Exchanges
  Substitutes for Leadership
  Situational Leadership Theory: Follower Maturity
    and Leadership Style

Special Sections

OB: A Research Perspective
  Charismatic Leaders: A Closer Look

OB: An International Perspective
  Getting on the Fast Career Track in Japan: The
  Role of Leader-Subordinate Exchanges

LEARNING OBJECTIVES

After reading this chapter, you should be able to:

1. Define *leadership* and indicate why being a leader and being a manager are not always the same.
2. Describe several key dimensions of leader behavior.
3. Summarize the main points of three major theories of leadership (*contingency theory, normative theory, path-goal theory*).
4. Indicate how leaders' relations with their subordinates can affect subordinates' performance and careers.
5. Describe the nature of *charismatic leadership* and indicate how such leaders influence followers.
6. Explain why leaders are not always essential for high levels of performance.
7. Explain why different styles of leadership may be required at different points in the development of work groups.

"Well, listen to this!" Jan Reynolds says to her husband, Kevin, as she peers over the business section of the morning paper. "Douglas Schmidt is through at REICO."

"No kidding," Kevin replies, lowering the section of the paper he's been reading. "But he just got there, didn't he? What is it, about six months ago?"

"Well, maybe more like a year, but it hasn't been long."

"So what happened, anyway? I thought he was Mr. Hot Shot himself."

"So did I. I'm glad I decided to leave last year. It sounds like things have gone from bad to worse. Just listen to this: 'Mr. Schmidt departs amid rumors that the company will soon report the largest drop in earnings in its history and a substantial decline in operating capital . . .' They just can't seem to get their act together."

"Yeah, that's for sure," Kevin agrees. "But let's get back to Schmidt. I thought they hired him to fix all that. He sure did a number for . . . what was that company he saved a couple of years ago?"

"Travco," Jan answers. "And you're right—he really turned it around in a hurry. We do business with one of their big customers, and they were really impressed. All their products improved, and they started shipping stuff out on schedule for a change."

"Well, that makes it even weirder," Kevin says, shaking his head. "How can a person do so well in one spot but totally bomb in another? What did he do, fall on his head or something?"

"Oh, be serious!" Jan answers, swatting at Kevin with the newspaper. "I think it has something to do with his style, and differences between the two companies."

"What do you mean? A style's a style. If it works in one place, it ought to work in another."

"Not necessarily. You know his reputation: he really likes to run the show—a take-charge guy if ever there was one. From what I heard, that's just what they needed at Travco. The whole operation was falling apart because there was no direction from the top and no one knew where the heck they were going."

"So?" Kevin asks, pushing his chair back from the table.

"So, Mr. Smart Aleck, that's just what they *didn't* need at REICO. They have a lot of senior people used to having their own way. Besides, most of them have solid technical backgrounds and lots of experience; they don't need anyone to tell them what to do."

"So why did they hire Schmidt in the first place? What did they expect, that he'd change overnight and fit in?"

"I don't know. They were pretty desperate. Maybe they just didn't think it through. They knew they needed *something,* quick . . . and he does have that great reputation."

"Well, they made a mistake, and now they'll have to pay for it."

"I guess so . . ." Jan agrees. She pauses for a moment, then continues. "You know, I think there's a message in here, somewhere. No one—no matter how good they are—is going to come into a company and work miracles unless there's a good match between what they've got to offer and what the company needs."

"Maybe so," Kevin replies, between sips of coffee, "but this is getting too philosophical for a Sunday morning. Why don't you quit trying to solve the mysteries of being a great leader and hand me the comics . . ."

If you surveyed one hundred executives working in a wide variety of jobs and asked them to name the single most important factor in determining organizational success, chances are good that many would reply "effective leadership." This answer reflects the existence of a strong and general belief, in the world of business, that leadership is a key ingredient in corporate effectiveness. And this view is by no means restricted to organizations; many people assume that leadership also plays a central role in politics, sports, and many other human activities.

Is this view justified? Do leaders really play such a crucial role in shaping the fortunes of organizations? More than fifty years of research on this topic suggest that they do.[1] Effective leadership, it appears, is indeed a key factor in organizational success (see Figure 11.1). Given this fact and its relevance to the field of OB, it seems appropriate for us to consider the topic of **leadership** in some detail. In this chapter, therefore, we will summarize current information about this complex process. One review of research on leadership published a few years ago cited more than 5,000 separate articles and books on this topic, so there is obviously quite a lot of ground to cover.[2]

To make the task of summarizing this wealth of information more manageable, we will proceed as follows: First, we will consider some basic points about leadership—what it is and how being a leader differs from being a manager. Second, we'll examine two basic views of leadership, one focusing primarily on the *traits* of leaders and the other focusing primarily on their *behaviors*. Third, we will describe several major theories of leadership. While these differ greatly in content and scope, all adopt a *contingency approach,* and recognize that there is no single best style of leadership. Rather, the key question they all consider is: under what specific conditions are various approaches or styles of leadership most (and least) effective? Finally, we'll examine several newer perspectives that provide additional insights into the nature and function of leadership.

LEADERSHIP: ITS BASIC NATURE

In one sense, at least, **leadership** resembles love: it is something most people feel they can recognize, but find difficult to define. What, precisely, is it? And how does being a leader differ from being a manager? We will now focus on these questions.

FIGURE 11.1 Effective Leaders: A Key Ingredient in Organizational Success

Strong, effective leaders such as Victor Kiam often contribute to the success of organizations.

Leadership: A Working Definition

Imagine that you accepted a new job and entered a new work group. How would you recognize its **leader?** One possibility, of course, is through the formal titles and assigned roles each person in the group holds. In short, the individual designated as Department Head or Project Manager would be the one you would identify as the group's leader. But imagine that during several staff meetings, it became apparent that this person was really not the most influential. While she or he held the formal authority, these meetings were actually dominated by another person who, ostensibly, was the top person's subordinate. What would you conclude about leadership then? Probably, that the real leader of the group was the person who actually ran things—not the one with the fancy title and the apparent authority.

In many cases, of course, the disparity we have just described does not exist. The individual possessing the greatest amount of formal authority is also the most influential. In some situations, however, this is not so. And in such cases, we typically identify the person who actually exercises the most influence over the group as its leader. These facts point to the following working definition of leadership—one accepted by many experts on this topic: *leadership is the process whereby one individual influences other group members toward the attainment of defined group or organizational goals.*[3]

Note that according to this definition, leadership is primarily a process involving *influence*—one in which a leader changes the actions or attitudes of several group members or subordinates. As we will see in chapter 12, many techniques for exerting such influence exist, ranging from relatively *coercive* ones—the recipient has little choice but to do what is requested—to relatively *noncoercive* ones—the recipient can choose to accept or reject the influence offered. In general, *leadership* refers to the use of relatively noncoercive influence techniques. This implies that leadership rests, at least in part, on positive feelings between leaders and their subordinates. In other words, subordinates accept influence from leaders because they respect, like, or admire them—not simply because they hold positions of formal authority.[4] As you can easily see, this makes sense, for when we describe a leader as being effective, we generally assume that positive feelings of loyalty and commitment on the part of subordinates are part of the total picture. (We'll return to various bases of influence or power in chapter 12.)

The definition presented above also suggests that leadership involves the exercise of influence for a purpose—to attain defined group or organizational goals. In other words, leaders focus on altering those actions or attitudes of their subordinates that are related to specific goals; they are far less concerned with altering actions or attitudes that are irrelevant to such goals.

Finally, please note that our definition, by emphasizing the central role of influence, implies that leadership is really something of a two-way street. Leaders do indeed influence subordinates in various ways. But since influence and power are always reciprocal in nature, at least to a degree, they do not operate in social isolation. On the contrary, as suggested by Figure 11.2, leaders are often influenced, in turn, by their subordinates. After all, one can't lead without followers!

Leaders and Managers: Why the Two Are Not Identical

In everyday speech, and also in some texts on management (!), the terms *leader* and *manager* are used almost interchangeably. While we understand the temptation to adopt this usage, we feel that, in fact, the two terms should be clearly distinguished. Many managers, of course, do function as leaders according to the definition offered above: they exert influence over their subordinates in order to attain organizational goals.

"Are you __ready__ for leadership?"

FIGURE 11.2 The Reciprocal, Two-way Nature of Leadership

As suggested by this cartoon, leadership is very much a two-way street. Leaders influence their followers but are also affected, in turn, by these persons. Or, to put it another way, no one can lead individuals who are not ready to follow (i.e., be influenced). (Source: Drawing by C. Barsotti; © 1979 The New Yorker Magazine, Inc.)

However, others do *not* function in this manner. Their jobs require that they devote most of their time to other management activities—planning, processing information, communicating with customers or suppliers. Such persons are not leaders in the sense indicated above. Indeed, they would reject this term as an apt description of their jobs or their activities.

Conversely, many persons who are leaders are not managers. They operate in contexts outside the world of business, and do not perform the basic functions usually associated with managerial roles (e.g., organizing, controlling, planning). In sum, while some managers are indeed leaders, others are not, so there is no simple or necessary link between these two roles. As indicated by Figure 11.3, not all managers are leaders, and not all leaders are managers. In view of these facts, we will distinguish between these two terms and the roles they describe throughout the present chapter, and in the remainder of this text.

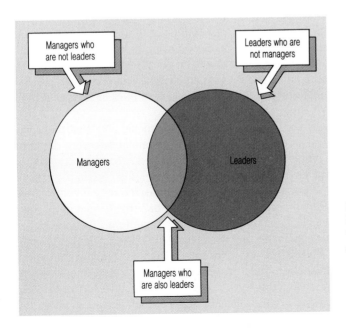

FIGURE 11.3 Leaders and Managers: Not Synonymous

While some managers act as leaders, others do not. Further, not all leaders are managers. For these reasons, it is useful to distinguish clearly between these two roles.

At one time or other, most persons have daydreams about being a leader. They have fantasies of taking charge of large groups and being viewed with great awe and respect. Despite the prevalence of such daydreams, however, relatively few individuals convert them into reality by becoming actual leaders. Further, among these, only a small proportion are considered effective in this role. This fact raises an intriguing question: what sets such persons apart from most others? Why, in short, do some persons, but not others, become effective leaders? Many answers have been proposed, but among these, two have received the most attention. These perspectives suggest, respectively, that effective leadership is largely a function of either the *traits* possessed by individuals, or the patterns or *behavior* they demonstrate.[5,6]

The Trait Approach: Leadership and Personal Characteristics

Are some people born to lead? Common sense suggests that this is so. Great leaders of the past such as Alexander the Great, Queen Elizabeth I, and Abraham Lincoln do seem to differ from ordinary human beings in several respects. For example, they all seem to have possessed high levels of ambition coupled with clear visions of precisely where they wanted to go. To a lesser degree, even leaders lacking in such history-shaping fame seem different from their followers. Top executives, some politicians, and even sports heroes or heroines often seem to possess an aura that sets them apart from others. On the basis of such observations, early researchers interested in leadership formulated a view known as the **trait** or **great person theory.** According to this approach, great leaders possess key traits which set them apart from most human beings. Further, the theory contends that these traits remain stable over time and across different groups. Thus, it suggests that all great leaders share these characteristics regardless of when and where they lived, or the precise role in history they fulfilled.

Certainly, these are intriguing suggestions, and seem to fit quite well with our own informal experience. You will probably be surprised to learn, therefore, that they have *not* been strongly confirmed. Decades of active research (most conducted prior to 1950) failed to yield a short, agreed upon list of key traits shared by all leaders.[7] A few consistent findings did emerge (e.g., leaders tend to be slightly taller and more intelligent than their followers), but these were hardly dramatic in nature or in scope.[8] Indeed, the overall results of this persistent search for traits associated with leadership were so disappointing that most investigators gave up in despair and reached the following conclusion: leaders simply do not differ from followers in clear and consistent ways.

While this conclusion is still widely accepted today, we should note that there has recently been renewed interest in the possibility that leaders and followers do differ in at least some measurable respects. Several types of evidence have contributed to this trend. First, research studies indicate that persons possessing certain patterns of motives (e.g., a high need for power coupled with a high degree of self-control) are more successful as managers than persons showing other patterns.[9] Second, political leaders appear to differ from nonleaders in ways we might expect (e.g., they are higher in self-confidence, need for achievement, and dominance).[10] Third, leaders who command tremendous respect, admiration, and excitement from their followers—often described as *charismatic*—do seem to differ in several respects from leaders who do not generate such reactions.[11] (Refer to our discussion of this topic on page 383.) Please don't misunderstand: none of these findings suggest that all leaders share the same traits, or that possession of these characteristics is required for leadership at all times and in all places. However, they do suggest that personal factors *can* play a role in leadership in some cases, and that in this respect, at least, there may be a small grain of truth in the *trait* approach.

Leader Behavior: Some Key Dimensions

When the search for a small list of key traits distinguishing leaders from followers or effective leaders from ineffective ones failed, researchers turned their attention to another possibility: perhaps the differences they sought would be apparent with respect to concrete *behaviors*. In other words, it seemed possible that effective and ineffective leaders differed not primarily with respect to specific traits, but rather with respect to their approaches to or styles of leadership. Research designed to investigate this possibility was much more successful, and added appreciably to our understanding of how leaders behave, and how their actions affect their followers.

Participative versus autocratic leaders: From directive autocrats to permissive democrats. Think about the different bosses you have had in your life or career. Can you remember one who wanted to control virtually everything—someone who made all the decisions, who told people precisely what to do, and who wanted, quite literally, to run the entire show? In contrast, can you recall a boss or supervisor who allowed employees greater freedom and responsibility—someone who invited their input before making decisions, who was open to suggestions, and who allowed them to carry out various tasks in their own way? If so, you already have first-hand experience with two sharply contrasting styles of leadership: **autocratic** and **participative.**

In the past, these styles were viewed as endpoints along a single continuum. However, as noted recently by Muczyk and Reimann, they actually seem to involve two separate dimensions.[12] The first is the extent to which leaders permit subordinates to take part in decisions; this is the *autocratic-democratic* dimension. The second involves the extent to which leaders direct the activities of subordinates and tell them how to carry out their jobs; this is the *permissive-directive* dimension. Combining these two variables yields four possible patterns, which Muczyk and Reimann label: (1) directive autocrat, (2) permissive autocrat, (3) directive democrat, and (4) permissive democrat. (These patterns are described in Table 11.1 on page 378.) While any attempt to divide human beings into discrete categories raises thorny issues, these patterns do seem to make good sense; many managers adopt a style of leadership that fits, at least roughly, within one.

But given that leaders differ along these two dimensions and can, as a result, be classified as falling into one of the four patterns listed above, do any of them have a clear-cut edge? In short, is one pattern superior to the others in many, if not most, situations? Existing evidence suggests that this is doubtful. All four styles seem to involve a mixed pattern of advantages and disadvantages. Moreover—and this is the crucial point—the relative success of each depends heavily on conditions existing within a given organization and its specific stage of development. For example, consider managers who might be described as *directive autocrats*. Such persons make decisions without consulting subordinates and supervise subordinates' work activities very closely. While it is tempting to view such a pattern as undesirable (it runs counter to the value of personal freedom), it may actually be highly successful in some settings (e.g., when employees are inexperienced or underqualified for their jobs; when subordinates adopt an adversarial stance toward management and must be closely supervised).

In contrast, consider the case of *permissive autocrats* (leaders who combine permissive supervision with an autocratic style of making decisions). This pattern may be

TABLE 11.1   Contrasting Styles of Leadership
According to Muczyk and Reimann, leaders often adopt one of the four distinct styles described here.

LEADERSHIP STYLE OR TYPE	DESCRIPTION
Directive Autocrat	Makes decisions unilaterally; closely supervises activities of subordinates
Permissive Autocrat	Makes decisions unilaterally; allows subordinates considerable latitude in carrying out assigned tasks
Directive Democrat	Makes decisions participatively; closely supervises activities of subordinates
Permissive Democrat	Makes decisions participatively; allows subordinates considerable latitude in carrying out assigned tasks

(Based on suggestions by Muczyk & Reimann, 1987; see Note 12.)

useful in dealing with employees who have a high level of technical skill and want to be left alone to manage their own jobs (e.g., scientists, engineers, computer programmers), but who have little desire to participate in routine decision making. In a similar manner, the remaining two patterns (directive democrat and permissive democrat) are also most suited to specific organizational conditions. The key task for leaders, then, is to match their own style to the needs of their organization, and to change as these needs shift and evolve. What happens when leaders in organizations lack such flexibility? Actual events in one company—People Express—are instructive.

Don Burr, the founder and CEO of this airline, had a very clear managerial style: he was a highly permissive democrat. He involved employees in many aspects of decision making, and emphasized autonomy in work activities. Indeed, he felt that everyone at People Express should be viewed as a "manager." This management style worked well while the company was young, but as it grew and increased in complexity, such practices created increasing difficulties. New employees were not necessarily as committed as older ones, so permissive supervision was ineffective with them. And as decisions increased in both complexity and number, a participative approach became less and less appropriate. Unfortunately, top management was reluctant to alter its style; after all, it seemed to have been instrumental in the company's early success. This poor match between the style of top leaders and changing external conditions seems to have contributed (along with many other factors) to People Express's mounting problems. Losses rose until finally the company was purchased by Texas Air, whose CEO, Frank Lorenzo, favors a much more directive leadership style.

To conclude, no single style of leadership is best under all conditions and in all situations.[13] However, recognizing the importance of differences in this respect can be a constructive first step toward assuring that the style most suited to a given set of conditions is in fact adopted.

Person-oriented versus production-oriented leaders: Consideration versus initiating structure. Now, think again about all the bosses you have had in your career. Divide these into two categories: those who were relatively effective and those who were relatively ineffective. How do the two groups differ? If you think about this issue carefully, your answers are likely to take one of two forms. First, you might reply: "My effective bosses helped me to get the job done. They gave me advice, answered my questions, and let me know exactly what was expected of me. My ineffective bosses didn't do this." Second, you might answer: "My effective bosses seemed to care about me as a person. They were friendly, listened to me when I had problems or questions, and seemed to help me toward my personal goals. My ineffective bosses didn't do this."

A large body of research, much of it gathered at the University of Michigan by Likert and his colleagues[14] and at Ohio State University by Stogdill and his associates[15] suggests that leaders do differ greatly along these dimensions. Those high on the first, known as **initiating structure,** are mainly concerned with production and focus primarily on getting the job done. They engage in such actions as organizing work, inducing subordinates to follow rules, setting goals, and making leader and subordinate roles explicit. In contrast, other leaders are lower on this dimension, and show less tendency to engage in these actions.

Leaders high on the second dimension, known as **consideration,** are primarily concerned with establishing good relations with their subordinates and being liked by them. They engage in such actions as doing favors for subordinates, explaining things to them, and assuring their welfare. Others, in contrast, are low on this dimension, and don't really care much about how they get along with subordinates.

At first glance, you might assume that these two dimensions (**initiating structure** and **consideration**) are closely linked. You might guess that persons high on one must, necessarily, be low on the other. In fact, this is not the case. The two dimensions actually seem to be largely independent.[16] Thus, it is possible for a leader to be high on both concern with production and concern for people, high on one of these dimensions and low on the other, moderate on one and high on the other, and so on (see Figure 11.4). Is any one of these possible patterns best?

Careful study indicates that this is a complex issue, for production-oriented and

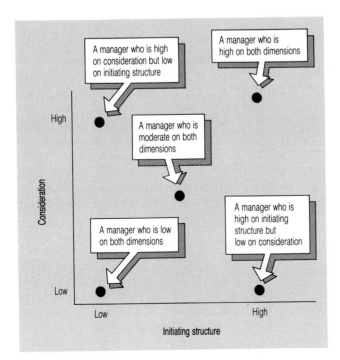

FIGURE 11.4 Key Dimensions of Leader Behavior

Leaders' behavior can vary from low to high with respect to *consideration* (person-orientation), and with respect to *initiating structure* (task-orientation). Various patterns of leader behavior produced by variations along these two dimensions are illustrated here. Research findings (refer to chapter 15) indicate that leaders who are relatively high on both consideration and initiating structure are often most effective.

people-oriented leadership styles both offer a mixed pattern of pluses and minuses. With respect to showing consideration (high concern with people and human relations) the major benefits center around improved group atmosphere and morale.[17] However, since leaders high on this dimension are reluctant to act in a directive manner toward subordinates and often shy away from presenting them with negative feedback, productivity sometimes suffers. Turning to initiating structure (high concern with production), efficiency and performance are indeed sometimes enhanced by this leadership style. If leaders focus entirely on production, however, employees may soon conclude that no one cares about them or their welfare. Then, work-related attitudes such as job satisfaction and organizational commitment may suffer.

Having said all this and pointed out the complexities, we should note that one specific pattern may indeed have an edge in many settings. This is a pattern in which leaders demonstrate high concern with both people and production.[18] As we'll see in chapter 16, encouraging such an approach (known as *team management*) is the goal of a popular form of organizational development, *grid training*.[19] An illustration of the potential benefits of this pattern is provided by a laboratory simulation carried out by Tjosvold.[20]

In this experiment, male and female students first worked with another person on a problem (rank ordering the survival value of items available after a plane crash). Subjects played the role of a subordinate, while another individual—actually an accomplice—served as their manager. During this period, the accomplice either behaved in a manner indicative of high concern with productivity (e.g., he or she told subjects precisely what to do; praised and criticized their performance), or showed low concern with productivity. In addition, the accomplice either demonstrated personal warmth (e.g., maintained a high level of eye contact with subjects and showed a friendly facial expression) or demonstrated personal coldness. Following completion of the first task, the accomplice asked subjects to work on a second task and then left the room, explaining that he or she had other work to perform at the moment. It was predicted that both variations in the accomplice's behavior would influence subjects' performance on this second task (which involved arithmetic and work problems). Specifically, Tjosvold hypothesized that subjects would work hardest when the leader was both warm and showed high concern with productivity, but would exert least effort when the leader was warm and showed low concern with productivity. (They would feel most free to goof off under this latter condition.) As you can see from Figure 11.5, results confirmed both predictions. In addition, it was found that subjects generally had more favorable impressions of the leader when this person acted in a warm and friendly manner than when he or she behaved in a cold and aloof fashion. They liked the leader more and expressed greater willingness to work with this person again.

These findings suggest that contrary to what common sense might suggest, high concern with people (showing consideration) and high concern with productivity (initiating structure) are *not* incompatible. On the contrary, skillful leaders can combine these orientations in their overall style to produce favorable results. Thus, while there is no one style of leadership that is best, it appears that leaders who combine these two concerns may often have an important edge over leaders who show only one or the other.

Organizational Constraints on Leader Behavior

In our discussion of leader behavior up to this point, we have focused on differences that stem primarily from the personal characteristics of individual leaders. At this point, we should note that this is only part of the total picture. While leaders' actions do stem,

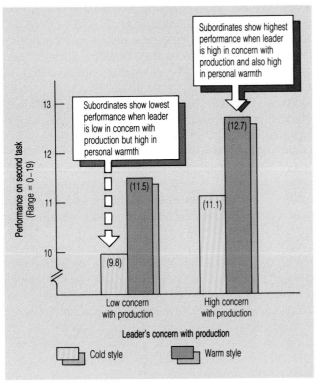

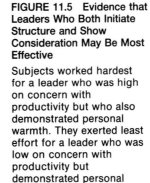

FIGURE 11.5 Evidence that Leaders Who Both Initiate Structure and Show Consideration May Be Most Effective

Subjects worked hardest for a leader who was high on concern with productivity but who also demonstrated personal warmth. They exerted least effort for a leader who was low on concern with productivity but demonstrated personal warmth. (Source: Based on data from Tjosvold, 1984; see Note 20.)

in part, from their traits, motives, and goals, they are also shaped by factors relating to their organizations—the environments in which they operate. In particular, such factors often determine how much time leaders devote to various tasks and how much authority they can exercise over subordinates. Direct evidence concerning the nature and scope of such effects has recently been reported by Hammer and Turk, in an especially revealing investigation.[21]

In this study, first-line managers in a large pharmaceutical plant (persons who often acted as leaders) reported on the amount of time they spent on several management functions described as *responsive management.*[22] (Such management involves processing information from the environment and responding to the demands it reveals. It differs from *discretionary* management in which leaders seek to change the environment in order to benefit the organization). Specifically, managers indicated the extent to which they engaged in *work group maintenance* (e.g., integrating new people into work units, explaining rules, resolving differences between new and older workers), *boundary spanning* or *networking* (e.g., negotiating relations between work units, being in contact with several departments), and *direct supervision.* In addition, the same managers indicated how much direct authority they exerted over subordinates (e.g., the extent to which they could determine the work pace in their unit, define work goals, distribute rewards and punishments).

In order to determine whether these aspects of leaders' behavior were affected by several variables relating to organizations, Hammer and Turk also obtained information on the *technology* used in each work unit, the proportion of employees who belonged to a labor union, the extent to which the plant was dependent on particular work sections (rated by section-level managers), and management philosophy (the extent to which managers were pressed by their supervisors to adopt an autocratic, directive style of management). When these organizational factors were used to predict the leaders' behavior, significant relationships were uncovered.

First, and perhaps most important, technology figured prominently in this regard. For example, managers in units that employed technology requiring routine, mass production work reported spending more time on work group maintenance than those in units that employed technology requiring complex, nonroutine tasks (e.g., two research labs, engineering units). These findings were consistent with initial predictions. Leaders in units performing routine, mass production work spent more time in work group maintenance because such units employ more low-skilled, entry level employees; such persons often require integration into existing work groups, explanation of plant rules, and so on. Correspondingly, leaders in units involved in nonroutine work spent more time in boundary spanning because in such work units, the complex, unpredictable nature of the work requires constant contact with other units. Finally, leaders in these units reported more authority because of the nonroutine nature of the work, and the need for leaders to exert more control over employees.

Additional findings also supported the view that conditions existing within an organization exert strong effects on the behavior of managers. Thus, leader behavior was also affected by union strength (managers reported engaging in more boundary spanning activities when union strength was high rather than low), and by management philosophy (leaders reported placing more emphasis on performance when management favored a philosophy of strict supervision).

In sum, the findings reported by Hammer and Turk indicate that organizational factors, as well as personal traits and dispositions, can strongly shape leaders' behavior. More concretely, when we observe a specific manager behaving in a relatively autocratic or participative manner, we should realize that such behavior may derive as much from such factors as technology, union strength, and the company's management philosophy as from this individual's personality or preferences (see Figure 11.6). (What accounts for the ability of some leaders to exert profound degrees of influence over their followers? In other words, what makes them *charismatic*? For information on this topic, please see the **Research Perspective** section opposite.)

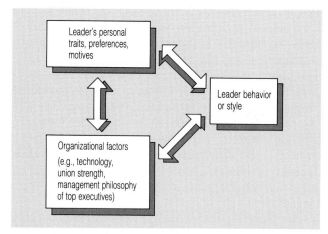

FIGURE 11.6 Organizational Factors and Leader Behavior

The style or specific behaviors adopted by a leader is affected by several organizational factors as well as by the personality, motives, and preferences of such leaders. (Source: Suggested by findings reported by Hammer & Turk, 1987; see Note 21.)

Charismatic Leaders: A Closer Look

Down through the ages, some leaders have been exceptionally successful in changing the attitudes or behavior of their followers. Indeed, it is not extreme to state that such persons have often served as key agents of social change, transforming entire societies through their visions of a new order or altered social structure.[23] Such individuals are often described as **charismatic leaders,** and they have constituted a persistent puzzle for scientists and others interested in the nature of leadership. What sets these persons apart from other leaders? How do they induce thousands or even millions of human beings to accept their views and directives willingly and without reservation? While no firm answers to such questions yet exist, a framework proposed recently by Conger and Kanungo offers intriguing insights into these matters.[24]

According to these researchers, charisma (which means *gift* in Greek) is best understood in terms of (1) specific patterns of behavior on the part of leaders, (2) attributions about the leaders by followers, and (3) specific social conditions that set the stage, so to speak, for the leaders' appeal. More specifically, Conger and Kanungo propose that because they behave in certain unusual ways, charismatic leaders come to be viewed by other persons as possessing a cluster of characteristics which, together, we label **charisma.** This attribution, in turn, contributes—along with such leaders' actual traits—to the powerful influence they exert on subordinates and other persons around them (please see Figure 11.7).

What specific forms of behavior contribute to followers' tendencies to attribute charisma to a given leader? Conger and Kanungo suggest that among the most important of these are the following: First, charismatic leaders describe the *status quo* within a society or organization as intolerable and, concurrently, propose a vision of another, better state which is highly discrepant from current conditions. Second, they willingly take high risks and engage in unconventional actions in order to reach these goals. (A good example of such behavior was provided by Lee Iacocca when he voluntarily reduced his salary to one dollar during his first year at Chrysler in order to demonstrate his personal commitment to the company.) Third, charismatic leaders express high levels of self-confidence, expertise, and concern with followers' needs. In short, they engage in many of the tactics of *impression management* described in chapter 4— tactics that greatly enhance their attractiveness and appeal to other persons. Fourth, such leaders exercise influence primarily through their personal qualities (e.g., deep commitment, high expertise) rather than through their formal position or through the attainment of consensus among their subordinates. Finally, charismatic leaders, although they favor radical change and offer idealized visions of future goals, are also quite realistic: they understand the resources available to them and the constraints of the environments in which they must operate. Thus, they often work to prepare the way for changes they wish to implement, or wait for the

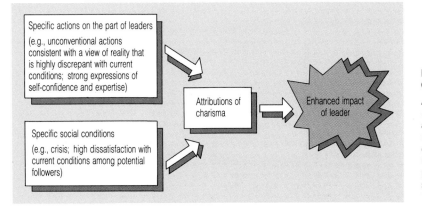

FIGURE 11.7 The Nature of Charisma: One View

According to Conger and Kanungo, *charismatic leadership* involves specific actions on the part of leaders that cause real or potential followers to attribute charisma to them. The leaders' profound impact on followers then flows, at least in part, from such attributions. (Based on suggestions by Conger & Kanungo, 1987, 1988; see Notes 23 and 24.)

appropriate time, place, and opportunities before beginning.

Obviously, charismatic leaders are not present in all settings at all times. Thus, another question relating to them is, when precisely do they emerge? Conger and Kanungo suggest that such leaders are most likely to appear—or to be labeled by followers as *charismatic*—at times of crisis; in short, when current conditions are so poor within a society or organization that radical change seems necessary.[25] At such times, charismatic leaders, because they possess high sensitivity to such contextual conditions, advocate change and engage in many of the other actions described above. The result: they encourage an image of charisma among potential followers and so enhance their own impact.

As you can readily see, all of these suggestions are quite consistent with the modern view of leadership described above. Charisma, it appears, is a function of the characteristics of specific leaders, perceptions of these characteristics among followers, and situational (contextual) factors that set the stage for the leaders' emergence. If a process as seemingly mysterious as charisma can be understood in these terms, it is clear that attention to such factors can indeed enhance our grasp of leadership as an organizational process. It is partly for this reason that we do not feel we were too optimistic in stating, earlier, that our current knowledge of leadership is indeed much more complete and sophisticated than was true in the past.

MAJOR THEORIES OF LEADERSHIP: THE CONTINGENCY MODEL, NORMATIVE THEORY, AND PATH-GOAL THEORY

By now, it should be obvious that leadership is indeed a complex process. It involves intricate social relationships and reciprocal influence between leaders and followers (see Figure 11.8). It is affected by a wide range of personal, situational, and organizational factors and it can be exercised in many different styles. Given all these complications, you may wonder why many researchers focus much of their time and energy on attempting to understand all of its intricacies. The answer, of course, is that effective leadership is an essential ingredient in organizational success. With it, organizations can grow, prosper, and compete. Without it, many simply cannot survive. Recognition of this basic point lies behind several modern theories of leadership. As will soon be clear, these theories differ sharply in their content, terminology, and scope. Yet, all are linked by two common themes. First, all adopt a *contingency approach* to this complex topic. All recognize that there is no single preferred style of leadership, and that the key task of OB researchers is determining which leadership styles will prove most effective under which specific conditions. Second, all are concerned with the issue of *leader effectiveness*. They seek to identify the conditions and factors that determine

FIGURE 11.8 Leadership: The Modern View

The modern view of leadership suggests that leaders both influence and are influenced by their followers. Moreover, this view calls attention to the fact that full understanding of leadership must consider the traits, motives, and perceptions of both leaders and followers, as well as a host of situational factors.

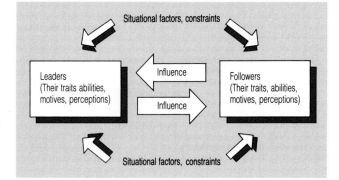

whether, and to what degree, leaders will enhance the performance and satisfaction of their subordinates.

Many theories of leadership exist, but among these, three have probably received the most attention within OB. These are Fiedler's **contingency theory,**[26] Vroom and Yetton's **normative theory,**[27] and House's **path-goal theory.**[28] We will now describe each of these theories.

Fiedler's Contingency Theory: Matching Leaders and Tasks

Leadership does not occur in a social or environmental vacuum. Rather, leaders attempt to exert their influence on group members within the context of specific situations. Since these can vary greatly along many different dimensions, it is only reasonable to expect that no single style or approach to leadership will always be best. Rather, as we have already noted, the most effective strategy will probably vary from one situation to another.

Acceptance of this basic fact lies at the core of a theory of leader effectiveness developed by Fiedler, who describes his theory as a *contingency* approach.[29] The term is certainly appropriate, for the theory's central assumption is as follows: a leader's contribution to successful performance by his or her group is determined both by the leader's traits and by various features of the situation. To fully understand leader effectiveness, both types of factors must be considered.

With respect to characteristics possessed by leaders, Fiedler identifies *esteem (liking) for least preferred coworker* (LPC for short) as most important. This refers to a leader's tendency to evaluate the person with whom she or he has found it most difficult to work in a favorable or unfavorable manner. Leaders who perceive this person in negative terms (low LPC leaders) seem primarily concerned with attaining successful task performance. In contrast, those who perceive their least preferred coworker in a positive light (high LPC leaders) seem mainly concerned with establishing good relations with subordinates. (As you can see, this dimension is related to two aspects of leader behavior described previously: initiating structure and showing consideration. These dimensions appear over and over again in systematic studies of leadership. Thus, there seem to be firm grounds for viewing them as very basic aspects of this process.)

Which of these types of leaders—low LPC or high LPC—is more effective? Fiedler's answer is: it depends. And what it depends on, of course, is several situational factors. Specifically, Fiedler suggests that whether low LPC or high LPC leaders are more effective depends on the degree to which the situation is *favorable* to the leader—provides this person with *control* over subordinates. This, in turn, is determined largely by three factors: (1) the nature of the leader's relations with group members (the extent to which he or she enjoys their support and loyalty), (2) the degree of structure in the task being performed (the extent to which task goals and subordinates' roles are clearly defined), and (3) the leader's position power (his or her ability to enforce compliance by subordinates). Combining these three factors, the leader's situational control can range from very high (positive relations with group members, a highly structured task, high position power) to very low (negative relations, an unstructured task, low position power).

Now, to return to the central question: when are different types of leaders most effective? Fiedler suggests that low LPC leaders (ones who are task-oriented) are superior to high LPC leaders (ones who are people-oriented) when situational control is *either* very low or high. In contrast, high LPC leaders have an edge when situational control falls within the moderate range (refer to Figure 11.9 on page 386).

The reasoning behind these predictions is as follows: under conditions of *low* sit-

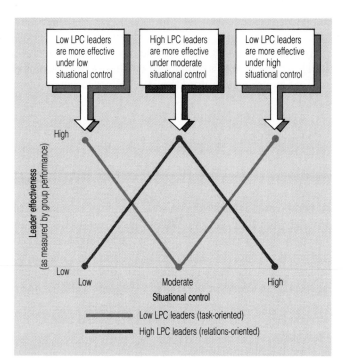

FIGURE 11.9   Contingency Theory: Some Major Predictions

Fiedler's *contingency theory* predicts that low LPC leaders (ones who are primarily task-oriented) will be superior to high LPC leaders (ones who are primarily person-oriented) when situational control is either very low or high. The opposite will be true when situational control is moderate.

uational control, groups need considerable guidance and direction to accomplish their tasks. Since low LPC leaders are more likely to provide such structure than high LPC leaders, they will usually be superior in such cases. Similarly, low LPC leaders also have an edge under conditions that offer the leader a *high* degree of situational control. Here, low LPC leaders realize that conditions are very good, and that successful task performance is virtually assured. As a result, they turn their attention to improving relations with subordinates, and often adopt a relaxed "hands off" style. Subordinates appreciate such treatment, and performance and morale are both enhanced. In contrast, high LPC leaders, feeling that they already enjoy good relations with their subordinates, may shift their attention to task performance. Their attempts to provide guidance in this respect may then be perceived as needless meddling by subordinates, with the result that performance is impaired.

Turning to situations offering the leader *moderate* situational control, conditions are mixed, and attention to good interpersonal relations is often needed. High LPC leaders, with their intrinsic interest in people, often have an important advantage in such cases. In contrast, low LPC leaders, who continue to focus on task performance, may become even more autocratic and directive. The negative reactions of subordinates to such behaviors may then have detrimental effects upon performance.

To repeat: Fiedler's theory predicts that low LPC (task-oriented) leaders will be more effective than high LPC (relations-oriented) leaders under conditions of either low or high situational control. In contrast, high LPC leaders will have an edge under conditions in which situational control is moderate.

Contingency theory: Its current status. Because it directs attention to characteristics of leaders, situational factors, and reactions among subordinates, Fiedler's theory is fully consistent with the modern view of leadership described earlier. Where any scientific theory is concerned, however, the ultimate question must be: how does it fare when put to actual test? For the contingency theory, the answer appears to be "moderately well." One review of more than 170 studies undertaken to test various aspects of Fiedler's theory indicates that most obtained positive results.[30] For example, consider one such study by Chemers and his colleagues.[31]

These investigators reasoned that leaders whose personal style did not match the conditions in their groups (i.e., low LPC leaders with moderate situational control or high LPC leaders with high or low degrees of control) would experience greater job-related stress than leaders whose personal style matched these conditions (i.e., low LPC leaders with high or low control, high LPC leaders with moderate control). To test this hypothesis, Chemers et al. had administrators at a large university complete questionnaires designed to measure their degree of situational control, their standing on the LPC dimension (high or low), and the level of job stress they experienced. As you can see from Figure 11.10, results offered support for the initial hypothesis. Leaders whose personal style did not match the level of situational control they enjoyed reported greater stress than those whose personal style matched this factor.

While such results are encouraging, and lend support to the theory, we should note that not all findings have been consistent with it. In fact, a more recent review suggests that while laboratory studies have tended to support Fiedler's view, field investigations (ones carried out with existing groups operating in a wide range of con-

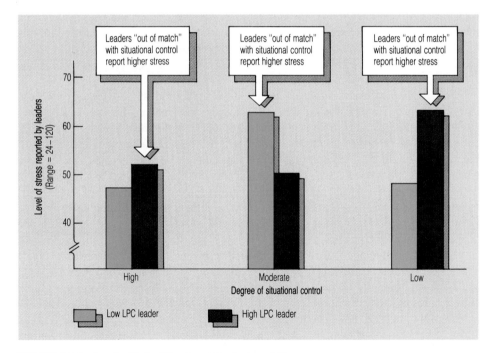

FIGURE 11.10 Leader Style, Situational Control, and Stress

Leaders whose personal style did not match their level of situational control (e.g., high LPC leaders with very low or high control) reported higher levels of stress than leaders whose personal style *did* match such control. (Source: Based on data from Chemers et al., 1985; see Note 31.)

texts) have not been as favorable.[32] Such investigations have sometimes yielded results contrary to what contingency theory would predict. In addition, the theory has been criticized on several important grounds. For example, a degree of ambiguity exists with respect to classifying specific situations along the dimension of situational control.[33] Unless situations can be accurately classified as very low, low, moderate, and so on in this regard, predictions concerning leader effectiveness are difficult to make. Similarly, some critics have questioned the adequacy of the questionnaire used to assess leaders' standing on the LPC dimension. In particular, the reliability of this measure does not seem to be as high as that of other widely used tests.[34]

Taking such criticisms plus existing evidence into account, the following tentative conclusion seems warranted. Contingency theory has indeed added to our understanding of key aspects of leadership and leadership effectiveness. However, several questions about its accuracy remain and require further, detailed attention. In sum, it should be viewed more as a theory still undergoing development and refinement than one that offers a fully valid framework for understanding leader effectiveness.

Cognitive resource theory: An extension of contingency theory to contingency leader abilities. Before concluding this discussion of contingency theory, we should note that Fiedler and Garcia have recently extended it to an issue largely ignored by most theories of leadership: the impact of leader cognitive abilities (e.g., intelligence, problem-solving skills).[35] Their theory, known as **cognitive resource theory,** does not follow directly or simply from contingency theory. However, it adopts the same general approach of seeking to determine under what conditions specific leader traits will or will not contribute to leaders' effectiveness. The basic question posed by cognitive resource theory is this: do leaders' cognitive abilities play a role in determining their success? Common sense seems to suggest a positive reply, but past evidence on this relationship has been mixed. Leader intelligence has been proven related to various measures of leader effectiveness, but only weakly (correlations in the range of .20 to .30). What accounts for these puzzling findings? Fiedler and Garcia suggest that the answer involves a complex interplay between several factors.

First, the relationship between leader intelligence and success depends on the extent to which leaders are *directive.* When they are high on this dimension, their intellectual abilities will be important. This is so because directive leaders issue clearcut instructions or orders to their subordinates. The more intelligent the leaders are, the better the plans, decisions, and strategies behind these directives. In contrast, when leaders are non-directive in style, their intelligence will be far less important in determining their success. This is because non-directive leaders issue few instructions or orders to subordinates. Since such leaders have little impact upon their subordinates, whether they are high or low in intelligence and formulate good or poor plans and decisions cannot matter very much.

Second, Fiedler and Garcia also reason that the link between leader intellectual abilities and group performance is strongly mediated by stress. When stress is low, leaders focus primarily on task-related issues. Then, their intellectual abilities will be closely related to performance. When stress is high, however, leaders' attention may be diverted to matters not directly linked to task performance (e.g., putting out various "fires"). Under such conditions, their intelligence will have little opportunity to affect group performance. Instead, other factors, such as their level of experience and degree of social skills, will be more important. (Please refer to Figure 11.11 for a summary of *cognitive resource theory*.)

Growing evidence supports the accuracy of these proposals. For example, in one study, Army infantry squad leaders reported on the level of stress they experienced with their supervisors.[36] In addition, measures of their intelligence (from Army records)

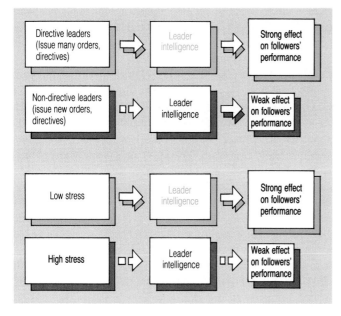

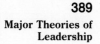

FIGURE 11.11 Cognitive Resource Theory: Some Major Predictions

According to *cognitive resource theory*, leaders' intelligence or other cognitive abilities will strongly affect the performance of their followers only when the leaders are directive and stress is low. When the leaders are non-directive and stress is high, their intelligence will have little impact on followers' performance. (Source: Based on suggestions by Fiedler & Garcia, 1987; see Note 34.)

and ratings of their performance (provided by their superiors) were also obtained. When these factors were correlated, the following pattern emerged. Under conditions of low stress, the squad leaders' intelligence was significantly correlated with their performance. Under conditions of high stress, however, this relationship totally vanished.

Such findings suggest that leaders' intellectual abilities do indeed affect the performance of the groups they head, but only under certain conditions. Thus, as is true with respect to many other aspects of life, high intelligence by itself is no guarantee of success where leadership is concerned. Other factors often determine when, and to what extent, it contributes to effectiveness in this important role.

Normative Theory: Decision Making and Leader Effectiveness

One of the major tasks performed by leaders is making decisions. Indeed, one defining characteristic of leadership positions is that they are where "the buck finally stops" and concrete actions must be taken. Since the decisions reached by leaders often have far-reaching effects on their subordinates, it is clear that one major determinant of leader effectiveness is the adequacy with which they perform this key task. Leaders who make good decisions will be more effective in the long run than leaders who make bad ones. We will consider various strategies leaders (and others) can employ to maximize their chances of making good decisions in chapter 14. Here, we will focus on a different, but equally important question: in reaching decisions, how should leaders behave with respect to their subordinates? Specifically, how much participation should they invite from these persons? As we noted earlier, participation in decision making is an important variable in many organizational settings—one with implications for job satisfaction, stress, and productivity. Thus, it is not surprising to learn that the manner in which leaders handle this issue can be crucial in determining their effectiveness.

But how much participation in decisions by subordinates should leaders allow? Perhaps the most useful answer to this question is provided by the **normative theory** developed by Vroom and Yetton.[37] After careful study of available evidence, these researchers concluded that leaders often adopt one of five distinct methods for reaching decisions. These are summarized in Table 11.2 and as you can see, they cover the entire range from decisions made solely by the leader in a totally autocratic manner through ones that are fully participative in nature.

Are any of these approaches strongly preferable to the others? Vroom and Yetton suggest not. Just as there is no single best style of leadership, there is no single best strategy for making decisions. On the contrary, each pattern offers a mixture of benefits and costs. For example, decisions reached through participative means stand a better chance of gaining support and acceptance among subordinates. However, such decisions require a great deal of time—often, more time than a leader or organization can afford. Similarly, decisions reached autocratically (by the leader alone) can be made more rapidly and efficiently. But such an approach can generate feelings of resentment among followers, and encounter difficulties with respect to actual implementation. According to Vroom and Yetton, then, a major task faced by leaders is selecting the specific decision-making approach that will maximize potential benefits but minimize potential costs. How can this be done? Again, they offer specific suggestions.

Vroom and Yetton propose that leaders should attempt to select the best approach (or at least eliminate ones that are not useful) by answering several basic questions about the situation. These relate primarily to the *quality* of the decision—the extent to which it will affect important group processes such as communication or production, and *acceptance* of the decision—the degree of commitment among subordinates needed for its implementation. For example, with respect to decision quality, a leader should ask such questions as: is a high quality decision required? Do I have enough information to make such a decision? Is the problem well structured? With respect to decision acceptance, he or she should ask: is it crucial for effective implementation that sub-

TABLE 11.2   Potential Strategies for Making Decisions

According to Vroom and Yetton, leaders often adopt one of the five strategies shown here in making decisions.

DECISION STRATEGY	DESCRIPTION
AI (Autocratic)	Leader solves problem or makes decision unilaterally, using available information
AII (Autocratic)	Leader obtains necessary information from subordinates but then makes decision unilaterally
CI (Consultative)	Leader shares the problem with subordinates individually, but then makes decision unilaterally
CII (Consultative)	Leader shares problem with subordinates in group meeting but then makes decision unilaterally
GII (Group Decision)	Leader shares problem with subordinates in a group meeting; decision is reached through discussion to consensus

(Source: Based on suggestions by Vroom & Yetton, 1973; see Note 27.)

ordinates accept the decision? Do subordinates share the organizational goals that will be reached through solution of this problem?

According to the normative model, by answering such questions, and applying specific rules such as those shown in Table 11.3, some of the potential approaches to reaching a given decision will be eliminated. Those that remain constitute a feasible set that can, potentially, be used to reach the necessary decision.

To simplify this process, Vroom and Yetton recommend use of a decision tree such as the one shown in Figure 11.12 (on page 392). To apply this diagram, a manager begins on the left side and responds, in turn, to the questions listed above each letter (A, B, C, and so on). As the manager replies to each question, the set of feasible approaches narrows. For example, imagine that the manager's answers are as follows:

Question A: Yes—a high quality decision is needed.
Question B: No—the leader does not have sufficient information to make a high-quality decision alone.
Question C: No—the problem is not structured.
Question D: Yes—acceptance by subordinates is crucial to implementation.
Question E: No—if the leader makes the decision alone, it may not be accepted by subordinates.
Question F: No—subordinates do not share organizational goals.
Question G: Yes—conflict among subordinates is likely to result from the decision.

As you can see, these replies lead to the conclusion that only one decision-making approach is feasible: full participation by subordinates. (The path leading to this conclusion is shown in color in Figure 9.12.) Of course, different answers to any of the seven key questions would have led to different conclusions.

The Vroom and Yetton model is highly appealing for several reasons. It takes full

TABLE 11.3 Decision Rules in Normative Theory
By using the rules suggested here, leaders can eliminate decision-making strategies that are likely to prove ineffective in a given situation.

RULES DESIGNED TO PROTECT DECISION QUALITY

Leader Information Rule   If the quality of the decision is important and you do not have enough information or expertise to solve the problem alone, eliminate an autocratic style.

Goal Congruence Rule   If the quality of the decision is important and subordinates are not likely to make the right decision, rule out the highly participative style.

Unstructured Problem Rule   If the quality of the decision is important but you lack sufficient information and expertise *and* the problem is unstructured, eliminate the autocratic leadership styles.

RULES DESIGNED TO PROTECT DECISION ACCEPTANCE

Acceptance Rule   If acceptance by subordinates is crucial for effective implementation, eliminate the autocratic styles.

Conflict Rule   If acceptance by subordinates is crucial for effective implementation, and they hold conflicting opinions over the means of achieving some objective, eliminate autocratic styles.

Fairness Rule   If the quality of the decision is unimportant but acceptance *is* important, use the most participatory style.

Acceptance Priority Rule   If acceptance is critical and not certain to result from autocratic decisions, and if subordinates are not motivated to achieve the organization's goals, use a highly participative style.

(Source: Based on suggestions by Vroom and Yetton, 1973; see Note 27.)

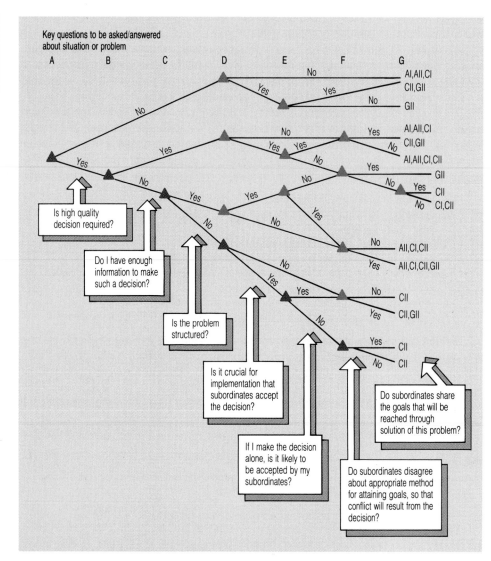

FIGURE 11.12 Choosing the Most Effective Strategy for Making Decisions
By answering the seven questions listed here and tracing a path through this *decision tree*, leaders can identify the most effective approaches to making decisions in a specific situation. Note: the path suggested by the answers to questions A–G provided on page 391 is shown by the rose-colored triangles. (Source: Based on suggestions by Vroom & Yetton, 1973; see Note 27.)

account of the importance of subordinate participation in decisions and offers leaders clear guidance for choosing among various methods for reaching decisions. As with any theory, though, the key question remains: is it valid? Are its suggestions concerning the most effective style of decision making under various conditions really accurate? The results of several studies designed to test the model have been encouraging in these respects.

First, it has been found that practicing managers rate their own past decisions as more successful when they are based on procedures falling within the set of feasible options identified by the model than when they fall outside this set of methods.[38] Second, when small groups of subjects reach decisions through methods falling within the feasible set identified by the model, these decisions are judged to be more effective by outside raters than when they are made through other methods.[39] Finally, store managers who made decisions in accordance with the basic principles of the model (even without formal training in its use) run more profitable operations than managers who do not seem to function in this manner.

Together, these findings suggest that the Vroom and Yetton model offers important insights into a key aspect of leader effectiveness. We should note, however, that other research findings suggest the need for adjustments in the theory. First, findings reported by Heilman and her colleagues suggest that most persons prefer a participative approach to decision making even under conditions where the model recommends a more autocratic approach.[40] Second, leaders and subordinates seem to differ in their reactions to various methods for reaching decisions. Leaders tend to prefer those methods suggested by the normative model in a given situation, while subordinates tend to prefer participative strategies in all cases.[41] Third, it appears that certain characteristics of leaders may play a key role in determining the relative effectiveness of various decision strategies. Evidence concerning this latter suggestion has recently been reported by Crouch and Yetton.[42]

These investigators focused on the *conflict rule* presented in Table 11.3. This rule suggests that in situations where conflicting opinions exist among subordinates over the means of reaching some goal, and acceptance of the decision is important for its implementation, a participative approach to decision making is best. Crouch and Yetton note that while many managers view this rule as accurate, others express reservations about its use. Specifically, such managers believe that the use of participative strategies in conflict laden situations can backfire, producing negative rather than positive effects (e.g., it may reduce subordinate performance). In view of these concerns, Crouch and Yetton reasoned that perhaps a personal characteristic of managers—their ability to handle interpersonal conflict—is crucial in such cases. When managers are high in this ability, a participative strategy is indeed useful, as the normative model suggests. However, when managers are low in this ability, a more autocratic approach, which avoids face-to-face confrontations, may be preferable.

To test these predictions, Crouch and Yetton asked a large group of employees to rate the conflict management skills of their managers. Ratings included items designed to assess each managers' skills in encouraging suggestions, maintaining an open mind, and willingness to listen to input from others. In addition, the managers rated the job performance of their subordinates. Finally, the same managers completed another measure which assessed their tendencies to employ participative rather than autocratic styles of decision making. Crouch and Yetton predicted that for managers relatively high in conflict handling skills, the greater their tendency to employ participative decision making, the higher their subordinates' performance. However, for managers low in conflict handling skills, the opposite would be true. As shown in Figure 11.13 (on page 394), both predictions were confirmed. These findings suggest that managers in the first group (ones with good conflict handling skills) would be wise to employ participative strategies for reaching decisions, while those in the second might attain greater success using more autocratic strategies.

To conclude: existing evidence suggests that the normative theory offers useful guidelines to leaders for choosing the most effective approach to decision making. However, adjustments in the model designed to take account of strong, general preferences for participative procedures, differences in the perspectives of leaders and subordinates, and the personal skills or traits of leaders seem necessary. With the incorporation of such modifications, the Vroom and Yetton model may prove very helpful in our efforts to understand this key aspect of leader effectiveness.

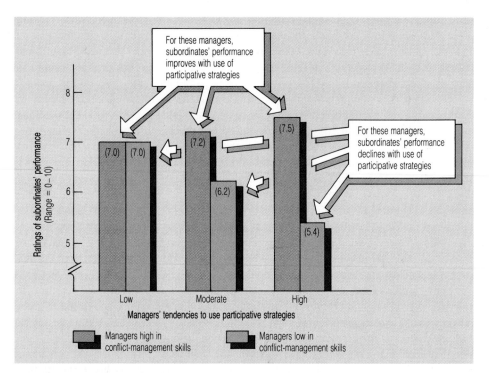

FIGURE 11.13   Conflict Handling Skills and Decision-Making Strategies

For managers rated by their subordinates as high in the ability to handle interpersonal conflict, the greater their tendencies to use participative strategies of decision making, the higher the subordinates' performance. For managers rated as low in ability to handle conflict, the opposite was true. These findings suggest that personal characteristics of leaders may play an important role in determining the most effective approach to making decisions. (Source: Based on data from Crouch & Yetton, 1987; see Note 42.)

Path-Goal Theory: Leaders as Guides to Valued Goals

Suppose you conducted an informal survey in which you asked one hundred people to indicate what they expect from their leaders. What kind of answers would you receive? While they would vary greatly, one common theme you might uncover would be, "I expect my leader to *help*—to assist me in reaching goals I feel are important." In short, many people would report that they expect their leaders to aid them in attaining valued goals.

This basic idea plays a central role in House's path-goal theory of leadership.[43] In general terms, the theory contends that subordinates will react favorably to a leader only to the extent that they perceive this person as helping them progress toward various goals by clarifying actual paths to such rewards. More specifically, the theory contends that actions by a leader which clarify the nature of tasks and reduce or eliminate obstacles will increase perceptions on the part of subordinates that working hard will lead to good performance and that good performance, in turn, will be recognized and rewarded. Under such conditions, House suggests, job satisfaction, motivation, and actual performance will all be enhanced. (As you can see, this **path-goal theory** of leadership is closely related to expectancy theory; refer to our discussion of this theory in chapter 3.)

How, precisely, can leaders best accomplish these tasks? The answer, as in other modern views of leadership, is, *it depends*. And what it depends upon is a complex interaction between key aspects of *leader behavior* and certain *contingency* factors. With respect to leader behavior, path-goal theory suggests that leaders can adopt four basic styles:

- *instrumental* (directive): an approach focused on providing specific guidance, establishing work schedules and rules
- *supportive:* a style focused on establishing good relations with subordinates and satisfying their needs
- *participative:* a pattern in which the leader consults with subordinates, permitting them to participate in decisions
- *achievement-oriented:* an approach in which the leader sets challenging goals and seeks improvements in performance

By the way, these styles are not mutually exclusive; in fact, the same leader can adopt them at different times and in different situations. Indeed, showing such flexibility is one important step toward being an effective leader.

Which of these contrasting styles is best for maximizing subordinate satisfaction and motivation? This depends on the *contingency factors* mentioned above. First, the style of choice is strongly affected by several *characteristics of subordinates.* For example, if followers are high in ability, an instrumental style of leadership may be unnecessary; instead, a less structured, supportive one may be preferable. On the other hand, if subordinates are low in ability, the opposite may be true; such persons need considerable guidance to help them attain their goals. Similarly, persons high in need for affiliation (i.e., close, friendly ties with others) may strongly prefer a supportive or participative style of leadership. Ones who are high in the need for achievement may strongly prefer an achievement-oriented leader.

Second, the most effective leadership style also depends on several aspects of *work environments.* For example, path-goal theory predicts that when tasks are unstructured and nonroutine, an instrumental approach by the leader may be best; much clarification and guidance is needed. However, when tasks are structured and highly routine, such leadership may actually get in the way of good performance, and may be resented by subordinates who think the leader is engaging in unnecessary meddling. (Please see Figure 11.14 for an overview of all these aspects of path-goal theory.)

Path-goal theory has been subjected to empirical testing in several studies.[44] In general, results have been consistent with major predictions derived from the theory,

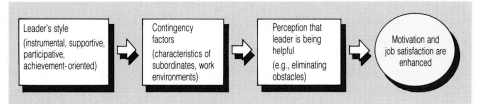

FIGURE 11.14 Path-goal Theory: An Overview
According to *path-goal theory*, perceptions among employees that leaders are helping them to reach valued goals enhance both their motivation and job satisfaction. Such perceptions, in turn, are fostered when a leader's style is consistent with the needs and characteristics of subordinates (e.g., their level of experience, achievement motivation) and aspects of the work environment (e.g., requirements of the tasks being performed). (Source: Based on suggestions by House, 1979; see Note 28.)

although not uniformly so. Thus, at present, path-goal theory appears to be another framework offering valuable insights into leadership and the many factors that determine the degree to which individual leaders are successful in this role.

ADDITIONAL PERSPECTIVES ON LEADERSHIP: THE VERTICAL DYAD LINKAGE MODEL, SUBSTITUTES FOR LEADERSHIP, AND SITUATIONAL LEADERSHIP THEORY

Because it is widely viewed as a central organizational process, leadership has long been the subject of extensive study in OB. Yet, recent years seem to have brought an acceleration in both the scope and volume of such work. In this final section, we will review several of the newer perspectives that have grown out of this research. Each is unique, but together they add appreciably to our understanding of the nature and impact of leadership.

The VDL Model: The Importance of Leader-Follower Exchanges

Do leaders treat all their subordinates in the same manner? Informal observation suggests that clearly, they do not. Yet many theories of leadership tend to ignore this basic fact. They discuss leadership style or behavior in terms that suggest similar actions toward all subordinates. The importance of potential differences in this respect are brought into sharp focus by the **vertical dyad linkage** model developed by Dansereau, Graen, and Haga.[45]

This theory suggests that leaders form distinct exchange relationships with each of their subordinates. Within these exchange relationships, leaders offer valued outcomes such as advice, support, inviting input into decisions, and open communication, while subordinates reciprocate with increased commitment, loyalty, and effort. While leaders form such relationships with all of their subordinates, the nature of these dyadic exchanges can differ sharply. At one extreme, the leader holds positive views about a subordinate who, in turn, feels that the leader understands his or her problems, appreciates his or her potential, and is willing to offer help and support when these are needed. At the other end of the continuum, the leader holds negative views about the subordinate who, in turn, has little faith or confidence in the leader. According to the VDL model, such differences in the quality of leader-member relations can have powerful effects on the performance, job satisfaction, and even career development of subordinates.[46]

To the extent this is true—and a growing body of research evidence suggests that it is—the next question is obvious: can any steps be taken to improve individual leader-member relations? The answer appears to be yes. For example, in one study on this topic, supervisors in a large government department underwent special training designed to equip them with skills that would help them establish positive relations with subordinates.[47] Before, and again after, the training was completed, the subordinates of these persons completed questionnaires on which they rated the quality of their relationships with their supervisors, their satisfaction with his or her leadership, and their satisfaction with their jobs. Results indicated that the special training did indeed help: subordinates reported higher satisfaction and better relations with their leaders after these persons had completed the training. In addition, as VDL theory suggests, the gains in these respects were greater for subordinates who initially reported poor relations with their supervisors than for those who initially reported good relations.

These findings, and those of related studies, suggest that attention to the relations (dyadic exchanges) between leaders and specific followers can be very useful. Such relations, it seems, vary greatly even within relatively small work groups. And their nature can strongly affect the morale, commitment, and performance of employees. Helping leaders to improve such relations, therefore, can be of practical value in several respects. (Do leader-subordinate relations have similar effects in different cultures? For evidence relating to this issue, please see the **International Perspective** section below.)

OB: AN INTERNATIONAL PERSPECTIVE

Getting on the Fast Career Track in Japan: The Role of Leader-Subordinate Exchanges

There is general agreement that managers in large Japanese corporations are among the very best in the world. In part, this view seems to derive from the fact that Japanese organizations are highly adept at selecting the best of their young employees for promotion to positions of increasing power and authority. How do they accomplish this task with such success? Or, turning the question around a bit, what factors are predictive of entering the "fast track" for promotion in Japanese companies? Revealing evidence on this important issue has recently been reported by Wakabayashi, Graen, and their colleagues.[48]

This study was actually part of a long-term, longitudinal investigation of the careers of Japanese managers. The study began in 1972, and is continuing at the present time. In it, a number of different variables have been examined as potential predictors of career success and performance. These include (1) the quality of leader-member exchanges (subjects' ratings of the extent to which their supervisor is approachable, uses his authority to help them solve problems, and shares social or leisure activities with them); (2) the managers' job performance (rated by their supervisors); (3) their assessed potential (when first hired); (4) the ranking (quality) of their university; and (5) their first job assignment. These and several other factors (all measured during the first three years after initial hiring) were used to predict the speed of promotion, rated promotability, and salaries of eighty-five male managers at two times: seven and thirteen years after their initial hiring. Two models of career development among Japanese managers were assessed in this manner. One model suggests that individuals are selected for the "fast" or "slow"

tracks relatively early in their careers (within the first few years). The other suggests that this selection does not occur until somewhat later—perhaps seven years or more after they enter the company.

The study itself was highly sophisticated, and results are, of necessity, quite complex. Here, we'll focus primarily on those that emerged most clearly or consistently. First, the total pattern of findings supported the early career choice model. Apparently, individuals are selected for fairly rapid or somewhat slower promotion quite early in their careers. Second, several factors seem to predict such outcomes. Perhaps the most important of these is, as VDL theory would suggest, the nature of leader-subordinate vertical exchanges. Individuals who indicated that such exchanges were largely positive attained promotion more rapidly than those who reported exchanges of a less favorable nature. Early job performance, too, was an important predictor of such outcomes, although its impact was somewhat less than that of vertical exchanges. Interestingly, the ranking of the managers' university and the nature of their first job added little to predictions of career development; apparently these are less important predictors of such outcomes.

Together, these and other findings suggest that individuals who are able to develop good working relations with their supervisors are the most likely to be selected, early in their careers, for entry into the "fast" managerial track. While good job performance or early rated potential can compensate for a lack of these skills to some degree, they are not, by themselves, sufficient to overcome this handicap. These findings, and others relating to VDL theory, offer an important message for persons interested in personal success in a managerial role: concentrate, as much as you can, on developing positive relations with your supervisor. To the extent you do, and succeed in this task, your career may well live up to your most optimistic predictions (see Figure 11.15).

FIGURE 11.15 Positive Vertical Exchanges: One Ingredient in Success

Growing evidence suggests that managers who enjoy positive exchange relations with their supervisors are more likely to attain success than managers whose relations with supervisors are less favorable. These findings are consistent with suggestions derived from VDL theory.

Substitutes for Leadership

Throughout this chapter, we have emphasized the following point: leaders are important. Their style, actions, and degree of effectiveness all exert major effects upon subordinates and, ultimately, upon organizations. In many cases, this is certainly true. Yet, almost everyone has observed or been part of groups in which the designated leaders actually had little influence—groups in which these people were mere figureheads with little impact on subordinates. One explanation for such situations involves the characteristics of the leaders in question: they are simply weak and unsuited for their jobs. Another, and in some ways more intriguing, possibility is as follows: in some contexts, other factors may actually *substitute* for a leader's influence, making it superfluous.

According to a framework developed by Kerr and Jermier, many different variables can produce such effects.[49] First, a high level of knowledge, commitment, or experience on the part of subordinates may make it unnecessary for anyone to tell them what to do or how to proceed. Second, jobs themselves may be structured in ways that make direction and influence from a leader redundant. Third, work norms and strong feelings of cohesion among employees may directly affect job performance and render the presence of a leader unnecessary. Fourth, the technology associated with certain jobs may strongly determine the decisions and actions of persons performing them, and so leave little room for input from a leader.

Evidence for these assertions has been obtained in several recent studies. For example, in an investigation conducted by Sheridan, Vredenburgh, and Abelson, nurses' job performance (as rated by their supervisors) was more strongly affected by many factors that might, potentially, serve as substitutes for leadership (e.g., the type of technology available, group norms concerning the quality of care) than by their supervisors' leadership style or behavior.[50]

If leaders are, in fact, superfluous in many situations, why has this fact often been overlooked? One possibility, suggested by Meindl and Erhlich, is that we have a strong tendency to "romanticize" leadership—to perceive it as more important and more closely linked to performance in many contexts than is actually the case.[51] To test this suggestion, Meindl and Ehrlich presented M.B.A. students with information about an imaginary firm, including a five year summary of selected indicators of its performance (e.g., total sales, profit margins, net earnings, stock price). Attached to these data was a paragraph describing the firm's key operating strengths. The content of this paragraph was varied, so that four different groups of subjects received four different versions. These attributed the firm's performance to its top-level management team, the quality of its employees, changing patterns of consumer needs and preferences, or federal regulatory policies, respectively.

After reading one of these paragraphs and examining other information about the firm, subjects rated two aspects of its overall performance: profitability and risk. Meindl and Ehrlich reasoned that because of the tendency to overestimate the importance of leadership, subjects would rate the firm more favorably when its performance was attributed to top-level management than when it was attributed to any of the other factors. As you can see from Figure 11.16, this was precisely what occurred. The imaginary company was rated as higher in profitability and lower in risk when subjects had read the leadership-based paragraph than when they had read any of the others.

These findings, plus others obtained by the same researchers, help explain why leaders are often viewed as important and necessary even when, to a large degree, they are superfluous. Please note: this in no way implies that leaders are usually unimportant. On the contrary, they often *do* play a key role in work groups and organizations. However, this is not always so, and their necessity should never be taken for granted.

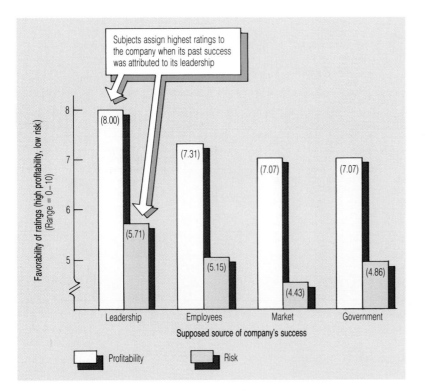

FIGURE 11.16 Leadership: Evidence that We Overestimate Its Importance

Subjects who received information suggesting that an imaginary company's past success was attributable to its top management rated the company more favorably (higher in profitability, lower in risk) than subjects who received information suggesting that the identical record had stemmed from other causes. These findings offer support for the view that we tend to perceive leadership as even more important than it actually is. (Source: Based on data from Meindl & Ehrlich, 1987; see Note 51.)

Situational Leadership Theory: Follower Maturity and Leadership Style

Consider an organization with a stable workforce. As time passes, many persons—including leaders and their subordinates—will work together for years or even decades. Since change is indeed the only constant where human beings are concerned, these individuals, and their relationships, will alter over time. One such change involves increasing maturity on the part of subordinates. As these persons grow older and obtain more job-related experience, they will become more mature in many respects. Will such shifts be reflected in their needs for various types of leadership? According to a theory proposed by Hersey and Blanchard, they will.[52] In a view known as **situational leadership theory,** these authors propose the following sequence. Initially, when subordinates' maturity is relatively low, their need for directive actions by the leader (initiating structure) will be high. Later, as they master their jobs, their need for emotional support (showing consideration) will increase. Finally, as they attain full maturity, the need for this, too, will decrease. Then, supervisory actions by their leader will become superfluous in many respects. (Refer to Figure 11.17 for a summary of these suggestions.)

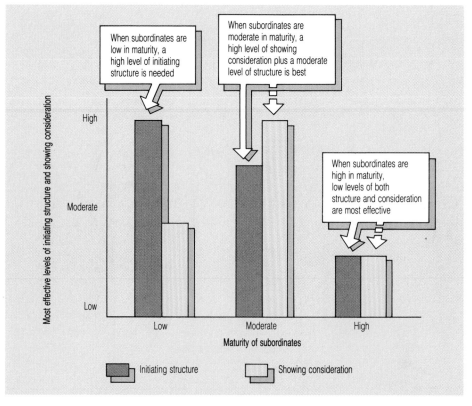

FIGURE 11.17 Situational Leadership Theory: A Summary

According to *situational leadership theory,* the most effective style of leadership changes as subordinates increase in maturity. At first, an approach high in initiating structure but low in showing consideration is best. Later, as subordinates become more mature, a style high in showing consideration but moderate in initiating structure is preferable. Finally, when subordinates attain a high degree of maturity, a leadership style low in both factors is best. (Source: Based on suggestions by Hersey & Blanchard, 1982; see Note 52.)

Are these assertions about the changing course of leadership requirements over time accurate? Situational leadership theory is quite new, so little evidence about it currently exists.[53] However, a study conducted by Vecchio offers at least some support for its usefulness.[54] In this investigation, Vecchio had several hundred high school teachers complete questionnaires designed to measure their perceptions of their leaders' (principals) behavior. Specifically, teachers indicated the extent to which the principals engaged in initiating structure and showing consideration. In addition, they also reported on the quality of their exchanges with their principals, and on their satisfaction with their principals' leadership. The principals also took part in the study. They rated the maturity and job performance of the teachers working under their supervision.

Situational leadership theory predicts that subordinates will demonstrate the highest performance and express the greatest satisfaction when their leader's style matches their own level of maturity. In order to test this prediction Vecchio divided the teachers into two groups: those whose leader's style matched their level of maturity and those whose leader's style did not match. Then, he compared the performance and self-rated satisfaction of teachers in the two groups. Consistent with predictions derived from the theory, teachers in the first category generally reported higher satisfaction, and received higher performance ratings, than those in the latter. However, these findings were clearest for teachers who were relatively low in maturity; they did not occur among those who were high in maturity.

Taken together, these findings suggest that situational leadership theory may be most applicable to newly hired employees—ones who require a high degree of structuring from their supervisors. However, it may be less applicable to more experienced, and more mature, individuals. Whatever its ultimate fate, the theory does emphasize an important fact: a style of leadership that is adaptive and successful at one point in time may not necessarily be so at others. Thus, once more, we are left with the same basic message for leaders or would-be leaders: *flexibility* is, perhaps, the most effective route to success.

SUMMARY AND REVIEW

Leadership: Some Basic Issues. Leadership is the process whereby one individual influences other group members toward the attainment of defined group or organizational goals. Leaders generally use noncoercive forms of influence and are influenced, in turn, by their followers. Not all managers function as leaders. Conversely, not all leaders are managers. Thus, the two terms should not be treated as synonyms.

Leader Traits and Leader Behaviors. In the past, it was assumed that leaders possessed key traits that set them apart from other persons. Efforts to identify such traits, however, generally failed. While leaders and followers may indeed differ in several respects, these differences are smaller and more subtle in nature than was once believed.

Leaders differ greatly in their style or approach to leadership. One key dimension involves the extent to which leaders are *directive* or *permissive* toward subordinates. Another involves the extent to which they are **participative** or **autocratic** in their decision making. Leaders also vary along two other key dimensions: concern with, and efforts to attain, successful task performance (**initiating structure**) and concern with maintaining favorable personal relations with subordinates (**consideration**). Organizational factors (e.g., technology, the presence and strength of unions) can strongly determine leaders' behavior.

Major Theories of Leadership. Major theories of leadership differ in many respects, but share a concern with the determinants of leader effectiveness. Fiedler's **contingency theory** suggests that both a leader's characteristics and situational factors are crucial. Task-oriented leaders are more effective than person-oriented ones under conditions where the leader has either high or low control over the group. In contrast, person-oriented leaders are more effective under conditions where the leader has moderate control. A second theory, Vroom and Yetton's **normative theory,** focuses on decision making as a key determinant of leader effectiveness. According to this theory, different situations call for different styles of decision making (e.g., autocratic, consultative, participative) by leaders. Recent evidence suggests that personal characteristics of leaders, too, are important in determining which of these styles is best. A third major theory of leadership, **path-goal theory,** suggests that leaders' behavior will be accepted by subordinates and will enhance their motivation, only to the extent that it helps them progress toward valued goals and provides guidance or clarification not already present in work settings.

Additional Theoretical Perspectives. The **vertical dyad linkage (VDL)** theory calls attention to the fact that leaders often have different relationships with different subordinates. These relationships, in turn, may strongly affect subordinates' satisfaction, performance, and perceptions of the leader. The quality of young managers' relations with their supervisors has been found to affect the course of their careers.

Growing evidence suggests that under some conditions (e.g., when subordinates are highly skilled or committed), directives or guidance from a leader may be superfluous. Such conditions are termed **substitutes for leadership.** The fact that leaders are unnecessary in at least some situations has often been overlooked because of our strong tendency to "romanticize" leadership—to perceive it as more important than it actually is. The **situational theory of leadership** calls attention to the fact that as they mature, followers may require different styles of leadership from their managers. Inexperienced subordinates may require a high level of structuring by their leaders. Ones who are moderately mature may require a high level of social and emotional support (showing consideration). However, those who are fully mature may require low levels of both types of behavior on the part of their leaders.

KEY TERMS

autocratic (leadership style): A style of leadership in which the leader makes all decisions unilaterally.

charisma: See charismatic leaders.

charismatic leaders: Leaders who exert powerful effects upon their followers and to whom special traits are attributed (e.g., possession of an idealized vision or goal, willingness to engage in unconventional behaviors to reach it).

cognitive resource theory: A theory of leadership concerned primarily with the impact of leaders' cognitive abilities upon the performance of their groups.

consideration: Actions by a leader that demonstrate concern with the welfare of subordinates and establish positive relations with them. Leaders who focus primarily on this task are often described as demonstrating a person-oriented style.

contingency theory: A theory suggesting that leader effectiveness is determined both by characteristics of leaders and by the level of situational control they are able to exert over subordinates.

great person theory: The view that leaders possess special *traits* that set them apart from others, and that these traits are responsible for their assuming positions of power and authority.

initiating structure: Activities by a leader designed to enhance productivity or task performance. Leaders who focus primarily on these goals are described as demonstrating a task-oriented style.

leaders: Individuals within groups or organizations who wield the most influence over others.

leadership: The process whereby one individual influences other group members toward the attainment of defined group or organizational goals.

normative theory: A theory of leader effectiveness focusing primarily on strategies for choosing the most effective approach to making decisions.

participative (leadership style): A style of leadership in which the leader permits subordinates to take part in decision making, and also permits them a considerable degree of autonomy with respect to the completion of routine work activities.

path-goal theory: A theory of leadership suggesting that subordinates will be motivated by a leader only to the extent they perceive this individual as helping them to attain valued goals.

situational approach (to leadership): A view suggesting that persons whose abilities and skills most closely meet the needs of a given situation are most likely to rise to positions of power and authority.

situational leadership theory: A theory suggesting that the most effective style of leadership varies with the maturity or experience of subordinates.

substitutes for leadership: The view that high levels of skill among subordinates or certain features of technology and organizational structure sometimes serve as substitutes for leaders, rendering their guidance or influence superfluous.

vertical dyad linkage (VDL): A theory suggesting that leaders form different relations with various subordinates and that the nature of such dyadic exchanges can exert strong effects on subordinates' performance and satisfaction.

QUESTIONS FOR DISCUSSION

1. It has often been said that "leaders are born, not made." Do you agree? If so, why? If not, why?

2. Are charismatic leaders really different from other leaders, or is this mostly just an illusion?

3. Under what conditions are person-oriented leaders more effective than task-oriented leaders and vice versa?

4. Suppose that a leader's personality or style of leadership does not seem to match the situation in which he or she must operate. Can the leader's style be changed so as to produce a better match?

5. Under what conditions would a leader obtain better results by making decisions in an autocratic rather than in a participative manner?

6. In your experience, do most leaders have a small "in-group"? If so, what are the effects of this clique upon other group members?

7. What style of leadership would be best for a newly formed group that was just "learning the ropes" with respect to its tasks and functions?

NOTES

1. Motowidlo, S. (in press). Leadership and leadership processes. In M. D. Dunnette (Ed.), *Handbook of industrial/organizational psychology* (2nd ed.). Palo Alto, CA: Consulting Psychologists Press.

2. Bass, B. M. (1981). *Stogdill's handbook of leadership: A survey of theory and research.* New York: Free Press.

3. Hollander, E. P. (1985). Leadership and power. In G. Lindzey & E. Aronson (Eds.), *The handbook of social psychology,* 3rd ed., (vol. 2, pp. 485–537). New York: Random House.

4. Cialdini, R. B. (1988). *Influence* (2nd ed.). Glenview, IL: Scott, Foresman.

5. Geier, J. G. (1969). A trait approach to the study of leadership in small groups. *Journal of Communication, 17,* 316–323.

6. Stogdill, R. (1974). *Handbook of leadership.* New York: Free Press.

7. See Note 5.

8. See Note 6.

9. McClelland, D. C., & Boyatzis, R. E. (1982). Leadership motive pattern and long-term succession management. *Journal of Applied Psychology, 67,* 737–743.

10. Costantini, E., & Craik, K. H. (1980). Personality and politicians: California party leaders 1960–1976. *Journal of Personality and Social Psychology, 38,* 646–661.

11. Conger, J. A., & Kanungo, R. N. (1987). Toward a behavioral theory of charismatic leadership in organizational settings. *Academy of Management Review, 12,* 637–647.

12. Muczyk, J. P., & Reimann, B. C. (1987). The case for directive leadership. *Academy of Management Executive, 1,* 301–311.

13. See Note 12.

14. Likert, R. (1961). *New patterns in management.* New York: McGraw-Hill.

15. See Note 4.

16. Weissenberg, P., & Kavanagh, M. H. (1972). The independence of initiating structure and consideration: A review of the evidence. *Personnel Psychology, 25,* 119–130.

17. Vroom, V. H. (1976). Leadership. In M. D. Dunnette (Ed.), *Handbook of industrial/organizational psychology.* Palo Alto, CA: Consulting Psychologists Press.

18. Blake, R. R., & Mouton, J. S. (1978). *The new managerial grid.* Houston: Gulf.

19. Blake, R. R., & Mouton, J. S. (1985). *The managerial grid III.* Houston: Gulf.

20. Tjosvold, D. (1984). Effects of leader warmth and directiveness on subordinate performance on a subsequent task. *Journal of Applied Psychology, 69,* 222–232.

21. Hammer, T. H., & Turk, J. M. (1987). Organizational determinants of leader behavior and authority. *Journal of Applied Psychology, 72,* 674–682.

22. Pfeffer, J., & Salancik, G. R. (1978). *The external control of organizations: A resource dependence perspective.* New York: Harper & Row.

23. See Note 11.

24. Conger, J. A., & Kanungo, R. N. (1988). *Charismatic leadership: The elusive factor in organizational effectiveness.* San Francisco: Jossey-Bass.

25. See Note 24.

26. Fiedler, F. E. (1978). Contingency model and the leadership process. In L. Berkowitz (Ed.), *Advances in experimental social psychology,* vol. 11. New York: Academic Press.

27. Vroom, V. H., & Yetton, P. W. (1973). *Leadership and decision-making.* Pittsburgh: Univ. Pittsburgh Press.

28. House, R. J., & Baetz, M. L. (1979). Leadership: Some generalizations and new research directions. In B. M. Staw (Ed.), *Research in organizational behavior.* Greenwich, CT: JAI Press.

29. See Note 26.

30. Strube, M. J., & Garcia, J. E. (1981). A meta-analytic investigation of Fiedler's contingency model of leadership effectiveness. *Psychological Bulletin, 90,* 307–321.

31. Chemers, M. M., Hays, R. B., Rhodewalt, F., & Wysocki, J. (1985). A person-environment analysis of job stress: A contingency model explanation. *Journal of Personality and Social Psychology, 49,* 628–635.

32. Peters, L. H., Hartke, D. D., & Pohlman, J. T. (1985). Fiedler's contingency theory of leadership: An application of the meta-analysis procedures of Schmidt and Hunter. *Psychological Bulletin, 97,* 274–285.

33. Ashour, A. S. (1973). The contingency model of leadership effectiveness: An evaluation. *Organizational Behavior and Human Performance, 9,* 339–355.

34. Fiedler, F. E., & Garcia, J. E. (1987). *Leadership: Cognitive resources and performance.* New York: Wiley.

35. Fiedler, F. E., & Leister, A. F. (1977). Leader intelligence and task performance: A test of a multiple screen model. *Organizational Behavior and Human Performance, 20,* 1–14.

36. See Note 27.

37. Vroom, V. H., & Jago, A. G. (1978). On the validity of the Vroom–Yetton model. *Journal of Applied Psychology, 63,* 151–162.

38. Field, R. H. (1982). A test of the Vroom–Yetton normative model of leadership. *Journal of Applied Psychology, 67,* 523–532.

39. See Note 27.

40. Heilman, M. E., Hornstein, H. A., Cage, J. H., & Herschlag, J. K. (1984). Reactions to prescribed leader behavior as a function of role perspective: The case of the Vroom–Yetton model. *Journal of Applied Psychology, 69,* 50–60.

41. See Note 40.

42. Crouch, A., & Yetton, P. (1987). Manager behavior, leadership style, and subordinate performance: An empirical extension of the Vroom–Yetton conflict rule. *Organizational Behavior and Human Decision Processes, 39,* 384–396.

43. See Note 28.

44. Schriesheim, C. A., & Denisi, A. S. (1981). Task dimensions as moderators of the effects of instrumental leadership: A two-sample replicated test of path-goal leadership theory. *Journal of Applied Psychology, 66,* 589–597.

45. Dansereau, G., Graen, G., & Haga, B. (1975). A vertical dyad linkage approach to leadership within formal organizations: A longitudinal investigation of the role making process. *Organizational Behavior and Human Performance, 13,* 45–78.

46. Graen, G. B., & Scandura, T. A. (1987). Vertical dyad linkages theory of leadership. In A. Kiesler, G. Reber, & R. Wunderer (Eds.), *Encyclopedia of Leadership* (pp. 378–390). Kernerstrasse, FRG: C. E. Paeschel Verlag.

47. Scandura, T. A., & Graen, G. B. (1984). Moderating effects of initial leader-member exchange status on the effects of a leadership intervention. *Journal of Applied Psychology, 69,* 428–436.

48. Wakabayashi, M., Graen, G., & Graen, M. (1988). Japanese management progress: Mobility into middle management. *Journal of Applied Psychology, 73,* 217–227.

49. Kerr, S., & Jermier, J. M. (1978). Substitutes for leadership: Their meaning and measurement. *Organizational Behavior and Human Performance, 22,* 375–403.

50. Sheridan, J. E., Vredenburgh, D. J., & Abelson, M. A. (1984). Contextual model of leadership influence in hospital units. *Academy of Management Journal, 27,* 57–78.

51. Meindl, J. R., & Ehrlich, S. B. (1987). The romance of leadership and the evaluation of organizational performance. *Academy of Management Journal, 30,* 91–109.

52. Hersey, P., & Blanchard, K. (1982). *Management of organizational behavior* (4th ed.). Englewood Cliffs, NJ: Prentice-Hall.

53. Hambleton, R. K., & Gumpert, R. (1982). The validity of Hersey and Blanchard's theory of leader effectiveness. *Group and Organization Studies, 7,* 225–242.

54. Vecchio, R. P. (1987). Situational leadership theory: An examination of a prescriptive theory. *Journal of Applied Psychology, 72,* 444–451.

Leadership by Example

Harry V. Quadracci often contemplated the qualities and actions necessary to be a successful leader. However, in his job as Vice President and Corporate Council of a large printing company, he had somewhat limited opportunity to implement his ideas. Despite his lack of leadership experience, Quadracci quit his job to start his own printing company. That company, now almost twenty years old and successful by all measures, is Quad/Graphics of Pewaukee, Wisconsin. Their primary customers are magazines such as *U.S. News & World Report, Newsweek,* and *Playboy.*[1]

Early in the firm's existence, crucial business decisions regarding operations and finance occupied most of Quadracci's time and energy. Soon, however, the situation stabilized and Quadracci's views on leadership were developed, tested, and successfully adopted. His most fundamental belief about leadership is that it must be based on the "concept of individual initiative and responsibility."[2] Numerous incidents illustrate that the employees of Quad/Graphics understand and accept this mandate. Perhaps the two examples that best illustrate the concept involve "Spring Fling" and the marijuana firings.

Spring Fling is an annual happening. Although it is now ritual, it started out almost by accident. At the time, May 1974, Quadracci had planned to shut down the printing plant for a day so that top management could have an opportunity to get together outside the office to do some strategic planning and socializing. However, when an unexpected order came in at the last minute, they decided to let the hourly employees run the presses. Now, every spring, a managerial retreat is deliberately planned and the shop operates as it normally would—except without any managerial personnel on hand to field questions or solve problems. The result of this is that employees have an opportunity to demonstrate their responsibility and autonomy. Not surprisingly, morale seems to rise after Spring Fling every year.

The "marijuana firings" happened when some of the managers who worked in the bindery discovered five employees who had been going out at lunch and smoking pot. All were fired. However, some time later, one of those involved requested his job back. Because Quadracci had come to believe that this person had been an innocent bystander, witnessing the smoking rather than participating, he departed from policy and let the bindery managers know that he thought it would be all right to rehire this individual. The managers, however, seized upon the Quadracci philosophy of individual initiative and responsibility. They refused to rehire the former employee because, "the kid had broken a cardinal rule—he had violated their trust. He had failed to assume responsibility for his own actions, so how could they trust him to assume responsibility for the success of the company?"[3]

While trust, initiative, and responsibility are the cornerstones of Quadracci's leadership style, he recognizes that these don't come easily. As a result, he developed numerous activities designed to help his employees become responsible and trustworthy. All new hires begin their employment with a two month probationary period during which time they are not allowed to wear the company uniform. Even after the two months, new recruits—most of whom are young men with little work experience—are put through a rigorous training program. This involves classes in such areas as job training (for example, "Intro to Printing" is taught by Quadracci himself), company values (for example, respect for people and property), and work ethic (for example, absenteeism will not be tolerated). Additionally, older and more experienced employees serve as role models and mentors. They carefully oversee all of the work done by the new recruits as well as instruct them in such areas as opening checking accounts, using their benefits wisely, and (where applicable) finishing their high school diploma. Quadracci explains, "They're raw recruits, and as far as we're concerned, they're in boot camp for about two years. They get indoctrinated, brainwashed—theirs is not to reason why. It's authoritarianism all the way, until they've proven they're adult enough to handle a participative management style. I mean, if you try to reason with an eight-year-old, he's gonna steal you blind."[4]

Quadracci varies the degree to which he gets involved in decision making depending on the situation. As revealed by the marijuana incident, he allowed the managers with the most direct knowledge of the circumstances, and who would be most affected by the decision, to use their own judgment about rehiring the former employee. However, when Quadracci believes his own special insight or expertise is relevant to a particular decision, he speaks out clearly—and sometimes overrides the decisions of others.

Even though Quad/Graphics seems to be informally operated, there is a clear order among the employees. There are vice presidents for finance, administration, manufacturing, production, press and bindery operations, and distribution. Under each vice president are two supervisors and a large number of line managers, all of whom are first pressmen responsible for running the printing presses. This structure partially serves as a substitute for leadership. As such, it helps organize employees around the tasks they are to accomplish and provides a mechanism through which Quadracci may implement his decentralized decision making. Hence, when a group of press operators decided to start the training program in printing they never asked or even told Quadracci what they had planned, they just did it. When asked how Quadracci found out about the program, Mike Collins, one of those involved said, "I really don't know . . . through the grapevine, I guess."[5]

Again, this experience illustrates Quadracci's leadership style and his heavy emphasis on employee participation. Even so, he recognizes that he can't force participation. In his words, "You have to accept the fact that every department is going to be run differently, depending on where the leader is on the authoritarian-participation scale. You can't change them. After all, imposing participative management on everybody would be as structured, or more so, as authoritarian management."[6]

Questions for Discussion

1. Is Quadracci a participative or authoritarian leader? Give examples to support your answer.

2. Use the Hersey-Blanchard situational leadership theory to explain Quadracci's apparently different leadership styles.

3. How does the path-goal theory help explain Quadracci's success as a leader?

4. Use Fiedler's model to analyze Quadracci's position power.

5. How does the Vroom-Yetton normative theory explain Quadracci's decision-making styles?

6. Is Quadracci more of a leader or manager? Explain.

Notes

1. Wojahn, E. (1983, October). Management by walking away. *Inc.,* pp. 68–76.
2. See Note 1, p. 68.
3. See Note 1, p. 76.
4. See Note 1, p. 72.
5. See Note 1, p. 74.
6. See Note 1, p. 76.

Leadership at Price Waterhouse

As we have noted repeatedly in this chapter, all leaders are certainly *not* alike in terms of personal style. While some focus primarily on maintaining friendly relations with subordinates, others direct their attention mainly to efficient task performance. Similarly, while some openly invite input and participation from organization members, others prefer to make decisions unilaterally.

The style of one successful leader is revealed by the PINNACLE interview of Joseph Connor. Mr. Connor is Chairman of Price Waterhouse, the largest accounting firm in the United States. In this interview, Mr. Connor makes the surprising point that from his perspective, *people skills* are far more important than technical skills, even in an accounting firm such as his. This suggests that he is something of a relations-oriented leader: in his opinion, good working relationships are a crucial ingredient for both individual and organizational success.

In addition, Mr. Connor describes several other key traits or characteristics that he feels are essential for successful leadership. Among these are the ability to evaluate one's own work objectively and the ability to unwind—to cope with the inescapable stress of top leadership through appropriate rest and relaxation.

As you watch the videotape of this interview, be on the lookout for other aspects of leadership discussed in this chapter. For example, notice any remarks by Mr. Connor that reflect his views about the responsibilities of leaders, how their effectiveness can be evaluated, and their reliance on support from subordinates. Do you think it is these views, and the ability to put them into practice, that has made Joseph Connor such a successful leader both at Price Waterhouse and in his profession?

Questions for Discussion

1. Do you agree with Joseph Connor? Are people skills more important than technical skills from the point of view of effective leadership?

2. Do you think such skills are more valuable in some types of organizations or businesses than others?

3. Has Mr. Connor's personal life played a role in shaping his preference for a particular style of leadership?

**EXPERIENCING
ORGANIZATIONAL
BEHAVIOR**

Can Everyone Be a Leader?

If you asked fifty people to indicate what the term *leadership* meant, the chances are good that you would receive a wide range of replies. Many individuals would focus on the traits or characteristics necessary for being an effective leader. Others would mention the benefits of serving as a leader—the power and prestige conferred by such roles. And a few, perhaps, would call attention to the responsibilities and cares that often fall on the shoulders of modern leaders. Despite these different definitions and perspectives, if you then asked the same fifty people whether they possessed the ability to serve as a leader, you would probably find much more uniform replies. The overwhelming majority would probably answer "Yes." In short, most persons believe that they possess considerable leadership potential, and that under the right circumstances, they could serve as an effective leader. To demonstrate this fact for yourself, follow the procedures outlined below.

Procedure

Ask ten people you know to answer the following questions. (Try to choose people who differ in age, occupation, and personal traits.)

1. How would you rate your own leadership ability?

Much Below Average						Much Above Average
1	2	3	4	5	6	7

2. To what extent could you serve as a leader if the need arose?

Definitely Could Not						Definitely Could
1	2	3	4	5	6	7

3. What are the chances that you will ever be called on to serve as a leader in some capacity in the future?

Very Low						Very High
1	2	3	4	5	6	7

Now, add the ratings provided by your subjects for each item, and obtain average scores.

Points to Consider

What did you find? Unless you have chosen a very unusual group of individuals, you will probably obtain ratings above the midpoint on each scale (i.e., above 4.0). In short, most people rate themselves as above average in leadership ability, and above average in the likelihood that they will actually become a leader in some context. Obviously, this can't be true: everyone can't be higher than average on these dimensions. Moreover, such beliefs are difficult to reconcile with the fact that humanity seems to suffer from a shortage of effective leaders—not an overabundance!

The key reason for this "tilt" in our thinking is obvious: *leadership* is a term with almost magical properties. The media, history, and even cultural folklore all join in emphasizing the importance of leadership and the powerful benefits conferred by this role. Little wonder that most people daydream at some time or other about being a leader, and that they tend to perceive themselves as above average in their capacity for leadership. Would we be better off if reality matched such wishful thinking? This is an intriguing issue you may wish to ponder.

CHAPTER TWELVE

POWER, POLITICS, AND ETHICS IN ORGANIZATIONS

CHAPTER OUTLINE

Power: The Capacity to Influence Others
Bases of Individual Power
Group or Subunit Power: Structural Bases

Organizational Politics: Power in Action
Organizational Politics: Where Does It Occur?
Political Tactics: Gaining the Power Advantage
Playing Political Games in Organizations
When Does Political Action Occur?

Ethics: Moral Constraints on Organizational Behavior
Political Behavior: What Makes It Ethical?
Why Does Unethical Behavior Occur in
  Organizations?

Promoting Organizational Morality: Some
  Strategies

Special Sections

OB: A Research Perspective
Using and Avoiding Power in Crisis Situations

OB: A Management Perspective
Coping with Organizational Politics: Some
Techniques

OB: An International Perspective
Corporate Morality: Facing the Challenge of the
Global Economy

LEARNING OBJECTIVES

After reading this chapter, you should be able to:
1. Describe the five bases of social power available to individuals.
2. Explain the factors that account for power differences between groups within organizations.
3. Identify the conditions under which political activity within organizations is most likely to occur.
4. Recognize different types of political tactics used in organizations and some techniques for overcoming them.
5. Distinguish between political activity that is ethical and unethical in nature.
6. Explain the forces leading to the occurrence of unethical behavior in organizations.
7. Describe strategies that might be used to encourage ethical behavior in organizations.

"I can't believe he's done it again," said Bud Martin as he shook his head in disbelief. "Mike Winetta's called another meeting of department managers. How the heck does he do it? He runs the smallest and least important unit in the whole place."

"Right, Bud," Roy D'Alfonso was quick to agree. "Besides, as long as I've been here at Playtime Toys, only Vice Presidents called department meetings."

"Well, maybe Jim Vorhees should've called a meeting to plan the new product introductions for Christmas, but he's so busy planning to take over the Presidency, he's not giving any attention to things. You'd never know he's our Vice President of Product Development."

Roy nodded as he sipped his coffee. "Jim's not doing his job, and Mike is anxious to take it over, don't you think?"

"Well," Bud noted, "the job does have to be done, but I don't like the way he's going about trying to get promoted to VP—by taking over a VP's job through the back door, one piece at a time. It's just not his responsibility. Who is he to call us together? If you ask me, he's really overstepping his bounds this time."

"Come to think of it, Bud, you're absolutely right," Roy replied. "You know, he can *try* to call a meeting—but if no one shows up, he might get the message that we're not going along with his little scheme."

"Good thinking, Roy." Bud smiled with all the confidence of a man with a plan. "I'll call Jackson in R & D and Hanover in Marketing; you call Freedman in Finance and Campbell in Purchasing. Let's all agree to be busy on the day he tries to call a meeting. Maybe he'll get the message that we're not going to let him take over."

"You can count on me," Roy agreed. "He can't be any more in charge than we let him. After all, he's not a Vice President just yet, so he can't do anything to us if we don't show up. No sense helping him pave the way to the top."

"It's not just that he'd make a crummy VP," Bud added, "but I don't like the way he's trying to take charge."

Roy nodded in agreement, but began looking a bit uncertain. "What's on your mind, Roy? Having second thoughts?" Bud asked.

"My only concern is that we might be getting so carried away with Mike's antics that we're losing sight of what's actually best for Playtime. Know what I mean?"

"Don't give it a second thought," Bud answered with confidence. "I'm as concerned for the company as the next guy; you know that. And you know that I'm more ethical than anyone around here. Don't you?"

Bud continued before Roy could answer. "Mike Winetta is not playing fair, and we don't have to help him take over. He's not the kind of guy we need at the top. So, as I see it, we're doing the company a favor by planning against him."

The longer Bud spoke, the more Roy nodded his head in agreement. "As they say, 'all's fair in love and war.' And, there's no doubt about it—this is war."

It looks like Mike's ambitions threaten Bud and Roy. He wants to make it to the top of the corporate ladder and they resent the way he's attempting to go about it. Now, Bud and Roy are planning to hinder Mike's efforts. At one time or another, most of us probably have been involved in some kind of situation like this—either trying to take charge of a group or organization when needed, or attempting to block someone else from doing so. It is a basic fact of organizational life that people seek to control the actions of others, to influence their behavior. Although few of us may experience

← RECEPTION
ELEVATORS →
← ACCESS TO
POWER

stevenson

FIGURE 12.1   Power: A Desired Organizational Goal

As suggested here, the attainment of power is one of the most commonly sought after goals of individuals in organizations. (Source: Drawing by Stevenson; © 1985 The New Yorker Magazine, Inc.)

this phenomenon at the top of the corporate ladder like Bud and Roy, efforts to alter the actions and beliefs of others are commonplace at all levels within organizations.

What we are alluding to here is the basic organizational process of trying to gain **power** and engaging in organized attempts to make those efforts pay off—**organizational politics.** It is easy to appreciate how power is an essential element of organizational success, and how gaining power is a desired goal of individuals in organizations (see Figure 12.1). Of course, the desire to control others' behavior raises serious questions about **organizational ethics.** Is it morally appropriate to use power against others? What factors encourage or discourage supervisors' ethical behavior while managing subordinates? These important questions will be examined in this chapter. Before considering the ethical questions that arise from the use of power and politics, we will take a closer look at these processes. Specifically, the first section of this chapter will focus on organizational power—how it is attained and used by individuals and work groups. The second section will examine the forms of political behavior that occur in organizations when someone attempts to use power. The final section will explore the ethical considerations involved in the use of organizational power and politics.

POWER: THE CAPACITY TO INFLUENCE OTHERS

If you imagine almost any interaction between people in organizations (including our opening story on page 410), you will realize how commonplace it is for one person to try to get another to do something he or she would rather not do. Consider these examples. An office manager seeks to get her secretarial staff to work overtime to complete an important project despite their interest in going home. A manager adds a new member to his staff in the face of protests from her colleagues. A professor requires a graduate student to rewrite a section of her doctoral dissertation, causing her to cancel a long-awaited vacation. Each of these examples reflects one person's capacity to successfully influence another's behavior—and in a manner that person did not desire. This is what social scientists refer to as **power.** More formally, power may be defined as *the capacity to change the behavior or attitudes of another in a desired manner.*[1]

As we have defined it, power involves the potential to influence others—either the things they do or the way they feel about something. In this section we will note that this capacity can reside in either individuals or groups. First, we will examine the bases of *individual power*—factors that give individuals the capacity to successfully alter the attitudes or behavior of others. Then, we will turn our attention to several bases of *group or subunit power*—aspects of organizational structure that determine the power of groups operating within them.

Bases of Individual Power

It is an inevitable fact of organizational life that some individuals can boast a greater capacity to successfully influence people than others. Within organizations, the distribution of power is typically unequal. Why is this so? What sources of power do people have at their disposal? Answers to these questions are provided in a classic framework developed by French and Raven.[2] This work identifies five different bases of social power derived from the characteristics individuals possess and the nature of the relationships between individuals with and without power. As we describe each of these interpersonal sources of power, it may be useful to refer to the summary presented in Table 12.1.

Reward power: Controlling valued resources. Imagine a supervisor in charge of twenty-five employees in a department of a large organization. As part of her job she is free to hire new staff members, set pay raises, control work assignments, and prepare budgets for department projects. It is easy to recognize how this kind of control over desired resources can provide a source of power for this supervisor. The resources at her disposal—access to jobs and money, in this case—are highly desired. Individuals with the capacity to control the rewards workers will receive is said to have **reward power** over them. Subordinates will often comply with their superior's wishes in hopes of receiving the valuable rewards they control.

The rewards at a manager's disposal may be tangible, such as raises, promotions, and time off, or intangible, such as praise and recognition. In either case, it is the access to these resources that often forms a source of individual power in organizations. Indeed, managers have been known to complain that they are left a powerless figurehead by not being able to control any important resources in their organizations. This is especially likely in the case of first-line supervisors, who often find themselves responsible for the actions of others but severely restricted by the incentives they can

TABLE 12.1 Individuals' Power: Five Major Bases

Individuals' power in organizations may be derived from any of the sources identified and described here.

Type of Power	Description of Base
Reward power	Based on the ability to control valued organizational rewards and resources (e.g., pay, information)
Coercive power	Based on control over various punishments (e.g., suspensions, formal reprimands)
Legitimate power	Based on the belief that an individual has the recognized authority to control others by virtue of his or her organizational position (e.g., the person is a high-ranking corporate official)
Referent power	Based on liking of the power-holder by subordinates (e.g., the superior is friends with a subordinate)
Expert power	Based on the accepted belief that the individual has a valued skill or ability (e.g., expert medical skills)

offer others for following their orders.[3] It is important to keep in mind (based on our discussion of the concepts of *reinforcement* in chapter 2 and *valence* in chapter 3) that resources may only enhance one's power to the extent that they are actually desired by the recipients. You also may recall from chapter 2 that for any rewards to be effective in changing people's behavior, it is necessary for the rewards to be closely tied to the desired behavior. Thus, whereas access to valued resources may enhance a manager's power base, the manager must administer them properly in order to be effective. Having resources at one's disposal and using them appropriately are obviously two different things.

Coercive power: Controlling punishments. In addition to controlling desired resources, managers often control the punishments of others—a capacity known as **coercive power.** Subordinates may do what their superiors desire because they fear the superior will punish them if they do not. Punishments may include pay cuts, demotions, suspension without pay, formal reprimands, undesirable work assignments, and the like. As in the case of reward power, it is important to note that punishments are effective only if used properly. In chapter 2 we noted that punishments may have undesirable side effects if they are too harsh or inconsistently administered (in extreme cases, employees may even rebel against an overly harsh supervisor by organizing their colleagues in protest, or by quitting their jobs).[4] Regardless, the capacity to administer punishment represents an important source of power in organizations.

Legitimate power: Recognized organizational authority. What would happen in your class if you learned that one of your classmates would be making the decisions about the final course grades? Someone might stand up and question this, asking, "Who is *he* to make those decisions?" If so, the speaker would be challenging the legitimacy of that individual's power. However, if the professor announced that she would be determining the final grades herself, no one would likely raise any questions. The difference between these two situations has to do with **legitimate power**—the recognized right of individuals to exercise authority over others because of their position in an organizational hierarchy. Students recognize the accepted authority of professors to determine their grades (i.e., professors have legitimate power in this regard), but reject as illegitimate the power of their classmates to make these same decisions.

Usually, legitimate power is derived from an individual's formal rank or position. Organizational members are likely to accept attempts to influence their behavior based on the fact that one has a higher position (see Figure 12.2 on page 414). This does not mean, however, that the higher-ranking individual can legitimately control all aspects of others' behavior. Managers only have authority over those aspects of others' behavior that fall under their accepted areas of organizational responsibility. For example, whereas secretaries may recognize the legitimate authority of their bosses to ask them to file and prepare office correspondence, they may reject as illegitimate that same boss's request to type his son's homework papers. Similarly, a plant manager may accept the authority of a Vice President of Production who directs him to increase inventories of certain items, but may question the authority of the very same order voiced by the Vice President of Finance. The key point is that legitimate authority applies only to the range of behaviors that are recognized and accepted as legitimate by the parties involved.

Referent power: Control based on admiration. "Joe, we go back over twenty years in this company, and I consider you a good friend. I'm in kind of a bind right now, and I could sure use your help. You see, what happened is. . . ." Joe is most certainly being set up to help the speaker, who is relying on the fact that he and Joe have a

FIGURE 12.2   Legitimate Power: Control Based on Formal Authority
One source of social power, *legitimate power*, is based on the idea that members of an organization recognize and accept the formal authority of individuals who have higher-ranking positions within the organizational hierarchy.

being set up to help the speaker, who is relying on the fact that he and Joe have a long-standing friendship. Out of his allegiance to that relationship and his liking and admiration for the speaker, Joe probably feels obligated to go along with whatever is being asked. Individuals who are liked and respected by others can get them to alter their actions in accord with their directives—a type of influence known as **referent power.** Senior managers who possess desirable qualities and a good reputation may find that they have referent power over younger managers who identify with them and wish to emulate them. Similarly, sports heros and popular movie stars often have referent power over their admiring fans (a fact advertisers often capitalize on when they employ these individuals as spokespersons to endorse their products).

Expert power: Control based on skills and knowledge. If a foreman tells one of his machine shop workers to readjust the settings on a certain piece of equipment, that person may well do it because he believes that the foreman is expert in the operation of the machine. To the extent that a subordinate recognizes a superior's advanced skill or knowledge and follows his orders because he realizes that the superior knows what's best, that superior is said to have **expert power.** The running of organizations often relies on experts who must be consulted frequently, and whose advice must be followed if an organization is to survive. The power of various experts is usually very narrowly defined, limited to the scope of their expertise. Accountants may have expert power when it comes to corporate taxes and investments, whereas market researchers may have expert power when it comes to deciding what type of advertising to use for a new product. Recent research has revealed that within teams of health care professionals (e.g., nurses, occupational therapists, etc.) it is the physician who tends to hold the most power—in part, a result of the greater professional expertise they are believed to have.[5]

Expert power can be a very successful way of influencing others in organizations. After all, it would be difficult to justify not following the directives of a trained professional who is better equipped than you are to know what to do. Given this, it is not surprising that problems often develop when younger, less experienced employees are given responsibility for a work crew. Until they have proven themselves with a record of success, many employees find it difficult to exercise power over others. By the same token, it is the recognized expertise of many managers, and the extreme power they wield as a result, that makes them highly sought after as employees.[6]

Uses of individual power bases. Although we have spoken about each base of power separately thus far, it is important to recognize that they are often closely related to each other.[7] For example, consider that the more someone uses coercive power, the less that person will be liked, and hence, the lower his or her referent power would be. Similarly, managers who have expert power are also likely to have legitimate power because it is accepted for them to direct others within their field of expertise. In addition, the higher someone's organizational position, the more legitimate power that person has, which is usually accompanied by greater opportunities to use reward and coercion.[8] Clearly, then, the various bases of power should not be thought of as completely separate and distinct from each other. They are often used together in varying combinations.

What bases of power do people prefer to use? Although the answer to this question is quite complex, research has shown that people prefer using expert power most and their coercive power least often.[9] Of course, a great deal depends on the individual's personality. In chapter 6 we described several personality characteristics of individuals that are likely to be related to the use of power. Most notably, the trait of *Machiavellianism* is relevant here. People who score high on this trait are likely to use whatever power they have at their disposal to manipulate others (please refer to chapter 6). Short of this extreme, it also is known that there are different personal preferences with respect to different forms of power. To help you learn about your own personal power style, complete the questionnaire shown in Table 12.2 and score it as described in the caption. This questionnaire is based on a sample of items recently developed by

TABLE 12.2   Social Power: What Kinds Do You Use?
A questionnaire like this is used to measure the kinds of power managers use over subordinates. To better understand your own use of power, complete these rating scales to indicate how often you use each of the behaviors indicated. Add your scores for questions 1 and 2 to reflect your use of reward power, 3 and 4 for coercive power, 5 and 6 for legitimate power, 7 and 8 for expert power, and 9 and 10 for referent power. Higher scores reflect greater degrees of each of these sources of power.

To control your subordinates during the last year, how often did you do each of the following?

	SELDOM				VERY OFTEN
1. Arrange for them to be promoted.	1	2	3	4	5
2. Nominate them for an award.	1	2	3	4	5
3. Recommend disciplinary action.	1	2	3	4	5
4. Punish them with extra work.	1	2	3	4	5
5. Tell them you expect your orders to be followed.	1	2	3	4	5
6. Explain that you're the boss and they have to do what you say.	1	2	3	4	5
7. Correct their work.	1	2	3	4	5
8. Give them advice and assistance.	1	2	3	4	5
9. Rely on your friendships with them to help get the job done.	1	2	3	4	5
10. Count on them to get the job done because they don't want to let you down.	1	2	3	4	5

(Source: Adapted from Frost and Stahelski, 1988; see Note 10.)

Frost and Stahelski to study the five bases of power in organizations.[10] Although the version of the scale shown here is an abbreviated and modified one, it will give you a good chance to appreciate the way you tend to use power in organizations.

Despite possible differences between individuals with respect to power, there are also certain situational factors that can greatly influence the use of various power tactics. One of these has to do with the target of influence attempts—who is being influenced. Whereas many different forms of power tend to be used to influence subordinates, research has shown that expert power is the preferred form used to influence peers and superiors.[11] After all, it is almost always appropriate to try to get others to go along with you if you justify your attempt on the basis of your expertise. (We also know that the way people use power depends on another important aspect of the situation—whether the setting is one in which a serious crisis is confronted, or just an everyday matter. For a detailed account of the research on this topic, please refer to the **Research Perspective** section below.)

OB: A RESEARCH PERSPECTIVE

Using and Avoiding Power in Crisis Situations

Imagine that you are a naval Commander in two different situations. In the first, you are at the helm of a huge warship in the middle of a ferocious battle deciding what weapons to use to destroy the enemy. In the second situation, you are talking to your crew about more day-to-day situations such as what the cook should prepare for dinner. Would you use your formal powers as Commander the same way in each of these situations? Probably not. Recent research suggests that group leaders may use their formal powers differently depending on whether or not their group is facing a crisis situation.

A recent investigation by Mulder and his associates surveyed the use of different powers by the managers of a bank in the Netherlands.[12] They were given a questionnaire asking them to describe the behaviors of their immediate supervisors in either a crisis situation or an everyday, noncrisis situation. (The executives were asked to think of crisis and noncrisis situations that actually occurred within their departments.) Among the types of power studied in the questionnaire were two of the bases of power identified by French and Raven which we noted earlier—*expert power* and *referent power*. Were the managers surveyed more likely to report that their supervisors used these forms of power under crisis or noncrisis situations? The answer is summarized in Figure 12.3.

As Figure 12.3 reveals, both expert power and referent power were more likely to be used in crisis situations than everyday situations. Apparently, when crises occurred, such formal powers were relied on

to get things done. Everyday situations were not as likely to call for reliance upon formal powers to manage. How, then, do superiors go about managing under noncrisis situations? The investigators found that under these circumstances supervisors relied instead upon *open consultation* with their subordinates. This refers to the tendency for managers to resolve problems by talking them out with their subordinates, and allowing themselves to be persuaded by subordinates' arguments. Supervisors using this approach do not use the power they could claim over subordinates, but instead, treat them as equals.

These findings point to some important conclusions regarding the use of power in organizations. Most importantly, they suggest that having power and using it are two different things. Just because a manager has certain powers at his or her disposal does not mean that they will be used automatically. Managers may prefer to rely on more open, two-way communication with their subordinates when dealing with everyday situations, in which using their influence would be unnecessarily severe. However, when crisis situations dictate the use of more formal powers, managers are apparently not reluctant to use the powers at their disposal. Accordingly, it is important to keep in mind that managers' use of power is likely to be based on the situations they face. (Please recall that a similar point was made in chapter 11 about the most effective leadership style for a given situation.)

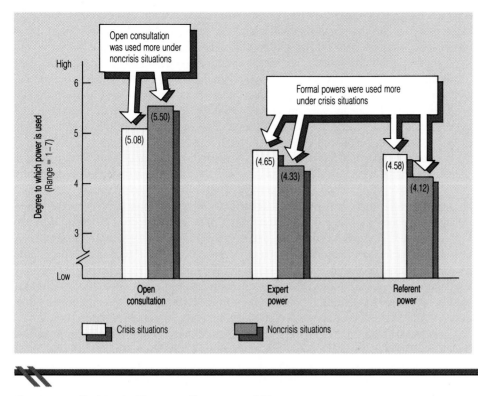

FIGURE 12.3 Power Use under Crisis and Noncrisis Conditions: An Experimental Comparison

When asked to report the types of power they used in crisis situations, Dutch bank managers noted using either their *expert power* or their *referent power*. Under noncrisis situations, in contrast, they reported a preference for openly consulting with their subordinates. (Source: Based on data reported by Mulder, de Jong, Koppelaar, & Verhage, 1986; see Note 12.)

Group or Subunit Power: Structural Bases

Thus far, this chapter has examined the uses of power by individuals. However, in organizations it is not only people acting alone, but groups that wield power. Organizations are frequently divided into *subunits* given responsibility for different functions such as finance, human resource management, marketing, and research and development. The formal departments devoted to these various organizational activities often must direct the activities of other groups, requiring them to have power. What are the sources of such power? By what means do formal organizational groups successfully control the actions of other groups? Two theoretical models have been proposed to answer these questions—the **resource-dependency model** and the **strategic contingencies model.** Our review of these approaches will help identify the factors responsible for subunit power and describe how they operate.

The resource-dependency model: Controlling critical resources. It is not too difficult to think of organizations as a complex set of subunits that are constantly exchanging resources with each other. By this, we mean that formal organizational departments may be both giving to and receiving from other departments such valued commodities as money, personnel, equipment, supplies, and information. These critical resources are necessary for the successful operation of organizations.

Various subunits are often dependent on others for such resources. Imagine, for example, a large organization that develops, produces, and sells its products. The Sales Department provides financial resources that enable the Research & Development Department to come up with new products. Of course, it cannot do so effectively without information from the Marketing Department about what consumers are interested in buying and how much they would be willing to pay. The Production Department has to do its part by manufacturing the goods on time, but only if the Purchasing Department can supply the needed raw materials—and at a price the Finance Department accepts as permitting the company to turn a profit. Without continuing this example, it is easy to see how the various organizational subunits are involved in a complex set of interrelationships with others. To the extent that one subunit controls the resources on which another subunit depends, it may be said to have power over it. After all, controlling resources allows groups to successfully influence the actions of other groups. Subunits that control more resources than others may be considered more powerful in the organization. Indeed, such imbalances, or *asymmetries*, in the pattern of resource dependencies occur normally in organizations. The more one group is dependent on another for needed resources, the less power it has (see Figure 12.4).[13]

In proposing their resource-dependency model, Pfeffer and Salancik note that a subunit's power is based on the degree to which it controls the resources required by other subunits.[14] Thus, while all subunits may contribute something to an organization, the most powerful ones are those that contribute the most important resources. Controlling the resources other departments need puts a subunit in a better position to bargain for the resources it requires. To illustrate this point, let's consider an important study by Salancik and Pfeffer.[15] Within a university, the various academic departments may be very unequal with respect to the power they possess. For example, some may have more students, be more prestigious in their national reputation, receive greater grant support, and have more representatives on important university committees than others. As such, they would be expected to have greater control over valued resources. This was found to be the case within the large state university studied by Salancik and Pfeffer. Specifically, the more powerful departments proved to be those that were most successful in gaining scarce and valued resources from the university (e.g., funds for graduate student fellowships, faculty research grants, and summer faculty fellowships). As a result, they became even more powerful, suggesting that within organizations, the rich subunits get richer.

The resource-dependency model suggests that a key determinant of subunit power is the control of valued resources. However, as we will now illustrate, it is not only control over resources that dictates organizational power, but also control over the activities of other subunits.

FIGURE 12.4 Power between Subunits: The Resource-dependency Model

The *resource-dependency model* of organizational power explains that subunits acquire power when they control critical resources needed by other subunits. In the example shown here, the Accounting Department would be considered more powerful than either the Production Department or the Marketing Department.

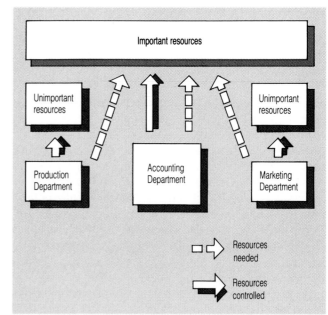

The strategic contingencies model: Power through dependence. The Accounting Department of a company might be expected to have responsibility over the approval or disapproval of funds requested by various departments. If it does, its actions greatly affect the activities of other units, who are dependent on its decisions—other department's operations are *contingent* on what the Accounting Department does. To the extent that a department is able to control the relative power of various organizational subunits by virtue of its actions, it is said to have control over *strategic contingencies*.[16] For example, if the Accounting Department consistently approved the budget requests of the Production Department but rejected the budget requests of the Marketing Department, it would be making the Production Department more powerful.

Where do the strategic contingencies lie within organizations? In a classic study, Lawrence and Lorsch found out that power was distributed in different departments in different industries.[17] Importantly, they found that within successful firms, the strategic contingencies were controlled by the departments that were most important for organizational success. For example, within the food processing industry, where it was critical for new products to be developed and sold, successful firms had strategic contingencies controlled by the Sales and Research departments. In container manufacturing firms, where the timely delivery of high quality goods is a critical determinant of organizational success, it was found that successful firms placed most of the decision-making power in the Sales and Production departments. Thus, successful firms were ones that focused the control over strategic contingencies within the subunits most responsible for their organization's success.

What factors give subunits control over strategic contingencies? The **strategic contingencies model** of Hickson and his associates suggests several key considerations.[18] Please refer to the summary of these factors in Figure 12.5.

Power may be enhanced by subunits that can help *reduce the levels of uncertainty* faced by others. Any department that can shed light on the uncertain situations organizations may face (such as those regarding future markets, government regulation, availability of needed supplies, financial security, and so on) can be expected to wield the most organizational power. Accordingly, the balance of power within organizations may be expected to change as organizational conditions change. Consider, for example, changes that have taken place over the years in public utility companies. Studying the

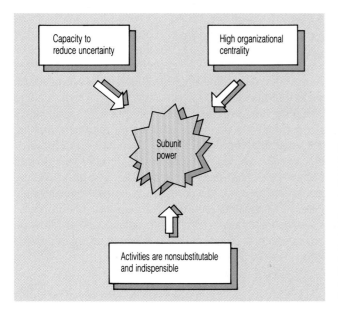

FIGURE 12.5 Strategic Contingencies Model: Identifying Sources of Subunit Power

The *strategic contingencies model* explains intraorganizational power in terms of the capacity of some subunits to control the actions of others. Subunit power may be enhanced by the factors shown here.

strategic contingencies in such organizations, Miles noted that a shift has occurred.[19] When public utilities first began, the engineers tended to wield the most power, but now that these companies have matured and face problems of litigation and governmental regulation (particularly over nuclear power), the power has shifted to lawyers. A similar shift toward the power of the Legal Department has occurred in recent years in the area of human resource management, where a complex set of laws and governmental regulations have created a great deal of uncertainty for organizations. Powerful subunits are those that can help reduce organizational uncertainty.

It has also been established that more powerful subunits are ones that have a *high degree of centrality in the organization*. Some organizational subunits perform functions that are more central, and others, more peripheral. For example, some departments—such as accounting—may have to be consulted by most others before any action can be taken, giving them a central position in their organizations. Centrality is also high when a unit's duties have an immediate effect on an organization. For example, the effects would be much more dramatic on an auto manufacturer if the production lines stopped than if market research activities ceased. The central connection of some departments to organizational success dictates the power they wield.

Third, a subunit controls power when its *activities are nonsubstitutable and indispensible*. If any group can perform a certain function, subunits responsible for controlling that function may not be particularly powerful. In a hospital, for example, personnel in Surgery are certainly more indispensable than personnel in Maintenance because fewer individuals have the skills needed to perform their department's duties. Because it is easier for an organization to replace some employees with others either within or outside it, those subunits composed of individuals who are most easily replaced tend to wield very little organizational power.

It is important to note that the strategic contingencies model has been tested and supported in several organizational studies.[20] For example, in one investigation conducted in several companies, it was found that a subunit's power within an organization was higher when it could reduce uncertainty, occupied a central place in the work flow, and performed functions that other subunits could not perform.[21] As such, it appears that the strategic contingencies model (summarized in Figure 12.5) should be considered a valuable source of information about the factors that influence the power of subunits within organizations.

ORGANIZATIONAL POLITICS: POWER IN ACTION

Our discussion of power focused on the *potential* to successfully influence others. When this potential is realized, put into action to accomplish desired goals, we are no longer talking about power, but **politics.** It is quite easy to imagine situations in which someone does something to accomplish his or her own goals, which do not necessarily agree with the goals of the organization (Mike's behavior in our story on page 410 provides a good example). This is what **organizational politics** is all about—*actions not officially sanctioned (approved) by an organization taken to influence others in order to meet one's personal goals.*[22] If you think we're describing something that is a bit selfish and appears to be an abuse of organizational power, you are correct. Organizational politics *does* involve placing one's self-interests above the interests of the organization. Indeed, it is this element of using power to foster one's own interests that distinguishes organizational politics from uses of power that are approved and accepted by organizations.

Organizational Politics: Where Does It Occur?

There can be little doubt that organizational politics is widespread. A survey of managers by Gandz and Murray revealed that political activities in organizations is one of the most common topics of conversation among employees.[23] However, political activity is not equally likely to occur throughout all parts of organizations.

The Gandz and Murray survey showed that the most likely areas of political activity involved those in which clear policies were nonexistent or lacking, such as interdepartmental coordination, promotions and transfers, and delegation of authority. However, when it came to organizational activities that had clearly defined rules and regulations, such as hiring and disciplinary policies, political activities were lowest. A survey of organizational political practices by Allen and his associates revealed similar findings.[24] Specifically, organizational politics was perceived to be greatest in subunits (such as Boards of Directors and members of the marketing staff) that followed poorly defined policies, whereas political activity was perceived to be lowest in those departments (such as production and accounting) in which clearly defined policies existed. Together, these findings help make an important point: *political activity is likely to occur in the face of ambiguity*. When there are clear-cut rules about what to do, it is unlikely that people will be able to abuse their power by taking political action. However, when people face highly novel and ambiguous situations in which the rules guiding them are unclear, it is easy to imagine how political behavior results.

Where in the organization is the political climate most active? In other words, at what organizational levels do people believe the most political activities are likely to occur? As shown in Figure 12.6, Gandz and Murray found that organizations were perceived to be more political at the higher levels, and less political at the lower man-

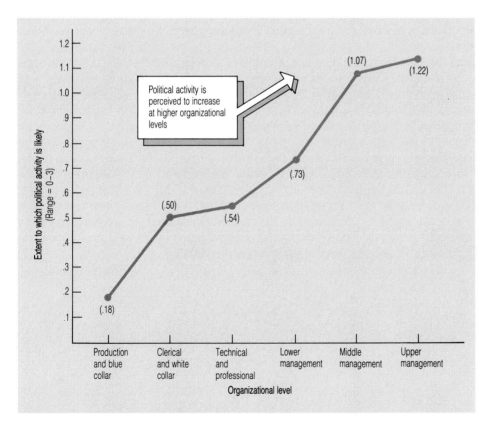

FIGURE 12.6 Organizational Politics: More Likely at the Top

Survey research has shown that employees believe political activity is more likely to occur at higher organizational levels (where the guiding rules are more ambiguous and the stakes are higher) than at lower levels. (Source: Based on data reported by Gandz & Murray, 1980; see Note 23.)

agerial and nonmanagerial levels of the organization.[25] Apparently, politics is most likely to occur at the top where, of course, the stakes are highest and power may corrupt.

Political Tactics: Gaining the Power Advantage

To understand organizational politics, it is important to recognize the various forms political behavior can take in organizations. In other words, we may ask: what are the techniques of organizational politics? When this question was asked of a group of managers surveyed by Allen and his associates, five techniques were identified as being used most often.[26]

1. Blaming and attacking others. One of the most popularly used tactics of organizational politics involves blaming and attacking others when bad things happen. A commonly used political tactic is finding a *scapegoat*, someone who could take the blame for some failure or wrongdoing. A supervisor, for example, may explain that the failure of a sales plan she designed was based on the serious mistakes of one of her subordinates—even if this is not entirely true. Explaining that "it's his fault," that is, making another "take the fall" for an undesirable event, gets the real culprit "off the hook" for it. Finding a scapegoat can allow the politically astute individual to avoid (or at least minimize) association with the negative situation. Although this practice may raise serious ethical questions, it is important to note that it goes on quite frequently in organizations.

2. Controlling access to information. As we noted in chapter 10, information is the lifeblood of organizations. Therefore, controlling who knows and doesn't know certain things is one of the most important ways of exercising power in organizations. Although outright lying and falsifying information may be used only rarely in organizations (in part because of the consequences of getting caught), there are other ways of controlling information to enhance one's organizational position. For example, you might: (a) withhold information that makes you look bad (e.g., negative sales information), (b) avoid contact with those who may ask for information you would prefer not to disclose, (c) be very selective in the information you disclose, or (d) overwhelm others with information which may not be completely relevant. These are all ways of controlling the nature and degree of information people have at their disposal. (For a whimsical look at information control in action, see Figure 12.7.) It is important to note how critical such information control can be. A recent analysis of the organizational restructuring of AT&T's Phone Stores revealed that control was transferred through the effective manipulation, distortion, and creation of information.[27] A Vice President's secret plan to feed incomplete and inaccurate information to the CEO was responsible for that Vice President's winning control over the stores.

FIGURE 12.7 Control over Information: A Critical Element of Organizational Politics

As demonstrated here, the selective use of information others need or wish to know is an important political tactic designed to give one a power advantage in organizations. (Source: Reprinted with special permission of NAS, Inc.)

3. Cultivating a favorable impression. It is not at all uncommon for persons interested in enhancing their organizational control to engage in some degree of "image building," an attempt to enhance the goodness of their impressions on others. Such efforts may take many forms, such as: (a) "dressing for success" (as discussed in chapter 10), (b) associating oneself with the successful accomplishments of others (or, in extreme cases, taking credit for others' successes), or (c) simply drawing attention to one's own successes and positive characteristics.[28] These are all ways of developing the "right image" to enhance one's individual power in organizations.

4. Developing a base of support. To be successful in influencing others, it is often useful to gain the support of others within the organization. Managers may, for example, "lobby" for their ideas before they officially present them at meetings, ensuring that others are committed to them in advance, thereby avoiding the embarrassment of being publicly rejected. They may also "scatter IOUs" throughout the organization by doing favors for others who may feel obligated to repay them in the form of supporting their ideas. The norm of *reciprocity* is very strong in organizations, as evidenced by the popular phrases "you scratch my back, and I'll scratch yours," and "one good turn deserves another." After all, when someone does a favor for you, you may say, "I owe you one," suggesting that you are aware of the obligation to reciprocate that favor. Calling in favors is a well-established and widely used mechanism for developing organizational power.

5. Aligning oneself with more powerful others. One of the most direct ways of gaining power is by connecting oneself with more powerful others. There are several ways to accomplish this. For example, a lower-power person may become more powerful if she has a very powerful mentor, a more powerful and better-established person who can look out for and protect her interests (recall our discussion of mentor-protege relationships in chapter 9). As another example, people may also agree in advance to form *coalitions*—groups that band together to achieve some common goal (e.g., overthrowing a current corporate CEO). Research has shown that the banding together of relatively powerless groups is one of the most effective ways they have of gaining organizational power.[29] Two relatively powerless individuals or groups may become stronger if they agree to act together, forming a coalition. It is also possible for people to align themselves with more powerful others by giving them "positive strokes" in the hope of getting more powerful persons to like them and help them—a process known as *ingratiation*.[30] Agreeing with someone who is more powerful may be an effective way of getting that person to consider you an ally. Such an alliance, of course, may prove to be indispensible when you are looking for support within an organization. To summarize, having a powerful mentor, forming coalitions, and using ingratiation are all potentially effective ways of gaining power by aligning oneself with others.

It is important to point out that the techniques of organizational politics noted here are just some of the many available means of gaining power in organizations.[31] The fact that there are so many techniques has led organizational scientists to view political behavior as a collection of games going on in a multi-ring circus. The idea is that many people or groups may be trying to influence many other people or groups simultaneously—as in playing a game. What, then, are the political games that unfold in organizations?

Playing Political Games in Organizations

One expert in the field of organizational power and politics, Henry Mintzberg, has identified four major categories of political games.[32] As we describe these games, it may be useful to refer to our summary of them in Table 12.3 (on page 424).

TABLE 12.3 Political Games: A Summary of Some Examples

Many political games are played in organizations, each involving different
individuals playing for different political goals.

GAME	TYPICAL MAJOR PLAYERS	PURPOSE
Authority Games		
Insurgency games	Lower-level managers	To resist formal authority
Counterinsurgency games	Upper-level managers	To counter resistance to formal authority
Power Base Games		
Sponsorship game	Any subordinate employee	To enhance base of power with superiors
Alliance game	Line managers	To enhance base of power with peers
Empire building	Line managers	To enhance base of power with subordinates
Rivalry Games		
Line vs. staff game	Line managers and staff personnel	To defeat each other in the quest for power
Rival camps game	Any groups at the same level	To defeat each other in the quest for power
Change Games		
Whistle-blowing game	Lower-level operators	To correct organizational wrongdoings
Young Turks game	Upper-level managers	To seize control over the organization

(Source: Adapted from Mintzberg, 1983; see Note 6.)

Authority games. Some games are played to resist authority—*insurgency games*—
while others are played to counter such resistance to authority—*counterinsurgency
games*. Insurgency can take forms that are quite mild (such as intentionally not doing
what is asked), to those that are very severe (such as organizing workers to mutiny
or sabotage their workplaces). Companies may try to fight back with counterinsurgency
moves. One way they may do so is by invoking stricter authority and control over
subordinates. Often unproductive for both sides, such games frequently give way to
the more adaptive techniques of bargaining and negotiation discussed in chapter 13.

Power base games. These are all games played to enhance the degree and breadth
of one's organizational power. For example, the *sponsorship game* is played with superiors. It involves attaching oneself to a rising or established star in return for a piece
of the action. A relatively unpowerful subordinate, for example, may agree to help a
more established person (such as his boss) by loyally supporting him in exchange for
getting advice and information from him, as well as some of his power and prestige.
Both benefit as a result. Similar games may be played among peers, such as the *alliance
game*. Here, workers at the same level agree in advance to mutually support each
other, gaining strength by increasing their joint size and power.

One of the riskiest power base games is known as *empire building*. In this game,
an individual or group attempts to become more powerful by becoming responsible for
more and more important organizational decisions. Indeed, a subunit may increase its
power by attempting to gain control over budgets, space, equipment, or any scarce
and desired organizational resource.

Rivalry games. Some political games are designed to weaken one's opponents. For example, in the *line versus staff game* managers on the "line," who are responsible for the operation of an organizational unit, clash with those on "staff," who are supposed to provide needed advice and information. For example, a foreman on an assembly line may attempt to ignore the advice from a corporate legal specialist about how to treat one of his production workers, thereby rendering the staff specialist less powerful. (We will have more to say about the distinction between "line" and "staff" positions in chapter 15.) Another rivalry game is the *rival camps game,* in which groups or individuals with differing points of view attempt to reduce the power of the other. For example, the Production Department of an organization may favor the goals of stability and efficiency whereas the Marketing Department may favor the goals of growth and customer service. The result may be that each side attempts to cultivate the favor of those allies who can support it, and who are less sensitive to the other side's interests. Of course, because organizational success requires the various organizational subunits to work in concert with each other, such rivalries are considered potentially disruptive to organizational functioning. One side or the other may win from time to time, but the organization loses as a result.

Change games. Several different games are played in order to create organizational change. For example, in the *whistle-blowing game* an organizational member secretly reports some organizational wrongdoing to a higher authority in the hope of righting the wrong and bringing about change. (We will have more to say about the phenomenon of whistle-blowing in chapter 13.) A game played for much higher stakes is known as the *young Turks game.* In it, camps of rebel workers seek to overthrow the existing leadership of an organization—a most extreme form of insurgency. The change sought by persons playing this game is not minor, but far-reaching and permanent. In governmental terms, they are seeking a "coup d'état."

As you review these various games (summarized in Table 12.3), it is clear that some political activities may readily coexist with organizational interests (e.g., the sponsorship game), while others are clearly antagonistic with organizational interests (e.g., the young Turks game). As such games are played out, it becomes apparent that although the existence of political activity may sometimes have little effect on organizations, more often they are quite harmful.[33] Now that we know what types of behavior reflect political activity in organizations, we are prepared to consider the conditions under which such behaviors take place.

When Does Political Action Occur?

Imagine the following situation. You are the director of a large charitable organization that administers funds supporting many charitable projects (e.g., saving endangered animals, providing shelter to the homeless, and so on). A wealthy philanthropist dies and his will leaves your organization $1 million to be spent in any desired manner. Hearing of this generous bequest, the directors of these various charitable groups are all interested in getting as much of this money as possible to support their projects. Several aspects of this situation make it liable to trigger political activity.[34]

For one, this situation is fraught with *uncertainty;* it is not obvious where the money should be spent. If the organization has no clearly prescribed priorities about how to spend its monies, various groups might very well try to get their share by any means possible. Second, this is clearly a matter in which there is an *important decision involving large amounts of scarce resources.* If the size of the gift were much smaller, say $500, or if it involved something trivial or readily available, such as paper clips, it is likely that the incentive for political action would be weak.

It is also important to note that the different groups in our example each have *conflicting goals and interests*. The save-our-wildlife group is intent on serving its interests; the shelter-for-the-homeless group has very different interests. Because such differing goals are sought, it is likely that political activity will result. Finally, we should note that this situation is potentially politically active because the different charitable groups are all approximately *equal in power*. If there were a highly asymmetrical balance of power (with one group having a lot more control over resources than others), political action would be futile because the most powerful group would simply make the decision.

As shown in Figure 12.8, political behavior is likely to occur when: (a) uncertainty exists, (b) large amounts of scarce resources are at stake, (c) organizational units (individuals or groups) have conflicting interests, or (d) the organizational units have approximately equal power.

It is important to note that because these conditions are likely to differ at various stages of an organization's life, contrasting degrees and types of political activities are expected. Organizations can be distinguished quite simply between those that are just being started by entrepreneurs (the *birth and early growth* stage), those that are fully developed (the *maturity* stage), and those that face decline and dissolution (the *decline or redevelopment* stage). As Gray and Ariss explain, different types of political activity are likely to occur during these various stages of an organization's life.[35]

When an organization is newly begun, it may have little or no structure, and be guided by the philosophy of the founder. During this stage, the entrepreneur gains political power by presenting his or her ideas as rational to the employees who accept this person's image of the corporate mission. The founder usually has complete access to information and makes decisions based on his or her own values. Explaining these decisions to subordinates is a way of inculcating these values to others in the organization, and thereby exercising power over them. Political activity is not particularly likely during this stage.

However, as organizations mature and become more complex, they tend to grow in size and to departmentalize, creating conditions in which the vested interests of different groups are likely to conflict. Political means may be used to gain an advantage in such a situation. Indeed, it is likely that the full range of political activities noted earlier may be employed when organizations are mature (e.g., forming coalitions, using information, etc.). It is particularly interesting to note that when organizations begin

FIGURE 12.8   What Triggers Political Activity in Organizations? A Summary

Several conditions are likely to stimulate political activity within organizations. A few of the key conditions are shown here.

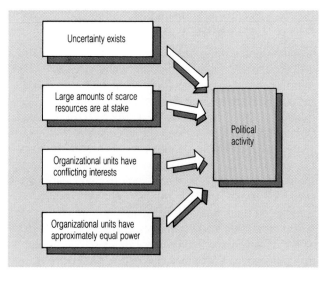

to decline, subunits may be quite insecure and the need for political action may be great as people and groups compete for the power to control (and perhaps turn around) the organization. A period of decline reflects a time of great uncertainty, and thus a period in which political activity is likely to be quite intense. For example, Hannan and Freeman found that staff members employed in California school districts experiencing decline tended to have more intense competitive interactions and to be at odds with each other more than members of similar organizations during periods of growth.[36] It is important to keep in mind that the use of political practices in organizations is likely to be affected by its degree of maturity.

As we conclude this section, it should be clear that the political behaviors enacted in organizations are both varied and complex. Accordingly, they provide some important challenges to managers who are likely to be involved in political activity in one form or another. (In the **Management Perspective** section below we will offer some suggestions for effectively managing political situations in organizations.)

OB: A MANAGEMENT PERSPECTIVE

Coping with Organizational Politics: Some Techniques

Given how fundamental the need for power appears to be among people, and how differences in power between employees are basic to organizations, it is safe to say that organizational politics is inevitable. This is not good news, however, as many of the effects of organizational politics are quite negative. Indeed, lowered corporate morale and diversion from key organizational goals (as employees pay closer attention to planning their attacks on others than to doing their jobs) are expected to result from political activity.[37] In view of this, it is critical for managers to consider ways of minimizing the effects of political behavior. Although it may be impossible to abolish organizational politics, there are several things managers can do to limit its effects.

1. Clarify job expectations. You will recall that political behavior is nurtured by highly ambiguous conditions. To the extent that managers help reduce uncertainty, they can minimize the likelihood of political behavior. For example, managers should give very clear, well-defined work assignments. They should also clearly explain how work will be evaluated. Employees who know precisely what they are supposed to do and what level of performance is acceptable will find it unnecessary to play political games to assert their power. Under such conditions, recognition will come from meeting job expectations, instead of from less acceptable avenues.

2. Open the communication process. It is difficult for people to try to foster their own goals at the expense of organizational goals whenever the communication process is open to scrutiny by all. Compare, for example, a department manager who makes budget allocation decisions in a highly open fashion (announced to all) and one who makes the same decisions in secret. When decisions are not openly shared and communicated to all, conditions are ideal for unscrupulous individuals to abuse their power. Decisions that can be monitored by all are unlikely to allow any one individual to gain excessive control over desired resources.

3. Be a good role model. It is well established that higher-level personnel set the standards by which lower-level employees operate. As a result, any manager who is openly political in her use of power is likely to create a climate in which her subordinates behave the same way. Engaging in dirty political tricks not only teaches subordinates that such tactics are appropriate, but also that they are the desired way of operating within the organization. Managers will certainly find it difficult to constrain the political actions of their subordinates unless they set a clear example of honest and reasonable treatment of others in their own behavior.

4. Do not turn a blind eye to game players. Suppose you see one of your subordinates attempting to gain power over another by taking credit for that individual's work. Immediately confront this individual and do not ignore what he did. If the person believes he can get away with it, he will try to do so. What's worse, if he suspects that you are aware of what he did, but didn't do anything about it, you are indirectly reinforcing his unethical political behavior—letting him know that he can get away with it.

In conclusion, it is important for practicing managers to realize that because power differences are basic to organizations, attempts to gain power advantages through political maneuvers are to be expected. However, it is a critical aspect of a manager's job to redirect these political activities away from any threats to the integrity of the organization. Whereas it may be unrealistic to expect to eliminate dirty political tricks, we believe the suggestions offered here provide some useful guidelines for minimizing their impact.

ETHICS: MORAL CONSTRAINTS ON ORGANIZATIONAL BEHAVIOR

Probably one of the most important effects of organizational power is that it invites corruption. Indeed, the more power an individual has at his or her disposal, the more tempted that person is to use that power toward some immoral or unethical purpose.[38] Obviously, then, the potential is quite real for powerful individuals and organizations to abuse their power and to behave unethically. Unfortunately, this potential is too frequently realized. Consider, for example, how greed overtook concerns about human welfare when the Manville Corporation suppressed evidence that asbestos inhalation was killing its employees, or when Ford failed to correct a known defect that made its Pinto vulnerable to gas tank explosions following low speed rear-end collisions.[39] Companies that dump dangerous medical waste materials into our rivers and oceans also appear to favor their own interests over public safety and welfare (see Figure 12.9). Although these examples are better known than many others, they do not appear to be unusual. In fact, the story they tell may be far more typical than we would like, as

FIGURE 12.9 Dubious Ethical Practices: Some Serious Consequences

When faced with the conflict between behaving in a manner that makes a company more profitable and powerful versus ensuring public health and safety, many organizations yield to the temptation of profit and power, and act unethically. The tragic aftermath of some such decisions is shown here.

one expert estimates that about two thirds of the 500 largest American corporations have been involved in one form of illegal behavior or another.[40]

The field of **organizational ethics** is concerned with applying moral and ethical standards to the behavior of individuals operating within organizations. Interestingly, the heads of large corporations believe that behaving in an ethically responsible fashion is in the best long-term interest of their organizations.[41] Despite this, the various political techniques described in this chapter suggest that unethical and dishonest behaviors may be common occurrences in organizations. Accordingly, we will devote the final section of this chapter to the important matter of ethical behavior in organizations. We will begin by attempting to describe the complex issue of what makes an act of organizational politics ethical or unethical. We will then explain some of the reasons why unethical decisions are made in organizations, and conclude by noting some strategies for enhancing ethical behavior.

Political Behavior: What Makes It Ethical?

Although there are obviously no clear-cut ways of identifying whether or not a certain organizational action is ethical, Velasquez and his associates suggest some useful guidelines for aiding us in considering this question.[42]

As a first consideration, we may ask: *will the political tactics promote purely selfish interests, or will they also help meet organizational goals?* If only one's personal, selfish interests are nurtured by a political action, it may be considered unethical. Usually, political activity fails to benefit organizational goals, but not always. Suppose, for example, that a group of top corporate executives is consistently making bad decisions that are leading the organization down the road to ruin. Would it be unethical in such a case to use political tactics to try to remove the power-holders from their positions? Probably not. In fact, political actions designed to benefit the organization as a whole (as long as they are legal) may be justified as appropriate and highly ethical. After all, they are in the best interest of the entire organization.

A second question in considering the ethics of organizational politics is: *does the political activity respect the rights of the individuals affected?* Generally speaking, actions that violate basic human rights are, of course, considered unethical. For example, dirty political tricks that rely on espionage techniques (such as wiretapping) are not only illegal, but also unethical in that they violate the affected individual's *right to privacy*. However, as you may know, police agencies are sometimes permitted by law to use methods that violate privacy rights under circumstances in which the greater good of the community at large is at stake. It is not easy, of course, to weigh the relative benefits of an individual's rights to privacy against the greater societal good. Indeed, making such decisions involves a potential misuse of power in itself. It is because of this that society often entrusts such decisions to high courts charged with the responsibility for considering both individual rights and the rights and benefits of the community at large.

Velasquez and his associates identified a third consideration in assessing the ethics of political action: *does the activity conform to standards of equity and justice; is it fair?* Any political behavior that unfairly benefits one party over another may be considered unethical. Paying one person more than another similarly qualified person is one example (as you may recall from our discussion of *equity theory* in chapter 3). It is important to realize that standards regarding the fair treatment of individuals are often unclear. Not surprisingly, more powerful individuals often use their power to convince others (and themselves!) that they are taking action in the name of justice (see Figure 12.10 on page 430). That is, they seek to implement seemingly fair rules that benefit themselves at the expense of others.[43] This, of course, represents an abuse of power. However,

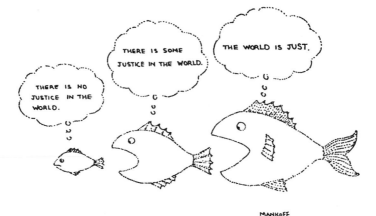

FIGURE 12.10   Is the World Fair? It Depends on How Powerful You Are
In view of the fact that standards of justice tend to be unclear, more powerful people (or fish, in this case) tend to use their power to convince others that their assessment of fairness is correct. (Source: Drawing by Mankoff; © 1981 The New Yorker Magazine, Inc.)

we must sometimes consider instances in which violating standards of justice may be considered appropriate. For example, it has been found that managers may sometimes give poorly performing employees higher pay than they deserve in the hope of stimulating them to work at higher levels.[44] Although the principle of equity is violated in this case (people should be paid in proportion to their job contributions), the manager may argue that the employee and the organization benefit as a result. Of course, the result may be considered unfair to the other individuals who are not so generously treated. Obviously, this is a complex issue that we will not be able to settle here. Our point is that although ethical behavior involves adhering to standards of justice, there may be instances in which violations of these standards are ethically acceptable.

As you can tell by now, most matters involving the resolution of moral and ethical issues are quite complex. Each time a political strategy is considered, its potential effects should be evaluated in terms of the questions outlined here. If the practice appears to be ethical based on these considerations, it may be acceptable in that situation. If ethical questions arise, however, alternative actions should be strongly considered. Unfortunately, many unethical political practices are followed in organizations despite their obvious violations of moral standards. We will now consider some of the underlying reasons for this.

Why Does Unethical Behavior Occur in Organizations?

As noted earlier in this chapter, unethical organizational practices are embarrassingly commonplace. It is easy to define such practices as dumping polluted chemical wastes into rivers, insider trading on Wall Street, and overcharging the government for Medicaid services as morally wrong. Yet these and many other unethical practices go on almost routinely in many organizations. Why is this so? In other words, what accounts for the unethical actions of people within organizations?

One answer to this question is based on the idea that *organizations often reward behaviors that violate ethical standards.* Consider, for example, how many business executives are expected to deal in bribes and payoffs, and how good corporate citizens blowing the whistle on organizational wrongdoings may fear being punished for their actions (refer to our discussion of whistle-blowing in chapter 13). Jansen and Von Glinow explain that organizations tend to develop *counternorms,* accepted organizational practices that are contrary to prevailing ethical standards.[45] Some of these are summarized in Figure 12.11.

The top of Figure 12.11 identifies being open and honest as a prevailing ethical norm. Indeed, governmental regulations requiring full disclosure and freedom of information reinforce society's values toward openness and honesty. Within organizations, however, it is often considered not only acceptable, but desirable, to be much more secretive and deceitful. The practice of *stonewalling,* willingly hiding relevant information, is quite common. One reason for this is that organizations may actually punish those who are too open and honest. Consider, for example, the disclosure that B. F. Goodrich rewarded employees who falsified data on the quality of aircraft brakes in order to win certification.[46] Similarly, it has been reported that executives at Metropolitan Edison encouraged employees to withhold information from the press about the Three Mile Island nuclear accident.[47] Both incidents represent cases in which the counternorms of secrecy and deceitfulness were accepted and supported by the organization.

As you can see from Figure 12.11, there are many other organizational counternorms that promote morally and ethically questionable practices. The fact that these practices are commonly rewarded and accepted suggests that organizations may be operating within a world that dictates its own set of accepted rules. This reasoning suggests a second answer to the question of why organizations act unethically—namely, because *managerial values exist that undermine integrity.* In a recent analysis of executive integrity, Wolfe explains that managers have developed some ways of thinking (of which they may be quite unaware) that foster unethical behavior.[48]

One culprit is referred to as the **bottom line mentality.** This line of thinking supports financial success as the only value to be considered. It promotes short-term solutions that are immediately financially sound, despite the fact that they cause problems for others within the organization or the organization as a whole. It promotes an unrealistic belief that everything boils down to a monetary game. As such, rules of morality are merely obstacles, impediments along the way to bottom line financial success.

Wolfe also notes that managers tend to rely on an **exploitative mentality**—a

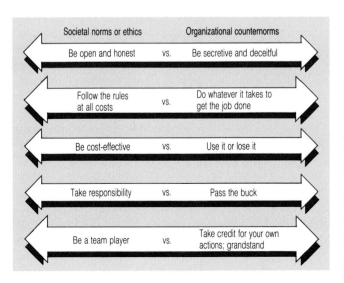

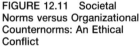

FIGURE 12.11 Societal Norms versus Organizational Counternorms: An Ethical Conflict

Although societal standards of ethics and morality dictate the appropriateness of certain actions, *counternorms* that encourage and support opposite practices often develop within organizations. (Source: Based on suggestions by Jansen & Von Glinow, 1985; see Note 45.)

view that encourages "using" people in a way that promotes stereotypes and undermines empathy and compassion. This is a highly selfish perspective, one that sacrifices concerns for others in favor of benefits to one's own immediate interests. In addition, there is a **Madison Avenue mentality**—a perspective suggesting that anything is right if the public can be convinced that it's right. The idea is that executives may be more concerned about their actions appearing ethical than by their legitimate morality— a public relations–guided morality. It is this kind of thinking that leads some companies to hide their unethical actions (by dumping their toxic wastes under cover of night, for instance) or to otherwise justify them by attempting to explain them as completely acceptable.

It is not too difficult to recognize the problems associated with such mentalities. Their overemphasis on short-term monetary gain may lead to decisions that not only hurt individuals in the long run, but threaten the very existence of organizations themselves. Although an organization may make an immediate profit by cutting corners, exploiting people, and convincing others that they have behaved appropriately, it is questionable whether such practices are in the long-term best interest of organizations. Just as people are learning that they cannot continue to exploit their natural environments forever without paying a cost (e.g., depletion of natural resources, and hazards allegedly caused by openings in the earth's ozone layer), the same may apply to business environments as well. Indeed, society appears to be increasingly less tolerant of organizations that continue to violate its moral standards in the name of short-term profit.[49] It has even been argued that when organizations continue to behave unethically, they may actually find that doing so is not profitable for them in the long run. Consumers who find the well-publicized unethical actions of various companies objectionable may cast their vote for greater social responsibility by not patronizing those organizations.[50] As such, the tendency for dubious ethical practices to be commonplace may be changing—although only time will tell.

Promoting Organizational Morality: Some Strategies

Because abuses of power in organizations are so objectionable, few would wish to sit back and allow organizations to hurt themselves and society by their sometimes unethical actions. Several suggestions have been made for encouraging ethical behavior in organizations.[51]

1. Integrity from the top down: Chief executives should promote ethical consciousness in their organizations. It is important to note that a sense of organizational morality does not develop automatically, but is communicated from the top down.[52] When top executives communicate their endorsement of high moral standards by way of their words and actions, lower-ranking organizational members can be expected to follow suit. This might be done by the CEO announcing that the company is interested in the free and open exchange of ideas (as we noted earlier, such a practice minimizes the occurrence of political activities). In a recent article, Raelin cites some examples of companies that have benefitted by acting this way.[53]

For example, the 3M Company implemented its Pollution Prevention Pays (3P) policy in 1975 to generate savings from the prevention of environmental pollution. Professionals within 3M were encouraged to submit suggestions for reducing pollution by changing their company's manufacturing processes. Through 1987, company scientists generated over 1,700 proposals that not only helped minimize environmental pollution, but also reportedly saved 3M some $300 million. Similar success stories have been reported at companies such as Polaroid and Atlantic Richfield (ARCO). Apparently, organizations that have the foresight to promote ethical consciousness starting at the highest corporate levels may reap large benefits for doing so. Indeed, it has been estimated that whereas $30,000 invested in Dow-Jones stocks in 1952 would have grown to $134,000 by 1986, the same money would have grown to over $1 million if invested in fifteen highly socially responsible companies.[54] Clearly, ethical behavior may pay off even more than unethical behavior!

2. Ethics through regulation: Develop formal procedures for addressing unethical behavior. Although executive pronouncements of morality may be helpful, to be most effective, they have to be backed up by specific procedures for handling unethical conduct. As we noted in our discussion of learning in chapter 2, desirable forms of organizational behavior may be effectively managed by appropriate disciplinary actions. Formal **codes of corporate ethics** may be especially helpful in this regard. For example, specific rules regarding such potentially unethical actions as conflicts of interest, political contributions, insider information, bribes and kickbacks, falsification of records, and misappropriation of corporate resources have been instituted into the formal ethical codes of many organizations.[55] Indeed, such codes are quite common. To quote one report appearing in the *New York Times:* "Over the last decade, nearly every major company has put together some form of written code of ethics, ranging from the Exxon Corporation's one-page 'Policy Statement on Business Ethics,' to Citicorp's 62-page booklet on 'Ethical Standards and Conflict of Interest Policy.' "[56] It is important that ethical codes be considered living documents, ones that can be reviewed periodically and changed to reflect developing societal standards and organizational conditions.

It is also considered useful for organizations to have an *appeals process,* some internal mechanism through which employees can voice their awareness of ethically inappropriate organizational behavior without fear of reprisal. The best systems are ones that have standardized mechanisms for receiving and impartially considering complaints. For example, in the aftermath of the Challenger spacecraft explosion in 1986, NASA created an Office of Safety, Reliability, Maintainability, and Quality Assurance staffed by engineers and astronauts. This group operates as an independent safety board that has authority to stop launches if it believes unsafe conditions prevail.

Together with ethical codes, appeals processes represent formal ways of promoting corporate social responsibility from within an organization. However, in view of the fact that such self-regulatory mechanisms do not always exist, some argue that the government should formally intervene in the creation of ethical policies.[57] Indeed, there are many governmental agencies in the United States that are responsible for overseeing the moral and ethical activities of different aspects of organizational functioning. For a summary of some of these, please see Figure 12.12 (on page 434). As the number of laws regulating business activities grows dramatically, many serious questions have been raised about the government's right to intervene, the high cost of such regulation, and the government's effectiveness as an agent promoting ethical behavior.[58] Regardless, the existence of governmental regulation provides a clear reminder that society will not tolerate unethical business activity.

3. Morality across the board: Incorporate ethical norms into jobs at all organizational levels. Raelin recommends that organizational ethics be institutionalized; that is, responsibility for moral behavior should not reside in any one person, but instead, should be incorporated into all aspects of all jobs. For example, financial resources should be made available in managers' budgets for testing the safety of equipment. In addition, performance appraisal forms should be modified to include consideration of employees' ethical behaviors as well as the more standard elements of their job performance. Moreover, employees should be rewarded for adhering to ethical

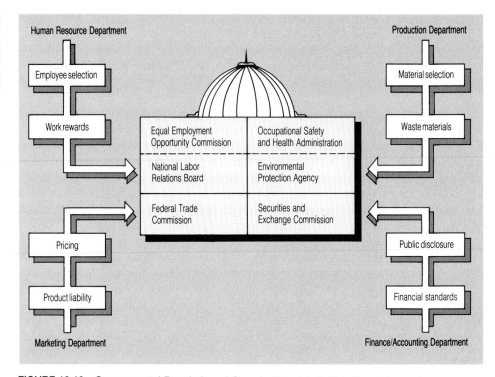

FIGURE 12.12   Governmental Regulation of Organizational Activities: Some Examples
In order to ensure that organizations operate in an ethical fashion, society has entrusted the government with responsibility for overseeing many aspects of their functioning. Some examples of U.S. government agencies that regulate business activities are indicated here. (Source: Based on information in Buchholz, 1989; see Note 39.)

standards. If they are not, as noted earlier, it is possible for counternorms to develop by which the organization (even if unknowingly) rewards unethical rather than ethical behavior. As a promising sign, it has been reported that many companies (including 44 percent of those in the *Fortune* 500) are instituting formal training programs in business ethics.[59] Many of these programs not only teach employees what's right and wrong as abstract concepts, but train them to think about the effects of their actions on others.

To summarize, many things can be done to combat the tendency for some individuals to abuse their power and behave unethically in organizations. Ethical practices should begin at the top, but be institutionalized at all organizational levels and regulated via internal mechanisms such as codes of ethical responsibility. (It is important to note, however, that the standards of moral and ethical behavior may not be universal. In fact, as we describe in the **International Perspective** section below, different standards of morality may exist in different nations. Understanding these differences can be a key to corporate success in this age of the multinational corporation.)

OB: AN INTERNATIONAL PERSPECTIVE

Corporate Morality: Facing the Challenge of the Global Economy

At the risk of directing your attention to thoughts of overwhelmingly negative events, we ask you to consider the following recent occurrences.

- Acid rain produced by various American companies threatens the ecological balance of the Canadian woodlands.

- Birth control devices ruled unsafe by American agencies are marketed to third-world nations by the large pharmaceutical companies that make them.
- An explosion at the Chernobyl nuclear power plant in the Soviet Union sends radioactive material into the atmosphere, threatening the health and safety of all living things on our planet for many years.
- Questionable money-saving safety practices of large foreign firms lead to disasters in those nations in which they employ workers, such as the explosion at a chemical plant in Bhopal, India.
- Private banks around the world are largely responsible for financing the debt, hence the security, of various third-world nations on the verge of bankruptcy.

Although they are clearly very different from each other, it is safe to say that these various incidents all have something in common. Namely, they each illustrate the increasingly tighter connections between the organizational activities of different nations. A business decision made in one nation can clearly have an impact on individuals in another nation—and, as these examples attest, that effect is not always positive. Thus, today's businesses face the prospect of *globalization*— realizing their part in a unified world economy,

instead of only their domestic base. As the examples above illustrate, one of the most pressing considerations of such a large-scale orientation to management involves recognition of the ethical and moral impact of their actions on others throughout the world. One important challenge to considering these effects is the possibility of different moral values within different cultures.

Adler and Bird recently reported some interesting data on this issue.[60] Business persons in eleven nations on four continents were asked to indicate how important it was for them to be *ethical* in their business dealings with others. The ratings could range from 1 ("most important") to 8 ("least important"). The results, summarized by continent, are shown in Figure 12.13. As you examine these findings, two interesting facts emerge. First, the ratings were approximately equal across the various continents. Apparently, the people of various nations were not any more or less concerned with ethical matters. Second, the expressed importance of ethics was only modest, at best. Individuals completing the survey tended to take ethical matters for granted, not believing that they were an important consideration in their business activities.

Despite the fact that ethical matters appear to be an equally modest concern of business persons

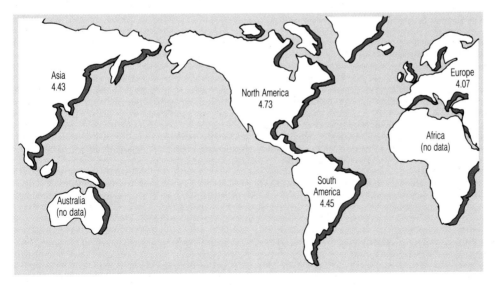

FIGURE 12.13 Concern about Organizational Ethics: A Universal Phenomenon

When business executives in eleven nations on four continents were asked how important it was for them to be ethical in their business interactions, their responses indicated a uniformly moderate level of concern for ethics all over the world (ratings could range from 1, "most important," to 8, "least important"). (Source: Based on data reported by Wolfe, 1988; see Note 48.)

around the world, it would be a serious mistake to suggest either that ethical issues don't really matter, or that what passes for ethical behavior is the same throughout different cultures. Adler and Bird make the point that although some ethical codes are universal (e.g., "thou shalt not kill"), others are not. For example, whereas it is considered dishonest in the United States for merchants to misrepresent the items they sell, the rule *caveat emptor* ("buyer beware") is considered completely acceptable in Hong Kong. Similarly, whereas bribery is considered a strictly illegal and immoral practice in many cultures, it is perfectly acceptable, and condoned, in others.

Such differences pose very serious dilemmas for individuals conducting business in cultures with widely differing moral values. In many cases, a conflict may be encountered between adopting the standards of the host nation (thereby risking allegations of unethical behavior at home) and not doing so (thereby risking failure in the business transactions). In either case, the individual is certain to face problems, and may be forced to choose between the lesser of two likely evils. In the interest of avoiding such situations, some observers have noted the need to develop ethics for a global society.

Because of deeply rooted cultural traditions, it would be very difficult and highly unrealistic to expect all cultures to adopt identical sets of moral values in conducting business. Yet, it has been argued that fostering a recognition of the interconnectedness between the organizations of the world's nations would help all nations prosper. Specifically, it has been recommended that businesses pay closer attention to the effects of their activities not just on the company's stockholders, but on the world as a whole, adapting a sense of "global community."[61] If you consider the far-reaching global consequences of the narrower views that led to the disasters described above, it is easy to understand the necessity of behaving with integrity. Clearly, moral behavior is more than an essential ingredient in the success of individual business enterprises; it is the key to a safe and prosperous world.

SUMMARY AND REVIEW

Organizational Power. The concept of **power** refers to the capacity to change the behavior or attitudes of others in a desired manner. Power may reside within individuals, and five bases of individual social power have been identified. **Reward power** and **coercive power** refer to an individual's capacity to control valued rewards and punishments, respectively. **Legitimate power** is the recognized authority that an individual has by virtue of his or her organizational position. **Referent power** is a source of control based on the fact that an individual is liked and admired by others. Finally, **expert power** refers to the power an individual has by virtue of the fact that he or she is recognized as having superior knowledge, skill, or expertise in some valued area.

Power may also reside within work groups, or subunits. The **resource-dependency model** explains that power resides within those subunits which control the greatest share of valued organizational resources. The **strategic contingencies model** explains power in terms of a subunit's capacity to control the activities of other subunits. Such power may be enhanced by the capacity to reduce the level of uncertainty experienced by another unit, having a central position within the organization, or performing organizational functions that other units cannot perform.

Organizational Politics. Behaving in a manner that is not officially approved by an organization in order to meet one's own goals by influencing others is known as **organizational politics**. Such activities typically occur under ambiguous conditions (such as in areas of organizational functioning in which clear rules are lacking). Political tactics may include blaming and attacking others, controlling access to information, cultivating a favorable impression, developing an internal base of support, and aligning oneself with more powerful others. This may involve the playing of political games, such as asserting one's authority, enhancing one's power base, attacking one's rivals, and trying to foster organizational change. Such actions typically occur under conditions in which organizational uncertainty exists, important decisions involving large amounts of scarce resources are made, and when the groups involved have conflicting interests, but are approximately equal in power.

Organizational Ethics. The study of **organizational ethics** is concerned with applying moral and ethical standards to the behavior of individuals within organizations. Although there are exceptions, political behavior may be considered ethical to the extent that it fosters organizational interests over individual greed, respects the rights of individuals, and conforms to prevailing standards of justice and fair play.

Unethical behavior occurs in organizations for several reasons. For one, organizations develop *counternorms* that reward individuals for behaving in a way that is not considered ethical in the outside world (e.g., being secretive and *stonewalling* instead of being open and honest with others). In addition, managerial values exist that undermine integrity, such as the **bottom line mentality** (a focus on short-term profit maximization), the **exploitative mentality** (selfishly using others for one's advantage), and the **Madison Avenue mentality** (convincing others that your unethical actions are actually moral).

Several strategies are recommended to promote organizational morality. First, chief executives should encourage ethical consciousness in their organizations from the top down—showing they support and care about ethical practices. Second, formal processes should be used to support ethical behavior. For example, internal regulation may involve the use of **codes of corporate ethics,** and the availability of appeals processes. Finally, it is recommended that ethical norms and practices be institutionalized—incorporated into all organizational levels.

KEY TERMS

bottom line mentality: The view that places the greatest importance on short-term financial gains of an organization. It considers ethics and morality obstacles in the path of financial gain.

codes of corporate ethics: Formal organizational rules identifying the ethical philosophy of a company, and specifying the unethical activities that will not be tolerated.

coercive power: The individual power base derived from an individual's capacity to administer punishment to another.

expert power: The individual power base derived from an individual's recognized superior skills and abilities in a certain area.

exploitative mentality: The selfish view that sacrifices concerns for others in favor of an individual's own immediate interests.

legitimate power: The individual power base derived from one's position in an organizational hierarchy; the accepted authority of one's position.

Madison Avenue mentality: The view suggesting that anything is right if others can be convinced that it's right; a public relations–guided morality.

organizational ethics: The application of moral and ethical standards to the behavior of individuals operating within organizations.

organizational politics: Actions not officially approved by an organization, taken to influence others in order to meet one's personal goals.

politics: See *organizational politics.*

power: The capacity to change the behavior or attitudes of others in a desired manner.

referent power: The individual power base derived from the degree to which one is liked and admired by others.

resource-dependency model: The view that power resides within those subunits which are able to control the greatest share of valued organizational resources.

reward power: The individual power base derived from an individual's capacity to administer valued rewards to others.

strategic contingencies model: A view explaining power in terms of a subunit's capacity to control the activities of other subunits. A subunit's power is enhanced when: (1) it can reduce the level of uncertainty experienced by other subunits, (2) it occupies a central position in the organization, and (3) its activities are highly indispensible to the organization.

Questions for Discussion

1. Suppose your professor asks you to redo a homework assignment. Explain the various bases of individual social power he or she may use to influence your behavior in this situation.

2. Using the *resource-dependency model* and the *strategic contingencies model* as the basis for your analysis, describe the relative power differences between groups in any organization with which you are familiar.

3. Suppose you are a corporate official on the lookout for places within your organization where political behavior is likely to occur. What places and conditions would you look for? Explain your answer.

4. Describe the political tactics and tricks that one person may use to gain a power advantage over another in an organization.

5. While it might not be possible to completely eliminate organizational politics, it might be possible to effectively manage political activity. Describe some of the things that can be done to effectively cope with organizational politics.

6. Explain why an organization's ethical norms may differ from ethical standards existing in the outside world.

7. Argue for or against the following statement: "Organizations engage in unethical behavior because such actions are in their own best interest."

Notes

1. Cobb, A. T. (1984). An episodic model of power: Toward an integration of theory and research. *Academy of Management Review, 9,* 482–493.

2. French, J. R. P., & Raven, B. (1959). The bases of social power. In D. Cartwright (Ed.), *Studies in social power* (pp. 150–167). Ann Arbor, MI: Inst. for Social Research, Univ. of Michigan.

3. Kanter, R. M. (1979). Power failure in management circuits. *Harvard Business Review, 57,* 65–75.

4. Arvey, R. D., & Jones, A. P. (1985). The use of discipline in organizational settings: A framework for future research. In L. L. Cummings & B. M. Staw (Eds.), *Research in organizational behavior,* vol. 7 (pp. 367–408). Greenwich, CT: JAI Press.

5. Fiorelli, J. S. (1988). Power in work groups: Team member's perspective. *Human Relations, 41,* 1–12.

6. Mintzberg, H. (1983). *Power in and around organizations.* Englewood Cliffs, NJ: Prentice-Hall.

7. Podsakoff, P. M., & Schriesheim, C. A. (1985). Field studies of French and Raven's bases of power: Critique, reanalysis, and suggestions for future research. *Psychological Bulletin, 97,* 387–411.

8. Huber, V. L. (1981). The sources, uses, and conservation of managerial power. *Personnel, 51*(4), 62–67.

9. Kipnis, D., Schmidt, S. M., Swaffin-Smith, C., & Wilkinson, I. (1984, Winter). Patterns of managerial influence: Shotgun managers, tacticians, and bystanders. *Organizational Dynamics,* 58–67.

10. Frost, D. E., & Stahelski, A. J. (1988). The systematic measurement of French and Raven's bases of social power in workgroups. *Journal of Applied Social Psychology, 18,* 375–389.

11. Kahn, R. L., Wolfe, D. M., Quinn, R. P., Snoek, J. D., & Rosenthal, R. A. (1964). *Organizational stress: Studies in role conflict and ambiguity.* New York: Wiley.

12. Mulder, M., de Jong, R. D., Koppelaar, L., & Verhage, J. (1986). Power, situation, and leaders' effectiveness: An organizational field study. *Journal of Applied Psychology, 71,* 566–570.

13. Mainiero, L. A. (1986). Coping with powerlessness: The relationship of gender and job dependency to empowerment-strategy usage. *Administrative Science Quarterly, 31,* 633–653.

14. Pfeffer, J., & Salancik, G. (1978). *The external control of organizations.* New York: Harper & Row.

15. Salancik, G., & Pfeffer, J. (1974). The bases and uses of power in organizational decision making. *Administrative Science Quarterly, 19,* 453–473.

16. Hickson, D. J., Hinings, C. R., Lee, C. A., Schneck, R. E., & Pennings, J. M. (1971). A strategic contingencies theory of intraorganizational power. *Administrative Science Quarterly, 15,* 216–229.

17. Lawrence, P. R., & Lorsch, J. W. (1967). *Organization and environment.* Cambridge, MA: Harvard Univ.

18. Hickson, D. J., Astley, W. G., Butler, R. J., & Wilson, D. C. (1981). Organization as power. In L. L. Cummings & B. M. Staw (Eds.), *Research in organizational behavior* (pp. 151–196). Greenwich, CT: JAI Press.

19. Miles, R. H. (1980). *Macro organizational behavior.* Glenview, IL: Scott, Foresman.

20. Saunders, C. S., & Scamell, R. (1982). Intraorganizational distributions of power: Replication research. *Academy of Management Journal, 25,* 192–200.

21. Hinings, C. R., Hickson, D. J., Pennings, J. M., & Schneck, R. E. (1974). Structural conditions of intraorganizational power. *Administrative Science Quarterly, 19,* 22–44.

22. Mayes, B. T., & Allen, R. T. (1977). Toward a definition of organizational politics. *Academy of Management Review, 2,* 672–678.

23. Gandz, J., & Murray, V. V. (1980). The experience of workplace politics. *Academy of Management Journal, 23,* 237–251.

24. Madison, D. L., Allen, R. W., Porter, L. W., Renwick, P. A. & Mayes, B. T. (1980). Organizational politics:

An exploration of managers' perceptions. *Human Relations, 33,* 79–100.

25. See Note 23.

26. Allen, R. W., Madison, D. L., Porter, L. W., Renwick, P. A., & Mayes, B. T. (1979). Organizational politics: Tactics and characteristics of its actors. *California Management Review, 22,* 77–83.

27. Feldman, S. P. (1988). Secrecy, information, and politics: An essay on organizational decision making. *Human Relations, 41,* 73–90.

28. Greenberg, J. (1990). Looking fair vs. being fair: Managing impressions or organizational justice. In B. M. Staw & L. L. Cummings (Eds.), *Research in organizational behavior,* vol. 12. Greenwich, CT: JAI Press.

29. Welsh, M. A., & Slusher, E. A. (1986). Organizational design as a context for political activity. *Administrative Science Quarterly, 31,* 389–402.

30. Liden, R. C., & Mitchell, T. R. (1988). Ingratiatory behaviors in organizational settings. *Academy of Management Review, 13,* 572–587.

31. Vredenburgh, D. J., & Maurer, J. G. (1984). A process framework of organizational politics. *Human Relations, 37,* 47–66.

32. See Note 6.

33. See Note 24.

34. Pfeffer, J. (1981). *Power in organizations.* Boston: Pitman.

35. Gray, B., & Ariss, S. S. (1985). Politics and strategic change across organizational life cycles. *Academy of Management Review, 10,* 707–723.

36. Hannan, M. T., & Freeman, J. H. (1978). Internal politics of growth and decline. In M. W. Meyer (Ed.), *Environment and organizations* (pp. 177–199). San Francisco: Jossey-Bass.

37. See Note 24.

38. Kipnis, D. (1976). *The powerholders.* Chicago: Univ. of Chicago.

39. Buchholz, R. A. (1989). *Fundamental concepts and problems in business ethics.* Englewood Cliffs, NJ: Prentice-Hall.

40. Gellerman, S. W. (1986, July–August). Why "good" managers make bad ethical choices. *Harvard Business Review,* pp. 85–90.

41. Ford, R., & McLaughlin, F. (1984). Perceptions of socially responsible activities and attitudes: A comparison of business school deans and corporate chief executives. *Academy of Management Journal, 27,* 666–674.

42. Velasquez, M., Moberg, D. J., & Cavanagh, G. F. (1983). Organizational statesmanship and dirty politics: Ethical guidelines for the organizational politician. *Organizational Dynamics, 11,* 65–79.

43. Greenberg, J. (1990). Looking fair vs. being fair: Managing impressions of organizational justice. In B. M. Staw & L. L. Cummings (Eds.), *Research in organizational behavior,* vol. 12. Greenwich, CT: JAI Press.

44. Greenberg, J. (1982). Approaching equity and avoiding inequity in groups and organizations. In J. Greenberg, & R. L. Cohen (Eds.), *Equity and justice in social behavior* (pp. 389–435). New York: Academic Press.

45. Jansen, E., & Von Glinow, M. A. (1985). Ethical ambivalence and organizational reward systems. *Academy of Management Review, 10,* 814–822.

46. Vandevier, K. (1978). The aircraft brake scandal: A cautionary tale in which the moral is unpleasant. In A. G. Athos, & J. J. Babarro (Eds.), *Interpersonal behavior: Communication and understanding relationships* (pp. 529–540). Englewood Cliffs, NJ: Prentice-Hall.

47. Gray, M., & Rosen, I. (1982). *The warning.* New York: Norton.

48. Wolfe, D. M. (1988). Is there integrity in the bottom line: Managing obstacles to executive integrity. In S. Srivastava (Ed.), *Executive integrity: The search for high human values in organizational life* (pp. 140–171). San Francisco: Jossey-Bass.

49. See Note 39.

50. Murray, K. B., & Montanari, J. R. (1986). Strategic management of the socially responsible firm: Integrating management and marketing theory. *Academy of Management Review, 11,* 815–827.

51. Raelin, J. A. (1987). The professional as the executive's ethical aide-de-camp. *Academy of Management Executive, 1,* 171–182.

52. Kelly, C. M. (1987, Summer) The interrelationship of ethics and power in today's organizations. *Organizational Dynamics,* pp. 5–18.

53. See Note 51.

54. Burns, S. (1987, April 15). Good corporate citizenship can pay dividends. *Dallas Morning News,* p. C1.

55. White, B. J., & Montgomery, B. R. (1980). Corporate codes of conduct. *California Management Review, 23,* 80–97.

56. Lewin, T. (1983, December 11). Business ethics' new appeal. *New York Times,* p. 4F.

57. Machan, T. R. (1984). Should business be regulated? In T. Regan (Ed.), *Just business: New introductory essays in business ethics* (pp. 200–215). New York: Random House.

58. Kangun, N., & Moyer, C. R. (1976). The failings of regulation. *MSU Business Topics, 24*(2), 10–18.

59. Center for Business at Bentley College (1986). Are corporations institutionalizing ethics? *Journal of Business Ethics, 5,* 77–89.

60. Adler, N. J., & Bird, F. B. (1988). International dimensions of executive integrity: Who is responsible for the world. In S. Srivastava (Ed.), *Executive integrity: The search for high human values in organizational life* (pp. 243–267). San Francisco: Jossey-Bass.

61. Wright, A. (1986). Toward the year 2000. *Issues, 1*(3), 1–8.

CASE
IN
POINT

Hollywood: Where Dreams Can Be Deadly

Hollywood—the dream factory. The place where this country's most popular and influential form of entertainment is made. As the power of television and movies to shape attitudes and values is remarkable, so too is the power of the few producers and directors who have bona fide hits to their credit. The motto in Hollywood is "you're only as good as your last picture," and few have had as many recent successes as John Landis.

Landis achieved his success at a very early age. He wrote and directed his first film at age twenty-one.[1] Although it was not a big box office smash, it achieved mild success and, partly because of his youth, he was highly acclaimed. By age thirty-six he had to his credit such hits as "An American Werewolf in London," "National Lampoon's Animal House," "The Blues Brothers," "Trading Places," and "48 HRS." He also had to his "credit" an indictment on three counts of involuntary manslaughter in connection with the deaths of actors Vic Morrow, age fifty-three, Renee Chen, age six, and Myca Dinh Le, age seven, during the shooting of a film he directed, "Twilight Zone: The Movie."[2]

A director on a movie set is akin to the CEO of a company. All final decisions about personnel, scheduling, and budgeting rest with this individual. In addition, the director is the creative force behind a film—the person who provides the artistic vision. Directors also take the role of counselor, coach, and advisor to the actors and actresses, many of whom are especially demanding in requiring this attention. Finally, the director is the coordinator of all activities that comprise the making of a motion picture.[3]

It was in his role as director that Landis made numerous decisions related to the accident that resulted in the three deaths. The most obvious decision was to order the shot in which Morrow was to carry the two children across a river while a set of a village was exploded in the background and a helicopter hovered above. Another decision was to hire the two children without first getting the necessary child-labor permits and without telling the parents about the potential dangers involved.[4,5] Patrick Henning, a former California Labor Commissioner, suggested that this was a "complete and absolute neglect of children bordering on obscenity. My guess is they were working on a schedule and didn't want to lose any time or money. They knew permits would not be issued because of the hazardous conditions. They just decided, 'the hell with it.' "[6] Landis also ordered the use of live ammunition in filming the scene in which the accident occurred. Although this practice is generally not employed and is frowned upon by the Screen Actors Guild and the photographers union, Landis felt that live ammo would provide a quicker and more dramatic shoot.[7] In addition, the placement of the ammunition, the helicopter, and the actors derived from Landis's artistic vision of what the scene should look like on film. It was generally agreed that the proximity of the helicopter to the explosions was partly responsible for the helicopter's spinning out of control, decapitating Morrow, and crushing the children. Finally, Landis repeatedly urged Morrow, the helicopter pilot, and the technical crew to proceed with the filming despite their repeated concerns about the safety conditions.[8]

Although in this particular case a jury acquitted Landis of the charges of manslaughter, the generally unsafe conditions highlighted in this case are all too often repeated on other motion picture and television sets.[9] For instance, in 1980–1981, three camera assistants were killed when vehicles collapsed on them during filming. Additionally, a stuntwoman was injured in an accident in which she claimed she warned the director that the car was unsafe—she is now a quadriplegic. More recently, four people were killed and five injured when a helicopter crashed during the filming of "Braddock: Missing in Action III," and a pilot lost his life during the filming of the hit movie "Top Gun."[10]

What leads to the conditions that create these accidents? Certainly many stunts are inherently dangerous. Additionally, mistakes are made. However, there is a feeling expressed by many stunt people and actors that some extremely dangerous stunts simply shouldn't be attempted. Yet, these stunts *are* attempted because these people feel pressure to perform or risk losing their jobs. It is also true that to keep within budgets and deadlines some corners are cut. Maintaining an "artistic vision" is also a contributing factor to some safety violations as directors are more immediately concerned with what the scene will look like than how safe it is. Finally, although worker safety is governed by federal and state regulations, when violations of regulations are found, imprisonments are extremely rare and fines are often negligible.[11]

Questions for Discussion

1. What bases of power does it appear Landis used in attempting to influence his cast and crew?

2. What factors contributed to Landis's decision to go ahead and shoot the scene that resulted in the accident?

3. How does the power of the motion picture and television industries contribute to the unsafe working conditions described?

4. Do you think Landis abused his power in ordering the shot that resulted in the accident? Do you think it was an ethical decision? Would you think the same thing had no accident occurred?

Notes

1. Black, S. (1983, December 4). Danger on the film set. *New York Times Magazine,* pp. 122–132.

2. Trippet, F. (1986, September 15). Twilight Zone: The trial. *Time.* p. 28.

3. Bach, S. (1985). *Final cut.* New York: Morrow.

4. See Note 1.

5. See Note 2.

6. See Note 1, p. 126.

7. See Note 1.

8. See Note 1.

9. See Note 1.

10. Farber, S. & Green, M (1988). *Outrageous conduct.* New York: Morrow.

11. See Note 1.

**EXPERIENCING
ORGANIZATIONAL
BEHAVIOR**

What Are Organizations Doing to Promote Corporate Ethics?

Although the popular press has made us well aware of the socially irresponsible and unethical activities of some organizations, it is also true that many other organizations are taking concrete steps to ensure that their employees strictly follow ethical principles (see pages 432–434). Not only do these organizations embrace a strong social conscience, they also seem to accept the idea that good ethics is good business. The purpose of this exercise is to uncover the variety of forms that concerns about ethics take in today's organizations.

Procedure

1. Each student in the class should research the attempts to promote ethical behavior on the part of any one particular organization. It can be an organization you've read about, one you've worked in, or one in which you have access to a high-ranking corporate officer who can answer your questions.

2. Based on what you have learned about the company (either through published materials, your own experiences, or an interview with a corporate official), give a report to the class addressing the following points.

    a. Does the company have an established code of corporate ethics? If so, describe its key features.

    b. Has the company made any attempts to promote ethical behavior from the top down? If so, describe these efforts.

    c. Does the company have any mechanisms in place that allow its employees to report the unethical actions of others? If so, describe them.

    d. Are the company's employees systematically rewarded for behaving ethically? If so, how?

3. Discuss the effectiveness of the various strategies described. With your instructor's guidance, outline a plan for improving them.

Points to Consider

1. What specific ethics-promoting actions were most commonly reported?

2. What types of organizations relied upon what approaches to promote ethical activities? Were any recurring patterns noted? Were the ethical practices found somehow related to governmental regulation?

3. What are the major trends with respect to instituting socially responsible organizational behaviors?

4. What experiences did you and your classmates encounter while attempting to collect the information in this exercise? Were the organizations contacted willing or unwilling to answer your questions?

5. Do you feel that organizations are interested in promoting ethical behavior, or does the "bottom line mentality" prevail?

CHAPTER THIRTEEN

COOPERATION AND CONFLICT: WORKING WITH OR AGAINST OTHERS

CHAPTER OUTLINE

Prosocial Behavior in Organizations: Beyond the Call of Duty
Cooperation: Mutual Assistance in Work Settings
  Individual Factors and Cooperation
  Organizational Factors and Cooperation
Conflict: Its Nature and Causes
  Conflict: A Modern Perspective
  Conflict: Its Major Causes
Conflict: Its Major Effects
  Conflict: The Negative Side
  Conflict: The Positive Side
Conflict: Its Effective Management
  Bargaining: The Universal Process

Third Party Intervention: Help from the Outside
The Induction of Superordinate Goals
Escalative Intervention: Intensifying Conflicts in Order to Resolve Them

Special Sections

OB: A Research Perspective
  Prosocial and Noncompliant Behavior at Work: Some Personal Factors
OB: An International Perspective
  Conflict in International Joint Ventures

LEARNING OBJECTIVES

After reading this chapter, you should be able to:

1. Define *prosocial behavior* and describe some of the forms it takes in organizations.
2. Identify key individual and organizational factors that determine the occurrence of *cooperation* in work settings.
3. Explain why *competition* rather than cooperation develops in many situations.
4. Define *conflict* and indicate how it can produce positive as well as negative effects.
5. Describe major organizational and interpersonal causes of conflict.
6. Indicate several techniques through which conflict can be *managed* so that it produces primarily positive outcomes.

Sandi Jackson, Director of Professional Publishing at Selkirk and Stevens (one of the largest book publishers in the country) is upset—and with good reason. Shoving the pile of papers in front of her away with a sigh, she turns to Ralph Kelsey, a senior member of her staff and her right-hand man in most respects. "Ralph, this has got to stop. What's wrong with those people anyway? Do they want to cut the ground out from under me—and themselves, too?"

"It sure looks that way," Ralph agrees. "And nothing we do seems to help."

"Just look at this stuff!" Sandi exclaims. "Social Sciences—down 13 percent; Chemistry—down 26 percent; Literature—down 19 percent. The only bright spot on the list is business, and that's up only marginally."

"I know," Ralph agrees. "We spend more, pump up everyone's budget, and lose market share. It just doesn't make sense."

"But we both know why, don't we?" Sandi comments, a grim smile on her face.

"Sure," Ralph answers at once. "They just *have* to do it. We tell 'em over and over again that we can't afford to compete against ourselves, but do they listen? No way!"

(Ralph is referring to the two major units under Sandi's authority. Despite repeated meetings, memos, and directives, the two companies continue to publish directly competing books. This is one major reason why total sales are down. Each year the two units publish books designed to sell in the same markets. Then, both divert large portions of their marketing efforts to these projects in a frenzied effort to assure that *their* text outsells the one produced by the other company. So far, results have been inconclusive: one year the first company wins; the next year, the other triumphs. No matter who comes out on top, though, the overall result remains the same: so much effort is spent on this internal struggle that the sales of many other books decrease, and the two companies lose total market share to outside competitors.)

"But *why* do they do it, that's what I want to know," Sandi continues. "You'd think they'd realize that we're all in this together, and that if I have to carry numbers like these to Harry Blumstein a few more times, we'll see major trouble—and I do mean *major*. He grumbled about our drop in total volume last year, but I managed to calm him down. This time there's no telling what he'll do."

"Sell off one or the other of those turkeys—or maybe both!" Ralph replies. "But you know, I really don't see any way out. Those guys competed with each other for so long before we bought 'em that they just can't seem to bury the hatchet."

"Yeah, that's part of the problem," Sandi agrees. "But it's more than that. They're such different outfits, it's like dealing with opposites."

"I'll say! And that makes it hard for them to trust each other—they're different and they know it, just like Brooke and Sam," Ralph says, referring to the Presidents of the two units. "It's tough to imagine two people with more different styles. They wouldn't spend five minutes in the same room if they didn't have to."

"I know. But we've just got to do something about it," Sandi answers with another sigh. "They've got to stop competing! Oh, shoot, let's get 'em in here for another meeting. Maybe this time we can get through."

"Okay," Ralph agrees as he rises to leave, "but I doubt it. Even if you can convince Brooke and Sam, they'll just go back to their separate little kingdoms and slip into the same old traps."

"Probably, but I'm going to get them to stop seeing each other as enemies if it's the last thing I do; and from the looks of things, it just might be!"

Does this situation strike you as strange? It should, for ultimately, all persons and groups within an organization are *interdependent;* what happens to one affects what happens to the others. If the organization prospers, increased rewards will be available. Everyone may not get an equal share of the pie (or even a share they consider fair), but at least the pie itself will be expanding. In contrast, if the organization does poorly, rewards will decrease for most if not all persons and groups within it (see Figure 13.1). Given these facts, it seems only reasonable to expect *cooperation* to be the byword or guiding principle in all work settings. Departments, divisions, units, and individuals should coordinate their efforts and work together as effectively as possible to maximize progress toward shared goals.

Yet, as you probably already know, reality often falls short of this basic ideal. Far from being benevolent places brimming with the spirit of mutual assistance, functioning organizations are just as likely to be filled with indifference, needless competition, smoldering feuds, and even open conflict. Why is this the case? What factors lead individuals and groups to compete (or worse) when they should, by all rational standards, be working closely together? And what steps can be taken to tip the balance away from such reactions and toward higher levels of coordination? We will focus on these and related questions in this chapter. In general terms, our concern will be with the conditions that shape or determine overall levels of *coordination* within a given organization. More specifically, we'll focus on three major processes reflecting different aspects of such coordination. The first of these is **prosocial behavior**—actions by individuals that assist others within the organization.[1] The second is **cooperation**—mutual, two-way assistance between individuals or groups. The third, and in some ways most important, is **conflict**—actions, by groups or individuals, that are perceived by others within an organization as having negative effects on their important interests.[2,3] Current knowledge relating to each of these processes will now be reviewed.

FIGURE 13.1   The Costs of Failing to Cooperate
Because all persons within an organization are *interdependent*, they should work together to achieve organizational goals. However, this is not always the case, and when internal coordination drops to low levels, the results can be disastrous for the organizations involved.

Prosocial Behavior in Organizations:
Beyond the Call of Duty

Is there such a thing as pure altruism—actions by one person that benefit one or more others under conditions where the donor expects absolutely, positively nothing in return? Philosophers have long puzzled over this question. More recently, social scientists have entered the debate.[4] Disappointingly, their research casts considerable doubt on the existence of totally selfless helping. Close examination of many instances in which individuals offer aid to others in a seemingly altruistic manner reveals that even in such cases, donors anticipate *some* form of compensation for their assistance. This return on their investment can be quite subtle (e.g., feelings of self-satisfaction resulting from the knowledge that they have acted benevolently; elimination of the negative emotions produced by exposure to others in need of assistance[5]). Yet, such gains are certainly real, and seem to provide at least a portion of the motivation behind seemingly altruistic acts. This is not to imply that instances of pure altruism cannot exist. A strong case can be made for the presence of such behavior in some contexts (e.g., self-sacrifice by parents for their children or by lovers for the objects of their affection). At the least, though, pure, selfless altruism seems to be far rarer and much more difficult to identify than was once assumed.

Regardless of whether such altruism exists, one basic fact is clear: human beings do frequently engage in **prosocial behavior.** They perform many actions which benefit others in various ways. Is such behavior common in work settings? Absolutely. As noted recently by Brief and Motowidlo many types of prosocial behavior occur in functioning organizations.[6] First, and most obviously, individuals who work together often assist each other with job-related matters. They pitch in and help those who have been absent, assist those experiencing especially heavy work loads, and take on tasks that are not necessarily part of their own jobs. In short, they demonstrate the kind of organizational *citizenship* behaviors we described in chapter 5.

Second, employees often assist coworkers with personal matters not directly related to their jobs. They provide emotional support, assist them with family matters, and generally offer a sympathetic ear for personal problems and difficulties. A third form of prosocial behavior often shown by organizational members involves services or products to people outside the organization with whom they do business (e.g., customers). Here, such actions as helping customers choose the right product for their needs or providing necessary service or information are part of the total picture. Additional forms of prosocial behavior involve suggestions for procedural or administrative improvements, putting forth extra effort on the job, volunteering for additional work assignments and representing the organization favorably to outsiders (e.g., saying positive things about it, its products or services).

All of the prosocial actions we have considered so far benefit an organization either directly or indirectly. It is important to note, however, that not all prosocial behaviors produce such effects. In some cases, individuals engage in actions which benefit specific persons but reflect negatively on the functioning of the organization itself. For example, consider employees who falsify records to conceal disapproved activities by friends, who offer special, costly deals to preferred customers, or who hire or promote people they know are unqualified for such rewards, but with whom they have some special relationship. Such persons are certainly behaving in a prosocial manner toward specific individuals—the beneficiaries of their actions. Yet, they are certainly *not* contributing to the well-being of their organization.

Other complexities are introduced into the equation by activities such as **whistle-blowing**—cases in which employees reveal an improper or illegal organizational practice to someone who may be able to correct it.[7] Is this a prosocial action? From the point of view of society, it usually is. The actions of whistle-blowers can protect the health, safety, or economic security of the general public. For example, an employee of a large bank who reports risky or illegal practices to an appropriate regulatory agency may protect thousands of depositors from large financial losses, or at least from considerable delay in recovering their savings. Similarly, an individual who blows the whistle on illegal dumping of toxic chemicals by his or her company may save many persons from serious illness.

From the point of view of the organizations involved, however, the situation is more complex. First, whether such actions are or are not prosocial in nature depends on the motivation underlying them. If a whistle-blower benefits from his or her actions while the organization suffers, it is reasonable to conclude that the whistle-blower did not intend to help the company. In such cases, it cannot be viewed as prosocial with respect to the organization. Second, much depends on how such whistle-blowing is carried out. If the potentially damaging information is revealed first to persons in authority *within* the organization who can take appropriate corrective actions, whistle-blowing is reasonably viewed as prosocial in nature. If the information is offered first to persons outside the organization, however, negative effects will probably follow, and such actions are not prosocial in nature, at least from the organization's point of view (see Figure 13.2). For example, one large brokerage house in the United States convicted of insider trading and related practices had to pay fines and damages totaling $650,000,000 when its illegal activities were made known to the Securities Exchange Commission.

In sum, whistle-blowing actions must be examined from the perspective of the motives underlying their performance and their ultimate effects before they can be

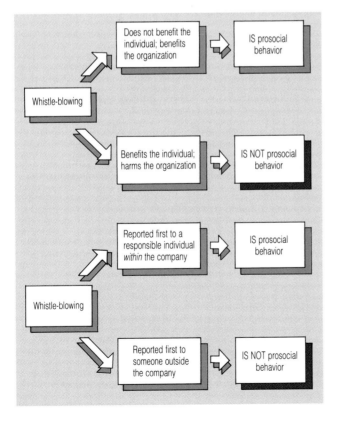

FIGURE 13.2 Whistle-blowing as a Prosocial Action toward An Organization

Whether *whistle-blowing* can be classified as prosocial in nature depends on the motives underlying it (see top panel), and the way in which it is handled (see lower panel). Thus, from an organization's point of view, the nature of this type of behavior depends strongly on the context in which it occurs.

classified as prosocial or not with respect to specific companies. (What factors lead individuals to engage in prosocial behavior in work settings? For intriguing evidence on this issue, please refer to the **Research Perspective** section below.)

OB: A RESEARCH PERSPECTIVE

Prosocial and Noncompliant Behavior at Work: Some Personal Factors

In any organization, some individuals show a high level of prosocial behavior, assisting coworkers, offering helpful suggestions for improving various activities, and volunteering to perform tasks over and above their regular duties. In contrast, others show low levels of prosocial behavior or may, in fact, engage in *noncompliant actions*—violations of widely accepted rules or norms. What personal factors or characteristics distinguish these two groups of persons? A study by Puffer provides some preliminary answers.[8]

Participants in this investigation were sales persons and managers in a chain of retail furniture stores. Managers rated the frequency with which the salespeople engaged in various *prosocial behaviors* they viewed as important (e.g., assisting other salespeople, keeping product displays and catalogs tidy, attaching sales tags to merchandise). In addition, they also rated the frequency with which these employees engaged in *noncompliant behavior* (e.g., being late, taking excessive breaks, complaining about the company or coworkers, taking customers away from other salespeople). In order to determine whether several personal characteristics were related to such behaviors, the salespeople were asked to complete questionnaires that assessed their need for achievement, need for autonomy (strong desires to be independent of authority), satisfaction with material rewards (e.g., pay), perceived competition from peers, and confidence in current management. Finally, to determine whether prosocial and noncompliant behavior and these personal characteristics were related to job performance, sales figures were obtained for each employee during the previous three months.

On the basis of previous research, Puffer predicted that need for achievement, satisfaction with material rewards, and confidence in management would be positively related to prosocial behavior, but negatively related to noncompliant behavior. In other words, the higher salespeople were on achievement, satisfaction, and confidence in management, the more prosocial behavior and the less noncompliant behavior

they would demonstrate. Conversely, she predicted that need for autonomy and perceived competition from peers would be positively related to noncompliant behavior but negatively linked to prosocial behavior. Finally, she also predicted that prosocial behavior would be positively related to job performance, while noncompliant behavior would be negatively related.

Results offered support for several, but not all, of these predictions. Employees' level of need for achievement, satisfaction with material rewards, and confidence in management did indeed predict their tendency to engage in prosocial behavior. However, prosocial behavior was only weakly related to job performance. Autonomy and perceived competition from peers were relatively weak predictors of the tendency to engage in noncompliant behavior, but such behavior, when it occurred, did undermine performance: the higher employees' tendencies to engage in such actions, the lower their sales performance. In sum, as shown in Figure 13.3, individuals high in need for achievement, confidence in management, and job satisfaction tended to perform prosocial behaviors. Such actions, however, did not necessarily enhance their on-the-job performance. In contrast, individuals low in need for achievement and confidence in management tended to perform noncompliant behaviors. And this tendency, in turn, reduced their job performance.

Taken as a whole, Puffer's findings suggest that the tendency to engage in prosocial behavior at work is indeed linked to several personal characteristics. However, contrary to what common sense suggests, the occurrence of such behavior does not necessarily result in enhanced job performance. Perhaps this latter finding stemmed, at least in part, from the context of Puffer's research—retail sales. In this setting, many prosocial actions by employees cannot, by themselves, generate increased business; only a steady flow of serious customers can yield such outcomes. Thus, the possibility remains that in other organizations, prosocial behavior is indeed closely linked to job performance. In any case, Puffer's

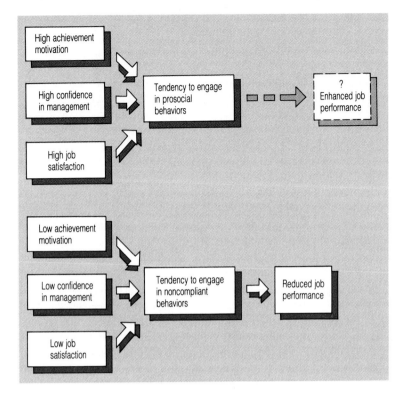

FIGURE 13.3 Causes and Effects of Prosocial and Noncompliant Behaviors

The higher salespeople were in need for achievement, confidence in management, and job satisfaction, the greater their tendency to engage in prosocial behaviors at work. However, such prosocial behaviors did not necessarily enhance their job performance. In contrast, the lower salespeople were in need for achievement, confidence in management, and job satisfaction, the greater their tendency to engage in noncompliant behavior. The greater this tendency, the poorer their job performance. (Source: Based on findings reported by Puffer, 1987; see Note 8.)

research suggests that the frequency of prosocial behavior can be increased, and the frequency of noncompliant behavior reduced, by encouraging need for achievement among employees and by increasing both their job satisfaction and confidence in management. This information may be valuable to many organizations in selecting employees, and in developing policies that contribute to their effectiveness.

COOPERATION: MUTUAL ASSISTANCE IN WORK SETTINGS

In prosocial behavior, individuals engage in actions designed to benefit other persons, groups, or the entire organization. As we have already noted, such actions are fairly common in work settings, and take many forms. While prosocial behavior is fairly common, another pattern known as **cooperation** is probably even more widespread.[9] Here, assistance is mutual, and two or more persons or groups work together to enhance progress toward shared goals. Such cooperation is a basic form of coordination in many work settings. To mention just a few examples, it occurs when several computer experts work together to debug a faulty program, when employees on a loading dock pool their physical efforts to lift a heavy package, and when members of a special project team consisting of experts from several different backgrounds combine their skills to develop a new product or service. In all these cases, the underlying principle is much the same: the persons, groups, or units involved coordinate their actions in order to reach goals or levels of performance they could not attain alone. Then, once the mutually desired goals are reached, the benefits are shared among the participants in some agreed upon manner. The result: cooperation yields positive outcomes for all concerned.

The obvious benefits yielded by this pattern raise a basic question: why, if it is so useful, does it often fail to develop? Why don't people, groups, or units seeking the same (or at least similar) goals always join forces? Several factors account for the puzzling lack of coordination, but by far the most important is this: cooperation simply cannot develop in many situations because the goals sought by the persons or groups involved cannot be shared. For example, two persons seeking the same job or promotion cannot join forces to attain it—the reward can go to only one. Similarly, if two companies are courting the same potential merger candidate, only one can succeed; it makes little sense for them to work together to assure that a merger does in fact take place, since only one will enjoy the benefits of this transaction.

In cases such as these, an alternative form of behavior known as **competition** often develops. Here, each person, group, or unit strives to maximize its individual gains, often at the expense of others. Indeed, as noted by Tjosvold, each side tends to view gains and losses by the other side as linked, so that their "wins" constitute the other side's "losses," and vice versa.[10] In many contexts, the occurrence of competition is both natural and understandable. People and departments do have to compete for scarce organizational resources and rewards. And organizations themselves must compete in the marketplace for supplies, government contracts, customers, and market share (see Figure 13.4). There are many instances, however, in which competition is *not* dictated by current conditions, and in which cooperation might develop instead. For example, consider the opening story at the start of this chapter. Couldn't the two publishing companies described coordinate their activities so that one focused on producing certain types of books while the other concentrated on different types? The answer is obvious: they could. And just as obviously, doing so might well have enhanced the profits and performance of both units. Why, then, did they choose head-on competition? As we suggested on page 445, the answer is complex, and involves many factors. To acquaint you with some of these, we'll now focus on the following question: what factors serve to tip the balance toward cooperation or competition in situations

FIGURE 13.4 Competition: A Fact of Life for Organizations
Organizations must often compete with one another for potential business. Fierce competition is readily understandable in these cases.

where either pattern is possible? As we'll soon note, both individual and organizational factors play a role in this regard.

Individual Factors and Cooperation

Several factors affecting the tendency to cooperate seem to function primarily through their impact on individuals. They influence the perceptions and reactions of specific persons and in this manner, shape individuals' decisions with respect to cooperating or competing with others. Among the most important of these are the principle of *reciprocity,* several aspects of *communication,* and the *personal orientation* toward working with others held by individuals.

Reciprocity: Reacting to others' behavior. Throughout life, we are urged to follow the "Golden Rule"—to do unto others as we would have others do unto us. Despite such exhortations, we usually behave in a different manner. Most people tend to treat others not as they would prefer to be treated, but rather as *they* have been treated in the past, either by these individuals or by others. In short, most individuals follow the principle of **reciprocity** much of the time. This tendency to behave toward others as they have acted toward us is quite powerful. It can be observed in actions as diverse as attraction, where individuals tend to like others who express positive feelings toward them, to aggression, where "an eye for an eye and a tooth for a tooth" seems to prevail.[11] The choice between cooperation and competition is no exception to this powerful rule. When others act in a competitive manner, we usually respond with mistrust and efforts to defeat them. In contrast, if they behave in a cooperative manner, we usually do the same.

The tendency to reciprocate cooperation is not perfect, however. In judging others' level of cooperation and adjusting our response to it, we tend to fall prey to the same type of *self-serving bias* described in chapter 4. We often perceive others' level of cooperation as lower than it really is, and our own level of cooperation as somewhat higher than reality would dictate. The result: in our dealings with others, we tend to *undermatch* the level of cooperation they demonstrate.[12]

This tendency aside, reciprocity does appear to be the guiding principle of cooperation. The key task with respect to establishing coordination in organizations then, seems to be getting it started. Once individuals, groups, or units have begun to cooperate, the process may be largely self-sustaining. Managers wishing to encourage cooperation, therefore, should do everything possible to get the process underway. After it begins, the obvious benefits cooperation confers, plus powerful tendencies toward reciprocity, may well maintain it at high levels.

Communication: Potential benefits, potential costs. In many situations where cooperation could potentially develop but does not, its absence is blamed on a "failure to communicate." It is suggested that better or more frequent contact between the persons or groups involved might have facilitated such coordination. Is this suggestion accurate? In one sense, it is. Some forms of communication do indeed seem to increase interpersonal trust, and so to enhance actual cooperation. For example, an open exchange of views may convince all parties that working together is the best strategy, and that a fair division of responsibilities and rewards is possible. Similarly, unless some minimal level of communication exists, close coordination of work activities may be impossible; after all, each individual or group will have little idea of what the others are doing.

It is also clear, however, that not all types of communication yield such beneficial outcomes. In fact, research findings indicate that at least one type of contact between persons or groups—communication involving the use of *threats*—can reduce rather than encourage cooperation.

Threats take many different forms, but they typically involve statements suggesting that negative consequences will be delivered if the recipient does not behave in a certain manner or refrains from acting in a certain manner. For example, a manager may warn her subordinate that if he continues to tie up the phones with personal calls, his phone privileges will be revoked. Similarly, during negotiations, representatives from one company may inform those from another that they will end the current discussions unless one of their requests is met. While the use of such tactics is tempting, they often produce mixed effects at best. In many cases, they anger recipients, stiffening their resolve to resist. Even in cases where threats appear to succeed and produce immediate yielding or surrender, they may leave a residue of resentment which can return on later occasions to haunt those who have issued threats. And of course, threats often stimulate counter-threats, and create a damaging spiral that can lead, ultimately, to open and costly conflict. A clear example of such effects is provided in a laboratory study conducted by Youngs.[13]

In this study, female students played a special type of game against a partner who issued either few or many threats, and whose threats, when delivered, were either small or large in magnitude. In this game, both players were asked to choose, on a number of occasions, between two options. If both selected Option 1 (the cooperative choice), each player won two points. (Points could be converted into money prizes at the end of the game.) If both selected Option 2 (the competitive choice), each lost two points. If a mixed pattern of choices occurred (one player selected Option 1 and the other Option 2), the player choosing Option 1 lost six points, while the player choosing Option 2 gained six points. This type of game has often been used in laboratory research on cooperation, for despite its obvious artificiality, it confronts players with a situation reminiscent of many real-life contexts: pressures toward both cooperation and competition exist, and operate concurrently. As you might guess, persons who participate in such games soon become highly involved in them, and do their best to outscore their opponents.

Returning to Youngs' study, at various points during the game, either participants or their opponent (but not both simultaneously) were allowed to send "warning messages" requesting that the other player select Option 1 (the cooperative choice). These messages served as threats, for in them, the players could indicate the number of points they would subtract from their opponent's score if she did not comply. In reality, participants' partner was actually fictitious, and was programmed by Youngs to issue either many or relatively few threats (on 50 percent of the game trials or 100 percent of these trials), and to issue threats of relatively small magnitude (losses of eight to twelve points to the subject) or relatively large magnitude (losses of sixteen to twenty points).

Consistent with the reciprocity principle described earlier, it was predicted that players in the game would generally tend to match the level of threat they received from their opponent, and as shown in Figure 13.5, this was indeed the case. Participants in the study issued more threats when they received many rather than few threats from their opponent, and they issued larger threats when their opponent used large rather than small ones. In addition, the overall level of cooperation during the game was low; participants chose the cooperative option only 33 percent of the time on those trials when the accomplices did not send a threat.

These findings, plus those of many other studies, suggest that threats are a very poor means of enhancing cooperation in a wide range of settings. While they may succeed in obtaining concessions and compliance in the short run, they tend to interfere with establishment of long-term, lasting patterns of coordination. For this reason, as

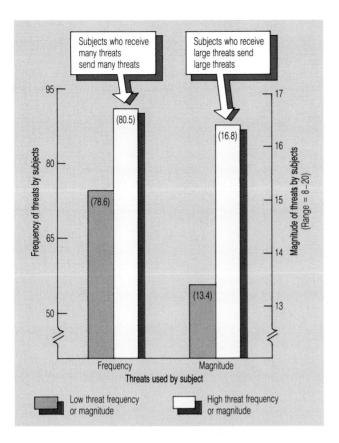

FIGURE 13.5   Threats and Cooperation

The more threats subjects received from an opponent while playing a Prisoner's Dilemma game, the more threats they returned. Similarly, the larger the threats subjects received, the larger the threats they returned. These findings suggest that the use of threats is a very poor tactic in situations where high levels of cooperation are desired. (Source: Based on data from Youngs, 1986; see Note 13.)

well as several others we will describe in a later section (see page 463), threats appear to be one type of communication managers should avoid on most occasions.

Personal orientations and cooperation. Think about the many people you have known during your life. Can you remember ones who were highly competitive—individuals who viewed most situations as contests in which they, or someone else, would triumph? In contrast, can you recall others who were highly cooperative—persons who preferred to minimize differences between their own performance or outcomes and those of others? Probably, you have little difficulty in bringing examples of both types to mind, for people differ greatly in terms of their tendencies to cooperate or compete. Such differences, in turn, seem to reflect contrasting perspectives toward working with others—perspectives individuals carry with them from situation to situation and over relatively long periods of time.[14] While both tendencies vary along continuous dimensions (from very low to very high), research findings suggest that many, if not most, persons fall into one of four distinct categories in this respect.

First, a sizeable proportion are **competitors.** These are persons whose primary motive is doing better than others—beating them in open competition. Indeed, in extreme cases competitors prefer negative outcomes that exceed those of their opponents to positive ones that are less than those attained by others. Second, some persons are concerned almost exclusively with maximizing their own gains. Such **individualists** have little interest in the outcomes of others, and don't really care whether others do better or worse than themselves. Their major focus is simply on gaining as much as possible in every situation. Third, a relatively small number of persons can be classified as **cooperators.** These are individuals who are primarily concerned with maximizing *joint outcomes*—the total received by themselves and others. They want everyone with whom they work to be satisfied with their rewards, and do not wish to beat or defeat them. Finally, a few persons can be described as **equalizers.** Their major goal is minimizing differences between their own performance or outcomes and those of others. In short, they wish to assure that everyone with whom they work receives the same basic results. (See Figure 13.6 for an overview of the motives of these four types of persons.)

At this point we should note that while many individuals seem to fall into one of these categories, others demonstrate a mixture of these perspectives. Substantial numbers seem to combine an individualistic orientation with a competitive one: they want to do as well as they can, but are also interested in surpassing others when this is possible. Similarly, some persons combine an individualistic orientation with a desire for equality. They want to do as well as they can, but don't want their outcomes to get too far out of line with those of others.

How common is each of these patterns? In other words, are there more competitors or cooperators? Do mixed patterns outnumber the simple ones? A study by Knight and Dubro provides information on this issue.[15] These researchers asked a large group of individuals (both males and females) to complete several tasks designed to reveal their orientation toward working with others. Results indicated that substantial proportions of the participants fell into each of the categories mentioned above. However, the pattern of these preferences differed somewhat for men and women. Among males, the single largest group was competitors; fully one-third showed this orientation, while another eighteen percent showed an individualistic pattern. In contrast, among females, the single largest group was cooperators (about twenty percent), followed closely by competitors (about fifteen percent). Only a relatively small proportion of each sex could be classified as equalizers.

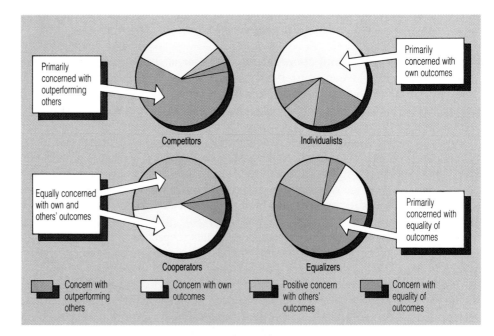

FIGURE 13.6 Motives and Personal Orientations toward Working With Others

As shown here, individuals with different orientations toward working with others demonstrate sharply contrasting patterns of motives.

As you might suspect, persons showing different perspectives toward working with others tend to behave quite differently.[16] Competitors frequently attempt to exploit the people around them, and cooperate only when they see no other choice. In contrast, cooperators prefer friendly ties with coworkers, and would rather work with them than against them. Individualists are flexible—they choose whatever strategy will succeed in a given situation. In addition, they often prefer to work alone, concentrating solely on their own outcomes rather than those of others. Persons with a mixed orientation are harder to predict; they often oscillate or adopt intermediate approaches in working with others.

From a practical point of view, managers should recognize the existence of these different patterns and should guard against assuming that all individuals are similar in their approach to exchange relations. Further, they should realize that such differences are relevant to several key personnel decisions (e.g., hiring, promotion, work assignments). For example, persons with a competitive orientation may be highly effective in situations where representatives of several organizations must compete against one another. However, they may wreak havoc in contexts requiring prolonged teamwork. In contrast, cooperators may shine as team players, but do poorly in some types of negotiations. Equalizers may excel in positions requiring the fair distribution of resources among various groups (e.g., scheduling space or equipment). But they may run into serious problems if, as managers, they must evaluate the performance of subordinates and recommend differential raises or promotions for them. In sum, individual differences with respect to such orientations are important and can affect performance in a wide range of positions.

Organizational Factors and Cooperation

That organizations differ greatly in terms of their internal levels of cooperation is obvious. Some—typically those that are quite successful—demonstrate a high degree of cooperation between their various units or departments.[17] Others—typically those that are *not* highly successful—show a lower level of such behavior. What accounts for these differences? We have already provided part of the answer: cooperation within an organization is affected by several factors relating primarily to individuals (e.g., communication, individual perspectives or preferences). In addition, several factors relating to an organization's internal structure and function also play a role.

Reward systems and organizational structure. Imagine the following situation. A large insurance company has two major divisions: Consumer Underwriting (which issues policies for individuals) and Commercial Underwriting (which issues policies for businesses). The company has a major bonus system and each year sizable bonuses are distributed to individuals in the division that is more profitable. This results in a high degree of competition between the units. At first glance, this might seem beneficial. However, it leads to situations in which sales personnel from one division actively interfere with the efforts of sales personnel from the other division. For example, while working hard to win a multi-million dollar policy with a large manufacturing concern, agents from the Commercial Underwriting division actually discourage top management within this company from seeking individual life and property policies from their company; after all, this will contribute to the sales of their archrival, Consumer Underwriting. And the opposite pattern is true as well. Agents for the Consumer Division discourage large clients from seeking policies for their businesses from the Commercial Division.

Although this might seem to be an extreme case, it reflects conditions that are all too common in many organizations. Reward systems are often "winner-take-all" in form.

This fact, coupled with internal differentiation, tends to reduce coordination between units or divisions, as each seeks to maximize its own rewards. This is not to imply that such internal competition is necessarily bad or counterproductive—far from it. Still, managers should take care to assure that it does not rise to the point at which it hinders the functioning and success of the entire organization.

Interdependence among employees: The nature of specific jobs. Imagine two organizations. In the first, the major tasks performed by employees can be completed alone; there is no need for individuals to work closely with others. In the second, the tasks performed by employees cannot be completed alone; they must work together closely to do their jobs. In which organization will higher levels of cooperation develop? The answer is obvious: in the second. The reason for this difference, too, is apparent. The level of cooperation attained is determined by the nature of the work performed. The greater the degree of interdependence among employees, the higher cooperation between them tends to be. This relationship has been verified in research studies, so it appears to be a useful principle to keep in mind.[18] To repeat: the level of cooperation within an organization is closely related to the level of interdependence among employees required by its major tasks.

Interorganizational coordination: Cooperation between independent organizations. When we think about relations between different organizations manufacturing the same products or providing similar services, the key word that comes to mind is *competition*. We tend to concentrate on the ways in which such organizations compete with one another and the strategies they adopt to improve their relative positions in the marketplace.[19] Yet, there are also situations in which independent organizations choose to coordinate their actions or efforts to attain mutual gains. In short, there are important instances of what might be termed *interorganizational coordination*. When does such coordination develop? Primarily under three sets of conditions.

First, interorganizational coordination occurs when several independent companies conclude that by joining forces, they can greatly increase their potential outcomes. A clear example of such coordination is provided by OPEC (the Organization of Petroleum Exporting Countries). Here, entire industries in highly diverse nations have chosen to coordinate their policies and actions in order to seize control of a crucial world market—petroleum. While the degree of coordination shown by these nations has varied, they have, by and large, succeeded in raising the price for this product to levels that, a few short decades ago, were totally unanticipated (see Figure 13.7).

Second, interorganizational coordination often occurs when new, external competitors enter a mature and previously stable market. This situation occurred in the United States in the late 1970s and early 1980s, when the sales of Japanese automobiles rose to unprecedented levels. In response to this external threat, major U.S. manufacturers who had competed with one another for decades joined forces to lobby for government action. They succeeded and legislation restricting the number of Japanese imports was quickly adopted. Certainly, this provides another good example of the benefits that may result when independent organizations coordinate their efforts.

Third, such coordination sometimes stems from rapidly changing environmental conditions. New patterns of trade, advances in technology, shifts in government policies, and similar trends combine to create an environment in which independent organizations find it difficult to continue "business as usual." One response to such conditions is merger: surrendering independence and becoming part of a larger company. Another is the formation of *consortiums*—confederations in which organizations maintain their formal independence, but agree to coordinate their activities through a central

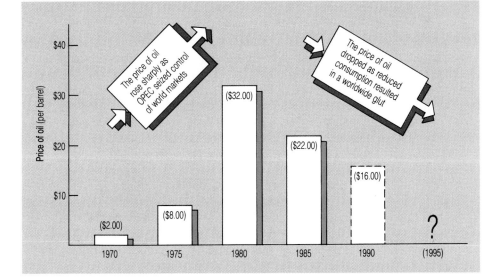

FIGURE 13.7   OPEC: A Dramatic Example of Interorganizational Coordination

OPEC (the Organization of Petroleum Exporting Countries) is one of the most impressive examples in history of *interorganizational coordination*. Before it began to exert its effect on world markets, oil sold for less than $2.00 per barrel. The price for this commodity rose sharply during the 1970s and peaked in the 1980s at almost $40.00 per barrel. After that, it fell as industrialized nations reduced their consumption of oil, thus creating a glut in world markets. Should the situation change, OPEC stands ready to profit once again from coordination between its members.

consortium management organization (CMO). Precisely such developments have taken place recently in the hospital industry in the United States where the growth of privately owned chains, the increasing complexity of medical technology, and the growing size of government programs have put mounting pressure on independent, nonprofit hospitals.[20] As a result, growing numbers have joined *multihospital consortia*. By doing so, they have been able to exert control over rising costs, provide a better mix of medical services, avoid duplication of personnel and equipment, and improve several aspects of their performance. Given such benefits, it is not surprising that this type of interorganizational coordination has increased dramatically in recent years.

Before concluding, we should note that interorganizational coordination can take several forms and operate in sharply contrasting ways.[21] In some cases, the groups responsible for such coordination are mandated by parent organizations and given specific tasks to perform. For example, a commission established by the federal government to eliminate duplication of function across several agencies would operate in this fashion. In other instances, the groups responsible for coordination are voluntary, and do not have a clearly structured agenda or set of tasks. The leaders of several independent lobby organizations who decide to meet to discuss ways of maximizing their impact on the political process are an example of this type of informal group. Their meetings are purely voluntary, and no definite tasks have been chosen when the leaders first convene. Mixed patterns (e.g., mandated groups with no fixed tasks or agenda; voluntary groups with fixed tasks or agenda) also exist. The main point to note is simply this: interorganizational coordination can take many forms, and these will reflect the nature of the organizations involved (large corporations, small citizen groups) and the environmental conditions that encourage such coordination.

If prosocial behavior and cooperation constitute one end of a continuum describing how individuals and groups work together in organizations, then **conflict** certainly lies at the other end. This term has many meanings and has been used to refer to events ranging from the inner turmoil produced by competing needs or desires (inner conflict) to open violence between entire societies (warfare). In the context of OB, however, conflict refers primarily to instances in which units or individuals within an organization work *against* rather than with one another.[22] More formally, according to one widely accepted definition, conflict is a process in which one party perceives that another party has taken some action which will exert negative effects on its major interests, or is about to take such action. In other words, the key elements in conflict seem to include: (1) opposing interests between individuals or groups, (2) recognition of such opposition, (3) the belief by each side that the other will thwart (or has already thwarted) these interests, and (4) actions that actually produce such thwarting (see Figure 13.8).

Unfortunately, conflict, defined in this manner, is all too common in modern organizations. Moreover, its effects are far too costly to ignore. Practicing managers report that they spend approximately *twenty percent of their time* dealing with conflict and its impact.[23] And the smoldering resentment and broken relationships that are the aftermath of many conflicts can persist for months or even years, continuing to exact a major toll in precious human resources long after the situation that initiated the conflict is itself merely a memory. For these and related reasons, **organizational conflict** is certainly an important topic for the field of OB, and one deserving of our careful attention. In the remainder of this section, we will provide you with an overview of current knowledge about this costly process. First, we will present a brief summary of an important and sophisticated model of conflict—one that helps place this process within a broader context of organizational and individual processes. Next, we'll describe some of the major causes of conflict, conditions and events that initiate its occurrence in work settings. Third, we'll examine its major effects. These, you may be surprised to learn, can be positive as well as negative. Finally, we'll focus on several tactics for resolving or *managing* organizational conflict—procedures for directing it into relatively constructive rather than destructive pathways.

Conflict: A Modern Perspective

Opposing interests, it is widely agreed, lie at the core of most conflicts. Indeed, it makes little sense to use the term *conflict* in the absence of incompatible interests or aspirations.[24] Yet conflict involves much more than this. Bitter disputes often erupt in

**FIGURE 13.8
Organizational Conflict: Its
Basic Nature**

Conflict involves opposing
or incompatible interests
between groups or
individuals, the recognition
of such opposing interests,
and the belief that others
will act on them. (Source:
Based on suggestions by
Thomas, 1989; see Note 25.)

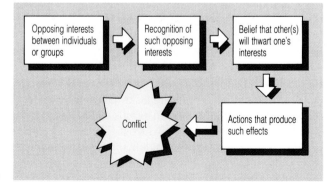

situations where the interests of the two sides are *not* clearly opposed, while in other cases, conflict fails to develop despite the existence of deep divisions between potential adversaries. Events such as these suggest that a full understanding of conflict will require much more than mere identification of opposing interests. Many other factors relating to the thoughts, feelings, and actions of the persons involved enter into the picture and must be carefully considered. How, then, should we conceive of organizational conflict? A model proposed recently by Thomas offers one intriguing answer.[25]

According to Thomas, it is important to view conflict as a *process*—a complex series of events over time that both *reflect* external conditions and, in turn, *affect* them. More specifically, Thomas notes that conflict episodes between individuals or groups stem from preceding events and conditions, and produce results and outcomes. In other words, conflict is part of a continuing, ongoing relationship between two or more parties, not an isolated event that can be considered in and of itself. What, then, are the key elements in this continuing process? Thomas calls attention to several.

The first of these involves *awareness of the conflict.* Thomas suggests that conflicts are, to a large extent, in the eye of the beholder—they occur only when the parties involved recognize the existence of opposing interests. This, of course, is why conflict sometimes fails to emerge in situations where outside observers notice deep divisions between potential opponents. The parties themselves do not notice (or care to notice!) these conditions, and if they do not, conflict remains only a possibility.

Second, once awareness of the conflict exists, both parties experience emotional reactions to it and think about it in various ways. These emotions and thoughts are crucial to the course of the developing conflict. For example, if the emotional reactions of one or both sides include anger and resentment from past wrongs or from contemplated future ones, the conflict is likely to be intense. If such reactions are absent, or if other emotions (e.g., fear over the potential costs) are dominant, it may be of lower intensity and will develop quite differently. Similarly, the parties' reasoning concerning the conflict can have profound effects on its form and ultimate resolution. Here, both *rational-instrumental reasoning* (e.g., thoughts concerning potential costs and benefits, the conflict's bearing on major goals) and *normative reasoning* (e.g., concerns about what is appropriate in the situation or how others would react) are important.

Third, on the basis of such thoughts and emotions individuals formulate specific *intentions*—plans to adopt various strategies during the conflict. These may be quite general in nature (e.g., plans to adopt a conciliatory, cooperative approach), or quite specific (e.g., decisions to follow specific bargaining tactics).

In the next step, such intentions are translated into actual behavior. Such actions then elicit some response from the opposite side, and the process recycles. That is, the opponent's reactions affect current thoughts and feelings about the conflict, intentions concerning further behavior, and so on. (Please see Figure 13.9 on page 460 for a summary of this process.)

Thomas's model of organizational conflict is quite sophisticated, and rests on a firm basis of empirical research. However, there can be little doubt that it will be modified in the years ahead as additional information about conflict and its components accumulates. Perhaps its main contribution, then, is that it calls attention to the following important facts: (1) organizational conflict is an ongoing *process,* one that occurs against a backdrop of continuing relationships and events; it is definitely not a short-term, isolated occurrence; (2) such conflict involves the thoughts, perceptions, memories, and emotions of the persons involved; these must be taken into account in any complete model of organizational conflict; and (3) conflict stems from a very wide range of conditions and events—ones relating to individuals and ones relating to the structure, norms, and functioning of organizations. It is to these factors—the major causes of conflict—that we turn next.

FIGURE 13.9   Conflict: A Modern Perspective

According to a model proposed by Thomas, conflict is a complex process involving the thoughts and emotions of participants, their intentions to behave in specific ways, and their overt actions.

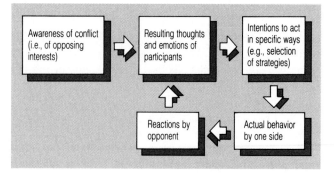

Conflict: Its Major Causes

As we noted above, conflict involves the presence or perception of opposing interests. Yet this condition, by itself, is neither a necessary nor a sufficient condition for the occurrence of actual conflict. Open confrontations sometimes fail to develop despite the existence of incompatible interests. And conflict does often emerge in situations where opposing interests are not present, or where, at least, ambiguity exists in this regard. Clearly, then, many factors and conditions contribute to its occurrence. These can be divided into two major groups: factors relating to organizational structure or functioning, and factors relating to interpersonal relations.

Organizational causes of conflict. Perhaps the most obvious organization-based cause of conflict is *competition over scarce resources*. No organization has unlimited resources, and conflicts often arise over the division or distribution of space, money, equipment, or personnel. Unfortunately, such conflicts are often intensified by the *self-serving bias* described in chapter 4. Each side tends to inflate its contribution to the organization, and therefore its fair share of available resources. The result can be intense, prolonged conflict.

Two closely related factors involve *ambiguity over responsibility* or *jurisdiction*. In the former case, groups or individuals within an organization are uncertain as to who is responsible for performing various tasks or duties. As a result, each involved party disclaims responsibility, and conflict can develop over this issue. In the latter instance, such uncertainty centers around who has jurisdiction or authority. Disputes over this issue, too, can be intense.

A third organizational factor that often plays a role in conflict is *interdependence* and events stemming from it. In most organizations, various units, groups, and individuals must depend on others for performance of their own jobs. They receive input from others, and cannot proceed without it. When such input is delayed or delivered in an incomplete or unsatisfactory form, strong conflict may result. This is hardly surprising; groups or individuals faced with this situation perceive (and rightly so) that their major goals are being blocked or interfered with by others. Little wonder that they then retaliate in kind and that productive work may grind to a halt (or at least slow appreciably) in the spiraling conflict that follows.

We have already described yet another organization-based cause of conflict: *reward systems*. When such systems pit one unit or group against another (as is often the case), a degree of conflict is practically guaranteed. This is especially likely if the persons involved perceive the system as somehow unfair or biased.[26] In such instances, the groups that fail to attain important benefits (e.g., bonuses, raises) may experience resentment, and unnecessary conflict may be the next step in the process.

Finally, conflict is sometimes a by-product of *differentiation* within an organization. As organizations grow and develop, many experience a trend toward an increasing number of departments or divisions. Individuals working in these groups become socialized to them, and tend to accept their norms and values. As they come to identify with these work groups, their perceptions of other members of the organization may alter. They view people outside their units as different, less worthy, and less competent than those within it. At the same time, they tend to overvalue their own unit and the people within it. Ultimately, this process may encourage costly conflicts.[27] After all, if individuals in each department or unit are fiercely loyal to their own turf, they may lose sight of shared organizational goals and tend to focus, instead, on pursuing their own self-interests. In sum, increasing differentiation within an organization encourages individuals within it to divide it into "us" (members of our own group) and "them" (people outside it), and this, in turn, can be a contributing factor in the initiation of conflict. (Please see Figure 13.10 for a summary of the organization-based causes of conflict discussed in this section.)

Interpersonal causes of organizational conflict. In the past, most research on organizational conflict focused on the type of organizational causes noted above. More recently, however, attention has been drawn to the possibility that in many instances, costly organizational conflicts stem as much (or perhaps more) from interpersonal factors—relations between specific individuals—as from organizational structure or underlying conflicts of interest. Many factors seem to be involved in this regard. First, consider the impact of lasting *grudges*. When individuals are angered by others, and especially when they are made to "lose face" (to look foolish publicly), they may develop strong, negative attitudes toward the persons responsible for these outcomes. The result: they spend considerable time and effort planning or actually seeking revenge for these wrongs. Unfortunately, such grudges can persist for years, with obvious negative effects for the organizations or work groups in question.

Second, conflict often stems from (or is intensified by) *faulty attributions*—errors concerning the causes behind others' behavior. When individuals find that their interests have been thwarted by another person, they generally try to determine *why* this person acted in the way he or she did. Was it malevolence—a desire to harm them or give them a hard time? Or did the provoker's actions stem from factors beyond his or her

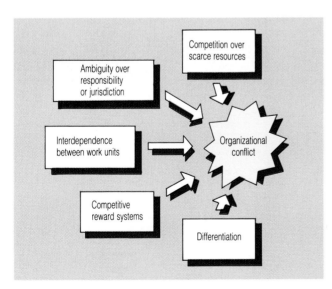

FIGURE 13.10
Organizational Causes of Conflict

Several organization-based factors contribute to the occurrence of conflict in work settings.

control? A growing body of evidence suggests that when people reach the former conclusion, anger and subsequent conflict are more likely and more intense than when they reach the latter conclusion.[28] For example, in one recent study on this issue, Baron had students engage in simulated negotiations with another person (actually an accomplice).[29] Both persons played the role of executives representing different departments within a large organization; they bargained over the division of $1,000,000 in surplus funds between their respective departments. The accomplice adopted a very confrontational stance, demanding fully $800,000 out of $1,000,000 in available funds for his or her own department, and offered only two small concessions during the negotiations. As the bargaining proceeded, the accomplice made several statements indicating that he or she had been ordered to behave in this "tough" manner by his or her constituents. In other words, the accomplice adopted a bargaining tactic often described as the "my hands are tied" strategy. In one condition, participants received information suggesting these claims were true (the opponent appeared to be *sincere* in his or her statements), while in another, they learned that these claims were false (the opponent appeared to be insincere). As predicted, participants reported more negative reactions to the accomplice, and stronger tendencies to avoid and compete with this person on future occasions, when they learned that he or she had misrepresented the causes behind his or her behavior (see Figure 13.11).

In related research, Bies, Shapiro, and Cummings asked a large group of employed individuals to describe a recent situation in which their boss had refused one of their requests.[30] Participants then rated the extent to which their boss offered a *causal account* for this behavior (an explanation attributing it to circumstances beyond his or her control). In addition, they rated the adequacy of the reasoning behind this account, its apparent sincerity, their anger at the refusal, and their disapproval of the boss. Results indicated that the mere presence of a causal account was not sufficient, by itself, to reduce anger or other negative reactions. However, the more adequate and

FIGURE 13.11 Insincerity as a Cause of Future Conflict

Subjects reacted more negatively to an opponent whose claims about the causes behind his or her "tough" bargaining stance seemed false than to one whose claims in this regard seemed true. These findings indicate that *attributions* often play an important role in organizational conflict. (Source: Based on data from Baron, 1988; see Note 29.)

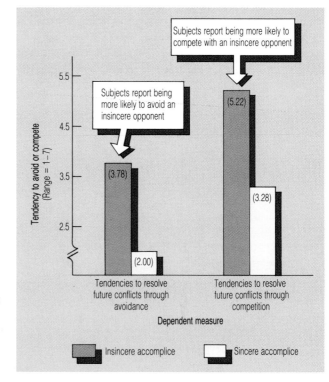

sincere such accounts seemed to be, the lower such reactions (e.g., the lower subjects' anger or disapproval of the boss). Together, the findings reported by Baron and by Bies and his colleagues suggest that attributions often play an important role in organizational conflict.

A third interpersonal factor of considerable importance in generating instances of organizational conflict might be termed *faulty communication*. This refers to the fact that often, individuals communicate with others in a way that angers or annoys them, even though it is not their intention to do so. Such faulty communication often involves a lack of clarity—for example, a manager is certain that she communicated her wishes clearly to a subordinate. In fact, however, the subordinate is confused about what he is supposed to do. When the manager later finds that the task has not been completed, she is annoyed. The subordinate, in turn, is angered by what he considers unfair treatment. In other cases, conflict centers around inappropriate *criticism*—negative feedback delivered in a manner that angers the recipient instead of helping this person to do a better job (see Figure 13.12). The negative effects of such *destructive criticism* have been demonstrated clearly in a study by Baron.[31]

In this investigation, subjects were asked to prepare an ad campaign for an imaginary product (a new shampoo), and then received feedback on their work from another person (an accomplice of the researcher). In one condition (*constructive criticism*), this feedback was negative, but was consistent with established principles for providing such feedback in an effective manner. Thus, it was considerate in tone, specific in content, contained no threats, and made no internal attributions for the supposedly poor performance. In a second condition (*destructive criticism*), this feedback was negative but, in addition, violated basic principles of effective feedback. It was harsh in tone, general rather than specific in content, contained threats, and placed the blame for poor performance squarely on the subject. After receiving one of these types of criticism, subjects rated their current feelings (anger, tension), and their likelihood of resolving future conflicts with the accomplice in each of five ways (through competition, compromise, collaboration, accommodation, or avoidance).

Results indicated that subjects who received destructive criticism reported being angrier and more upset than those who received constructive criticism. In addition, those who received destructive criticism, reported being more likely to resolve future conflicts through avoidance or competition, and less likely to resolve them through collaboration (see Figure 13.13 on page 464). In a follow-up study, it was found that destructive criticism also reduced subjects' self-set goals and feelings of self-efficacy

DUFFY®   **by BRUCE HAMMOND**

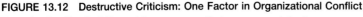

FIGURE 13.12 Destructive Criticism: One Factor in Organizational Conflict
Negative feedback delivered in a manner that angers recipients or causes them to lose face (*destructive criticism*) can contribute to costly organizational conflicts. (Source: DUFFY copyright 1985 Universal Press Syndicate. Reprinted with permission. All rights reserved.)

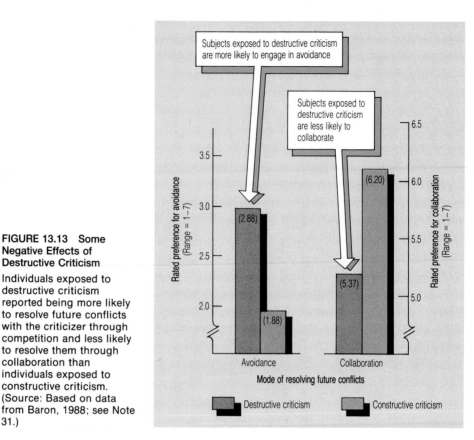

FIGURE 13.13 Some Negative Effects of Destructive Criticism

Individuals exposed to destructive criticism reported being more likely to resolve future conflicts with the criticizer through competition and less likely to resolve them through collaboration than individuals exposed to constructive criticism. (Source: Based on data from Baron, 1988; see Note 31.)

(i.e., perceived ability to perform various tasks). Together, the findings reported by Baron and others[32] suggest that harsh, destructive criticism is one type of communication managers (and others) would do well to avoid. Such criticism induces feelings of anger, may contribute to the occurrence of costly conflicts, and may also exert negative effects on motivation and self-efficacy. Truly, this seems to be a devastating combination!

Finally, several personal characteristics, too, seem to play a role in organizational conflict. For example, Type A persons report becoming involved in conflict with others more frequently than Type B persons (refer to our discussion of this characteristic in chapter 6).[33] Conversely, persons who are high in *self-monitoring* (ones who are highly aware of how others are reacting to them) report resolving conflict in more productive ways (e.g., through collaboration or compromise) than persons who are low in self-monitoring.[34]

In sum, considerable evidence suggests that conflict in work settings often stems from the relations between individuals and from their personal characteristics, as well as from underlying structural (organization-based) factors. At first glance, this finding might appear to be quite pessimistic in its implications for the reduction or management of such conflict; after all, it adds several potential causes to those that have traditionally been viewed as important in this respect. In fact, however, it can actually be interpreted as quite optimistic. Interpersonal behavior, and even many personal characteristics, can readily be modified. Indeed, in many cases, these may be easier to change than organizational structure, and easier to modify than built-in underlying conflicts of interest. For this reason, understanding the interpersonal causes of organizational conflict may offer important, practical benefits. (In recent years, growing numbers of organizations have entered into international joint ventures. To what extent does conflict occur in such settings? And when it does, what factors contribute to its presence? For information on these issues, see the **International Perspective** section below.)

OB: AN INTERNATIONAL PERSPECTIVE

Conflict in International Joint Ventures

In order to maximize their efficiency or exploit various natural resources, many large companies have entered into multinational joint ventures. Such ventures are most common in the oil, chemical, and petrochemical industries, but occur in others as well. Because such joint ventures involve two or more organizations, the potential for conflict within them seems quite high. After all, individuals from different cultures (both organizational and national) must work together, perhaps for the first times in their careers. Is actual conflict common in such ventures? And when it occurs, what issues does it involve? To answer these questions, Habib conducted an extensive survey study.[35] The first task he faced was identifying potential causes of conflict in such organizations. Habib accomplished this by carrying out a thorough search of the literature, plus preliminary research with a relatively small sample (ten companies). On the basis of this work he then selected fourteen factors which appeared to be most important in provoking conflict in international joint ventures (see Table 13.1). Once these factors were chosen, Habib wrote to the presidents of 258 multinational ventures, asking that they have the person in their company most familiar with the joint venture rate the frequency and intensity of disagreements over these issues. Only a small proportion of the companies responded, but the information obtained in this manner is at least suggestive.

First, Habib found that conflict over these issues was in fact quite common. Indeed, on a scale ranging from 1 (never) to 6 (constantly), the persons responding indicated that conflict in the joint venture was quite frequent (a mean rating of 4.61). Second, he found that when such conflicts occurred, they were relatively intense. Thus, on a scale ranging from 1 (very low) to 5 (very high), respondents rated the intensity of the conflicts as 3.65. Finally, Habib correlated these ratings of conflict frequency and intensity with respondents' ratings of satisfaction with

TABLE 13.1   Causes of Conflict in International Joint Ventures
The issues listed here appear to be important potential causes of conflict in international joint ventures.

Potential Causes of Conflict in International Joint Ventures
Separating operations of the joint venture from those of parent companies
Prudence of committing a large proportion of joint venture's outputs to a parent company
Prudence of obtaining needed inputs from parent companies
Partner's attempt to make changes in terms of joint venture contract
Partner's attempt to control key decisions in joint venture
Differences of opinion regarding amount of profit to be retained
Differences of opinion regarding expansion of joint venture
Differences regarding accessibility to new technology from parent company
Differences regarding pricing of an input provided by partner
Differences of opinion regarding product proliferation
Differences regarding roles and functions of each partner
Differences regarding hiring policies
Differences regarding interpretation of terms of joint venture contract
Differences regarding division of benefits between partners

(Source: Adapted from Habib, 1987; see Note 35.)

their joint ventures and the number of changes in them that they desired. As expected, the higher the rated frequency and intensity of conflict, the lower subjects' satisfaction with the joint ventures and the larger the number of changes in them they desired.

Together, the findings reported by Habib suggest that multinational joint ventures do indeed encounter serious problems with respect to conflict. Given the increasing economic importance of such organizations, further research focused on the task of developing means for reducing or managing conflict in joint ventures would appear to be well justified.

In everyday speech, the term *conflict* has strong negative connotations. It seems to imply anger, direct confrontations, and harsh, damaging behavior. In fact, however, conflict, in work settings, actually operates like the proverbial "double-edged sword." Depending on why it occurs and how it develops, it can yield beneficial as well as harmful effects.

Conflict: The Negative Side

Some of the negative effects produced by conflict are too obvious to require much comment. For example, it often produces strong negative emotions and, in this regard, can be quite stressful. Conflict frequently interferes with communication between individuals, groups, or divisions. In this way, it can all but eliminate coordination between them. Third, it diverts attention and needed energies away from major tasks and efforts to attain key organizational goals. In all these ways, conflict can seriously interfere with organizational effectiveness.

Other negative effects of conflict are somewhat more subtle and are sometimes easily overlooked. First, it has been found that conflict between groups often encourages their leaders to shift from participative to authoritarian styles.[36] The reason for this is as follows: groups experiencing stress require firm direction. Recognizing this fact, their leaders adopt more controlling tactics when conflict develops. As a result of such changes, groups experiencing conflict tend to provide less pleasant work environments than ones not faced with this type of stress.

Second, conflict increases the tendency of both sides to engage in negative stereotyping. As we noted earlier, the members of opposing groups or units tend to emphasize the differences between them. Moreover, these differences are interpreted in a negative light, so that each side views the other in increasingly unfavorable terms.

Finally, conflict leads each side to close ranks and emphasize loyalty to their own department or group. Anyone who suggests, even tentatively, that the other side's position has some merit is viewed as a traitor and is strongly censured. As a result, it becomes increasingly difficult for opponents to take each other's perspective—a development that sharply reduces the likelihood of an effective resolution of their differences,[37] and increases the likelihood of *groupthink* (see chapter 14).

Conflict: The Positive Side

The overall picture is not entirely bleak, however. While conflict often has a disruptive impact on organizations, it can, under some conditions, also yield important benefits. First, conflict serves to bring problems that have previously been ignored out into the open. Since recognition of such difficulties is a necessary first step to their solution, conflict can sometimes be useful in this respect.

Second, conflict often encourages the consideration of new ideas and approaches. In short, it facilitates innovation and change. This is so because once open conflict erupts, an organization or work unit simply cannot continue with "business as usual." The need for hard decisions, new policies, major shifts in personnel, or even a new internal structure is driven home, and appropriate change may follow.

Third, because conflict enhances group loyalty, it can increase motivation and performance within the groups or units involved. Each strives to attain even higher levels of excellence than before, both to outdo its rival and confirm its own positive self-image.

Finally, conflict encourages both sides to carefully monitor one another's performance in order to see exactly what the opponent is up to. This, too, can increase motivation and performance.

In these ways, conflict can actually contribute to organizational effectiveness. It is important to note, however, that such benefits will occur only when conflict is carefully managed and does not get out of control. If it is permitted to become extreme, rationality—and the potential benefits just described—tend to quickly disappear. Assuming that such pitfalls are avoided, however, conflict *can* sometimes play a useful role.

CONFLICT: ITS EFFECTIVE MANAGEMENT

If conflict can indeed yield benefits as well as costs, then the key task organizations face with respect to this process is *managing* its occurrence. In short, the overall goal should not be eliminating conflict; instead, it should be adopting procedures for maximizing its potential benefits while minimizing its potential costs. Fortunately, a number of approaches have been found useful in this regard. Several of these will now be reviewed.

Bargaining: The Universal Process

By far the most common strategy for resolving organizational conflicts, and therefore for managing them effectively, is **bargaining** or **negotiation.**[38] In this process, opposing sides to a dispute exchange offers, counteroffers, and concessions, either directly or through representatives (see Figure 13.14). If the process is successful, a solution acceptable to both sides is attained, and the conflict is effectively resolved, perhaps with such "extras" as enhanced understanding and improved relations between the two sides. If, instead, bargaining is unsuccessful, costly deadlock may result and the conflict may intensify. What factors determine which of these outcomes occurs? Given the importance of bargaining, and its occurrence in virtually all spheres of life, this question has been the subject of intensive study for decades. The answer that has

FIGURE 13.14   Bargaining: The Most Common Approach to Resolving Conflicts
During *bargaining*, two sides in a dispute exchange offers, counteroffers, and concessions in an attempt to reach a settlement acceptable to both.

emerged from such research would fill several volumes, so we can do no more than touch on it briefly here. (If you are particularly interested in this topic, please refer to recent volumes by Lewicki and Litterer[39] or Lewicki, Sheppard, & Bazerman.[40])

One group of factors that strongly affects the outcomes of negotiations involves the specific tactics adopted by bargainers. Many of these are designed to reduce opponents' aspirations—to convince them that they have little chance of reaching their goals and should, instead, accept offers that are actually quite favorable to the side proposing them. Many specific strategies can be used for this purpose. For example, one side can suggest that it has other potential partners and will withdraw from the current negotiations if its proposals are not accepted. Similarly, one party to a dispute can claim that its break-even point is much lower than it really is—a procedure known as the "big lie" technique.[41] If the other side accepts this information, it may make sizeable concessions. Third, the course of negotiations, and final settlements, are often strongly affected by the nature of initial offers. Relatively extreme offers seem to put strong pressure on opponents to make concessions, resulting in settlements favorable to the side adopting such positions.[42] On the other hand, if initial offers are too extreme, opponents may be angered and decide to seek other negotiating partners.

A second group of factors that determines the nature and outcomes of bargaining involves the cognitive set or focus adopted by negotiators. Several studies suggest that when bargainers adopt a *positive frame*—focusing on the potential benefits of negotiations and of the settlements that may result—bargaining is facilitated. In contrast, when they adopt a *negative frame*—focusing on potential losses or costs, bargaining is impaired.[43] In short, expectations or cognitive sets shape reality, determining the nature and course of actual bargaining.

Perhaps the single most important factor determining the success of negotiations in producing settlements satisfactory to both sides, however, involves participants' overall orientation toward this process. Almost three decades ago, Walton and McKersie pointed out that persons taking part in negotiations can approach such discussions from either of two distinct perspectives.[44] On the one hand, they can view negotiations as "win-lose" (*distributive*) situations in which gains by one side are necessarily linked with losses for the other. On the other hand, persons can approach negotiations as potential "win-win" situations—ones in which the interests of the two sides are not necessarily incompatible and in which the potential gains of both can be maximized. Not all situations offer the potential for such agreements, but many that at first glance seem to involve simple head-on clashes between the two sides do, in fact, provide such possibilities. If participants are willing to explore all options carefully, and exert the effort required to identify creative potential solutions, they can attain **integrative agreements**—ones that offer greater joint benefits than simple compromise (splitting all differences down the middle).

How can such integrative agreements be attained? Pruitt and his colleagues suggest the possibilities summarized in Table 13.2.[45] As you can see, these involve several distinct tactics. In *nonspecific compensation,* one side receives certain benefits and the other is compensated for providing these in some unrelated manner (e.g., by concessions or some other issue). In *logrolling,* each side makes concessions on relatively unimportant issues in order to attain concessions on issues it views as more central to its needs. For example, consider a dispute between scientists and management in a research department of a large organization. The scientists want to be free to order any equipment they want, to pursue projects they feel are important, and to do as little paperwork as possible. Management wants to hold costs to a minimum, wants the scientists to pursue only company-chosen projects, and requires many reports and forms. Under the strategy of logrolling, the scientists might agree to doing more paperwork (a relatively unimportant issue to them, but one that is very important to

TABLE 13.2 Techniques for Attaining Integrative Agreements

Several strategies can be used to attain *integrative agreements* through bargaining.

TYPE OF AGREEMENT	DESCRIPTION
Broadening the Pie	Available resources are broadened so that both sides can obtain their major goals
Nonspecific Compensation	One side gets what it wants; the other is compensated on an unrelated issue
Logrolling	Each party makes concession on low priority issues in exchange for concessions on issues that are of higher value to it
Cost Cutting	One party gets what it desires and the costs to the other party are reduced or eliminated
Bridging	Neither party gets its initial demands, but a new option that satisfies the major interests of both sides is developed

(Source: Based on suggestions by Pruitt et al., 1983; see Note 44.)

management), and to paying more attention to costs (another issue of great importance to management). However, they would gain more freedom to pursue at least some projects of their own choosing (a central issue to the scientists).

Research findings suggest that when disputing parties strive for integrative agreements, joint outcomes do indeed increase. Moreover, the nature of their discussions changes. *Contentious tactics* such as threats or taking firm, unyielding positions decrease, and the open exchange of accurate information between the two sides increases. Thus, not only does integrative bargaining increase the outcomes of both sides—it may enhance their relationships, too. Given such benefits, it seems clear that encouraging such an approach to negotiations is one highly effective strategy for managing real or potential conflicts.

Third Party Intervention: Help from the Outside

Despite the best efforts of both sides, negotiations sometimes deadlock. When they do, the aid of a third party, someone not directly involved in the dispute, is often sought. Such *third party intervention* can take many forms, but the most common are **mediation** and **arbitration**.[46] In mediation, the third party attempts, through various tactics, to facilitate voluntary agreements between the disputants. Mediators have no formal power and cannot impose an agreement on the two sides. Instead, they seek to clarify the issues involved and enhance communication between the opponents. Mediators sometimes offer specific recommendations for compromise or integrative solutions; in other cases, they merely guide disputants toward developing such solutions themselves. In sum, their role is primarily that of *facilitator*—helping the two sides toward agreements they both find acceptable.

In contrast, *arbitrators* do have the power to impose (or at least strongly recommend) the terms of an agreement. In *binding arbitration,* the two sides agree in advance to accept these terms. In *voluntary arbitration,* though, the two sides retain the freedom to reject the recommended agreement (although the personal stature and expertise of the arbitrator may make it difficult for them to do so). In *conventional* arbitration, the arbitrator can offer any package of terms he or she wishes. However, in *final offer* arbitration, the arbitrator merely chooses between final offers made by the disputants.

Both mediation and arbitration can be helpful in resolving organizational conflicts. However, both suffer from certain drawbacks. Because it requires voluntary compliance by the disputing parties, mediation often proves ineffective. Indeed, it may simply serve to underscore the depth of the differences between the two sides. Arbitration suffers from several potential problems. First, it may exert a *chilling effect* on negotiations, bringing voluntary progress to a halt. Since both sides know the arbitrator will resolve the dispute for them, they see little point in engaging in serious bargaining which, after all, is hard work. Second, one or both sides may come to suspect that the arbitrator is biased. The result: disputants become increasingly reluctant to agree to arbitration. Finally, there is some indication that commitment to arbitrated settlements is weaker than that to directly negotiated ones.

In most instances, mediation and arbitration are relatively formal procedures involving the services of persons from outside an organization. Are they also used by practicing managers to resolve disputes between persons under their authority? Research by Sheppard suggests that this is not usually the case.[47] Sheppard asked a large number of practicing managers to describe how they intervened in disputes between their subordinates. Careful analysis of their replies indicated that managers usually adopt one of three approaches in such situations, and none of these closely resemble traditional mediation. In the first and most common form, managers actively question both sides about the nature of the dispute and their opposing positions. Then, they impose a solution that they believe will meet the needs of both sides.

In a second approach, managers don't actively question both sides—they simply listen to their respective points of view and then impose a solution. Finally, in a third pattern, managers make a quick, informal diagnosis of the nature of the conflict. After doing so, they tell both sides to negotiate directly with each other and reach a solution, warning them that if they don't succeed, the manager will impose one. Why are these approaches different from standard mediation or arbitration? Many factors probably play a role in this regard, but two seem most important. First, time constraints are often intense in such situations. Conflict between subordinates must be quickly resolved, so little opportunity exists for the institution of formal procedures. Second, managers have established relationships with the persons involved. Thus, their approach to resolving conflicts between subordinates must occur within this context. Whatever the precise factors involved, it is clear that managers often seek to resolve conflicts between their subordinates in ways other than standard mediation or arbitration.

The Induction of Superordinate Goals

At several points in this chapter, we have noted that individuals often divide the world into two opposing camps: *us* and *them*. They perceive members of their own group as quite different from, and usually better than, people belonging to other groups. These dual tendencies to magnify the differences between one's own group and others and to disparage outsiders are very powerful and are as common in organizations as in other settings.[48] Further, they seem to play a central role in many conflicts between various departments, divisions, and work groups. How can they be countered? One answer, suggested by research findings, is through the induction of **superordinate goals**—ones that tie the interests of the two sides together. The basic idea behind this approach is simple: by inducing both parties to a conflict to focus on and work toward common objectives, the barriers between them—ones that interfere with communication, coordination, and agreement—can be weakened. Then, the chances for cooperation rather than conflict are enhanced.

One example of this process is provided by events occurring in the U.S. automobile industry during the early 1980s. Faced with growing competition from foreign companies, labor and management—traditional opponents with a long-standing history of bitter conflicts—agreed to adopt a different strategy. They would join forces (at least temporarily) to attain a common goal: turning back the wave of foreign imports that threatened their joint livelihood. Employees agreed to reductions in pay and other benefits while management agreed to use such savings to retain as many jobs as possible. The results were dramatic: within a few years, the companies involved were generating record-setting profits instead of record-breaking losses. The total situation was more complex than suggested here, and many other factors played a role (e.g., government-established quotas on imports). However, there is little doubt that the recognition of shared, superordinate goals was important.

Escalative Interventions: Intensifying Conflicts in Order to Resolve Them

Perhaps the most intriguing approach to managing organizational conflict suggested in recent years is one that seems, at first glance, to fly in the face of common sense. This approach, known as **escalative intervention,** seeks to intensify existing conflicts as a means of resolving them and attaining several related goals as well.[49] The reasoning behind this strategy is as follows: increasing the intensity of a conflict brings matters to a head. The underlying causes of friction or disagreement are clarified, and the motivation to search for effective, integrative solutions is increased. Then, instead of continuing to smolder beneath the surface, conflicts emerge into the open, and can be resolved to the satisfaction of those involved.

According to Van de Vliert, several tactics can be used to intensify ongoing conflicts.[50] First, steps may be taken to add to the existing causes of conflict. For example, present channels of communication may be blocked, or the incompatibility of various goals can be emphasized. Similarly, various barriers to open conflict can be removed or lessened (e.g., direct contacts between the opposing sides can be increased; both sides may be urged to express negative feelings about one another). Second, the range of issues on which the conflict is based can be extended by calling attention to additional matters about which the disputants disagree. Third, additional parties can be added to the conflict, thus fueling its scope or intensity. In a fourth strategy, actions that serve to escalate the conflict can be encouraged (e.g., one side is urged to prove to the other that it is right, or to cause the other to lose face). Finally, the two sides may be encouraged to perceive hostile intentions in each others' actions, or to express strong disapproval of one another's proposals.

To the extent such tactics succeed, ongoing conflict is intensified. Thus, strong pressures toward reaching a resolution are generated, and several benefits may follow. First, and most important, faced with mounting tension and a situation that is fast becoming intolerable, the two sides may increase their efforts to reach effective, integrative agreements. In addition, other benefits, such as the stimulation of major change, discouragement of avoidance behaviors, and a clearer diagnosis of underlying problems within an organization may also result (see Figure 13.15 on page 472). However, these favorable outcomes are certainly *not* guaranteed. They will follow only when the individuals managing such an intensification of conflict are skilled in this task, and are able to direct the growing tensions and friction into constructive channels.

Is it actually possible to direct escalating conflicts in this fashion? Research evidence suggests that it is, and that escalative interventions are indeed helpful in several contexts (e.g., in marital disputes as well as organizational ones).[51] Thus, in this context, there appears to be a favorable trade-off between controlled, temporary escalation of conflict and its effective long-term management.

FIGURE 13.15 Escalative Interventions: Some Potential Benefits

In some instances, increasing the intensity of ongoing conflicts through *escalative interventions* may be a useful technique for managing conflict. Several potential benefits of such procedures are shown here. (Source: Based on suggestions by Van de Vliert, 1984; see Note 49.)

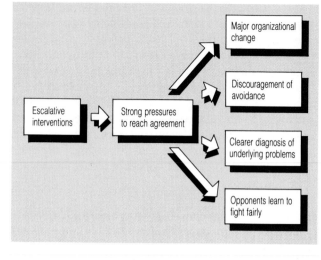

SUMMARY AND REVIEW

Prosocial Organizational Behavior. Individuals often engage in **prosocial behavior** in work settings, performing actions that benefit others in the organization. For example, they may assist others with their jobs or with personal matters, and provide suggestions for procedural or administrative improvements. Such actions may benefit the organization but in some instances, they may actually harm it (e.g., when an individual provides rewards to persons who are not qualified to receive them or engages in **whistle-blowing** to outsiders).

Cooperation and Competition. Cooperation involves mutual assistance or coordination between two or more persons or groups. Its occurrence in work settings is affected by several factors relating to individuals (e.g., strong tendencies toward **reciprocity,** communication, personal orientations and preferences). It is also affected by several organizational factors (e.g., reward systems, interdependence among employees). Coordination also occurs between independent organizations when they form interorganizational groups such as *consortia*.

The Nature and Causes of Conflict. Conflict is a process that begins when one person or group perceives that another person or group has taken or is about to take some action inconsistent with the perceiver's major interests. Conflict is indeed a process, and involves the perceptions, thoughts, feelings, and intentions of all participating parties. **Organizational conflict** stems from both organization-based and interpersonal factors. Included in the first category are such conditions as competition over scarce resources, ambiguity over responsibility or jurisdiction, interdependence between individuals or groups, and reward systems that pit persons or units against one another. Included in the second category are grudges, errors in discerning the causes behind others' actions, faulty communication, and several personal characteristics. Conflict appears to be quite common in multinational joint ventures, stemming from many issues and causes.

The Effects and Management of Conflict. While conflict often exerts negative effects on organizations (e.g., it interferes with communication and coordination), it sometimes produces positive outcomes as well (e.g., it brings smoldering problems to a head and encourages change). Thus, the key task with respect to conflict is managing its occurrence, not eliminating it entirely. Several tactics have proven useful in this regard.

Bargaining is the most common procedure for resolving organizational conflicts. *Third-party intervention* (e.g., **mediation, arbitration**) can also prove helpful in resolving many conflicts. A third approach to managing conflict involves the induction of **superordinate goals**—ones shared by both sides. Finally, conflict can sometimes be resolved through **escalative interventions**—actions that intensify current conflicts in order to resolve them more effectively.

KEY TERMS

arbitration: A form of third-party intervention in disputes in which the intervening person has the power to determine the terms of an agreement.

bargaining: A process in which two or more parties in a dispute exchange offers, counteroffers, and concessions in an effort to attain a mutually acceptable agreement.

competition: A process in which individuals or groups seek to attain desired goals at the expense of others seeking the same goals.

competitors: Individuals who are primarily concerned with exceeding the outcomes of others.

conflict: See *organizational conflict.*

cooperation: A process in which individuals or groups work together to attain shared goals.

cooperators: Individuals who are primarily concerned with maximizing joint outcomes.

equalizers: Individuals primarily concerned with assuring equality of outcomes among all persons who work together on joint projects.

escalative interventions: Techniques for managing conflict that seek to increase conflict as a means of resolving it effectively.

individualists: Persons primarily concerned with maximizing their own outcomes.

integrative agreements: Agreements between negotiators that maximize the joint outcomes of all parties.

mediation: A form of third-party intervention in disputes in which the intervener does not have the authority to dictate an agreement. Mediators simply attempt to enhance communication between opposing sides and to provide conditions that will facilitate acceptable agreements.

negotiation: See *bargaining.*

organizational conflict: A process which begins when individuals or groups perceive that others have taken or will soon take actions incompatible with their own major interests. Conflict involves awareness of opposing interests, the thoughts and emotions of all involved parties, their strategies and intentions, and their overt actions.

prosocial behavior: Actions that benefit others within an organization. Such behaviors may or may not benefit the organization as well.

reciprocity: The principle that we should treat others as they have treated us in the past.

superordinate goals: Goals shared by the parties in a conflict or dispute.

whistle-blowing: One form of *prosocial behavior* in organizations. Whistle-blowing involves calling attention to actions or practices that are inconsistent with established organizational norms or policies.

QUESTIONS FOR DISCUSSION

1. Whistle-blowing can be a prosocial action with respect to society, yet produce harmful effects for an organization. How?

2. What steps can organizations take to encourage good *citizenship* behaviors and other prosocial actions among their employees?

3. Under what conditions does communication enhance cooperation? Under what conditions does it interfere with cooperation?

4. For what kind of jobs would highly competitive persons be best? For what kind of jobs would very cooperative persons be a better choice?

5. "Conflict doesn't exist until it is recognized by the parties involved." Do you agree with this statement? If so, why? If not, why?

6. Do you believe that conflict in organizations stems primarily from structural factors (e.g., competition for scarce resources) or primarily from interpersonal ones (e.g., grudges, poor communication)?

7. Many persons approach bargaining as a "win-lose" situation. Why is a "win-win" approach often better?

1. Brief, A. P., & Motowidlo, S. J. (1986). Prosocial organizational behaviors. *Academy of Management Review, 4,* 710–725.

2. Pondy, L. R. (1967). Organizational conflict: Concepts and models. *Administrative Science Quarterly, 12,* 296–320.

3. Thomas, K. W. (1989). Conflict and negotiation processes in organizations. In M. D. Dunnette (Ed.), *Handbook of industrial/organizational psychology* (2nd ed.). Palo Alto, CA: Consulting Psychologists Press.

4. Eisenberg, N. (1985). *Altruistic emotion, cognition, and behavior.* Hillsdale, NJ: Erlbaum.

5. Schaller, M., & Cialdini, R. B. (1988). The economics of empathic helping: Support for a mood management motive. *Journal of Experimental Social Psychology, 24,* 163–181.

6. See Note 1.

7. Dozier, J. B., & Miceli, M. P. (1985). Potential predictors of whistle-blowing: A prosocial behavior perspective. *Academy of Management Review, 11,* 823–836.

8. Puffer, S. M. (1987). Prosocial behavior, noncompliant behavior, and work performance among commission salespeople. *Journal of Applied Psychology, 72,* 615–621.

9. Forsyth, D. R. (1983). *An introduction to group dynamics.* Monterey, CA: Brooks/Cole.

10. Tjosvold, D. (1986). *Working together to get things done.* Lexington, MA: Lexington Books.

11. Gouldner, A. W. (1960). The norm of reciprocity: A preliminary statement. *American Sociological Review, 25,* 161–178.

12. Youngs, G. A., Jr. (1986). Patterns of threat and punishment reciprocity in a conflict setting. *Journal of Personality and Social Psychology, 51,* 541–546.

13. See Note 12.

14. Knight, G. P., & Dubro, A. F. (1984). Cooperative, competitive, and individualistic social values: An individualized regression and clustering approach. *Journal of Personality and Social Psychology, 46,* 98–105.

15. See Note 14.

16. Khulman, D. M., & Marshello, A. F. J. (1975). Individual differences in game motivation as moderators of preprogrammed strategy effects in prisoner's dilemma. *Journal of Personality and Social Psychology, 32,* 922–932.

17. Peters, T. J., & Waterman, R. H., Jr. (1982). *In search of excellence: Lessons from America's best-run companies.* New York: Warner Books.

18. Cheng, J. L. (1983). Interdependence and coordination in organizations: A role-system analysis. *Academy of Management Journal, 26,* 156–162.

19. Oliva, T. A., Day, D. L., & Macmillan, I. C. (1988). A generic model of competitive dynamics. *Academy of Management Review, 13,* 387–389.

20. Provan, K. G. (1984). Interorganizational cooperation and decision making autonomy in a consortium multihospital system. *Academy of Management Review, 9,* 494–504.

21. Schopler, J. H. (1987). Interorganizational groups: Origins, structure, and outcomes. *Academy of Management Review, 12,* 702–713.

22. See Note 3.

23. Thomas, K. W., & Schmidt, W. H. (1976). A survey of managerial interests with respect to conflict. *Academy of Management Journal, 10,* 315–318.

24. Pruitt, D. G., & Rubin, J. Z. (1986). *Social conflict: Escalation, stalemate, and settlement.* New York: Random House.

25. See Note 3.

26. Greenberg, J. (1987). A taxonomy of organizational justice theories. *Academy of Management Review, 12,* 9–22.

27. Blake, R. R., & Mouton, J. S. (1984). *Solving costly organizational conflicts.* San Francisco: Jossey-Bass.

28. Johnson, T. E., & Rule, B. G. (1986). Mitigating circumstance information, censure, and aggression. *Journal of Personality and Social Psychology, 50,* 537–542.

29. Baron, R. A. (1988). Attributions and organizational conflict: The mediating role of apparent sincerity. *Organizational Behavior and Human Decision Processes, 41,* 111–127.

30. Bies, R. J., Shapiro, D. L., & Cummings, L. L. (in press). Causal accounts and managing organizational conflict: Is it enough to say it's not my fault? *Communication Research.*

31. Baron, R. A. (1988). Negative effects of destructive criticism: Impact on conflict, self-efficacy, and task performance. *Journal of Applied Psychology, 73,* 199–207.

32. Larson, J. R., Jr. (1986). Supervisors' performance feedback to subordinates: The impact of subordinate performance valence and outcome dependence. *Organizational Behavior and Human Decision Processes, 37,* 391–408.

33. Baron, R. A. (in press). Personality and organizational conflict: Effects of the Type A pattern and self-monitoring. *Organizational Behavior and Human Decision Processes.*

34. See Note 33.

35. Habib, G. M. (1987). Measures of manifest conflict in international joint ventures. *Academy of Management Journal, 30,* 808–816.

36. Fodor, E. M. (1976). Group stress, authoritarian style of control and use of power. *Journal of Applied Psychology, 61,* 313–318.

37. See Note 27.

38. Lewicki, R. J., & Litterer, J. A. (1985). *Negotiation.* Homewood, IL: Irwin.

39. See Note 38.

40. Lewicki, R. J., Sheppard, B. H., & Bazerman, M. (Eds.). (1986). *Research on negotiation in organizations,* vol. 1. Greenwich, CT: JAI Press.

41. Chertkoff, J. M., & Baird, S. L. (1971). Applicability of the big lie technique and the last clear chance doctrine to bargaining. *Journal of Personality and Social Psychology, 20,* 298–303.

42. Chertkoff, J. M., & Conley, M. (1967). Opening offer and frequency of concessions as bargaining strategies. *Journal of Personality and Social Psychology, 7,* 181–185.

43. Huber, V. L., Neale, M. A., & Northcraft, G. B. (1987). Decision bias and personnel selection strategies. *Organizational Behavior and Human Decision Processes, 40,* 136–147.

44. Pruitt, D. G., Carnevale, J. D., Ben-Yoav, O., Nochajski, T. H., & Van Slyck, M. R. (1983). Incentives for cooperation in integrative bargaining. In R. Tietz, *Aspiration levels in bargaining and economic decision making.* Berlin: Springer-Verlag.

45. See Note 44.

46. Carnevale, P. J. D., & Conlon, D. E. (1988). Time pressure and strategic choice in mediation. *Organizational Behavior and Human Decision Processes, 42,* 111–133.

47. Sheppard, B. H. (1984). Third party conflict intervention: A procedural framework. In B. Staw and L. Cummings (Eds.), *Research in Organizational Behavior,* vol 6 (pp. 141–190). Greenwich, CT: JAI Press.

48. Fiske, S. T., & Taylor, S. E. (1984). *Social cognition.* Reading, MA: Addison-Wesley.

49. Van de Vliert, E. (1984). Conflict: Prevention and escalation. In Drenth, P. J. D., Thierry, H., Willems, P. J., & de Wolff, C. J. (Eds.), *Handbook of work and organizational psychology.* New York: Wiley.

50. Van de Vliert, E. (in press). Escalative intervention in small-group conflicts. *Journal of Applied Behavioral Science.*

51. See Note 50.

Unfriendly Skies/Friendly Freeways

During the winter and early spring of 1988–1989, business magazines and newspapers were filled with reports of a head-on clash between two exceptional and unbending adversaries: Frank Lorenzo, CEO of Texas Air, the parent company of Eastern Airlines, and Charlie Bryan, the head of Eastern's powerful International Association of Machinists (IAM). Both men claimed that they wanted to see Eastern, the center of this storm of conflict, survive.[1] Yet both took actions that, looking back, seemed to doom it to its likely eventual fate: a place in the dustbin of failed corporations.

The conflict between Eastern's unions (particularly the IAM) and its management has a long history. In fact, the conflict had grown so intense during the time Frank Borman was Eastern's CEO, that the union was instrumental in calling for the sale of the troubled airline to Texas Air. Following this deal, Borman was replaced as CEO by Lorenzo.[2]

Lorenzo had quite a reputation in the airline industry. His holding company, Texas Air Corp., owned not only Eastern but also Continental, and what were formerly Frontier Airlines, New York Air, and People Express. He received a great deal of publicity when, in 1983, he took Continental into bankruptcy, cancelled its union contracts, and slashed fares. Lorenzo is described by colleagues and enemies alike as brilliant, pragmatic, and crafty.[3] He admits that he wants to be in control and often acts in a manner designed to assure that he gets his way. The long-standing dispute with Eastern's unions finally came to a boil when Lorenzo requested that the machinists take a 28 percent pay cut and agree to work rule reforms including cross-utilization of employees as well as hiring part-time personnel.[4] The union's outraged response brought the conflict to a crisis, and moved Eastern rapidly along the road to corporate oblivion.

Bryan, head of the IAM, also developed a well-known reputation. He is described as extremely stubborn, cautious, and above all, mistrustful of management. He strongly believed that he had his union's best interests at heart and that by sticking to his plan— no givebacks or rules changes—he would win the final victory.[5]

During the dispute, both Lorenzo and Bryan used numerous ploys to get the other side to "see the light." Lorenzo engaged in a great deal of financial maneuvering. He stopped service to fourteen cities and slashed 4,000 jobs. He sold Eastern's reservation system to Texas Air for $100 million. Then, he negotiated the sale of Eastern's prize property, its Shuttle, for $365 million. It was widely believed that with this money and profits from Texas Air, Lorenzo planned to accumulate almost $1 billion with which to fight off the unions.[6] Meanwhile, Bryan steadfastly refused to agree to pay cuts. He tried to raise support from Eastern's other unions, and his success in gaining the cooperation of its pilots was instrumental in bringing the airline to its knees. Bryan also helped launch a safety campaign that resulted in the FAA's review of Eastern's fleet and operations. Although the FAA ultimately gave Eastern a clean bill of health, the publicity surrounding the investigation created a great deal of consumer distrust and defection. Partly as a result of this series of events, both Lorenzo and Bryan filed numerous lawsuits against each other's units.

As history now records, this contentious climate finally carried Eastern to the brink of bankruptcy—and over, into near insolvency.[7] The airline, which was once numbered among the largest and most successful in the United States, is now mainly a memory. And if it ever re-emerges, it will certainly be a far different organization than the proud and profitable airline that once existed.

The United Auto Workers (UAW) and General Motors (GM) used to have relations as poor as those between the IAM and Eastern. Recently, however, they have embarked on a program of "jointness" whereby management and labor meet and work together to solve problems. They have established a "twenty-two acre 'jointness' park, a thirteen-room 'joint education' wing, a plantwide 'joint communications network' with forty-four TV monitors, a 'joint' newsletter, and 200-plus 'joint employee involvement groups.' "[8] In addition, special programs ranging from AIDS education to remedial math have been established.

In some places the results of such programs have been extraordinary. At one plant in Toledo, Ohio management estimates that these cooperative programs have resulted in savings of $20 million in production costs in one year alone. They have seen an improvement in quality also, as reflected by a 90 percent drop in the number of defective parts. In other areas, however, it isn't quite clear how these programs directly affect the bottom line. Even so, the idea is that by continuing the joint programs, the UAW and GM are fostering increased trust between labor and management—an increased trust they believe will pay off in the future.

To maintain this trust, GM and the UAW work very hard to demonstrate equality in the administration of the programs. Each program is administered by two directors, one representing labor and one representing management. Logos from both the UAW and GM appear on all correspondence. Even the headquarters offices of the program directors are of equal size.

By all appearances these programs are working to increase cooperation. Alfred Warren, GM's top contract negotiator says, "We don't pound the table anymore like we used to, or yell and shout and call people names."[9] At some plants workers have become so flexible that management doesn't feel the need to ask for work-rule changes. And even in acrimonious times (for example, following a six-day strike at the Kokomo, Indiana plant), these programs have helped labor and management to come together to settle their disputes more quickly.

Questions for Discussion

1. Why is it necessary for labor unions and management to cooperate with one another?

2. Use Thomas' conflict model to explain the positions taken by Lorenzo and Bryan.

3. Use the concepts of reciprocity, communication, and personal orientation to explain the positions Lorenzo and Bryan take relative to one another.

4. Can you imagine any potential problems arising from the GM and UAW "jointness" programs? What might these problems be? Why might they develop?

Notes

1. Stockton, W. (1988, November 6). Tearing apart Eastern Air Lines. *New York Times Magazine*, pp. 36–39, 82–87.

2. Engardio, P., & Bernstein, A. (1988, November 21). Charlie Bryan has ideas—and Lorenzo is listening. *Business Week*, pp. 88–93.

3. See Note 1, p. 38.

4. See Note 1.

5. See Note 2.

6. See Note 1.

7. See Note 2.

8. Schlesinger, J. M. (1987, August 25). Auto firms and UAW find that cooperation can get complicated. *Wall Street Journal*, pp. 1, 20.

9. See Note 8, p. 20.

EXPERIENCING ORGANIZATIONAL BEHAVIOR

Personal Styles of Conflict Management

Conflict with others is a common and probably inescapable part of life. Given this fact, an important task we all face is *managing* conflict effectively when it arises. How do *you* deal with such situations? What is your preferred mode of handling disagreements and conflicts with others? For some insight into this important issue, please follow the instructions below.

Procedure

First, recall three recent events in which you have experienced conflict with other persons. Describe each briefly below, and then answer the following questions for each.

Incident #1:

To what extent did you try to resolve this conflict through *avoidance*—sidestepping the issue, withdrawing from the situation?

Did Not Do This						Did Do This
1	2	3	4	5	6	7

To what extent did you try to resolve this conflict through *accommodation*—giving in to the other person, yielding to his or her point of view?

Did Not Do This						Did Do This
1	2	3	4	5	6	7

To what extent did you try to resolve this conflict through *competition*—trying to win, standing up for your rights or views?

Did Not Do This						Did Do This
1	2	3	4	5	6	7

To what extent did you try to resolve this conflict through *compromise*—finding the middle ground between your position and the other person's?

Did Not Do This						Did Do This
1	2	3	4	5	6	7

To what extent did you try to resolve this conflict through *collaboration*—working with the other person to find some solution that would satisfy both of your basic needs or concerns?

Did Not Do This						Did Do This
1	2	3	4	5	6	7

Incident #2:

To what extent did you try to resolve this conflict through *avoidance*—sidestepping the issue, withdrawing from the situation?

Did Not Do This						Did Do This
1	2	3	4	5	6	7

To what extent did you try to resolve this conflict through *accommodation*—giving in to the other person, yielding to his or her point of view?

Did Not Do This						Did Do This
1	2	3	4	5	6	7

To what extent did you try to resolve this conflict through *competition*—trying to win, standing up for your rights or views?

Did Not Do This						Did Do This
1	2	3	4	5	6	7

To what extent did you try to resolve this conflict through *compromise*—finding the middle ground between your position and the other person's?

Did Not Do This						Did Do This
1	2	3	4	5	6	7

To what extent did you try to resolve this conflict through *collaboration*—working with the other person to find some solution that would satisfy both of your basic needs or concerns?

Did Not Do This						Did Do This
1	2	3	4	5	6	7

Incident #3:

To what extent did you try to resolve this conflict through *avoidance*—sidestepping the issue, withdrawing from the situation?

Did Not Do This						Did Do This
1	2	3	4	5	6	7

To what extent did you try to resolve this conflict through *accommodation*—giving in to the other person, yielding to his or her point of view?

Did Not Do This						Did Do This
1	2	3	4	5	6	7

To what extent did you try to resolve this conflict through *competition*—trying to win, standing up for your rights or views?

Did Not Do This						Did Do This
1	2	3	4	5	6	7

To what extent did you try to resolve this conflict through *compromise*—finding the middle ground between your position and the other person's?

Did Not Do This						Did Do This
1	2	3	4	5	6	7

To what extent did you try to resolve this conflict through *collaboration*—working with the other person to find some solution that would satisfy both of your basic needs or concerns?

Did Not Do This						Did Do This
1	2	3	4	5	6	7

Points to Consider

Now, examine your reactions in all three situations. Do you notice any consistencies? Did you tend to prefer one basic mode of resolving conflict over the others? Research on this topic suggests that many persons possess relatively clear preferences in this regard: they tend to approach many conflict situations in a similar manner. While such preferences are understandable, they can be the cause of serious difficulties. Each conflict situation we encounter is, to some extent, unique. Thus, the most adaptive approach is probably one emphasizing *flexibility:* choose the approach that best fits the current circumstances. Keeping this point firmly in mind may help you to manage conflicts more effectively.

CHAPTER FOURTEEN

DECISION MAKING IN ORGANIZATIONS

CHAPTER OUTLINE

Organizational Decision Making: Its Basic Nature
A General Model of Decision Making
Varieties of Organizational Decisions

Individual Decision Making in Organizations: An Imperfect Process
Two Approaches to Individual Decision Making: The Rational-Economic Model and the Administrative Model
Impediments to Optimal Individual Decisions

Group Decisions: Do Too Many Cooks Spoil the Broth?
Comparing Group and Individual Decisions: When Are Two (or More) Heads Better Than One?

Obstacles to Effective Group Decisions: Groupthink and Group Polarization
Improving the Effectiveness of Group Decisions: Some Techniques

Special Sections

OB: A Research Perspective
Identifying Differences in Decision Styles

OB: A Management Perspective
Guidelines for Improving Group Decisions: A Checklist

LEARNING OBJECTIVES

After reading this chapter, you should be able to:
1. Identify the general steps in the decision-making process.
2. Describe different types of organizational decisions.
3. Distinguish between the rational-economic model and the administrative model of decision making.
4. Describe the barriers to high quality individual decisions.
5. Compare the advantages and disadvantages of using groups and individuals as decision makers.
6. Describe the conditions under which groups make better decisions than individuals.
7. Identify the major obstacles to effective group decisions.
8. Describe ways of improving group decisions.

It was a good year for Mama's Restaurants, a small chain of family-style Italian restaurants with eight units in two midwestern states. Profits were up by 12.4 percent, almost twice as much as the industry average. This really pleased Tony Lagucci, the company's founder and Chief Executive Officer. After a few rough years, the company could now grow and greatly expand its share of the market.

One Friday night after closing time, Lou Chambers, the company's comptroller and Tony's trusted financial advisor, entered Tony's office. "Hey, Tony," said Lou with an edge of excitement to his voice, "I understand the Luigi's Ristorante chain is going under and will be up for sale soon."

"Really?" Tony responded with raised eyebrows. "With them out of the way we can pick up some new customers."

"We can do a lot better than that," Lou countered, "if we buy them out at a bargain price. Just think—we'd be able to double our size overnight. Twice as many units can mean twice as much profit—or even more!"

"I'm all for that," said Tony, "but can we afford it?"

"Leave it to me," Lou replied. "We have some cash, and Luigi will be willing to finance some of the price. I think we can put together a deal if you want to. It's up to you. The partners will go along with whatever you want, as long as I can convince them there's money to be made in the deal."

"Well, I'll have to think about it," Tony said as Lou left his office. There was a lot to think about, and the weight of the decision made Tony uneasy. What would it mean if the business got too big? It was already much more than Tony could comfortably handle by himself. Expansion would surely mean hiring new managers to run the new restaurants, and perhaps even district managers to coordinate and oversee operations. The Mama's chain was already much larger than Tony ever thought it would be when he opened his first thirty-seat restaurant just ten years earlier. The business was good to him, but the prospect of doubling the size of the chain was troubling. What would it mean for Tony himself? Would he be happy? And what would it mean for the business? Could it be run successfully at such a large scale?

These were the unknowns Tony pondered. But he did not have the luxury of taking his time in considering the possibility of buying Luigi's. Once it was up for sale, it could be sold to a competitor, thereby threatening Mama's. What to do? Tony could not afford to ignore an opportunity like this. There was risk associated with making the move—and with not doing anything.

I've got it! Tony thought. *I'll ask everyone affected by the decision what they think. After all, my current managers would be called on to train new managers. Could they do it? What do they think of the markets in which the Luigi's units operate?*

I'll ask Rosa, too. Tony thought of his wife of almost thirty years. How would she feel about the extra hours, the greater responsibility, and the risk of making it really big or losing it all?

Sunday the restaurants were closed, and so Tony called all of his closest aides and his various restaurant managers. There was no time to bring these people together for a meeting, but they had to be consulted before Tony could make a move. A tele-conference was set up and Tony led the meeting.

"Friends," he began, "Mama's Restaurants is facing a great opportunity. How great it really is will depend on you. I come to you today seeking advice about a decision I can't and shouldn't make alone. . . ."

With these words, Tony Lagucci began the process of changing the future of Mama's Restaurants.

Although you may not be in a position to take over a chain of restaurants, you can probably appreciate Tony's dilemma. Anyone who has ever worked through a complex decision is aware of how difficult it is to consider everything. Deciding which college or university to go to probably wasn't easy for you, since there were many factors to take into account. As our story suggests, Tony also has many things to consider. He resolved to make his decision with the assistance of others who would be affected by it—a common practice. Will this way of decision making help Tony—will it lead to the best possible decision? We cannot say. But one thing is clear: if you have ever been involved in committee work, you are probably all too familiar with how difficult it may be for a group of people, no matter how well-intentioned, to reach a decision. Thinking about the problems involved in making decisions in your own life may help you appreciate the importance of understanding **decision making** in organizations, where the stakes—both personal and financial—may be much greater.

This chapter will examine theories, research, and practical managerial techniques concerned with organizational decision making. We will explore the ways individuals make decisions, and then look at the decision-making processes of groups. Specifically, we will review the basic characteristics of individual decisions and group decisions. For each, we will identify factors that may adversely affect the quality of decisions, and ways of combatting them—that is, techniques for improving the quality of decisions. We will compare the quality of individual and group decisions on a variety of tasks and note the conditions under which individuals or groups are better suited for making decisions. But first, we will begin by taking a closer look at the general process of decision making and the varieties of decisions made in organizations.

ORGANIZATIONAL DECISION MAKING:

ITS BASIC NATURE

It is safe to say that decision making is one of the most important—if not *the* most important—of all managerial activities.[1] Management theorists and researchers agree that decision making represents one of the most common and most crucial work roles of the executive. In fact, organizational scientist Herbert Simon, who won a Nobel prize for his work on decision making, has gone so far as to describe decision making as *synonymous* with managing (see Figure 14.1).[2]

FIGURE 14.1 Decision Making: A Common Managerial Work Role

This manager's job requires her to make many decisions. Experts agree that making decisions is one of the most basic elements of managerial work.

Given the central importance of decision making in organizational life, we will begin our discussion by highlighting some of the basic steps in the decision-making process and considering the characteristics of organizational decisions.

A General Model of Decision Making

Many scientists find it useful to conceptualize the process of decision making as a series of steps through which groups or individuals go to solve problems.[3] A general model of the steps in the decision-making process can help us understand the complex nature of organizational decision making (see Figure 14.2).[4] As we present this model, it is important to note that not all decisions fully conform to the neat, eight-step pattern described (e.g., steps may be skipped and/or combined).[5] However, for the purpose of pointing out the general way the decision making process operates, we think the model is quite effective.

The first step in decision making is *problem identification*. In order to decide how to solve a problem, it must first be recognized and identified as a problem. For example, an executive may identify the fact that the company cannot meet its payroll obligations

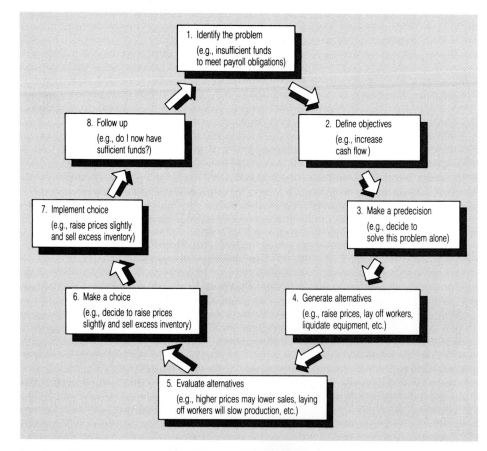

FIGURE 14.2 The Decision-making Process: A Basic Model
The process of decision making tends to follow the eight steps outlined here. Note how each step may be applied to a hypothetical organizational problem: having insufficient funds to meet payroll obligations. (Source: Based on information in Wedley & Field, 1984; see Note 4).

as a problem. This step isn't always as easy as it sounds. In fact, research reviewed by Cowan has shown that people often distort, omit, ignore, and/or discount information around them that provides important cues regarding the existence of problems.[6] You may recall from our discussion of the social perception process (see chapter 4) that people do not always accurately perceive social situations. It is easy to imagine that someone may fail to recognize a problem if doing so makes him or her uncomfortable. Denying a problem may be the first impediment on the road to solving it!

After a problem is identified, the next step is to *define the objectives to be met in solving the problem.* It is important to conceive of problems in such a way that possible solutions can be identified. The problem identified in our example may be defined as not having enough money, or in business terms, "inadequate cash flow." By looking at the problem in this way, the objective is clear: increase available cash reserves. Any possible solution to the problem should be evaluated relative to this objective. A good solution is one that meets it.

The third step in the decision-making process is to *make a predecision.* A **predecision** is a decision about how to make a decision. By assessing the type of problem in question, the style of the decision-maker, and other aspects of the situation, managers may opt to make a decision themselves, delegate the decision to another, or have the decision made by a group. Decisions about how to make a decision should be based on research that tells us about the nature of the decisions made under different circumstances—many of which will be reviewed later in this chapter. For many years managers have been relying on their own intuition, or better yet, on empirically-based information about organizational behavior (contained in books like this), for the guidance needed to make predecisions. Recently, however, computer programs have been developed summarizing much of this information in a form that gives practicing managers ready access to a wealth of social science information that may help them decide how to make decisions.[7] We should note, of course, that such *decision support systems,* as they are called, can only be as good as the social science information that goes into them.

The fourth step in the process is *alternative generation,* the stage in which possible solutions to the problem are identified. In attempting to come up with solutions, people tend to rely on previously used approaches that might provide ready-made answers for them.[8] In our example, some possible ways of solving the revenue shortage problem would be to reduce the work force, sell unnecessary equipment and material, or increase sales.

Because all these possibilities may not be equally feasible, the fifth step calls for *evaluating alternative solutions.* Which solution is best? What would be the most effective way of raising the revenue needed to meet the payroll? The various alternatives need to be identified. Some may be more effective than others, and some may be more difficult to implement than others. For example, although increasing sales would help solve the problem, that is much easier said than done. It is a solution, but not an immediately practical one.

Next, in the sixth step, a *choice* is made. After several alternatives are evaluated, one that is considered acceptable is chosen. As we will describe shortly, different models of decision making offer different views of how thoroughly people consider alternatives and how optimal their chosen alternatives are. Choosing which course of action to take is the step that most often comes to mind when we think about the decision-making process. (For a humorous example of making choices, see Figure 14.3 on page 486.)

The seventh step calls for *implementation of the chosen alternative.* That is, the chosen alternative is carried out. The eighth and final step is *follow-up.* It is important to the success of organizations to monitor the effectiveness of the decisions they put into action. Does the problem still exist? Have any new problems been caused by

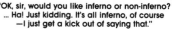

**FIGURE 14.3   Selecting among Alternatives: A
Key Aspect of the Decision-making Process**
Although this example is whimsical, it illustrates
the importance of selecting among alternatives
in decision making. (Source: The Far Side
copyright 1986 Universal Press Syndicate.
Reprinted with permission. All rights reserved.)

"OK, sir, would you like inferno or non-inferno?
... Ha! Just kidding. It's all inferno, of course
—I just get a kick out of saying that."

implementing the solution? In other words, it is important to seek feedback about the
effectiveness of any attempted solution. For this reason, the decision-making process
is presented as circular in Figure 14.2. If the solution works, the problem may be
considered solved. If not, a new solution will have to be attempted.

As you might imagine, the decision-making process just outlined may be applied
to many kinds of decisions. To better appreciate the various types of decisions that
are made, we will now consider some of the basic characteristics of organizational
decisions.

Varieties of Organizational Decisions

Consider, for a moment, the variety of decisions likely to be made in organizations.
Some decisions have far-reaching consequences (such as Tony Lagucci's decision regarding Mama's Restaurants in our story on page 482), and others are more mundane
(such as the decision to reorder office supplies). People sometimes make decisions in
situations in which the likely outcomes are well-known (e.g., the decision to underwrite
life insurance on the basis of actuarial data), while other times the outcomes are much
more uncertain (e.g., the decision to invade a hostile nation for purposes of freeing
hostages). These examples are reflective of the two major characteristics of organizational decisions: how structured or unstructured is the situation, and how much certainty or risk is involved in the decision?

**Programmed versus non-programmed decisions: How well structured is the
decision setting?** Think of a decision that is made repeatedly, according to a pre-
established set of alternatives. For example, a word processing operator may decide
to make a backup diskette of the day's work, or a manager of a fast food restaurant
may decide to place an order for hamburger buns as the supply starts to get low.
Decisions such as these are known as **programmed decisions**—they are routine
decisions, made by lower-level personnel, that rely on predetermined courses of action.

By contrast, we may identify **non-programmed decisions**—ones for which there
are no ready-made solutions. The decision-maker confronts a unique situation in which

the solutions are novel. The research scientist attempting to find a cure for a rare disease faces a problem that is poorly structured. Unlike the order clerk whose course of action is clear when the supply of paper clips runs low, the scientist in this example must rely on creativity rather than pre-existing answers to solve the problem at hand. A special type of non-programmed decisions is known as *strategic decisions.*[9] These decisions are typically made by coalitions of high-level executives and have important long-term implications for the organization. Strategic decisions reflect a consistent pattern for directing the organization in some specified fashion—that is, according to an underlying organizational philosophy or mission. For example, an organization may make a strategic decision to grow at a specified yearly rate, or to be guided by a certain code of corporate ethics. Both of these decisions are likely to be considered "strategic" because they guide the future direction of the organization.

Table 14.1 summarizes the differences between programmed and non-programmed decisions with respect to three important questions. First, *what type of tasks* are involved? Programmed decisions are made on tasks that are common and routine, whereas non-programmed decisions are made on unique and novel tasks. Second, *how much reliance is there on organizational policies?* In making programmed decisions, the decision-maker can count on guidance from statements of organizational policy and procedure. However, non-programmed decisions require the use of creative solutions that are implemented for the first time; past solutions may provide little guidance. Finally, *who makes the decisions?* Not surprisingly, non-programmed decisions typically are made by upper-level organizational personnel, whereas the more routine, well-structured decisions are usually relegated to lower-level personnel.[10]

Certain versus uncertain decisions: How much risk is involved? Just think of how easy it would be to make decisions if we knew what the future held in store. Making the best investments in the stock market would simply be a matter of looking up the changes in tomorrow's newspaper. Of course, we never know exactly what the future holds, but we can be more certain at some times than others. Certainty about the factors on which decisions are made is highly desired in organizational decision making.

Degrees of certainty and uncertainty are expressed as statements of *risk.* All organizational decisions involve some degree of risk—ranging from complete certainty (no risk), to complete uncertainty, "a stab in the dark" (high risk). What makes an outcome risky or not is the *probability* of obtaining the desired outcome. Decision-makers attempt to obtain information about the probabilities, or odds, of certain events occurring given that other events have occurred. For example, a financial analyst may report that a certain stock has risen 80 percent of the time that the prime rate has

TABLE 14.1 Programmed and Nonprogrammed Decisions: A Comparison

The two major types of organizational decisions—*programmed decisions* and *nonprogrammed decisions*—differ with respect to the types of tasks on which they are made, the degree to which solutions may be found in existing organizational policies, and the typical decision-making unit.

	TYPE OF DECISION	
VARIABLE	PROGRAMMED DECISIONS	NONPROGRAMMED DECISIONS
Type of task	Simple, routine	Complex, creative
Reliance on organizational policies	Considerable guidance from past decisions	No guidance from past decisions
Typical decision-maker	Lower-level workers (usually alone)	Upper-level supervisors (usually in groups)

dropped, or a TV weather person may report that the precipitation probability is 50 percent (i.e., in the past it rained half the time certain meteorological conditions existed). These data may be considered reports of *objective* probabilities because they are based on concrete, verifiable data. Many decisions are also based on *subjective* probabilities— personal beliefs or hunches about what will happen (please see Figure 14.4). For example, a gambler who bets on a horse because it has a name similar to one of his children, or a person who suspects it's going to rain because he just washed his car, is basing these judgments on subjective probabilities.

Obviously, uncertainty is an undesirable characteristic in decision-making situations. We may view much of what decision-makers do in organizations as attempting to reduce uncertainty so that better decisions can be made. How do organizations respond when faced with highly uncertain conditions, when they don't know what the future holds for them? Studies have shown that decision uncertainty can be reduced by establishing linkages with other organizations. The more an organization knows about what another organization will do, the greater certainty it will have in making decisions.[11]

Research on this topic also has revealed that organizational uncertainty influences decisions regarding whether to make or buy components needed in the manufacturing process. When highly competitive conditions exist between organizations, a high degree of uncertainty regarding the availability of required technology leads organizations to buy the components they need rather than making them.[12] Apparently, executives do not wish to bog their organizations down by investing in the technology for manufacturing needed components when an uncertain future and the prospect of high competition conspire to make organizational change likely. Under such conditions, organizations that simply buy the needed components can respond more quickly to change (for more on organizations' adaptations to technological changes, please see chapter 16). Not surprisingly, the faster an organization has to change to operate effectively in the market, the more uncertainty it faces, and the greater difficulty it confronts in making decisions. A good example of this is today's rapidly changing microcomputer business. Winners and losers in this market will depend, in part, on how well they can predict what products will succeed. Clearly, organizations must be sensitive to conditions of uncertainty when making decisions; uncertain conditions qualify the nature of organizational decisions.

In general, what reduces uncertainty in decision making situations? The answer is

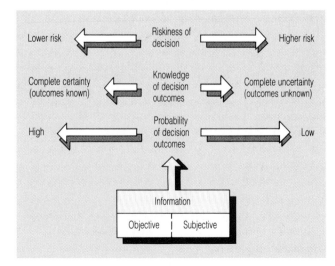

FIGURE 14.4   The Riskiness of a Decision: A Summary

Decisions differ with respect to their degree of riskiness, based on how certain (high probability) or uncertain (low probability) various outcomes may be. Information—both objective and subjective—is used as the basis for estimating the probability of a decision outcome.

information. Knowledge about the past and the present can be used to help make projections about the future. A modern executive's access to data needed to make important decisions may be as close as the nearest computer terminal. Indeed, computer technology has greatly aided managers' ability to make decisions quickly, using the most accurate and thorough information available.[13] Indeed, a variety of on-line information services are designed to provide organizational decision-makers with the latest information relevant to the decisions they are making. Of course, not all information needed to make decisions comes from computers. It is well-established that many managerial decisions are also based on the decision-maker's past experiences and intuition.[14] This is not to say that top managers rely on subjective information in making decisions (although they might), but that their history of past decisions—successes and failures— is often given great weight in the decision-making process. In other words, *information*—either in the form of currently available data, or the collective wisdom of past decisions—is the key to reducing organizational uncertainty, and thereby enhancing the quality of organizational decisions.

INDIVIDUAL DECISION MAKING IN ORGANIZATIONS:
AN IMPERFECT PROCESS

Decision making is one of the most common processes in which we engage. We are always making decisions—whether they are simple ones, such as which television show to watch, or more complex ones with far-reaching consequences, such as who a presidential candidate should select as his vice presidential running mate. Organizations represent a context within which decisions may be particularly important (see Figure 14.5). As such, it would be useful to examine some of the most basic characteristics

FIGURE 14.5   Individual Decisions in Organizations: Some Examples

Shown here is just one example of a situation in which an individual makes important decisions (e.g., what colors to use in packaging various products) in the course of a work day.

of individual decision processes and how organizational variables influence them. Specifically, this section will analyze the process of individual decision making in organizations and some of the major impediments to high quality individual decisions.

Two Approaches to Individual Decision Making: The Rational-Economic Model and the Administrative Model

We all like to think that we are "rational" people who make the best possible decisions. What does it mean to make a *rational* decision? Organizational scientists view **rational decisions** as ones that maximize the attainment of goals, whether they are the goals of a person, a group, or an entire organization.[15] In this section we will present two approaches to decision making that derive from different assumptions about the rationality of individual decision-makers.

The rational-economic model: In search of the ideal decision. What would be the most rational way for an individual to go about making a decision? Economists interested in predicting market conditions and prices have relied on a **rational-economic model** of decision making which assumes that decisions are perfect and rational in every way. An economically rational decision-maker will attempt to maximize his or her profits by systematically searching for the best possible solution to a problem. For this to occur, the decision-maker must have complete and perfect information, and be able to process all this information in an accurate and unbiased fashion.[16]

In many respects, rational-economic decisions follow the same steps outlined in our general model of decision making (see Figure 14.2). However, what makes the rational-economic approach special is that it calls for the decision-maker to recognize *all* alternative courses of action, and to accurately and completely evaluate each one. As such, it views decision-makers as attempting to make *optimal* decisions.

Of course, the rational-economic approach to decision making does not fully appreciate the fallibility of the human decision-maker. It is based on the assumption that people have access to complete and perfect information and use it to make perfect decisions. As such, the model can be considered a *normative* (also called *prescriptive*) approach—one that describes how decision-makers ideally ought to behave to make the best possible decisions. It does not describe how decision-makers actually behave in most circumstances. This task is undertaken by the next major approach to individual decision making, the *administrative model*.

The administrative model: Exploring the limits of human rationality. Not only are some people incapable of acting in a completely rational-economic manner, but the cost of such so-called rationality may be very high. In fact, research has shown that it may be more rational not to try to be so rational after all. For example, in one study, Fredrickson and Mitchell found that considering all possible solutions to problems might not be such an effective way of solving them.[17] They surveyed over one hundred executives in the forest products industry concerning how comprehensive and exhaustive their organizations were likely to be in making different types of decisions. It was found that using this seemingly rational strategy was not linked to organizational prosperity. In fact, the more comprehensive the executives reported their organizations' decision strategies were, the poorer their organizations performed financially. Particularly when organizations operate in very unstable environments (ones in which there is a great deal of change), the effort involved in making completely rational decisions can actually interfere with economic progress. In other words, the costs of attempting to make a seemingly rational economic decision may sometimes be so high that they cut into economic gains.

For example, consider how a personnel department might go about deciding on hiring a new receptionist. After several applicants are interviewed, the personnel director might select the best candidate seen so far and stop the selection process. Had the interviewer been following a rational-economic model, he or she would have had to interview all possible candidates before deciding on the *best* one. However, by ending the search after finding a candidate that was just *good enough,* the manager was using a much simpler approach. The decision strategy used by the personnel manager in this example typifies an approach to decision making known as the **administrative model.**[18] This conceptualization recognizes that decision-makers may have a limited view of the problems confronting them. The number of solutions that can be recognized or implemented is limited by the capabilities of the decision-maker and the available resources of the organization. Also, decision-makers do not have perfect information about the consequences of their decisions, so they cannot tell which one is best.

So, how are decisions made according to the administrative model? Instead of considering all possible solutions, as suggested by the rational economic model, the administrative model recognizes that decision-makers consider solutions as they become available. Then, they decide on the first alternative that meets their criteria for acceptability. As such, the decision-maker selects a solution that may be just good enough, although not optimal. Such decisions are referred to as **satisficing decisions.** Of course, it is much easier for a decision-maker to make a satisficing decision than an optimal decision. In most decision-making situations, March and Simon note, satisficing decisions are acceptable and are more likely to be made than optimal ones.[19] They use the following analogy to compare the two types of decisions: *making an optimal decision is like searching a haystack for the sharpest needle, but making a satisficing decision is like searching a haystack for a needle just sharp enough with which to sew.*

As we have noted, it is often impractical for people to make completely optimal, rational decisions. The administrative model recognizes the **bounded rationality** under which most organizational decision-makers must operate. The idea is that people lack the cognitive skills required to formulate and solve highly complex business problems in a completely objective, rational way.[20]

It should not be too surprising that the administrative model does a better job than the rational-economic model of describing how decision-makers actually behave. As such, the approach is said to be *descriptive* (also called *proscriptive*) in nature. This interest in examining the actual, imperfect behavior of decision-makers rather than specifying the ideal, economically rational behaviors that decision-makers ought to engage in lies at the heart of the distinction between the administrative and rational-economic models (please refer to the summary of these two approaches in Table 14.2). Our point is not that decision-makers do not want to behave rationally, but that restrictions posed by the innate capabilities of the decision-makers themselves and the

**TABLE 14.2   The Administrative Model versus The Rational-Economic Model:
A Summary Comparison**

The *rational-economic model* and the *administrative model* of individual decision making are based on a variety of assumptions about how people make decisions.

ASSUMPTION	RATIONAL-ECONOMIC MODEL	ADMINISTRATIVE MODEL
Rationality of decision-maker	Perfect rationality	Bounded rationality
Information available	Complete access	Limited access
Selection of alternatives	Optimal choice	Satisficing choice
Type of model	Normative	Descriptive

social environments in which decisions are often made sometimes discourage "perfect" decisions. With this in mind, we will now explore some of the factors limiting optimal decisions.

Impediments to Optimal Individual Decisions

The picture of an imperfect decision-maker operating in a complex world is supported by many studies that point to the seemingly confused and irrational decisions people make. The imperfections of decision-makers take many forms, several of which will be reviewed here.

Cognitive biases in decision making: Framing and heuristics. Probably the most obvious limitation on people's ability to make the best possible decisions is imposed by their restricted capacity to process information accurately and thoroughly (like a computer). For example, it has been established that people often focus on irrelevant information in making decisions.[21] They also fail to use all the information made available to them.[22] Obviously, limitations in people's abilities to process complex information adversely influences their decisions. Beyond this general limitation in information-processing capacity, we may note the existence of systematic biases in decision making.[23]

Framing: One well-established decision-making bias has to do with the tendency for people to make different decisions based on how the problem is presented to them— that is, the **framing** of a problem. Specifically, Kahneman and Tversky have noted that problems framed in a manner that emphasizes the positive gains to be received tend to encourage conservative decisions (i.e., decision-makers are said to be *risk averse*), whereas problems framed in a manner that emphasizes the potential losses to be suffered lead to *risk seeking* decisions.[24] Consider the following example.

> The government is preparing to combat a rare disease expected to take 600 lives. Two alternative programs to combat the disease have been proposed, each of which, scientists believe, will have certain consequences. *Program A* will save 200 people, if adopted. *Program B* has a ⅓ chance of saving all 600 people, but a ⅔ chance of saving no one. Which program do you prefer?

When Kahneman and Tversky presented such a problem to people, 72 percent expressed a preference for Program A, and 28 percent for Program B. In other words, they preferred the "sure thing" of saving 200 people over the ⅓ possibility of saving them all. However, a curious thing happened when the description of the programs were framed in negative terms. Specifically:

> *Program C* was described as allowing 400 people to die, if adopted.
> *Program D* was described as allowing a ⅓ probability that no one would die, and a ⅔ probability that all 600 would die. Now which program would you prefer?

Compare these four programs. Program C is just another way of stating the outcomes of Program A, and Program D is just another way of stating the outcomes of Program B. However, Programs C and D are framed in negative terms, which led to almost opposite preferences: 22 percent favored Program C and 78 percent favored Program D (for a summary, please see Figure 14.6). In other words, people tended to avoid risk when the problem was framed in the "lives saved" version (i.e., in positive terms), but to seek risk when the problem was framed in the "lives lost" version (i.e., in negative terms). Findings such as these suggest that people are not completely rational decision-makers, but are systematically biased by the aversiveness of the outcomes they confront as a result of their decisions.

when organizations face crisis situations requiring immediate decisions. In crisis situations, decision-makers have been found to limit their search for information that may help them make optimal decisions.[34]

The quality of many organizational decisions also may be limited by *political "face saving" pressure.* In other words, decision-makers may make decisions that help them save face at work, although the resulting decisions might not be in the best interest of their organizations. Imagine, for example, how an employee may distort the available information needed to make a decision if the correct decision would jeopardize his job. Unfortunately, such misuses of information to support desired decisions are common (recall our discussion of the problem of distorted communication in chapter 10). One study on this topic reported that a group of businessmen working on a group decision-making problem opted for an adequate—although less than optimal—decision rather than risk generating serious conflicts with their fellow group members.[35] In an actual case, a proponent of medical inoculation for the flu was reported as having decided to go ahead with the inoculation program on the basis of only a 2 percent chance of an epidemic.[36] What we are saying is that people may make the decisions they *want* to make even though these may not be the optimal ones for the organizations involved.

Besides the time constraints and political pressures that limit the quality of organizational decisions, we should also note the limitations imposed by moral and ethical constraints—what is known as *bounded discretion.*[37] According to this idea, decision-makers limit their actions to those that fall within the bounds of current moral and ethical standards. So, although it may optimize an organization's profits to engage in illegal activities such as stealing, ethical considerations may discourage such actions.

All of the variables we have been discussing so far suggest that people are far from perfect in their decision-making skills. The road to the best possible decisions is booby-trapped with many impediments. Yet, although individual decisions are likely to be imperfect, it would be a mistake to think that all decision-makers are equally likely to be influenced by the various impediments we have discussed in this section. Indeed, important individual differences exist between decision-makers that tend to make some people better suited to making good decisions than others. (As we describe in the **Research Perspective** section below, the greater flexibility of approaches taken by some decision-makers helps improve the quality of their decisions.)

OB: A RESEARCH PERSPECTIVE

Identifying Differences in Decision Styles

Do all individuals go about making decisions the same way, or are there differences in the typical approaches taken to making decisions? In general, research has shown that there are meaningful differences between people with respect to their orientation toward decisions, known as their **decision style.** Whereas some people are primarily concerned with achieving success at any cost, others are more concerned about the effects of their decisions on others. Furthermore, some individuals tend to be more logical and analytical in their approach to problems, whereas others are more intuitive and creative. Clearly, important differences exist in the approaches decision-makers take to problems.

A *decision-style model* proposed by Rowe, Boulgaides, and McGrath classifies four varieties of decision styles.[38]

1. The *directive style* is characterized by people who prefer simple solutions and prefer avoiding ambiguity. They tend to make decisions rapidly because they use little information and do not consider many alternatives. They tend to rely on existing rules to make their decisions and aggressively use their status to achieve results.

2. By contrast, people with an *analytical style* tend to be more willing to consider complex solutions based on ambiguous information. They tend to carefully analyze their decisions using as much data as possible. Such individuals enjoy solving problems. They want the best possible answers and are willing to use innovative methods to achieve them.

3. Compared to the directive and analytical styles, people with a *conceptual style* tend to be more socially oriented in their approach to problems. Their approach is humanistic and artistic. They tend to consider many broad alternatives when approaching problems and value commitments and creativity in finding solutions. They have a strong future orientation and like initiating new ideas.

4. Finally, individuals with a *behavioral style* may be characterized as having a deep concern for the organization in which they work and the personal development of their coworkers. They are highly supportive of others and very concerned about others' achievement, frequently helping them meet their goals. They tend to be open to suggestions from others, and therefore tend to rely on meetings for making decisions.

It is important to point out that although most managers may have a dominant style, they use many styles. In fact, those who can shift between styles—in other words, those who exhibit *flexibility* in their approach to decision making—have complex, highly individualistic styles of their own. Despite this, people's dominant style reveals a great deal about the way they tend to make decisions. As a result of these styles, conflicts often occur between individuals with different styles. For example, a manager with a highly directive style may have a hard time accepting the slow, deliberate actions of a subordinate with an analytical style.

Rowe and his associates argue that being aware of a person's decision style is a potentially useful way of understanding the interactions between individuals in organizations. With this in mind, they have developed an instrument known as the *decision-style inventory,* designed to reveal the relative strength of people's decision styles. The higher an individual scores with respect to a given decision style, the more likely that style is to predominate that individual's decision making. To give you a feel for how the various decision styles are measured, we have prepared a version of the decision-style inventory for you to take and score yourself (see Table 14.3).

Research using this instrument has revealed some interesting findings.[39] For example, when the decision-style inventory was given to a sample of

---

TABLE 14.3   Assessing Your Decision Style: A Self-Test

This short questionnaire is adapted from a longer survey known as the *Decision-Style Inventory* used to identify people's decision styles. Complete this self-test to shed light on your own decision style by following the instructions shown. Score the test as follows: Give yourself a point in the *directive* category for each *a* you select, *analytical* for each *b*, *conceptual* for each *c*, and *behavioral* for each *d*. The points reflect the relative strengths of your preferences for each decision style.

Directions: For each of the following questions, select the one alternative that best describes how you see yourself in your typical work situation.

1. When performing my job, I usually look for:
   a. practical results
   b. the best solutions to problems
   c. new ideas or approaches
   d. pleasant working conditions

2. When faced with a problem, I usually:
   a. use approaches that have worked in the past
   b. analyze it carefully
   c. try to find a creative approach
   d. rely on my feelings

3. When making plans, I usually emphasize:
   a. the problems I currently face
   b. attaining objectives
   c. future goals
   d. developing my career

4. The kind of information I usually prefer to use is:
   a. specific facts
   b. complete and accurate data
   c. broad information covering many options
   d. data that is limited and simple to understand

5. Whenever I am uncertain about what to do, I:
   a. rely on my intuition
   b. look for facts
   c. try to find a compromise
   d. wait, and decide later

6. The people with whom I work best are usually:
   a. ambitious and full of energy
   b. self-confident
   c. open-minded
   d. trusting and polite

7. The decisions I make are usually:
   a. direct and realistic
   b. abstract or systematic
   c. broad and flexible
   d. sensitive to others' needs

(Source: Adapted from material appearing in Rowe, Boulgaides, & McGrath, 1984; see Note 38.)

corporate presidents, their scores on each of the four categories were approximately equal. Apparently, they had no one dominant style, but were able to switch back and forth between categories with ease. Further research has shown that different groups tend to have, on average, different styles that dominate their decision making. For example, top executives and military officers tend to have high conceptual style scores. It is interesting to note that military officers were *not* highly domineering in their decision style; instead, they tended to be highly conceptual and people-oriented in their approach. Such findings paint a far more humanistic and less authoritarian picture of military officers than many would guess.

In conclusion, research on decision styles suggests that people tend to take very different approaches to the decisions they make. Their personalities, coupled with their interpersonal skills, lead them to approach decisions in consistently different ways—that is, using different decision styles. Although research on decision styles is just beginning, it is already clear that understanding such stylistic differences is a key factor in appreciating the potential conflicts likely to arise between decision-makers.

GROUP DECISIONS: DO TOO MANY COOKS SPOIL THE BROTH?

Decision-making groups are a well-established fact of modern organizational life. Groups such as *committees, study teams, task forces,* or *review panels* are often charged with the responsibility for making important business decisions. They are so common, in fact, that it has been said that some administrators spend as much as 80 percent of their time in committee meetings.[40] Given this, it is important to consider the strengths and weaknesses of using groups to make organizational decisions. Please refer to our summary of these factors in Figure 14.7.

There is little doubt that there is much to be gained from using decision-making groups. Several potential advantages of this approach may be identified. First, bringing people together may increase the amount of knowledge and information available for making good decisions. In other words, there may be a *pooling of resources.* A related

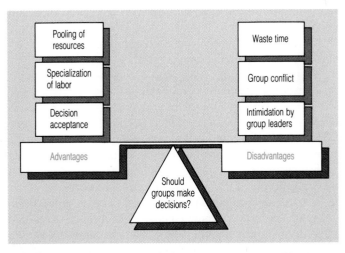

FIGURE 14.7 Group Decision Making: Advantages and Disadvantages
Should groups be used to make decisions? There are both advantages and disadvantages associated with using groups rather than individuals to make decisions.

benefit is that in decision-making groups there can be a *specialization of labor*. With enough people around to share the work load, it becomes possible for individuals to perform only those tasks at which they are best, thereby potentially improving the quality of the group's efforts. Another benefit is that group decisions are likely to enjoy *greater acceptance* than individual decisions. People involved in making decisions may be expected to understand those decisions better and be more committed to carrying them out than decisions made by someone else.[41]

Of course, there are also some problems associated with using decision-making groups—ones that are probably familiar to you. One obvious drawback is that groups are likely to *waste time*. The time spent socializing before getting down to business may be a drain on the group and be very costly to organizations. Another possible problem is that potential disagreement over important matters may breed ill-will and *group conflict*. While constructive disagreement can actually lead to better group outcomes, highly disruptive conflict may interfere with group decisions (see chapter 13). Indeed, with corporate power and personal pride at stake, it is not at all surprising to find that lack of agreement can cause bad feelings to develop between group members. Finally, we may expect groups to be ineffective sometimes because of members' *intimidation by group leaders*. A group composed of several "yes" men or women trying to please a dominant leader tends to discourage open and honest discussion of solutions. Given these problems, it is no wonder we often hear the old adage, "a camel is a horse put together by a committee."

Given the several pros and cons of using groups to make decisions (see the summary in Figure 14.7), we must conclude that neither groups nor individuals are always superior. Obviously, there are important trade-offs involved in using either one to make decisions.

Comparing Group and Individual Decisions: When Are Two (or More) Heads Better Than One?

Since there are advantages associated with both group and individual decision-makers, a question arises as to *when* each should be used. That is, under what conditions might individuals or groups make superior decisions? Fortunately, research has addressed this important question.[42]

When are groups superior to individuals? Imagine a situation in which an important decision has to be made about a complex problem—such as whether one company should acquire another. This is not the kind of problem about which any one individual working alone would be able to make a good decision. Its highly complex nature may overwhelm even an expert, thereby setting the stage for a group to do a better job.

Whether or not it actually will depends on several important considerations. For one, we must consider who is in the group. Successful groups tend to be composed of *heterogeneous group members with complementary skills*. So, for example, a group composed of lawyers, accountants, real estate agents, and other experts may make much better decisions on complex problems than one composed of specialists in only one field. Indeed, research has shown that the diversity of opinions offered by group members is one of the major advantages of using groups to make decisions.[43]

As you might imagine, it is not enough simply to have skills. For a group to be successful, its members must also be able to freely communicate their ideas to each other in an open, non-hostile manner (see chapter 10). Conditions under which one individual (or group) intimidates another from contributing his or her expertise can easily negate any potential gain associated with composing groups of heterogeneous experts (see chapter 8). After all, *having* expertise and being able to make a contribution by *using* that expertise are two different things. Indeed, research has shown that only when the contributions of the most qualified group members are given the greatest weight does the group derive any benefit from that member's presence.[44] Thus, for groups to be superior to individuals, they must be composed of a heterogeneous collection of experts with complementary skills who can freely and openly contribute to their group's product.

In contrast to the complex decision task of determining whether or not a merger is appropriate, imagine a situation in which a judgment is required on a simple problem with a readily verifiable answer. For example, imagine that you are asked to translate a phrase from a relatively obscure language into English. Groups might do better than individuals on such a task, but probably only because the odds are increased that someone in the group knows the language and can perform the translation task. However, there is no reason to expect that even a large group will be able to perform such a task better than a single individual who has the required expert skills. In fact, the expert working alone will probably do better than a group. In other words, for groups to benefit from a pooling of resources, there must be some resources to pool! The pooling of ignorance does not help.

People can help each other perform abstract problems by pooling and integrating their resources and by correcting each others' errors. As a result, they may perform better than the average group member, but certainly not the *best* group member. As noted in chapter 8, an individual with a correct answer to a problem faces the challenge of convincing others of the correctness of his or her solution. It is quite possible that a good answer will be challenged or ignored by the group. Such dynamics work against the group. Therefore it has been concluded that an exceptional individual may be expected to perform a relatively simple task better than a committee.[45]

To summarize, groups *may* perform better than individuals depending on the nature of the task performed and the expertise of the people involved. We have summarized some of these key considerations in Figure 14.8.

When are individuals superior to groups? As we have described thus far, there are conditions under which groups may be expected to perform better than the average

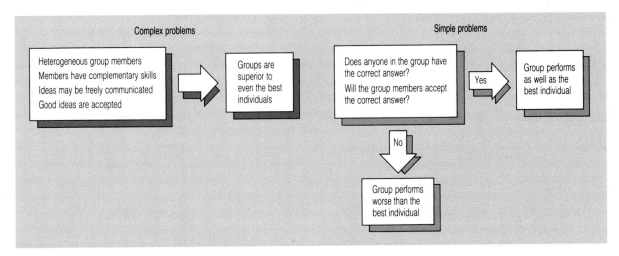

FIGURE 14.8 Group Decisions: When Are They Superior to Individual Decisions?
When performing complex problems, groups are superior to individuals if certain conditions prevail (i.e., group members have heterogeneous, complementary skills, they can freely share ideas, and good ideas are accepted). However, when performing simple problems, groups will only perform as well as the best individual in the group, and then only if that person has the correct answer and that response is accepted by the group.

or even the exceptional individual. However, there are also conditions under which individuals are superior to groups.

Most of the problems faced by organizations require a great deal of creative thinking. A company deciding how to use a newly-developed adhesive in its consumer products is facing decisions on a poorly-structured task. Similarly, the decision faced by Tony of Mama's Restaurants in our opening story (see page 482) is also poorly structured. Although you would expect that the complexity of such creative problems would give groups a natural advantage, this is *not* the case. In fact, research has shown that on poorly-structured, creative tasks, individuals perform better than groups.[46]

An approach to solving creative problems commonly used by groups is **brainstorming.** This technique was developed by advertising executive Alex Osborn of the Madison Avenue agency Batten, Barton, Durstine, and Osborn as a tool for coming up with creative, new ideas.[47] The members of brainstorming groups are encouraged to present their ideas in an uncritical way and to freely and openly discuss all ideas on the floor. Specifically, members of brainstorming groups are required to follow four main rules:

1. avoid criticizing others' ideas,
2. share even far-out suggestions,
3. offer as many comments as possible, and
4. build on others' ideas to create your own.

Does brainstorming help improve the quality of creative decisions? In order to answer this question, Bouchard and his associates conducted a study in which they compared the effectiveness of individuals and brainstorming groups working on creative problems.[48] Specifically, participants were given thirty-five minutes to consider the consequences of everybody suddenly going blind. Comparisons were made of the number of solutions generated by groups of four or seven people and a like number of individuals working on the same problem alone. As shown in Figure 14.9, individuals were far more productive than groups.

FIGURE 14.9
Brainstorming: Unsuccessful for Creative Problems

Research comparing the number of solutions to creative problems generated by brainstorming groups (of four or seven members) and a like number of individuals working alone has shown that individuals are more productive. (Source: Based on data in Bouchard, Barsaloux, and Drauden, 1974; see Note 48.)

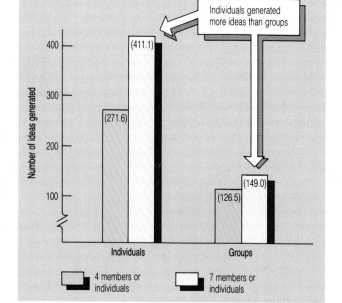

In sum, groups perform worse than individuals when working on creative tasks. A great part of the problem—and it *is* a problem, given the prevalence of decision-making groups in organizations—is that some individuals feel inhibited by the presence of others even though it is a rule of brainstorming that even far-out ideas may be shared. To the extent that people wish to avoid feeling foolish as a result of saying silly things, their creativity may be inhibited when in groups. Similarly, groups may inhibit creativity by slowing down the process of bringing ideas to fruition. Thus, although groups may be expected to help stimulate the creative process, it is clear that any such benefits of groups are more than offset when it comes to creative problems.

Although we have noted in passing several of the problems underlying the relatively poor performance of groups compared to individuals, we have neglected two of the most important contributing factors—*groupthink* and *group polarization*.

Obstacles to Effective Group Decisions: Groupthink and Group Polarization

Given the mixed findings regarding the effectiveness of decision-making groups, it is important to consider some of the factors that may potentially limit their operation. In other words, we may ask: what characteristics of group functioning may disrupt or bias the group decision-making process?

Groupthink: When too much cohesiveness is a dangerous thing. One reason groups may fare so poorly on complex tasks lies in the dynamics of group interaction. As we have already noted in chapter 8, when members of a group develop a very strong group spirit—or a high level of *cohesiveness*—they sometimes become so concerned about not disrupting the like-mindedness of the group that they may be reluctant to challenge the group's decisions. When this happens, group members tend to isolate themselves from outside information, and the process of critical thinking deteriorates. This phenomenon is referred to as **groupthink**.[49]

The concept of groupthink was proposed initially as an attempt to explain the ineffective decisions made by U.S. government officials that led to such fiascoes as the Bay of Pigs invasion in Cuba and the Vietnam war. Analyses of these cases have revealed that the President's advisors actually *discouraged* more effective decision making in each case. More recent analyses of the business policies of such large corporations as Lockheed and Chrysler have suggested that it was the failure of top management teams to respond to changing market conditions that at one time led them to the brink of disaster.[50] The problem is that members of very cohesive groups may have greater confidence in their group's decisions than in their own doubts about these actions (i.e., "the group seems to know what it's doing"). As a result, they may suspend their own critical thinking in favor of conforming to the group. When group members become fiercely loyal to each other they may ignore potentially useful information from other sources that challenges the group's decisions. The result of this process is that the group's decisions may be completely uninformed, irrational, or even immoral.[51] For a more precise description of groupthink (and a practical guide to recognizing its warning signals), see Table 14.4 (on page 502).

So as not to conclude on an entirely pessimistic note, we should point out that there are several strategies for effectively combatting groupthink.

1. Promote open inquiry. Remember: groupthink arises in response to group members' reluctance to "rock the boat." Group leaders should encourage members to be skeptical of all solutions and to avoid reaching premature agreements. It sometimes helps to play the role of "devil's advocate"; that is, to intentionally find fault with a

TABLE 14.4 Groupthink: Its Warning Signals

Sometimes in highly cohesive groups the members become more concerned about maintaining positive group spirit than about making the most realistic decisions—a phenomenon known as *groupthink*. The major symptoms of groupthink are identified and described here.

SYMPTOM	DESCRIPTION
Illusion of *invulnerability*	Ignoring obvious danger signals, being overly optimistic, and taking extreme risks
Collective *rationalization*	Discrediting or ignoring warning signals that run contrary to group thinking
Unquestioned *morality*	Believing that the group's position is ethical and moral and that all others are inherently evil
Excessive negative *stereotyping*	Viewing the opposing side as being too negative to warrant serious consideration
Strong *conformity pressure*	Discouraging the expression of dissenting opinions under the threat of expulsion for disloyalty
Self-censorship of dissenting ideas	Withholding dissenting ideas and counterarguments, keeping them to oneself
Illusion of *unanimity*	Sharing the false belief that everyone in the group agrees with its judgments
Self-appointed *mindguards*	Protecting the group from negative, threatening information

(Source: Adapted from Janis, 1982; see Note 49.)

proposed solution.[52] Although leaders should not be argumentative, raising a non-threatening question to force discussion of both sides of an issue can help.

2. Use subgroups. Because the decisions made by any one group may be the result of groupthink, basing decisions on the recommendations of two groups is a useful check. If the two groups disagree, a spirited discussion of their differences is likely to raise important issues. However, if the two groups agree, you can be relatively confident that they are not both the result of groupthink.

3. Admit shortcomings. When groupthink occurs, group members feel very confident that they are doing the right thing. Such feelings of perfection discourage people from considering opposing information. However, if group members acknowledge some of the flaws and limitations of their decisions, they may be more open to corrective influences. Try to keep in mind that no decision is perfect. Asking others to point out their misgivings about a group's decisions may help avoid the illusion of perfection that contributes to groupthink.

4. Hold second-chance meetings. Before implementing any decision, it may be a good idea to hold a *second-chance meeting* during which group members are asked to express any doubts and propose any new ideas they may have. Alfred P. Sloan, the former head of General Motors, is known to have postponed acting on important matters until some group disagreement developed.[53] As people get tired of working on problems they may hastily reach agreement on a solution. A second-chance meeting can be useful to see if the solution still seems as good after "sleeping on it."

Given the extremely adverse effects groupthink may have on organizations, we encourage practicing managers to put these simple suggestions into action. The alternative—facing the consequences of groupthink—certainly suggest the need for serious consideration of this issue.

Group polarization: The extreme nature of group decisions. Imagine that you are an investor considering diversifying your portfolio. Your present holdings yield a modest appreciation each year. Although the stocks you own are safe and very conservative, they are unlikely to produce any great gains. Now you have an opportunity to buy an interest in a new company that has a highly uncertain future. If the company succeeds, the payoff will be enormous. But you don't know how well it will do. Should you consider converting your safer investments into this much riskier, but potentially more lucrative one?

What would the odds of the new company's success have to be before you would decide to "go for it" and make the investment? If you said that there would have to be a 90 percent chance of the company's succeeding before you would advocate making the investment, we could safely characterize your stance as conservative or cautious. However, if you were willing to make the investment when there was only a 10 percent chance of success, we would consider your stance quite risky. Now, suppose we asked a group of investors (e.g., an investment club) to consider this same decision. The question we are interested in is: would the group make a riskier or a more conservative decision than an individual?

You might think that the give-and-take going on in a group's discussion sessions would cause more middle-of-the-road, neutral decisions to be made by groups—ones that shy away from risk. However, a considerable amount of research seriously challenges this popular belief. In fact, systematic studies have shown that groups tended to make riskier decisions than individuals.[54] So, for example, if four individuals recommended that the riskier courses of action be taken if the odds of success were 40 percent, a group composed of these same individuals might recommend that the riskier course of action be taken if the odds of success were lower, say 20 percent. Because of this shift in the direction of riskiness by groups compared to individuals, the phenomenon became known as the **risky shift.**

Scientists quickly became interested in the risky shift phenomenon. Their curiosity was not only sparked by the surprising nature of the effect, but also, no doubt, by the interesting implications that decision-making groups (such as juries, or business and governmental committees) might be biased toward making risky—perhaps even dangerous—decisions. As researchers continued to study the decisions made by groups, it became apparent that they were not only riskier—they were more extreme along several other dimensions as well. For example, studies have shown that liberal judges tend to hand down more liberal decisions when they convene in panels of three than when they decide cases alone.[55] Other studies have found that jury members who believe a defendant is innocent or guilty before deliberations tend to be even more certain of these convictions after joint discussions. Apparently, the risky shift is part of a more general tendency for group members to shift their individual views in a more extreme direction, a phenomenon known as **group polarization.**[56] Specifically, the group polarization effect refers to the tendency for group members to shift their views about a given issue to ones that are more extreme in the same direction as the views they held initially. This effect is summarized in Figure 14.10 (on page 504). As you can see, someone who is initially in favor of a certain decision will be *more favorable* toward it following group discussion, and someone who is initially opposed to a certain decision will be *more opposed* to it following group discussion.

Apparently, the group interaction makes people more extremely disposed to their initially held beliefs. Why does this happen? In other words, what causes group polarization? One major explanation, the *social comparison* view, suggests that group members may want to make a positive impression on their fellow group members, and do so by strongly endorsing predominant cultural values. People wanting to impress their fellow group members (or at least, to not embarrass themselves in front of them) will

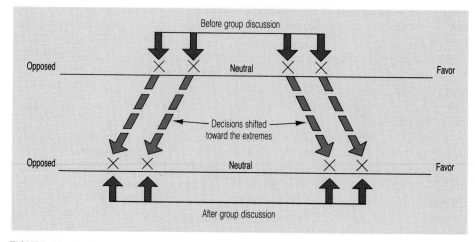

FIGURE 14.10 The Group Polarization Effect: A Summary

The *group polarization effect* refers to the tendency for individuals initially in favor of or against a certain decision to become even more in favor of it or against it following group discussions.

embrace the predominant cultural value—wanting to appear to do the right thing in front of others, therefore going to the extreme with respect to whatever perspective seems right. This explanation suggests that group polarization represents a serious bias in group decision-making processes.

Another possible explanation of the group polarization effect is that *persuasive information* is exchanged during the course of group deliberations. As deliberations progress, some group members may be exposed to arguments they had not previously considered. Since most of these arguments will favor the views initially held by the majority of the group members, there is a gradual shift toward extremity as more and more dissenters change their minds and "jump on the bandwagon." It is difficult to say which explanation of the group polarization effect is best since both are supported by research.[57]

Regardless of the precise basis for the group polarization effect, its existence has important implications for managers and organizations. Potentially, groups may make increasingly extreme decisions, which can be very dangerous. If this occurs, the results for both organizations and individuals can be disastrous. Clearly, the group polarization effect is a phenomenon worthy of careful consideration. Along with groupthink, it is a potentially important negative influence on group decisions. Given these serious problems, it is clearly worthwhile to consider ways of overcoming such obstacles to effective group decision making.

Improving the Effectiveness of Group Decisions: Some Techniques

As we have made clear in this chapter, there are certain advantages to be gained from using individuals or groups to make decisions. What would be ideal is a decision-making technique that combines the best features of groups and individuals while minimizing the disadvantages. Several techniques designed to realize the "best of both worlds" have been widely used in organizations. These include techniques that involve the structuring of group discussions in special ways, as well as improving the skills individuals may bring to the decision-making situation.

The Delphi technique: Decisions by expert consensus. According to Greek mythology, persons interested in seeing what fate the future held for them could seek the counsel of the Delphic oracle. Today's organizational decision-makers sometimes consult experts to help them make the best decisions as well. A technique developed by the Rand Corporation, known as the **Delphi technique,** represents a systematic way of collecting and organizing the opinions of several experts into a single decision.[58] The steps in the process are summarized in Figure 14.11.

The Delphi process starts by enlisting the cooperation of experts and presenting the problem to them, usually in a letter. Each expert then proposes what he or she believes is the most appropriate solution. The group leader compiles all of these individual responses and reproduces them so they can be shared with all the other experts in a second mailing. At this point each expert comments on the others' ideas and proposes another solution. These individual solutions are returned to the leader, who compiles them and looks for a consensus of opinions. If a consensus is reached, the decision is made. If not, the process of sharing reactions with others is repeated until a consensus is eventually obtained.

The obvious advantage of using the Delphi technique to make decisions is that it allows the collection of expert judgments without the great costs and logistical difficulties of bringing many experts together for a face-to-face meeting. However, there are also limitations that need to be considered. As you might imagine, the Delphi process can be very time consuming. Sending out letters, waiting for everyone to respond, transcribing and disseminating the responses, and repeating the process until a consensus is reached can take quite a long time. Experts have estimated that the minimum time it would take to use the Delphi technique would be over forty-four days. In one case,

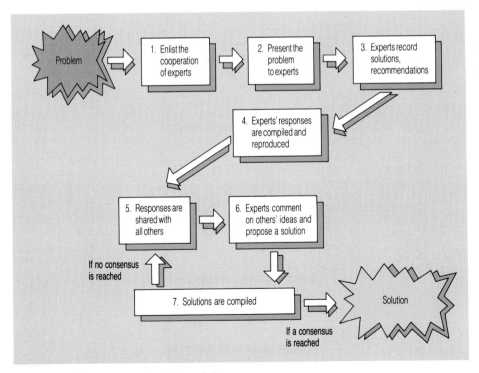

FIGURE 14.11   The Delphi Technique: A Summary

The *Delphi technique* allows decisions to be made by several experts without encountering many of the disadvantages of face-to-face group interaction.

the process took five months to complete.[59] Obviously, the Delphi approach would not be appropriate for making decisions in crisis situations, or whenever time is of the essence. However, the approach has been successfully employed to make decisions such as what items to put on a conference agenda and what the potential impact of implementing new land use policies would be.[60]

The nominal group technique: A structured group meeting. When there are only a few hours available to make a decision, group discussion sessions can be held, in which members interact with each other in an orderly, focused fashion aimed at solving problems. The **nominal group technique (NGT)** brings together a small number of individuals (usually about seven to ten) who systematically offer their individual solutions to a problem and share their personal reactions to others' solutions.[61] The technique is referred to as *nominal* because the individuals involved form a group *in name only*. The participants do not attempt to agree as a group on any solution, but rather, vote on all the solutions proposed. For an outline of the steps in the process, please see Figure 14.12.

As shown in Figure 14.12, the nominal group process begins by gathering the group members together around a table and identifying the problem at hand. Then, each member writes down his or her solutions. Next, one at a time, each member presents his or her solutions to the group and the leader writes these down on a chart. This process continues until all the ideas are expressed. Following this, each solution is discussed, clarified and evaluated by the group members. Each member is given a chance to voice his or her reactions to each idea. After all the ideas have been evaluated,

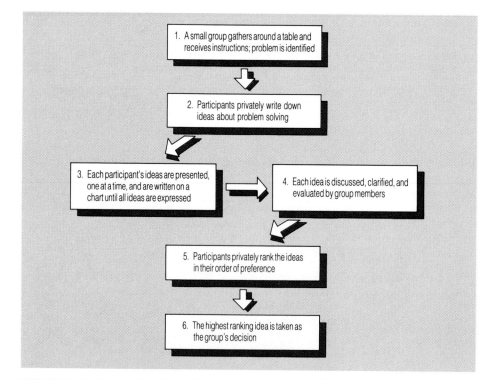

FIGURE 14.12 The Nominal Group Technique: A Summary of Steps

The *nominal group technique* structures face-to-face group meetings in a way that allows for the open expression and evaluation of ideas.

the group members privately rank order their preferred solutions. The idea that receives the highest rank is taken as the group's decision.

Although nominal groups traditionally meet in face-to-face settings, advances in modern technology have made it possible for nominal groups to meet even when its members are far away from each other. Specifically, a technique known as **automated decision conferencing** has been used in which individuals in different locations participate in nominal group conferences by means of telephone lines or direct satellite transmissions.[62] The messages may be sent either via characters on a computer monitor or images viewed during a teleconference. Despite their high tech look, automated decision conferences are really just nominal groups meeting in a manner that approximates face-to-face contact.

The NGT has several advantages and disadvantages.[63] We have already noted that this approach can be used to arrive at group decisions in only a few hours. The benefit of the technique is that it discourages any pressure to conform to the wishes of a high status group member because *all* ideas are evaluated and the preferences are expressed in *private* balloting. The technique must be considered limited, however, in that it requires the use of a trained group leader. In addition, using NGT successfully requires that only one narrowly defined problem be considered at a time. So, for very complex problems, many NGT sessions would have to be run—and only *if* the problem under consideration can be broken down into smaller parts.

It is important to consider the relative effectiveness of nominal groups and Delphi groups over face-to-face interacting groups. In general, research has shown the superiority of these special approaches to decision making in many ways on a variety of decision problems.[64] For example, the effectiveness of both techniques has been demonstrated in a study by Van de Ven and Delbecq in which seven-member groups (nominal, Delphi, and interacting) worked on the task of defining the job of a dormitory counselor.[65] Nominal groups tended to be the most satisfied with their work, and made the best quality judgments. In addition, both nominal groups and Delphi groups were much more productive than interacting groups. As we have noted earlier, however, there is a potential benefit to be derived from face-to-face interaction that cannot be realized in nominal and Delphi groups—that is, acceptance of the decision. Groups are likely to accept their decisions and be committed to them if members have been actively involved in making them. Considering this, it is not surprising to find that the more detached and impersonal atmosphere of nominal and Delphi groups sometimes makes their members less likely to accept their groups' decisions. We may conclude, then, that there is no one best type of group used to make decisions. Which type is most appropriate depends on the trade-offs decision-makers are willing to make between speed, quality, and commitment.[66]

The nominal group technique and the Delphi technique represent two very useful and effective ways of improving group performance. The problem with using these techniques, however, is that they go outside the normal decision-making channels and utilize special procedures requiring the use of specialists to run group meetings. It may not always be feasible, of course, to conduct such meetings, suggesting that a need exists for improving the quality of group decisions on a more regular basis. What else can be done to help improve the quality of group decisions? One promising answer appears to lie in the area of training individual decision-makers to work more effectively in groups.

Training individuals to improve group performance. As we noted earlier in this chapter, how well groups solve problems depends in part on the composition of those groups. If there is at least one group member who is capable of coming up with a solution, then groups may benefit by that individual's expertise. Based on this reasoning, it follows that the more qualified individual group members are to solve problems, the better their groups as a whole will perform.

In a recent study, Bottger and Yetton found that individuals trained to avoid four common types of errors were able to significantly reduce the number of mistakes made by their groups when attempting to solve a creative problem.[67] Specifically, participants in the study were asked to be aware of and to try to avoid four common problems.

1. Hypervigilance. This state involves frantically searching for quick solutions to problems, going from one idea to another out of a sense of desperation that one idea isn't working and that another needs to be considered before time runs out. A poor, "last chance" solution may be adopted to bring relief from anxiety. This problem may be avoided by keeping in mind that it is best to stick with one suggestion and work it out thoroughly, and reassuring the person solving the problem that his or her level of skill and education is adequate to perform the task at hand. In other words, a little reassurance may go a long way toward keeping individuals on the right track and avoiding the problem of hypervigilance.

2. Unconflicted adherence. Many decision-makers make the mistake of sticking to the first idea that comes into their heads without more deeply evaluating the consequences. As a result, such persons are unlikely to become aware of any problems associated with their ideas or to consider other possibilities. To avoid unconflicted adherence, decision-makers are urged to: (a) think about the difficulties associated with their ideas, (b) force themselves to consider different ideas, and (c) consider the special and unique characteristics of the problem they are facing and avoid carrying over assumptions from previous problems.

3. Unconflicted change. Sometimes people are too quick to change their minds and adopt the first new idea to come along. To avoid such unconflicted change, decision-makers are encouraged to ask themselves about: (a) the risks and problems of adopting that solution, (b) the good points of the first idea, and (c) the relative strengths and weaknesses of both ideas.

4. Defensive avoidance. Too often decision-makers fail to solve problems effectively because they avoid working on the task at hand. To minimize this problem, they should do three things. First, they should attempt to *avoid procrastination*. Just because you cannot come up with a solution right away, don't let it get to you by putting off the problem indefinitely. Continue to budget some of your time on even the most frustrating problems. Second, *avoid disowning responsibility*. It is easy to minimize the importance of a problem by saying "it doesn't matter, so who cares." Avoid giving up so soon. Finally, *don't ignore potentially corrective information*. It is tempting to put your nagging doubts about the quality of a solution to rest in order to be finished with it. Good decision-makers would not do so. Rather, they use their doubts to test and potentially improve the quality of their ideas.

The encouraging aspect of Bottger and Yetton's findings is that merely having members of problem-solving groups consider these four potential pitfalls was an effective way of improving the quality of their groups' solutions. Apparently, how well groups perform depends to a great extent on the problem-solving skills of the individual group members. Attempting to avoid the four major pitfalls described here appears to be an effective method of improving individual decision-making skills—and hence, the quality of group decisions. Obviously, this is only one approach that can be taken to improve organizational decision making. Overall, how effectively decisions are made will depend on a variety of factors that have been addressed in this chapter. The **Management Perspective** section below summarizes many of these key considerations.

Guidelines for Improving Group Decisions: A Checklist

This chapter has identified and described many factors that influence group decision making. By summarizing several of our major conclusions in the form of rules, we present a checklist to guide managers in improving the quality of group decisions.

___ 1. *Is the group's task a creative one?* If so, keep in mind that individuals tend to perform creative tasks better than groups. So avoid using groups to make these decisions; use individuals instead.

___ 2. *Check for group composition.* Groups should be composed of members with a heterogeneous blend of skills needed to perform the tasks and solve the problems they face. Make sure that members of the group are qualified to make the decisions confronted.

___ 3. *How cohesive is the group?* A group should be cohesive enough to be able to coordinate its efforts and work together, but it should not be so highly cohesive that it loses sight of outside influences that could improve its work (i.e., it should not be prone to groupthink).

___ 4. *Discourage intimidation by high-status persons.* If group members are likely to be intimidated by the presence of high-status persons, these individuals should be absent from the discussion process, or their contributions should be controlled through structured group interactions (e.g., the nominal group technique).

___ 5. *Train individuals in the skills needed to make a decision.* Remember that good decisions are made by groups composed of individuals trained in avoiding the pitfalls of problem solving. If possible, train individuals to avoid the four pitfalls described on page 508—namely, hypervigilance, unconflicted adherence, unconflicted change, and defensive avoidance.

___ 6. *If commitment to a decision is important, involve individuals in the decision-making process.* Keep in mind that people are most likely to be committed to a course of action when they have been involved in deciding it. If it is important that group members accept the decisions made, the members should be consulted in the decision-making process.[68]

___ 7. *Is time of the essence?* If a decision has to be made right away, as in an emergency situation, there might not be adequate time to use groups to make decisions. If a timely decision has to be made, and a group decision is needed, the nominal group technique allows the group's ideas to be presented and considered most efficiently.

___ 8. *Make sure the group has adequate resources to make its decision.* Remember, information is the key to reducing the uncertainty behind decisions. Groups should be given access to as much information as possible in order to recommend the best possible courses of action.

___ 9. *Encourage decisions to be made without political pressures.* Too many times group judgments are flawed because they do not really represent the collective best judgment of the individuals charged with making a decision. Instead, they reflect what the members believe someone in power wants them to decide. Such politically sensitive judgments make a mockery of the group and insult all those participating in it. If a group is created to render a decision, it should be free to make its decision without bias.

Please note that this is not an exhaustive list. There are many other considerations involved in making good group decisions. However, this list provides a useful starting point for any manager interested in avoiding some of the most common impediments to group decision making.

SUMMARY AND REVIEW

The Nature of Decision Making. Decision making is the multi-step process through which a problem is identified, solution objectives are defined, a *predecision* is made (i.e., a decision about how to make the decision), alternatives are generated and evaluated, an alternative is chosen, implemented, and then followed up.

The decisions made in organizations can be characterized as **programmed**, routine decisions made in accordance with pre-existing guidelines, or **nonprogrammed**, decisions requiring novel and creative solutions. Decisions also differ with respect to the amount of risk involved, ranging from those in which the decision outcomes are relatively *certain* to those in which the outcomes are highly *uncertain*. Uncertain situations are expressed as statements of probability based on either objective or subjective information.

Individual Decision Making. Two major approaches to individual decision making have been identified. The **rational-economic model** characterizes decision-makers as thoroughly searching through perfect information to make an *optimal* decision. In contrast, the **administrative model** recognizes the inherent imperfections of decision-makers and the social and organizational systems within which they operate. Limitations imposed by people's ability to process the information needed to make complex decisions (**bounded rationality**) restrict decision-makers to making **satisficing decisions,** solutions that are not optimal but good enough.

Impediments to optimal individual decisions include cognitive biases (such as **framing** and **heuristics**), the tendency for decision-makers to escalate their commitment to failing courses of action, and various organizational factors (such as time constraints, and political face-saving pressures).

Group Decision Making. In comparing the decisions made by groups and individuals, the results are mixed. Groups have proven superior to individual members when they are composed of a heterogeneous mix of experts who possess complementary skills. However, groups may not be any better than the best member of the group when performing a task that has a simple, verifiable answer. Compared to individuals, groups tend to make inferior decisions on creative problems.

Two major obstacles to good group decisions may be identified. One of these, **groupthink,** is the tendency for strong conformity pressures within groups to lead to the breakdown of critical thinking and to encourage premature acceptance of potentially questionable solutions. Another possible obstacle is known as **group polarization**—the tendency, following group discussions, for group members to shift their opinions to more extreme positions in the direction they initially favored. As a result, groups tend to make more extreme decisions than individuals.

The quality of group decisions can be enhanced by using the **nominal group technique**—a method of structuring group meetings so as to systematically elicit and evaluate all opinions—and the **Delphi technique**—a method in which solutions to problems proposed by experts are solicited through the mail. The quality of group decisions has also been shown to improve following individual training on problem-solving skills.

Key Terms

administrative model: A model of decision making that recognizes the *bounded rationality* that limits the making of optimally rational–economic decisions.

automated decision conferencing: A technique in which decision-making groups are formed by connecting people in different locations via satellite transmissions or telephone lines.

availability heuristic: The tendency for people to base their judgments on information that is readily available to them, although it may be potentially inaccurate, thereby adversely affecting decision quality.

bounded rationality: The major assumption of the administrative model—that organizational, social, and human limitations lead to the making of *satisficing* rather than optimal decisions.

brainstorming: A technique designed to foster group productivity by encouraging interacting group members to express their ideas in a noncritical fashion.

decision making: The process through which a problem is identified, solution objectives are defined, a *predecision* is made, and alternatives are generated and evaluated, an alternative is chosen, implemented, and followed up.

decision style: The orientation people have toward making decisions, including the *directive style, analytic style, conceptual style,* and *behavioral style.*

Delphi technique: A method of improving group decisions utilizing the opinions of experts, which are solicited by mail and then compiled. The expert consensus of opinions is used to make a decision.

escalation of commitment phenomenon: The tendency for individuals to continue to support previously unsuccessful courses of action.

framing: The presentation of a problem to an individual, either in negative terms (leading to *risk seeking*) or positive terms (leading to *risk aversion*).

group polarization: The tendency for group members to shift to more extreme positions (in the direction they initially favored) following group interaction.

groupthink: The tendency for members of highly cohesive groups to so strongly conform to group pressures regarding a certain decision that they fail to think critically, rejecting the potentially correcting influences of outsiders.

heuristics: Simple decision rules (rules of thumb) used to make quick decisions about complex problems. (See *availability heuristic* and *representativeness heuristic.*)

nominal group technique (NGT): A technique for improving group performance in which small groups of individuals systematically present and discuss their ideas before privately voting on their preferred solution. The most preferred solution is accepted as the group's decision.

non-programmed decision: A decision made about a highly novel problem for which there is no pre-specified course of action.

predecision: A decision about what process to follow in making a decision.

programmed decision: A highly routine decision made according to pre-established organizational routines and procedures.

rational decisions: Decisions that maximize the chance of attaining an individual's, group's, or organization's goals.

rational-economic model: The model of decision making according to which decision-makers consider all possible alternatives to problems before selecting the optimal solution.

representativeness heuristic: The tendency to perceive others in stereotypical ways if they appear to be typical representatives of the category to which they belong.

risky shift: The tendency for groups to make riskier decisions than individuals.

satisficing decision: A decision made by selecting the first minimally acceptable alternative as it becomes available.

Questions for Discussion

1. Apply the eight-step model of decision making described in the text to any decision you may have recently made.

2. Distinguish between *programmed decisions* and *non-programmed decisions,* giving an example of each in an organization with which you are familiar.

3. Describe the various barriers to effective decision making recognized by the *rational-economic model.* Give an example of each.

4. Suppose you were hired as a consultant to improve the decision-making skills of an organization's personnel. Outline the things you would do, and justify these measures.

5. Imagine that you are a manager facing the problem of not attracting enough high-quality personnel to your organization. Would you attempt to solve this problem alone or by committee? Explain your reasoning.

6. *Groupthink* is a potentially serious impediment to group decision making. Describe this phenomenon, and review some things that can be done to avoid it.

7. Give an example of *group polarization* operating in any group in which you have been a member.

8. Suppose you find out that a certain important organizational decision has to be made by a group, but you suspect that a better decision might be made by an individual. How could you structure a group so as to derive its advantages while avoiding its disadvantages?

9. Describe how individuals can be trained to improve the quality of group decisions.

Notes

1. Mintzberg, H. J. (1988). *Mintzberg on management: Inside our strange world of organizations.* New York: Free Press.

2. Simon, H. (1977). *The new science of management decisions* (2nd ed.). Englewood Cliffs, NJ: Prentice-Hall.

3. Harrison, E. F. (1987). *The managerial decision-making process* (3rd ed.). Boston: Houghton Mifflin.

4. Wedley, W. C., & Field, R. H. G. (1984). A predecision support system. *Academy of Management Review, 9,* 696–703.

5. Nutt, P. (1984). Types of organizational decision processes. *Administrative Science Quarterly, 29,* 414–450.

6. Cowan, D. A. (1986). Developing a process model of problem recognition. *Academy of Management Review, 11,* 763–776.

7. Dennis, T. L., & Dennis, L. B. (1988). *Microcomputer models for management decision making.* St. Paul, MN: West.

8. Stevenson, M. K., Busemeyer, & Naylor, J. C. (1990). Judgment and decision-making theory. In M. D. Dunnette (Ed.), *Handbook of industrial/organizational psychology* (2nd ed.). Palo Alto, CA: Consulting Psychologists Press.

9. Hill, C. W. L., & Jones, G. R. (1989). *Strategic management.* Boston: Houghton Mifflin.

10. See Note 3.

11. Provan, K. G. (1982). Interorganizational linkages and influence over decision making. *Academy of Management Journal, 25,* 443–451.

12. Walker, G., & Weber, D. (1987). Supplier competition, uncertainty, and make-or-buy decisions. *Academy of Management Journal, 30,* 589–596.

13. Parsons, C. K. (1988). Computer technology: Implications for human resources management. In G. R. Ferris & K. M. Rowland (Eds.), *Research in personnel and human resources management* (vol. 6, pp. 1–36). Greenwich, CT: JAI Press.

14. Simon, H. A. (1987). Making management decisions: The role of intuition and emotion. *Academy of Management Executive, 1,* 57–64.

15. Linstone, H. A. (1984). *Multiple perspectives for decision making.* New York: North-Holland.

16. Simon, H. A. (1979). Rational decision making in organizations. *American Economic Review, 69,* 493–513.

17. Fredrickson, J. W., & Mitchell, T. R. (1984). Strategic decision processes: Comprehensiveness and performance in an industry with an unstable environment. *Academy of Management Journal, 27,* 399–423.

18. March, J. G., & Simon, H. A. (1958). *Organizations.* New York: Wiley.

19. See Note 18.

20. Simon, H. A. (1957). *Models of man.* New York: Wiley.

21. Gaeth, G. J., & Shanteau, J. (1984). Reducing the influence of irrelevant information on experienced decision makers. *Organizational Behavior and Human Performance, 33,* 263–282.

22. Ginrich, G., & Soli, S. D. (1984). Subjective evaluation and allocation of resources in routine decision making. *Organizational Behavior and Human Performance, 33,* 187–203.

23. Abelson, R. P., & Levi, A. (1985). Decision-making and decision theory. In G. Lindzey & E. Aronson (Eds.), *Handbook of social psychology,* 3rd ed. (vol. 1, pp. 231–309). Reading, MA: Addison-Wesley.

24. Kahneman, D., & Tversky, A. (1984). Choices, values, and frames. *American Psychologist, 39,* 341–350.

25. Nisbett, R. E., & Ross, L. (1980). *Human inference: Strategies and shortcomings of social judgment.* Englewood Cliffs, NJ: Prentice-Hall.

26. Dubé-Rioux, L., & Russo, J. R. (1988). An availability bias in professional judgment. *Journal of Behavioral Decision Making, 1,* 223–237.

27. Kahneman, D., & Tversky, A. (1973). On the psychology of prediction. *Psychological Review, 80,* 251–273.

28. Taylor, R. N. (1984). *Behavioral decision making.* Glenview, IL: Scott, Foresman.

29. Staw, B. M., & Ross, J. (1987). Behavior in escalation situations: Antecedents, prototypes, and solutions. In L. L. Cummings & B. M. Staw (Eds.), *Research in organizational behavior* (vol. 9, pp. 39–78). Greenwich, CT: JAI Press.

30. Ross, J., & Staw, B. M. (1986). Expo 86: An escalation prototype. *Administrative Science Quarterly, 31,* 274–297.

31. Staw, B. M. (1981). The escalation of commitment to a course of action. *Academy of Management Review, 6,* 577–587.

32. Whyte, G. (1986). Escalating commitment to a course of action: A reinterpretation. *Academy of Management Review, 11,* 311–321.

33. Bowen, M. G. (1987). The escalation phenomenon reconsidered: Decision dilemmas or decision errors? *Academy of Management Review, 12,* 52–66.

34. Tjosvold, D. (1984). Effects of crisis orientation on managers' approach to controversy in decision making. *Academy of Management Journal, 27,* 130–138.

35. Johnson, R. J. (1984). Conflict avoidance through acceptable decisions. *Human Relations, 27,* 71–82.

36. Neustadt, R. E., & Fineberg, H. (1978). *The swine flu affair: Decision making on a slippery disease.* Washington, DC: U.S. Department of Health, Education, & Welfare.

37. Shull, F. A., Delbecq, A. L., & Cummings, L. L. (1970). *Organizational decision making.* New York: McGraw-Hill.

38. Rowe, A. J., Boulgaides, J. D., & McGrath, M. R. (1984). *Managerial decision making.* Chicago: Science Research Assocs.

39. See Note 38.

40. Delbeq, A. L., Van de Ven, A. H., & Gustafson, D. H. (1975). *Group techniques for program planning.* Glenview, IL: Scott, Foresman.

41. Murninghan, J. K. (1981). Group decision making: What strategies should you use? *Management Review, 25,* 56–62.

42. Hill, G. W. (1982). Group versus individual performance: Are N + 1 heads better than one? *Psychological Bulletin, 91,* 517–539.

43. Wanous, J. P., & Youtz, M. A. (1986). Solution diversity and the quality of group decisions. *Academy of Management Journal, 29,* 149–159.

44. Yetton, P., & Bottger, P. (1983). The relationships among group size, member ability, social decision schemes, and performance. *Organizational Behavior and Human Performance, 32,* 145–149.

45. See Note 42.

46. See Note 42.

47. Osborn, A. F. (1957). *Applied imagination.* New York: Scribner's.

48. Bouchard, T. J., Jr., Barsaloux, J., & Drauden, G. (1974). Brainstorming procedure, group size, and sex as determinants of the problem-solving effectiveness of groups and individuals. *Journal of Applied Psychology, 59,* 135–138.

49. Janis, I. L. (1982). *Groupthink: Psychological studies of policy decisions and fiascoes* (2nd ed.). Boston: Houghton Mifflin.

50. Janis, I. L. (1988). *Crucial decisions: Leadership in policy making and crisis management.* New York: Free Press.

51. Morehead, G., & Montanari, J. R. (1986). An empirical investigation of the groupthink phenomenon. *Human Relations, 39,* 399–410.

52. Schweiger, D. M., Sandberg, W. R., & Ragan, J. W. (1986). Group approaches for improving strategic decision making: A comparative analysis of dialectical inquiry, devil's advocacy, and consensus. *Academy of Management Journal, 29,* 51–71.

53. Sloan, A. P., Jr. (1964). *My years with General Motors.* New York: Doubleday.

54. Pruitt, D. G. (1971). Choice shifts in group discussion: An introductory review. *Journal of Personality and Social Psychology, 20,* 339–360.

55. Walker, T. G., & Main, E. C. (1973). Choice-shifts in political decision making: Federal judges and civil liberties cases. *Journal of Applied Social Psychology, 2,* 93–98.

56. Lamm, H. & Myers, D. G. (1978). Group-induced polarization of attitudes and behavior. In L. Berkowitz (Ed.), *Advances in experimental social psychology* (vol. 11, pp. 145–195). New York: Academic Press.

57. See Note 56.

58. Dalkey, N. (1969). *The Delphi method: An experimental study of group decisions.* Santa Monica, CA: Rand Corporation.

59. Van de Ven, A. H., & Delbecq, A. F. (1971). Nominal versus interacting group processes for committee decision-making effectiveness. *Academy of Management Journal, 14,* 203–212.

60. See Note 39.

61. Gustafson, D. H., Shulka, R. K., Delbecq, A., & Walster, W. G. (1973). A comparative study of differences in subjective likelihood estimates made by individuals, interacting groups, Delphi groups, and nominal groups. *Organizational Behavior and Human Performance, 9,* 280–291.

62. See Note 38.

63. Ulshak, F. L., Nathanson, L., & Gillan, P. B. (1981). *Small group problem solving: An aid to organizational effectiveness.* Reading, MA: Addison-Wesley.

64. Willis, R. E. (1979). A simulation of multiple selection using nominal group procedures. *Management Science, 25,* 171–181.

65. Van de Ven, A. H., & Delbecq, A. L. (1974). The effectiveness of nominal, Delphi, and interacting group decision making processes. *Academy of Management Journal, 17,* 605–621.

66. Stumpf, S. A., Zand, D. E., & Freedman, R. D. (1979). Designing groups for judgmental decisions. *Academy of Management Review, 4,* 589–600.

67. Bottger, P. C., & Yetton, P. W. (1987). Improving group performance by training in individual problem solving. *Journal of Applied Psychology, 72,* 651–657.

68. Cotton, J. L., Vollrath, D. A., Froggatt, K. L., Lengnick-Hall, M. L., & Jennings, K. R. (1988). Employee participation: Diverse forms and different outcomes. *Academy of Management Review, 13,* 8–22.

CASE
IN
POINT

Coke's Fizzled Decision Making

On April 23, 1985, the Coca-Cola Company, led by Chief Executive Officer Roberto Goizueta, made an announcement that surprised Coca-Cola employees, bottlers, investors, and the American public.[1] Calling it "the most significant soft drink development in the company's history,"[2] Goizueta announced that Coca-Cola Co. had decided to change their extremely successful 99 year old formula for Coca-Cola and replace it with a newer, sweeter Coke—"New Coke." Saying, "the best has been made better," Goizueta believed that great times and increased market share lay ahead for Coca-Cola.[3]

Consumers felt differently, though. In fact, the response to this decision is unparalleled in U.S. marketing history. Consumers formed protest groups demanding the return of "old Coke." One such group even planned to file a class action law suit to demand that the original formula Coke be returned.[4] Coca-Cola headquarters in Atlanta was besieged with angry letters and phone calls—1,500 angry phone calls per day, in fact.[5] A black market in "old Coke" imported from foreign distributors resulted in cases of soda being sold for ten times their normal price. Distributors and bottlers complained bitterly to headquarters. Even Goizueta's father told him he had made a mistake.[6]

Given this reaction, why didn't the top officials at Coca-Cola realize that they had made a serious error? The answer lies, in part, in the fact that they felt they were making a good decision. Their share of the national sugared cola market was slipping to arch-rival Pepsi, and officials were concerned that their product seemed to always lose the "Pepsi Challange"—a blind taste test sponsored by Pepsi. Because of their belief that their market share would continue to decline, Coca-Cola management decided to investigate the possibility of introducing a new formula for their flagship soda.

This investigation took four and a half years and was generally acknowledged to be "one of the most exhaustive research projects ever for a consumer goods company."[7] The company spent $4 million and taste-tested 200,000 people on three different new formulas. (However, interestingly, less than 40,000 of these people actually tasted the formula selected to replace the old Coke.)[8] Consumers were also polled as to their likely behavior if a new Coke was introduced. Ad agencies and outside consultants helped participate in the decision. Based on all the taste-test data, and the projected financial earnings, Coca-Cola brass decided to introduce their new product with much fanfare.

Soon after the introduction, however, it was clear that the American public was unhappy—complaints began pouring in and sales slumped. The people at headquarters believed that sales would soon pick up as people grew accustomed to the new flavor. But sales continued to plummet and the complaints grew louder and louder.

Despite all their research, it seems the officials at Coca-Cola didn't account for Coke's biggest attraction for consumers—not necessarily its taste, but its symbolic value and emotional ties. Coca-Cola customers, and particularly those who so vocally wanted the "old Coke" back, thought of Coke as more than a soda for quenching their thirst. They thought of it as a way of life, a reminder of times gone by, of youth. According to Robert Antonio, a sociology professor at the University of Kansas, "some people felt that a sacred symbol had been tampered with."[9] All the market research failed to account for this attraction as people were only asked a series of yes/no questions about the new formula and were not asked anything about their feelings or attachments to Coke. Additionally, consumers participating in the market research were not told that by choosing the taste of the "new Coke" over the "old" they would forever be choosing a new formula.[10]

The response of consumers greatly surprised the Coca-Cola officials responsible for making the decision to switch "new" for "old" Coke. But it shouldn't have been such a surprise. Since taking over as CEO in 1981, Goizueta had introduced many changes to the company. One large change was the use of the Coca-Cola logo on products other than the flagship brand of soft drink (e.g., Diet Coke, Cherry Coke). The Coke trademark was even used on clothing. Managerially unlike his predecessor, Goizueta believed in the value of debt, and growth through acquisition. He also believed in management by consensus. Additionally, Goizueta and many top officials at Coke came to their posts through international operations and perhaps weren't as familiar with U.S. perceptions of their product as they might have been. As one Southern bottler said, "If we still had some of these Southern good ol' boys running this company instead of this international crew, maybe this never would have happened."[11]

Less than three months after introducing the new formula for Coca-Cola, on July 11, 1985 CEO Goizueta announced the return of the original Coke as "Coca-Cola Classic." The newly formulated soda would simply be called "Coca-Cola." This decision was clearly made much more hastily than the decision to introduce the new formula. It was based on the complaints of consumers, bottlers, and the plummeting sales figures. Six months later Coke Classic was outselling Coke by large margins in big cities (eight to one in Dallas and New York; nine to one in Minneapolis) and by at least two to one overall.[12] Interestingly, the overall market share of both old and new Coke combined was equal to that before the announcement of the new product.[13]

Questions for Discussion

1. Use the model of the decision-making process to examine how Coca-Cola officials decided on a new formula for Coke.

2. Was the decision to introduce a new formula a programmed or non-programmed decision? Why?

3. Is there any evidence for the existence of group polarization or groupthink operating among Coca-Cola executives during the time in which the decision was made to change the formula for Coke?

4. Use the model of the decision-making process to examine how Coca-Cola officials decided to reintroduce "old Coke" as Coca-Cola Classic.

5. After Coke Classic was "introduced" there was some speculation that the Coca-Cola Company had deliberately planned this fiasco to create market awareness for their product. In response, Donald Keough, President of Coca-Cola said, "Some critics will say Coca-Cola has made a marketing mistake. Some cynics say that we planned the whole thing. The truth is, we're not that dumb, and we're not that smart."[14] Evaluate this statement in light of your knowledge of decision making.

Notes

1. Greenwald, J. (1985, July 22). Coca-Cola's big fizzle. *Time*, pp. 48–52.
2. See Note 1, p. 49.
3. See Note 1, p. 49.
4. Fisher, A. B. (1985, August 5). Coke's brand-loyalty lesson. *Fortune*, pp. 44–46.
5. See Note 4.
6. Ellis, J. E., & Brown, P. B. (1985, July 29). Coke's man on the spot. *Business Week*, pp. 56–59.
7. Koten, J., & Kilman, S. (1985, July 15). How Coke's decision to offer two colas undid 4½ years of planning. *Wall Street Journal*, pp. 1, 8.
8. Gelb, B. D., & Gelb, G. M. (1986, Fall). New Coke's fizzle—Lessons for the rest of us. *Sloan Management Review*, pp. 71–76.
9. See Note 1, p. 48.
10. See Note 8.
11. See Note 6, p. 57.

12. Giges, N. (1986, January 27). Coke family' sales fly as new Coke fizzles. *Advertising Age,* pp. 1, 91.

13. See Note 8.

14. See Note 1, p. 49.

Making Decisions in Nominal Groups

One of the most effective ways of systematically gathering the opinions of several different people is the *nominal group technique*. This method of group decision making allows individuals to vote privately on their own decisions after participating in a group discussion of various alternatives (see pages 506–507). The following exercise will give you first-hand experience with nominal group decision making.

Procedure

1. Divide the class into groups of approximately seven to ten students. Each group selects one person to be its leader.

2. Each group selects a different question on which to focus. The most appropriate questions are those about which there exists a diversity of opinions. Some examples: (a) Why should people go to college? (b) What are the most important problems faced by society today? (c) What topics should be covered in an OB class? (d) What are your instructor's major responsibilities?

3. Review the rules for conducting nominal group sessions (see Figure 14.13).

4. Groups meet in separate parts of the room and run their own nominal group sessions for approximately forty-five minutes to one hour. Your instructor will walk around the room checking to make sure you are proceeding properly.

5. When time is up, someone from each group reports to the class on the question they considered, and what answers they derived using the nominal group technique. Group members will also report any problems or interesting experiences they encountered.

Points to Consider

1. Were the groups properly set up for decision making? Specifically, was the group size appropriate? Was there enough time to consider the questions carefully?

2. How did the group leaders perform? What did they do well? What could they have done better?

3. Did any one person try to dominate the group discussions? Was the leader effective in controlling this individual?

4. Do you think the nominal group technique is a useful way of making group decisions? Identify some specific questions for which you believe it would be particularly appropriate.

CHAPTER FIFTEEN

ORGANIZATION DESIGN: ENVIRONMENT, STRATEGY, TECHNOLOGY

CHAPTER OUTLINE

Organizational Structure: Its Basic Dimensions
Specialization: How Tasks Are Divided
Formalization: Rules and Documentation
The Span of Control: Flat Structures and Tall Ones
Centralization versus Decentralization: Who Makes Decisions?
Complexity: Internal Differentiation
Line versus Staff: Production or Support?
Putting the Basic Dimensions Together: Mechanistic and Organic Structures

Basic Organization Designs: Functional, Product, Matrix
Functional Designs: When Tasks Determine Structure
Product Designs: When Outputs Determine Structure
Matrix Designs: A Hybrid Approach

Environment: How External Conditions Shape Structure, Function, and Strategy
The External Environment: Some Key Domains

The External Environment: Some Basic Dimensions
External Environments: Their Major Effects
Turning the Tables: Techniques for Changing the Environment

Technology: How Tools Shape Structure
Technology and Structure in Manufacturing Companies: The Woodward Studies . . . and Beyond
Work-flow Integration: The Aston Studies
Technology and Interdependence

Special Sections

OB: A Research Perspective
Strategy and Structure in Large Manufacturing Firms: When Divisionalization Affects Diversification

OB: An International Perspective
The Present and Future Form of Organizations: Convergence or Divergence?

LEARNING OBJECTIVES

After reading this chapter, you should be able to:
1. Describe several basic dimensions of organizational structure, including formalization, centralization, and complexity.
2. Explain the difference between organic and mechanistic internal structures.
3. Describe the major features of three types of organizational design: functional, product, and matrix.
4. List and define the major dimensions along which external environments often vary.
5. Explain how the external environment shapes the internal structure and strategies of organizations.
6. Indicate how technology shapes the internal structure of organizations.
7. Differentiate between three basic types of interdependence in organizations.

For thirty years, Granex Corp. existed in what seemed to be a largely unchanging world. Granex manufactured a line of protective coatings (e.g., varnishes, rust-proofing), and sold these products only to commercial customers. Sales rose modestly in most years, and return on investment remained fairly stable. Recently, however, the situation has changed radically. First, a number of new competitors—many of them foreign—have entered the market. Their sales strategies, rapidly shifting product mix, and aggressive pricing policies caught Granex off guard. Second, recent breakthroughs in chemical engineering have led to a virtual technological revolution in Granex's industry. Using the new technology, it is now possible to custom design new products with the precise mix of features and properties demanded by specific customers. Finally, several of Granex's competitors have expanded their operations to include direct marketing to consumers. Fearing that it would be shut out of this potentially profitable market if it did not follow suit, Granex has found it necessary to deal with very new kinds of customers.

In response to these changing conditions, Granex has undergone a major shake-up in its top management team. The new CEO (a grandson of the original founder of the company) has established new strategies for the company—ones designed to cope with the changing world in which it does business. Further, he has invested large sums in product development and in new equipment designed to benefit from the new, improved technology. One result: Granex's facilities are now moving toward state-of-the-art status. Despite all these changes, the company continues to experience serious problems. It is still being beaten to the punch—and to lucrative contracts—by some of its key competitors. In fact, just last week it lost a major deal on which management had pinned many hopes. It is to discuss this recent setback that Charles Hall, Granex's CEO, has called this meeting.

"Okay, we've had the bad news. There's no sense going over *that* again. What's more important is figuring out exactly *why* we lost this one. We've got to learn from these situations if we expect to do better next time around. So tell me, people, why couldn't we give them that June 1st delivery date when Carter-Stein could?"

There's a moment of pained silence and then Lola Singh, one of the company's senior Vice Presidents, answers. "I don't have any simple answers Charlie—we all know there aren't any. But if you want it straight, I think it all boils down to the way we operate."

"What do you mean?" Hall asks, clearly perplexed. "We've got the best marketing strategies in the industry. And I'd match our new Beaver River plant with anyone's. Come on, lay it out for me; I don't follow."

"Okay, I will. You're right—we *do* have first-rate strategies. And our facilities *are* top notch. But somehow, we still seem to do things the old way. You want a 'for instance?' Take our project teams. Setting them up was a great idea; it gets the right people and the right talent just where we need it. But then what do we do? We make the project managers report back to their Department Heads."

"So?" Phil Grodini breaks in. "What else would you do—have 'em go off on their own, without any controls?"

"No," Lola replies, "but it sure slows them down when they have to work through channels for almost every decision—even ones that are downright trivial."

"You know," Kate Abell, another Vice President, interjects, "I think Lo's onto something. It *does* slow things down when project people have to work through the departments. I think it would help a lot if Project Managers had more authority. The way things are moving out there in the market these days, every week on their schedules counts."

"Right," Lola agrees. "And another thing: haven't you noticed the way Department Heads dig in their heels about letting their top people move into projects? They seem to see every one as some kind of raid on their turf. No wonder we have so many start up problems."

"Okay, okay," Charles comments, waving his hands in the air to signify that he's heard enough. "I'm beginning to get the picture. We've changed our strategies, changed our tactics, and changed our products, but we're still functioning in the same old way. So let's get on it. I don't care if we have to take this company apart and put it back together upside down. We've *got* to start winning in these situations or everything we've done will go right down the drain. Let's get a task force together right away, to figure out what needs to be changed. Hmm . . . who should head it up . . . ?"

Let's begin with four basic facts:

1. All organizations have some kind of **internal structure**—some formal arrangement that allocates tasks, responsibilities, and authority among individuals or departments. Such structure is intended to help the organization attain its major goals, whatever these may be.[1]

2. All organizations are affected by the **external environment** in which they operate. They are part of a specific society with many values and traditions; they are affected by shifting economic conditions and patterns of competition, government regulations, changes in the availability of raw materials and human resources, plus a host of other factors.

3. All organizations employ some type of **technology**—various means for converting input (e.g., raw materials, information) into output (products, services).

4. All organizations adopt some type of **strategy**—a plan (or plans) for matching the organization's skills and resources with opportunities (and threats) in the external environment.[2]

Now, consider the most crucial fact of all: important relationships exist between these factors—between an organization's internal structure, the environment in which it functions, the strategy (or strategies) it adopts, and the technology it employs. Moreover, such relationships tend to be *reciprocal* and *interactive* in nature.[3] Thus, an organization's internal structure is shaped, in part, by the external environment in which it operates, and also by the technology it uses. Similarly, internal structure often affects an organization's strategy and is affected, in turn, by such strategy. We could go on and on, for the links between these factors are complex and varied. The key point, however, is this: in order to fully understand organizations and the processes that occur within them, we must pay careful attention to the ways in which they are put together (their **internal structure**) and the relationships between this structure and the external environment, technology, and various business strategies (see Figure 15.1).

The complex interplay between structure, environment, technology, and strategy is illustrated by our chapter-opening story. Granex, Inc. has made many changes in response to altered conditions in the marketplace and rapid shifts in technology. These have involved updating its production facilities, expanding the market for its products, and adopting several new business strategies. Yet so far, changes in its internal structure have failed to keep pace with such moves—a fact that seems responsible, at least in part, for serious strains within the company and for its continued inability to compete effectively. Clearly, major shifts in internal structure are needed if Granex is to survive and prosper. But what form should such changes take? And how should they reflect

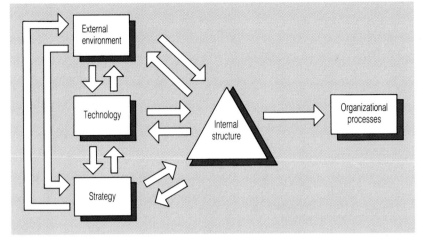

FIGURE 15.1   Key Components in Organizational Processes
In order to understand the complex processes occurring within organizations, we must comprehend the reciprocal, interactive relationships between the external environment, strategy, technology, and internal structure.

changing external conditions and the company's new strategies? We will focus on questions such as these in this chapter. Specifically, we will provide an introduction to *organization design*—the formal system of communication, authority, and responsibility adopted by organizations which constitutes their internal structure. This discussion will include a description of the basic dimensions along which internal structure can vary and an overview of several of the basic forms it takes in organizations. In addition, we'll consider the nature of the *external environment* in which organizations operate, and how the environment shapes both their structure and strategies. Finally, we'll examine *technology* and its relationship to the structure of organizations and of the jobs within them.

As you can see, the questions we'll address in this chapter are very different from those examined in earlier portions of this book. Instead of focusing on individuals or groups and the ways in which they shape organizations, we'll consider organizations themselves, and how *they* are shaped by external factors and events. Thus, we will shift from a **micro perspective,** which seeks to understand organizations by understanding the individuals and groups of which they are comprised, to a **macro perspective,** which seeks to understand organizations by comprehending the manner in which they fit into, and are affected by, external events and larger social systems (see Figure 15.2 on page 522). We trust that as we proceed, it will become increasingly clear that these perspectives are in no way contradictory or inconsistent. As we noted in chapter 1, each adds to our total comprehension of organizations and organizational behavior and each is valid in its own right; they simply approach key issues and questions from different directions.

ORGANIZATIONAL STRUCTURE: ITS BASIC DIMENSIONS

Organizations vary tremendously in size, scope, and purpose. However, differences in their internal structure seem to fall mainly along several key dimensions. Understanding the nature of these dimensions, therefore, is a very useful first step in comprehending the internal structure of most, if not all, organizations. Several of the most important are described below.

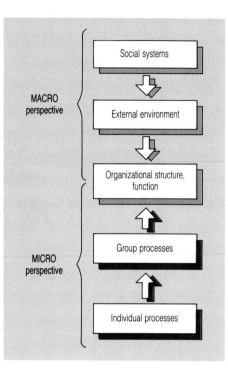

FIGURE 15.2 Micro and Macro Perspectives: Alternative Routes to Knowledge about Organizations

The *macro* and *micro perspectives* represent different approaches to understanding organizations and organizational processes. The macro approach is a "top-down" perspective, which works from social systems to groups and individuals. The micro approach is a "bottom-up" perspective, which works from individuals through groups, to entire organizations.

Specialization: How Tasks Are Divided

One important way in which organizations differ concerns the extent to which tasks are subdivided. At the high end of this dimension of **specialization** are organizations (usually large ones) in which each person (or each subunit) performs a very narrow range of activities—one operation on the assembly line, entering one type of information into the company's information systems. At the low end are organizations (usually smaller ones) in which employees (or subunits) perform a wide range of tasks or jobs—many steps in the manufacture of a product, processing many types of information about the company's operations.

Because it can improve overall efficiency, a high degree of specialization (or *division of labor*) was strongly recommended by early management experts, especially Frederick Taylor and other adherents of *scientific management* (see chapter 1).[4] However, when carried to extremes, it can yield intense feelings of boredom (qualitative underload; see chapter 7), thus reducing job satisfaction and creating stress. For this reason, specialization is far from the unmixed blessing some of its advocates once proposed.

Formalization: Rules and Documentation

A second key dimension of organizational structure involves **formalization**—the extent to which an organization relies on written documentation and formal rules. At the low end of this dimension are organizations with little written documentation and few formal rules. People in these organizations "play it by ear" most of the time, proceeding in whatever way seems best at the moment. At the high end are organizations in which rules governing virtually every aspect of the organization's functioning are contained in printed handbooks or manuals. For example, many government agencies publish manuals for new managerial-level personnel that run to several hundred pages. Such manuals attempt to touch on virtually every activity persons holding these jobs might perform and every set of circumstances they might conceivably encounter (see Figure

FIGURE 15.3   Formalization: An Extreme Case
As suggested by this cartoon, governments often show a high degree of formalization.
(Source: Reprinted with special permission of NAS, Inc.)

15.3). Such a high level of formalization reduces uncertainty; after all, it clearly delineates authority, responsibility, decision-making procedures, who should report to whom, and almost every other aspect of organizational functioning you can imagine. However, it can lead to a situation in which organizations literally drown in their own documentation or rules, and lose the capacity to respond rapidly and effectively to changing environmental conditions.

The Span of Control: Flat Structures and Tall Ones

A third important aspect of organizational structure is the **span of control.** This refers to the number of persons reporting to a single supervisor. In some cases, this number is fairly large (e.g., twenty or more). Such conditions result in what is termed a *flat organizational structure*—one in which relatively few levels separate top management from persons on the shop or office floor (see Figure 15.4 on page 524). In other instances, the span of control is *narrow.* Here, only a few individuals report to each supervisor. This often results in what is known as a *tall organizational structure,* one in which many levels intervene between the top and bottom of the organization.

In the past it was often recommended that the span of control be kept quite narrow (e.g., no more than four to six subordinates under each supervisor). Now, however, it is recognized that the ideal span for a given organization or unit depends on the tasks it performs and the goals it seeks.[5] For example, the span may be greater when work is routine or repetitive than when it is not, because under these conditions, employees need relatively little direction and assistance from managers. Similarly, it can be greater when employees are highly trained or experienced. Several other variables, too, may play a role. In view of these complexities, it is apparent that there can be no simple, hard-and-fast rule for setting this important aspect of organizational structure.

Centralization versus Decentralization: Who Makes Decisions?

In some organizations, important decisions are made only by top-level managers. In others, decision making (and the authority it implies) is shared quite widely, so that even persons at relatively low levels in the hierarchy can offer input or participate in some manner. Organizations falling into the first category are described as showing a

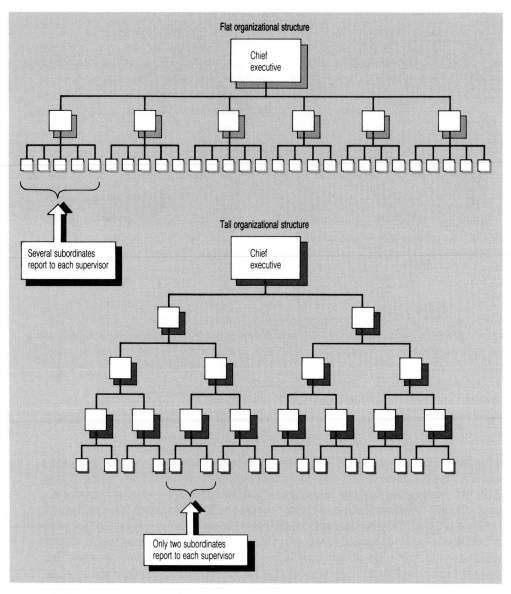

FIGURE 15.4   Flat and Tall Organizational Structures
In a *flat* organizational structure (top illustration), a relatively small number of steps exists between the lowest and highest levels of authority in an organization, and several subordinates report to each supervisor. In a *tall* organizational structure, many steps separate the lowest and highest levels and only a few subordinates report to each supervisor.

high degree of **centralization;** those in the latter are described as demonstrating **decentralization.**

At several points in this book, we have called attention to the benefits of permitting organization members to participate in decisions (e.g., increased motivation, higher job satisfaction, reduced stress).[6] As we noted in chapters 5 and 7, such benefits do not always occur and are by no means automatic. Still, under many circumstances, permitting employees to participate in decisions affecting their jobs can be quite beneficial. Given this fact, it seems reasonable to assume that a decentralized structure is often preferable to a centralized one. Yet, here too, there are complexities to consider.

First, decentralization can sometimes contribute to jurisdictional disputes, since different individuals or groups feel equally responsible for key decisions. Second, it can actually work to *reduce* coordination between various departments or groups, since each becomes accustomed to making its own decisions and operating in an independent fashion. Third, as we noted earlier, participative decision making is often relatively inefficient—it takes a long time for all concerned parties to have their say and express their views. For these and other reasons, decentralization is not always a plus in organization design, and its potential effects must be evaluated on a case-by-case basis.

Complexity: Internal Differentiation

An additional aspect of organizational structure with important effects is **complexity.** This refers to the degree of internal differentiation (*divisionalization*) present within an organization along two key dimensions: *vertical* and *horizontal*. Organizations are vertically complex to the extent that there are many levels in their **chain of command.** Many large corporations (e.g., General Electric) have a long chain of command: many levels separate top management from production-line employees. Other organizations (especially newer or smaller ones), have much shorter chains of command.

Organizations are *horizontally complex* to the degree that they contain many departments or units. As they grow in size and scope, complexity, too, usually increases. This in itself is not necessarily a problem, provided that additional attention is directed to the task of maintaining coordination. When growing complexity is not matched by the development or refinement of various *integrating mechanisms* (mechanisms for enhancing communication and coordination among the many different departments), negative effects can result. Indeed, at extreme levels, decision making, satisfaction, and overall efficiency can all be adversely affected.

Line versus Staff: Production or Support?

As organizations grow in size and scope, they often discover that they require the services of individuals possessing specialized knowledge or skills not directly linked to their principal work flow—not directly related to the products or services they produce. For example, a company that manufactures audio equipment may find that it needs the full-time service of legal experts to advise it on matters relating to patents and increasingly complex contracts with suppliers or customers, and the services of labor relations experts to handle dealings with a newly formed employee union. Such persons occupy **staff positions**—their primary task is offering advice and expertise to top management and so, indirectly, to persons in **line positions**—jobs directly linked to the company's primary business.

Unfortunately, conflict between line and staff personnel is far from rare. Individuals directly concerned with the production of goods or services (line personnel) often feel that they know more about the organization's business and how it should be run than the "experts" occupying staff positions. Yet, top management often accepts the advice of such persons over their own. Conversely, staff personnel may conclude that individuals in line positions have a narrow perspective and lack the training or sophistication needed to see beyond the confines of their own jobs or daily activities. In any case, the line-staff distinction is an important one, and should be carefully considered in efforts to understand an organization's internal structure.

Putting the Basic Dimensions Together: Mechanistic and Organic Structures

Admittedly, we have now covered a lot of ground and described many aspects of organizational structure. Is there any way to combine these so as to simplify the task

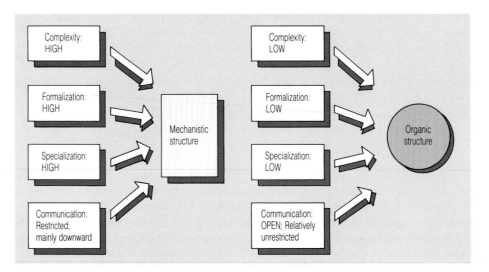

FIGURE 15.5 Mechanistic and Organic Structures

Several basic dimensions of organizational structure combine to form internal structures that are relatively *mechanistic* or relatively *organic* in nature.

of thinking about, and discussing, organizational structure? One scheme for doing so involves the classification of organizational structure into two major categories: **mechanistic** or **organic.**[7]

An organization can be viewed as possessing a mechanistic structure to the extent it is high in formalization, high in complexity, has a restricted flow of information (mostly downward), and permits little participation in decision making by employees below its top levels (i.e., centralization is high). In contrast, an organization can be described as possessing an organic structure to the extent it is low in complexity and formalization, possesses an extensive communication network (with lateral and upward as well as downward communication) and permits a high degree of participation in decision making by employees (see Figure 15.5, above).

Organizations are complex, and perfect types rarely exist. A given company may combine elements of both organic and mechanistic structure. In general, though, organizations tend to demonstrate one pattern or the other, so the mechanistic-organic distinction is often a useful heuristic (rule of thumb) for conceptualizing major differences in internal organizational structure. (Does the structure of an organization shape its business strategy? Or does strategy shape structure? For revealing evidence on this issue, please see the **Research Perspective** section below.)

OB: A RESEARCH PERSPECTIVE

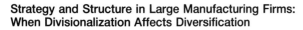

Strategy and Structure in Large Manufacturing Firms: When Divisionalization Affects Diversification

No organization can be all things in all markets. Rather, each must actively choose its domain of action or business (e.g., the specific market for its products), the types of competitive tactics it will adopt (e.g., pricing, marketing, uniqueness), and the opportunities for growth it wishes to pursue.[8] In many cases, such **strategy** is consciously chosen by

top management after a careful assessment of the organization's resources and the environment in which it must operate; indeed, the term *strategy* itself implies an active choice.[9] It is possible, however, that these decisions may be shaped by an organization's internal structure.

As noted by several experts on business

strategy, internal structure may provide a cognitive framework within which strategic decisions are reached.[10,11] For example, in an organization with a high degree of centralization, top management may be reluctant to adopt a strategy requiring the dispersal of decision-making responsibilities to lower levels of the organization. This is simply not the way in which the organization has operated in the past, and managers may be quite uncomfortable with this type of approach. Similarly, an organization which has previously hired few persons for staff positions may find a business strategy that requires a large influx of staff persons relatively unappealing. Thus, such an organization might decide to avoid expanding its operations into areas subject to intense government regulation, since doing so would necessitate hiring staff personnel who specialize in such matters.

Perhaps the clearest potential link between organizational structure and strategy exists with respect to *diversification*—the extent to which an organization chooses to enter different businesses and produce a wide range of products or services. It seems reasonable to suggest that a strong link may exist between adoption of such strategy and the degree of *divisionalization* within an organization. Briefly, to the extent an organization already possesses many divisions, each operating in a relatively independent manner, the move to an explicit strategy emphasizing diversification may prove congenial and relatively easy to implement. After all, in several ways, such a strategy represents an extension of procedures and conditions already existing within the company. Each division would simply expand the scope of its operations to include a wider range of products or services, and perhaps to absorb formerly independent companies as these are acquired.

Does such a link between internal complexity (divisionalization) and diversification actually exist? A recent study by Keats and Hitt suggests that it does.[12] As part of a larger project, these researchers gathered data on the degree of divisionalization existing in more than 250 large *Fortune* 500 companies. Differences along this dimension were assessed by ratings (by the researchers) of each company on a five-point scale ranging from simple functional structure, in which each department or division performed a single function, to decentralized holding company form, in which a small head office had the task of overseeing several largely independent businesses. In addition, Keats and Hitt measured the extent to which each company had adopted a diversification strategy. This was measured by means of a ten-point scale ranging from a single business to a portfolio of many unrelated businesses (and therefore, many unrelated products). Statistical analyses indicated a strong relationship between these factors. Specifically, the greater the companies' degree of internal complexity (i.e., the greater their level of divisionalization), the greater their tendency to adopt diversification. Moreover, additional findings suggested that the causal direction of this relationship was from internal structure to strategy rather than the reverse. In short, as Keats and Hitt note (1988, p. 589), "Structure affected strategy, in contrast to . . . the thesis that structure follows strategy."

These findings, and those of related studies, suggest that the adoption of new strategies may sometimes be constrained by existing organizational structure.[13] If it is difficult for managers to see how a new strategy will fit with existing internal structure, its appeal, as well as the probability of its adoption, may be lowered. Thus, an important first step in developing and then actually implementing a new business strategy may be to carefully examine current internal structure. Before an organization can adopt bold, new strategies and put these into operation, it may first find it necessary to redesign its component parts and the ways in which these fit together. In short, for organizations as well as individuals, internal change must often occur before major external change can follow.

BASIC ORGANIZATION DESIGNS: FUNCTIONAL, PRODUCT, MATRIX

Suppose that as the CEO of a newly-formed company, you faced the task of choosing an internal structure for your organization. How would you proceed? Since internal structure can vary along many dimensions, this job might seem, at first, to be an especially challenging one. To a degree, this is certainly true; indeed, there are probably as many unique organization designs as there are functioning organizations. Despite this fact, the internal structure of most organizations seems to fit, at least roughly, into one of three major categories: **functional, product,** or **matrix** designs. The nature and key characteristics of each of these major types is described below.

Functional Designs: When Tasks Determine Structure

Because it is the type of internal structure adopted by many organizations when they are first established, **functional designs** can be viewed as the most basic type. Within such designs, departments, divisions, and work groups are based on the performance of specific tasks or functions. For example, in a manufacturing concern, separate departments might exist for basic tasks such as sales, maintenance, production, and accounting. Similarly, in an insurance company, the functional departments might include sales, claims investigation and adjustment, underwriting, customer service, and accounting (see Figure 15.6).

As a particular organization grows, develops, and becomes more complex, additional departments are created as the need for them arises. For example, consider a small high-tech firm which initially produces only one type of software. If it is successful, it may expand into several other product lines and begin offering information services as well. As these developments unfold, new departments, each concerned with a specific task or function, may be created. This ability to meet new needs as they arise is one of the key benefits offered by functional designs.

In addition, such designs offer other pluses as well. Since all employees performing the same or similar functions work together and share facilities, they encourage the economies of scale available in such situations. Similarly, functional designs encourage work units and individuals to specialize and to develop a high degree of skill in their respective areas of expertise.

Partly offsetting these advantages, however, are several potential weaknesses. The most important of these stems from the fact that such designs encourage separate units to go their own way and develop their own perspectives. Since all (or at least most) individuals working in a given unit share the same tasks, and often similar training, they tend to confirm each other's views—especially of other parts of the organization. As a result, the "us versus them" phenomenon described in chapters 4 and 13 may intensify, making it increasingly difficult to attain interunit coordination.[14] Second, top

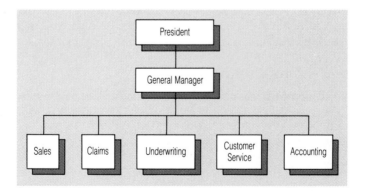

FIGURE 15.6   A Simple Functional Design
In a *functional design,* departments or divisions are based on the tasks performed by each unit.

management, which has the task of integrating various activities, may soon find itself overloaded in a functional design. Specific departments, with their limited, focused views of the organization's activities, can offer little help in this regard. Finally, functional designs encourage organization members to focus on routine tasks within their own units. As a result, the likelihood of innovations is reduced, and the organization as a whole may be relatively slow in responding to environmental challenges or opportunities. In sum, while functional designs are certainly logical in nature and have proven useful in many contexts, they are by no means a perfect solution to the problem of effective organization design.

Product Designs: When Outputs Determine Structure

Successful organizations do not stand still; on the contrary, they continue to grow in both size and scope. They develop new products, seek new customers, and adopt new strategies. As they do, the strain on a functional design may become intense. The production department may find it increasingly difficult to oversee the manufacture of a wide range of items; sales may find the task of promoting seemingly unrelated products unwieldy; and accounting may discover that keeping track of a growing number of local tax and business regulations, which impinge on the company as it expands its operations, is pushing it to its limits. When such strains develop, organizations often shift to a **product design.**

Here, self-contained divisions concerned with specific products or product groups are established. Each of these units contains all the resources and departments necessary for handling these products—everything from obtaining needed supplies and personnel to production, marketing, and delivery. Thus, in a sense, a single organization is divided into several autonomous units, each capable of operating as an entity by itself. Of course, the heads of each of these units still report to top management within the company. Moreover, some functions are generally performed at the organization's central headquarters, rather than in the individual product units (e.g., public relations, overall market research, establishment of strategic policy). On a day-to-day basis, though, each unit operates in a largely independent fashion. (Please see Figure 15.7 on page 530 for a concrete example of a product design.)

At this point, we should note that several variations on this basic theme exist. Self-contained operating units are sometimes established on the basis of specific markets, geographic regions, and even customers, rather than on the basis of different products or services. Thus, a retail chain might establish separate units in different regions, states, or provinces. Similarly, a publisher might establish largely independent divisions to sign, develop, and publish books for the general public and books of a more technical nature. Regardless of the precise reasons for moving to a product design, the basic rationale remains the same: divide the organization's operations in a way that enhances efficiency.

Product designs offer several major advantages. Perhaps the most important of these is increased flexibility and ability to respond to changing external conditions.[15] Since each unit specializes in a particular product line, service, or market, it can be sensitive to shifts in competition, customer needs, and related matters. Second, since each unit is largely self-contained, product designs heighten concern with overall results. Indeed, a degree of competition between an organization's operating units may develop, with each attempting to attain a better record of profits and sales than the other. This can contribute to overall effectiveness. Third, because divisions or units are held to manageable size, coordination with them may be enhanced.

On the other hand, product designs suffer from several drawbacks. The most obvious of these is the loss of economies of scale stemming from the duplication of

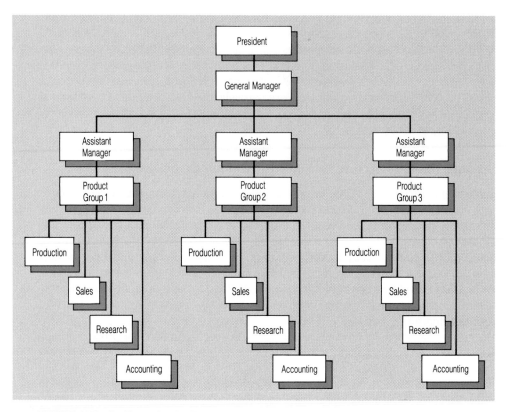

FIGURE 15.7   An Example of a Product Design

In a *product design,* separate units are established to handle different products or product lines. Each of these divisions contains all of the departments necessary for operating as an independent unit.

various departments within operating units. For example, if each unit carries out its own research and development functions, the need for costly equipment, facilities, and personnel may be multiplied. Another problem associated with product designs involves the organization's ability to attract and retain talented employees. Since each department within operating units is necessarily smaller than a single combined one would be, opportunities for advancement and career development may suffer. This, in turn, may pose a serious problem with respect to the long-term retention of talented employees. Finally, problems of coordination across product lines may arise. In fact, in extreme cases, actions taken by one operating division may have adverse effects on the outcomes of one or more others.

A clear example of such problems was provided by Hewlett-Packard, a major U.S. manufacturer of computers and a wide array of test and measurement equipment. During most of its history, Hewlett-Packard adopted a product design: it consisted of scores of small, largely autonomous divisions, each concerned with producing (and selling) certain products. As it grew in size and complexity, the company found itself in an increasingly untenable situation in which sales representatives from different divisions sometimes attempted to sell different lines of equipment, often to be used for the same basic purposes, to the same customers! To deal with such problems, top management at Hewlett-Packard decided to restructure the company into sectors based largely on the markets they served (business customers; scientific and manufacturing customers). In short, Hewlett-Packard switched from a fairly traditional product design to an internal structure driven by market considerations.[16] While it's too soon to determine whether the effects of this reorganization will be as positive as top management hopes, initial results, at least, are promising.

Matrix Designs: A Hybrid Approach

As we have already seen, both functional and product designs offer important advantages. Is there any way of combining these approaches so as to obtain the best of each, while holding associated disadvantages to a minimum? Such a strategy is provided by **matrix designs.**[17] Basically, matrix designs are the result of superimposing a product structure on a functional one. In the organization design that results, a dual system of authority is established. On the one hand, there are managers for various functional areas—individuals with authority over production, engineering, marketing, and so on. On the other hand, there are also *product managers*—ones whose authority extends to all processes connected with a specific product or project. The result is that some persons actually report to two bosses—one in their functional department and one who is in charge of the particular project to which they are currently assigned. (Please see Figure 15.8 for an illustration of a matrix design.) It is important to note, however, that this is the case only for a relatively small number of persons located near or at the top of the organization. Below this level, employees usually have only one supervisor, based either on functional or product considerations.

Perhaps our comments so far can be clarified by noting that within matrix designs, three major roles exist. There is the *top leader*—the person who has authority over

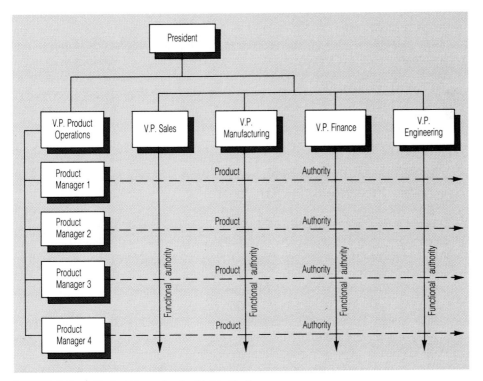

FIGURE 15.8   A Typical Example of a Matrix Design

In a *matrix design*, a product structure is superimposed on a basic functional structure. This results in a dual system of authority in which some managers report to two bosses—a project (product) manager and a functional (departmental) manager.

both lines (the one based on function and the one based on product or project). It is this individual's task to enhance coordination between functional and project managers and to maintain an appropriate balance of power between them. Second, there are the *matrix bosses*—people who head functional departments or specific projects. Since neither of these persons have complete authority over subordinates, they must work together to assure that their efforts mesh rather than conflict. In addition, they must agree on such issues as promotions and raises for specific persons working under their joint authority. Finally, there are *two-boss managers*—people who must report to both product and functional managers, and attempt to balance the demands of each.

Organizations are most likely to adopt matrix designs when they confront certain conditions. These include a complex and uncertain environment (one with frequent changes), and the need for economies of scale in the use of internal resources. Specifically, a matrix approach is often adopted by medium-sized organizations with several product lines, which do not possess sufficient resources to establish fully self-contained operating units. Under such conditions, a matrix design provides a useful compromise. Some companies that have adopted this structure, at least on a trial basis, are TRW Systems Group, Liberty Mutual Insurance, and Citibank.[18]

Key advantages offered by matrix designs have already been suggested by our discussion so far. First, they permit flexible use of an organization's human resources. Individuals within functional departments can be assigned to specific products or projects as the need arises and then return to their regular duties when this task is completed. Second, matrix designs offer medium-sized organizations an efficient means of responding quickly to a changing, unstable environment. Third, such designs often enhance communication among managers; indeed, they literally force matrix bosses to discuss and agree on many matters. Disadvantages of such designs include the frustration and stress faced by two-boss managers in reporting to two different supervisors, the danger that one of the two authority systems (functional or product) will overwhelm the other, and the fact that in order to succeed, it requires consistently high levels of cooperation from the persons involved. As we noted in chapter 13, this is sometimes far easier to imagine than to achieve! In situations where organizations must stretch their financial and human resources to meet challenges from the external environment or take advantage of new opportunities, however, matrix designs can often play a useful role.

ENVIRONMENT: HOW EXTERNAL CONDITIONS SHAPE STRUCTURE, FUNCTION, AND STRATEGY

As we noted earlier, organizations do not exist in social, economic, or political vacuums. On the contrary, they are affected by a host of factors and forces that impinge on them from the larger society in which they operate. Together, such forces are described as the **external environment.** More formally, this term refers to all elements outside the boundary of an organization that have the potential to affect it, or its component parts, in some manner.[19] In principle, virtually any aspect of the external world might exert such effects. For example, the intense heat and drought of the summer of 1988 raised the cost of raw materials for many companies, increased their energy consumption, and even adversely affected the health and motivation of some of their employees. Correspondingly, recent political shifts in China and the USSR have created new opportunities and challenges for many organizations existing in those nations (see Figure 15.9). While such events and trends are certainly dramatic, they are only the tip of the proverbial iceberg—a small, if impressive, sample of the many ways in which the external environment can affect the nature and functioning of organizations.

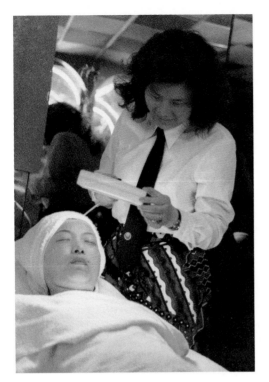

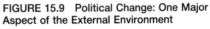

FIGURE 15.9   Political Change: One Major Aspect of the External Environment

Changes in long-standing government policies in several nations (e.g., China, the USSR) have created both opportunities and problems for organizations operating in them. Shown here is the first privately-owned, full-service beauty shop in Shanghai.

In the discussion which follows, we will first identify a number of key *environmental domains*—specific aspects of the external environment that have been found to exert important effects on a wide range of organizations. Next, we will describe several dimensions often useful in classifying external environments and their impact on organizations.[20] Finally, we will examine the impact of these environmental factors and dimensions on organizational structure and performance.

The External Environment: Some Key Domains

At various times and under various conditions, many aspects of the external environment can influence organizations. However, careful study of such effects suggests that nine factors are most important. The first of these is often summarized by the term *industry*. This refers primarily to the level and nature of competition experienced by a given organization. It determines how much an organization's resources must be directed to marketing, the specific competitive tactics it adopts, the size of its profit margins, and many other important outcomes.

A second key environmental factor is *raw materials*—the essential inputs required by an organization for completing its major work. This can range from various commodities, in the case of manufacturing concerns, to entering students in universities. The availability and cost associated with such raw materials can strongly affect the nature, operations, and survival of any organization.

A third important aspect of the external environment is *financial resources*. This factor includes the availability of funds required by normal operations (e.g., procurement, production, maintenance, sales), as well as resources for expansion and growth. It encompasses interest rates, insurance premiums, current conditions in capital markets (e.g., the selling price of the company's stock), and many other issues.

The fourth factor on our list, *human resources,* might, at first, appear to be located within the organization. To an extent, it is; but given that every organization experiences some degree of turnover (both voluntary and involuntary), the supply of appropriate personnel in the labor market is an external factor of major importance.

A fifth factor, *market,* refers primarily to customer demand for the goods and services produced by an organization. Since this can fluctuate greatly in response to many factors other than the quality or price of an organization's output, it is another important aspect of the external environment.

A sixth factor involves the actions and policies of *government.*[21] Safety regulations, minimum wage, tax codes, affirmative action guidelines—these are just a few of the many ways in which government actions impinge on and strongly affect the operations of many organizations. *General economic conditions,* too, are important. If these are favorable, an organization may prosper; if they are unfavorable, it may have difficulty making a profit or even surviving. Another aspect of the external environment that is often of major importance involves the *culture* or society in which an organization operates. Values can shift (e.g., from no concern with protecting the physical environment to major concern with this issue), and these, in turn, can strongly affect an organization's outcomes. Similarly, changes in the ethnic makeup of the work force, shifts in average age, changes in birth rates, and related factors can all have profound long-term effects on organizations in many fields. Finally, organizations are strongly affected by *technology*—tools, techniques, and methods used in their major work flow. Since many of these are imported into an organization from the outside, technology can be viewed as another way in which the external environment influences organizations. (A summary of these nine major environmental domains is provided in Figure 15.10.)

The External Environment: Some Basic Dimensions

In a sense, every organization confronts a unique external environment. Because of differences in products, goals, work procedures, market niche and a host of other factors, no two organizations can ever exist in precisely the same external context. How then, can we hope to establish the existence of general links between environmental conditions on the one hand and organizational structure or function on the other?

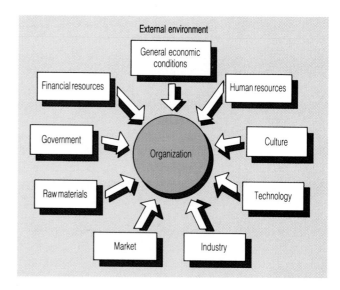

FIGURE 15.10 Key Domains of the External Environment

Organizations are affected by many aspects of the external environment.

One answer lies in the following fact: while specific environments are indeed unique, most, if not all, can be classified according to their position along several underlying dimensions. The most important of these involve variations in what have been termed the **complexity,** and **uncertainty, stability,** and **munificence** of external environments.

Complexity. The complexity dimension involves the heterogeneity of environmental elements that are relevant to, or play a role in, an organization's operations.[22] In a simple environment, few outside elements impinge on the organization; in a complex one, many exert such effects. For example, consider a company that rents umbrellas and lounge chairs on the beach. Few environmental conditions (aside from the weather!) influence its operations. It has no competitors on its particular stretch of beach, high school students provide a steady source of inexpensive labor, and the organization is affected to a small degree, if at all, by such factors as technology, government regulations, or the availability and cost of raw materials.

In contrast, consider an organization that runs day care centers for the children of working families. The external environment it confronts is probably considerably more complex. The company must react to an ever-changing pattern of government standards and regulations, wide swings in the availability of trained personnel, general economic conditions that increase or reduce the number of spouses entering the labor force, shifting societal views about what activities should occur in day care centers, and even changes in the cost of raw materials (e.g., toys, food for lunches, and even cookies!). Clearly, the external environment is considerably more complex for such an organization than it is for the simple seaside business described previously (see Figure 15.11).

Stability. A second key dimension of the external environment is the extent to which it (or key aspects of it) change over time. In a stable environment, few shifts occur, even over substantial periods of time. In an unstable one, major shifts occur frequently and often rapidly. Companies in the petroleum industry have recently faced a very unstable external environment; indeed, they have been rocked to their very foundations by the winds of political change, international conflicts, and the actions of cartels bent on controlling the price of this strategic commodity. In contrast, the environment has

FIGURE 15.11 Environmental Complexity: Extremes on the Dimension
The external environment is relatively simple for a company that sells ice cream by the roadside. However, it is considerably more complex for an organization that builds airplanes.

been more stable (although certainly not static) for manufacturers of plumbing supplies and fixtures. While change has occurred, both with respect to shifting public taste and rising foreign competition, the speed and magnitude of these shifts has been much less pronounced than in other industries.

Uncertainty. A third dimension along which external environments vary, often greatly, involves **uncertainty**.[23] This refers to the inability to predict some aspect of the external environment accurately, and takes three basic forms.[24] First, there is uncertainty with respect to the current or future *state* of the environment—an inability to understand the environment at present or to predict what events or trends may develop in the months or years ahead. For example, such uncertainty might involve an inability to predict the actions of key competitors, future actions by state or national governments, or the actions and policies of labor unions. Second, there is uncertainty with respect to the *impact* of environmental events or changes on the organization. What will be the effect of a political victory by one party? How will a rise in the number of older persons affect the organization's central business? These are the kind of questions reflective of such uncertainty. Third, there is uncertainty with respect to the response options open to the organization, and the consequences that may follow from each. How should a company respond to rising demands from a labor union—by yielding to its requests? By moving its operations to another geographic location? By increasing its degree of automation, and so reducing the size of its labor force? And what results, in turn, will follow from each of these options?

As you can readily see, all three types of uncertainty have important implications for an organization. The specific impact of the three types, however, can differ appreciably. Uncertainty about the state of the environment may lead administrators to seek more information—to spend lots of time attempting to scan and forecast the environment. Uncertainty concerning the potential impact of environmental change may encourage the adoption of diversification strategies; in this way, the organization is prepared for most contingencies. In contrast, uncertainty with respect to appropriate responses to environmental change may lead to tendencies to adopt the strategies of other organizations, or to delay the implementation of new strategies altogether (see Figure 15.12). Whatever its source or form, uncertainty is one environmental dimension most organizations seek to minimize.

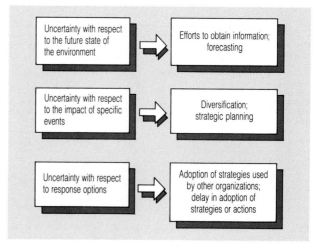

**FIGURE 15.12
Environmental Uncertainty:
Three Basic Types**

According to Milliken, three types of *uncertainty* exist with respect to the external environment. As shown here, each type of uncertainty leads to different reactions on the part of managers. (Source: Based on suggestions by Milliken, 1987; see Note 23.)

Munificence. Finally, it has recently been suggested that external environments can also be classified in terms of their **munificence**—the degree to which they provide the resources an organization needs for further growth.[25] In other words, environments vary in terms of the extent to which they are relatively favorable or unfavorable for a specific organization. As you might expect, there is a strong relationship between environmental munificence and organization size. Organizations that find themselves in a favorable, supportive environment seem to capitalize on their opportunities, and increase in size. Moreover, this relationship exists even if they are relatively inefficient in their operations.

External Environments: Their Major Effects

Earlier, we noted that organizations are strongly affected by the external environments in which they operate. Given the constant interaction between organizations and various environmental domains, this is hardly surprising. Perhaps somewhat more unexpected is the systematic nature of these effects. A considerable body of evidence suggests that the internal structure of organizations is shaped, at least to a degree, by environmental factors.[26] We will now review some of the research illustrating this important point.

The environment and structural complexity. The modern world, it is widely agreed, grows more complex with each passing year. To the extent this is true, the external environment surrounding many organizations, too, tends to increase in complexity. How do organizations respond to such conditions? The answer seems to be: with growing internal complexity of their own. As a growing number of environmental elements impinge on an organization, it tends to add departments, new job titles, and levels within its authority hierarchy.[27] The basic reason for this is straightforward: these new units or positions are needed to deal with an ever-increasing array of external factors. So, in sum, growing external complexity is reflected, in many organizations, in corresponding internal adjustments.

Environmental uncertainty and boundary-spanning activities. All organizations must make contact with important groups beyond their boundaries. Relationships with suppliers, customers, banks, government regulatory agencies, and many other entities are essential to the performance of their major work and functions. In addition, in large organizations, different units or divisions may have sharply different perspectives or even cultures. Maintaining effective relationships with groups outside the organization, and between groups within it, is an important task. For this reason, many organizations charge specific individuals or units with this responsibility. They act as *boundary spanners,* and perform several key activities. First, they obtain and process information about environmental conditions. Second, they represent the organization in its dealings with other persons and entities. Third, they facilitate communication and coordination between different parts of the organization, especially ones with different functions and contrasting outlooks.

While all organizations show some degree of boundary spanning, it appears that the resources invested in such activities increase with environmental uncertainty.[28] As the external environment becomes less stable and more complex, organizations assign more and more employees to these tasks. For example, as government regulations become increasingly complex, a company may increase the size of its legal department or hire lobbyists to present its views to legislators. Similarly, as market conditions become more competitive, an organization may add staff to its marketing department or perhaps establish new units to deal directly with the task of forecasting future market trends.

That increased attention to boundary-spanning activities is often worth the effort is suggested by the findings of a study by Dollinger.[29] He examined the relationship between boundary-spanning activities by the owners of eighty-two small businesses and the success of their organizations. Boundary spanning was assessed by asking participants to record the number of hours per week during which they had contact with people outside their company (e.g., customers, suppliers, potential new employees, bankers, union officials). Financial success was measured through data on current sales and growth in net earnings. Results indicated that boundary-spanning activity was positively related to financial performance. The greater the proportion of time spent by these entrepreneurs in contact with people outside their organizations, the more successful their businesses tended to be.

The external environment and management style: Organic and mechanistic structures revisited. Another way in which the external environment influences organizations is illustrated by a famous investigation carried out nearly three decades ago by Burns and Stalker.[30]

These researchers examined the organizational structure of twenty industrial firms in England. Included in their sample, and of special interest, were a rayon manufacturer, an engineering company, and a newly formed electronics development firm. The external environment confronted by each of these organizations differed sharply. While environmental stability was high for the rayon manufacturer, it was lower for the engineering firm, and lowest of all for the electronics company. Burns and Stalker predicted that these differences in environmental stability would be reflected in the structure of the organizations, and results offered support for this prediction. The rayon company showed a relatively formal structure involving a high degree of specialization and centralization, a strict hierarchy of authority, and vertical (mostly downward) patterns of communication. In contrast, the engineering company demonstrated a more flexible structure. Tasks were not as clearly defined, and less emphasis was placed on the chain of command.

Finally, the electronics firm showed the least formal structure of all. Decision making was more participative in nature and there was less specialization. Communication, too, was more open. Further, study of additional companies confirmed these observations, leading Burns and Stalker to a general conclusion: many organizations tend to adopt either a relatively *organic* or a relatively *mechanistic* structure (or style of management). Moreover, which of these contrasting approaches is more effective depends on the nature of the external environment. When conditions are relatively stable, a mechanistic approach may prove desirable. However, when they show rapid change, an organic approach may be more effective. In short, neither is necessarily better than the other; their relative success is contingent on key aspects of the external environment.

Environment, structure, and performance: The mediating role of strategy. So far, we have seen that the external environment shapes certain aspects of an organization's internal structure, some of its major functions (e.g., boundary spanning), and even the overall style of management it adopts. Given the existence of such diverse and far-reaching effects, it seems only reasonable to raise the following question: does the external environment, through these effects, also influence an organization's overall level of performance? While this question itself seems straightforward, the answer emerging from recent research is quite complex.[31] In fact, to accurately address the relationship between the external environment, internal structure, and performance, it seems we must also consider the crucial role of **strategy.** Why should this be the case? Primarily, it appears, for the following reasons.

First, as noted earlier (page 532), the environment often exerts strong effects on an organization's strategy. Uncertain, rapidly changing environments call for specific types of strategy (e.g., innovation, diversification). Thus, the only way in which a software producer can hope to prosper and grow is through the development of an unceasing flow of new and innovative products. In contrast, stable, predictable environments call for other strategies, such as efforts to attain price leadership. For example, producers of chocolate bars, such as Hershey's or Nestle, cannot hope to capture much larger shares of the existing market through the development of creative new products. Thus, they tend to focus on differentiating their products and on building brand loyalty.

Second, different strategies may call, in turn, for different types of internal structures.[32] For example, if a company decides to seek success through innovation and unique products, it will, of necessity, hire many technical experts and give them considerable latitude to manage their own work and make many decisions. Then, structural techniques designed to increase communication between these otherwise isolated groups of experts, and between them and top management, may be needed.

Third, the relationship between internal structure and strategy is probably reciprocal. Strategy shapes structure, we have just noted, but structure, in turn, shapes strategy (recall our earlier discussion, page 526). For example, once many technical experts have been hired, they may push for even less centralization or formalization within the organization; after all, scientists, engineers, and other professionals generally dislike rules and prefer to take direct responsibility for their own work.

In view of these points, the following conclusion about the relationship between environment, structure, strategy, and performance seems warranted: in general, successful organizations are ones in which there is a high degree of *congruence* (match) between these various elements. In short, effective performance by an organization occurs when its business strategies are appropriate to current environmental conditions, and when its internal structure facilitates implementation of these strategies (see Figure 15.13).

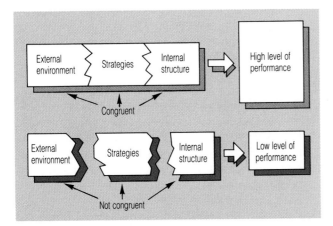

FIGURE 15.13 Strategy, Structure, the Environment, and Performance
Growing evidence suggests that successful organizations (ones with a high level of performance) adopt strategies appropriate to existing environmental conditions, and an internal structure that enhances implementation of such strategies. In contrast, unsuccessful organizations fail to show such *congruence* between strategy, the environment, and internal structure. (Source: Based on findings reported by Miller, et al. 1988; see Note 32.)

Evidence for this view is provided by a series of highly sophisticated investigations conducted by Miller and his colleagues.[33] For example, in one of these studies, Miller had the top management of eighty-nine companies complete a questionnaire designed to measure: (1) key aspects of the external environments in which their firms operated (e.g., its degree of stability, unpredictability), (2) their companies' internal structure (e.g., degree of formalization, specialization, integration), and (3) their business strategies (e.g., marketing or innovative differentiation, cost leadership). In addition, several measures of each company's actual business performance were also gathered (e.g., five year return on investment and growth in net income). On the basis of these latter measures, the companies were divided into two groups—ones that were successful and ones that were relatively unsuccessful.

Analysis of all these data offered support for the suggestions noted above. Specifically, while there were no simple, direct relationships between specific types of structure, strategies, or types of environments, successful firms appeared to be ones in which internal structure matched business strategy, and in which such strategy, in turn, reflected existing environmental conditions. In sum, a company was most successful when, in a sense, these three important components meshed—when what a company was trying to accomplish made sense in the context of its external environment, and its internal structure fit closely into this overall picture. (As the world moves toward a single, unified economy, all organizations, wherever they are located, are being exposed to similar environmental conditions. Are they therefore converging toward a uniform internal structure? For some thoughts on this intriguing issue, please see the **International Perspective** section below.)

OB: AN INTERNATIONAL PERSPECTIVE

The Present and Future Form of Organizations: Convergence or Divergence?

Throughout this discussion, we have noted that various features of the external environment exert powerful effects on the structure and function of organizations. Such conditions certainly vary from region to region and from nation to nation. Yet, as we approach a new century, it is also apparent that many features of the environment are becoming increasingly worldwide in scope. Commodities, products, technology, and information flow so readily between the continents that their availability and cost are becoming relatively uniform all over the globe. Similarly, the internationalization of trade, and of organizations, has reached unprecedented levels—ones which tend to blur distinctions based on national boundaries. Given such trends, it seems reasonable to suggest that all organizations, wherever they exist, are probably moving toward a single, uniform model. In short, it might be predicted that all will soon adopt similar forms of internal structure and similar methods of doing business. Is this actually the case? Surprisingly, existing evidence suggests that it is not.

Perhaps the clearest indication that all organizations are *not* moving toward *convergence* in

structure and function is provided by studies of highly successful Japanese companies.[34] At one time, it was suggested that the differences between these companies and those in other countries (e.g., Western Europe, the United States), were a vestigial remnant of irrelevant cultural factors, and would soon fade away. However, this has not proven to be the case. Japanese firms operating in Japan continue to differ in important ways from their competitors in other nations. For example, they maintain different relationships with key stakeholders (government bodies, financial institutions), working more closely and cooperatively with them than is true in other nations. Second, they continue to demonstrate more centralized power structures, and have *not* moved toward the decentralization observed in U.S. or European companies.

Third, they retain a distinctive manufacturing philosophy, which emphasizes quality to a much greater degree than is true elsewhere. And finally, they have maintained distinct personnel practices, such as an emphasis on decision making through consensus, and delaying initial evaluation of new employees' work until several years after they join the company. In sum, Japanese companies have not converged toward the model adopted by successful Western companies; rather, they have continued to go their own way in several respects.

What accounts for this uniqueness among Japanese companies? No clear-cut answer as yet exists, but several factors seem to contribute. First, even now, Japan remains a much more culturally homogeneous nation than most others. This, in turn, makes shared Japanese culture a more powerful force for uniformity than in other nations. Second, the managerial and political elites in Japan seem to have selected from foreign competitors those business practices which are simultaneously conducive to corporate goals and strategies (e.g., long-term rather than short-term growth) *and* consistent with basic cultural values. The result: cherished cultural values serve to legitimize and reinforce preferred business practices rather than work against them.

In sum, it appears that organizations throughout the world are *not* converging toward a single, uniform model. On the contrary, cultural differences, coupled with conscious choices by top management, seem to be maintaining existing contrasts between organizations located in various nations. And judging from the success of many Japanese companies, at least, these differences may well contribute to overall effectiveness.

Turning the Tables: Techniques for Changing the Environment

One of the main points we have made so far in this chapter can be simply stated: organizations are often shaped by the external environment. They respond to shifting conditions in the markets and societies around them through changes in their internal structure and in their strategies. But, as we're sure you realize, organizations do more than simply react to the environment. In many cases, they attempt to change it—to render it more favorable through active means. Such change can be accomplished in several different ways.

Political action. One of the most important of these is some form of political action. This can involve contributions to the campaigns of candidates viewed as friendly to an organization's goals, contributions to *political action committees* (PACs), which then use these funds to support the election campaigns of specific candidates or promote various views, or hiring professional lobbyists, whose full-time job is influencing the views of lawmakers in certain directions. Whatever the specific tactics followed, the major goals remain the same: producing shifts in government policies that are favorable to the interests of the organizations involved. These can range from establishing trade barriers designed to blunt the assault of foreign competition, to the removal of various regulations and restrictions, and even changes in current tax codes. That efforts along these lines often pay—and pay quite handsomely—is readily apparent. Japanese consumers pay far more for many items than their American counterparts. This difference is due largely to tariffs and other barriers established by the Japanese government to protect native producers of such items.

Contracts and mergers. Another strategy organizations often employ to produce a more favorable external environment is somehow attaining control over important (but uncertain) environmental domains. This can be accomplished through negotiated contracts, which secure long-term access to needed raw materials, markets or financial resources. For example, a furniture manufacturer, concerned about the availability of certain types of wood required for its products, might sign a long-term agreement with a forestry products company to guarantee supplies of this important raw material.

A second strategy for controlling important aspects of the external environment is mergers or acquisitions. Through this tactic, successful organizations can eliminate key competitors, assure supplies of needed inputs, and even develop outlets for their products.

Public relations: Building the right image. A third strategy for improving the external environment involves efforts to enhance an organization's public image. Examples of this approach are provided by safe driving campaigns sponsored by the liquor industry and energy conservation tips from public utilities. Through these and many other means, specific organizations attempt to generate good will among consumers or the general public. Presumably, such positive attitudes translate into increased business and, ultimately, favorable legislation.

In sum, organizations often take an active approach to the environment. Rather than merely adapting to external conditions, they seek to change them—to assure that they operate in an environment that is relatively favorable to their interests and goals. To the extent such tactics are effective, the organizations that adopt them may well contribute to their own success.

TECHNOLOGY: HOW TOOLS SHAPE STRUCTURE

Organizations differ tremendously with respect to **technology**—the means by which they transform inputs into outputs.[35] These can vary from the simplest of tools used by single individuals, to huge machines and complex, automated equipment. Clearly, the technology employed by a given organization is closely linked to the work it performs and the major tasks it seeks to accomplish. But growing evidence indicates that this relationship, too, is something of a two-way street. Organizations not only choose the technology they will employ; they are also affected by such tools once they are selected. In short, just as the design of a specific building reflects the activities that take place within it, the structure of many organizations, too, tends to mirror the technologies they employ. In the discussion that follows we will describe several major studies that point to this conclusion. As you will soon see, these investigations classify technology in contrasting ways and focus on a wide range of issues. Thus, their findings are often difficult to compare in a simple or direct manner. Generally, though, all point to the same basic conclusion: technology plays an important role in shaping both the design and performance of many organizations.

Technology and Structure in Manufacturing Companies: The Woodward Studies . . . and Beyond

Perhaps the best-known study on the effect of technology is one conducted in England during the 1950s by Woodward.[36] At that time, it was widely assumed that the performance of virtually any organization could be maximized by following certain *universal principles of management*—by adopting a specific span of control, a particular degree of centralization, and so on. To determine if these principles are indeed universal, Woodward and her associates collected information about one hundred manufacturing firms. Data on many *structural characteristics* in these companies (e.g., span of control, management style, chain of command) as well as information on their success (e.g., profitability, market share) were gathered. Initially, Woodward expected that organizations classified as highly successful would share similar structural characteristics, while those classified as relatively unsuccessful would share other characteristics. Surprisingly, this was not the case. Instead, various aspects of organization structure appeared to be just as common in successful and unsuccessful companies. Thus, there was little if any support for the accuracy of universal principles of management.

At this point, Woodward and her colleagues considered the possibility that technology might serve as a *mediating factor,* somehow determining the impact of various aspects of structure on performance. To see if this was indeed the case, they developed a system for classifying the firms in their study in terms of the complexity of the technology they employed. Three major categories were established. In the first, labeled **small-batch production,** custom work was the norm. Capital equipment (machinery) was not highly mechanized, and the companies involved typically produced small batches of products to meet specific orders from customers. Employees were either skilled or unskilled, depending on the tasks they performed. Firms included in this category made such items as specialized construction equipment or custom-ordered electronic items. Other examples include dressmaking and printing.

Companies in the second category, known as **large-batch** or **mass production,** used basic assembly-line procedures. These organizations typically engaged in long production runs of standardized parts or products. Their output then went into inventory from which orders were filled on a continuous basis. Employees were mainly unskilled or semi-skilled, with a sprinkling of research and engineering personnel. The third category, known as **continuous-process production,** was the most technologically complex. Here, there was no start and no stop to production, which was automated and fully integrated. Employees were skilled workers or engineers. Among the organizations employing such advanced technology were oil refining and chemical companies.

When companies using these various types of technology were compared, important differences were noted. First, as expected, they demonstrated contrasting internal structures. For example, the span of control (of first-level supervisors), formalization, and centralization were higher in companies employing mass production than in ones using small-batch or continuous-process technologies. Similarly, chains of command were longest in organizations using continuous-process production, and shortest in those using small-batch methods. Complexity, too, varied with technology; companies using continuous-process production were highest on this dimension, while those using small-batch procedures were lowest. In short, it appeared that the type of technology employed in production was in fact an important variable in shaping organization structure. As Woodward herself put it: "Different technologies imposed different kinds of demands on individuals and organizations, and those demands had to be met through an appropriate structure."[37]

Perhaps even more important than these findings was the fact that the characteristics distinguishing highly successful from unsuccessful companies also varied with technology. At the low and high ends of the technology dimension described above, an *organic* management approach seemed best; companies showing this strategy were more successful than those demonstrating a *mechanistic* approach. In contrast, in the middle of the technology dimension (mass production), the opposite was true. Here, companies adopting a mechanistic approach tended to be more effective. Another finding was that successful firms tended to have structures suited to their level of technology. Specifically, those with above average performance showed structural characteristics similar to most other firms using the same type of production methods; in contrast, those with below average records tended to depart from the median structure shown by companies in the same technology category. In sum, the results of Woodward's study indicated that there are important links between technology and performance.

Additional support for these conclusions was later obtained in several other studies. For example, in a project involving fifty-five U.S. firms, Zwerman found that organizations employing small-batch or continuous-process technology tended to adopt an organic management approach.[38] Those employing mass production generally showed a mechanistic approach. We should note, however, that other findings seem to suggest that *size* may sometimes be a more important determinant of both internal structure and performance than technology.[39] Such possibilities aside, Woodward's findings were quite important in the following respect: they called attention to the fact that there is no single best type of organization structure. On the contrary, the characteristics that will prove most effective vary with (are *contingent on*) technology and several other factors. This *contingency approach* to organization design has guided most subsequent research on this topic and remains influential today. In this regard, certainly, the value of Woodward's research can hardly be overstated.

Technical batch production: An extension of Woodward's findings. When Woodward conducted her research, in the early and mid 1960s, most organizations fell under one of the three categories she described (small-batch, mass production, continuous-process). More recently, though, another type seems to have emerged. Organizations in this category produce customized, high-performance products in relatively small runs. However, because these products are technologically advanced and complex, they are produced by highly automated, computer-controlled equipment. Moreover, the persons involved in their manufacture must often possess a high level of professional or technical knowledge. In short, such companies share some characteristics with the traditional small-batch firms studied by Woodward, but share others with the technologically advanced continuous-process firms at the other end of her continuum. What type of internal structure do such *technical batch* organizations demonstrate? Evidence on this issue has been provided by Hull and Collins.[40]

These researchers examined the internal structure of 110 separate companies operating in the United States. On the basis of careful examination of their methods of production, Hull and Collins divided these organizations into four categories—traditional batch, technical batch, mass production, and process production. Then they compared the companies' internal structure along several key dimensions (e.g., supervisory span of control, occupational specialization, decentralization, formalization). As shown in Figure 15.14, the four types differed in various ways. As predicted, organizations classified as traditional batch or technical batch in their methods of production showed contrasting structure in several respects. For example, the traditional batch companies possessed a larger supervisory span of control. In contrast, the technical batch companies showed a greater degree of occupational specialization and more decentralization. Further, and perhaps most important, the technical batch companies showed a much higher level of innovative activity (e.g., a higher percentage of employees involved in research and development activities.)

In sum, expanding Woodward's original categories to reflect recent developments in methods of production yielded additional evidence for the powerful impact of technology on internal structure. Additional research along similar lines may help us to sharpen our knowledge of this important relationship still further.

Work-flow Integration: The Aston Studies

As the heading of the preceding section suggests, Woodward's project, and several subsequent investigations, focused primarily on the links between technology and structure in manufacturing companies. Thus, as thorough as this work was, it left a basic issue unresolved: would similar findings be observed in other types of companies as well? Evidence on this question was provided by another team of British researchers affiliated with the University of Aston.[41] After studying a wide range of both manufacturing and service organizations (e.g., savings banks, insurance companies, department stores), these researchers concluded that technology can be described in terms of three basic characteristics: *automation of equipment*—the extent to which work activities are performed by machines, *work-flow rigidity*—the extent to which the sequence of work activities is inflexible, and *specificity of evaluation*—the degree to which work activities can be assessed by specific, quantitative means. Since these three factors appeared to be highly associated, they were combined into a single scale labeled

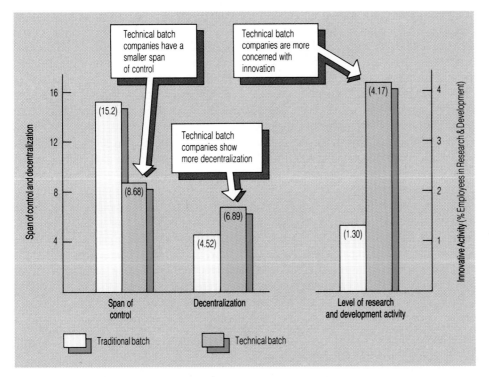

FIGURE 15.14   Technology and Internal Structure: Some Recent Findings
Organizations employing technical batch technology differ in several respects from ones
employing traditional batch technology. (Source: Based on data from Hull & Collins, 1987;
see Note 40.)

work-flow integration. The higher an organization's score on this scale, the more
likely it was to employ automation, rigid task sequences, and quantitative measurement
of its operations. The work-flow integration scores obtained by various companies are
shown in Table 15.1. As you can see from this table, manufacturing firms generally
score higher than those whose primary output is service.

When work-flow integration was related to structural characteristics in the orga-

TABLE 15.1   Work-Flow Integration in Different Organizations
Manufacturing firms generally score higher on work-flow integration than
service organizations (e.g., banks, stores).

Organization	Classification (Manufacturing or Service)	Work-Flow Integration Score
Vehicle manufacturer	Manufacturing	17
Metal-goods manufacturer	Manufacturing	14
Tire manufacturer	Manufacturing	12
Printer	Service	11
Local water department	Service	10
Insurance company	Service	7
Savings bank	Service	4
Department stores	Service	2
Chain of retail stores	Service	1

(Source: Based on data from Hickson, Pugh, and Pheysey, 1969; see Note 41.)

nizations studied, no strong or general links were uncovered. Thus, at first glance findings seemed contradictory to those reported by Woodward. Closer analysis of the data obtained, however, revealed that technological complexity *was* related to structural features in at least some ways. For example, as work-flow integration increased, so did specialization, standardization, and decentralization of authority. The magnitude of these findings was small, and they seemed to involve mainly those aspects of structure closely connected to actual work flow. Moreover, *size* exerted stronger effects on several aspects of structure than technology.

These findings, plus those obtained in later studies, point to two conclusions. First, while technology does indeed seem to affect the internal structure of organizations, it is only one of several influences. As a result, the so-called *technological imperative*—the view that technology always has a compelling influence on organizational structure—clearly overstates the case. Indeed, as noted by Singh, close examination of recent evidence for this view suggests that it is far from strong or consistent.[42] Second, technology probably exerts stronger effects on structure in small organizations, where such characteristics impinge directly on work flow, than in large ones, where structure is complex and often far removed from actual production. In any case, taken as a whole, the findings of the Aston studies can be interpreted as indicating that the impact of technology on organization structure is not restricted to manufacturing concerns. Under certain conditions, it can be observed in other types of companies as well.

Technology and Interdependence

Another aspect of technology with important implications for organization structure is **interdependence.** This refers to the extent to which individuals, departments, or units within a given organization depend on each other in accomplishing their tasks. Under conditions of low interdependence, each person, unit, or group can carry out its functions in the absence of assistance or input from others. Under high interdependence, in contrast, such coordination is essential. A framework proposed by Thompson helps clarify the various types of interdependence possible in organizations, and also the implications of this factor for effective structural design.[43]

The lowest level within this framework is known as **pooled interdependence.** Under such conditions, departments or units are part of an organization, but work does not flow between them. Rather, each carries out its tasks independently. One example of pooled interdependence is provided by the branches of a clothing retailer with stores in many large shopping malls. Each contributes to the total earnings of the parent company, but there is little if any contact or coordination between them.

The next higher level suggested by Thompson is **sequential interdependence.** Here, the output of one department or subunit becomes the input for another. For example, the marketing department of a food company cannot proceed with promotional campaigns until it receives information about new products from the product development unit. Similarly, in a company that manufactures electronic toys, final assemblers cannot perform their jobs unless they receive a steady supply of component parts from other work units or outside suppliers. Note that in sequential interdependence, information, products, and components flow in one direction. Thus, units further along the chain of production are dependent on ones that precede them, but the reverse is not true.

The highest level in Thompson's model is known as **reciprocal interdependence.** Here, the output of each department or unit serves as the input for other departments or units in a reciprocal fashion. Thus, the output of Department A provides input for Department B, while the output of Department B serves as the input for Department

A. An example of such reciprocal interdependence is provided by the operations of the marketing and production departments of many companies. Marketing, through appropriate surveys, may develop a profile of new products or product innovations attractive to potential customers. This serves as input for Production, which considers the feasibility of actually making such products and suggests modifications. The appeal of these modifications is then assessed by Marketing and the results obtained serve as the basis for further planning by Production. This process may repeat until a plan for product innovations acceptable to both units is devised (see Figure 15.15).

These three forms of interdependence require varying levels of coordination between the units involved. The need for coordination is quite low under conditions of pooled interdependence, since each of the departments involved is relatively independent. Rules and standard operating procedures usually suffice. In contrast, sequential interdependence requires substantially greater coordination. Here, formal meetings and vertical communication are often needed. Finally, reciprocal interdependence calls for concerted efforts at coordination, including many meetings and a high level of horizontal communication.[44]

The level of interdependence existing between various units within an organization also has important implications for internal structure. Special attention should be directed in organization design to departments or units that are reciprocally interdependent. These should be grouped together so that they can engage in continuous, mutual adjustment (e.g., they should be close to each other physically and should fall under the authority of the same person). Further, specific mechanisms for assuring a high degree of coordination between them (e.g., daily meetings, the creation of special liaison positions) should be developed. While top priority in devising internal structure should be devoted to reciprocal interdependence, efforts to establish effective communication between units that are sequentially interdependent is important, too. These should have ready access to one another so that work flow between them can proceed in a smooth and orderly manner.

In sum, the kind of work activities performed within an organization, and the specific technologies it employs, often determine the level of interdependence between its various units. Such interdependence, in turn, should be taken into careful account when planning internal structure.

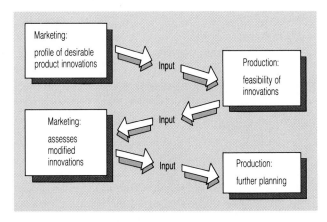

FIGURE 15.15   Reciprocal Interdependence: An Example

Under conditions of *reciprocal interdependence,* the output of two or more departments serves as the input for each other in a reciprocal fashion. (Source: Based on suggestions by Thompson, 1967; see Note 43.)

Summary and Review

Basic Dimensions of Organizational Structure. The **internal structure** of organizations varies along many dimensions. Among the most important of these are **specialization, formalization, span of control,** degree of **centralization,** and overall **complexity.** Together, several of these dimensions determine whether an organization's internal structure can be described as relatively **organic** or relatively **mechanistic** in nature.

Basic Organization Designs. In **functional designs,** departments, divisions, and work groups are based on the tasks they perform (e.g., marketing, production, maintenance). In **product designs,** self-contained internal divisions are responsible for specific products or product lines. **Matrix designs** result when a product design structure is superimposed on a functional design. One key aspect of such designs is that within them, some individuals (*two-boss managers*) report to two supervisors. All three types of design offer advantages, and all suffer from certain drawbacks.

Impact of the External Environment. The **external environment** refers to all factors or forces beyond an organization's boundary that affect it or its component parts. Among the most important *environmental domains* are the industry in which an organization operates, raw materials, financial resources, human resources, market factors, general economic conditions, technology, and government policy or legislation.

External environments vary with respect to their **complexity, uncertainty, stability,** and **munificence.** They affect the structural complexity of organizations and the prevalence of boundary-spanning activities within them. In addition, external environments shape general management approach and, through their impact on **strategy,** overall organizational performance.

Organizations do not simply respond to the external environment. In addition, they often take steps to affect it. This can involve political action, the negotiation of long-term contracts, mergers, and public relations activities.

Technology. The **technology** employed by an organization often affects its internal structure. Companies employing **small-batch, large-batch (mass production),** and **continuous-process** technologies often differ with respect to their internal structure. In recent years, companies employing small-batch production coupled with a high level technology have emerged. The internal characteristics of such companies are different from those of traditional small-batch organizations, which typically employ simpler means of production.

Organizations vary with respect to the level of **interdependence** between departments or other work units. The higher such interdependence, the greater the need for structural components that enhance coordination.

Key Terms

centralization: The extent to which authority and decision making are reserved for individuals high in an organization's hierarchy.

chain of command: The division of authority in an organization; also the number of steps between highest and lowest levels of authority in an organization.

complexity: A composite index of the number of separate job titles and departments within an organization, plus the number of levels separating its highest- and lowest-ranking members.

continuous-process production: A highly automated form of production which is continuous in nature and highly integrated in terms of component steps and processes.

decentralization: The extent to which authority and decision making are spread throughout all levels of an organization rather than being reserved for top management.

external environment: All elements outside the boundary of an organization that have the potential to affect it in some manner.

formalization: The extent to which an organization possesses, and operates in accordance with, written documentation.

functional design: A basic type of *organization design,* based on activities or functions.

interdependence: The extent to which units or departments within an organization depend on each other to accomplish tasks.

internal structure: The manner in which an organization divides work, authority, responsibility, and decision making among various groups or individuals.

large-batch (mass) production: Technology based on long production runs of standardized parts or products.

line positions: Positions in an organization directly concerned with its major work flow.

macro perspective: An approach which emphasizes the impact of social systems on organizations, and organizations on groups and individuals.

matrix designs: A form of *organization design,* in which a product or project structure is superimposed on a functional design.

mechanistic structure: An internal organizational structure characterized by high formalization, specialization, and complexity, together with a restricted communication flow (primarily downward).

micro perspective: An approach which emphasizes the impact of individuals and groups on organizations and organizational processes.

munificence (environmental): The extent to which the external environment offers an organization opportunities for growth, or for achieving its major goals.

organic structure: An internal organizational structure characterized by low formalization, specialization, and complexity, together with a relatively open communication flow.

pooled interdependence: A relatively low level of interdependence in which units within an organization operate in a largely independent manner.

product designs: A basic form of *organization design* based on products or lines of products.

reciprocal interdependence: A high level of interdependence in which the output of each unit within an organization serves as the input for other units, and vice versa.

sequential interdependence: An intermediate level of interdependence in which the output of one unit serves as input for another.

small-batch production: A technology in which products are custom-produced in response to specific customer orders.

span of control: The number of subordinates in an organization who are supervised by managers.

specialization: The extent to which tasks performed by an organization are subdivided and assigned to different units or individuals.

stability (environmental): The extent to which key aspects of the external environment in which an organization operates change over time.

staff positions: Positions in an organization not directly concerned with its major work flow.

strategy: Plans adopted by an organization to facilitate the attainment of its major goals.

technology: The knowledge, tools, and procedures used by an organization to perform its major work.

uncertainty (environmental): The extent to which the impact of the external environment on an organization cannot be readily or accurately predicted.

work-flow integration: A measure of technology that takes account of the degree of automation, work-flow rigidity, and specificity of evaluation within an organization.

QUESTIONS FOR DISCUSSION

1. Under what conditions are organizations with a mechanistic internal structure likely to be more successful than ones with an organic internal structure? Under what conditions will the opposite be true?

2. As organizations grow in size, they often increase in complexity. Is this necessarily a bad thing? How can the potentially adverse effects of increased complexity be reduced?

3. From the point of view of individual employees, what are some of the advantages of a matrix design? What are some of the disadvantages?

4. "An organization's strategic plans should reflect projected shifts in its operating environment." Do you agree or disagree with this statement? Why?

5. What steps can organizations take to change their external environments so as to make them more favorable?

6. At one point, it was widely believed that technology is the single most important determinant of an organization's internal structure. Is this true? What evidence either supports or tends to refute this suggestion?

7. As international trade increases and large organizations become more international in scope, it might be assumed that they will all become increasingly similar in internal structure, regardless of their national origins. Is this actually occurring? If not, why?

NOTES

1. McKenna, D. G., & Fry, L. (in press). Organization design. In M. D. Dunnette (Ed.), *Handbook of industrial/organizational psychology* (2nd ed.). Palo Alto, CA: Consulting Psychologists Press.

2. Porter, M. (1980). *Competitive strategy.* New York: Free Press.

3. Miller, D. (1987). The structural and environmental correlates of business strategy. *Strategic Management Journal, 8,* 55–76.

4. Taylor, F. W. (1911). *The principles of scientific management.* New York: Harper & Brothers.

5. Robbins, S. P. (1987). *Organization theory: Structure, design, and applications* (2nd ed.). Englewood Cliffs, NJ: Prentice-Hall.

6. Locke, E. A. & Schweiger, D. M. (1979). Participation in decision making: One more look. *Research in Organizational Behavior, 1,* 265–339.

7. See Note 5.

8. Rumelt, R. P. (1974). *Strategy, structure, and economic performance.* Cambridge, MA: Harvard Graduate School of Business Administration.

9. Miller, D., & Friesen, P. H. (1977). Strategy making in context: Ten empirical archetypes. *Journal of Management Studies, 14,* 259–280.

10. Pitts, R. (1980). The strategy-structure relationship: An exploration into causality. Paper presented at the annual meetings of the Academy of Management, Detroit.

11. Miller, D., & Droge, C. (1986). Psychological and traditional determinants of structure. *Administrative Science Quarterly, 31,* 539–560.

12. Keats, B. W., & Hitt, M. A. (1988). A causal model of linkages among environmental dimensions, macro organizational characteristics, and performance. *Academy of Management Journal, 31,* 570–598.

13. Daft, R. L. (1986). *Organizational theory and design* (2nd ed.). St. Paul, MN: West.

14. See Note 13.

15. Davis, R., & Lawrence, P. R. (1977). *Matrix.* Reading, MA: Addison-Wesley.

16. Uttal, B., (1985, June 29). Mettle test time for John Young. *Fortune,* pp. 242–244, 248.

17. See Note 13.

18. Wall, W. C., Jr. (1984, February). Integrated management in matrix organization. *IEEE Transactions on Engineering Management,* EM31a, pp. 30–36.

19. Dess, G. G., & Beard, D. W. (1984). Dimensions of organizational task environments. *Administrative Science Quarterly, 29,* 52–73.

20. Ungson, G. R., James, C., & Spicer, B. H. (1985). The effects of regulatory agencies on organizations in wood products and high technology electronics industries. *Academy of Management Journal, 28,* 426–445.

21. See Note 20.

22. Thompson, J. D. (1967). *Organizations in action.* New York: McGraw-Hill.

23. Milliken, F. J. (1987). Three types of perceived uncertainty about the environment: State, effect, and response uncertainty. *Academy of Management Review, 12,* 133–143.

24. See Note 9.

25. Duncan, R. (1973). Multiple decision making structures in adapting to uncertainty. *Human Relations, 73,* 273–291.

26. See Note 13.

27. See Note 22.

28. Tushman, M., & Scanlan, T. (1981). Boundary-spanning individuals: Their role in information transfer and their antecedents. *Academy of Management Journal, 4,* 289–305.

29. Dollinger, M. J. (1984). Environmental boundary spanning and information processing effects on organizational performance. *Academy of Management Journal, 27,* 351–368.

30. Burns, T., & Stalker, G. M. (1961). *The management of innovation.* London: Tavistock.

31. Miller, D. (1987). Strategy making and structure: Analysis and implications for performance. *Academy of Management Journal, 30,* 7–32.

32. Miller, D., Droge, C., & Toulouse, J. M. (1988). Strategic process and content as mediators between organizational context and structure. *Academy of Management Journal, 31,* 544–569.

33. Miller, D. (1988). Relating Porter's business strategies to environment and structure: Analysis and performance implications. *Academy of Management Journal, 3,* 280–308.

34. Dunphy, D. (1987). Convergence/divergence: A temporal review of the Japanese enterprise and its management. *Academy of Management Review, 12,* 445–459.

35. Fry, L. W., & Slocum, J. W., Jr. (1984). Technology, structure, and work-group effectiveness: A test of a contingency model. *Academy of Management Journal, 27,* 221–246.

36. Woodward, J. (1965). *Industrial organization: Theory and practice.* London: Oxford Univ. Press.

37. See Note 36.

38. Zwerman, W. L. (1970). *New perspectives on organizational theory.* Westport, CT: Greenwood.

39. Grinyer, P. H., & Hasai-Ardekani, M. (1980). Di-

mensions of organizational structure. *Academy of Management Journal, 24,* 471–486.

40. Hull, F. M., & Collins, P. D. (1987). High-technology batch production systems: Woodward's missing type. *Academy of Management Journal, 30,* 786–797.

41. Hickson, D., Pugh, D., & Pheysey, D. (1969). Operations technology and organization structure: An empirical reappraisal. *Administrative Science Quarterly, 26,* 349–377.

42. Singh, J. V. (1986). Technology, size, and organizational structure: A reexamination of the Okayama study data. *Academy of Management Journal, 29,* 800–812.

43. See Note 22.

44. See Note 13.

Organization Design for Effectiveness: Promoting Teamwork

Imagine going to work and being asked to put all your belongings on your desk chair then being asked to shove your chair to a new office down the hall or on another floor. Imagine 500 people all doing this at once! This "organized chaos" actually took place at noon on August 14, 1987 at the headquarters of AAL's (Aid Association for Lutherans) insurance operations in Appleton, Wisconsin.[1] By requiring employees to become physically involved in moving their offices, AAL hoped to increase their personnel's acceptance of and commitment to the restructuring.

The reason for the reorganization—that is, change in organization design—was that the insurance company had grown large and inefficient over its eighty-four years. Under the pre-August 14, 1987 structure, AAL's insurance subsidiary was divided into three sections: health insurance, life insurance, and support services. Each of these areas was split into two further divisions (e.g., health insurance comprised both processing and underwriting divisions). As a result of this setup, the procedure for claims processing was complex and time consuming as it involved numerous people coordinating across the different areas. For example, if a customer wanted to use the cash value of his or her life insurance policy to purchase additional health and life insurance coverage, at least eight separate transactions would be required to process the request. In this case, a different person in each of the six divisions would need to complete appropriate paperwork on the customer request and forward their recommendation to the others. "A case would get lost in the maze and sometimes take thirty days to find,"[2] said Vice President of Insurance Operations, Jerome H. Laubenstein. Actually, a complex case took an average of twenty days—still a lengthy delay. Additionally, the former organizational scheme had developed many unnecessary layers of bureaucracy that slowed decision making and claims processing and increased personnel costs.

When the employees of AAL got to their new offices on the day of the company restructuring, they discovered that AAL was no longer divided along product lines. Instead, they found they had been regrouped into teams. Each team consisted of twenty to thirty people. The teams were selected to include members who had skills in processing various types of claims. In this way, each team could be self-sufficient—that is, no matter how complex a claim, each team would have enough expertise to complete its processing. To further reduce dependence on some team member's highly specialized skills, employees are being trained in various aspects of claims processing. Teams are organized in groups of three or four which are assigned to serve the agents and consumers in different geographic areas. This allows the agents and field service representatives to develop close working relationships with their assigned team thereby reducing the frictions that had developed when they felt they had to deal with faceless bureaucrats.

The team structure has proven very effective. Claims processing time is down, in some cases by 75 percent. Complex claims that formerly took twenty days to process are now being completed in five days. Productivity has increased by 20 percent while the number of services provided has increased by 10 percent. Three layers of supervision have been eliminated, resulting in substantial savings in personnel costs.[3]

Questions for Discussion

1. What type of organizational structures did AAL use before and after 1987?

2. Why is the team organization so effective for AAL's insurance division? Would it be effective for all organizations?

3. By reducing the number of levels of bureaucracy, what happens to the chain of command?

4. Is AAL's insurance division organic or mechanistic in structure?

Notes

1. Hoerr, J. (1988, November 28). Work teams can rev up paper-pushers, too. *Business Week,* p. 64–72.

2. See Note 1, p. 68.

3. See Note 1.

Casey at the Bat: Prodding the Post Office to Efficiency

Oh, how we love to complain about the postal service. It is practically an American sport! As the cost of postage has risen dramatically while the level of service has fallen, most of us feel justified in voicing our complaints. Albert V. Casey, the U.S. Postmaster General from January to August, 1986 agreed that the Postal Service had become inefficient and ill-managed. Casey had a long and distinguished career in numerous other industries (railroads, publishing, airlines) prior to heading the Postal Service. When he took over as Postmaster General, he knew he would have a short time in which to implement changes (he had already accepted a teaching appointment for the fall of 1986 when he was approached for this position). As a result, he only had a small window of opportunity in which to make drastic changes in the organization of the U.S. Postal Service.

Upon arrival at his Washington, D.C. office, Casey's first act was to examine the management structure of the Postal Service. This exploration revealed a huge bureaucracy. At the top, the Postmaster General reported to a politically appointed Board of Governors. Reporting to the Postmaster General were six divisional heads in charge of different functional areas (e.g., finance, legal), as well as a Deputy Postmaster General. Additionally, Casey discovered that the Postal Service divided the country into five geographic regions, each employing about 580 staff at headquarters. Reporting to the regional offices were forty-two sectional offices employing about another 1,000 people. Two hundred and twenty-two management sectional centers reported to these regional centers. The 30,000 individual post offices in turn reported to the management sectional centers.[1] Based on interviews with his top advisers and his prior experience as CEO of large companies, Casey determined "that the work force offered a wealth of talent which was being wasted in an inefficient management structure, outmoded procedures and inadequate technology."[2]

Because Casey knew he only had a short time in the job he decided to focus his efforts on changing the organizational structure. He realized that by changing the reporting relationships, eliminating a layer of management, and decentralizing the decision making process, the Postal Service would be able to respond more quickly to changes in its environment and thereby provide improved service. Casey recognized that many of the changes he wanted to implement would make him unpopular. After all, in any organization with 780,000 employees, change is likely to have an adverse effect on many. He knew, however, that in order for change to take hold he would have to call for dramatic and sweeping reforms. This resulted from the sheer size of the postal service. The 780,000 employees (all but thirty of whom were union members) were spread across 30,000 post offices.

By the first of February 1986, one month after assuming his duties, Casey ordered the five regional Postmasters to cut the size of their regional offices from 580 employees to eighty-five. Next, he entirely eliminated the forty-two sectional offices. The seventy-four largest management sectional centers were reclassified as divisions with the 148 smaller centers reporting to them. The people who ran these seventy-four centers were given the new title of "General Manager." Accompanying this title was the authority for all operating and capital spending that had previously only been allowed those at the regional or sectional levels. Casey's plan was that the newly formed divisions would be similar in spirit to "wholly owned subsidiaries" found in the private sector and would act autonomously. To help reinforce his vision, he arranged for $12,000 of each Division Manager's pay to be held "at risk," and only distributed *if* the manager's performance was satisfactory.

Although Casey's tenure with the organization was very brief, it was long enough to determine that some of the changes had worked just as he planned. For instance, under the old organizational design, it had taken between ten and twelve years to have a new post office authorized and constructed. This resulted from the fact that final approval for a new post office was granted only after each level of management (i.e., management sectional center, sectional office, regional office, Deputy Postmaster General, and functional division heads) had been consulted and had determined a new facility was necessary. Thus, the local post office would identify the need to expand operations and seek permission from the sectional level. Once this level had granted permission, the next level would be contacted and the process repeated. By the time all levels of management had agreed to a new post office, many years had passed—and only then could the process of looking for real estate and developing site plans by undertaken! By eliminating the necessity of gaining the approval of higher level management, the new structure was expected to cut this time by 80 percent. As a result, the Postal Service could respond more quickly to changing demographic conditions. In addition, a new program of expanded hours and services (e.g., express mail) was implemented more quickly than had been anticipated.

In summarizing the actions that led to his success Casey claimed:

"The secret is that you must be willing to act without asking for permission. However, you must be equally prepared to defend your actions, as following the Postal Service reorganization, I was investigated by both the Congress and the Board of Governors."[3]

Questions for Discussion

1. Draw an organizational chart depicting the structure of the Postal Service both before and after Casey's reorganization.

2. How did this change make the Postal Service more organic?

3. Do you think Casey could have continued to be effective if he had remained in the position of Postmaster General for a longer period of time? How long? Why or why not?

Notes

1. Casey, A. V. (1986, November 13). Remarks by Albert V. Casey to Audit Bureau of Circulation. Unpublished manuscript.
2. See Note 1, p. 8.
3. See Note 1, p. 17.

Internal Structure in a Changing Organization

Apple Computer, which began its existence in a garage, experienced tremendous early success. Within a few short years of its founding, it was selling more than $1 billion worth of personal computers. The future looked bright, and Apple planned to take on "Big Blue" (IBM) with its new Macintosh line. Unfortunately, for a variety of reasons this strategy backfired, and by 1985 Apple was in deep trouble. Profits evaporated, and the company found it necessary to cut more than 20 percent of its labor force. It was during this period that major friction developed between the young and charismatic Steven Jobs, Apple's founder and largest stockholder, and John Sculley, the high-powered executive Jobs had hired in 1983 to serve as Apple's CEO.

As John Sculley testifies in this interview, he found himself in a difficult position, to say the least. As Chairman of the Board, Steven Jobs had authority over him. But Jobs, in his role as head of the Macintosh Division, reported *to* John Sculley. More important, the two men disagreed on how to handle the company's present problems. Sculley, drawing on his long career as a top executive, wanted to reorganize Apple along the lines of other large corporations. Jobs objected to such change; he wanted Apple to retain the informal structure it had used throughout its short history. The outcome was that Steven Jobs resigned and ultimately left the company.

As you watch this videotape, be on the alert for information indicating why, in John Sculley's view, the reorganization at Apple was necessary. Was this merely an attempt by Sculley to increase his own power at Jobs's expense? Or were his plans for reorganization based on his expert knowledge of the internal structure of companies, and how such structure must change as organizations themselves grow and confront an ever-shifting external environment? Why do you think Sculley was successful in wresting control of Apple from Steven Jobs? And do you predict success for him in the years ahead as Apple continues to grow and develop?

Questions for Discussion

1. Do organizations really need different types of leaders at different points in their history?

2. What are some of the advantages of the informal structure adopted by Apple during its early years?

3. Why was this informal structure no longer effective when the company became a $1 billion-plus business?

Competition, Strategy, and Structure: A Personal Perspective

557

Experiencing
Organizational
Behavior

**EXPERIENCING
ORGANIZATIONAL
BEHAVIOR**

There can be no doubt that for many organizations, the external environment has become increasingly complex and competitive. Since organizations must, of necessity, adapt to such changes, they are mirrored in the organizations' internal structure and competitive strategies. Have you observed such relationships yourself? Chances are good that you have. To increase your awareness of the complex links between various aspects of the environment and the internal workings of organizations, please follow these procedures.

Procedure

First, think about an organization in which you have worked. (Select one in which you were employed for at least six months to a year.) Now, answer the following questions:

What was the major *competitive strategy* adopted by this organization—the basic way in which it sought to maintain and expand its business in the face of growing competition? (Check one or more as appropriate.)

_____ Cost Advantage (The company tried to keep the cost of its products or services below that of competitors)

_____ Product Quality (The company tried to make its products or services higher in quality than those of its competitors)

_____ Innovation/Differentiation (The company tried to develop new products or to differentiate its current products from those of competitors)

Now, consider one aspect of the internal structure and functioning of the organization—its *human resource systems* (systems designed to attract, train, and retain individuals with the skills and abilities the organization needs). Where did the organization stand on each of the following dimensions?

Source of new hires

Mainly outside company						Mainly inside company
1	2	3	4	5	6	7

Performance appraisals cover short periods of time						Performance appraisals cover long periods of time
1	2	3	4	5	6	7

Rewards on basis of individual performance						Rewards on basis of work group performance
1	2	3	4	5	6	7

Little training and development of employees						Much training and development of employees
1	2	3	4	5	6	7

Points to Consider

Now, consider the possibility of links between the competitive strategy/strategies chosen by the organization and these human resource practices. Research on this topic indicates that competitive strategies do indeed shape this aspect of an organization's internal operations.[1,2] For example, companies that choose a strategy based on cost reduction cannot afford to invest a great deal in training employees. Similarly, they prefer to reward employees on the basis of individual effort and output. In contrast, organizations that adopt a strategy based on innovation face an opposite situation. They must attract and retain highly skilled, creative individuals. Thus, employee training and development are high-priority items for them. Similarly, since teamwork is important for new breakthroughs, reward systems based on group rather than individual output may be most appropriate.

Do you perceive similar relationships in the organization you chose to consider and in which you have worked? In all probability, you can. To the extent you do, you will have gained first-hand evidence for the existence of important links between strategy and several aspects of internal structure.

Notes

1. Schuler, R. S., & Jackson, S. E. (1987). Linking competitive strategies with human resource management practices. *Academy of Management Executive, 1,* 207–219.

2. Sonenfeld, J. A., & Peiperl, M. A. (1988). Staffing policy as a strategic response: A typology of career systems. *Academy of Management Review, 13,* 588–600.

CHAPTER SIXTEEN

ORGANIZATIONAL CHANGE AND DEVELOPMENT

CHAPTER OUTLINE

Organizational Change: Some Determining Factors
Planned Internal Change
Planned External Change
Unplanned Internal Change
Unplanned External Change

The Process of Organizational Change: Some Basic Issues
Targets of Organizational Change: What Is Changed?
Readiness for Change: When Will Organizational Change Occur?
Resistance to Change: Will Organizational Change Be Accepted?

Organizational Development: The Implementation of Planned Organizational Change
OD Interventions: Major Techniques
The Effectiveness of Organizational Development: Does It Really Work?

Special Sections

OB: A Management Perspective
Overcoming Resistance to Organizational Change: Some Guidelines

OB: An International Perspective
Cultural Barriers to Effective OD Interventions: The Importance of Matching OD Values and National Culture

LEARNING OBJECTIVES

After reading this chapter, you should be able to:
1. Identify the major factors responsible for organizational change.
2. Describe the primary targets of organizational change efforts.
3. Identify the conditions under which organizational change is likely to occur.
4. Explain the major factors making people resistant to organizational change and some ways of overcoming them.
5. Describe the major techniques of organizational development.
6. Evaluate the effectiveness of organizational development efforts.
7. Explain the potential cultural barriers to effective organizational development.

"Maybe ten years isn't such a long time to be in business," Paul Sanders said with a combination of exuberance and fatigue, "but it's been a decade with one change after another—always something to stay on top of."

The hotel ballroom was almost empty now, as the employee celebration for Sanders Electronics' tenth year in business had just ended. Only Paul, his wife, Marilyn, and his good friend and partner, Sol Morrison lingered in the ballroom, shoes off and bow ties loosened, as the cleaning crew began folding the chairs. They couldn't help reminiscing as they prepared to enter their second decade in business.

"Remember when we started out," Sol recalled. "We were taking on the big guys—Sparky's TV & Appliance, and Transistor City."

"Yeah, they're long gone now," Marilyn observed. "It's funny," she added, "we were so afraid of them, but in the long run, we made it and they didn't."

"Don't suppose for a second that I don't think about that every day," Paul responded. "Why did we succeed while our competitors folded?"

Sol was quick to respond. "In my opinion," he began, "we were always first to give the consumers what they wanted—instant financing, good service, fair prices."

"I agree," Paul added, "but there's more. We were quick to read the market demands and were smart enough to buy up popular goods like CD players and fax machines at good prices. Our competitors waited to gauge the demand, but we knew our customers would want them, and we made a name for ourselves by having lots of this stuff around."

"You're right, Paul," Marilyn agreed. "I remember a few Christmas seasons ago we were the only one in town with CD players in stock."

"Yeah," Sol noted. "It seems so strange now, because they're everywhere—and at prices far lower than our cost back then."

"There's no doubt about it," said Paul, "we made some good decisions. We saw the market changing, and we responded quickly—and wisely. The big guys were slower, and we got the jump on them."

"It's amazing when you think how different our inventory is today than it was when we first opened," Sol observed. "Computers, laser discs, digital audio tape recorders, camcorders—things sure have changed a lot."

"Yeah, but it's more than just our merchandising style and our product mix that's changed," Paul interjected.

"What do you mean?" Marilyn asked.

"We've changed in other ways too. When we first started out, I did everything from painting the store and hooking up the TV sets to paying the bills. Now, I just look around and see everyone else doing things I used to do—only much better."

"Sure, Paul," Sol was quick to respond, "that's what happens when you grow from a small business to a more mature one."

Paul continued. "Even the way we treat our employees has changed. We give them bonuses, liberal insurance plans, we train them carefully, and we allow them to take leaves for maternity. We involve them in almost every decision we make. We didn't seem to care as much at first, I don't think. But now, we treat everyone like family."

"That really *is* a big change." Marilyn agreed. "After we lost some of our best salespeople, we knew we were doing something wrong. We knew electronics, but we didn't know people."

"You're both right," said Sol, jumping on the bandwagon. "That's an area where we learned the hard way. But, we did it; we changed—and successfully, too."

"Here, here," Paul interjected, his champagne glass raised in a toast. "But you know, it's true what they say: 'the more things change, the more they stay the same.' "

"How's that?" Marilyn asked.

"Simple," Paul replied, "I'm just as overworked now as I was back then."

There is no doubt about it, Sanders Electronics has been through many changes in its decade of existence. Some of the changes may have improved business, and some may have hindered it. Many were very carefully and strategically planned by top management, while others were imposed on the company from the outside. You may even say that "the one constant the organization has always faced is change." It is certainly an inevitable part of life in organizations. As organizations face changes in the environments within which they operate, they must adapt to new circumstances. History reveals that such adaption is critical for organizations: those that successfully adapt thrive, while those that do not, eventually die out (see Figure 16.1).

It is on this process of **organizational change** that we will focus in this chapter. Specifically, we will begin by considering four varieties of organizational change: ones that are either planned or unplanned in nature, in conjunction with those that are imposed from within the organization, or those coming from outside it. Next, we will examine some of the major issues involved in the organizational change process. Specifically, these involve: what is changed (i.e., organizational structure, technology, or people), the conditions under which change will occur, and the willingness of people to accept

FIGURE 16.1 Adaptation to Change: A Key to Organizational Survival

As organizations confront the need for change in their environments, it is essential to their survival that they adapt accordingly. Shown here are examples of companies that were unsuccessful (above) and successful (below) in responding to the need for change.

organizational change. Following this, we will review some of the major techniques used to implement planned organizational change, approaches known as **organizational development** techniques. In closing, we will review the effectiveness of these organizational development efforts, considering what may be expected of them.

ORGANIZATIONAL CHANGE: SOME DETERMINING FACTORS

As you look around you today, the sight of portable computers is hardly uncommon. Indeed, the fact that they can be easily transported from home to car to airplane to office is a major reason for their popularity. Given this, it is hard to understand why the developers of the first portable computers, Osborne Computer, found itself $45 million in debt and was forced to declare bankruptcy just two years after its first portable computer was introduced in January, 1981. This is especially surprising in view of the fact that the company enjoyed sales of nearly $100 million in the two years of its existence.[1]

How does a company go from boom to bust so quickly? Although there are undoubtedly many reasons for Osborne's failure, one of the key factors was its inability to manage the rapid growth and complex changes brought about by the introduction of such giants as IBM into the field. As the market for computer products changed, along with the technology needed to make them, other companies, such as the much larger IBM, and the highly aggressive upstart, Apple Computers, found themselves better suited to making the changes necessary to create and meet the growing demand for home computers. As you might imagine, Osborne is hardly alone in its inability to adapt to change. Companies such as Xerox, Texas Instruments, American Motors, and Eastman Kodak, to name just a few, have encountered difficulties at various times in their histories meeting rapidly changing technological and marketing conditions. Sometimes, as in the case of Osborne Computers, the inability to respond to changing conditions leads to organizational decline and eventual dissolution. Indeed, as shown in Figure 16.2, the survival rate of U.S. corporations tends to be rather low, with 62 percent failing within their first five years of operation.[2]

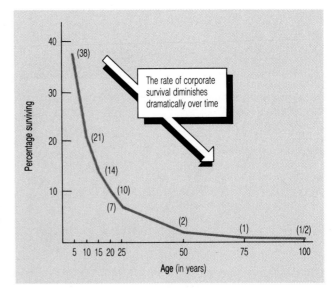

FIGURE 16.2   Survival Rates of American Corporations: The Grim Picture

As these data reveal, only 38 percent of organizations survive their first five years in business—and even fewer make it longer than that. The failure to successfully make needed changes is undoubtedly one key reason behind these statistics. (Source: Based on data reported by Nystrom & Starbuck, 1984; see Note 2.)

Obviously, ever-changing conditions present a formidable challenge to organizations, which must learn to be flexible and adapt to them. However, not all organizational changes are the result of unplanned, externally-imposed factors. Some organizational changes are planned, and quite intentional. Indeed, there are a large variety of determinants of organizational change, forces dictating change. Because there are many such factors, it is helpful to organize them into four major categories. These categories are created by combining two key distinctions: (a) whether the organizational change is *planned* or *unplanned* by the organization, and (b) whether they come from factors *internal* or *external* to the organization. The taxonomy that results from combining these two dimensions—as shown in Table 16.1—provides a useful way of summarizing the major determinants of organizational change.

Planned Internal Change

A great deal of organizational change comes from the conscious decision to alter the way an organization does business or the very nature of the business itself. For example, when one company takes over another, it has to plan how it is going to change its operations and management to accommodate the new acquisition. Two examples of planned organizational change may be identified—changes in products or services, and changes in administrative systems.

Changes in products or services. Imagine that you and a friend begin a small janitorial business. The two of you divide the duties, each doing some cleaning, buying supplies, and performing some administrative work. Before long, the business grows and you expand, adding new employees, and really begin "cleaning up." Many of your commercial clients express interest in window cleaning, and so you and your partner think it over and decide to expand into the window cleaning business as well. This decision to take on a new direction to the business, to add a new, specialized service, will require a fair amount of organizational change. Not only will new equipment and supplies be needed, but also new personnel will have to be hired and trained, new insurance will have to be purchased, and new accounts will have to be secured. In short, the planned decision to change the company's line of services necessitates organizational change. As you are undoubtedly well aware, the rash of new products and services offered to consumers each year is staggering. Unfortunately, many new prod-

TABLE 16.1 Categories of Organizational Change: A Taxonomy and Some Examples

Organizational changes may be either planned or unplanned, and based on either internal or external causes. Some examples of changes within each of the four categories are listed here.

	PLANNED CHANGE	UNPLANNED CHANGE
INTERNAL CHANGE	Changes in products or services Changes in administrative systems	Changing employee demographics Performance gaps
EXTERNAL CHANGE	Introduction of new technologies Advantages in information processing and communication	Governmental regulations External competition

ucts and services are unsuccessful, with only about one out of every eight ever becoming profitable. Why is this so, and what can be done to improve these odds?

Some valuable insight into this question is provided by the **horizontal linkage model.**[3] In brief, this model specifies that the success of a new product is based on the success of the *marketing* and *research* departments in interacting with their external environments, and with each other. The marketing and research areas are singled out because these are typically the ones most concerned with affecting change. Moreover, experts in these fields are expected to keep close tabs on the environment external to the organization. Specifically, employees involved in research are expected to make themselves aware of new technological developments and advances in areas relevant to the organization as soon as they occur. Analogously, people involved in marketing are expected to be able to monitor changes in consumers' preferences and the product introductions by competitors. In short, both departments are expected to serve important *boundary-spanning* roles—that is, to connect the organization to its external environment (see chapter 15).

However, it is not sufficient that these two units only gather information; they must also establish *horizontal linkages* between themselves. In other words, they must coordinate their efforts, sharing the information they receive, and giving each other advice. The absence of such communication can not only cause a great deal of confusion within the organization (see chapter 10), but is also greatly responsible for the failure of many organizations to successfully change as desired. Organizations whose critical marketing and research subunits not only function effectively with the outside world, but with each other as well, tend to be ones whose products are best accepted. By carefully paying attention to the advice of the horizontal linkage model (summarized in Figure 16.3), organizations can increase the odds that they will be effectively—and profitably—able to change the products and services they offer.

Changes in administrative systems. Although an organization may be forced to change its policies, reward structure, goals, and management style in response to outside competition, governmental regulation, and economic changes (as we will note later), it is also quite common for changes in administrative systems to be strategically planned in advance. Such changes may stem from a desire to improve efficiency, to change the company's image, or to gain a political power advantage within the organization (see chapter 12).[4]

Typically, the pressure to bring about changes in the administration of organizations (i.e., to coordinate activities, set goals and priorities, etc.) comes from upper man-

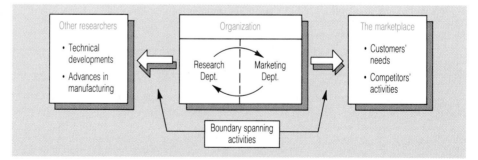

FIGURE 16.3   The Horizontal Linkage Model: A Summary

According to the *horizontal linkage model,* new products and services will be successful if they result from the boundary spanning activities of an organization's marketing and research staffs, and from the coordinated interaction between these two units. (Source: Based on suggestions by Daft, 1986; see Note 3.)

agement—that is, from the top down. In contrast, pressure to change the central work of the organization (i.e., the production of goods and services) comes from the technical side of the organization, from the bottom upward.[5] This is the idea behind the **dual-core model** of organizations. Many organizations, especially medium-sized ones, may be characterized by potential conflicts between the administrative and the technical cores—each faction wishing to change the organization according to its own vested interests.

Which side usually wins? Research suggests that the answer depends on the design of the organization in question (please refer to chapter 15). Organizations that are highly *mechanistic* as opposed to *organic* in their approach (i.e., they are highly formal and centralized) tend to be successful in introducing administrative changes.[6] The high degree of control wielded by the administrative core tends to facilitate the introduction of administrative change. Obviously, the issue is made more complex by factors such as the need to make administrative changes in order to support the technical changes required for organizational success. Regardless, it remains clear that changes in the administrative systems of organizations represent a good example of planned internal change.

Planned External Change

In addition to planning changes in the ways organizations are run, it is often possible to plan which change variables originating outside the organization will be incorporated into it. Introductions of new technology and advances in information processing and communication fall into this category. Both of these advances typically originate outside the organization and are introduced into it in some planned fashion.

Introduction of new technologies: From slide rules to computers. There can be little doubt that advances in technology produce changes in the way organizations operate. Scientists and engineers, for example, can probably tell you how their work was drastically altered in the mid 1970s when their ubiquitous plastic slide rules gave way to powerful pocket calculators. Things changed again only a decade later when calculators were supplanted by powerful desktop microcomputers. As you are probably well aware, the use of computers has revolutionized the way documents are prepared, transmitted, and filed in an office. Manufacturing plants have also seen a great deal of growth recently in the use of computer-automated technology.[7] Each of these examples represents an instance in which technology has altered the way people do their jobs (for a humorous example of this, see Figure 16.4).

"I never use my crystal ball anymore."

FIGURE 16.4 Technology: A Major Source of Organizational Change

It's hard to tell if the gypsy's crystal ball will ever be made obsolete by a computer. However, the availability of sophisticated technological equipment has changed the way many jobs are performed. (Source: From *The Wall Street Journal*—Permission, Cartoon Features Syndicate.)

Technological changes may take various forms in organizations. For one, technological advances are commonly applied in the cockpits of airplanes, where computer-based devices are commonly used to guide, assist, or take over many functions performed by pilots. This is in keeping with a prediction by John Naisbitt, in his best-selling book, *Megatrends,* that high-tech devices would become friendlier and easier to use.[8] Anyone who has used computer software packages to make complex mathematical calculations during the last several years will surely recognize how much easier modern programs are to use than older programming languages (e.g., FORTRAN).

In keeping with this ease-of-use theme, we should also note that technological advances applied to the shop floor have been responsible for the introduction of complex microelectronic, computer-based devices—*robots.* The use of robots has clearly taken hold in manufacturing industries, especially in the performance of monotonous or dangerous jobs. Such devices are commonly used in automobile manufacturing (see Figure 16.5), as well as in other industries. For example, the use of robots has reportedly helped the General Electric Company produce 20 percent more dishwashers in 20 percent less floor space in its Louisville, Kentucky plant. Robots have also helped the Walgreen's drugstore chain increase the rate of packing shipments from its distribution center to its stores by over 800 percent.[9] As you may expect, because robots are so efficient, they pose a challenge to workers who fear being replaced by them. (As we will describe later in this chapter, such a fear represents one especially potent source of workers' resistance to organizational change.) Obviously, the introduction of new technology poses an important challenge to today's businesses.[10]

Advances in information processing and communication. Although it is easy for us to take for granted such everyday events as television transmissions and long distance telephone calls, it really wasn't too long ago that these things were merely exotic dreams. If you've ever seen an old Western film in which the Pony Express rider struggled through uncharted territories in order to deliver messages to people in distant western cities, you are well aware of the difficulties that had to be faced—and in the not too distant past—to communicate over long distances. Of course, with

FIGURE 16.5 Robots: An Important Source of Technological Change
The use of robots has replaced many of the monotonous or dangerous jobs that used to be performed by people on automobile assembly lines. Such a change not only relieves people from undesirable jobs, but also dramatically improves the quality of manufacturing—hence, organizational functioning.

today's sophisticated satellite transmission systems, fiber-optic cables crisscrossing the planet, facsimile machines, portable telephones, tele-conferencing facilities (see chapter 10) and the like, it is easier than ever for businesses to communicate with each other and with their clients. The key point is that as such communication systems improve, opportunities for organizational growth and improvement immediately follow.[11] One of the keys to organizational success is to selectively incorporate advances in communication technology that allow organizations to share vast amounts of information faster and more widely than ever before.

Unplanned Internal Change

In contrast to the forces noted above, which encourage planned changes in organizations, not all forces for change are the result of strategic planning. Indeed, organizations must often be responsive to changes that are unplanned—especially those derived from factors internal to the organization. Two such forces are changes in the demographic composition of the work force, and performance gaps.

Changing employee demographics. It is easy to see how, even within your own lifetime, the composition of the work force has changed. Consider these statistics.[12]

- There are more women working now than ever before. By 1995, it is estimated that 60.3 percent of American women will be working, and will be doing so at all stages of their lives.
- Minority group representation in the labor force rose from 10.7 percent in 1954 to 12.8 percent in 1982. The figure is expected to rise to 14.5 percent by 1995.
- Union affiliation has been declining steadily, from a peak of 35 percent in 1955 to less than 20 percent today.
- American workers are now better educated than ever. The percentage of the labor force that completed four years of college rose from 14.7 percent in 1970 to 24.2 percent in 1983. Today's figures are even higher.

These are, of course, only some of the major demographic changes that have occurred in the labor force in recent years. If you think about it, it is not difficult to imagine how such shifting conditions force organizations to change in many varied and important ways. Baby boomers are becoming more of an economic force than ever— their high income and educational levels have forced organizations to make a wide variety of comfort and convenience items available (e.g., luxury cars, convenience foods and microwave ovens in which to cook them).[13] With more female employees of childbearing age in the work force than ever before, organizations have been forced to make child-care facilities available, and to allow many employees to work on a part-time basis or to "share" jobs. As workers grow older, they will soon put an increasing burden on pension systems. If they live longer lives, and work farther into their lives, the drain on health insurance may become severe. Even if higher levels of affluence allow people to retire earlier than ever before, the lack of experienced personnel may pose a formidable organizational problem.[14] Scientists are just beginning to understand how the ever-changing composition of the work force is influencing the operation of organizations. Although the exact nature of the changes forced by shifting demographics is complex and not yet fully understood, one thing is certain—changes in the composition of the work force demand corresponding changes in organizations.

Performance gaps. If you've ever heard the phrase, "if it's not broken, don't fix it," then you already have a good feel for one of the most potent sources of unplanned internal changes in organizations—performance gaps. A product line that isn't moving, a vanishing profit margin, a level of sales that isn't up to corporate expectations—these are all examples of gaps between real and expected levels of organizational performance. Few things force change more than sudden and unexpected information about poor organizational performance. While organizations often stay with a winning course of action, they often change in response to failure; in other words, they follow a *win-stay/lose-change rule*. Indeed, several research projects have shown that a performance gap is one of the key factors providing an impetus for organizational innovation.[15] Those organizations that are best prepared to mobilize change in response to unexpected downturns may well be the ones that succeed.

Unplanned External Change

One of the greatest challenges faced by an organization is its ability to respond to changes from the outside world over which it has little or no control. As the environment changes, organizations must follow suit. Research has shown that organizations that can best adapt to changing conditions tend to survive.[16] Two of the most important unplanned external factors are governmental regulation and economic competition.

Governmental regulation. One of the most commonly witnessed unplanned organizational changes results from governmental regulations. In the late 1980s restaurant owners in the United States have had to completely change the way they report the income of waiters and waitresses to the federal government for purposes of collecting income taxes. Similarly, any change in the minimum wage law greatly influences organizations, forcing them to revise the amount they pay their lowest-paid employees. In recent years the U.S. federal government has been involved in both imposing and eliminating regulations in industries such as commercial airlines (e.g., mandating inspection schedules, but no longer controlling fares) and banks (e.g., restricting the amount of time checks can be held before clearing, but no longer regulating interest rates). No doubt, such activities have greatly influenced the way business is conducted in these industries.

An excellent example of how governmental activities drive organizational change is provided by the 1984 divestiture of AT&T. A settlement of antitrust proceedings dramatically rearranged the activities of almost one million Bell System employees—a company with $103 billion in assets. Among other things, the agreement led to the creation of seven new independent companies. At Southwestern Bell, CEO Zane Barnes remarked that the divestiture forced them to "rethink the functions of some 90,000 employees," a process that was like "taking apart and reassembling a jumbo jet while in flight."[17] Not surprisingly, the company relied on its expertise in satellite and communications technology to provide information about the change process to 55,000 employees in fifty-seven locations.

Governmental regulations are often imposed on organizations following some crisis of public health or safety. Such was the case when the Nuclear Regulatory Commission (NRC) imposed safety standards on nuclear power plants following the 1979 accident at Three Mile Island. Among other things, the NRC imposed a set of guidelines for improving the safety of all nuclear power plants. A recent study by Marcus compared the safety records of power plants that responded to the NRC's guidelines either exactly as established (i.e., they were *rule-bound*), or by customizing the regulations to their individual circumstances (i.e., they were *autonomous*).[18] As shown in Figure 16.6, the autonomous power plants operated significantly more safely than the rule-bound ones (they had one third as many human-caused errors), and more profitably, too.

As Marcus explains, a good safety record encouraged the use of discretion in following the NRC's rules, whereas a poor safety record encouraged the NRC to require

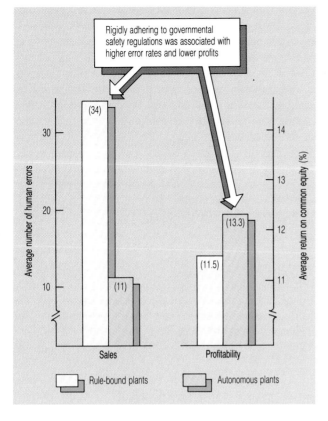

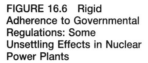

Rigidly adhering to governmental safety regulations was associated with higher error rates and lower profits

FIGURE 16.6 Rigid Adherence to Governmental Regulations: Some Unsettling Effects in Nuclear Power Plants

Research comparing several nuclear power plants found those that adapted governmental safety guidelines to their own operations (i.e., *autonomous* plants) operated more safely and at a higher profit margin than those that adhered rigidly to the guidelines (i.e., *rule-bound* plants). (Source: Based on data reported by Marcus, 1988; see Note 18.)

stricter adherence to its policies. Unfortunately, because plants that were allowed to customize the rules performed more safely than those that did not, insisting on close adherence to the rules may have only kept the dangerous power plants performing dangerously. These self-defeating actions are clearly responsible for the mixed effectiveness of governmental regulation in this case. Regardless, this research is useful in providing a clear example of the organizational changes created by governmental regulation in one important industry.

Economic competition. It happens every day: someone builds a better mousetrap—or, at least a cheaper one, or one that's marketed more effectively. As a result, companies must often fight to maintain their share of the market, advertise more effectively, and produce products more inexpensively. This kind of economic competition not only forces organizations to change, but demands that they change effectively if they are to survive.

Although competition has always been crucial to organizational success, today competition comes from all over the world. As it has become increasingly less expensive to transport materials around the world, the industrialized nations (e.g., the United States, Canada, Japan, and the nations of western Europe) have found themselves competing with each other for shares of the marketplace in nations all over the world. In other words, there is an ever-growing *global marketplace*. This situation is made more complex by the newly developing economic powers of the third world (e.g., Mexico, and South Korea). These nations are not only exploited by corporations from other nations for their vast natural resources and their pool of inexpensive labor, but are also developing their own multinational corporate giants ready to take their place in the world's market.[19]

This extensive globalization of the economy presents a formidable challenge to all organizations who wish to compete within the world's economic system. The primary challenge is to meet the ever-present need for change—to be innovative. For example, consider how the large American automobile manufacturers suffered by being unprepared to meet the world's growing demand for small, high-quality cars—products their Japanese (and now, Korean) competitors were only too glad to supply an eager marketplace. One thing is certain: as the stakes get higher and the number of players increases, the world marketplace becomes an arena where only the most adaptive organizations can survive.

THE PROCESS OF ORGANIZATIONAL CHANGE: SOME BASIC ISSUES

Clearly, organizations change in many ways and for many reasons. However, as you might imagine, the process of changing organizations is not haphazard; rather, it proceeds according to some well-established, orderly pattern. It is well known, for example, what the targets of organizational change efforts may be. It is also known under which conditions organizational change is likely to occur, and when people will be most likely to resist making such changes. It is these basic issues that concern us in this section.

Targets of Organizational Change: What Is Changed?

Imagine that you are an engineer responsible for overseeing the operation of a large office building. The property manager has noted a dramatic increase in the use of heat in the building, causing operating costs to skyrocket. In other words, a need for change exists—specifically, a reduction in the building's heat usage is deemed necessary. You cannot get the power company to lower its rates, so you realize you must bring about changes in the use of heat. How do you do this? Working with the manager, you consider some ways of achieving this goal. One possibility calls for rearranging job responsibilities so that only maintenance personnel are permitted to adjust thermostats. Another possibility is to put timers on all thermostats so that the building temperature is automatically lowered during periods of nonuse. Finally, you considered the idea of putting stickers next to the thermostats, requesting that occupants refrain from turning the heat up beyond 68 degrees. Although there are clearly other possibilities, these three options represent excellent examples of the three potential targets of organizational change we will consider here--changes in *structure, technology,* and *people.*

Changes in organizational structure. In chapter 15 we described in detail the key characteristics of organizational structure. Here, we wish to note that altering the structure of an organization may be a reasonable way of responding to a need for change. In the above example, a structural solution to the heat regulation problem came in the form of reassigning job responsibilities. Indeed, modifying rules, responsibilities, and procedures may be an effective way of managing change. Changing the control of heat from a highly decentralized design (whereby anyone can adjust the thermostats) to a centralized design (whereby only maintenance personnel may do so) may be one way of implementing organizational change in response to a problem. This particular structural solution called for changing the power structure (i.e., who was in charge of a particular task).

Different types of structural changes may take other forms.[20] For example, changes can be made with respect to an organization's span of control, altering the number of employees over which supervisors are responsible. Structural changes may also take the form of revising the basis for creating departments—such as from product-based departments to functional departments (see chapter 15). Other structural changes may be quite simple, such as clarifying someone's job description or the written policies and procedures followed.

It is important to note that structural changes are not uncommon in organizations. Consider, for example, some changes reported in recent years at the huge consumer products company, Procter & Gamble.[21] In response to growing competition, the company was forced to make a number of changes that streamlined its highly bureaucratic organizational structure. For example, the decision-making process used to be so centralized that many decisions that could have been made at lower levels were being made by top corporate personnel (such as the color of the cap on the can of decaffeinated instant Folgers coffee). Now, decentralized business teams have been instituted and are permitted to make all the necessary decisions about developing, manufacturing, and marketing products. These represent good examples of structural changes made in organizations.

Changes in technology. In the example used to open this section we noted that one possible solution to the heat conservation problem would be to use thermostats that automatically reduce the building's temperature while it is not in use. This is an example of a technological approach to the need to conserve heat in the building. It would also be possible to place regulating devices on the thermostats that would thwart attempts to raise the temperature. They also may be encased in a locked box, or simply removed altogether. A new, modern, energy-efficient furnace could also be installed in the building. All of these suggestions represent technological approaches to the need for change.

The underlying idea is that technological improvements can lead to more efficient work. Indeed, if you've ever prepared a term paper on a typewriter, you know how much more efficient it is to do the same job using a word processor. Technological changes may involve a variety of alterations, such as changing the equipment used to do jobs (e.g., robots), substituting microprocessors for less reliable mechanical components (e.g., on airline equipment), or simply using better-designed tools (e.g., chairs that conform to one's body). Each of these changes, large or small, may be used effectively to bring about improvements in organizational functioning.

Changes in people. You've probably seen stickers next to light switches in hotels and office buildings asking the occupants to turn off the lights when not in use. These are similar to the suggestion in our opening example to affix signs near thermostats asking occupants to refrain from turning the thermostats up beyond 68 degrees. Such efforts represent attempts to respond to the needed organizational change by altering the way people behave. The basic assumption is that the effectiveness of organizations is greatly dependent on the behavior of the people working within them. To the extent that employees are motivated to meet organizational goals (see chapter 3), and are rewarded for working efficiently (see chapter 2), organizations will be able to change as necessary.

As you might imagine, the process of changing people is not an easy one—indeed, it lies at the core of most of the topics discussed in this book. However, theorists have identified three basic steps that summarize what's involved in the process of changing people.[22,23] The first step is known as *unfreezing*. This refers to the process of recognizing that the current state of affairs is undesirable and in need of change. Realizing that change is needed may be the result of some serious organizational crisis (e.g., a serious profit loss, a strike, or a major lawsuit), or simply becoming aware of the fact that current conditions are inadequate (e.g., antiquated equipment, inadequately trained employees, etc.). After unfreezing, *changing* may occur. This step occurs when some planned attempt is made to create a more desirable state for the organization and its members. Change attempts may be quite ambitious (e.g., an organization-wide restructuring), or only minor (e.g., a change in a training program). (A thorough discussion of such planned change techniques will be presented in the next major part of this chapter.) Finally, *refreezing* occurs when the changes made are incorporated into the employees' thinking and the organization's operations (e.g., mechanisms for rewarding behaviors that maintain the changes are put in place). Hence, the new attitudes and behaviors become a new, enduring aspect of the organizational system. For a summary of these three steps in the individual change process, please see Figure 16.7. Despite the simplicity of this model, it does a good job of identifying some of the factors that make people willing to change their behavior—thereby potentially improving organizational effectiveness.

It is important to close this section with the reminder that organizational change efforts may be directed at the organizational structure, the technology used, or the people involved. As you might imagine, however, changes made with respect to one of these targets may very well necessitate changes with respect to another. As a simple example, imagine how a change in the machinery used to perform a job requires changes in the skills needed by the employees who operate it. In fact, almost any change, be it in organizational structure or technology, may be expected to have profound effects on the way people do their jobs. For this reason, it is important to pay careful attention to the kinds of factors that may make people more or less willing to accept organizational changes.

Readiness for Change: When Will Organizational Change Occur?

As you might imagine, there are times when organizations are likely to change, and times during which change is less likely. Even if the need for change is high and resistance to change is low (two important factors), it does not automatically follow that organizational change will occur. There are, obviously, other factors involved. We have summarized some of the key variables in Figure 16.8.

As Figure 16.8 summarizes, change is likely to occur when the people involved believe that the benefits associated with making a change outweigh the costs involved.

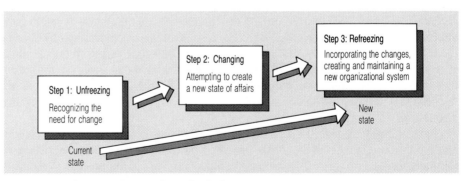

FIGURE 16.7 Changing People: Some Basic Steps

Many planned organizational change efforts are directed at changing people. Generally speaking, the process of changing people goes through the steps outlined here. (Sources: Based on ideas suggested by Lewin, 1951, see Note 22; and Schein, 1968; see Note 23.)

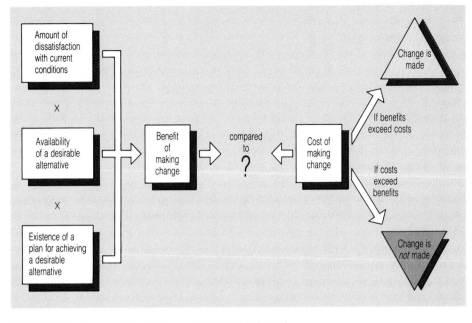

FIGURE 16.8   Organizational Change: When Will It Occur?
Whether or not an organizational change will be made depends on members' beliefs regarding the relative benefits and costs of making the change. The benefits are reflected by three considerations reviewed here. (Source: Based on suggestions by Beer, 1980; see Note 24.)

The factors contributing to the benefits of making a change are: (a) the amount of dissatisfaction with current conditions, (b) the availability of a desirable alternative, and (c) the existence of a plan for achieving that alternative. Theorists have claimed that these three factors combine multiplicatively to determine the benefits of making a change.[24] The implications of this are that if any one of these factors is very low (or zero), then the benefits of making a change, and the likelihood of change itself, are very low (or zero). If you think about it, this will begin to make sense to you. After all, people are unlikely to initiate change if they are not at all dissatisfied, or if they don't have any desirable alternative in mind (or any way of attaining that alternative, if they do have one in mind). Of course, for change to occur, the expected benefits must outweigh the likely costs involved (e.g., disruption, uncertainties, etc.). Professionals in the field of organizational development pay careful attention to these factors before they attempt to initiate any formal, ambitious organizational change programs. Only when the readiness for change is high will organizational change efforts be successful.

However, the likelihood that any planned attempt at organizational change will be effective depends to a great degree on the extent to which several formidable barriers to organizational change can be overcome. As we will now see, there are many such barriers that must be considered before organizations may be effectively changed in a systematic, planned manner.

Resistance to Change: Will Organizational Change Be Accepted?

Although people may be unhappy with the current state of affairs confronting them in organizations, they may be afraid that any changes will be potentially disruptive and will only make things worse. Indeed, fear of new conditions is quite real; it creates unwillingness to accept change (as demonstrated in Figure 16.9). Organizational scientists have recognized that **resistance to change** comes from both individual and organizational variables.

Individual barriers to change. Researchers have noted several key factors that are known to make people resistant to change in organizations.[25]

   1. Economic insecurity. Because any changes on the job have the potential to threaten one's livelihood—either by loss of job or reduced pay, some degree of resistance to change is inevitable unless job security can be assured.

   2. Fear of the unknown. It is well accepted that employees derive a sense of security from doing things the same way, knowing who their coworkers will be, and who they're supposed to answer to from day to day. Disrupting these well-established, comfortable, familiar patterns creates unfamiliar conditions, a state of affairs that is often rejected.

   3. Threats to social relationships. As people continue to work within organizations, they form strong social bonds with their coworkers. Many organizational changes (e.g. the reassignment of job responsibilities) threaten the integrity of friendship groups that provide an important source of social rewards for many employees.

   4. Habit. Jobs that are well learned and become habitual are easy to perform. The prospect of changing the way jobs are done challenges workers to relearn their jobs and to develop new job skills. Doing this is clearly more difficult than continuing to perform the job as it was originally learned.

   5. Failure to recognize need for change. Unless employees can recognize and fully appreciate the need for changing things in organizations, any vested interests they may have in keeping things the same may easily overpower their willingness to accept change.

Organizational barriers to change. As we noted earlier, resistance to organizational change arises not only from individual forces, but also from several factors associated with the organization itself.[26]

FIGURE 16.9 Resistance to Change: An Example

Because of their uncertainties about new ways of doing things, people (and perhaps seals, too) are often reluctant to accept changes. (Source: The BIZARRO Cartoon by Dan Piraro is reprinted by permission of Chronicle Features, San Francisco, CA.)

1. Structural inertia. Organizations are designed to promote stability. To the extent that employees are carefully selected and trained to perform certain jobs, and rewarded for performing them, the forces acting on individuals to perform in certain ways are very powerfully determined—that is, jobs have **structural inertia.**[27] In other words, because jobs are designed to have stability, it is often difficult to overcome the resistance created by the many forces that create the stability.

2. Work group inertia. Inertia to continue performing jobs in a specified way comes not only from the jobs themselves but from the social groups within which many employees work. Because of the development of strong social norms within work groups (see chapter 8), potent pressures exist to perform jobs in certain ways, and at certain accepted rates. Introducing change causes disruption in these established normative expectations, which imposes formidable barriers to change.

3. Threats to existing balance of power. If changes are made with respect to who's in charge and how things are done, a shift in the balance of power between individuals and organizational subunits is likely to occur (see chapter 12). Those units that now control the resources, have the expertise, and wield the power may fear losing their advantageous positions as a result of any organizational change.

4. Previously unsuccessful change efforts. Anyone who has lived through a past disaster may be understandably reluctant to endure another attempt at the same thing. Similarly, groups or entire organizations that have been unsuccessful in introducing change in the past may be understandably reluctant to accept further attempts at introducing change into the system.

Having summarized some of the barriers to organizational change, it is important to consider some of the ways to overcome resistance. After all, unless these barriers to change can be effectively overcome, any attempts to systematically change organizations may be doomed to failure. With this in mind, the material in the **Management Perspective** section below outlines some of the major methods used to overcome resistance to organizational change.

OB: A MANAGEMENT PERSPECTIVE

Overcoming Resistance to Organizational Change: Some Guidelines

Whether we are talking about change that is unplanned and forced on a company or change that follows from a carefully planned strategic effort, one thing is certain: organizational change is inevitable. A key factor in making sure that organizational change is for the better is how well change is managed. Given the many sources of resistance to change likely to be encountered, it is imperative that managers attempt to take steps to overcome such barriers. Several useful approaches have been suggested and are summarized here.[28,29]

1. *Shape political dynamics.* Earlier in this book (chapter 12), we described the important role of organizational politics in achieving desired goals. Political variables are crucial when it comes to getting organizational changes accepted. Politically, resistance to change can be overcome by winning the support of the most powerful and influential individuals. Doing so builds a critical internal mass of support for change. Demonstrating clearly that key organizational leaders support the change is an effective way of getting others to go along with it— either because they share the leader's vision, or because they fear the leader's retaliation. Either way, political support for change will facilitate acceptance of change.

2. *Educate the work force.* Sometimes, people are reluctant to change because they fear what the future has in store for them. Fears about economic security, for example, may be easily put to rest by a few reassuring words from organizational powerholders. As part of educating employees about what organizational changes may mean for them, it is imperative for top management to show a considerable amount of emotional sensitivity. As we described in chapter 10 (see especially pages 360–362), communicating exactly what an organizational change means for the work force can help allay the fears that are a key source of resistance to change. Doing so makes it possible for the people affected by the change to become instrumental in making it work. This philosophy of educating employees, providing them with information that helped them better understand organizational goals, has been cited as one of the elements responsible for successfully implementing the large-scale organizational changes at Honeywell which were needed to make it competitive with IBM.[30]

3. *Involve employees in the change efforts.* It is well established that people who participate in making a decision tend to be more committed to the outcomes of the decision than those who are not involved.[31] Accordingly, employees who are involved in responding to unplanned change, or who are made part of the team charged with planning a needed organizational change, may be expected to have very little resistance to change. Organizational changes that are "sprung" on the work force with little or no warning might be expected to encounter resistance simply as a "knee jerk reaction," until employees have a chance to assess how the change affects them. In contrast, employees who are involved in the change process are better positioned to understand the need for change, and are therefore less likely to resist it. It is precisely these kinds of efforts at participative management that are credited with the successful changes in Southwestern Bell in the aftermath of the breakup of AT&T.[32]

4. *Reward constructive behaviors.* One rather obvious, and quite successful, mechanism for facilitating organizational change is rewarding people for behaving in the desired fashion (recall our discussion of organizational rewards in chapter 2). Changing organizational operations may necessitate a change in the kinds of behaviors that need to be rewarded by the organization. This is especially critical when an organization is in the transition period of introducing the change. For example, employees who are required to learn to use new equipment should be praised for their successful efforts. Feedback on how well they are doing not only provides a great deal of useful assurance to uncertain employees, but also goes a long way in shaping the desired behavior (see chapter 2).

Although these four suggestions may be easier to state than to implement, it is clear that any effort to follow them will be well rewarded. Given the many forces that make employees resistant to change, it is important for managers to keep these guidelines in mind. If organizational change is to be beneficial, it is critical that all employees work toward accepting the change rather than using it as a rallying point around which organizational conflict may focus.

ORGANIZATIONAL DEVELOPMENT: THE IMPLEMENTATION OF PLANNED ORGANIZATIONAL CHANGE

Now that we have shed some light on the basic issues surrounding organizational change, we are ready to look at planned ways of implementing it—collectively known as techniques of **organizational development** (or, **OD**). More formally, we may define organizational development as: *a set of social science techniques designed to plan and implement change in organizational work settings for purposes of enhancing the personal development of individuals and improving the effectiveness of organizational functioning.*[33] By planning organization-wide changes involving people, OD seeks to enhance organizational performance by improving the quality of the work environment and the attitudes and well-being of employees.

Over the years, a vast array of strategies for implementing planned organizational change (referred to as *OD interventions*) have been used by specialists attempting to improve organizational functioning (referred to as *OD practitioners*).[34] We will begin this section by summarizing several major OD techniques. Following this, we will conclude by assessing their overall effectiveness, addressing the important question: do they work?

OD Interventions: Major Techniques

All the major methods of organizational development attempt to produce some kind of change in individual employees, work groups, and/or entire organizations. This is the goal of the six well-known OD techniques we will review—*survey feedback, sensitivity training, team building, grid training, quality of work life programs,* and *management by objectives.*

Survey feedback: Inducing change by sharing information. In order for effective organizational change to occur, it is necessary for employees to understand the organization's current strengths and weaknesses. That's the underlying rationale behind the **survey feedback** method.

This technique follows three simple steps (summarized in Figure 16.10).[35] First (usually with the help of an outside consultant retained by top management), data is collected that provides information about matters of general concern to the employees, such as organizational climate, leadership style, degree of satisfaction, and similar themes. This may take the form of intensive interviews or structured questionnaires (either standardized, or developed specifically for the organization studied), or both. Because it is important that this information be as accurate as possible, employees providing feedback are assured that their responses will be kept confidential.

The second step calls for reporting the information obtained to the employees during small group meetings. Typically, this consists of summarizing the average scores on the various work-related attitudes measured in the survey. Profiles are created of feelings about the organization, its leadership, the work done, and related topics. Discussions also focus on why the scores are as they are, and what problems are revealed by the feedback. The third and final step involves analyzing problems dealing with communication, decision making, and other organizational processes in order to make plans for dealing with them. Such discussions are usually most effective when they are carefully documented and a specific plan of implementation is made (with someone put in charge of carrying it out).

Survey feedback is a widely used OD technique.[36] This is not surprising in view of the advantages it offers. It is efficient, allowing a great deal of information to be collected relatively quickly. Also, it is very flexible, and can be tailored to the needs of different organizations facing a variety of problems. However, the technique can be no better than the quality of the questionnaire put together by the outside consultant— it must measure the things that really matter to the employees. Of course, to derive the maximum benefit from survey feedback, it must have the support of top management. Specifically, the plans developed by the small discussion groups must be capable of implementation with the full approval of the organization. When these conditions are met, survey feedback can be a very effective OD technique.

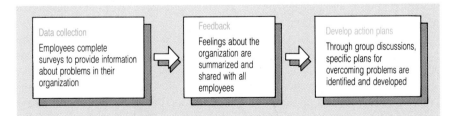

Data collection
Employees complete surveys to provide information about problems in their organization

Feedback
Feelings about the organization are summarized and shared with all employees

Develop action plans
Through group discussions, specific plans for overcoming problems are identified and developed

FIGURE 16.10 Survey Feedback: An Overview
The *survey feedback* technique of organizational development follows the three stages outlined here.

Sensitivity training: Developing personal insight. Sensitivity training is a method by which small, face-to-face group interaction experiences are used to give people insight into themselves (who they are, the way others respond to them, etc.). Developed in the 1940s, sensitivity training groups (also referred to as *encounter groups, laboratory groups,* or *T-groups*) were among the first OD techniques used in organizations (such as Standard Oil and Union Carbide).[37]

The rationale behind sensitivity training is that people are usually not completely open and honest with each other, a condition which thwarts insights into oneself and others. However, when people are placed in special situations within which such open, honest communication is allowed and encouraged, such personal insights may be gained. To do this, small groups (usually of about eight to fifteen) are created and meet away from the pressures of the job site for several days. An expert trainer (referred to as the *facilitator*) guides the group at all times, helping assure that the proper atmosphere is maintained.

The sessions themselves are completely open with respect to what is discussed. Often, to get the ball rolling, the facilitator will frustrate the group members by not getting involved at all, and appearing to be passively goofing off. As members sit around and engage in meaningless chit-chat, they begin to feel angry at the change agent for wasting their time. Once these expressions of anger begin to emerge, the change agent has created the important first step needed to make the session work—he or she has given the group a chance to focus on a current event. At this point, the discussion may be guided into how each of the group members expresses his or her anger toward the others. They are encouraged to continue discussing these themes openly and honestly, and not to hide their true feelings as they would often do on the job. The rule is to openly and honestly share your feelings about others. So, for example, if you think someone is goofing off and relying too much on you, this is the time to say so. Participants are encouraged to respond by giving each other *immediate feedback* to what was said. By doing this, it is reasoned, people will come to learn more about how they interrelate with others, and will become more skilled at interpersonal relations. These are among the major goals of sensitivity groups.

It probably comes as no surprise to you that the effectiveness of sensitivity training is difficult to assess. After all, measuring insight into one's own personality is clearly elusive. Even if interpersonal skills seem to be improved, it is not always the case that people will be able to successfully transfer their newly-learned skills when they leave the artificial training atmosphere and return to their jobs.[38] As a result, sensitivity training tends not to be used extensively by itself for OD purposes. Rather, as we will see, it is often used in conjunction with, or as part of, other OD techniques.

Team building: Creating effective work groups. Team building is a technique that developed in an attempt to apply the techniques and rationale of sensitivity training to work groups. The approach attempts to get members of a work group to diagnose how they work together, and to plan how this may be improved.[39] Given the importance of group efforts in effective organizational functioning, attempts at improving the effectiveness of work groups are likely to have profound effects on organizations. If one assumes that work groups are the basic building blocks of organizations, it follows that organizational change should emphasize changing groups instead of individuals.[40]

Team building begins when members of a group admit that they have a problem, and gather data to provide insight about it. The problems that are identified may come from sensitivity training sessions, or more objective sources, such as production figures or attitude surveys. These data are then shared, in a *diagnostic session,* to develop a consensus regarding the group's current strengths and weaknesses. From this, a list of desired changes is created, along with some plans for implementing these changes.

In other words, an *action plan* is developed—that is, some task-oriented approach to solving the group's problems as diagnosed. Following this step, the plan is carried out, and its progress is evaluated to determine whether the originally identified problems still remain. If the problems are solved, the process is completed, and the team may stop meeting. If not, the process should be restarted. (Please see Figure 16.11 for a summary of these steps.)

Work teams have been used effectively to combat a variety of important organizational problems.[41] For these efforts to be successful, however, it is important that all group members participate in the gathering and evaluating of information as well as in the planning and implementing of action plans. Input from group members is also especially crucial in evaluating the effectiveness of the team building program.[42] It is also important to keep in mind that because the team building approach is highly task-oriented, interpersonal problems between group members may be disruptive, and need to be neutralized by an outside party. With such interpersonal strain out of the way, the stage is set for groups to learn to effectively solve their own problems. However,

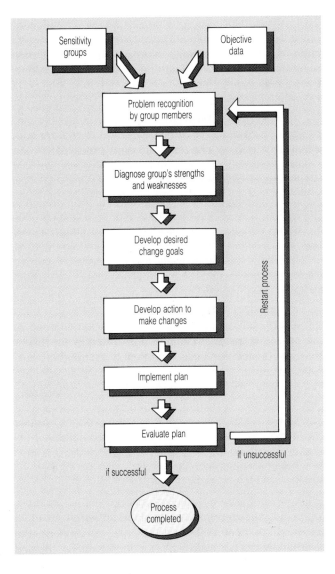

FIGURE 16.11 Team Building: An Overview

Team building, a popular technique of organizational development, follows the steps outlined here.

this does not happen overnight. To be most effective, team building should not be approached as a one-time exercise undertaken during a few days away from the job. Rather, it should be thought of as an ongoing process that takes several months (or even years) to develop. Given the great impact effective groups can have on organizational functioning, efforts at building effective work teams seem quite worthwhile.

Grid training: Improving managerial effectiveness. Improving the total organization on a long-term basis is the goal of **grid training.** This approach, developed by Blake and Mouton, seeks to promote organizational excellence by fostering concern for both production and people.[43] Working on the premise that most organizational problems stem from poor communication and inadequate planning, Blake and Mouton propose a multi-step process for improving organizations by attempting to cultivate these skills.

The initial step consists of a *grid seminar*—a session (usually beginning on a Sunday night and ending the following Friday at noon) in which an organization's line managers (who have been previously trained in the appropriate theory and skills) help organization members analyze their own management styles. This is done using a specially designed questionnaire that allows managers to determine how they stand with respect to two important dimensions of effective management—their *concern for production* and their *concern for people* (you may recall similar dimensions identified in several approaches to leadership discussed in chapter 11). Each participant's approach on each dimension is scored using a number ranging from 1 (low) to 9 (high). Managers who score low on both concern for production and concern for people are scored *1,1*—evidence of *impoverished management.* A manager who is highly concerned about production, but shows little interest in people, the *task management* style, scores *9,1.* In contrast, ones who show the opposite pattern—high concern with people but little concern with production—are described as having a *country club* style of management; they are scored *1,9.* Managers scoring moderately on both dimensions, the *5,5* pattern, are said to follow a *middle-of-the-road management* style. Finally, there are individuals who are highly concerned with both production and people, those scoring *9,9.* This is the most desirable pattern, and represents what is known as *team management.* These various patterns are represented in a diagram like that shown in Figure 16.12, known as the *managerial grid.*®

After a manager's position along the grid is determined, training begins to improve concern over production (planning skills) and concern over people (communication skills) in order to reach the ideal, *9,9* state. This training consists of organization-wide team training aimed at helping work group members interact more effectively with each other. Then, this training is expanded to help reduce conflict between groups that have to work with each other. Additional phases of training include efforts to identify the extent to which the organization is meeting its strategic goals, and then comparing this performance to an ideal. Next, plans are made to meet these goals, and these plans are implemented in the organization. Finally, progress toward the goals is continuously assessed, and problem areas are identified.

As you can tell, full implementation of grid training involves many changes, making it difficult to tell which aspects of the program may be responsible for improved organizational functioning. Some skeptics would argue that because grid training is prepackaged, and designed to be used in all organizations, it may not meet the special development needs of any particular organization. Specifically, it always assumes that being concerned about both people and production is the best management style. However, as we described in chapter 11, there are many situations in which effective leadership requires much more of one of these skills than the other. Regardless, the technique has been identified as a successful mechanism for implementing planned

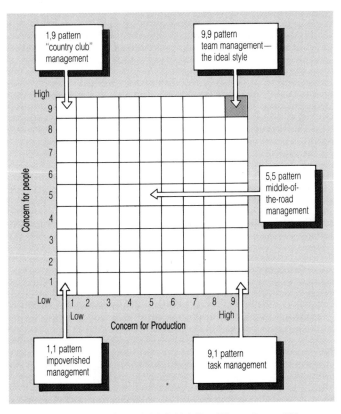

FIGURE 16.12 The Managerial Grid:® Key Dimensions of Management
A manager's standing along two key dimensions—concern for production, and concern for
people—can be illustrated by means of a diagram such as this one, known as the *managerial
grid.*® Blake and Mouton, the developers of the popular organizational development
technique, *grid training,* suggest that organizational effectiveness results when managers are
trained to score high on both dimensions. (Source: Based on suggestions by Blake and
Mouton, 1969; see Note 43.)

organizational change in several studies.[44] Because the grid approach trains managers
to train their coworkers, it has been widely used—allowing several hundred thousand
people to reap its benefits.

Quality of work life programs: Humanizing the work place. When you think
of work, do you think of drudgery? Although many people believe these two terms go
together naturally, it has become increasingly popular in recent years to systematically
improve the quality of life on many jobs. As more and more people demand satisfying
and personally fulfilling places to work (a movement that became popular in the 1970s),
OD practitioners have attempted to systematically create work situations that enhance
employees' motivation, satisfaction, and commitment—factors which may contribute
to high levels of organizational performance. Such efforts are known collectively as
quality of work life (or **QWL) programs.** Specifically, such programs are ways of
increasing organizational output and improving quality by involving employees in the
decisions that affect them on their jobs. Typically, such programs encourage highly
democratic treatment of employees at all levels, and encourage their participation in
decision making. Although there are many approaches to improving the quality of work
life, they all share the common goal of humanizing the work place.[45]

One popular approach to improving the quality of work life involves *work restruc-*

turing—the process of changing the way jobs are done so as to make them more interesting to workers.[46] If this sounds familiar to you, it might be because we already discussed several such approaches to redesigning jobs—including as *job enlargement, job enrichment,* and the *job characteristics model*—in our discussion of motivation in chapter 3. In the present context, it is important to note that such techniques represent effective ways of improving the quality of work life for employees.

Another approach to improving the quality of work life, and an increasingly popular one in recent years, has been imported from Japan—**quality circles** (or **QCs**). These are small groups of volunteers (usually, around ten) who meet regularly (usually, weekly) to identify and solve problems related to: (a) the quality of the work they perform, and (b) the conditions under which people do their jobs.[47] An organization may have several QCs operating at once, each dealing with a particular work area about which it has the most expertise. To help them work effectively, the members of the circle usually receive some form of training in problem solving. Such large companies as Westinghouse, Hewlett-Packard, and Eastman Kodak, to name only a few, have included QCs as part of their QWL efforts.[48] Groups have dealt with such issues as how to reduce vandalism, how to create safer and more comfortable working environments, and how to improve product quality. Research has shown that while quality circles are very effective at bringing about short-term improvements in quality of work life (i.e., those lasting up to eighteen months), they are less effective at creating more permanent changes.[49] As such, they may be recognized as useful temporary strategies for enhancing organizational effectiveness.

As you might imagine, there are a variety of benefits (if even short-term ones) that might result from QWL programs—both work restructuring and QCs. These fall into three major categories.[50] The most direct benefit is usually increased job satisfaction and organizational commitment among the work force. A second benefit is increased productivity. Following from these two is the third benefit—increased organizational effectiveness (e.g., profitability, goal attainment, etc.). Many companies, including such industrial giants as Ford, General Electric, and AT&T have active QWL programs and are reportedly quite pleased with their results.[51]

Achieving these benefits is not automatic, however. There are two major potential pitfalls that must be avoided for QWL programs to be successfully implemented. For one, it is essential that both management and labor cooperate in designing their program. Should any one side believe that the program is really just a method of gaining an advantage over the other, it is doomed to fail. Second, it is essential that the plans agreed to by all concerned parties be fully implemented. It is too easy for action plans developed in QWL groups to be forgotten amidst the hectic pace of daily activities. It is the responsibility of employees at all levels—from the highest-ranking manager to the lowest-level laborer—to follow through on their part of the plan.

Management by objectives: Clarifying organizational goals. You may recall that in chapter 3 we detailed the positive motivational benefits of setting specific goals. As you might imagine, it is not only individuals but also entire organizations that stand to benefit from setting specific goals. For example, an organization may strive to "raise production" and "improve the quality" of its manufactured goods. These goals, noble and well intentioned though they may be, may not be as useful to an organization as more specific ones, such as "increase production of widgets by 15 percent" or "lower the failure rate of widgets by 25 percent." After all, as the old saying goes, "it's usually easier to get somewhere if you know where you're going." Peter Drucker, consulting for General Electric during the early 1950s, was well aware of this idea, and is credited with promoting the benefits of specifying clear organizational goals—a technique known as **management by objectives** (or **MBO**).[52]

The MBO process, summarized in Figure 16.13, consists of three basic steps. First, goals are selected that employees will try to attain in order to best serve the needs of the organization. The goals should be selected by managers and their subordinates together. It is important that the goals be set mutually, not imposed on subordinates by their managers. Further, these goals should be directly measurable and have some time frame attached to them. Goals that cannot be measured, or that have no time limits (e.g., "make the company better"), are useless. As part of this first step, it is crucial that managers and their subordinates work together to plan ways of attaining the goals they have selected—what is known as an *action plan*.

After goals are set and action plans have been developed to attain them, the second step calls for *implementation*—carrying out the action plan and regularly assessing its progress. Is the plan working? Are the goals being approximated? Are there any problems being encountered in attempting to meet the goals? Such questions need to be considered while implementing an action plan. If the plan is failing, a mid-course correction may be in order—changing the plan, the way it's carried out, or the goal.

After monitoring progress toward the goal, the third step may be instituted, *evaluation*—that is, assessing goal attainment. Were the organization's goals reached? If so, what new goals should be set to improve things still further? If not, what new plans can be initiated to help meet the goals? Because the ultimate assessment of the extent to which goals are met helps determine the selection of new goals, the MBO process is shown in Figure 16.13 as a continuous one.

As described here, MBO represents a potentially effective source of planning and implementing strategic change for the organization. Individual efforts designed to meet organizational goals get the individual employee and the organization itself working together toward common ends. Hence, system-wide change results. Of course, for MBO to work, everyone involved in the process has to buy into it. Because the program typically entails a great amount of participation by lower-level employees, top managers must be willing to accept and support the cooperation and involvement of all employees. Making MBO work also requires a great deal of time—anywhere from three to five

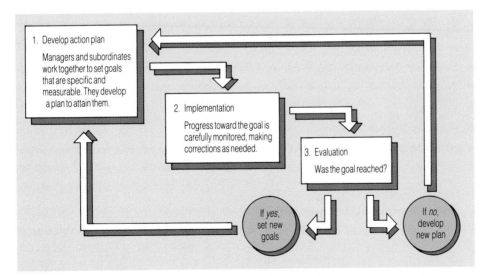

FIGURE 16.13.   **Management by Objectives: Developing Organizations through Goal Setting**
The organizational development technique of *management by objectives* requires managers and their subordinates to work together on setting and trying to achieve important organizational goals. The steps in the process are outlined here.

years.[53] Hence, MBO may be inappropriate in organizations that do not have the time to commit to making it work. Despite these considerations, MBO has become one of the most widely used techniques for affecting organizational change in recent years. It is not only used on an ad hoc basis by many organizations, but constitutes an ingrained element of the organizational culture in some companies, such as Hewlett-Packard and IBM. Given the successes MBO has experienced (not only as an OD technique, but also as a motivational tool and an aid to effective performance appraisals), it is not surprising that it is still widely used.[54]

The Effectiveness of Organizational Development: Does It Really Work?

Thus far, we have described some of the major techniques used by OD practitioners to improve organizational functioning. As is probably clear, carrying out these techniques requires a considerable amount of time, money, and effort. Accordingly, it is appropriate to ask if the investment involved in implementing OD interventions is worth it. In other words, does OD really work? Given the increasing popularity of OD in a wide variety of organizations, the question is more important than ever.[55]

Research has revealed that the answer to the question is a qualified *yes*. In other words, although many studies have revealed beneficial effects associated with OD programs, the findings are far from unanimous. Consider, for example, research on quality circles. While many researchers have found that quality circles help reduce organizational costs and improve employees' attitudes, many other studies reported no such beneficial effects.[56] Mixed results have also been obtained in many studies assessing the effectiveness of sensitivity training programs. For example, whereas such programs often lead to temporary differences in the way people interact with others, the results tend to be short-lived on the job, and are not related to permanent changes in the way people behave.[57] Thus, whereas OD may have many positive effects, not all desired outcomes may be realized.

A recent review by Porras, Robertson, and Goldman compared the results of forty-nine OD studies published between 1975 and 1986.[58] Among the different types of OD interventions studied were those we have described, specifically: *grid training, MBO, QWL, survey feedback, sensitivity groups,* and *team building*. The investigators categorized the research with respect to whether they found the effects of the interventions to be beneficial, negative, or nonexistent. The outcomes studied were both individual (e.g., job satisfaction) and organizational (e.g., profit, productivity) in nature. The results, summarized in Figure 16.14, reveal some interesting findings.

It is important to note that a sizeable percentage of the studies found effects of the various interventions beneficial. However, these beneficial results were not as impressive for individual outcomes (where the vast majority of the studies demonstrated no effects of any of the interventions) as they were for organizational outcomes (where many studies found positive effects). Accordingly, the benefits of OD techniques are more firmly established with respect to improving organizational functioning than with respect to improving individuals' job attitudes.

We hasten to add, however, that this conclusion needs to be qualified in several important ways. For one, research has shown that OD interventions tend to be more effective among blue-collar employees than among white-collar employees.[59] Second, it has been found that the beneficial effects of OD can be enhanced by using several techniques instead of just one. Specifically, studies in which four or more OD programs were used together yielded positive findings more frequently than those in which fewer techniques were used.[60] Thus, it appears that the effectiveness of OD efforts can be enhanced by not relying on any one single technique, but rather, a combination of several.

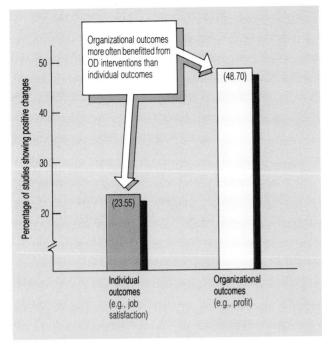

**FIGURE 16.14
Organizational Development:
Evidence of Its Effectiveness**

In reviewing forty-nine
studies of organizational
development (OD)
techniques published
between 1975 and 1986,
Porras, Robertson, and
Goldman found that
organizational outcomes
(e.g., productivity) benefited
more often than individual
outcomes (e.g., job
satisfaction). (Source:
Based on data reported by
Porras et al., in press; see
Note 33.)

Despite the importance of attempting to evaluate the effectiveness of OD interventions, a great many of them go unevaluated. Although there are undoubtedly many
reasons for this, one of the key factors has to do with the difficulty of assessing change.
Because many factors can cause people to behave differently in organizations, and
because such behaviors may be difficult to measure, many OD practitioners avoid the
problem of measuring change altogether. In a related vein, political pressures to justify
OD programs may discourage some OD professionals from honestly and accurately
assessing their effectiveness. After all, in doing so, one runs the risk of scientifically
demonstrating one's wasted time and money (a similar point was made in chapter 2
regarding the assessment of organizational training programs).

In cases where OD has been studied, however, the research is more often than
not conducted in a manner that leaves its conclusions seriously open to question.[61] In
particular, it is often very difficult to isolate exactly which aspects of an organizational
intervention were responsible for the changes noted. Also, because OD practices are
a novelty to most employees, there may be a tendency to produce temporary improvements (recall our discussion of the Hawthorne effect in chapter 1).[62] In other
words, serious questions may be raised about the true effectiveness of organizational
development efforts as revealed in existing research.

As such, we may conclude that organizational development is an approach that
shows considerable promise in its ability to benefit organizations and the individuals
working within them. With further refinements in assessing the benefits of OD programs, a great many benefits may be derived—benefits for the OD practitioner who
seeks to improve organizations, for the organizational scientist who seeks to understand
organizational behavior, and ultimately, of course, for the people who make up the
organizations themselves.

(Given the widespread popularity of organizational development techniques in the
United States, it seems reasonable to ask whether these techniques may be used in
other nations. Moreover, given the proliferation of multinational organizations, the
question of whether this social technology can be effectively imported to these orga-

nizations is extremely important.[63] As shown in the **International Perspective** section below, American OD practitioners may be in for some serious surprises and disappointments when they try to practice their work in different nations.)

OB: AN INTERNATIONAL PERSPECTIVE

Cultural Barriers to Effective OD Interventions: The Importance of Matching OD Values and National Culture

Warren Bennis, an expert in OD, recounts an incident in which a large Swiss company terminated a group development program after the company president found the program's egalitarian values inconsistent with the values of his Swiss Army training—that authority is based on one's position in an organizational hierarchy.[64] Steele tells a similar story of his failed experiences at attempting to introduce OD to Great Britain.[65] Apparently, there was a clash between the expectations of openness underlying the OD techniques and British norms encouraging the avoidance of "unsuitable" topics. These examples suggest that the underlying assumptions behind many OD interventions may clash with cultural values operating in organizations. Thus, OD practitioners apparently require a great deal of knowledge about the culture of the nations in which their techniques are to be used before they can be expected to have beneficial results.

What elements of social culture are most likely to account for cross-national differences in organizational functioning? Based on a questionnaire administered to 116,000 employees of a large multinational corporation working in forty countries, Hofstede identified four critical elements of culture.[66]

1. *power distance:* the degree to which the unequal distribution of power within organizations is accepted by members of society.
2. *uncertainty avoidance:* how much members of a society are threatened by uncertain and ambiguous situations.
3. *individualism-collectivism:* the tendency to take care of oneself and one's family versus the tendency to work together for the collective good of everyone.
4. *masculinity-femininity:* the extent to which highly assertive values predominate (e.g., acquiring money and goods at the expense of others) versus showing sensitivity and concern for others' welfare.

In recent years, organizational scientists have disclosed some very interesting and important findings regarding these cultural dimensions. For example, Kedia and Bhagat reviewed literature revealing that new technologies were most likely to be accepted by nations when certain cultural elements prevailed.[67] Specifically, among other things, they note that technology is likely to be accepted and successfully implemented by nations that have an individualistic orientation (e.g., West Germany), than those with a collective one (e.g., Venezuela). The point is that cultural values operating within nations are expected to influence the likelihood that new technology will be adapted. To the extent that a culture's prevailing norms and values are threatened by a new technology, it is unlikely to be accepted (e.g., a machine that enables workers' jobs to be more equal might not be accepted in a culture like India's, where high degrees of power distance are culturally embraced). In fact, in the case of developing nations, cultural factors may be even more important than the strategic value of the technology itself when it comes to the willingness to import new technology.

Given that Hofstede's four key cultural dimensions are critical to the successful adoption of new technologies, it is not surprising that they may likewise be an important part of any planned organizational change efforts. With this in mind, Jaeger argued that the values underlying most OD techniques may be described as: low on power distance, uncertainty avoidance and masculinity, and moderate on individualism.[68] He reasoned that countries whose national values come closest to this pattern (e.g., the Scandinavian nations) may be the most successful in using OD techniques, whereas those that are highly different (e.g., most Latin American nations) may be most unsuccessful (see summary in Figure 16.15).

However, because not all OD techniques are alike, Jaeger analyzed specific intervention techniques with respect to their underlying cultural values. For example, MBO, a very popular OD technique in the United States, may have caught on because it promotes the American values of willingness to take

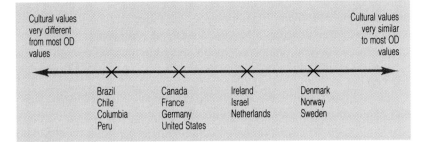

FIGURE 16.15 Organizational Development: Its Fit With Cultural Values
Organizational development (OD) techniques tend to be more successful when the underlying values of the technique match the cultural values of the nation in which it is used. General OD values tend to conform more to the cultural values of some nations, shown on the right (where OD is more likely to be accepted) and less to others, shown on the left (where OD is less likely to be accepted). (Source: Based on suggestions by Jaeger, 1986; see Note 68.)

risks and working aggressively at attaining high performance. However, because MBO also encourages superiors and subordinates to negotiate freely with each other, the technique has been generally unsuccessful in France, where high power distance between superiors and subordinates is culturally accepted.[69] Following similar reasoning, one may expect such OD techniques as survey feedback to be unsuccessful in the southeast Asian nation of Brunei, where the prevailing cultural value is such that problems are unlikely to be confronted openly.[70] These and other examples illustrate an important point: *the effectiveness of OD techniques will depend, in part, on the extent to which the values of the technique match the underlying values of the national culture in which it is employed.*

Given this, we may conclude that OD practitioners must fully appreciate the cultural norms of the nations where they are operating. Failure to do so may not only make OD interventions unsuccessful, but may even have dangerous negative consequences. Therefore, as part of planning an OD intervention, it is strongly recommended that OD practitioners carefully match the techniques they use to the values of the host culture. The most rigidly held values of a culture should never be challenged by the OD techniques. Remember: these techniques are designed to improve the functioning of the organization *within its culture*. Therefore, any techniques that clash with prevailing cultural norms should be avoided.

SUMMARY AND REVIEW

Forces Behind Organizational Change. Changes in organizations may be either planned or unplanned, and they may be based internal or external to the organization. Planned internal changes may include changes in products or services and changes in administrative systems. Planned external changes include the introduction of new technologies and advances in information processing and communication. Unplanned internal changes include shifts in the demographic characteristics of the work force and responses to performance gaps. Unplanned external change may result from governmental regulation as well as from economic competition.

The Process of Organizational Change. Organizations may change with respect to their organizational structure (responsibilities and procedures used), the technology used on the job, and the people who perform the work. Change is likely to occur whenever the benefits associated with making a change (i.e., dissatisfaction with current conditions, the availability of desirable alternatives and the existence of a plan for achieving that alternative) outweigh the costs involved. Generally speaking, people are resistant to change because of individual factors (e.g., economic insecurity and fear of the unknown) and organizational factors (e.g., the stability of work groups, and threats to the existing balance of power). However, resistance to change can be overcome in several ways, including educating the work force about the effects of the changes and involving employees in the change process.

Techniques of Organizational Development. Techniques for planning organizational change in order to enhance personal and organizational outcomes are collectively known as **organizational development** practices. For example, *survey feedback* uses questionnaires and/or interviews as the basis for identifying organizational problems, which are then addressed in planning sessions. *Sensitivity training* is a technique in which group discussions are used to enhance interpersonal awareness and reduce interpersonal friction. *Team building* involves using work groups to diagnose, and develop specific plans for solving, problems with respect to their functioning as a work unit. *Grid training* focuses on efforts to improve managers' concerns for people and their concern for production by training them on communication skills and planning skills. *Quality of work life* programs attempt to humanize the work place by involving employees in the decisions affecting them (e.g., through *quality circle* meetings) and by restructuring the jobs themselves. Finally, *management by objectives* focuses on attempts by managers and their subordinates to work together at setting important organizational goals and developing a plan to help meet them. The rationale underlying all six of these techniques is that organizational functioning may be enhanced by involving employees in identifying and solving organizational problems.

The effectiveness of most organizational development programs is not systematically assessed in practice, and the few studies that do attempt to measure the success of such programs are not carefully conducted. However, those studies that have systematically evaluated organizational development programs generally find them to be successful in improving organizational functioning and, to a lesser degree, individual satisfaction.

KEY TERMS

dual-core model: The theory recognizing that changes in the administration of organizations come from upper management (i.e., from the top, down), whereas changes in the work performed come from the technical specialists within organizations (i.e., from the bottom, up).

grid training: The OD technique designed to strengthen managers' communication skills (their concern for people) and their planning skills (their concern for production).

horizontal linkage model: The theory specifying the importance of the marketing and research functions of organizations in the introduction of new products and services.

management by objectives (MBO): The technique by which managers and their subordinates work together to set, and then meet, organizational goals.

organizational change: Alterations in the operations of organizations that are either planned or unplanned, and are a result of either internal or external influences.

organizational development (OD): A set of social science techniques designed to plan change in organizational work settings, for purposes of enhancing the personal development of individuals and improving the effectiveness of organizational functioning.

quality circles (QCs): An approach to improving the quality of work life, in which small groups of volunteers meet regularly to identify and solve problems related to the work they perform and the conditions under which they work.

quality of work life (QWL): An OD technique designed to improve organizational functioning by humanizing the workplace, making it more democratic, and involving employees in decision making.

resistance to change: The tendency for employees to be unwilling to go along with organizational changes, either because of individual fears of the unknown, or organizational impediments (such as *structural inertia*).

sensitivity training: An OD technique that seeks to enhance employees' understanding of their own behavior and its impact on others. Such changes, it is believed, will reduce the interpersonal conflicts that interfere with organizational effectiveness.

structural inertia: The organizational forces acting on employees, encouraging them to perform their jobs in certain ways (e.g., training, reward systems), thereby making them resistant to change.

survey feedback: An OD technique in which questionnaires and interviews are used to collect information about issues of concern to an organization. This information is shared with employees and is used as the basis for planning organizational change.

team building: An OD technique in which employees discuss problems related to their work group's performance. On the basis of these discussions, specific problems are identified and plans for solving them are devised and implemented.

QUESTIONS FOR DISCUSSION

1. Some changes in organizations are unplanned, while others are the result of deliberate, planned actions. Give examples of each of these varieties of change and explain their implications for organizational functioning.

2. Suppose you are having difficulty managing a small group of subordinates who work in an office 1,000 miles away from your home base. What kinds of changes in *structure, technology,* and *people* can be implemented to more closely supervise these distant employees?

3. Under what conditions will people be most willing to make changes in organizations? Explain your answer and give an example.

4. Suppose you are a top executive of a large organization about to undertake an ambitious restructuring involving massive changes in job responsibilities for most employees.

Explain why people would be resistant to such changes and what steps might be taken to overcome this resistance.

5. Imagine that you are supervising ten employees who are not getting along. Their constant fighting is interfering with their job performance. Identify any two different *organizational development* techniques that might be employed to address this problem. Explain why they may help. Describe the steps taken to implement these techniques.

6. Overall, how effective is organizational development in improving organizational functioning? With respect to what factors does it work or not work?

7. Argue for or against the following statement: "Organizational development techniques are universally effective, and may be effectively applied in any culture."

NOTES

1. Barczak, G., Smith, C., & Wilemon, D. (1987, Autumn). Managing large-scale organizational change. *Organizational Dynamics,* 23–35.

2. Nystrom, P. C., & Starbuck, W. H. (1984, Spring). To avoid organizational crises, unlearn. *Organizational Dynamics,* 44–60.

3. Daft, R. L. (1986). *Organization theory and design* (2nd ed.). St. Paul, MN: West.

4. Cobb, A. T., & Marguiles, N. (1981). Organizational development: A political perspective. *Academy of Management Review, 6,* 49–59.

5. Daft, R. L. (1982). Bureaucratic versus nonbureaucratic structure and the process of innovation and change. In S. B. Bachrach (Ed.), *Research in the sociology of organizations,* vol. 1 (pp. 56–88). Greenwich, CT: JAI Press.

6. Gaertner, G. H., Gaertner, K. N., & Akinnusi, D. M. (1984). Environment, strategy, and implementation of administrative change: The case of civil service reform. *Academy of Management Journal, 27,* 525–543.

7. Majchrzak, A., & Cotton, J. (1988). A longitudinal study of adjustment to technological change: From mass to computer-automated batch production. *Journal of Occupational Psychology, 61,* 43–66.

8. Naisbitt, J. (1982). *Megatrends.* New York: Warner.

9. Foulkes, F. K., & Hirsch, J. L. (1984, January–February). People make robots work. *Harvard Business Review,* 94–102.

10. Ettlie, J. E. (1988). *Taking charge of manufacturing: How companies are combining technological and organizational innovations to compete successfully.* San Francisco: Jossey-Bass.

11. Keen, P. G. W. (1988). *Competing in time: Using telecommunications for competitive advantage* (rev. ed.). Cambridge, MA: Ballinger.

12. Best, F. (1985, January). The nature of work in a changing society. *Personnel Journal,* pp. 37–42.

13. Colvin, G. (1984, October 15). What baby boomers will buy next. *Fortune,* pp. 28–34.

14. Dennis, H. (1988). *Fourteen steps in managing an aging work force.* Lexington, MA: Lexington Books.

15. Wheelen, T. L., & Hunger, J. D. (1989). *Strategic management and business policy* (3rd ed.). Reading, MA: Addison-Wesley.

16. Singh, J. V., House, R. J., & Tucker, D. J. (1986). Organizational change and mortality. *Administrative Science Quarterly, 31,* 587–611.

17. Barnes, Z. E. (1987). Change in the Bell System. *Academy of Management Executive, 1,* 43–46. (quote from p. 43).

18. Marcus, A. A. (1988). Implementing externally induced innovations: A comparison of rule-bound and autonomous approaches. *Academy of Management Journal, 31,* 235–256.

19. Kilmann, R. H., & Covin, T. J. (1987). *Corporate transformation: Revitalizing organizations for a competitive world.* San Francisco: Jossey-Bass.

20. Glueck, W. F. (1979). *Personnel: A diagnostic approach.* Dallas, TX: Business Publications.

21. Solomon, J. B., & Bussey, J. (1985, May 20). Cultural change: Pressed by its rivals, Procter & Gamble is altering its ways. *Wall Street Journal,* p. 1.

22. Lewin, K. (1951). *Field theory in social science.* New York: Harper & Row.

23. Schein, E. H. (1968). Organizational socialization and the profession of management. *Industrial Management Review, 9,* 1–16.

24. Beer, M. (1980). *Organizational change and development: A systems view.* Glenview, IL: Scott, Foresman.

25. Nadler, D. A. (1987). The effective management of organizational change. In J. W. Lorsch (Ed.), *Handbook of organizational behavior* (pp. 358–369). Englewood Cliffs, NJ: Prentice-Hall.

26. Katz, D., & Kahn, R. L. (1978). *The social psychology of organizations* (2nd ed.). New York: Wiley.

27. Hannan, M. T., & Freeman, J. (1984). Structural inertia and organizational change. *American Sociological Review, 49,* 149–164.

28. Kotter, J. P., & Schlesinger, L. A. (1979, March–April). Choosing strategies for change. *Harvard Business Review,* pp. 106–114.

29. See Note 25.

30. Reiner, J. J. (1987). Turnaround of information systems at Honeywell. *Academy of Management Executive, 1,* 47–50.

31. Cotton, J. L., Vollrath, D. A., Froggatt, K. L., Lengnick-Hall, M. L., & Jennings, K. R. (1988). Employee participation: Diverse forms and different outcomes. *Academy of Management Review, 13,* 8–22.

32. See Note 17.

33. Porras, J. I., Robertson, P. J., & Goldman, L. (in press). Organization development: Theory, practice, and research. In M. D. Dunnette (Ed.), *Handbook of industrial/organizational psychology* (2nd ed.). Palo Alto, CA: Consulting Psychologists Press.

34. Huse, E. F., & Cummings, T. G. (1985). *Organization development and change* (3rd ed.). St. Paul, MN: West.

35. See Note 34.

36. Franklin, J. L. (1978, May–June). Improving the effectiveness of survey feedback. *Personnel,* pp. 11–17.

37. Golembiewski, R. T. (1972). *Renewing organizations: A laboratory approach to planned change.* Itasca, IL: Peacock.

38. Campbell, J. P., & Dunnette, M. D. (1968). Effectiveness of T-group experiences in managerial training and development. *Psychological Bulletin, 70,* 73–104.

39. See Note 24.

40. Sherwood, J. J. (1972). An introduction to organization development. In J. W. Pfeiffer, & J. E. Jones (Eds.), *The 1972 handbook for group facilitators* (pp. 122–168). La Jolla, CA: Univ. Assoc.

41. Beckhard, R. (1972, Summer). Optimizing team-building efforts. *Journal of Contemporary Business,* pp. 23–32.

42. Vicars, W. M., & Hartke, D. D. (1984). Evaluating OD evaluations: A status report. *Group and Organization Studies, 9,* 177–188.

43. Blake, R. R., & Mouton, J. S. (1969). *Building a dynamic corporation through grid organizational development.* Reading, MA: Addison-Wesley.

44. Porras, J. I., & Berg, P. O. (1978). The impact of organization development. *Academy of Management Review, 3,* 249–266.

45. Burke, W. W. (1982). *Organization development: Principles and practices.* Boston: Little, Brown.

46. Hackman, J. R., & Oldham, G. R. (1980). *Work redesign.* Reading, MA: Addison-Wesley.

47. Munchus, G. (1983). Employer-employee based quality circles in Japan: Human resource implications for American firms. *Academy of Management Review, 8,* 255–261.

48. Meyer, G. W., & Scott, R. G. (1985, Spring). Quality circles: Panacea or Pandora's box? *Organizational Dynamics,* 34–50.

49. Griffin, R. W. (1988). Consequences of quality circles in an industrial setting: A longitudinal assessment. *Academy of Management Journal, 31,* 338–358.

50. Suttle, J. L. (1977). Improving life at work—problems and prospects. In J. R. Hackman, & J. L. Suttle (Eds.), *Improving life at work: Behavioral science approaches to organizational change* (pp. 1–29). Santa Monica, CA: Goodyear.

51. Jick, T. D., & Ashkenas, R. N. (1985). Involving employees in productivity and QWL improvements: What OD can learn from the manager's perspective. In D. D. Warrick (Ed.), *Contemporary organization development: Current thinking and applications* (pp. 218–230). Glenview, IL: Scott, Foresman.

52. Drucker, P. (1954). *The practice of management.* New York: Harper & Row.

53. Kondrasuk, J. N., Flager, K., Morrow, D., & Thompson, R. (1984). The effect of management by objectives on organization results. *Group and Organization Studies, 9,* 531–539.

54. Kondrasuk, J. N. (1981). Studies in MBO effectiveness. *Academy of Management Review, 6,* 419–430.

55. French, W. L., Bell, C. H., Jr., & Zawacki, R. A. (1989). *Organization development: Theory, practice, & research* (3rd ed.). Homewood, IL: BPI/Irwin.

56. Steel, R. P., & Shane, G. S. (1986). Evaluation research on quality circles: Technical and analytical implications. *Human Relations, 39,* 449–468.

57. See Note 38.

58. See Note 33.

59. Nicholas, J. M. (1982). The comparative impact of organization development interventions on hard criteria measures. *Academy of Management Review, 7,* 531–542.

60. See Note 44.

61. Nicholas, J. M., & Katz, M. (1985). Research methods and reporting practices in organization development: A review and some guidelines. *Academy of Management Review, 10,* 737–749.

62. White, S. E., & Mitchell, T. R. (1976). Organization development: A review of research content and research design. *Academy of Management Review, 1,* 57–73.

63. Egelhoff, W. G. (1988). *Organizing the multinational enterprise.* Cambridge, MA: Ballinger.

64. Bennis, W. (1977). Bureaucracy and social change: An anatomy of a training failure. In P. H. Mirvis, & D. N. Berg (Eds.), *Failures in organizational development and change: Cases and essays for learning* (pp. 191–215). New York: Wiley.

65. Steele, F. (1977). Is culture hostile to organization development? The UK example. In P. H. Mirvis, & D. N. Berg (Eds.), *Failures in organization development and change: Cases and essays for learning* (pp. 23–31). New York: Wiley.

66. Hofstede, G. (1980). *Culture's consequences.* Beverly Hills, CA: Sage.

67. Kedia, B. L., & Bhagat, R. S. (1988). Cultural constraints on transfer of technology across nations: Implications for research in international and comparative management. *Academy of Management Review, 13,* 559–571.

68. Jaeger, A. M. (1986). Organizational development and national culture: Where's the fit? *Academy of Management Review, 11,* 178–190.

69. Trepo, G. (1973, Autumn). Management style *a la française. European Business, 39,* 71–79.

70. Blunt, P. (1988). Cultural consequences for organization change in a southeast Asian state: Brunei. *Academy of Management Executive, 2,* 235–240.

Changing Agendas

The Aluminum Company of America, commonly known as Alcoa, was founded in 1888 with a $20,000 loan from the Mellon family. From the company's birth, its sole product has been aluminum. In fact, they were so successful at mining and manufacturing aluminum and had grown so large that in 1961 the U.S. government declared them a monopoly and demanded divestiture of their Canadian holdings. Even after this forced shrinkage and the appearance of competitors in the marketplace, Alcoa remained the industry leader. Nonetheless, when Charles W. Parry was named CEO of Alcoa in 1983, he thought he had been selected to implement changes at the nearly 100 year old aluminum giant. This belief developed from many circumstances. For instance, growth in the aluminum industry looked weak and profits were declining. Additionally, Parry's predecessor and mentor, William Henry Krome George, had initiated changes by cutting staff and closing manufacturing facilities. Parry assumed he was to continue this process so that long-term profitability would improve.[1]

Parry's main strategy for change was to develop new business. He increased research and development spending by 36 percent, with plans for further increases, in an attempt to generate new aluminum products. These products, such as aluminum hybrid ceramics and plastics, were believed to have large growth potential in industries such as packaging and aerospace. Parry also shopped around for new businesses to acquire. He was particularly fond of aerospace companies since he thought these would provide good opportunities for the expanded use of Alcoa aluminum products in the manufacture of aircraft. He projected that by 1995 fully half of Alcoa's revenues would come from non-aluminum ventures. As the search for new products and companies progressed, Parry continued to make changes at headquarters. Through layoffs, he and his chief operating officer, C. Fred Fetterolf, continued to reduce staff size. Additionally, they began to decentralize the decision-making process.

Although the board of directors generally was supportive of diversification, they seemed unaware of the extent to which Parry planned to move into other businesses. Said board member William S. Cook, "There was a new idea every few board meetings . . . He wanted to buy this and he wanted to buy that."[2] The board wasn't the only group to express concern. Customers were uneasy about Alcoa's diversification and its implications for the continued service of their aluminum needs. Similarly, Wall Street showed little support for this program of change as the value of Alcoa shares declined approximately 20 percent. Finally, Alcoa's employees were uncertain about the new directions suggested by Parry. Morale had become so low that when Parry held a barbeque to show his support for employees, one staffer remarked, "It was more like a wake."[3]

Within two years of his appointment as CEO, the board of directors had secretly begun to look for a replacement for Parry. They felt that the idea of 50 percent growth in non-aluminum business was not in the best interest of the company. Interestingly, although Parry had been very vocal in his support for acquisitions, his actions hardly followed his words. In the three years he had been at the helm, Parry had only engineered twelve acquisitions worth $500 million (about 3.5 percent growth). In searching for a new CEO, the board decided to look for an outsider with senior management and public policy experience. Parry had spent his entire career with Alcoa and the board reasoned that a "fresh set of eyes" would be valuable.

By 1987, four years after Parry took the top job, he retired early, thereby leaving his job open for the board's replacement, Paul H. O'Neill. O'Neill, who had been president of International Paper, had served on the Alcoa board for fifteen months and was well known to the directors. Although it was once speculated that O'Neill was brought in to implement Parry's vision, that has not turned out to be the case. In fact, in his letter to shareholders in the 1987 annual report, O'Neill made clear Alcoa's continued reliance on their core aluminum business.

Not all management appointments result in such poor acceptance of change. Like Parry at Alcoa, Robert R. Kiley believed he was brought to his job as head of the Metropolitan Transit Authority (MTA) in New York to implement change. The MTA, consisting of 230 miles of subway lines, 3,964 buses, and multiple commuter rail lines, had long been plagued with problems. The most obvious of these, about which complaints were most vocal, concerned the subways—they were late, dirty, broken, and dangerous. This resulted in part from MTA employees working only minimum time according to archaic work rules. Additional contributions to these problems arose from insubordination of employees and on-the-job alcohol consumption. Poor management further aggravated the problems. In this case, supervisor's participation in the labor union greatly diminished their effectiveness in applying necessary discipline. Finally, due to the fiscal crisis suffered by New York City in the mid 1970s, for many years little money was invested in equipment such as trains and track. This lack of financial support contributed to the overall run-down nature of the subway system. Given the severe state of disrepair of the MTA system, as well as the fact that each day 5.7 million people (an amount equivalent to one-third of the nation's mass transit riders) relied on the system for transportation, Kiley clearly felt the pressure for change.[4]

Kiley took many actions to improve the system. He raised money to pay for repairs to the system. Specifically, he began by paying to fix miles of broken and degenerating track. Also, new subway cars were purchased and old ones were refurbished. Kiley took controversial action to help improve the management of the system. To release 25 percent of the supervisors from their union contract, he paid $1.8 million to the union's health and welfare funds. Once these managers were placed under contract to the MTA, Kiley implemented performance appraisal systems whereby managers were responsible for improving the performance of their subordinates. Managers who, themselves, did not perform risked losing their jobs. New performance standards were also issued to workers. Sleeping and drinking on the job would no longer be tolerated. A new employee cafeteria was set up to discourage employees from storing beer in hidden refrigerators and bringing hot plates on which to prepare meals. Kiley also deftly handled the public. He began by providing realistic expectations about what could be accomplished in any time frame. He also publicized system improvements.

Kiley managed these changes in two ways. First, he decentralized decision making. He gave greater authority to middle and lower levels managers. In this way, when they saw problems, they were free to implement their own solutions. Additionally, Kiley instituted a system of setting both short and long term goals. These helped direct the work of MTA employees. They also served as a measuring device against which to assess achievements.

Kiley carefully managed the intricate political structure of New York City and State. Through a combination of cooperation and confrontation he achieved some remarkable gains for the MTA system. Among these were a 50 percent reduction in the breakdown rate of trains. Graffiti, which once covered almost the entire fleet, is gone from about 90 percent of the trains. Of the 6,250 subway cars, 1,425 have been newly purchased. The number of train repair employees has been reduced from 1,000 to 630 and productivity has risen 35 percent. Ridership rose to the highest levels in thirteen years.

Despite these impressive improvements, Kiley still has a great many changes to implement in order to get the MTA back to a smoothly functioning, efficient system. Many more trains still need replacement. The security of riders must be improved through better surveillance and police protection. New rail lines need to be installed to handle the ever-increasing amount of commuter traffic. Many new employees will be required after an expected wave of retirements in the near future. All in all, it appears that the pressures for change will continue for quite some time.

Questions for Discussion

1. What were the internal and external sources of pressure for change at Alcoa? At the MTA?

2. What were the organizational barriers to change at Alcoa? At the MTA?

3. Why do you think Parry was relatively unsuccessful in implementing changes at Alcoa?

4. Why do you think Kiley has been relatively successful in implementing changes at the MTA?

5. What changes in technology, structure, and people did Kiley make at the MTA?

Notes

1. Schroder, M. (1988, June 27). The quiet coup at Alcoa. *Business Week,* pp. 58–65.
2. See Note 1, p. 61.
3. See Note 1, p. 65.
4. Machalaba, D. (1988, October 14). Transit manager shows New York subway isn't beyond redemption. *Wall Street Journal,* pp. 1, A9.

Keeping Xerox Successful: Changing, Not Copying

If this chapter made only one point, it is surely that organizational change is inevitable, and that successful organizations are ones that adapt to changing conditions. As the PINNACLE interview with David Kearns, the Chairman of Xerox, clearly shows, Xerox confronted several serious conditions that prompted changes within the operation of this corporate giant.

Probably the major force for change Xerox confronted was the intense competition it faced from low-cost machines marketed by Japanese competitors. (In fact, Mr. Kearns notes that at one point, other companies were selling copy machines for what it cost Xerox to manufacture them!) To enable Xerox to price its products competitively, Mr. Kearns sought to simplify the company's corporate structure. Specifically, he eliminated layers of corporate hierarchy that previously interfered with communication between top management and manufacturing. Although this involved cutting 15,000 jobs in 1982, streamlining its operation to a leaner, more efficient one was necessary for the company's survival.

Not only changes in economics, but changes in technology dictate change within Xerox. Here, though, the changes are sometimes more carefully planned and intentional. For example, by spending $750 million a year on research and development, Xerox plans to be a leader in newly developing fields, and to constantly produce the best photocopying equipment. Thus, it is clearly Xerox's intention not to merely respond to change, but to be a leader in innovation, causing its competitors to change.

It is interesting to note the seeds for long-term change Mr. Kearns is planting. By investing large sums of money in educational programs, Xerox may be seen as preparing future generations of literate employees to run the company—and to use its products. After all, literacy is a necessary skill for a thriving "information business."

Questions for Discussion

1. Describe the major force dictating unplanned organizational change at Xerox and the steps taken in response to the changing conditions.

2. What is Xerox doing to plan for future organizational change?

3. What long-term steps is Mr. Kearns taking to help ensure the future success of Xerox? Do you think these measures will be successful?

EXPERIENCING ORGANIZATIONAL BEHAVIOR

Facing Resistance to Change

If there's one thing you can count on in organizations, it's change. As technology advances, the composition of the work force shifts, and new markets evolve, people confront the reality of organizational change. Such changes are often quite threatening to employees, and pose serious challenges to managers attempting to implement the changes needed for organizations to survive (see pages 573–575). This exercise will help you appreciate the resistance to change many supervisors encounter.

Procedure

1. Consider each of the following organizational change situations: (a) A secretarial staff that did typing will shift to word processing; (b) An older, well-liked supervisor is retiring and will be replaced by a younger person hired from outside the company; (c) In response to shifting consumer preferences, a vinyl record stamping plant will convert to compact disc manufacturing.

2. For each of these situations, discuss the following questions: (1) What impediments to change are likely to arise? (2) What can be done to overcome employees' resistance to change?

3. On the board, your instructor will record everyone's answers to both questions for all three situations.

Points to Consider

1. How are the three organizational change situations similar or different?

2. How are the impediments to change and the methods of overcoming them similar or different for the various organizational change situations?

3. Do you think the organizational change situations considered in this exercise are unique or are they typical of others likely to be encountered?

NAME INDEX

Abelson, M. A., 398
Adler, N. J., 435, 436
Alderfer, C., 81
Allen, R. W., 421, 422
Andrews, B., 110
Antonio, R., 514
Ariss, S. S., 426

Baker, D. D., 232
Bandura, A., 204
Barnard, C. I., 333
Barnes, Z., 568
Baron, R. A., 197, 233, 462, 463, 464
Baron, R. S., 280
Bass, B. M., 337
Bateman, T. S., 173, 174
Bazerman, M., 468
Bennis, W., 586
Berkowitz, L., 165
Berreth, R., 31, 32
Betz, E. L., 81
Beyer, J. M., 58
Bhagat, R. S., 586
Bies, R. J., 462, 463
Biggers, K., 245
Bingley, J., 233
Binning, J. F., 131, 133
Bird, F. B., 435, 436
Blake, R. R., 580
Blanchard, K., 400
Borman, F., 476
Bottger, P. C., 508
Bouchard, T. J., Jr., 500
Boulgaides, J. D., 495
Boyatzis, R. E., 208
Brief, A. P., 446
Brooke, P. B., Jr., 174
Bryan, C., 476
Burke, J., 367
Burns, T., 538
Burr, D., 378

Callahan, A. L., 162
Cardy, R., 135
Carlzon, J., 329
Carrera, S., 195, 196
Carsten, J. M., 171
Casella, D. F., 201
Casey, A. V., 554
Cato the Elder, 77
Chang, K., 148
Chemers, M. M., 387
Cochran, S., 165
Cody, D., 185
Cohen, B., 326
Collins, P. D., 544
Conger, J. A., 383, 384
Connor, J., 407
Cook, W. S., 592

Cooke, R. A., 270
Cooper, C. L., 242
Costanza, R. S., 230
Cowan, D. A., 485
Cox, C. E., 337
Creel, W., 253, 254
Crouch, A., 393
Cummings, L. L., 462
Curry, J. P., 174

Daft, R. L., 341
Delbecq, A. L., 507
Dansereau, G., 396
DeNisi, A. S., 304
Derlega, V. J., 230
Dollinger, M. J., 538
Drake, M. F., 337
Drucker, P., 582
Dubro, A. F., 454
Dunnette, M. D., 84
Dyer, W. G., Jr., 299

Earley, P. C., 55
Ellis, R. A., 205, 206
Erhlich, S. B., 398, 399
Evans, G. W., 195, 196

Feldman, D. C., 271, 303
Fetterolf, C. F., 592
Feynman, R., 291, 292
Fiedler, F. E., 385, 386, 387, 388, 402
Fields, D., 218, 219, 297
Forsythe, S., 337
Fraser, S., 165
Frederickson, J. W., 490
Freeman, J. H., 427
French, J. R. P., 412, 416
Fried, Y., 167, 171
Friedman, H. S., 201
Frost, D. E., 416

Gandz, J., 420, 421
Garcia, J. E., 388
Garvin, D. A., 17, 18
Gaugler, B. B., 212
George, W. H. K., 592
Gilbert, G., 31, 32
Gillett, G., 112
Goizueta, R., 514, 515
Goldman, L., 584
Graen, G., 396, 397
Graham, W., 291
Grams, R., 180
Granrose, C. S., 321
Graves, L. M., 138, 180
Gray, B., 426
Greenberg, J., 85, 87, 339
Greenfield, J., 326

Gutek, B. A., 167
Gyllenhammar, P. G., 96

Habib, G. M., 465
Hackman, J. R., 165, 266, 267
Haga, B., 396
Hammer, T. H., 381, 382
Hannan, M. T., 427
Hanson, J. K., 31, 32
Heilman, M. E., 178, 393
Hersey, P., 400
Herzberg, F., 96, 162–164, 180
Hickson, D. J., 419
Hill, D. R., 194
Hitt, M. A., 527
Hoffman, J., 98
Hofstede, G., 586
Hogan, E. A., 139, 140
Holmes, T. H., 233, 234
Hopkins, A. B., 148
House, R. J., 385, 394
Huber, V., 161
Hull, F. M., 544

Iacocca, L., 157, 383
Isabella, L. A., 360, 361
Ivancevich, J. M., 245

Jackson, D. N., 192
Jackson, S. E., 241
Jaeger, A. M., 586
Jansen, E., 431
Jermier, J. M., 398
Jobs, S., 556
Jones, A. P., 133
Jorgenson, D. O., 84

Kahneman, D., 492
Kanter, R. M., 355
Kanungo, R. N., 383, 384
Kapor, M., 315
Kearns, 595
Keats, B. W., 527
Kedia, B. L., 586
Keenan, A., 228
Keinan, G., 239
Kerr, S., 398
Kirmeyer, S. L., 245
Klauss, R., 337
Klein, K. J., 175
Knight, G. P., 454
Knowlton, W. A., Jr., 124
Koroda, T., 149
Krackhardt, D., 349
Krzystofiak, F., 135

Lam, D., 148
Landis, J., 440
Landy, F. J., 164

Lardner, J., 108
Larkin, J. E., 203
Latané, B., 281
Latham, G. P., 46, 48
Laubenstein, J. H., 552
Lawler, E. E., III, 88, 172
Lawrence, P. R., 419
Lazarus, R. S., 234
Leffingwell, W. H., 352
Lengel, R. H., 341
Lewicki, R. J., 316, 468
Liden, R. C., 270
Liederman, D., 218, 219
Likert, R., 379
Litterer, J. A., 468
Locke, E. A., 164, 180
Lombardo, M. M., 318
Lorenzo, F., 329, 378, 476
Lorsch, J. W., 5, 419

McCall, M. W., Jr., 318
McCarty, P. A., 178
McClelland, D. C., 208
McGrath, M. R., 495
Machiavelli, N., 197, 198, 199
Machungwa, P. D., 163
McKersie, 468
Malloy, J. T., 337
Manning, M. R., 237
Mao Tse-tung, 78
March, J. G., 491
Marcus, A. A., 568
Marshall, J., 242
Martin, J., 300
Martin, R. A., 238, 239
Maslow, A., 79, 80, 81, 102, 103, 164, 263
Masuda, M., 233
Matteson, M. T., 245
Mayo, E., 12, 13
Meglino, B. M., 304, 305
Meindl, J. R., 398, 399
Miles, R. H., 420
Miller, D., 540
Miller, K. I., 171
Mintzberg, H., 423
Mitchell, T. R., 124, 270, 490
Mobley, W. H., 170
Monge, P. R., 171
Morrell, E., 253
Morrow, V., 440
Motowidlo, S. J., 237, 446
Mouton, J. S., 580
Muczyk, J. P., 377
Mueller, C. W., 174
Mulder, M., 416
Murray, V. V., 420, 421
Mustari, E. L., 282, 283

Naisbitt, J., 566
Newman, J., 135
Newton, T. J., 228
Nixon, R. M., 77, 276
Noe, R. A., 310
Numerof, R. E., 241

Oberman, S. M., 192
Oldham, G. R., 165, 166, 171, 353
O'Neill, P. H., 592

Organ, D. W., 173
Ornstein, S., 360, 361
Osborn, A. F., 500
Ouchi, W. G., 16, 17
Oullette-Kobasa, S. C., 230, 244

Packard, J. S., 237
Palsane, M. N., 195, 196
Parry, C. W., 592
Paunonen, S. V., 192
Pavlov, I., 38–39
Peiperi, M. A., 319
Peters, L. H., 180
Peters, T. J., 300
Pfeffer, J., 418
Porras, J. I., 584
Porter, L. W., 81, 88, 172, 349
Portwood, J. D., 321
Powell, G. N., 138, 180
Price, J. L., 174
Pritchard, R. D., 84
Pruitt, D. G., 468
Psarouthakis, J., 108
Pucetti, M. C., 230, 244
Puffer, S. M., 448

Quadracci, H. V., 405, 406

Raelin, J. A., 432, 433
Rahe, R. H., 233, 234
Raven, B., 412, 416
Reimann, B. C., 377
Reynolds, P. C., 301
Richardson, S., 242
Riggio, R. E., 201
Ringelmann, 281
Riskind, J. H., 227
Robertson, P. J., 584
Rogers, W. P., 291, 292
Ronen, S., 77
Rothman, M., 270
Rousseau, D. M., 270
Rowe, A. J., 295, 296
Russell, D. W., 174

Saari, L. M., 46, 48
Saffold, G. S., III, 300
Salancik, G., 418
Scarpello, V., 161
Schein, E. H., 312, 315
Schlenker, J. A., 167
Schmitt, N., 163
Schoorman, F. D., 141
Schuler, R. S., 241
Schwab, D. P., 180
Schwab, R. L., 241
Sculley, J., 340, 556
Seashore, S. E., 277
Seltzer, J., 241
Selye, H., 224
Shapiro, D. L., 462
Shapiro, S., 177
Shaw, J. B., 227
Shenkar, O., 77
Sheppard, B. H., 468, 470
Sheridan, J. E., 398
Sherif, M., 275
Siehl, C., 300
Simon, H., 483, 491

Skinner, B. F., 40, 51
Sloan, A. P., Jr., 502
Sonnenfeld, J. A., 319
Spector, P. E., 171
Stahelski, A. J., 416
Stalker, G. M., 538
Staw, B. M., 494
Steele, F., 586
Steinberg, R., 177
Stogdill, R., 379
Strasser, S., 174
Sutton, R. I., 162

Tang, E., 242
Taylor, F. W., 11, 95, 522
Taylor, M. S., 205, 206
Terkel, S., 317
Terpstra, D. E., 232
Thomas, K. W., 459
Thompson, J. D., 546
Tjosvold, D., 380
Treasure, F. P., 165
Trevino, L. K., 341
Trice, H. M., 58
Triplett, N., 278
Tso, J., 148
Turban, D. B., 133
Turke, J. M., 381, 382
Tversky, A., 492

Vandenberg, R. J., 161
Van de Ven, A. H., 507
Van de Vliert, E., 471
Van Maanen, J., 306
Van Zelst, R. H., 264
Vecchio, R. P., 401
Velasquez, M., 429
Von Glinow, M. A., 431
Vredenburgh, D. J., 398
Vroom, V. H., 88, 385, 389, 390, 391, 393, 402

Wakabayashi, M., 397
Wakefield, D. S., 174
Walton, 468
Wang, K. L., 149
Warren, A., 477
Waterman, R. H., 300
Weiss, B., 255
Weldon, E., 282, 283
Whyte, W. F., 274
Wilkins, A. L., 299
Williams, K. D., 283
Williams, K. J., 304
Winstead, B. A., 230
Winter, D. G., 209
Wolfe, D. M., 431
Woodward, J., 542, 543, 545, 546
Wyble, R., 110

Yetton, P. W., 385, 389, 390, 391, 393, 402, 508
Youngblood, S. A., 304
Youngs, G. A., Jr., 452

Zajonc, R. B., 278, 279, 280
Zuboff, S., 352
Zwerman, W. L., 543

SUBJECT INDEX

AAL, 552
Absenteeism, 170–171
Achievement motivation, 97, 207–208, 214
Action plan, 579, 583
Additive tasks, 281, 284, 287
Ad hoc committees, 262
Administrative model, 490, 510
Affiliation motivation, 207, 208, 214
Affirmative action, 159
Ageism, 135, 177
Air Florida, 345
Alarm reaction, 224
Alcoa, 592–593
Alliance game, 424
Alternative generation, 485
American Airlines, 85
American Can, 91
American Motors, 562
Appeals process, 433
Apple Computers, 562
Arbitration, 469–470
  binding, 469
Arousal, 75, 224, 279–280
Asian-Americans, 148–149
Assembly line, 31, 108
Assessment Centers, 211–212, 214
Assignment flow, 319
Aston studies, 544–546
Asymmetries, 418
AT&T, 212, 358, 568, 582
Atlantic Richfield (ARCO), 432
Attention, 42, 118–119, 126
Attitudes
  changing, 156–160, 180
  defined, 155
  motives and, 118
  nature of, 154–160, 180
  negative, 176–180
  toward organizations, 173–176
  work-related, 153–155, 160–173, 180
Attribution, 121–125, 144
  causal, 123–125
  errors in, 130–131
  faulty, 461
  performance appraisal and, 140
Audience, 278
Authority, 10
Authority games, 424
Autocratic leadership, 377–378, 401
Automated decision conferencing, 507
Autonomy, 78, 99, 174, 315, 448
Availability heuristic, 493
Avoidance, *see* Negative reinforcement

Bank Wiring Room study, 12, 13
Bargaining, 462, 467–469, 472. *See also* Negotiations
Batten, Barton, Durstine, and Osborn, 500

Behavioral reproduction, 42
Behavioral sciences, 4
Ben & Jerry's Homemade, Inc., 326–327
Benefit plans, 91
B. F. Goodrich, 431
Bias
  arbitrator, 470
  in decision making, 492–494
  in interviews, 138
  in reward systems, 460
  self-serving, 130–131, 144, 206, 451, 460
  sources of, 133, 141, 142
Binding arbitration, 469
Biological clock, 314
Boards, 262–263
Bottom line mentality, 431, 437
Boundary spanning, 203, 381, 382, 537–538, 564
Bounded discretion, 495
Bounded rationality, 491, 510
Brainstorming, 500
Burnout, 240–242, 249, 255, 316

Cafeteria-style benefit plans, 91
Career anchors, 315, 323
Career development, 312
  fostering, 320–322
  in Japan, 397
  life stages and, 312–314
  personal factors in, 296
Career management (assistance) programs, 317, 320–322, 323
Career plateaus, 316–317
Careers, 296
  changes in, 311–322
  defined, 311
  issues, 314–319
  managing strategies, 319–320
  planning, 315
Career systems, 296, 312, 319–320, 323
Case method, 19
Causal account, 462–463
Causal attribution, 123–125
Cause and effect relationships, 21–22
Caveat emptor, 436
Centralization, 346, 571
  versus decentralization, 323–325
Centralized networks, 346, 362
Chain of command, 9, 525
Challenge, 165, 244
Challenger disaster, 291, 433
Change, job, 296. *See also* Organizational change
Change games, 425
Charisma, 383
Charismatic leaders, 376, 383–384
Chilling effect, 470
Chrysler Corporation, 383
Citibank, 532

Citicorp, 433
Citizenship behaviors, 172–173, 181, 446
Classical conditioning, 38–39
Coactors, 278
Coalitions, 423
Coca-Cola company, 514
Codes of corporate ethics, 433, 436, 437
Coercive power, 413, 415, 436
Cognitive appraisals, 194, 225, 248
Cognitive dissonance, 158–160, 169, 180
Cognitive frameworks, 216–217
Cognitive resource theory, 388
Cohesiveness, 274–278, 287
  benefits and costs of, 276–278, 501
Command group, 261
Commissions, 262–263, 291
Commitment
  job, 244
  organizational, 173–176, 181
Communication, 333
  advances in, 566–567
  barriers, 354–360, 451–453
  channels of, 10, 334
  defined, 334–336
  downward, 344, 360
  faulty, 463
  flow of, 358–360
  horizontal, 345
  improving, 355–360, 427
  informal, 349
  major influences on, 342–354
  media, 335, 340–341
  model, 334–336
  nature of, 334–342, 362
  nonverbal, 128, 337–340, 362
  overload, 359
  persuasive, 157–158
  upward, 345, 357
  verbal, 336–337, 340–342
  and work environment, 352–354
  written, 340–342
Communication networks, 346–349, 359, 362
  informal, 349–351, 363
Compensation
  expectations, 187
  nonspecific, 468
Compensatory tasks, 284, 287
Competition, 450, 472
  between organizations, 456
  economic, 569–570
  foreign, 471, 569–570
  group cohesiveness and, 274–275
  noncompliant behavior and, 448
  over scarce resources, 460
Competitors, 453, 454, 455
Complexity, 525, 535
Compresence, 280
Compromise, 284
Computers, 489, 562, 565–566, 571

Conditioned response, 38, 64
Conditioned stimulus, 38, 63
Conflict, 445, 472
  in goals and interests, 426
  group, 498
  handling skills, 393
  interrole, 269, 287
  intrarole, 269, 270, 287
  organizational, *see* Organizational conflict
  role, 227–228, 269–270
Conflict rule, 393
Confrontation meetings, 162
Congruence, 539
Conjunctive tasks, 285–286, 287
Consensus, 123
Consideration, 379, 401
Consistency, 123, 191
Consortium management organization
  (CMO), 457
Consortiums, 456–457
Contingencies of reinforcement, 41, 48,
  50
Contingency approach, 15–16, 28, 373,
  384, 544
Contingency factors, in leadership, 395
Contingency theory, 385–389, 402
Continuous process production, 543
Continuous reinforcement, 45, 47, 48
Contracts, long-term, 541–542
Contrast effects, 134, 144
Control group, 23
Control systems, 8
Convergence, in structure, 540
Cooperation, 445, 449–457, 472
  between organizations, 456–457
  communication and, 451–453
  individual factors and, 451–455
  nature of work and, 456
  organizational factors and, 455–457
  personal orientation and, 453–455
Cooperators, 454, 455
Core job dimensions, 98–99
Corporate hotlines, 358
Corporate morality, 434–436
Corporate relocation, 360–362
Correlational method, 20
Correlation coefficient, 20
Counterinsurgency games, 424
Counternorms, 431, 433–434, 437
Country club management, 580
Credibility, 157
Creel Morrell Inc., 253–254
Critical incidents, 160, 162, 163, 180
Critical psychological states, 98
Criticism, 463–464
Cultural differences, 55–56
  in corporate morality, 434–436
  in negotiations, 128–129
  in organizational development, 586–587
  in stress, 242–243
  in Type A behavior, 195–196

Decentralization, 248, 571
  versus centralization, 523–525
Decentralized networks, 346, 347, 362
Decision making, 483
  bias in, 492–494
  in equity theory, 87
  ethics in, 495

group, 497–508, 510
  individual, 489–497, 510
  individual versus group, 498–501
  lack of participation in, 230–231
  and leader effectiveness, 389–393, 498
  models of, 484–486, 490–492
  obstacles to, 501–504
  organizational impediments to, 494–495
  process, 483–489, 509
  risk in, 487–488
  stress and, 239–240
  subordinate participation in, 392
  techniques for improving, 504–508
  varieties of decisions, 486–492
Decision style, 495–496
Decision-style inventory, 496
Decision support systems, 485
Decision training, 143
Decoding, 336, 362
Deeper levels of processing, 143
Deere & Company, 108
Defenders, 319
Defensive avoidance, 508
Deficiency needs, 80, 81
Delphi technique, 505–506, 510
Demographic similarity, 133
Departments, creating, 571
Dependent variable, 23
Descriptive approach, 491
Diagnostic session, 578
Diamond International, 50
Differentiation, 461
Direct supervision, 381
Discipline, 58–63, 64
  impact of, 59–63
  progressive, 59
  types of, 58–59
  uses of, 58–59
Discretionary management, 381
Disjunctive tasks, 284–285, 287
Dissonance, 158–160
  cognitive, 158–160, 169, 180
  post-decision, 159
Distinctiveness, 124
Distraction-conflict model, 280, 287
Diversification, 527
Divestiture, 307, 568
Divisionalization, 525, 526–527
Division of labor, 522
Documentary approach, 55
Dress, style of, 337–338, 340
Drive theory of social facilitation, 279
Dual-core model, 565

Eastern Airlines, 476
Eastman Kodak Company, 358, 562, 582
Economic conditions, 534
Emery Air Freight, 45
Empire building, 424
Employee Stock Ownership Plans
  (ESOPs), 175–176
Encoding
  in communications, 334, 362
  in memory, 125, 126
Entry shock, 303
Environment, state of, 536. *See also*
  External environment
Equal Employment Opportunity
  Commission, 232

Equalizers, 454, 455
Equitable payment, 82
Equity
  perceptions of, 83, 165
  principle of, 430
Equity theory, 82–86, 87, 102, 103, 429
ERG theory, 79, 81–82
Escalation of commitment, 140, 160
  in decision making, 494
  in performance appraisal, 140–141
Escalative interventions, 471, 472
Esteem needs, 81
Ethics, *see* Organizational ethics
Evaluation, 57–58
Evaluation apprehension, 280, 287
Exhaustion, 225, 240
Existence needs, 81–82
Expectancy, 39, 88, 89, 103
Expectancy theory, 88–91, 102, 103, 394
Expectations
  job, 427
  in performance appraisal, 139–140
  role, 268
  of women, 178
Experimental method, 22–25
Experimentation, 22–25, 28
Expertise, 157
Expert power, 414–415, 416, 436
Exploitative mentality, 431–432, 437
External environment, 9, 520, 521, 532–
  542
  dimensions and classification of, 534–
  537
  impact of, 537–540, 548
  key domains, 533–534, 548
  management style and, 538
  techniques for changing, 541–542
Extinction, 41, 48, 64
Exxon Corporation, 433

Facilitator, 578
Fair procedure, 87–88, 429
Federal Bankruptcy Code, 162
Feedback, 54
  in communication, 336, 357–358
  effective, 99, 142
  and goal attainment, 94–95
  immediate, 578
  negative, 140, 142, 204, 463–464
  and self-confidence, 179
Field studies, 23
Figure-ground relationships, 119–121
Financial resources, 533
Firestone Tire and Rubber Company, 361
Fixed interval schedule, 45
Fixed ratio schedule, 45–46
Fixed programs, 307
Flexibility, 401, 480, 496
Formal groups, 261–263
Formalization, 522–523
Ford Motor Company, 428, 582
Frame of reference training, 143
Framing, 492, 510
Functional design, 528–529, 548
Fundamental attribution error, 130

Gatekeepers, 359
General Electric Company, 92, 98, 566,
  582

General Mills, 68–70
General Motors, 110, 344, 476–477, 502
Giant Food supermarkets, 85
Gillett Group, 112
Global economy, 434–436, 569–570
Goal setting, 91–95, 102, 103
    feedback in, 94–95
    logic behind, 94
    and job performance, 93
    personal, 113
    worker participation in, 93
Government regulations, 534, 568–569
Grapevine, 10, 350–351
Great person theory, 376
Grid seminar, 580
Grid training, 380, 580–581, 588
Group conflict, 498
Group decisions, 497–508, 510
Group dynamics, 260
Grouping, 121
Group polarization, 503–504, 510
Groups
    characteristics of, 260–261, 287
    defined, 260–261, 287
    formal, 261–263
    informal, 261, 263–264
    norms in, 92
    power and, 417–420, 426
    stages of development, 264–265
    stress and, 388
    tasks, 284–287
    within organizations, 261–264
Group structure, 267, 287
Groupthink, 277, 466, 501–502, 510
Growth needs, 81, 99, 163

Halo effects, 131–133, 144
Hardiness, 234, 244, 249
Hassles, daily, 234–235, 249
Hawthorne studies, 11–13, 585
Health, stress and, 235–236
Helplessness, 230–231
Heuristics, 492, 510
Hewlett-Packard, 148, 530, 582, 584
Hierarchy of needs, 79–81, 82, 102, 164
Honeywell, 576
Horizontal linkage model, 564
Horizontally complex, 525
Human relations approach, 13, 27
Human resources, 533–534
Human resources model, 15, 28
Human rights, 429
Hygienes, 163
Hypervigilance, 508
Hypothesis, 20, 26

IBM, 80, 93, 297, 319, 556, 562, 576, 584
Illumination, and productivity, 11–13
Image building, 423
Immune system, 236
Implicit personality theories, 134–135, 144
Impression management, 383
Impressions, 423
Independent variable, 23
Individual decisions, 489–497, 510
Individualists, 453

Industry, 533
Inequities, 82. *See also* Equity theory
Inflection point, 237
Influence
    in leadership, 374, 401
    in politics, 411
Informal groups, 261, 263–264
Information
    controlling access to, 422
    and decision making, 489
Information processing
    advances in, 566–567
    in performance appraisal, 143
Ingratiation, 423
Initiating structure, 379, 401
Inputs, 7
    in equity theory, 82
In Search of Excellence (Peters and Waterman), 300
Instrumental conditioning, *see* Operant conditioning
Instrumentality, 88, 89, 91, 103
Insurgency games, 424
Integrating mechanisms, 525
Integrative agreements, 468
Integrity, 432
Intentions, 459
Interdependence, 445, 456, 460
    level of, 547, 548
    technology and, 546–547
Interest group, 263
Internal structure, 9, 520, 543, 544
    changing, 556
    planning, 547
International Association of Machinists (IAM), 476
Interorganizational coordination, 456–457
Interpersonal approach, 55
Interpersonal relations, 196–197
Interrole conflict, 269, 287
Intervention, control, 25
Interviewer, 117
Interviews
    appraisal, 142
    employment, 136
    job satisfaction, 160, 162
    social perception and, 136–138
Intrarole conflict, 269, 270, 287
Inventories, 210
Invisible college, 351
Isolation, 230

Japan
    culture of, 128, 541
    imports from, 456, 582
    management styles, 16–17, 397–398, 540
    product quality in, 17–18
Jargon, 355, 363
Jenkins Activity Survey, 193, 196, 245
Job characteristics model, 97–102, 103, 165, 582
Job description, 254
Job Descriptive Index (JDI), 161, 173
Job design, 11, 91, 95–102, 103
    examples of, 108–109
Job Diagnostic Survey (JDS), 100
Job enlargement, 95–97, 103, 164, 248, 582

Job enrichment, 95–97, 100, 103, 164, 248, 582
    acceptance, 97
    implementation, 97, 101
Job expectations, 427
Job performance, *see* Performance
Job satisfaction, 160–173, 180–181
    causes of, 164–167
    effects of, 169–173
    loss of, 167–168
    measuring, 160–162
    and performance, 171–173
    prevalence of, 168–169
    theories of, 162–164
Job succession, 318
Johnson & Johnson, 366–367
Joint outcomes, 454
Joint ventures, conflict in, 465
JP Industries, 108

K.I.S.S. principle, 356

Large-batch (mass) production, 543
Law of Effect, 40
Leader effectiveness, 384–385, 389–393
Leaders, 401
    charismatic, 376, 383–384
    and decision making, 389–393, 498
    intelligence of, 388–389
    and managers, 374–375
    organizational constraints on, 380–382
    personal characteristics, 376–377
    person-oriented, 378–380
    production-oriented, 378–380
Leadership, 373, 405–406
    autocratic, 377–378, 401
    behavior, 377–380
    contingency factors in, 395
    defined, 374
    nature of, 373–375
    participative, 377–378, 401
    personal motives and, 209–210
    substitutes for, 398–399, 402
    theories of, 384–401, 402
    trait approach to, 376–377, 401
Leadership motivation pattern (LMP), 208, 214
Learning, 37, 63
    theories of, 38–43, 63
Learning curve, 53
Least preferred coworker (LPC), 385, 386, 387
Legitimate power, 413, 436
Liberty Mutual Insurance, 532
Life satisfaction, 167
Life stages, and careers, 312–314
Line positions, 525
Line versus staff game, 425
Listening, attentive, 356–357, 369
Locus of control, 199–201
Logrolling, 468–469

McDonald's, 351
Machiavellianism, 197–199, 214, 415
Mach scale, 197–198
Macro perspective, 521
Madison Avenue mentality, 432, 437

Management by objectives (MBO), 582–584, 586–587, 588
Managerial competence, 315
Managerial grid®, 580
Managerial talent, 211–212
Managers
    leaders and, 374–375
    training, 55–56
Manufacturing firms, 526–527
Manville Corporation, 428
Market, 534
Marketing, 564
Matrix bosses, 532
Matrix designs, 531–532, 548
Mechanistic structure, 525–526, 538, 543, 548, 565
Mediation, 469–470
Megatrends (Naisbitt), 566
Memory, 125, 126, 127
Mentors, 309–311, 316, 322, 423
Mergers, 456, 541–542
Merit systems, 48, 91, 110
Merrill, Lynch, Pierce, Fenner & Smith, 149
Meta-analysis, 212
Metropolitan Edison, 431
Micro perspective, 521
Middle-of-the-road management, 580
Minnesota Satisfaction Questionnaire (MSQ), 161
Minorities, 148–149, 169
Modeling, *see* Observational learning; Role models
Morale, employee, 169
Moral issues, *see* Organizational ethics
Motivating potential score (MPS) 100
Motivation, 42
    components of, 76
    defined, 75–76
    and job performance, 76, 89, 90
    nature of, 75–78, 103
    techniques for enhancing, 91–102, 103
    theories of, 78–91, 103
    through language, 102
    in the work environment, 88, 447
    and the work ethic, 77
Motivator-hygiene theory, *see* Two-factor theory
Motivators, 163
Motives
    attitudes and, 118
    competitive, 453
    and leadership, 209–210
    and persuasion, 157
    work-related, 206–210
MTA, New York, 593
Munificence, environmental, 535, 537

National Aeronautics and Space Administration (NASA), 433
Natural observation, 19, 28
Needs assessment, 52
Needs theories, 79–82, 103, 164
Negative correlation, 20
Negative frame, 468
Negative reinforcement, 41
Negotiations, 117, 122, 452, 455
    cultural differences in, 128–129
    factors affecting, 468

simulated, 462
third party intervention, 469
    see also Bargaining
Networking, 381
New Jersey Bell Telephone, 333
Noise, 336, 362
Nominal group technique (NGT), 506, 517
Noncommon effects, 122
Noncompliant actions, 448–449
Noncontingent rewards, 62
Nonprogrammed decision, 486–487, 509
Nonspecific compensation, 468
Nonverbal communication, 128, 337–340, 362
    in negotiations, 128–129
Nonverbal cues, 136–137
Normative approach, 490
Normative reasoning, 459
Normative theory, 385, 389–393, 402
Norms, 270–272
    defined, 270
    development of, 271–272
    ethical, 431, 433–434
    influence on behavior, 270–271
    organizational culture and, 297
    prescriptive and proscriptive, 270
    of reciprocity, 423
Nuclear Regulatory Commission (NRC), 568–569

Objective probabilities, 488
Observation
    natural, 19, 28
    systematic, 19–22, 28
Observational learning, 42–43, 56–57, 64
Observational skills, training in, 143
Office design, 353–354
Older employees, 174, 318
OPEC (Organization of Petroleum Exporting Companies), 456
Open consultation, 416
Open-plan office, 353, 363
Open system, 7–8, 27
Operant conditioning, 39, 40–41, 64
Optimal decisions, 490
Optimism, 243–244
Organic structure, 525–526, 538, 543, 548, 565
Organization, perceptual, 118, 119–121
Organizational behavior (OB)
    field of, 3–10, 27, 75
    historical perspective, 10–17, 27
    levels of analysis, 5
    overview, 14–18
    research methods in, 18–26, 28
Organizational behavior management, 45, 48–51, 64
Organizational behavior modification (OB Mod), 48
Organizational change, 299, 561
    determining factors, 562–570, 587
    implementation of, 576–586
    individual barriers to, 574
    organizational barriers to, 574–575
    planned external, 565–567, 587
    planned internal, 563–565, 587
    process, 570–575, 587
    readiness for, 572–573

resistance to, 176, 562, 573–575, 588, 596
stress of, 233
in structure, 248, 570–571
targets of, 570–572
unplanned external, 568–570, 587
unplanned internal, 567–568, 587
Organizational chart, 9, 10, 343, 344–346, 362
Organizational commitment, 173–176, 181
    effects of, 176
    factors affecting, 174–175
    job satisfaction and, 174
Organizational conflict, 204, 445, 472
    awareness of, 459
    effects of, 466–467, 472
    interpersonal causes of, 461–465
    in joint ventures, 465
    line and staff, 525
    management of, 467–471, 472, 478
    model of, 458–459
    nature of, 458–465, 472
    organizational causes of, 460–461
    see also Conflict
Organizational culture, 10, 296–302, 322
    changes in, 299
    classifying, 299
    effects of, 299–302
    imposing of, 301–302
    origins, 297–299
Organizational development (OD), 156, 576–586, 588
    cultural barriers to, 586–587
    defined, 576
    evaluation of, 584–586, 588
    interventions, 577, 586–587
Organizational ethics, 51, 411, 428–436, 437
    codes of, 433, 436, 437
    field of, 429
    global economy and, 434–436
    norms and counternorms, 431, 433–434, 437
    and politics, 422, 429–430
    and power, 428
    promoting morality, 432–434, 442
    unethical behavior, 430–432, 433, 437
Organizational politics, 411, 420–428, 436
    ethics in, 422, 429–430
    games, 423–425, 427
    occurrence of, 420–422, 425–427
    tactics, 422–423, 429
    techniques for coping with, 427–428
Organizational seduction, 316, 323
Organizational socialization, 10, 296, 302–311, 322
    defined, 302
    effective programs in, 307–308
    mentors and, 309–311
    occurrence of, 306–307
    stages of, 302–306, 322
Organizations, 7
    cooperation between, 456–457
    distinguishing, 426
    nature of, 7–10, 27
Organizational structure
    basic dimensions, 9, 10, 521–526, 548
    changing, 554
    impact on communication, 342–344, 362

Organizational structure (*Continued*)
  and performance, 538–540
  and reward systems, 455–456
Organization designs, 521, 527–532, 548, 552
Orientation programs, 305
Osborn Computer, 562
Outcomes, 82, 85
Output, 7
Overload, 228, 359, 363
Overpayment inequity, 82, 84

Parkdale Mills, Inc., 92
Partial (intermittent) reinforcement, 45, 48
Participant observation, 19
Participation, 53
Participative leadership, 377–378, 401
Path-goal theory, 385, 394–396, 402
Pavlovian conditioning, 38–39
Pay-for-performance systems, 48, 91
Pay Satisfaction Questionnaire (PSQ), 161
People Express, 378
Perceived similarity, 133
Perception
  basic features of, 117–121, 143
  defined, 116
  organizing principles in, 119–121
  selectivity in, 118–119
  see also Social perception
Perceptual congruence, 133
Perceptual grouping, 121
Performance
  attainable, 90
  effects of groups on, 278–279
  goal setting and, 93
  level of, 124, 172, 538
  job satisfaction and, 171–173
  motivation and, 76, 89, 90
  organizational culture and, 300
  rewards and, 91
  role perception and, 90
  self-efficacy and, 204
  stress and, 236–239
  Type A behavior and, 194–196
Performance appraisal, 124, 131, 144
  accuracy in, 142–143
  hidden traps in, 148–149
  information processing approach, 143
  interviews, 142
  response to, 205
  social perception and, 138–142
  stress of, 232–233
Performance gaps, 567–568
Personality, 189
  defined, 190
  implicit theories of, 134–135
  measuring, 194, 210–213, 214
  nature of, 190–192, 213
  and OB, 192–210, 213
  origins, 191–192
Persuasion, 156–158
Pessimism, 243
Physical environment, 165–166
  leadership and, 395
  organizational commitment and, 175
  stress of, 233
Physical fitness programs, 80, 246, 248, 249

Physiological needs, 79
Piecework pay system, 46
Polaroid, 432
Political action committees (PACs), 541
Politics, 420
  presidential, 209–210, 276
  see also Organizational politics
Pooled interdependence, 546
Pooling of resources, 497–498
Positive correlation, 20
Positive frame, 468
Positive reinforcement, 40, 41, 51, 71
Postal Service, U.S., 554–555
Power, 411–420, 436
  abuse of, 429, 432, 434
  balance of, 419–420
  in crisis situations, 416–417
  defined, 411
  ethics in, 428
  group, 417–420, 426
  individual, bases of, 412–416
  subunit, 417–420
Power base games, 424
Power motivation, 207, 208, 214
Pragmatic, 198
Predecision, 485, 509
Prediction, 20, 25
Prejudice, 176–180, 181
Price leadership, 298
Price Waterhouse, 148–149, 407
Prince, The (Machiavelli), 197
Principles of Scientific Management, The (Taylor), 11
Problem-focused coping, 243
Problem identification, 484–485
Procedural justice, 87–88
Procter & Gamble, 340, 571
Product designs, 529–531, 548
Product managers, 531
Product quality, 17–18
Programmed decision, 486–487, 509
Progressive discipline, 59
Projective techniques, 210–211, 214
Promotion, 159, 319
  on basis of merit, 159
  denial of, 148
Prosocial behavior, 445, 446–448, 472
  forms of, 446
  and job performance, 448
  motivation and, 447
  personal factors in, 448–449
Prospectors, 319
Psychological contracts, 93
Public relations, 542
Punishment, 40–41, 58, 64
  controlling, 413
  effective, 59–63
  guidelines for using, 60–62
  observing, 62–63
  see also Discipline

Quad/Graphics, 405
Qualitative overload, 228–229
Qualitative underload, 228–229
Quality circles (QCs), 582
Quality of work life (QWL), 581–582, 588
Quantitative overload, 228–229
Quantitative underload, 228–229

Questionnaires, 160, 161, 210, 357
Queuing, 359, 363

Racism, 135, 148–149, 177
Rand Corporation, 505
Rating scales, 160, 161
Rational decisions, 490
Rational-economic model, 490, 491, 510
Rational-instrumental reasoning, 459
Raw materials, 533
Realistic job previews, 303, 304, 322
Reassignments, office, 85, 86, 167
Reciprocal interdependence, 546–547
Recruiting, 319
Reduction in staff, 167
Redundancy, 360
Referent power, 413–414, 416, 436
Reflexive, 39
Refreezing, 572
Regression analysis, 21
Reinforcement, 44–58, 413
  contingencies of, 41, 48, 50
  continuous, 45, 47, 48
  negative, 41
  partial, 45, 48
  positive, 40, 41, 51, 71
  schedules of, 45–48, 64
  see also Rewards
Reinforcer, 44, 64
Relatedness needs, 81
Relaxation training, 246–247, 249
Relay Room experiments, 12, 13
Reliability, 213
Repetition, 53
Representativeness heuristic, 493–494
Research, 18–26, 28, 564
  use of college students in, 24–25
Resistance to change, 176, 562, 573–575, 588, 596
Resistance to extinction, 48
Resource-dependency model, 417–418, 436
Resources, control of, 418
Responsibility
  ambiguity over, 460
  level of, 174
  for others, 229–230
Responsive management, 381
Retention, 42
Retirement, 314, 319
Reward power, 412–413, 436
Rewards, 40–41, 89
  bias in, 460
  and job performance, 91
  and job satisfaction, 164–165
  noncontingent, 62
  organizational structure and, 455–456
  patterns of administering, 45–48
  social approval, 71
  for unethical behavior, 430
Right to privacy, 429
Risk seeking decisions, 492
Risky shift, 503
Rival camps game, 425
Rivalry games, 425
Robots, 566
Rogers Commission, 291
Role ambiguity, 228, 268
Role conflict, 227–228, 269–270

Role differentiation, 268–269
Role expectations, 268
Role incumbent, 267
Role models, 427
Role perception, 90
Roles, 267–270, 287
  self-oriented, 268, 287
  socio-emotional, 268, 287
  task-oriented, 268, 287
Role senders, 269
Rorschach Ink Blot Test, 211
Rules, 87, 522–523
Rumors, 351

SAAB, 97
Safety needs, 79–80
Sales performance, improving, 68–70
Salience, 118
SAS, 329
Satisficing decision, 491, 510
Saturation, 347
Scapegoat, 422
Schedules of reinforcement, 45–48, 64
Schemas, 126–127, 144
  implicit personality theories as, 135
  persuasion and, 158
  and stereotypes, 127–128
Scientific management, 10–11, 27, 95, 522
Scientific method, 4–5, 18
Second-chance meetings, 502
Selectivity, in perception, 118–119
Self-actualization needs, 81
Self-concept, 205
Self-confidence, 178
Self-control, 208
Self-efficacy, 204–205, 214
Self-esteem, 131, 205–206, 214
  and job satisfaction, 166, 205
Self-managed reinforcement plans, 51
Self-monitoring, 202–204, 214, 220, 464
Self-oriented role, 268
Self-perception, 315
Self-regulating work groups, 263
Self-serving bias, 130–131, 144, 206, 451, 460
Sensitivity training, 578, 588
Sequential interdependence, 546
Sexism, 135, 177–180
Sex role stereotypes, 128, 137–138, 148, 178
Sexual harassment, 231–232, 248
Shaping, 49
Similarity
  demographic, 133
  perceived, 133
Similar-to-me effects, 133, 144
Situational leadership theory, 400–401, 402
Skills and abilities, 89, 90
Skill variety, 98–99
Small-batch production, 543
Snowball effect, 349
Social cognition, 125–126, 158
Social comparison view, 503
Social desirability, 122
Social environment, 166
Social facilitation, 278–280, 287
  drive theory of, 279
  model of, 279

Social impact theory, 282
Social information processing, 121
Socialization, see Organizational
  socialization
Social loafing, 281–284, 287, 293
  on judgmental tasks, 282–283
  strategies for overcoming, 283–284
Social needs, 80–81
Social perception, 117, 121–129, 144
  cognitive factors in, 125–128
  errors in, 129–136, 144
  and OB, 136–143, 144
Social skills, 214
  components of, 201
  individual differences in, 201–202
  measuring, 202
Social support, lack of, 230, 243
Social systems, 11–14
Space, use of, 339, 340
Span of control, 523, 571
Specialization, 522
Specialization of labor, 498
Sponsorship game, 424
Stability, environmental, 535–536
Staff positions, 525
Standing committees, 262
Status
  formal and informal, 272–273
  in groups, 272–274
  influence on OB, 273–274
  loss of, 167–168
Status symbols, 272–273
Stereotypes, 135, 144
  effects of, 135–136
  and job interviews, 137–138
  negative, 135, 158, 318, 466
  racial, 148–149
  schemas and, 127–128
  sex role, 128, 137–138, 148, 178
Stimulus, 38–39
Stonewalling, 431
Strategic contingencies model, 417, 419–420, 436
Strategic decisions, 487
Strategy, 520, 548
  in manufacturing firms, 526–527
  mediating role of, 538–540
Stress, 223
  causes of, 226–235, 248
  conflict and, 466
  cultural differences in, 242–243
  and decision making, 239–240
  defined, 226
  effects of, 235–243, 249
  group, 388
  managerial, 242–243
  managing, 245–248, 249, 257
  nature of, 224–226, 248
  and performance, 236–239
  physiological aspects of, 224, 226, 229, 235–236, 247
  resistance to, 243–245, 249, 256
  stages of, 224–225
  of success, 253–254
  Type A behavior and, 194, 244–245, 247
Stressful life events, 233, 249
Stressors, 225
Stress-resistant, 234

Structural inertia, 575
Structure, see Internal structure
Subcultures, 297
Subgroups, 502
Subjective probabilities, 488
Substitutes for leadership, 398–399, 402
Subunits
  politics in, 421
  power bases, 417–420
Suggestion systems, 357–358
Superordinate goals, 470–471, 472
Supervision
  burnout and, 241
  perceived quality of, 165
Supervisory support, 93
Supply flow, 319
Survey feedback, 577, 588
Surveys, 20, 357
Systematic observation, 19–22, 28

Task forces, 262
Task group, 262
Task identity, 99
Task management, 580
Task-oriented role, 268
Task performance, 284–287. See also
  Performance
Task significance, 99
Team building, 578–580, 588
Team management, 380
Technical batch production, 544
Technology, 9, 548
  changes in, 571
  classification of, 543, 544
  computer, 489, 565–566, 571
  effect of organizations, 534, 542–544, 566
  and interdependence, 546–547
  introduction of new, 565–566, 586
  manager's use of, 381–382
  organizational use of, 352, 520, 521, 542
Tension discharge rate, 245, 249
Texas Air, 329, 476
Texas Instruments, 562
Thematic Apperception Test (TAT), 211
Theory, 25–26, 28
Theory X, 15
Theory Y, see Human resources model
Theory Z (Ouchi), 16
Threats, 452, 469
3-M Company, 432
Three Mile Island accident, 431, 568
Time
  constraints, 494–495
  use of, 338–339, 340
Time and motion studies, 11
Top leader, 531
Training, 45, 51, 52–58, 64
  managers, for overseas assignments, 55–56
  principles, 53–54
  through observational learning, 56–57
Training programs, 305
Traits
  inferring, 122, 178
  lasting, 189, 190
  leadership, 376–377, 401

Transference, 54
TRW Systems Group, 532
Turnover, 170–171
Two-boss managers, 532
Two-career family, 317
Two-factor theory, 162–164, 180
Two-tier wage, 84–85
Tylenol, 366–367
Type A behavior pattern, 193–197
  assessing, 210
  conflict and, 464
  cultural differences in, 195–196
  health and, 194
  and interpersonal relations, 196–197
  performance and, 194–196, 213

Uncertainty, environmental, 535, 536,
    537–538, 539
Unconditioned response, 38, 63
Unconditioned stimulus, 38, 63
Unconflicted adherence, 508
Unconflicted change, 508
Underload, 228
Underpayment inequity, 82, 83
Unethical behavior, 430–432, 433, 437
Unfair procedure, 87–88
Unfreezing, 571
Union strength, 382
United Airlines, 85

United Auto Workers (UAW), 476–477
Universal principles of management, 542
U.S. Air Force, 94, 108–109

Valence, 88, 89, 103, 413
Values, shifting, 534
Value theory, 164, 180
Variable interval schedule, 45
Variable programs, 307
Variable ratio schedule, 46, 47
Variables, 20
Variety, in work, 165
Verification, 360
Vertical dyad linkage (VDL), 396–397,
    402
Vertical job loading, 96
Vicarious experiences, 204
Volvo, 96–97

Walgreen's, 566
Walt Disney World, 185–186
Watergate conspirators, 276
Western Electric, 12
Westinghouse, 582
Whistle-blowing
  game of, 425
  prosocial aspects, 446–447
Winnebago Industries, Inc., 31–33

Women
  expectations of, 178, 187
  mentors and, 311
  self-confidence in, 179
  sexual harassment and, 231–232
  in work force, 567
  see also Sexism
Work, challenging, 165
Work ethic, 5, 77
Work-flow integration, 544–546
Work force, demographics, 567
Work group maintenance, 381, 382
Work groups
  self-regulating, 263
  structure of, 267–278
Work load, 165
Work-related attitudes, 153–154, 155,
    160–173, 180
Work restructuring, 581–582
Work settings, see Physical environment
Work teams
  guidelines for creating effective, 266–
    267
  use of, 579
World economy, 6–7

Xerox, 562, 595

Young Turks game, 425

A TIMELINE OF MILESTONES IN THE

(Continued from inside front cover)

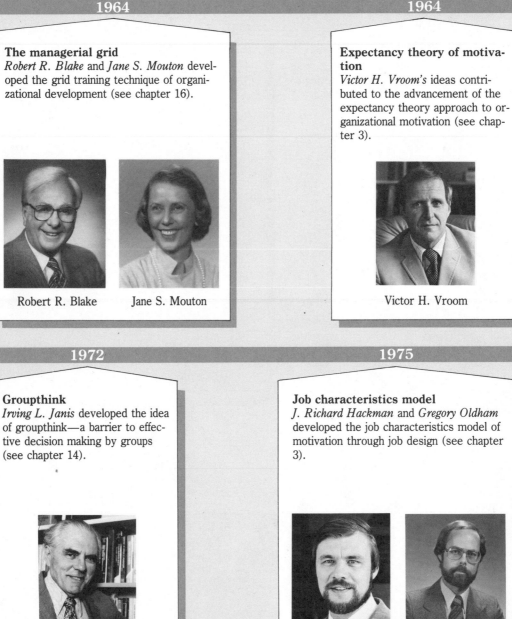

1964

The managerial grid
Robert R. Blake and *Jane S. Mouton* developed the grid training technique of organizational development (see chapter 16).

Robert R. Blake   Jane S. Mouton

1964

Expectancy theory of motivation
Victor H. Vroom's ideas contributed to the advancement of the expectancy theory approach to organizational motivation (see chapter 3).

Victor H. Vroom

1972

Groupthink
Irving L. Janis developed the idea of groupthink—a barrier to effective decision making by groups (see chapter 14).

Irving L. Janis

1975

Job characteristics model
J. Richard Hackman and *Gregory Oldham* developed the job characteristics model of motivation through job design (see chapter 3).

J. Richard Hackman   Gregory Oldham

Note: These events were selected on the basis of suggestions in the following sources:

Lawrence, P.R. (1987). Historical development of organizational behavior. In J.W. Lorsch (Ed.), *Handbook of organizational behavior,* (pp. 1–9). Englewood Cliffs, NJ: Prentice-Hall.
Pugh, D.S., Hickson, D.J., & Hinings, C.R. (1985). *Writers on organizations*.